A Surplus of Memory

A CENTENNIAL BOOK

One hundred books
published between 1990 and 1995
bear this special imprint of
the University of California Press.
We have chosen each Centennial Book
as an example of the Press's finest
publishing and bookmaking traditions
as we celebrate the beginning of
our second century.

UNIVERSITY OF CALIFORNIA PRESS

Founded in 1893

A Surplus of Memory

Chronicle of the Warsaw
Ghetto Uprising

Yitzhak Zuckerman ("Antek")

TRANSLATED AND EDITED BY
Barbara Harshav

UNIVERSITY OF CALIFORNIA PRESS
Berkeley   Los Angeles   Oxford

The Publisher gratefully acknowledges the generous
contributions provided by the following organizations:

The Associates of the University of California Press
The Lucius N. Littauer Foundation
The "1939" Club
The Roth Family Foundation

Originally published in Hebrew as *Those Seven Years: 1939–1946*, Copyright 1990 by
Hakibbutz Hameuchad Publishing House and Bet Lochamei Hagetaot, Tel Aviv.

University of California Press
Berkeley and Los Angeles, California

University of California Press
Oxford, England

Library of Congress Cataloging-in-Publication Data

Zuckerman, Yitzhak, 1915–1981.
    [Sheva' ha-shanim ha-hen. English]
    A surplus of memory: chronicle of the Warsaw Ghetto uprising /
Yitzchak Zuckerman ; translated and edited by Barbara
Harshav.
        p. cm.
    Includes bibliographical references (p.) and index.
    ISBN 0-520-07841-1 (cloth)
    1. Zuckerman, Yitzhak, 1915–1981.   2. Holocaust, Jewish
(1939–1945)—Poland—Personal narratives.   3. World War, 1939–1945—
Underground movements, Jewish—Poland.   4. Warsaw (Poland)—
History—Uprising of 1943.   I. Harshav, Barbara, 1940–
II. Title.
D804.3.Z8613   1993
940.53'18—dc20   92–31230
                                                              CIP

Printed in the United States of America

1   2   3   4   5   6   7   8   9

CONTENTS

Warsaw 1946

preparing their members to migrate to Eretz Israel to build workers' settlements there. Now these groups formed the backbone of the resistance organizations in the ghettoes of Eastern Europe. Their members were imbued with a national sense of meaning and destiny, and instilled with a discipline that would stand them in good stead during the Nazi ordeal. In addition, movement membership also served a tactical function during the uprisings when fighting units were composed of members of youth movements who knew one another before the ghetto; hence it was almost impossible to infiltrate spies or agents provocateurs.

Finally, this is a book about heroes and heroism. We have no standards to measure the Warsaw Ghetto and its heroes, for history offers us no parallels. Sometimes, when we want to focus on the helplessness of the Jews, to emphasize their ultimate powerlessness in the face of the Nazi juggernaut, we reduce the event to practically nothing. Historians point out that, in fact, only a handful of German soldiers were actually killed in the Uprising and that, when the Nazis finally got tired of the game, they simply burned down the ghetto and finished it. In the "overall scheme of things," they argue, the Warsaw Ghetto Uprising really wasn't very important. At other times, the event is elevated to mythical proportions and those who carried it out are transformed into Titans, demigods.

The truth of the Warsaw Ghetto Uprising does not lie "somewhere in between," as the cliché would have it. The truth is in another sphere altogether, at that place where human beings push their human potential beyond anything we've known, out to what looks like the breaking point. And there, they are transformed into heroes; there they expand our definition of human possibility. This is the reality of the Warsaw Ghetto, and what preceded it and what followed it. We didn't have a yardstick to measure that behavior until they came along and provided it.

The people in this book are heroes. Not because they smuggled guns or manufactured Molotov Cocktails or shot Nazi soldiers or defended their positions against tanks and machine guns. But because, in that hell they lived in, they've maintained a human image. Because they stared the reality of their situation directly in the face and took control of their own lives, holding onto their definition of who they were and what they valued—difficult enough in the best of circumstances; well-nigh impossible under Nazi occupation. Risking their lives every single minute, they lived in constant tension and fear, yet they demonstrated a generosity and a capacity for self-sacrifice we seldom find anywhere in history. If the Nazis represent the ultimate evil that human beings are capable of, the cast of this drama demonstrate the ultimate dignity we can also attain.

At the twenty-fifth anniversary of the Warsaw Ghetto Uprising, Antek was interviewed in the Israeli press. The final question he was asked was

When the war was over, some Poles went on murdering Jews, notably in the pogrom in Kielce in the summer of 1946; but it was also the Polish regime that arranged for the rescue and evacuation of Jews from there. What is apparent in Antek's account is the extraordinary complexity of these relations and the treachery of any superficial blanket judgments: they too were human beings.

Like everyone else in the book, and despite all the "I's," Antek also keeps his own dimensions human. This is no pasteboard hero of a shoot-em-up between the Jews and the Nazis, not the swaggering ghetto fighter of popular legend. The Antek presented in this account is more complex and, hence, more courageous: he admits to being frightened almost all the time, humiliated on occasion, on the verge of a breakdown a few times, and often wrong, when mistakes were measured in terms of lives. Like other resistance leaders, his most salient characteristic was his ability to confront the Nazi threat directly without taking refuge in any consolations about the possibility of evading the impending fate of the Jews. Both he and Abba Kovner in Vilna drew the awful conclusion from the massacre of the Vilna Jews in Ponar in the autumn of 1941 that the Nazis meant to liquidate *all* the Jews. Henceforth, all their efforts were devoted to preparing for resistance, knowing full well what the outcome had to be.

The emotional and spiritual toll of living this dangerous paradox was enormous:

> Anyone with eyes in his head understood we were walking a very thin tightrope. The only other choice was to hide, because you could have thought differently: Why endanger yourself? Why be among the wolves when I'm only a dog? Why walk around tense all the time? What good will come from this? You don't know what other people are thinking deep down, and that makes it hard for someone who has to make decisions.

All these resistance fighters were good children of middle-class homes, with no training in weapons or clandestine operations or military tactics. And children they were! Antek, born in 1915, was one of the "old timers" in the group. Most of them were in their late teens and early twenties; they were studying in gymnasia or preparing to immigrate to Palestine when the war caught them and transformed their lives. They had to learn as they went along, under conditions which were hardly conducive to education; and the lessons could be—and most often were—at the cost of their lives. Most of them had been members of one of the various Jewish youth movements which flourished in the inter-war period.[1] Those movements, particularly the Zionist Halutz movements, had aimed at

1. See below.

ANTEK

I want you to know something about Yitzhak. I'm his wife and we were together there in everything, and you can say that whatever I say is subjective. . . . What can I do . . . I'm convinced it's the objective truth. By now, there are no witnesses left except me and I say [. . .]: if it weren't for Yitzhak, we Halutzim would not have had the Warsaw Ghetto Uprising! Only one step—and we would have been swallowed up in the darkness of the Holocaust without a trace.

—Zivia Lubetkin

Yitzhak Zuckerman (1915–1981; known by his underground pseudonym Antek) was one of the organizers and leaders of the Jewish Fighting Organization (ZOB—Zydowska Organizacja Bojowa) that led the Uprising in the Warsaw Ghetto. After the ghetto revolt was crushed and Jürgen Stroop, the Nazi general in charge of the operation, declared Warsaw *"judenrein,"* Antek directed clandestine ZOB operations on the "Aryan" side of the city, where about 20,000 Jews were hiding. In August 1944, he commanded a unit of Jewish fighters in the Polish Uprising.

After the Liberation, Antek remained in Poland until late in 1946 to help the Jewish survivors returning from the concentration and death camps as well as Jewish refugees and exiles coming back from the Soviet Union. He was one of the major figures of Brikha, the organization to smuggle illegal Jewish immigrants to Palestine. And, after the horrifying massacre of Jews in Kielce, in "liberated" Poland, in 1946, he was in charge of evacuating Jews from there.

In the spring of 1947, he immigrated to Palestine and was one of the founders of the Ghetto Fighters' Kibbutz and a moving force in the establishment of the important Holocaust museum and research center, Beit Katznelson, located there.

This book is an account of his activities during "those seven years" (as the book is titled in Hebrew), from 1939 to 1946, which spanned the greatest catastrophe in Jewish national history. What is significant about this time frame is that it does not lift the event out of its time; the book neither begins with the ghetto and the resistance nor ends with their demise. Rather, it sets them in the specific social and political context that preceded them and goes on to recount the continuation of resistance activity after the liquidation of the ghetto and after the end of the war.

But it is not a "typical" memoir; Antek did not sit down and write a continuous narrative of that time. It emerged out of the dedicated efforts of a group of friends connected with Beit Katznelson, the Holocaust Museum at Kibbutz Lohamei Ha-Getaot. Yoske Rabinovitch describes the inception of the project in his introduction to the Hebrew edition:

> Antek's close friends who frequently met with him in friendly gatherings of two or three [. . .] during the evening—would hear him tell each time another tale, another episode, another fragment of an experience, and another portrait of a friend—and each time they were surprised; sometimes they heard expressions of grief and pain, and even rage and rebuke. And you clearly sensed how deep was the well and how heavy the burden, the burden of memory he bore on his shoulders. "I feel in my soul that I'm a thousand years old, since ever hour *there* counts for a year in me," he once told me. He tried to get rid of this burden with his constant energetic activity, devotion and initiative, to expand the museum, renew its exhibits, publish witness accounts and research, produce documentary films, establish a school to teach the Holocaust and the Uprising. . . .
>
> We knew he wouldn't yet release his personal book, stored up inside him. So we kept begging him—and he kept rejecting it as if he were retreating from it.

It was not until the Yom Kippur War in late 1973, which shook the foundations of Israeli confidence, that Antek agreed to record his book on tape with his friend Yoske Rabinovitch. The project was begun in January 1974, and Antek imposed two conditions. The first was his proposal that he himself would not refer to any documents, sources or books on the period, but would rely solely on his own memory. As he put it, "Maybe I'll succeed in preserving the climate of those days, the experience of then; not to tell anything new, but to tell what I thought and what I felt then."

Hence, on one level, this is a study of the nature of memory and remembering. Clearly, Antek had a prodigious memory capable of presenting hosts of people and situations often with an extraordinary vividness and density of detail and affect. (Although he refrained from consulting documents while the discussions were being taped, he had spent several years engaged in articulating the history of the resistance in Nazi-occupied Poland.)

Antek claimed that he "suffered from a surplus of memory," whereas others tended to forget. Perhaps one reason for the copiousness of his memory is that what he had to remember about himself in the past didn't impair his identity in the present. That is, except for one or two relatively minor incidents he reports, Antek didn't suffer the kind of humiliation and degradation we have come to expect in survivor accounts of the Holocaust. Although he spent a short time in a labor camp near Warsaw,

he had almost no direct contact with the Germans. He led a life of fear
and hiding and tension; but it was not the emotional and physical deg-
redation of the camps.

The resistance fighters, whose lives were completely and self-con-
sciously devoted to revolting against the Nazi regime, succeeded throughout all the horror they experienced in maintaining their integrity. Hence,
they can afford to remember the quality of those events in detail.

Antek's second condition was more serious: he demanded that the
tapes not be transcribed and certainly not published until after his death.
Yoske Rabinovitch asked him for an explanation of this stipulation:

> These were his main reasons: he claimed that as long as he was sure that
> things would remain hidden for a long time, he would be freer in his tale;
> thus he could lift the prohibitions and perhaps tell maybe "ninety percent
> and maybe ninety-five percent of what he had." Whereas "five percent of
> the things should better go down to the grave with me. But these are things
> that can't change or add anything to the main thing, since they are things
> that are only between me and myself." And the second reason, in his words:
> "You know me and you know that I'm like that 'famous humble man.' But
> the real truth is that I was among the few who knew 'everything,' or 'almost
> everything,' and I had a hand in almost everything that was done, through-
> out those years. And if I talk freely—I would have to talk in the first person,
> in sentences that begin with the word 'I': I said, I went, I did, and so on.
> And just imagine that the book appears while I'm still alive, with all those
> I's. Could I hold my head up and look people in the eye? No, I couldn't!

The taping continued throughout 1974 and, when it ended, there were
thirty-eight tapes with almost sixty hours of conversation, recorded in
forty sessions with Yoske Rabinovitch and Yudke Helman. After Antek's
death in June 1981, the tapes were transcribed and a decision was made
to extract the questions and present the text as a continuous narrative,
with as little editing of the material as possible. This unorthodox composition technique accounts for occasional repetitions in the text as well
as for some seemingly peculiar shifts of time in the narrative. However,
it also lends a quality of immediacy not often found in autobiographical
narratives where the author is in control of the image of himself that he
presents. Antek was talking with friends about the past and the man
comes through with a rare force.

Hence, though this is a book of history, it is not a history book. As
Rabinovitch says,

> this is not a systematic, consistent and objective history book, . . . Certainly
> it isn't scientific research on the period, . . . This book is itself a *source*. It
> is an historic and specifically human source of someone who was at the heart
> of events and acts of that period.

It is an invaluable contribution to our knowledge of what is still an obscure corner of Holocaust history. Despite the avalanche of material that has appeared in recent years chronicling the destruction of the Jews in Europe, the history of Jewish resistance movements has not received a great deal of attention especially in English, and has remained primarily in the realm of myth and popular culture. There is precious little material on the day to day activities, the cast of characters, the small and large failures, and successes, the exhaustion, the despair, the shock and the horror. It is this texture of their lives that fills Antek's book.

Antek was not interested in a "judicious account," did not strive for some kind of "objectivity," made no attempt to be even, balanced, fair. He was biased and passionate, deeply and personally involved in the events of the period; he was fond of some people, disliked others, admired some and loathed others. He was devoted to his Dror (He-Halutz Ha-Tza'ir) youth movement; but that did not blind him to its deficiencies and failures. He was dedicated to Zionism and profoundly wounded by the silence emanating from leaders of the Yishuv in Eretz Israel. But most often, with a remarkable generosity, he could see both flaws and heroism in the same person. He was *there*, so the myths that have emerged from the Warsaw Ghetto don't impress him: Mordechai Anielewicz, leader of the fighting forces in the Warsaw Uprising, was a boy whose mother sold fish; the historian Emmanuel Ringelblum, who conceived and directed the enterprise of the ghetto archives, gave boring lectures. This hardly denigrates the enormous achievements of these characters, but it does bring them down from the Olympus where they reside in most other accounts and locates them in the realm of humanity.

He also brings the Poles into the sphere of the human. From April 1942 until he left Poland in 1946, Antek served as the top-level liaison between the Jewish and Polish undergrounds, and later between the Jews and the Polish government officials. What emerges in his account is a generous and well-balanced picture of what were very complex relations. He rejects the demonization of the Polish nation as a whole; yet he does not overlook the crimes committed by the Poles against the Jews. In this book, there are extraordinarily brave and devoted Poles who risked their lives to save Jews; and there are Poles who saved Jews to spirit them off to convents and monasteries where they could be spiritually saved by conversion to Catholicism; and sometimes the same Poles did both. There are Poles who died savings Jews, and Poles who made sure more Jews died. There were two Polish undergrounds: the right-wing Armia Krajowa, which was the stronger force during the war; and the Communist Armia Ludowa, which was weak during the war, but strong afterward. Much of the leadership of Armia Krajowa was antisemitic, but many of its members were friendly to the Jews; the situation was more or less reversed in the Armia Ludowa.

what were the military and strategic lessons to be learned from the Ghetto Uprising. He replied:

> I don't think there's any need to analyze the Uprising in military terms. This was a war of less than a thousand people against a mighty army, and no one doubted how it was likely to turn out. This isn't a subject for study in a military school. Not the weapons, not the operations, not the tactics. If there's a school to study the *human spirit,* there it should be a major subject. The really important things were inherent in the force shown by Jewish youths, after years of degredation, to rise up against their destroyers and determine what death they would choose: Treblinka or Uprising. I don't know if there's a standard to measure *that.*

EDITOR'S NOTE

Since this book was dictated by its author, and since the published Hebrew text has no vowels, it was necessary to track down the precise spelling of various places and names. Place names and Polish names are spelled in their Polish orthography; Yiddish and Hebrew names are transcribed phonetically or as they are most commonly written; German names are spelled in German. Often, people spelled their names differently in the different languages, but I tried to keep one consistent spelling for each name.

About one-fifth of the footnotes come from the Hebrew edition. I have added the rest to provide the American reader with necessary information and occasionally with variant accounts of events found in other sources (listed in the References).

ACKNOWLEDGMENTS

Such an enormous project necessarily involves the cooperation of several people. From the beginning, Yudke Helman of Kibbutz Gvat has shown steadfast devotion to this English edition, often from a hospital bed or a wheelchair. Yehiel Yanai of Kibbutz Ma'agan Michael took a great deal of time and effort going over the text and making excellent editorial recommendations. Stanley Holwitz, my indomitable editor at the University of California Press was, as always, more than helpful and patient. Paula Cizmar did an intelligent and sensitive job of editing. Yitzhak Mais of Yad Vashem and Nava Schreiber helped with pictures.

Funding for this project was provided by the indefatigable and loving efforts of Bernard and Shelly Tenzer. Many thanks to Congregation Anshe Chesed of Manhattan which administered the fund-raising endeavor.

Most of all, thanks to my husband, Benjamin Harshav, who makes everything possible.

Barbara Harshav

ON JEWISH PARTIES
AND YOUTH MOVEMENTS

A gamut of ideologies emerged in Jewish society in Eastern Europe from the end of the nineteenth century, resulting in several political parties, active in Jewish political life in Poland in the interwar period. There were also many youth movements, some affiliated with parties, others not. Since these movements were such a vital part of the resistance organizations in the ghettoes, we present here a brief outline of the spectrum, moving from left to right:

1. The illegal Communist Party.
2. The *Bund*—short for "General Jewish Workers' Union." A strong Jewish socialist-democratic party, founded in 1897, which advocated Yiddish language and culture and secular Jewish nationalism in the Diaspora (*Doyigkeyt*—"Hereness"); opposed to Zionism.
3. *Po'alei Zion Left*—a small left-Marxist Zionist party, sympathizing with the Soviet Union, but not accepted by the Communist Party. Supported the Yiddish language, even in Eretz Israel.
4. *He-Halutz*—an umbrella organization which included the following Zionist youth movements (along with several smaller ones) which aimed at personal realization through building kibbutzim in Israel:
   A. *Ha-Shomer Ha-Tza'ir*—"Young Guard." A Marxist-Freudian Zionist youth movement, demanding personal realization at the age of eighteen by immigration to a kibbutz in Eretz Israel; hence it had no political party. It attracted members from the upper economic strata and the intellectual youth; was oriented to Polish and Hebrew, not Yiddish.

B. *He-Halutz Ha-Tza'ir*—"Young Pioneer."
   Frayhayt (Dror)—"Freedom."
   Zionist-socialist youth movements affiliated with the so-
   cial-democratic Zionist Party Po'alei Zion (Z.S.) and Ha-
   Kibbutz Ha-Meuchad kibbutz movement in Israel. Whereas
   Frayhayt was more Yiddish-oriented and appealed to the
   masses, He-Halutz appealed to youth in the Gymnasia and
   promoted Hebrew. These two movements united before the
   outbreak of World War II in 1939 under the name Dror-
   He-Halutz Ha-Tza'ir, but tensions remained between the
   youth movement which advocated Aliya to Eretz Israel at
   the age of 18 on the one hand, and the party which was
   content to be Zionist in Poland, on the other.

C. *Gordonia*—A non-Marxist socialist youth movement promoting Aliya to a kibbutz in Israel.

5. Two *General Zionist* parties, one liberal and one conservative, and
   the youth movement, *Ha-Oved Ha-Tzioni* ("Zionist Work").

6. Two religious parties: the Zionist *Mizrakhi* and the anti-Zionist
   Agudas Yisroel, and their respective youth movements.

7. The radical rightist *Revisionist* party, which split from the World
   Zionist Organization, and its paramilitary youth movement *Betar.*

ONE

The War

[World War II broke out with the invasion of Poland by the German armies in the early morning hours of September 1, 1939. At the time, Zuckerman was a leader of the He-Halutz Ha-Tza'ir (Young Pioneer) Zionist socialist youth movement, which had recently united with Frayhayt (Freedom, later known as Dror), a youth movement with similar ideals. Both belonged to the He-Halutz (Pioneer), an umbrella organization of all pioneering Zionist youth movements, striving to realize their ideals on kibbutzim in Eretz Israel.]

On September 1, 1939, I was in Klebań, a small village in Wołyń, near Rowno, where we were holding seminars of He-Halutz Ha-Tza'ir and later of the united movement of Frayhayt–He-Halutz Ha-Tza'ir. Why was I in Klebań at that time? The twenty-first Zionist Congress was taking place in Geneva and most of the Shlikhim from Eretz Israel who worked with our Movement in Poland were in the delegation to the Congress, along with many from the local leadership cadre. There were very few of us left in Poland in this season of summer camps, symposia, and similar activities. A month-long seminar for the leaders of the united movement from Wołyń and Polesie was going on in Klebań, which began on August 11 with thirty-eight participants.

I opened the seminar with lectures on literature and other subjects. Haim Shechter and Edek Golowner were with me.[1] I stayed a week, delivered a course of lectures, and returned to Warsaw at the end of August. Arriving in Warsaw, before I had a chance to bask in the sun—the weather was very nice—I was informed that the English Consul in Warsaw had called on English citizens, including residents of Eretz Israel who had British Mandatory citizenship, to leave Poland immediately.

One of the first things I did when I heard this was to return to Klebań to replace Yudke Helman, a Shaliah from Eretz Israel who had succeeded me there.[2] I did that to keep the seminar from dispersing, for Yudke had

1. Yitzhak (Edek) Golowner: Born in Vienna in 1915, educator; one of the founders of the He-Halutz and Frayhayt (Dror) underground in the Soviet zone in December 1939. Imprisoned in Luck by the Soviets and murdered at the age of twenty-seven when the Germans captured that city. (Details of his death are unknown.)

2. Yudke Helman: Born in Pinsk. Immigrated to Israel as a Halutz. Sent to Poland in 1939 by Ha-Kibbutz Ha-Meuchad and the Histadrut; established the Dror underground in

to rush to Warsaw with the other Shlikhim returning from the Congress until the issue of their return to Eretz Israel was clarified.

At that time, I was Secretary General of the united movement, Frayhayt–He-Halutz Ha-Tza'ir. Edek Golowner was in Klebań with me. As a result of the parity arrangement in the Movement, after unification, Moshe Novoprutzki, a member of Frayhayt, was supposed to be with me; but he was also a delegate to the Congress.[3] He was supposed to "keep an eye on" me, in case I "went too far" in shifting the Movement onto the tracks of Halutziut,[4] Hebrew, and such, so that Frayhayt wouldn't assimilate, God forbid, into He-Halutz Ha-Tza'ir. When He-Halutz had told me they didn't want to add Novoprutzki to the delegation to the Congress, I thought it was unfair to him; I discussed it with Abraham Gewelber of the He-Halutz Central Committee and Nowoprutski was ultimately added to the delegation.[5] The Zionist Pioneer movement in Warsaw was almost bereft of its central activists and I remained practically alone.

So, at the outbreak of the war, on September 1, I was back in Klebań. We assembled the students for a discussion and tried to prepare them for the future in terms of our naïve understanding. First, we made sure everyone would return home. Edek and I stayed behind. The two of us belonged to the Polish "Patriot" branch—we overlooked the injustices and hatred of the Polish state against the Jews and reported to the local authorities to enlist in the army. But the authorities didn't know what to do with us. The next day, September 2, we decided to return to Warsaw, which we did by traveling a roundabout route, in a train and a taxi. The great turmoil had not yet reached eastern Poland. We even took a taxi, which was expensive. On the way, in Miedzyrzec, I think, we came upon an army unit commanded by a Polish officer. We reported to the officer, a pleasant young man, who told us he wished he knew what to do with his own soldiers, let alone civilians.

I must say that I didn't serve in the Polish army. I was the youngest of four children in my family, two boys and two girls. The family did

---

the Soviet zone and worked there until his return to Eretz Israel in February 1940. Currently a member of Kibbutz Gvat.

3. Moshe Novoprutzki: A member of the Central Committee of Frayhayt–He-Halutz. Immigrated to Eretz Israel from Vilna in 1941.

4. I.e., "pioneering," striving to realize the ideals of the Movement by joining a kibbutz in Eretz Israel.

5. Abraham Gewelber: Secretary of He-Halutz Ha-Tza'ir in Poland from 1937 on. Active in the Soviet zone after the outbreak of the war. Moved to Vilna, where he represented He-Halutz Ha-Tza'ir in Jewish welfare organizations. Immigrated to Eretz Israel in 1941.

everything to keep my oldest brother, Abraham, from serving in the army. The night before he reported for the draft, he and his friends sat up all night drinking coffee. When my brother appeared the next day, his heart was pounding and the doctor sent him to rest. After an hour's rest, his strength was restored. But, finally, he was released with a bribe. I didn't allow my parents to do the same for me and reported on time for the military examination. He-Halutz was against shirking Polish army duty, and that was my personal position, too. But by law, high school graduates could not serve as simple soldiers and were sent to officer's school; yet, except for physicians, Jews weren't accepted to those schools. This dragged on for a year, two, three, and I wasn't called to the army. Finally, I was called in and informed that I wasn't accepted. So I was exempt from military service.

Now, when we got to Warsaw, I reported again for the draft, for the third time. They took Edek but not me. Since the Halutzim on Dzielna[6] and Gęsia[7] considered me a "patriot," I tried to do something. Not everyone understood what war with the Germans meant. There was a certain apathy. I argued not only the anti-German aspect, but also the pro-Polish angle.

On September 2, by the time I returned from Klebań, the Shlikhim who had returned from the Congress were in Warsaw, and everything was confused and in a turmoil. As we made our way to Warsaw, we saw bombing, and Warsaw itself had already been bombed. The war began on Friday, September 1; many cities were bombed that day, there were serious casualties, and everything was in an uproar.

We gathered to discuss the situation. By then we knew from the radio about the German advance. We figured that our Movement would retreat eastward, but it didn't occur to us that Poland wouldn't hold out at all, not even a few months. We assumed our men would be drafted, and a "cabinet of girls" was set up for that eventuality.

All this happened within a few days. The situation deteriorated from day to day and, at one meeting in which we discussed the Shlikhim, the local members proposed that the Shlikhim from Eretz Israel leave Poland at once because both the front and the Movement would probably move east and the men would be mobilized. The Shlikhim were citizens of a foreign country and, although we locals probably couldn't do anything, they certainly couldn't; and, in any case, the entire burden would fall on the girls. And if something could be done—it would be done by us Polish

6. For many years, Dzielna Street 34 was the Warsaw address of the Kvutsa, a commune of Shlikhim and activists in He-Halutz and He-Halutz Ha-Tza'ir. The apartment was the center of all Zionist operations, and Dzielna turned into a proper name.
7. Gęsia Street 14: Address of the offices of He-Halutz and the Po'alei Zion party.

citizens. Nor did we think the Shlikhim could contribute anything to the Movement; on the contrary, we thought they would be a burden. Fay-vush Ben-Dori was against our position and was supported by Yudke Helman.[8] I was strongly in favor of sending the Shlikhim back to Eretz Israel. Perhaps our position was arrogant, but experience in the long run proved us right. We thought we could work by ourselves; we were ambitious young people and thought we could do everything.

I was young; I had come to Warsaw in 1936 and joined the central staff of He-Halutz Ha-Tza'ir. I was supposed to live in the leadership commune on Dzielna, but, as the youngest one, I didn't feel comfortable there. I was depressed and so I fought to be transferred to our training farm in Grochów,[9] which is what happened. I worked in Landau's workshop and became friendly with him.[10] After work or on my days off, I would come to central Warsaw. Only after the unification of Frayhayt and He-Halutz Ha-Tza'ir did I have to move to the commune on Dzielna and serve as one of the two secretaries of the Movement. Unhappily, I left Grochów and moved to Dzielna 34.

I was also a member of the Central Committee of the umbrella organization, He-Halutz, but my position there was that, for example, if there were twelve people at a meeting and only eleven chairs, I was the one who sat on the floor. (And if there was another chair missing, Zivia would also sit on the floor.[11]) At any rate, the group at Dzielna was young, and even though I had come before the others and had been in the commune longer, I still regarded myself as one of them.

That emergency meeting with the Shlikhim was the first time I talked aggressively, insolently. I demanded that we locals do the work in the Movement and said that if we weren't drafted into the army, we would probably have to move east someday. At that time, we thought Poland was likely to take a stand on some line of defense in the east; we thought in terms of World War I. It didn't occur to us that Poland would completely

8. Fayvush Ben-Dori (1900–1956): Key member of the Eretz-Israeli delegation to the Polish He-Halutz.

9. The training farm of He-Halutz was located in a Warsaw suburb, Praga, on Grochów Street.

10. Alexander Landau: Born in Galicia. Engineer. Came to Warsaw after living in Vienna. Friendly to He-Halutz and the underground. Owner of a wooden products factory, where many activists found shelter during the Great *Aktsia* of July 1942; crossed to the Aryan side in April 1943, sent to Vittel Camp in occupied France and from there to Auschwitz, where he was murdered.

11. Zivia Lubetkin (1914–1978): Born in Bitan, Polesie, Poland. Active in Dror (Frayhayt); central figure in ZOB; leader in the January and April uprisings in the Warsaw Ghetto and prominent in subsequent activity. Wife of Antek Zuckerman. Immigrated to Israel in 1946; was a member of Kibbutz Lohamei Ha-Getaot.

collapse in three weeks. Warsaw was conquered and surrendered on the twenty-seventh of that month!

This meeting took place on September 6. The girls assigned to run things were Zivia Lubetkin, the sisters Frumka[12] and Hancia Plotnitzka,[13] and Leah Perlstein.[14]

In the first days of the war, even before the decision about the departure of the Shlikhim, "Commissars" were appointed by the central committee for various areas of the country: Yudke [Helman], for example, was to go to Vilna and I was to be the "Commissar" of Białystok—a real Commissar! This was preceded by another development. On the third day of the war, I think, a He-Halutz delegation, which included Fayvush Ben-Dori and Dr. Meir Pecker, reported to the Polish authorities.[15] There was something in the press about it, and the document about the delegation was re-published a few years ago by the Poles in a collection of documents of September 1939.[16] This delegation informed the military authorities of Zionist support for the Polish army and announced that all our training groups, workshops, sewing shops, in Łódz, as well as everywhere else, were at the disposal of the war effort. This was received very positively.

That delegation also informed the authorities that we were sending special emissaries to various places to mobilize all Zionist forces. These emissaries received special permits along with an appeal for help to all local institutions. I also received such a document, which turned out to be very useful and saved a lot of our people.

One night, I went to the railroad station with Yukde. Train traffic was disrupted; we sat in the station all night long and finally went

12. Frumka Plotnitzka: Born in Plotnica, near Pinsk. Active member of He-Halutz and ZOB, member of the ZOB delegation on the Aryan side of Warsaw, brought the first weapons into the ghetto. Sent to Będzin-Sosnowiec in September 1942 to organize the local defense there. Was killed in the ZOB uprising in Będzin on August 3, 1943.

13. Hancia Plotnitzka: Born in Plotnica, near Pinsk. Outstanding figure in He-Halutz and Frayhayt. Active in the underground, first in the Soviet zone and later in the Nazi area. Sent to the Aryan side of Warsaw; caught and murdered by the Germans at the age of twenty-five.

14. Leah Perlstein: Born in Sokolka. A teacher and one of the organizers of the Frayhayt and He-Halutz underground in the Generalgouvernement. Active in the ZOB on the Aryan side. Captured by the Germans during the January Uprising and sent to Treblinka. Details of her death are unknown.

· 15. Dr. Meir Pecker: Physician of the Palestine office in Warsaw; worked for He-Halutz in the official institutions of Poland. Went to Vilna, where he immigrated to Eretz Israel in 1941.

16. The delegation reported to the Polish Welfare Minister, Marjan Zyndram-Kościałkowski. A dispatch of the Polish information agency, PAT, of September 2, 1939, was published in the Polish-Jewish newspaper *Nasz Przegląd*, September 3. See Dobroszyski, 1964:17.

back home. Hancia Plotnitzka was sent to Łódz and Natan Blizowski to Wołyń.[17] I was supposed to remain in Białystok, while Yukde was to go on to Vilna, but both of us got stuck. Two days later, the trains stopped running altogether. At that meeting, it was decided that the Shlikhim would leave Warsaw for Romania on the way to Eretz Israel; and that very night they moved out, except for Yukde who stayed with us a while longer.

That night, Mayor Starzyński made a radio appeal to all civilian men to report to the suburbs with tools, to dig defense trenches.[18] I mobilized my friends Gewelber and Mulka Barantshuk, and we worked all night in Wola, one of the suburbs of Warsaw.[19] We worked hard and the Poles were nice to us. We didn't sense a whiff of antisemitism in those hours. At daybreak, we returned exhausted and found the house on Dzielna empty. We didn't know that, on that night, Colonel Umiastowski, on behalf of the army staff, broadcast a dramatic appeal to all able-bodied armed men to go east.[20] To this day, I don't know exactly what that announcement meant. It might have been an act of German provocation since it resulted in hundreds of thousands of people streaming eastward, blocking the roads to Polish army traffic, the few tanks and the cavalry. The next day, they were exposed to aerial bombings.

A group of us, including Mulka Barantshuk, Avreml Gewelber, and I, were hungry and set out for Grochów, where we learned that the members of the training farm who had been there had gone. By decision of the Central Committee, they left at night for the eastern border, guided by Frumka. The gentiles in the area had plundered the farm, but we did find a horse and cart left for our escape. I told my comrades I would go to a hut I had seen, perhaps to check out if anyone was left. When I came back, there was no cart and no comrades. So I remained alone without food or a horse, with just my own two feet.

I started walking with the masses streaming on the roads at the height of the bombings. I think I reached Mińsk-Mazowiecki at nightfall. I was hungry and worn out after a night of work, mad at myself, and without a cent; I was close to passing out. I sat down against some fence, and

17. Natan Blizowski: Member of the Central Committee of He-Halutz in Poland; active in the Soviet zone and later in Vilna. Immigrated to Eretz Israel in 1941.

18. Stefan Starzyński: Appointed mayor of Warsaw in 1934. Mobilized into the Polish army with the rank of major, but remained in the city, he said, to provide the population with necessary services. Arrested by the Germans in October; executed in Dachau.

19. Mulka (Shmuel) Barantshuk: Member of the Central Committee of He-Halutz in Poland and editor of *Yediyer*. Immigrated to Eretz Israel in 1940.

20. I.e., the night of September 6. Colonel Umiastowski was chief of propaganda in the headquarters of the Polish Supreme Command. His appeal resulted in a mass exodus, panic, and confusion; he committed suicide.

suddenly Oskar Hendler appeared, like a guardian angel.[21] He dragged me into some courtyard where all the comrades were, the members of the He-Halutz Central Committee as well as others from the Central Committee of Po'alei Zion–Z.S.; the comrades with the horse and wagon were also there. I didn't ask any questions. To this day, I don't know why they went off and left me. I think it was because of the general chaos and panic; at least that's how I tried to explain it to myself; I was young, inclined to joke and not to bear a grudge. I wasn't angry for more than a few minutes. Apparently, we met by chance, since I had started walking on a different road from the one they took. And so, for example, Zivia and Edek Golowner, who were in charge of the evacuation of our resthome in Jósefów outside Warsaw, had also taken another road.[22]

So, at dawn on September 8, I was back with the group. I ate my fill and rested. We got hold of another wagon and, in the early morning, we set out for the east. We had ridden about half an hour when I suddenly saw some of the people from Grochów. There was a group of children from Zbąszyn who had been expelled from Germany and were studying in Grochów.[23] They were in a woods with Frumka, but with nothing to eat and helpless; so, they went to look for food. I got out of the wagon, which would continue with the other comrades, while I joined the members of the Grochów training program.

We did have money because we had had time to withdraw most of the money in the He-Halutz account from the PKO Bank. In Mińsk-Mazowiecki, we distributed the money to our comrades in case we were separated. I got some too, but not much, maybe enough to pay for a haircut. (Later, when I got to Kowel, I got some more.) Yet, I remember that we bought wine, got hold of a bag of bread somewhere, and brought it all to the woods, where it was a cause of great joy. Yitzhak

21. Oskar Hendler (1911–1978): Born in Germany, active in the Central Committee of He-Halutz in Berlin. Deported to Poland by the Nazis and joined He-Halutz in Warsaw. One of the founders of the Frayhayt and He-Halutz underground in the Soviet zone. Was arrested by the Soviet authorities and sent to a labor camp in the Urals. Returned to Poland in 1945 and resumed activity in Dror. Immigrated to Eretz Israel in 1948 and settled on Kibbutz Lohamei Ha-Getaot.

22. The central rest home of He-Halutz in a suburb of Warsaw. On September 8, 1939, a unit of the German army arrived there and arrested the patients and nurses. The men were forced to precede the advancing unit over the frontline in the suburbs of the city. Most of those arrested were killed by the Polish defense. When Warsaw surrendered on September 29, the Nazi army took over the resthome and turned it into a military hospital.

23. In 1938, the Germans expelled German Jews of Polish origin from the Reich to the Polish border near Zbąszyn, where they were stuck in no-man's land until the war. The "children of Zbąszyn" were a group of youths from the German He-Halutz who had been kept for a long time in the border town of Zbąszyn until just before the war, when they were allowed to go to Grochów to train at the He-Halutz farm there.

Perlis[24] rode on the wagon that went on and I returned to Frumka, who remained there alone, near Kałuszyn.[25] When we got back to the woods that evening, we didn't know there were two more groups of people in the same woods: one, a Polish army unit that had explosives; and the other, a group of gypsies. Nor did we know German spies were also swarming around there, signaling to German pilots that the Polish army was camping there, and they began bombing the woods. Trees fell down right before my eyes; I ordered the young people to cover their heads and not to look; but I did look and I saw how the woods burned down. The heavy bombing went on for hours, and it was extraordinary luck that we weren't hit. The Polish army group was hit. What saved me and our group afterward was the "commissar document" we had gotten from the Polish authorities. For, as darkness came on, Polish gendarmes surrounded the woods searching for spies and caught us. Many of our young people didn't know a single word of Polish and spoke only German. I was their spokesman, and the documents I had received from the central authorities helped us get away from the gendarmes. Many fell victim to that bombing, but none of us was hit. After that we decided to travel only at night and to hide during the day off the road. We continued walking until we reached the River Bug. It was the eve of Rosh Hashana when we came to the town of Włodowa on the River Bug.[26] We were exhausted and looked for a place to rest. We found a place and got an extraordinary welcome from the local youths, who weren't even members of the Movement, just young Jews.

The daughter of the rich man of the town took us home and offered us a straw pallet in the attic. We rested there until the rich man himself appeared; he was terrified that the place would be bombed because of us and gruffly ordered us out of the attic. We came down and lay on the lawn. We were very tired and waited for night. There's one picture I remember clearly. It was dusk; I was wearing a black coat, and I went into the rich man's house. Candles were lit inside the house, since it was a holiday eve. I found him drinking tea. I thanked him for the "welcome" and took some money out to give him. He asked for what. I said: "For hospitality, since you welcomed us so nicely." "In a few more hours," I said, "more Jews might pass by here, and I'm paying for them in advance so that you'll welcome them nicely too." He got up

24. Yitzhak Perlis: Member of the He-Halutz Central Committee and editor of *He-Halutz Ha-Tza'ir.*

25. Kałuszyn: A Jewish town of 6,000 between Warsaw and Siedlce. Served as transit point at the outbreak of the war for masses of refugees streaming east.

26. In September 1939, the River Bug became the boundary between the German and Soviet zones of occupation of defeated Poland.

and started weeping with remorse and invited me to tea. But I refused. The place wasn't far from the River Bug, close to the town of Domcowa. We had to shoe the horse we bought on the way, along with a wagon; and we had to cross the Bug; and we needed help with both. I told the rich man: "If you want to help us, we've got two requests: shoe our horse and guide us across the river." He asked some locals to take the horse to the blacksmith to be shoed and to find a peasant to help us across the river. So, in about an hour and a half, we crossed the Bug. There was no bridge at that place, but there was a crossing where we passed safely.

We were a big group and there wasn't room on the wagon for everybody, so some rode and some walked behind the wagon. Frumka claimed that we couldn't go on like that, since those who were riding could travel faster. She suggested dividing the group in two, and I agreed. But then there was a "war" between us over the horse and wagon. Frumka argued that she couldn't manage them and wanted to walk; I should take the horse and wagon. (In time, the army would have confiscated the horse and wagon anyway.) So I took the horse and wagon and became a driver. It was a big wagon I had paid a lot for; and with that horse, if I'm not mistaken, we arrived in Kowel a few days later.[27] Frumka and her group were still walking toward Kowel. She walked with the older ones, and I rode with the weak and the young and the girls. I think Frumka reached Kowel a day after me.

On the way, before we got to Kowel, we had a single casualty and I found out about that only later. I protected the youths from every patrol. We tried to circumvent any place Polish soldiers were liable to be since these youths spoke German; so we traveled dozens of extra kilometers. Before we had a horse and wagon, we used to walk on foot at night. I didn't know whether to walk at the head of the line or to bring up the rear. These were youngsters and you had to watch them. I used to run back and forth, from one end of the line to the other.

I mentioned the first casualty we had on the way: one of the youths had relatives in Brisk [Polish: Brześć], and he asked permission to go to his relatives, but I forbade him to go. Nevertheless, he left the ranks and went to Brisk, where Polish soldiers captured him; and, because he didn't know Polish, they thought he was a German spy and executed him. We learned about this later. The rest of the group reached Kowel safely.[28]

27. Kowel: A city in western Wołyń, in the Soviet occupation zone, not far from the German-Soviet line, which served as a transit point and shelter for Polish refugees.

28. Later, they learned of a few other victims among the Zbąszyn Halutzim. (See Yehuda Helman 1969:74.)

When we reached Kowel on September 16, I found all the others who had preceded us, including the members of Grochów and other kibbutzim who had found a shelter in Kibbutz "Kłosowa" in Kowel, while we found a place in the apartment of Zvi Melnitzer (now Netzer).[29]

On the day we reached Kowel, the Germans bombed the city and a meeting of the Central Committee of He-Halutz was held in Zvi's apartment by all the members of the Central Committee who were there. They decided that, first of all, the young people had to be evacuated from Kowel to a small town further east, Mielnica, and that I would take them. I asked if any of the comrades was willing to go with me and Nehemia Gross agreed to come along.[30] It was at dawn on September 17, 1939, the day the Soviets entered those areas. On our way, we saw airplanes and thought they were German. We hadn't heard the radio and didn't know about the new partition of Poland according to the Ribbentrop-Molotov Pact.[31]

I spent only one night in bombed-out Kowel. We got to Mielnica with the group, me at the head, riding a horse—a real cavalryman. I could ride well since we had had a small mill when I was young, and in summer I would go there and ride for pleasure. I also knew how to swim and to trade blows with the gentile boys.

By the time we got to Mielnica, it was empty. We entered one house, opened the windows, went into the cellar and found jars of preserves. Mielnica was empty because the Jews didn't know what we knew by then—that the Russians would soon enter that area. The very next day, the Soviets appeared in the area and the *baleboste*[32] also returned and found us eating everything she had stored in the cellar. She cursed us to kingdom come and threw us out. We settled the youngsters in all kinds of places, since the Jews were compassionate and took care of us. We bought sacks of flour and left them for the locals. Then I returned to

---

29. Zvi Melnitzer (now Netzer): Educated in He-Halutz Ha-Tza'ir, a member of Kibbutz Grochów. After the Soviet-German war broke out in Vilna in 1941, he was arrested by a Soviet patrol on the road from Vilna to the Soviet zone. In 1943, he arrived in Eretz Israel through Teheran. After the war, he worked with Brikha in Poland; after the establishment of the State of Israel, he was Israeli ambassador to Poland.

30. Nehemia Gross (1917–1970): Born in Leipzig, Germany. Worked in the He-Halutz underground in the Soviet zone; arrested by the Soviets and imprisoned in a forced labor camp for five years. Returned to Poland after the war and was active in Brikha; arrested again by the Soviets and imprisoned in Leipzig. Died in Israel.

31. Ribbentrop-Molotov Pact: A secret agreement between Germany and the Soviet Union which divided Poland: the western and central part went to the Germans, and eastern Poland to the Soviets. The Red Army crossed the border and incorporated the eastern parts of Poland into Soviet Byelorussia and the Ukraine. Vilna was given to Lithuania, which was an independent state until May 1940.

32. Lady of the house.

Kowel with Nehemia Gross and, since I was a "Polish patriot," as I said, I would stop on the way, despite the danger, and take wounded Polish soldiers to Kowel.

Two Central Committees were then formed: one of He-Halutz Ha-Tza'ir and Frayhayt in Kowel, and another one of Ha-Shomer Ha-Tza'ir in Rowno. Kowel became a transit city for masses of refugees, including the leaders of the Jewish and Zionist parties, such as Bundists Erlich[33] and Alter,[34] general Zionist leaders of Et livnot and Al Ha-Mishmar factions and the heads of Po'alei Zion–Z.S. and Po'alei Zion Left. Everyone was looking for a way out. In Kowel, Yitzhak Perlis, Abraham Gewelber, Mulka Barantshuk, and I shared an apartment. I was up to my old tricks. What could you buy in those days? Wine! So I bought wine. I would come to Frumka, who was in charge of supplies, and tell her that Dr. Pecker, the He-Halutz doctor, was "dying of hunger" and needed food packages and she would give them to me. Later I told her the truth, that we ate the food ourselves. My comrades put me up to it, and I was tempted even though, morally, it wasn't nice. But they wanted to eat, and, as we know, hunger isn't the best counselor in matters of morality.

In the evenings we would discuss serious matters: what to do? The first question was how to find a way to Eretz Israel. Then the decision was made that Mulka and I would go to Vilna, our hometown, cross the border of Lithuania and, from there, get in touch with Eretz Israel.[35] So I left for Lithuania to pave the way. I had relatives around Vilna, in Troki, which was perhaps four or five kilometers from the Lithuanian border. I had spent a lot of time in Troki, in summers, when I was a boy. There were big, beautiful orchards there, leased by my uncle on my mother's side, Shimon Kotz, the rich man of the town. He was a "State Appointed Rabbi." Now, as when I was in school, I contacted the chairman of Keren Kayemet and consulted with him about how to cross the border to Lithuania.[36] He found a gentile who was supposed to take me across. Vilna was then under Soviet control.

At that time, Mulka and I were the only members of the Central Committee of He-Halutz in the area. On the day I was supposed to cross the border, the Zionist activist in charge of Keren Kayemet came to me

33. Henryk Erlich (1882–1941): Journalist and Bundist leader in Poland. Editor of the party's Yiddish daily newspaper, *Di Folkstzaytung*. Executed by the Soviets in December 1941.

34. Viktor Alter (1890–1941): Bundist leader in Poland; member of the Warsaw city council for twenty years. Executed by the Soviets in December 1941.

35. Prior to the outbreak of the war, Vilna had been part of Poland, close to the Lithuanian border. Between September 17 and October 10, 1939, the city was controlled by the Soviets, who then ceded it to the Lithuanians.

36. Keren Kayemet: Jewish National Fund, the land purchase and development fund of the Zionist Organization, founded December 29, 1901, at the Fifth Zionist Congress.

and said he had heard that Vilna was ceded to Lithuania by the Soviets. So I decided there was no point crossing the border, but it was better to return to Vilna and consult with Mulka about what to do. I went back to Vilna. We decided not to cross: why cross to the Lithuanians if the Lithuanians would come to us? But it took a long time.

After we had been in Vilna for two weeks, the members of the Central Committee began arriving, including Kozibrodski and Perlis.[37] Abraham Gewelber remained in Kowel. I lived with my parents, but I spent all day in the training kibbutz Shahariya on Subocz Street.[38] At one of the meetings, I was informed that, at a meeting of the Central Committee in Kowel, the decision was made that most of the members would go to Vilna, while Yitzhak Zuckerman and David Kozibrodski would return to Kowel to work in the Soviet zone.

The decision was made on the afternoon of September 20. We can determine almost with certainty the day I left Vilna. On September 17, the Soviets crossed the Polish border. A few days before I left, there were rumors of possible pogroms in Vilna upon the Lithuanians' arrival, and our first idea was to establish a self-defense organization. Mulka Barantshuk and I went to consult with the old leader, Dr. Jacob Wygodski, a personage universally admired by the Jews of Vilna, who had also been a member of the Polish Parliament, the *Sejm*, and he encouraged us. Dr. Wygodski was a poor man and was old by that time. It was the first time I had ever been in his home, and I still recall how poor it was, with shabby chairs and peeling walls; but it was a large flat.[39]

After that visit to Wygodski, I returned to my father's house to say goodbye. I didn't know then it was forever.

Let me say a few words here about my family:

My father was a tall man with a small beard, and he held himself erect. I think it was Mordechai Tennenbaum who told me that if you had put a bucket of water on his head, not a single drop would have fallen to the ground. He was an observant Jew, but I suspect that he neglected a prayer every now and then. Aside from Yiddish, he spoke Polish and Russian and knew Hebrew.

---

37. David Kozibrodski: Born in Prusków. Active in He-Halutz and Dror in Vilna; escaped from there to the United States during Soviet control of the city. Immigrated to Israel.

38. A center for He-Halutz members from all over occupied Poland. As one of them said: "Our kibbutz in Vilna, which had a small number of members, began to increase daily . . . and became a kibbutz of 600 members by the time the Lithuanians entered." (Quoted in Arad 1982:15.)

39. Jacob Wygodski: A prominent leader of Vilna Jewry. Head of the Jewish Community Council formed in July 1928. A member of the Judenrat in the ghetto; arrested by the Nazis on August 24, 1941, and died in Lukiszki Prison a few days later.

My grandfather, Rabbi Yohanan Zuckerman, was a rabbi who didn't want to make his living at it. In terms of the Hasid-Misnaged [40] conflict, I'm the child of a mixed marriage. On my father's side, I'm "Ukrainian" from the area of Kiev or from Kiev itself; on my mother's side, I'm a real "Litvak," from a small town in Lithuania. My mother's maiden name was Frenkel.

I was born in Vilna in December 1915, during World War I, when the city was occupied by the Germans and Mother was alone at home. Father had gone with his mother and my two sisters to Moscow (he had relatives there and in Kiev) and was still there when the Germans occupied Vilna. I can only imagine the problems caused by my birth.

How did the "Ukrainian" side meet the "Lithuanian" side? How did Mother and Father meet? I learned the details of that only recently. My aunt, my father's sister, died a year ago in Israel. I had taken care of her when she was ill, and she had always been very fond of me. When she was sick, she told me a lot of things I didn't know.

Apparently, Father had been something of a "hippie" in his youth. His father, Rabbi Yohanan Zuckerman, came from the town of Lebedova where he owned a small flour mill. He was a rabbi and ritual slaughterer; but, as I said, he didn't want to make a living at it and he hated the sight of blood; so he set up a flour mill. My father was his oldest son and Grandfather loved him very much; but one day Father got fed up and disappeared, taking some money without permission. Apparently he went to Russia, where he wandered around. One day, he came to Vilna, hungry and tattered, not knowing where to spend the night. At a bakery, he saw a Jewish Lithuanian girl who had left her native village and had come to the big city of Vilna where she worked for her relatives.

She took the handsome lad under her wing, brought him home, and fed him. Thus began the love that was to produce me. At first, Grandfather refused to come to the wedding—because of the theft and other "favors" his son had done him. But since Father was the only son from his first wife, his second wife made him go to the wedding. Grandfather came to live in Vilna later, and, when I visited home in 1939, he still lived there and was very old, about 90, I think.

In my childhood, the commandment to Honor thy Father and thy Grandfather was the law in our home. When Grandfather came in, everyone would stand up and no one sat down before he did, in a chair Father would clear for him. They loved each other very much, and I too loved Grandfather. On my last visit in 1939, I came home by surprise. Grandfather could still read without glasses, but I didn't yet know that

40. The conflict between the populist Hasidic sects, primarily based in Poland and the Ukraine, and the rationalist Misnagdim faction, centered in Lithuania.

changes had taken place in him. On my way, I had bought a volume of the Talmud for Grandfather from the Rom Printers.[41] The Soviets were in control of Vilna by then. Grandfather came into the dining room and everyone stood up. "What's new, *Dyedushka* [Grandfather, in Russian]?" I called out. And he said: "The French entered Vilna."[42] I knew he was old, but I didn't imagine he had reached such a state. That was the first time I saw a smile on the faces of Father, Mother, and my sister. I was furious: how dare they smile? When Grandfather left after the meal, I exploded. They explained and told me for the first time of the changes in him: he thought "the French have come." And they were used to his eccentricities. He died a natural death at the age of 90-plus, old and senile.

Long before that, some time after I was born, when Father was in Moscow, a fire started in the house when I was alone in my cradle. Mother had begun working for her relatives as a housekeeper. And one of their daughters saved me from the fire. When I came to Israel, I met that woman, who lived in Haifa, and she loved to tell how she rescued me from the fire and how I wet her lap.

Let's go back to that part in my parents' story when Father was in Russia and World War I divided him from Mother, who was in German-occupied Vilna. Homeless after the fire, Mother decided to cross the border to look for her husband. I was the only one with her at the time, since the other three children were with Father. The Germans let her cross the border (apparently they were "different Germans" then).

After the family was united, they returned to Vilna, lived in another house, and began restoring their fortune. That was when I started talking, and what I said amazed the family. I told what we had gone through on the road: my fears, riding in a wagon, and the shooting we heard. I said that Mother held me in her arms, and I wanted Father awfully and he didn't come. That was all true. I remember a wagon covered with a tarpaulin. I recall shots across the border, horses rearing, and Father holding them by the reins, and I wanted Father to come to me. I was born in a war, and we escaped from the Russian Revolution of 1917. The Germans saved us. I was two years old.

Once, when I was five years old, I lay in bed and the *"Hallerczyki"* (the unit of General Haller of the newly created Polish army who was notorious for pogroms against Jews) came looking for Father, but he had run away and they didn't find him. I was terribly scared they would hit me, but they didn't do anything to me. That was during the pogroms, in 1920

41. Rom Printers: Publishing house and printing press famous for its classical editions of the Babylonian Talmud, distributed all over the Jewish Diaspora.
42. Allusion to the vivid memory of Napoleon's sojourn in Vilna in 1812.

[when the Poles took over the city from the Red Army], and the fear of Poles remained engraved on my heart ever after.

From that early period, I remember the big fire when everything burned down; and I remember a flour mill (near Bratslav) and big lakes. I would go there every year, between the ages of eleven and thirteen. I learned to ride horses and I felt like a kind of Taras Bulba, riding on the steppes.[43]

My parents' home was in Vilna, and when I visited there in 1939, that home no longer existed. I hadn't come to my sister's wedding because I didn't have money for the trip. I was a member of the Central Committee of He-Halutz and I didn't want to ask my relatives for money. I didn't have a proper suit either.

My sister bought a big apartment, a two-story house on Ponarska Street, and brought Father and Mother to live there. She and her husband worked hard and strictly observed the commandment to Honor thy Father and Mother. My sister's family lived on the top floor, and everyone else was downstairs, including Grandfather and my widowed sister.

My father was a Zionist, but I don't think he belonged to any Zionist organization, although I think he leaned to Mizrakhi.[44] Our home was a Zionist home. Zalman Kleinstein, a famous Zionist leader in Vilna in the 1920s, was a member of our family. When I was a child, Father made incessant and unsuccessful efforts to immigrate to Eretz Israel. In those years long before my Bar Mitzva, I was promised a Bible as a gift.

I completed seven grades in a religious grammar school, *Ezra*, where Yiddish was the basic language. It was a school run by Mizrakhi, which had an educational system in Poland. Then Father sent me to the Hebrew secular Gymnasium, an aristocratic institution, whose very high tuition posed a heavy financial burden on the family, especially since all four of us children (my brother, my two sisters, and I) were in school at the same time. Almost all the teachers in the Gymnasium were Zionists. Some were adherents of labor Zionist ideals,[45] like Dr. Riger and Dr. Yosef Shuster, who was later a teacher in Ben-Shemen. I was friendly with him (I saw him a lot when I came to Israel).

I was outstanding in my attitude toward Yiddish culture in the Gymnasium. It was not a matter of spoken Yiddish (most students spoke

43. Taras Bulba: A Cossack leader and Ukrainian national hero who perpetrated pogroms against Jews, as described in Gogol's novel of the same name.

44. Mizrakhi: Religious Zionist movement, founded in 1902, whose motto was "The Land of Israel for the People of Israel according to the Torah of Israel." Later renamed the National Religious Party.

45. Eretz Israel Ovedet: A federation of Socialist Zionist parties and various social organizations for material and political support of the Labor Movement in Eretz Israel. Founded in 1930.

Yiddish at home), but of literature: I was perhaps the only one in the
Hebrew Gymnasium who constantly read and kept up with Yiddish
literature. I read a lot—that was my weakness, and because of it, I used
to put off doing my homework and sometimes neglected it altogether so
I could read. I first read Yosef-Haim Brenner[46] when I was in Gymnasium, and read all eight volumes in Hebrew (published by "Stybel"[47]) by
the time I left home. I continued to read both Hebrew and Yiddish
(Scholem Asch,[48] for example). Thus, I came to He-Halutz with a great
love for the Yiddish language and went to Lida[49] for training in a unit
in the Kłosowa work brigade.

When I was active in the League for Workers' Eretz Israel on behalf
of the students, I met with members of He-Halutz and with members of
Po'alei Zion and Ha-Shomer Ha-Tza'ir. In my last two years of school, I
was chairman of the student organization of the Gymnasium and chairman of the League for Workers' Eretz Israel. There I met Dr. M.
Dworzecki[50] and the father of Professor Kolat (Kopelovitsh). I had
friends both in Ha-Shomer Ha-Tza'ir and in Betar, but I myself didn't
belong to any movement. I was a Zionist first of all and also had roots in
the Yiddish language and its literature. I wasn't a member of a party until
I was forced to by the merger of Frayhayt–He-Halutz Ha-Tza'ir. What
kept me out of party affiliation was a group of Po'alei Zion I knew, part
of which was militantly anti-Hebrew and against Zionist realization. Although my world view was close to theirs, and I was far from Z.S. and
Hitahdut,[51] I remained only a member of the general He-Halutz.

I graduated from the Hebrew Gymnasium in 1933, passed the government matriculation examinations, and applied for admission to the
university in Vilna. I also applied to the university in Jerusalem and was
accepted there too. I don't know the meaning of the turn I took—instead
of studying, I joined the He-Halutz training kibbutz on Subocz Street in
Vilna. I think I was the only one in my class who went to He-Halutz. And
I also tried to establish a movement of He-Halutz Ha-Tza'ir, which didn't
exist in Vilna up to then. I didn't have much success, but a small branch

46. Yosef-Haim Brenner (1881–1921): Major Hebrew writer of the Second Aliya. Born
in the Ukraine, lived in Białystok, Warsaw, and London. Immigrated to Eretz Israel in 1909.
Was murdered in the Arab riots in Jaffa on May 2, 1921.

47. Stybel (German: Stiebel): Publishing house founded in 1917 in Moscow by Abraham
Yosef Stybel for the advancement of Hebrew literature, later moved to Warsaw.

48. Sholem Asch: Prominent Yiddish novelist and dramatist. Born in Poland, lived in
the United States during both World Wars. Spent his last years in Bat Yam, Israel.

49. Lida: A small town near Vilna.

50. Dr. Mark Dworzecki: Physician in Vilna, author of the well-known *Jerusalem of
Lithuania in Struggle and Death,* a history of the Vilna Ghetto (in Yiddish), Paris, 1948.

51. Small Zionist Socialist (non-Marxist) parties, which eventually merged with Po'alei
Zion.

was set up. The regional council of He-Halutz for the Vilna district was located in the training kibbutz on Subocz Street. They knew me and, when I came, they drew me into activities in He-Halutz Ha-Tza'ir. My path in He-Halutz was the opposite of the normal one: not from the youth movement to the general He-Halutz, but vice-versa.

I don't remember how I got to the kibbutz on Subocz Street the first time; but I do remember a visit to Krupnicza 9, where Ha-Shomer Ha-Tza'ir had their club. It was a group of intellectuals, and they had a big branch. Ze'ev (Velvl) Shapiro, a member of the district council, was the one who brought me to He-Halutz. I joined the student group as "an unaffiliated Halutz." I was seventeen and a half at the time, in 1933–1934, and He-Halutz had a very nice branch in Vilna.

I remember May Day 1934 in Vilna: a thousand Halutzim paraded through the city. That year, I was elected secretary of He-Halutz in Vilna; Ze'ev (Velvl) Shapiro and Ruvke Tshirlin were on the council; and for a time, Yafa Broide, a Shaliah from Eretz Israel, also worked in the training program on Subocz. I was also appointed to the district council of He-Halutz at that time, and I started visiting small towns around Vilna, participating in symposia and such. At that period, Moshe Carmel[52] was a Shaliah to He-Halutz Ha-Tza'ir in Poland. One winter day, we went together to lecture at a symposium. Many years later, Moshe told me he was amazed to hear a boy from the Diaspora lecture on Hebrew literature, on Brenner and Berditshevski.[53]

I already mentioned coming to Warsaw in 1936. I was sent to work in He-Halutz Ha-Tza'ir and I was put on the Central Committee of the Movement. Then I moved to Grochów, as I said, and was sent from there for operations in the He-Halutz Ha-Tza'ir movement. We called that activity "winning the educated youth" for He-Halutz Ha-Tza'ir, which previously consisted mostly of uneducated youth. The first attempt was in Kowel, where I met Zvi Melnitzer (Netzer), Sheindl Schwartz,[54] and the whole Kowel group. That was the first time we penetrated the circles of young Jewish intelligentsia. In Kowel, the students' parents, led by Zvi Melnitzer's father, made a fuss. Melnitzer was a big shot, with a typical

52. Moshe Carmel was later a general in the Israeli army.
53. Micha Yosef Berditshevski (1865–1921): Hebrew writer and thinker. One of the most seminal figures in modern Hebrew literature and Jewish thought, embodying the difficult ambivalence between traditional Judaism and European culture.
54. Sheindl Schwartz: Born in Kowel. Active in the He-Halutz Ha-Tza'ir; joined the Grochów kibbutz in June 1938. One of the founders of the Dror underground in Nazi-occupied Kowel. Murdered by the Germans at the age of twenty-three. One of four signers (with Leah Fish, Rachel Fogelman, and David Eisenberg) of the inscription on the synagogue wall in Kowel.

rich man's house. Sheindl Schwartz was also from the "Kowel aristocracy." I would come to the Gymnasium to talk with the students and, one day, the students in the junior and senior classes stopped doing homework. So the teachers decided to ban me from the Gymnasium and from working with the students. In response, the students declared a strike and stopped studying, forcing the Gymnasium to allow me back, but on condition that I work in the Gymnasium only in the presence of a teacher. I remember one teacher of literature who sat there while I lectured on Brenner and "At the Railroad Station" by David Bergelson.[55] He was amazed, shook my hand, and after that, no longer came to class during my discussions. The group I worked with was a very good group and later filled important functions in the Movement.

That was my early Kowel period, and there is a sequel to the tale. I said that, in 1939, in Vilna, the comrades decided that I and David Kozibrodski, who was about to go to Kowel, had to go to the Soviet zone because of the transfer of Vilna to the government of Lithuania. Since it was underground activity, young counselors had to be sent to Kowel and not Movement veterans, who were widely known. I didn't accept this argument, since although I was young I was already known in Poland, especially in Polesie and Wołyń, where I had worked in the youth movement and participated in seminars; I had worked in Kowel, Luck, and Ostrog. However, I did accept the argument that I had to do this work, because I was one of the young people.

That hasty departure from Vilna to Kowel haunted me for a long time. I didn't know it would be the last time I would see my parents and our home. Father said he didn't understand the point of my trip this time. He would have understood if I had gone closer to Eretz Israel. But to go farther away! I couldn't tell him I was going to do clandestine work. I shall never forget the picture: Mother didn't know anything. I went into the kitchen, came from behind her, picked her up, kissed her, and told her I was leaving. She started weeping. There was an atmosphere of pogrom in the streets, so I tried to convince Father not to accompany me. I begged but he wouldn't yield. It was night and he accompanied me to the train. I still imagine I hear the echo of his footsteps. There were few people in the street. This was how I left.

55. David Bergelson (1884–1952): Major Russian Yiddish writer; arrested in 1949 by the Stalinist regime and executed in August 1952.

TWO

Underground in the Soviet Zone

[The Hebrew language was forbidden in the Soviet Union on the grounds that it was a "clerical language," and Zionism was considered an anti-Soviet activity. Zuckerman goes from the still-free state of Lithuania to organize the Frayhayt (Dror) underground in the Soviet zone of occupation.]

The next day, I arrived in Kowel. There were only a few hours between the committee's decision and my departure from Vilna. I decided that the faster I went the safer it would be, and I left without David Kozibrodski. I waited for David a few days, but he didn't come. Later, after the war, friends told me he had left Warsaw and had gone everywhere, even Kowel, didn't find a single one of us, and returned to Vilna. I doubt that he was in Kowel. I don't think he left Vilna. (Afterward, he managed to get out to safety.)

Later on, Yudke and Zivia arrived and we started going to see what was happening in the small towns, what effect the Russians were having; I was known everywhere, since my students were there. I went to Afiszy and to Ostrog—wherever I could go to get a picture of the situation. I decided not to work with adults but with young people. There were cases of members leaving the Movement to join the Communists; even teachers in Hebrew schools forgot their learning overnight. But there were no denunciations. The fact is that I continued working. But they did warn me. I thought we should start all over with a younger, more ideological generation, who were more willing to sacrifice, that we should start all over and not endanger the generation of activists I knew.

There was one person who deserted us and did outrageous things. At a certain period, this person worked on Gęsia Street. His name was Gele; he showed up at the end of the war, in 1945, in Warsaw; but I didn't see him then. At the He-Halutz Central Committee, at Gęsia 14, he worked in provisions and lived at Dzielna 34. Later I heard harsh things about him.

Some people worked in the Soviet militia. But we didn't hear of deserters from our ideological cadres, those who attended our seminars.

There were some from Ha-Shomer Ha-Tza'ir, where there was a serious collapse.[1] Apparently, our education innoculated against such desertion more than theirs.

Nevertheless, not everyone was immune and some succumbed to social demands and opportunism: this happened even before we knew the hardships we faced. One of the first things I discovered was that Zionism had begun to be outlawed. At that time, our training kibbutzim in both Kowel and Białystok were still legal, and there was some Russian activity to persuade them to become Communist, without coercion. I had no experience in underground work, except for all the literature I had read—memoirs of revolutionaries, which were not so appropriate for this new situation. I didn't know where to start.

Zivia returned from a meeting with the Shlikhim who were stuck in Husiacin on the border. I met her afterward, and she told me explicitly that our most important Shaliah made her swear that we wouldn't set up an underground in the Soviet Union since it might end badly; but, of course, we were deaf to that and decided to act. We didn't have any illusions that we could act legally for long; we knew that that wouldn't go on for more than a few months. Dr. Meir Pecker was the only one who tended to believe in those delusions. He was the only one left of the Central Committee of Po'alei Zion–Z.S., and he refused to leave for Vilna immediately, like the others. We saw how Polish prisoners were accompanied by armed patrols and dogs; and I would say to myself: "Some day, they'll probably lead me away like that, too." I had no delusions. I decided to start by building the Movement. I was the oldest of the young comrades left there, and I had to set up the educational movement. Oscar Hendler and Edek Golowner were there, along with Zivia, and Nehemia Gross who was younger. Zvi Mersik was also there, but he wasn't active.[2] Even if he had wanted to be active, I wouldn't have called on him—not because I didn't trust him but because his emotional makeup didn't fit such revolutionary times. He had deep cultural roots, was too delicate and fragile. There was also Sheindl Schwartz, whom I was once in love with and who had been my student. I started organizing the youth from all over. Dov Berger and others were in Luck and some were in Kowel.[3] They would show up after traveling around in trains with no windows in the cold

1. Though a Zionist Pioneer movement, Ha-Shomer Ha-Tza'ir was far to the left, and at various periods, some of its members switched to Communism.
2. Zvi Mersik (1916–1943): Born in Mielnica, near Kowel; joined the Halutz Ha-Tza'ir at the age of fourteen. Went to Białystok in 1942, where, with Mordechai Tennenbaum, he set up the Dror Secret Archives. Died of typhus in January 1943.
3. Dov Berger: One of the founders of the Dror underground in the Soviet zone. He was conscripted into the Red Army and died in battle.

Polish autumn. Sometimes, when I set out, I didn't know if or when I would get someplace.

One day, I was lying on the sofa in my room, and one of our young people came and said he couldn't bear this work and couldn't stand this tension. I told him: I don't care if you lie on the sofa and spit at the ceiling, that doesn't interest me in the least; but the work has to be done! From that work emerged a coterie of young people who had been in the youth groups of the Movement.

Sheindl Schwartz was one of the girls I trusted. She was my first courier. She got paper for the first newspaper, and I managed to edit six issues of it. At first it wasn't called *Dror,* but I don't even remember the name. *Dror* (Hebrew for *Frayhayt,* Freedom) was the name later on. At great risk, we sent issues to Vilna to be sent to Eretz Israel for preservation. Our comrades had a sense of history, but I don't know if the issues were received there or in Eretz Israel.

Our first unity meeting with Ha-Shomer Ha-Tza'ir was in Rowno, with two of their members, Yosef Kaplan and Shaike Weiner.[4] I proposed setting up a unified underground youth movement or else maximum collaboration. I said: if we can set up an underground movement that would maintain a relationship to Eretz Israel and its members would sing a Hebrew song—that's enough for us. Moreover, the Movement would not be anti-Communist; if it were Zionist, Halutz, that was good enough for me; more than that I didn't ask. I was willing to accept such unity. I had decided this on my own, since everyone else was traveling around and we didn't meet. Only later, in Lwów, did we start organizing as a Central Committee.

At first, Ha-Shomer Ha-Tza'ir answered my proposal by saying that they had to consult; then they said no. So we started organizing as a Frayhayt Central Committee. We did some work in education and tried to set up a framework for young people in the training kibbutzim. We instructed the members of the branches not to stay where they were, but to leave for Vilna or Romania and they obeyed. The idea was that anyone who wasn't necessary for work in a place should leave. There were some attempts to go to Romania, but first of all they set out for Vilna. Because of the responsibility involved with this, I couldn't set up an underground movement with sixteen-year-olds.

4. Yosef Kaplan (1913–1942): Born in Kalisz. Prominent in He-Halutz and Ha-Shomer Ha-Tza'ir. One of the founders and first commanders of the ZOB. Arrested by the Gestapo and killed on September 11, 1942. Shaike Weiner (1912–1979): At the start of the war, he was in the Halutz center in Vilna. Member of the first steering committee of Ha-Shomer Ha-Tza'ir in the Warsaw Ghetto. Active in the underground in the Soviet zone. Immigrated to Eretz Israel in 1941. Was the first Shaliah of Ha-Kibbutz Ha-Artzi to Poland after the war.

Yudke Helman, Zivia, and Oskar Hendler were with me; Edek Golowner was at the Romanian border. Nehemia Gross was sent to Lida for activities beyond the Lithuanian border. Mulka Barantshuk and Yitzhak Perlis were in Vilna. The last one to leave for Vilna was Avreml Gewelber. Very few of us were left. At that time, I was the only adult leader in the youth movement. I had to start gathering young members, establishing and building; I considered this an extraordinarily important mission. Others did important work at the borders. Within a few months, we set up a Central Committee, a general headquarters, which was in fact responsible for everything—for escapes beyond the borders and for the youth movement; it was responsible for carrying out decisions.

In Kowel and Luck, before January 1940, we managed to print one or two issues of our newspaper, thanks to Sheindl Schwartz who supplied the paper—and I don't know where she got it. One day in Kowel she told me that there were rumors that the authorities knew about my activity, and so I had to get out of there. So I left and went to Luck where I stayed with a Jew whose sister I knew in Łódz. He gave me a room where I lived until I left for Lwów. That man visited me in Israel about ten years ago, at Kibbutz Lohamei Ha-Getaot. I was at home, recuperating from a heart attack; he showed up and I recognized him immediately. At that time, he told me he remembered that I would go to sleep alone, and, in the morning, he would see ten people jumping out the window and he pretended not to know. I was such a "great conspirer" that my room was famous and people would come and go. I could easily have been captured. In time, I learned that you didn't behave like that.

One day, Dov Berger came to warn me to stop my activity and get out of Luck. The source of the warning was one Ochs, a Communist leader in Luck and mayor of the city; he had a position in Poland after the war, too. This Ochs had a brother in He-Halutz and he asked him to warn me before they arrested me. It turns out that that Communist saved me from prison. After the war, he returned to Poland from Russia and played a central role in propaganda in Poland.

I left Luck on December 25, 1939, and didn't return to live there. I remember that trip: a creeping train, snow falling outside. Dark. I found a seat. My boots hurt and I took them off. I was tired from the long trip. Some time later, I stood up to look out the window. Next to me stood a young man in a Russian fur hat. Suddenly the man started speaking Russian to me. My sister and I had learned Russian in school, but I understood only a few words. I said, "I don't understand," or something like that, and he asked if I was Polish. I said no. And he asked: "*Yevrei?* (Jew?)," and I said yes. He said: "*Ya tozhe yevrei.* (I'm also a Jew.)" I asked him if he spoke Yiddish and he replied in broken Yiddish. I said to him: "*Ayer yidish shlept zikh vi a tsug.* (Your Yiddish crawls like this train.)" And he said: "But I remember the names: Bialik, Tshernikhovski, Shneur."[5] "From where?" I asked. From his father's library, he said. I didn't know who the man was and that worried me. As we neared Lwów, he came to me, shook my hand, and said: "Remember December 25, we'll meet again. . . ."[6]

That was an extraordinary event for me. I was so excited I told the story to Yudke and other friends, who were also excited: an ember was still stirring in the Soviet Union! We started dreaming about finding a way to get in touch with the Jews there.

I reached Lwów, the third place in my underground wanderings, after Kowel and Luck. We lived in a room (on Rozodowski Street) we rented from an old woman. Yudke and I slept in a double bed, and I finally had somebody to talk to. I was never registered anywhere as a tenant. I would come late and give the gatekeeper some hush-money, and my rule was not to show my face. We knew that gatekeepers, barbers, and such are the first to denounce you to the authorities. But this guy had no interest in turning me in since he profited a bit from me, and it was better for me not to be registered.

I had only school documents. First, I asked all the activists to spread the rumor that Yitzhak Zuckerman had left the Movement and was at the university. In fact, the news of my "treason" came back to me later. I created the image of a man with no connection with the Movement, and I began acting increasingly through contacts. If I could avoid any trip, I didn't travel. I withdrew.

In Lwów, I was assisted in the underground work and in printing the newspaper by two girls who might have helped me without knowing it. And by Edek Golowner's father. They all helped me get paper and set up a primitive printing press.

Edek's father had two sons; one was a Communist and Edek was a Zionist. Under Polish rule, the Communist had been in jail and the father provided him with what he needed. Now the Communist son rose to power, and Edek was in distress and his father helped him, sometimes

5. Haim Nakhman Bialik (1873–1934); Shaul Tshernikhovski (1875–1943); Zalman Schneur (1887–1959): Considered the greatest figures of modern Hebrew poetry.

6. Yudke Helman, who was in close contact with Zuckerman in those days and shared a room with him in Lwów, notes that the date December 25, 1939, which Zuckerman mentions twice, cannot be the date Zuckerman left Luck under the conditions he mentions here (after Ochs's warning, etc.), since, to the best of Helman's knowledge, Zuckerman reached Lwów from Luck earlier. This is supported by Zuckerman himself, who says that, after he came to Lwów, there were a few more weeks in December, which were used to shape the Movement and to prepare for the convention in Lwów he discusses at length. Hence he apparently left Luck earlier in December, and the trip described as occurring on December 25 took place *after* he had moved to Lwów and would occasionally travel to branches of Dror underground in the Soviet zone.

without the other son knowing. So, "things were topsy-turvy" and, after
Edek was arrested, his father would send him packages. I avoided meeting the father and he didn't know me. I had already learned not to meet
with people unnecessarily, not to appear in public in restaurants and
public places.

I had the money I had received when it was distributed on the way from
Mińsk-Mazowiecki. I had taken it to Vilna when we decided to turn it over
to me for financing the underground. I myself never was a treasurer. I
gave all the money to Oskar and would take what I needed.

Oskar lived in an apartment at Dunin-Borkowski Street 4, and I would
come to him every single day. We liked the place a lot. Oskar would make
sandwiches (tiny ones) and give us wine; he had enough to last a week.
His landlord had a crazy daughter, and they lived in the outskirts of the
city. Altogether, a good underground setup.

We decided at that time to call a meeting for December 31, 1939,
disguised as a New Year's Eve party, to reorganize the Movement underground. The participants were Dov Berger, Rachel Fogelman,[7]
Sheindl Schwartz, Oskar Hendler, Nehemia Gross, Leah Fisch,[8] Hershel
Plotnitzki,[9] Yudke Helman, Zivia Lubetkin, Edek Golowner.[10] Because
our address in Lwów was secret, we decided that those who attended the
assembly would gather at a café, and, from there, they would be taken to
the meeting. Two days before the conference, Zivia, Oskar Hendler, and
Edek were in Oskar's apartment one night when Soviet police suddenly
appeared. There was an interrogation, but they emerged from it safely.
This led to a quarrel between Oskar and me. He claimed that the police
came because of a denunciation; I argued that if there had been a
denunciation, they would have come two days later, during the confer-

7. Rachel Fogelman: Born in Lachowicz. One of the founders of the Dror underground
in the Soviet zone and of the Jewish resistance movement under the Nazis. Arrested by the
Germans at the age of twenty-six. Her name was engraved with three others (Sheindl
Schwartz, Leah Fisch, and David Eisenberg) on the wall of the synagogue in Kowel under
a Hebrew inscription: "Greetings from the members of the group of Halutzim who are going
to die. We kept faith with our ideals to the end. Avenge our blood." The details of their
deaths are unknown.

8. Leah Fisch: Born in Horochów, Wołyń. Active in Dror underground in the eastern
region. Under the Nazis, she attempted to establish a partisan base in the Kowel area.
Captured by the Germans at the age of twenty-four.

9. Hershel Plotnitzki: Born in Pinsk. Younger brother of Frumka and Hancia. One of
the founders of the Dror underground in the Soviet zone; organized movement activities
in Polesie region. Murdered by the Germans at the age of twenty-two.

10. According to Zivia Lubetkin (1981) and Zuckerman (Institute for Contemporary
Judaism 14/59), Abraham Leibowicz (Laban), Zvi Mersik, Nesha Zucker, and Yakov Zvi-
dovitsh also attended the convention. Along with Zuckerman and Yudke Helman, there
were fifteen people altogether at that meeting, including a few young people and new
members.

ence. I thought the visit was accidental. He insisted and so did I. In the argument, I didn't mince any words (later I regretted my words) and told him: "The line between caution and cowardice is very thin." He was deeply offended. I said such things because I was afraid they would call off the conference. And I also thought it stupid for the Soviets to warn us in advance. Nevertheless, the conference could not be postponed, since it was set for New Year's Eve of 1940 when people get together and drink, so we could sit together, sing, talk, and discuss, even aloud. If we had put off the conference, we would have had to look for another place to hold it, since we knew the Soviets were experts in such things and we might be caught. We were "at odds" for a long time, and I had to work very hard to appease Oskar. He was a sensitive lad and I behaved coarsely. I loved Oskar. If I had been a drinking man in those days, I would have had a drink with him and put an end to the quarrel. He loved liqueurs; he had twenty bottles. There was some man there with two sons, refugees from Germany, and to help them, Oskar would buy wine from them and put the bottles under his bed; so dozens of bottles were piled up there.

The convention lasted a night and a day and was a great success. The speakers included Oskar Hendler, Edek Golowner, Yudke Helman, and myself. The first issue of the convention was to set a path—what to do?—including the fundamental aspect of our relation to the Soviet Union, and education for Eretz Israel. There were no minutes but, a year later, in an issue of *Dror* I edited in Warsaw,[11] an article was published titled "*A yor nokh der lemberger conferentz.* (A Year After the Lwów Conference.)" Among other things, I wrote about our relations with the Soviet Union and its traditional position on the Jewish question, a position we disagreed with completely. And, in fact, we also differed with Ha-Shomer Ha-Tza'ir about this. For some reason, they believed in a "Marxist rapprochement" with the Soviet Union, which would exist by dint of a certain adaptation of the Halutz movement, especially Ha-Shomer Ha-Tza'ir, to certain lines in the Soviet ideology. That was reminiscent of the delusion once held by Po'alei Zion Left who believed it was possible to integrate into the Soviet regime without giving up Zionism. We however posed this issue very sharply so there wouldn't be any delusions. We thought we should not seek a common language, for Moscow would certainly not go along with that, since the Zionist solution is not the Communist solution. In our opinion, there could be no concessions on this issue.

In Lwów, I happened to meet again with the members of Ha-Shomer Ha-Tza'ir who also set up an underground organization in the Soviet zone. They also came from Vilna, which is where they had gone from Rowno. I have already told about my first meeting with the members of

11. *Dror* 5 (9), January-February 1941.

Ha-Shomer Ha-Tza'ir in Rowno. Later, there were many more meetings in Lwów. Negotiations with them didn't result in anything. When our Central Committee was in Kowel, theirs was in Rowno, where they had a training kibbutz. They had more faith in the Soviet regime. They believed you could convince Moscow. We didn't. We didn't intend to prove our revolutionary nature to the regime, but we did want to emphasize what distinguished the youth we wanted to save for Eretz Israel. This was expressed in simple things: Hebrew, the tie to the land of Israel, self-realization.[12] Ha-Shomer Ha-Tza'ir, however, stressed ideological principles. Our response to the Soviet regime was a positive attitude to its ideals as a way of socialist realization, but strong disagreement on the solution of the Jewish issue. We didn't yet know the full meaning of the dictatorship in the Soviet Union and thought it was a dictatorship of the proletariat. But there were already heretics among us who claimed that it wasn't a dictatorship *of* the proletariat but *over* the proletariat. We in the Movement generally weren't interested in such questions, but some of the conference in Lwów was devoted to the question of our attitude toward the Soviet Union.

In Lwów, the capital of eastern Galicia, we also met and negotiated with the members of Akiba and Gordonia, movements which had once been strong in Galicia and now were very weak. Only a few members were left and those movements were falling apart.

Yosef Rondstein was the central person in Akiba at that time, its Shaliah to Poland. He told me explicitly at our meeting that he hadn't agreed before the war, and didn't agree now, with the Frayhayt–He-Halutz Ha-Tza'ir platform, since Akiba was neither Marxist nor Borokhovist, and they had a different political and educational system.[13] But, if the choice was between abandoning the young people to the Soviet regime or saving them for Zionism, he chose the second option. Neither Akiba nor Gordonia was strong enough to set up its own movement. Akiba members were instructed to join Frayhayt. We took them in Warsaw, too. It wasn't a big movement, but a very good one. (Don't confuse Akiba with Bnai Akiba.[14] Akiba was part of He-Halutz. It wasn't a big movement, and it wasn't religious, but it did preserve the Jewish tradition; it wasn't affiliated with any party. It had a general Zionist education, was very liberal, close to the Labor Movement, didn't go with the Ha-No'ar Ha-Tzoni, which wasn't part of He-Halutz.)

12. Self-realization: Personally implementing the goals of Halutz Zionism through *Aliya* and working the land in a communal framework.

13. Ber Borokhov (1881–1917): Socialist Zionist leader and theoretician; influenced the Jewish labor movement with concepts of the organic unity between scientific socialism and Jewish nationalism.

14. A religious youth movement.

The members of Akiba were very pleasant. I wasn't a party man either, not a fanatic on the subject. For me, all those debates—whether to call it "Frayhayt–He-Halutz Ha-Tza'ir" or "He-Halutz Ha-Tza'ir–Frayhayt"— were like medieval scholastic debates. I didn't care. I was freer and more open in this matter than other members. One of the things I suggested at that conference was that we stop being called Frayhayt–He-Halutz Ha-Tza'ir. My reason was very simple: when one of our agents came to a town, by the time he'd managed to say the name "Frayhayt–He-Halutz Ha-Tza'ir"—he'd be arrested. I proposed the name "Dror" for everyday use; and for formal occasions, the letters HNHS: Histadrut Noar Halutzit Socialistit–Dror. Our newspaper would also be called Dror. At that conference, it was decided that the Movement would be called Dror. I later brought that name with me from the Russian to the German zone.

The Gordonia movement went through the same process as Akiba. Their leadership had also been depleted. Wherever they had members they tried to find a way to survive. We suggested they join us and they did.

Once again I have to deny the rumor that spread after the war that there was a unification between Dror, Akiba, and Gordonia. There was no unification. Akiba and Gordonia were a part of the Movement that we absorbed without any difficulty because, in those days, we weren't interested in Marxism or Borokhovism; we simply wanted to preserve the ember. For us, that was the essential thing. And I want to emphasize that the "unity" was valid only in the Soviet occupation zone.

But, let's go back to the conference in Lwów and its results.[15] There was a farewell party that evening. Zivia left for Warsaw, following a decision made previously, before Vilna (it was after Hancia Plotnitzka came from the German zone with an explicit demand from Frumka that only Zivia should come help her). So, we decided that Zivia would go to Warsaw and join Frumka who had gone to Warsaw as soon as the siege was lifted, after the city fell to the Germans (September 27, 1939). She was sent to check on what was happening. We were sure the Movement still existed, and we knew that members of the kibbutzim in western Poland who hadn't reached the Soviet zone were still there (the whole command cadre went east). Frumka assumed that mission even before the Lwów Conference, then Hancia came from Łódz asking Zivia to come help Frumka. Our policy was not to reinforce any of the activities unless

15. In his testimony in the publication of the Institute of Contemporary Jewry 19 (59), Zuckerman defined the Lwów Conference as "a meeting that laid the ideological foundation for continuing action as much as possible, imposed historic responsibility, encouraged agents and gave them courage, nourished and supported the participants for a long time after the conference. The conference is remembered in our movement as an historic meeting which laid the foundation for the underground movement."

they asked for it. Frumka sent people from Warsaw across the border and the Soviet zone to Vilna, and agents came and told us what was happening in Warsaw. We knew the situation.

Frumka was the first to go to the German occupation zone and was followed by Tosia Altman of Ha-Shomer Ha-Tza'ir,[16] while we worked in the Soviet zone setting up the young underground. We also organized whomever we could to send them to the border to Vilna in independent Lithuania. We also tried to break through to Romania but we didn't succeed in that.

At that Lwów Conference we parted, as I said, from Zivia, who left the next day, January 1, 1940, but she stayed with us till the evening. When the meeting was over, she said goodbye and went west through Białystok. She left with the clear knowledge that she had witnessed the historical conference of the Movement and she knew that there was Dror, and a division into districts, and that everyone was responsible for his own place: someone was responsible for Białystok and the surrounding area, someone for Galicia and Wołyń. As I recall, we divided the country into five districts so people would be independent and would set up youth groups.[17]

We of the Central Committee started our visits to the district centers and cells. Later, I stopped visiting the small towns and would appear only occasionally in Białystok or some other place to meet people. It was the great ambition, perhaps even the great insolence of young people to make a "revolution" in the country of revolution. There were many people from many places in the Movement. Nourishment came from the small towns of Wołyń and we were strong in and around Białystok. Hershel Plotnitzki lived in Pinsk; he was a courier and set up an illegal organization in the schools.[18] Activity and publicity were in Yiddish. There were student cells in the schools and an organization headed by the "five" of

16. Tosia Altman: Born in Włocławek. One of the founders of Ha-Shomer Ha-Tza'ir in the Soviet zone and leader of its underground in the German occupied territory. A member of the ZOB in Warsaw on the Aryan side, she was trapped in the ghetto during the April uprising. She escaped through the sewers to the Aryan side, was badly burned in the fire in the celluloid factory (see below). Captured by the Germans and tortured to death at the age of twenty-five.

17. Rachel Fogelman and Dov Berger were in Białystok. Edek Golowner—in Wołyń. Hershel Plotnitski in Polesie (stayed in Pinsk). Yudke moved between Kowel and Lwów and sometimes also visited Kolomea. Nehemia Gross was in Lida during the crisis, in the Lithuanian area. Oskar Hendler was in Lwów. Leibowicz (Laban) was our man in Kraków. All those assisted in the activity, although their main activity was searching for a breach in the Lithuanian and Romanian borders. (From the protocol of the testimony in the Institute of Contemporary Jewry.)

18. The underground organization was built on the principle of "fives," small cells concentrated in the hands of the person responsible for the city or town.

the district council. The students would put their hands in their coat pocket and take out a proclamation. This is exactly what the Communists had done under the Polish regime (before 1939). The Communists knew we existed and were active. So, one day, they started arresting us.

I already said that I intentionally gave myself a bad name, but I think that that was good. People who knew me treated me like a leper; they saw a member of the Central Committee of He-Halutz who left everything and didn't go to Vilna. There had to be some explanation for this. Even back in Vilna, they began to say that I was steeped in the [Communist] "World of Tomorrow," that I had gone away, was studying at the university in Lwów, and didn't want to know anything about the Movement. Of course all that reached me. In my heart of hearts, it hurt me a little that people were so quick to believe. I had a great desire for life. I loved nothing more than life. I was twenty-four years old, in the prime of life. But I had no illusions. I was almost sure they'd catch me one day. My heart was heavy and I lived in uncertainty. Sober consideration said we would go to Siberia. But, in comparison to the information we got from Warsaw, we were really living in paradise! I was a free man. I could move around. In this period anyway. Whereas Warsaw under the Nazis scared me to death. I felt free from the blows, the persecution of Warsaw. We didn't know that, at some distance, there was a concentration camp and hangings and Siberia. We still thought the Soviet regime was a liberating regime. But there were Communists who knew Jewish society and did denounce us. In the cities and towns, this was the first time in their lives they could be policemen. Moreover, there were a lot of Jewish Communists, not organized in a party, who did make trouble. Anyone who remained loyal to Zionism or the Halutz movement had to flee from his small town to other places. Yitzhak Perlis knew someone in his town who warned him to get out. And he did. Zvi Melnitzer (Netzer) was in Vilna at that time. He was sent on an errand from Vilna to the Russian side and was supposed to come to me; but on the way they caught him and one of the things they found on him was a compass. They took him straight to prison and from there to Russia, thus ending his activity after he had organized a few groups. He was arrested in December and didn't participate in the Lwów Conference. He was a wonderful fellow. He was carrying a letter and, when he was captured, he ate the letter without even knowing what was in it.

The Central Committee of He-Halutz concentrated on sending people to Vilna from the German and Soviet occupation zones, searching for ways to the south, to Romania. I include Ha-Shomer Ha-Tza'ir in this as well as the Gordonia representative who was operating in conjunction with us within the general He-Halutz framework. The youth movements were different and their activities were separate.

There were no training kibbutzim in the Soviet zone. The kibbutzim in Białystok, Kowel, Luck, Rowno, Pinsk, and Baranowicz existed for only a few weeks. There was Communist pressure on the kibbutzim: their system was first to use the carrot and—only later—the stick. On the one hand, we took the members of the kibbutzim out of the Russian zone and transferred them to Vilna, since we didn't believe the kibbutzim had a future in the Soviet zone. On the other hand, we operated among the young generation and set up the new youth movement.

The name *kibbutzim* was no longer as respectable as it had been. The last time I visited Białystok, two weeks before Passover, I met members who didn't brag about being in a kibbutz; everyone knew there was no future for the kibbutz, the commune, in the Soviet regime. A few people were left in the kibbutz in Kowel; there were some sewing machines there, and the property had to be guarded. We sent all those people to Vilna; only a few of them remained with their parents in the Russian occupied zone.

We didn't unite with Ha-Shomer Ha-Tza'ir, as I said. In Lwów, we had ideological debates. I can't say that there were any in Rowno. There, they really were still stunned and didn't know what to do. I'm not bragging if I say that we were the first to stand the educational movement on its feet. And this influenced others, too. I don't recall the circumstances of my meeting with Rudstein, whether he looked for me or I found him. And it's really important for me to know because, if he found me, that proves I was a poor underground man. I know I had a lot to learn about conspiratorial methods. And we did learn a little over the years. But anyway, in the dark and fog that enshrouded us, we found a place to meet; later, we tried to get to wherever there were branches of Akiba and Gordonia; I knew they weren't strong enough for operations and that they didn't have people. But I can't testify to anything after I left the Soviet zone.

At that time, I went deeper underground and met less with the cells. I would come to the Central Committee, to the districts, to our top staffs, in Białystok and Kowel, but I wouldn't come to small towns like Wyszi-nowka, for example.[19] In the early days, as I went to places, I was careful not to let some renegade turn me in. Then I stopped traveling altogether. But because of my activity in recent years in the educational movement in Wołyń and Polesie, I maintained contact with the guides and the students of the last course in Klebań. Thus, I didn't have to respond to the issue of our attitude toward the Soviet Union. But, as I said, our attitude was positive. I'm sure that, if I had known in 1940 what I knew in the 1950s, my attitude would have been different. We simply lacked information.

19. A town in the Białystok district; once a branch of He-Halutz Ha-Tza'ir existed there.

Henceforth, I stayed in Lwów, would go visiting for a week or ten days, and return to Lwów. On these trips, I always bribed someone to have a reserved seat on the train, and I was never without a seat. Sometimes, I even traveled in a sleeping compartment. The train workers everywhere would help. We would pay some man and get a ticket. Interestingly, the cars were mostly empty, but they would say there were no tickets. But for a bribe, you could get anything, even a ticket in a sleeping compartment. The Russian railroad workers could easily be convinced with a bribe. That was one of the astounding and disgusting things. Never mind the Poles, who sold tickets on the side because they weren't loyal to the regime; but it was amazing that, even from the Russians, you could get a ticket to anywhere for a bribe. When I returned to Lwów, I would bring books for the library. I bought maybe five to six hundred books, since books were cheap. This was how I got to know Soviet Yiddish literature. One of the books I came across was Shmuel Halkin's drama *Bar-Kokhba*.[20] The difference between Tshernikhovski's *Bar-Kokhba* and Halkin's *Bar-Kokhba* was considerable; Halkin emphasized the social struggle, while not ignoring the national struggle of the Jewish people. What did we do? We sent people to buy dozens of copies of the book for the cells of the Movement. We didn't have books in Hebrew, but we found meaning in Halkin's *Bar-Kokhba*. Later on there wasn't much literature like that on national themes published in the Soviet Union, whereas during the war, it was allowed. That was in 1940. This was the period when they were somewhat contemptuous of Jewish history and scorned the Jewish ethnic lifestyle. And it was precisely this play, praising and glorifying the Jewish past, that we liked. And of course, there is also value to the social aspects and the struggles.

In those days, I read a lot. I remember having an antipathy for Itsik Fefer.[21] I would buy books for pennies, practically nothing. Of course, I can tell more about myself than about others, but until I left Lwów, I seemed to be the only one on the Central Committee concerned with the educational movement. The other members were scattered in various places. Dov Berger was with us and so was Rachel Fogelman, who stayed in Białystok. Zvi Mersik moved to Vilna. At that time, they were busy organizing border crossings.

Nehemia Gross worked for He-Halutz (not Dror) as coordinator for sending people from the Soviet zone to Vilna. Edek Golowner worked for He-Halutz on the Romanian border. Yudke Helman participated in

20. Shmuel Halkin (1897–1960): Yiddish poet in the Soviet Union. Exiled to Siberia (1949–1955). Rehabilitated in 1958.
21. Itsik Fefer (1900–1952): Born in Shpola. Prominent Soviet Yiddish poet, arrested in 1948 and executed by Stalin.

meetings. Oskar Hendler coordinated all activities and was also the treasurer. He had a very comfortable apartment and all our meetings were
held there. That period is described in Nehemia Gross's memoirs, as is
the period of his arrest, until he returned to Łódz in 1945. At our
conference in Lwów (at the end of December 1939, in the dead of winter),
he asked permission to go to Vilna to visit, see, and return. We authorized
his trip to Vilna. On the way, he fell into the hands of the Soviets, after
he himself had sent dozens of people who got through.

Edek was fearful because of our failures on the Romanian border,
since we managed to get only very few people across. Every week brought
more failures. The Romanian border was being sealed off relatively early.
You could only get to Vilna somehow. Shmuel Brider was the first to be
captured at the Romanian border.[22] When I was sent to Vilna, he was sent
to Romania. Very few of our people or of Ha-Shomer Ha-Tza'ir ever
made it to Romania. We learned of Brider's fate later from one of the
newspapers. He was killed in the Soviet Polish army, in 1945, in Prussia;
in the same newspaper where his obituary appeared, there was a special
mention of Shmuel Brider's heroism. I immediately wrote to the staff of
the Polish army, requesting details, but I didn't get any answer. How he
got to the Polish army, I don't know. We learned later that he had been
in prison and later sent to Russia. I wasn't sure they were talking about
the same man, so I contacted the Polish army, but I didn't hear any more
about him since. A lot of people were killed in Prussia; perhaps he
received the medal posthumously. If he had remained alive, he would
certainly have tried to find his comrades in Poland.

Now, a slight digression:

All the documents repeat the conventional wisdom that Ha-Shomer
Ha-Tza'ir members formed the majority in the youth movement in Vilna.
They were, indeed, very strong in Vilna, because of their branch in that
city. He-Halutz had pretty much collapsed in Vilna back in 1936 and
1937. With the unification of Frayhayt–He-Halutz Ha-Tza'ir, I was sent
to Vilna to establish a branch of our Movement there; but Dobkirer and
Burstein of Po'alei Zion–Z.S., didn't help me with that because I was not
a member of their party and they didn't trust me.

Anyway, when I arrived, I found a branch that couldn't carry on
educational or any other activity, a branch that lacked Halutz enthusiasm
and a guiding ideal. The only thing we had left there was the training
kibbutz Shaharia on Subocz Street. When the war broke out, many members of our kibbutz wanted to see their families, and many of those at
Subocz went to the Russian zone to visit their parents. In Vilna, there were

22. Shmuel Brider: Member of a kibbutz named for Borochov in Kielce and one of the
central Movement activists in Poland.

hundreds of local *Shomrim,* and that was significant later, when the area was occupied by the Germans.

When the Germans entered, we didn't have any people in Vilna. But there were dozens of activist members of Ha-Shomer Ha-Tza'ir there, local people; and they were the ones who absorbed the refugees. Almost all our people were refugees themselves who came to Vilna from someplace else. Ilya Sheinbaum was a refugee;[23] Mordechai Tennenbaum[24] was a refugee; Tema Schneiderman was a refugee;[25] Zvi Mersik was a refugee. We didn't have anyone like Abba Kovner who was a Vilna-ite, and that's just one example.[26] I wasn't in Vilna at that time and it was the local people who determined the situation. Because of that, they achieved what they did and that was to the credit of Ha-Shomer Ha-Tza'ir in Vilna.

As for their opposition to unity, it might well have been organic. The emotional makeup of their members might not have been the same as ours. But that wasn't expressed. They didn't say they didn't want unity with us because we *were* such-and-such, but because we *thought* thus-and-so; that is, they opposed unity because of ideological differences. We were "not Soviet enough" for their taste; we emphasized the Jewish element too much. And in this Jewish matter, we wouldn't agree to any compromise. We didn't think the regime would make compromises either. Both of us lost people. Later, we got information in Warsaw about arrests and about the trial of Ha-Shomer Ha-Tza'ir members. I heard that they made a brave and proud appearance at the trial. I know precise details about our people; there were arrests. Edek Golowner was also jailed. There were other kinds of losses too, of members who joined the Komsomol. That was

23. Ilya (Yehiel) Sheinbaum: He-Halutz Ha-Tza'ir–Dror leader in Vilna Ghetto. His group did not join the Vilna FPO (United Partisan Organization) and formed an independent organization. Sheinbaum proposed sending fighters to the forest to form partisan units instead of mounting a revolt in the ghetto. He was killed by the Germans in a skirmish in Vilna Ghetto on September 1, 1943. (See Arad 1982:263ff., 411ff.)

24. Mordechai Tennenbaum: Born in Warsaw. Came to Vilna at the outbreak of the war and returned to Warsaw in 1942. Was active in the Dror underground. In late 1942, was sent to Białystok by the ZOB and became the local ZOB commander. Led the uprising there on August 17, 1943; details of his death are unknown; it is believed he took his own life at the age of twenty-seven.

25. Tema Schneiderman: Born in Warsaw. ZOB and Dror liaison between General-gouvernement, the territories annexed by the Reich, Ostland, and the Ukraine. Came to Vilna with her boyfriend, Mordechai Tennenbaum. When the city fell to the Germans, she returned to Warsaw. Spent some time in Białystok and came back to Warsaw in January 1943; was captured by the Germans in the January Uprising and sent to Treblinka. Details of her death are unknown. She was about twenty-five years old.

26. Abba Kovner (1918–1987): Leader of the Ha-Shomer Ha-Tza'ir in Vilna; commander of FPO in Vilna Ghetto (after the death of Itsik Wittenberg) and partisan leader in Rudnicka Forest. Immigrated to Israel; Hebrew poet and designer of the Diaspora Museum in Tel Aviv.

a widespread phenomenon; it was more prevalent in Ha-Shomer Ha-Tza'ir, but I suppose we gave our share too. I think that if one of our members went to them, it wasn't for ideological reasons, but out of opportunism and weakness. In Ha-Shomer Ha-Tza'ir they went to the Communists for ideological reasons; that is, they had an emotional penchant for that. They were more willing than we were to accept the Soviets. In their literature, they write that they supposedly had some mission. They thought that, since they were Marxists, they would succeed in influencing the Bolsheviks. It's interesting to read the memorandum they prepared to send to the Supreme Soviet.[27] Echoes of that position can be found in the underground press of that time, even in Warsaw. They scolded us for "not being revolutionary enough" in our attitude toward the Soviet Union; they said we were misled about the issue. This is documented.

Another matter is whether the mission to the Jews of Russia was an ideological problem. It's hard to say; I don't think so. This again reminds me of that meeting on the train with the Jew from the Soviet Union who hinted that there was some spark there. We were convinced that, if Stalin really wanted to solve the "Jewish problem," he should have invited the members of the Halutz movement. We were the only ones who could have solved the problem. Although certainly not in the Soviet Union or in Birobidzhan.[28] I don't think we had any illusions about building an underground movement inside Russia. The area of activity I kept talking about was the western Ukraine and western Byelorussia. That is, the area where we had invested decades of Halutz work and knew we had a reservoir of loyal young people.

The children in our ranks, those who studied in the Hebrew secular *Tarbut* schools or in the Polish grammar schools, became members of the underground and, in these terms, there was no difference between the Yiddish secular school on the one hand and the Hebrew *Tarbut* school and the Polish state grammar school. When Sovietization was fully carried out, they studied in Yiddish, in the small town schools, where there were more Jews than gentiles. Naturally, not all Jewish teachers and principals were loyal. It was our children who preserved the spark, who engaged in activities: proclamations stuck in coat pockets, and so forth. That is, in the schools, they knew about the Halutz underground. Some day, arrests would be made; but, by that time, I was no longer in the Soviet zone.

We put out pamphlets and guidance manuals for our group leaders. In every issue, we tried first of all to present something from Eretz Israel,

27. The memorandum they prepared in response to the document called the "Ivanov Letter," published in the Soviet press, ultimately was not sent.

28. Region in the far east of the Soviet Union officially designated as the "Jewish Autonomous Region," established in 1930.

which had come to us, either through Vilna or through couriers. At that time, we still had contacts with Warsaw and Vilna. In the Soviet zone, you were still allowed to listen to the radio and we could pick up broadcasts. I don't know what happened afterward, but we would get information. In the Movement newspaper, we presented items we heard about Eretz Israel or the kibbutz; marginal items in Eretz Israel were central for us. We presented some Hebrew literature. We knew that anyone who had Hebrew books in the town probably hid them, and, where there was a public library, Hebrew books were probably banned from it. We tried to use material with ideological significance and sent it to various places. We gave information about the Movement in Vilna and conditions of activity in the Soviet zone. Things were handwritten and printed very primitively.

Now I come to a painful and stormy matter.

Zivia left us and went to Warsaw, under German occupation. (That was in January, before Yudke left for Eretz Israel in February.) One day, a messenger from Zivia came from Warsaw with a letter describing life and conditions there: the decrees, the "patch" (in Warsaw, it wasn't actually a patch, but a white armband with a blue Magen-David). In her letter, she told of labor camps for men between the ages of fourteen and sixty, to "rehabilitate parasitic Jews" and train them for work. She wrote very graphically that there was talk of "concentrating" all the men. And she added wisely that an educational movement was the most imperative requirement in the German zone and someone should be sent for that. She also recommended that the person should know German. Why? I didn't understand it either then or when I got to Warsaw. But that's what the letter said.

Yudke, Edek, Oskar, and I discussed the needs of our educational activities and whether it was possible to meet them. Two people were considered for a mission to the German zone: Edek and me; but if the knowledge of German had to be factored in, Edek was the right person. Our emphasis always had been on educational activity. Perhaps my meetings with people from Warsaw, from the German occupation zone, who had been on the road for weeks or months, made me think of Warsaw as an abyss, so I was depressed. Edek, on the other hand, was really happy about it. He volunteered and the members supported him. But I was opposed to sending Edek.

I didn't usually act like that, but I didn't have enough emotional strength to send him. The memories stirred by Warsaw and the rumors about what the Germans were doing and all the information we got made it hard for me. And, in addition, to see him run merrily to it! I couldn't do it; I was against sending him and there was a sharp debate between us. I wasn't afraid for Edek; in fact, I was afraid for myself. In the hard years, when I was younger and had to decide to send a person, the question I always asked was: am I myself willing to take on this mission? In some cases, I could figure that I was willing to do it, but some operations had to be done by a woman, whose pants wouldn't be checked; or I might decide that some specific operation had to be done by someone who wasn't so well known, or whose Polish was more fluent than mine. But the emotional test—"Am I willing to do this?"—was the essential test. I was then in my twenties and I couldn't send a person to do something I couldn't do myself. This issue was perhaps one of the greatest crises in my life: I didn't know if I had the emotional strength to go to Warsaw. And there was a big fight between us, despite our great love for one another. Apparently, I wasn't careful about what I said, which sometimes happens to me in the heat of argument.

I argued that, in terms of education, I was as fit as Edek, that I had always been involved with education. Of course I could find all sorts of excuses. Edek was an outstanding counselor, a profound thinker, who loved to read: a person in touch with young people. In this debate, I resorted to demagoguery, arguing that, though he had taken care of youth from Germany in Warsaw, here, in the Soviet underground, he was involved with getting people across the border. Whereas I had always been concerned only with education.

Yudke left for Eretz Israel and weeks passed; February went by. Edek and I would meet and talk, but we weren't close anymore. For weeks we didn't talk to each other. Each of us stuck to his guns. At first, our comrades supported Edek. But in fact, neither he nor Oskar could oppose me. Edek went back to Kolomea, his center, on the Romanian border; and I continued my work. We were upset, but we went on working. Around Passover, a second messenger arrived, begging for help in Warsaw to set up the educational movement. Edek's name wasn't mentioned this time either. I went to Oskar's apartment, where I found Edek. Apparently, they had agreed to give in to me. The argument was over.

In less than forty-eight hours, I transferred everything to Edek and was ready to leave. I left the new suit I had ordered before the war and dressed like a refugee—in the shabbiest suit I had and an old overcoat. I got a gift from Oskar: a towel, which almost cost me my life. Then we parted. The comrades in the area didn't know I was leaving. Edek was the only one who came with me to the train. We sat in the station all night, since you never knew when the train would leave. When we learned that the train was leaving in an hour, there was enough time for me to tell Edek why I opposed his going. We kissed goodbye, and that was the last time I saw him. Someone denounced him and he was arrested a while later. The details of his death are unknown.

THREE

To the German Hell

When I got to Białystok, I found Rachel Fogelman and Dov Berger there (they were already a couple). I wrote my "Last Will and Testament," and we started looking for a way to the German side. One fellow there was a student of mine I had known back in Warsaw, Yehuda Mankuta (now Manor), whose family lived in Zaromb, where the border passed between the Russians and the Germans.[1] He was well versed in sneaking back and forth from the Soviet side to the German side; but at that time, people didn't usually sneak across the border from Warsaw to the Soviet zone, not to mention the opposite direction. Anyway, it was forbidden to approach the border two stations beyond Białystok. One night, Yehuda Mankuta took me from Białystok, and we boarded a train going west.

Yehuda rode in a passenger car, but there were also freight cars with elevated cabins where the train guards were stationed. He put me in a car, after he checked the area and found that no one was watching. At every stop, Yehuda would get off and talk in a loud voice to deflect attention away from me and let me know he was on guard. So we came to the first station, Czyzew, which was out of bounds because of its proximity to the border. We got off and I saw a destroyed town. It was a snowy night, and we walked in a ghost town. Either there weren't any more inhabitants there or they weren't in the streets we passed.

Suddenly we were stopped by two Soviet border guards. Their first question was: where are you going? Yehuda took out his documents and

---

1. Yehuda Manor adds that, as a member of the He-Halutz training kibbutz in Białystok, he was assigned to help guide a group of Halutzim going east from the German occupation zone to Vilna. Yitzhak Zuckerman went the opposite way—to Warsaw. Having family and friends in Zaromb, where the border was, made it easier for Manor.

began responding. It was dark; I took out matches to illuminate the papers, but I had nothing to show them and nothing to say to explain what I was doing in an abandoned town close to the border. He said something and named some local watchmaker. His relatives lived in a town near Zaromb (Zaręby Kościelne). His explanation must have been convincing because they let us go.

We continued walking a long time until we came to Zaromb. It was still night; Yehuda Mankuta took me into an apartment belonging to Jews. From now on, his job was to find someone to help me sneak across the border, to the next town, Malkinia, not far from Treblinka. As I recall, Malkinia was divided in two: the town itself was in the hands of the Russians, whereas the railroad station was in the German zone. Anyway, the border passed through there.

I waited one day and another. The third day came and the longer I sat, the closer I felt to collapse. There was a young woman there, a rabbi's wife, who was very depressed. Her neighbors told me that the Germans had raped her and killed her husband. The many rumors I heard—and there were some I didn't need to hear—depressed me. I saw that in another day or two, I wouldn't have any emotional strength left to hold out.

When Yehuda Mankuta came back and told me that the gentile hadn't yet come and it would take time until he did, I gave him an ultimatum: if he didn't take me across within twenty-four hours, I would go by myself. Apparently, he looked for an escort and didn't find one; so he decided to take me across himself. And he himself made the plan to sneak across the border. We set out to walk a few kilometers to the last village, closest to the border. We didn't walk on side roads but on the main highway and, as we walked, we talked aloud. He told me about the village and the name of a gentile girl who "took in men," so, in case we were stopped, we could tell where we were going. On the way, he told me to act natural, talk and whistle, so as not to look out of place. So we went on walking.

It was dusk; in the twilight, when we passed the last border patrol, I saw lights in the distance. We entered the most dangerous area. This was a few days before Passover, the snow was melting fast, and it was dark. Physically, I was quite sturdy, but I was falling on my feet. I learned two things then: I needed a lot of physical strength, and I wouldn't be a scout in the partisans. I was amazed at Yehuda's senses: how he led me in the darkness and mud; how he would bend down over the ground to listen to rustling; how he knew every tree, every bush! He was shorter and thinner than me. I wanted to stop and rest, but he didn't let me. Danger was lurking, and there was no way he would let us rest. Not on this Soviet side, and not on the other side. I begged him just to let me sit down for

a minute and he absolutely refused. He kept moving constantly, indefatigably toward the border.

It went on like this most of the night. We must have gone seven or eight
kilometers. We weren't walking on paved roads now, but tramping in the
mud, through fields of melting snow. When we reached the border, I saw
a straight line of barbed-wire fence in front of me, with wire triangles next
to it, which, Yehuda said, were connected to an alarm system of bells—I
don't think there were electrical alarms then. Crossing the Russian fence
was extremely dangerous. But Yehuda found the place where the barbed-
wire fence was cut and we crossed over to the German side. Now the
German danger began.

Yehuda Mankuta crossed with me and stayed with me until he brought
me to Warsaw, even though, except for a short section, I didn't need him
on the other side of the border. We went on walking a few more hours;
every ruined house I saw on the way winked at me to come in and rest,
but Yehuda wouldn't let me. At night—I think it was near dawn, but still
dark—we came to the hut of a peasant named Mikołajczyk, which I
remember because it was a famous name.[2] He didn't know Yehuda
Mankuta but he gave us a very nice welcome. We were exhausted and wet.
He lit his coal or wood oven for us, brought some straw into the hut, and
covered it with a sack. We undressed, lay down stark naked, and fell asleep
on the spot. Meanwhile, our clothes dried.

Yehuda agreed with our host that we would leave for Warsaw on the
early morning train from the German station of Malkinia. I didn't yet
know about the existence and purpose of nearby Treblinka, which was
just a railroad station for me, held by the Germans, whereas Mankuta and
the gentile knew only that Malkinia was a dangerous place, with a German
border patrol and police, and anyone who passed by or came to the
railroad station was risking his life.[3] So they decided that the gentile would
go buy two tickets in the morning, and we would then come to the railroad
station. But to be absolutely sure, we would wait behind a fence a little bit
away, and, when the train moved about 200 or 300 meters out of the
station, we would jump on since it would still be moving slowly, because
of a curve in the track. They knew that place well. So we had to jump. The
two of us waited and, when the train moved, we ran up to it, but my guide
forgot one thing: behind the curve was a two-story building where the
Gestapo was located. I jumped on the train, with Yehuda behind me, and

2. Stanisław Mikołajczyk (1901–1966): Polish statesman, co-organizer and leader of the
Peasants' Party (1931–1939), and member of the Sejm. Fled to London in 1939 and was
Minister of the Interior and Prime Minister (1943–1944) in the Polish Government-in-
Exile.

3. In fact, the death camp of Treblinka began operations only in the spring of 1942.

when I grabbed the door handle of the car, shots were heard. A Polish railroad worker called to me: "Throw away your bundle!" (Oscar's towel was in the bundle.) After I threw the bundle, both my hands were free. I opened the door of the car and jumped inside and immediately lay down on the floor; the rest of the passengers in the car were also lying on the floor. After we had gone about a kilometer, I went to the door and found the bullets stuck in it close to the place where Yehuda's head had been as he climbed into the car behind me. At every station, peasants with baskets boarded the train and the car filled up. No one asked me anything and no one apparently noticed that I was a Jew. The police who came were interested in those carrying baskets.

On a lovely spring day, I reached Praga, a suburb of Warsaw. We rented a carriage (I remember that the driver was a Jew) and went to the Jewish streets of the city. This was the first time I saw Jews wearing the Magen-David armband.

We came to the apartment at Dzielna Street 34, where a new chapter began in my life, the Warsaw chapter. Yehuda Mankuta, on the other hand, after bringing me safely to Warsaw, returned to the Soviet zone, where he was arrested and held a few days. (Yehuda immigrated to Eretz Israel in 1947.[4]) This was April, three or four days before Passover and just before the pogrom.[5] The Germans incited the Poles to attack the Jews and those attacks were filmed, with the Nazis playing the saviors of the Jews against the Poles. Those were very hard times for me. I had brought stocks of experiences from a country occupied by the Soviets. Say what you want about the Soviets, but in their occupation zone you walked around like a free person. At least that had been the feeling of those who didn't know that thousands of people had been arrested on dark nights and sent to Siberia or tortured in jails; and, when I lived there, I didn't know that. I would sometimes see groups of people led by a patrol, but I didn't know the great horror they experienced. In contrast to the situation I came on now, Lwów was a dream. Here, when I went into the street in the morning with my young comrades, I saw the ruins of Warsaw, and German soldiers hunting Jews. In that situation, you had to learn to run to the highest floor in the house in order to escape; a few days later, we were to see a pogrom, with Poles and Germans abusing Jews. Of course, it wasn't so awful in comparison with later times, and someone who had been in Warsaw all the time might have been used to it. But for me it was a difficult and shocking experience, and it took me days to adjust to the new conditions.

4. Yehuda Manor (Mankuta), a resident of Israel, lived in Kiryat Motzkin.
5. On March 28, 1940, gangs of Polish youth (incited by the Nazis) made a pogrom against the Jews of Warsaw. For an account, see Chaim Kaplan 1973:134–135.

There was not yet a ghetto or a wall, you could still ride the trolleys and cabs, you could still go back and forth to Praga, and Jews lived all over the city. Of course, Jews were treated cruelly, but the harsh decrees hadn't yet been issued. But even in this period, going through the streets was very hard. The ruins and the sight of the Jews, the humiliation, and the German pilots—young, handsome fellows, who suddenly turned into beasts. They would grab Jews for forced labor in the air force. That was the background of Yitzhak Katznelson's Yiddish poem, "A Jew Went into the Street."[6] The most important group of movement activists was concentrated at Dzielna 34. These were Frumka Plotnitzka, Yosef Kornianski,[7] and Zivia; the younger ones were Berl Broyde,[8] Muniek Reingewirtz,[9] Leah Perlstein, Hancia Plotnitzka. When I came to Dzielna, Leah Perlstein and Frumka Plotnitzka were on a reconaissance mission in Zeglębie, the coal mining region in Polish Silesia. It was a very serious and active group. What was lacking was a young person to restore the ruins of the educational movement. We had a few apartments on Dzielna Street. Our main apartment was at Dzielna 34 (Apartment 8); on the top floor, beyond the kitchen, we now had one or two rooms. In time, we rented a few apartments in the same big courtyard of Dzielna Street.

After we responded to the call of Colonel Umiastowski and abandoned the house and the city, our comrades came from the kibbutz in Łódz and moved into the apartment on Dzielna. The closets were still full since they hadn't yet been plundered, and the apartment was salvaged for the Movement. Some of the comrades moved to Vilna, but new people from different places kept coming to that address. There was Yosef Kornianski who escaped from Łódz when he learned they were looking for him. Other people came with him, and one of them played a vital role in that

6. Yitzhak Katznelson: Born in Karelitsh, Byelorussia. Writer, poet, teacher, playwright in Hebrew and Yiddish; principal of a Hebrew Gymnasium in Łódz. After the German occupation of Łódz, he fled to Warsaw where he worked in the Dror underground press. Was sent to internment camp in Vittel, France, in 1943, where he wrote his diary in Hebrew and the famous epic poem, "The Song of the Slaughtered Jewish People," in Yiddish. From there, he was shipped to Drancy and, on March 18, 1944, was transported to Auschwitz, where he died in early May. The final version of the above-mentioned poem was written in Camp Vittel. See Katznelson 1956:17–18 (Hebrew).

7. Yosef Kornianski: Born in Białystok. Active in He-Halutz underground. Went to Slovakia in spring 1941 and helped establish He-Halutz underground in Hungary. Reached Eretz Israel in January 1944.

8. Berl Broyde: Born in Słonim. One of the founders of Dror underground. Caught during the January Uprising in 1943 and sent to Treblinka; escaped and returned to Warsaw. Was Dror unit commander in the Central Ghetto during the April Uprising. Committed suicide in the bunker at Miła 18, at the age of twenty-five.

9. Muniek Reingewirtz: Born in Radomsk. Active in the commune at Dzielna 34 and in the Dror underground. Member of the group sent to the forests near Hrubieszów during the Great *Aktsia*. Murdered by the Germans; aged about twenty-six.

first period. This was a simple fellow, Hirshke Kutsher, a native of Vilna, who was later in Grochów.[10] Even before the war, he set up a workshop for weapons and ammunition in Warsaw in the apartment of Yehuda Arzi, who was sent from Eretz Israel by the Hagana; he and Hillel Schwartz were the main directors of that workshop.[11] Later, when I came to Dzielna, they told me about the heroism of that Hirshke Kutsher, who saved the apartment on Dzielna several times from firebombs that fell on the house. He was a very innovative fellow.

So there was a group of activists in the place we could be proud of. I knew almost all of them from our pre-war activity. Now I started meeting the people on the periphery. One of the new people I met at Dzielna 34 was Havka Folman's[12] brother, a fellow more or less my age, Marek Folman, who was later principal of the Gymnasium in the ghetto.[13] Zivia told me he was eager to start working with youth. He had studied mathematics at the University of Warsaw; but I don't think he graduated. In the last year, he had contacts with youth groups; but who would organize them now? There was nobody around. Frumka, who was also busy with the educational movement, was mainly on the road [between the cities]. Leah Perlstein and Zivia Lubetkin were in charge of social welfare. Yosef Kornianski was one of the pillars of the commune at Dzielna 34; Gedalia Gershuni, scion of the family of the Russian Soviet Revolutionary Gershuni, was there too.[14] But none of them had worked in the youth movement. Marek Folman knew Hebrew. I got to know and respect him; and we began discussing and considering what we faced. We had to start doing something. And we did. In Warsaw, there was no branch of Dror. We had to work hard to set it up. In the last issue of *Bleter far geshikhte*, published in Poland on the thirtieth anniversary of the Uprising, there is a lot of material on the youth movement. Someone did research on the youth movement in the Warsaw Ghetto and one of the things he

10. Zvi Kutsher: Born in Vilna. In charge of supplies for the Dzielna kibbutz. Deported to Treblinka in January 1943. Details of his death unknown. Aged about twenty-nine.

11. The activists of the workshop to create weapons and ammunition for Eretz Israel also included Yakov Burstein. Hillel Schwartz, of Ramat Ha-Kovesh, fell in a clash with an Arab gang from Tira, not far from his kibbutz.

12. Havka Folman: Born in Warsaw. Student in Dror underground Gymnasium; became Dror and ZOB courier. Arrested by the Nazis in 1942 and sent to Auschwitz. Immigrated to Israel.

13. Marek Folman: Born in Miechów. Active in Dror and founder of Dror underground Gymnasium. Caught by the Nazis in the January Uprising in 1943 and sent to Treblinka; escaped and returned to Warsaw. With the ZOB on the Aryan side. Participated in the April Uprising. Shot and killed in the railroad station in Czestochowa at the age of twenty-seven.

14. Gedalia Gershuni (1914–1942): Born in Białystok. Secretary of the commune at Dzielna 34. In August 1942, during the Great *Aktsia*, he organized a partisan unit that left Warsaw for Hrubieszów. Shot along with his comrades at the age of twenty-eight.

mentions is that the largest movement was Dror, with eight hundred members. Then came Ha-Shomer Ha-Tza'ir, with five hundred. The other movements, Gordonia, Akiba, and others, had between one and two hundred. These are statistical, factual data. A lot of people worked very hard to set up the youth movement. The conditions of poverty of our youth, up to 1939, were well known; at some period before the war, I worked in the Warsaw branch of He-Halutz Ha-Tza'ir and I knew it was a very small, miserable branch. Now, in a year and a half, we reached new strata of youth, youth in school, and working circles of youth—youth who finished school, that is, who were sixteen years old when the war broke out. We got into many different circles and became a large educational operation.

Our members, the refugees who came from the west of Poland, from our training kibbutzim, led by the members of the Łódz and Będzin kibbutzim, saved the Dzielna house physically, and Dzielna itself was the physical salvation of hundreds of people. When Frumka came, she breathed life into the place, gave it a mission. Many people came after her. Of course, what arose on Dzielna was not the work of one person. Frumka came to Warsaw right after the surrender, and Zivia came in January 1940. From October to January, Frumka played a central role; they called her Mother. She was a "mother" not only of He-Halutz; people got to know her in the corridors of the Joint and in the Jewish social centers that formed.[15] For a time, Hirshke Kutsher was Frumka's boyfriend, but there was a big difference in the public appearance of the two. There are periods that make people grow, and vice versa, there are periods of degradation. Frumka grew and rose with events. There are people who aren't distinguished and don't prove themselves, if they don't have an appropriate opportunity. No doubt Frumka had a great personality. If she had immigrated to Eretz Israel in 1938, as planned, she would certainly have been a blessing to the kibbutz. But she reached the height of her personality in the new situation that emerged, with the new challenges. Conditions demanded and she gave herself without stinting. There's a moral in that: this is how people grow—you have to let them grow. People who stand at the helm of state and sometimes think they're indispensable are wrong and should learn that lesson.

Dzielna also had the warmth of a big family. I remember how they all welcomed me. I had known many of them from before and there were also new ones. I had last seen Frumka in Kowel; I had parted from Zivia

15. Joint (American-Jewish Joint Distribution Committee), founded November 27, 1914, as the Joint Distribution Committee of American Funds for the Relief of Jewish War Sufferers, chaired by Felix Warburg. Between 1939 and 1945, a total of $78,878,000 was spent mainly on relief and rescue schemes in Europe, including relief in the ghettoes.

in Lwów; I had met Yosef Kornianski, Leah Perlstein, and others in mid-December 1939 in Łódz; I knew almost everybody. I also knew a few of the young people, and I started observing, examining, talking, and taking the first practical steps. The social work staff didn't need reinforcement; but we had to take elementary steps to reorganize the underground educational movement. There were some initial activities, but they were random. For example, Frumka and Leah Perlstein went to towns where there were no branches, to introduce themselves. But when they departed, they left a vacuum. We had to have a continuation. We started organizing the first Seminar for counselors. I had some reservations about the old-time members in He-Halutz and the training kibbutzim, who had stayed there until 1940. I started trying to bring younger people into the operation. We became an underground movement within Warsaw. Officially, Dzielna was a soup kitchen and a station for refugees, under the aegis of the social aid committee. Everyone could and had to integrate into this framework and live a Movement life.

We sought a framework that would not be apparent on the outside at all and would be an underground in every respect. We needed new people for that. In the first assemblies held at Dzielna, I saw the abyss gaping between the vital demands of the living person who wanted to keep eating, and the need to set up an underground educational movement, which would deduct this money from food and invest it in things that were of dubious value, at least in the short run. But this is how an underground movement is built. And there was also another conception, which was basically a concern for giving the comrade the best soup. For example, I still see a comrade from Będzin, an old-timer in the Movement, loyal and important; but, in my heart, I didn't think he was fit for an underground youth movement. You might set up a training kibbutz with him, but not an underground. I'm talking about everybody from the Movement, whose talents, for example, were in management or economics, even if he had been in educational work in his hometown. Conditions in 1940 were different and special and demanded different qualities. Of course, there were also exceptions; for example, such men as Yosl Kornianski, who was an outstanding Movement person even though he also was busy with all sorts of organizational matters, like establishing a sewing workshop, a barbershop, and such institutions.

The treasurer, that is, the one who kept the money, was Munia Reingewirtz; but the one who took care of our livelihood was Zivia. I was new, and she was widely known then. I would go with her to the institutions. Sometimes, I would accompany her to the Joint, which was how I got to know the area. There was nothing special in my relations with Zivia yet. Before that, back in Kowel, she was sick and I went out, like a martyr, to bring her some fish and cake. It was autumn and on the way, I had to go through all the mud of Kowel. I went in to her, and she started scolding me: "Look at your muddy pants." I didn't answer; I was amazed at her nerve; she was talking like a wife. I didn't know that a few months later, she would "be legitimate." That was before there was anything between us. We were puritans in every respect.

Frumka had previously taken care of money matters, but when Zivia came it was she who started mobilizing financial means; she haunted corridors, went to meetings, began to be known in the institutions. Later, Zivia was the representative of the "coordinating committee" of the Halutz movement in the various institutions, and I was very impressed with her. Back in 1936, I once came from Warsaw to Kielce, where there was a branch with hundreds of members. I remember the assembly in the hall of pillars. In the middle was a table and next to it stood a young girl who spoke and banged the table with every sentence. I noticed her and I saw her like that again in 1940. What force! And, even though she is my wife, and I shouldn't spoil her with compliments, I must say she showed great sense and earned everyone's respect. So with her help, I got acquainted with Warsaw organizations; it took me time to master the situation.

Marek Folman was the first to come up with ideas: he told about groups of young people on the left and academic youth circles he had met back before the war; they wanted to meet and he began to bring them. I was surprised by that phenomenon, since we hadn't previously known that kind of young people in Warsaw. Now they were adults, eighteen-year-olds. But there were also sixteen-year-olds. Some of them later integrated into our underground Gymnasium. Our idea was to teach them, since the war would end some day—we didn't think about Treblinka then—and someone would be needed to take up the burden.

These were groups of youth expelled to Warsaw from the towns: Plock, Gostynin, Konin, and elsewhere. We began searching for them among the expatriates, and we started the Movement with them. It was an underground movement from the first day; at first it was secret even from the Dzielna people. We worked in groups; we didn't yet set up fives, as in the Russian zone, but there were also small groups here. They would gather in houses and various other places. The underground in Warsaw was established by locals, groups that had already met before. Not all our activity was underground, but our "Gymnasium" was; its existence wasn't a secret, but classes were held in all kinds of secret places. Only the Movement Seminars took place at Dzielna 34. Nowhere else but Dzielna could we seat forty people for classes. There was also Dzielna 12, nearby, where the party later set up a kitchen (Po'alei Zion–Z.S.). Before the war, the kitchen was at Gęsia 14, but it was hit by a bomb. At Gęsia 9, there was an official teachers' college. Haim Zelmanowski was a teacher there.[16] Some of the people from the Warsaw branch of He-Halutz Ha-Tza'ir were my students and I can certainly be proud of them, like Saul Dobuchna, whom I loved,[17] and Gura Zelazna[18] and David Eisenberg[19] who later played central roles in Białystok and Kowel. These are young people I had met back in 1936/1937 in He-Halutz Ha-Tza'ir in Warsaw. I knew them well, and they were loyal to me.

I started activity by sending people to the various communes. In those days (1940), you could still move around in Poland as Jews, but it wasn't wise to do too much traveling, and men and women who didn't look Jewish could be used for this. I had to select people for missions. One night, I left for my big trip to the cities of the German occupation zone. I went through nineteen places and met several people. Another trip lasted five weeks. At first, when you could still travel, I would go back and forth; it would take a few days, but I visited every possible place. I found remnants of our members in various towns. In one place, I met someone who later played a very important role in the German zone. This was Abraham Leibowicz (Laban).[20] He was with us in the Soviet underground for some time and took care of us there. He was my age. In the Soviet zone, it was due to him that we ate our fill and had bread and even

16. Haim Zelmanowski: Born in Nowogródek. Biologist; one of the directors of the Dror Gymnasium in the ghetto. Deported to a concentration camp near Lublin during the April Uprising. Lewin tells of seeing him deported on August 26, 1942 (Lewin 1989:162). Survived the war and immigrated to Israel. According to Zivia Lubetkin, he was "a superb biology teacher and a brilliant educator" (Lubetkin 1981:69).

17. Saul Dobuchna: Born in Warsaw. Prominent Dror activist; later organized underground activities in Hrubieszów district. Killed September 1942; aged nineteen. According to Zivia Lubetkin he was "physically weak but displayed a moral strength beyond description" (Lubetkin, 1981:281).

18. Gura Zelazna: Born in Siedlce, Poland. At the outbreak of the war, he escaped to the Soviet occupation zone. After the German invasion of the Soviet Union, he went to Białystok, where he became one of the important figures in ZOB and was killed in the battles of August 1943 at the age of twenty-four.

19. David Eisenberg: Born in Warsaw. Active in Dror underground. One of those who signed the inscription on the synagogue wall with Sheindl Schwartz, Leah Fish, and Rachel Fogelman.

20. Abraham Leibowicz (Laban): Born in Kraków. Established Dror underground in the Soviet zone and later in the Generalgouvernement. Appointed commander of ZOB in Kraków in September 1942. Caught by the Gestapo in December 1942. Described by Gusta Dawidsohn ("Justyna") as "A huge, broad-shouldered fellow, with an extraordinary gift of directness, . . . He looked as though the world around him did not concern him, as though nothing in the world could ever terrify him or upset his balance. At the same time he viewed everything from a humorous point of view and his sense of humour was the most pleasant feature of his personality." (Quoted in Ainsztein 1974:830–831.) Killed trying to escape in April 1943 at the age of twenty-six.

sausage, and shoes. That was not just because he was a local, but because he had initiative and knew how to get along in every situation. In this respect, we had "two left hands." He combined warmth and great concern for friends. First he was with us in Lwów and then was one of the pillars of our Movement in Kraków. He moved to the German zone after Zivia, in February 1940. With somebody like Laban, we could start activity in Kraków, search for, and organize people.

Hanna'le Gelbart was one of our first couriers but you couldn't always make do with couriers.[21] In this respect, Lonka Kozibrodska played a different role from Frumka;[22] Frumka was a courier but, after she reached someplace, she would invoke movement authority and solve whatever problems had arisen there. There were other courier-emissaries, whose job was to assess the situation and convey information, and there was a difference between these two. After the information was collected, I would go see what was done; I would travel and return to Warsaw, in those pre-ghetto days. I would travel as a gentile. The first name I used in the Soviet zone was Witold Kimstaczas; I didn't have any documents there. I would sign letters: Yefim.

(Later, in Warsaw, I had a forged document as Stanisław Bagniewski.) In Praga, a house on Stalowa Street 13 (or maybe 19) was destroyed, and an official stamp somehow remained in the hands of a woman member of Ha-Shomer Ha-Tza'ir.[23] This stamp wound up in the hands of Yosef Kaplan, and I used it. I made a photograph and a document, not an identity document, but an identity picture. On the other side of the picture was a confirmation that I was called thus-and-so, by the porter, who was supposed to know. I didn't use it in Warsaw; but I did use it a few times on the roads. The guards on duty examined the document to ascertain if the identity was correct, and it worked.

21. Hannah Gelbart: Born in Pruszków. Active in Dror underground; counselor in youth groups. Courier between Central Committee in Warsaw and the provinces. Immigrated to Israel; member of Kibbutz Dafna.

22. Lonka Kozibrodska: Born in Pruszków. One of the main couriers in Poland for Dror and He-Halutz. Her Polish appearance and her knowledge of languages enabled her to travel throughout Poland. Arrested in June 1942 in Malkinia and sent from there to Pawiak Prison in Warsaw; transported to Auschwitz (as a Pole). Died of typhus on March 18, 1943, aged twenty-six. Ruzka Korczak (1965:45) describes her vividly: "A tall girl who didn't look at all Jewish. When I first saw her . . . I was sure she was a native born Pole. Apparently the Germans she came upon in her frequent travels also thought so. They usually thought she was a *Volksdeutschin* because of her knowledge of German. . . . She had great stores of energy and vitality. As a courier between the ghettoes, she experienced great dangers. Her boldness and coolness always stood her in good stead. Her friends used to say that 'Lonka wouldn't burn even in a fire!' She believed that, too, and that faith in her power kept her spirits up."

23. Apparently it was the stamp of the house committee authorizing residents.

The document I used in the early days was my picture in the name of Antoni Wilczyński. I don't remember how I got to that name. One of the historians failed to identify that name. Later, in 1941, when I came back from the Kampinos Labor Camp,[24] I published an article about the camp in *Dror* and signed it, A. Wilecz. I couldn't write Yitzhak Zuckerman because I was registered with the Judenrat in my real name. Years later, Professor Ber Mark selected that article, published in *Yediyes* by A. Wilecz, for his anthology of ghetto literature[25] and put me into the classics of Yiddish literature. Professor Mark thought the article had been written by Wilczyński, a well-known literary critic. I read a lot of Yiddish all the time and I remember Wilczyński's book, *The Tragedy of the Jewish Woman in Polish Literature* (in Yiddish). I don't know what happened to that Wilczyński but we can guess. Professor Mark published his book in Poland in the dark Stalinist period of the 1950s. If he had known it was Yitzhak Zuckerman, he surely wouldn't have mentioned it. Others followed suit and, in various lexicons, A. Wilecz appears as a pseudonym for Wilc- zyński. Since I was friendly with Ber Mark, I wrote him from Israel and pointed out his mistake, and you can imagine what an impression my letter made on him. In any event, "Antoni Wilczyński" was the first name I used and A. Wilecz is me.

This was how we began setting up the Movement. One of the first things we decided to do was organize a Counselors' Seminar. About two weeks after I came, I published the first issue of *Dror* in Yiddish. We hid whatever was preserved of that material in a few places. What was buried at Dzielna 34 was found after the war, but not what was in Grochów and Czerniaków. The material Eliahu Gutkowski[26] took from me and gave to the Ringelblum Archive was preserved.[27] Issues of both *Dror* and *Yediyes* are missing, and we found only one copy of *El Ha-Madrikh*.[28] *Payn un gvure* was later found in Warsaw in the Jewish Historical Archive.[29] We

24. See below, chapter 4.

25. *Tsvishn lebn un toyt (Between Life and Death)*, Ber Mark, ed., Warsaw 1955.

26. Eliahu Gutkowski: Born in Kalwaria, Lithuania. Active in Po'alei Zion-Z.S.; history teacher in Dror underground Gymnasium. Worked with Emmanuel Ringelblum to estab- lish and develop the Warsaw Ghetto Secret Archive. Died in the sewers after the April Uprising at the age of forty-three.

27. Ringelblum Archive (*Oneg Shabbat*): Collection of materials documenting various aspects of life (and death) in the Warsaw Ghetto founded and directed by Dr. Emmanuel Ringelblum (see below). A selection of this material is in *To Live with Honor and Die with Honor!*. . . . *Selected Documents from the Warsaw Ghetto Underground Archives "O.S. [Oneg Shabbath]*," ed. and annotated by Joseph Kermish, Jerusalem: Yad Vashem, 1986.

28. A periodical collection for group leaders of the Dror movement, including material for activity and discussion, 1941, Yiddish, 20 mimeographed pages.

29. *Payn un gvure in dem yidishn over, in likht fun der kegnvart (Suffering and Heroism in the Jewish Past in Light of the Reality of our Time)*—an anthology on the martyrology of the Jewish

have only one copy of it in Beit Katznelson in Kibbutz Lohamei Ha-Getaot.

Back to the Seminar, and now I come to Tuvia Borzykowski.[30] In that summer of 1939, before I came to Klebań for the Seminar, I had been in a place near Radomsk. It was a very tough time and I was practically alone, since those who were scheduled to lecture at the Seminar that summer didn't show up. One of the activists there was a young fellow named Sinai Okrent, a member of Frayhayt, from Radomsk (today a member of Kibbutz Lohamei Ha-Getaot). One day, he saw I was in distress and said there was a member in Radomsk who was a "little old" and didn't know Hebrew, but who lectured on the labor movement and might be a great help. I asked him to bring the man and that was Tuvia Borzykowski. He was amazing. Short, proletarian, a tailor. He was a typical self-taught man who had things all jumbled up in his "suitcase." But a lot of things. He knew Borokhov well and would talk about all of Yiddish literature. He lectured very well on the pioneers of Yiddish proletarian poetry, Yosef Bovshover[31] and Dovid Edelshtat.[32] So I used him in that Seminar before the war. Now I remembered Tuvia Borzykowski as a lecturer. Frumka, a member of Frayhayt, knew him better than I did, went to Radomsk, and brought him to Warsaw. We brought in more than forty young people we saw as builders of the Movement in the towns and cities.

Those were days of debate for our group at Dzielna 34. There was an extraordinary and loving friendship between the people there. Even bitter debates about fundamental issues—and there were some—didn't weaken our friendship. When I came to Warsaw, Frumka and Leah Perlstein were in the kibbutz in Będzin. In those days, the Zionist groups in Warsaw were very busy making lists of endorsements for Certificates they had been supposedly promised to be submitted to the "Lloyd Triestino [Adriatic]" travel company in Italy (there were several different promises).[33] Several people did manage to get out legally, including Ze'ev

people since the Exile from its land, (Yiddish) by Y. Zuckerman, for the Dror movement, in 400 copies, mimeographed. It was the first book to appear in the ghetto.

30. Tuvia Borzykowski: Born in Łódz. Active in Dror and ZOB in the January and April Uprisings; escaped to the Aryan side and fought in the Polish Uprising. Immigrated to Israel in 1949. Died in 1959, aged forty-eight. Author of *Between Tumbling Walls*.

31. Yosef Bovshover (1873–1915): American Yiddish poet (immigrated from Riga to the U.S. in 1891). Wrote revolutionary, anarchist poetry; published essays on Heine, Emerson, and Whitman; translated Shakespeare's *Merchant of Venice* into Yiddish.

32. Dovid Edelshtat (1866–1892): One of the first Yiddish socialist poets in the U.S., editor of the New York anarchist newspaper *Fraye Arbeter Shtime*. Died of tuberculosis at the age of twenty-six and became a romantic legend to the Jewish labor movement.

33. Certificates: Certificates of legal entry to Eretz Israel, limited by the British Mandatory authorities to about 20,000 a year.

Hering, one of our party members, Professor Weiss of Mizrakhi, and others. But no one from He-Halutz went.

As I said, the two girls, Frumka Plotnitzka and Leah Perlstein, were then in Zagłębie. At that time, there was a debate among the veteran activists: who was first to go in the legal Aliya. These were Certificates they expected in the spring and summer of 1940. The disagreement between the Halutz movements and the "party veterans" was whether the Halut-zim would be included in the list of those receiving certificates. Abraham Gewelber wrote the same things about Vilna, where the veteran party activists also controlled Aliya and did what they wanted with it.[34]

At that time, members from Germany contacted us, but not only members of Ha-Bonim.[35] One of them, for example, Benno Rosenberg, of Bahad (Brit Halutzit Datit), a religious Zionist movement in Germany which was very close to us, and refugees from their movement found shelter in the Polish He-Halutz.[36] They were very fine people, very moral, but they were observant Jews. I can't tell how pious they were; apparently it was what was usual among Orthodox German Jewry. He-Halutz still existed there, an Eretz-Israeli office operated and corresponded with Berlin. A man named Munik Merin, who later won notoriety as a member of the Judenrat in Sosnowiec, traveled from Zagłębie to Berlin; when he returned, he told our members in the training kibbutz we still had there that he was taking care of Aliya, and Halutzim might be able to go to Eretz Israel from Poland through Germany.[37] Frumka and Leah Perl-stein left for Będzin to look into the matter and to talk with Merin, to find out what it was all about. But he procrastinated. Apparently the man was also a liar, who told all kinds of stories. When they returned, the debate began.

By then I was in Warsaw. The debate was about whether there would be a big Aliya and we knew that, even if there was an Aliya of Halutzim, there would be a bitter battle over every Certificate. And so we concluded that we should start leaving via underground ways. One enthusiastic supporter of that idea was Shlomo Cygielnik who volunteered to go and examine that possibility himself on the border of Slovakia.[38]

34. See Yehuda Helman 1969:65–118 (Hebrew).

35. Ha-Bonim: A labor Zionist youth movement.

36. See Yitzhak Schwersantz 1969.

37. Moshe Merin: Chairman of the Judenrat in Sosnowiec. An unscrupulous character who was opposed to the underground movement and "spared no effort to stop the un-derground activities of the youth organizations." Killed in Auschwitz in June 1943. See Isaiah Trunk 1977:459 & passim.

38. Shlomo Cygielnik: Came to Warsaw from Białystok in spring 1940; active in Dror. Organized a route from Poland to Slovakia for illegal immigration. Was sent back to Poland by the Slovakian authorities in spring 1942 and was rumored to have been killed in Belzec at the age of twenty-six.

I was one of those who didn't believe in legality, but I was naïve and thought we should first contact our members in Vilna since there was an opening to Eretz Israel (through Shlikhim in various European countries). I sent a letter to Israel Idelson,[39] then secretary of Ha-Kibbutz Ha-Meuchad (as I recall, through Shlomo Tamar-Lipski who was still in Hungary then). In our letters, we asked where we should go or if we should just go—because our goal was not just to leave the German occupation zone, but also to try to get someplace. We wasted months on that. Our position in Geneva was abandoned. Pino Ginzburg returned to Eretz Israel and Natan Schwalb stayed there.[40] We waited for weeks; Shlomo Cygielnik argued for going on our own, but I still believed we had to appeal to our members. I didn't believe in legal means, but I did think we needed a clear destination. Should we go to the Balkans? Someone had to take the people in, we needed a place to be accepted on the other side. We didn't get an answer to any of our letters. That was one of the things that made us mad. Our dear friend Yosef Kaplan of Ha-Shomer Ha-Tza'ir said he once got a letter or a cable from Switzerland saying: "We're with you." He replied: "Better I should be with you." We didn't even get that. That contact with Geneva never yielded anything. But I won't get into that now. That went on a few months, and before Shlomo Cygielnik departed, I left for Kraków. Hence the episode of Laban's role in opening a route to Slovakia. Shlomo Cygielnik was the first to go the route of Warsaw–Kraków–Tarnów–Nowy Sącz; he got across the border to a place called Bardejov, sent messengers and communicated with Bratislava, and even got an answer that there was someone there to take them in.

Another argument between us young people and members of Po'alei Zion flared up when the party Central Committee (of Po'alei Zion) learned of our plan to establish a Seminar for counselors, and they forbade us to do it. We told them to go to hell. They forbade us in the name of the Central Committee of the party and thought if they put it that way, we would fall into line. I remember that morning: I was living at that time in a room with Zivia and some of the young people who weren't at Dzielna 34, but on Nowolipki Street, where we had an apartment; in the same building there was also a Polish police station. You had to get home every night before curfew at nine. After two weeks in that

39. Israel Idelson-Bar Yehuda (1895–1965): Israeli labor leader; served in the Knesset and as Minister of the Interior (1955–1959).

40. Pino Ginzburg: Shaliah of Histradrut and Ha-Kibbutz Ha-Meuchad in Western Europe. Natan Schwalb: Shaliah of Histradrut and world coordinator of He-Halutz in Geneva during the war. Apparently in other cases he was highly instrumental in providing relief to concentration camp inmates and in rescue efforts. (See *The "Gordonia" Press in the Warsaw Ghetto Underground*, ed. Arieh Avnon, Israel: "Gordonia-Maccabi Hatzair" Archives in Hulda, 1966:10–11.)

apartment on Nowolipki, I saw that it wasn't acceptable for us members of the Movement. Several young people who were supposed to be leaders in the educational movement couldn't live apart from the group, cut off every night. It made no sense. I didn't recommend returning to Dzielna 34. But, not to endanger those who weren't involved in underground educational work, we rented another room in the same courtyard on Dzielna. And, as coordinator of that operation, it was decided that I should live in a separate room. For various reasons, it took a while until Zivia—who was already my "common-law girlfriend"—dared to move into that room with me.

We gave the apartment on Nowolipki to Gordonia when we brought Israel Zelcer[41] from Lublin to restore the Gordonia movement. The apartment on Dzielna was a center for the whole Halutz movement.

I remember that day in my room at Dzielna 34. I was in one bed and Zivia was in the other; it was after curfew and suddenly Yohanan Morgenstern showed up.[42] He apologized for not telling us the day before, and now told us, in the name of the party, that we could not establish the Seminar, under any circumstance. I told him that the Seminar participants were already in Warsaw and that the Seminar was about to begin in two hours. He was stunned and furious.

The first Seminar of summer 1940 went on for five or six weeks[43] and we argued about it with the veteran members. About that time, Frumka and I were appointed to the Po'alei Zion Central Committee. Zivia, Frumka, and I were dissatisfied with the Po'alei Zion party mentality, but we kept quiet about it. The central man in the party was Yosef Sak,[44] but

41. Israel Zelcer (1913–1942): Born in Zdolbrinow. One of the founders of Gordonia in his hometown. Sent with a Dror partisan group to the forests of Hrubieszów in August 1942. The group was captured and almost all were murdered; Zelcer was taken to Pawiak Prison where he was executed in September 1942.

42. Yohanan Morgenstern: Born in Zamość. One of the founders of Po'alei Zion–Z.S. underground in Warsaw; responsible for the finances of ZOB. Escaped to the Aryan side after the April Uprising and was killed by the Gestapo on May 6, 1943 at the age of thirty-eight.

43. The first Seminar took place in June-July 1940. Forty-five members of twenty-three branches participated, as a result of the visits made to the branches. The second Seminar was in January 1941, with thirty-two participants, mainly from the Warsaw branch. The third Seminar was in December 1941–January 1942, with the participation of forty-two members from eight cities; it began after information had arrived about the annihilation of the Jews of Vilna and the surrounding areas.

44. Yosef Sak: Born in Przemyśl. Teacher of literature in Częstochowa; social activist in the Warsaw Ghetto; one of the founders and directors of the Dror underground Gymnasium and member of the Anti-Fascist Bloc. Died in Israel in 1965 at the age of sixty-seven.

the one with moral authority was Leyzer Levin.[45] Morgenstern and Leyzer Levin acted as chairmen. The youngest one in the group was Stefan Grajek.[46] There were one or two others—Abraham Fishelson and somebody else whose name I forgot.[47] As I recall, they didn't invite us to every meeting, as for example, when the subject was distributing money from abroad. It was like this throughout the years, even in very hard times when we were starving. Later, we found out about money the party received.

So we set up the Seminar; and I want to say, to the credit of those members who were against it, that they came to lecture despite their opposition: Morgenstern, for example, Leyzer Levin, Yosef Sak, and others who were friendly with us. There was also Dr. Haim Zelmanowski, Dr. Meir Morgenstern of Łódz,[48] Michael Landau,[49] who later became a member of the leftist Moshe Sneh group in Israel, and Eliahu Gutkowski, a history teacher and a loyal friend to the Dzielna group. He later worked with Ringelblum in the Ghetto Archive but wasn't one of his subordinates.[50] Eliahu Gutkowski was my close friend throughout the years and we did a great deal together. He was older than I (I think he was close to forty); but despite the age gap, we were good friends and addressed each other in Yiddish in familiar terms, (using the singular "thou," instead of the more distant and formal plural "you"). We got to Zelmanowski through Saul Dubochna; first we brought him to the Seminar, then to our Gymnasium. Back when he was my student, Saul had told me about a biology teacher he admired, who

45. Leyzer Levin: One of the organizers of Po'alei Zion–Z.S. in the underground; active in the Jewish Self-Help Society (YISA) and supervisor of soup kitchens. Escaped to the Aryan side during the April Uprising. Died in Israel in 1967 at the age of seventy-six.

46. Stefan Grajek: Born in Warsaw. One of the founders of the Po'alei Zion–Z.S. underground in Warsaw. Escaped to the Aryan side after the April Uprising; fought in the Polish Uprising; participated in Brikha. Immigrated to Israel.

47. Abraham Fishelson: Born in Warsaw. Member of Po'alei Zion–Z.S. underground in the Warsaw Ghetto and one of the founders of his party's soup kitchens; member of the Anti-Fascist Bloc. Deported to Treblinka in June 1942 at the age of thirty-two.

48. Meir Morgenstern: Active in Po'alei Zion–Z.S. underground and maintained close ties with Dror underground. Details of his death unknown.

49. Michael Landau: Born in Łódz. Lawyer. Member of Po'alei Zion–Z.S. underground. After the Great *Aktsia* of July-August 1942, he escaped to the Aryan side. Died in Israel in 1971 at the age of fifty-nine.

50. Emmanuel Ringelblum: Born in Buczacz, Galicia. Historian; active in Po'alei Zion Left. One of the leaders of the Jewish underground in the Warsaw Ghetto. Best known for establishing and directing the underground archives that bear his name. Murdered by the Gestapo in March 1944 at the age of forty-four. See *To Live with Honor and Die with Honor! . . . Selected Documents from the Warsaw Ghetto Underground Archives "O.S. [Oneg Shabbath],"* ed. and annotated by Joseph Kermish, Jerusalem: Yad Vashem, 1986.

had once said during a class in the Polish Gymnasium: "I'm a socialist because I'm a biologist." I really liked such things in an official Polish institution. When I came to Warsaw, I met Saul Dubochna and I also visited his parents' home and saw their terrible poverty; they eventually died of hunger. We brought Saul to Dzielna, and when he told me the story of Zelmanowski and what he said, I asked him to bring the biologist to us; that's how I met Zelmanowski. Later I learned that he had once been one of the first members of He-Halutz (back in 1916). He hadn't continued in their way of self-realization in Israel, but went his own way instead. He lectured—first in Łódz, later in Warsaw. I met him in 1940, and apparently the sympathy was mutual. He was a man with vision who was devoted to underground work, since both our Gymnasium and Seminar were held underground. I was very friendly with him, his wife, and his old mother.

We brought Janusz Korczak[51] to the Seminar through Stefa Wilczyńska,[52] whom Zivia met in the corridors of various offices where they were both trying to get money, Stefa for her orphanage, and Zivia for her orphans. Stefa admired Zivia very much and so she started coming to us. The idea of bringing Korczak to the Seminar came up, and I asked Zivia to ask Stefa to bring him. Leyzer Levin also came to us. We constructed the curriculum of the Seminar with those people.

I lectured on literature and would fill any "hole." Later, in 1945, when the Ringelblum Archive was discovered, the schedule of lectures, in my handwriting, was in it. Why? My dear friend, Eliahu Gutkowski, of blessed memory, took everything he could from me, even the diary and that schedule. I'm not sure what happened to my diary—he might have taken it or it might have gotten lost; it wasn't full. I had to write my outlines in it, to keep them secret. I relied a lot on my memory; I thought I could decode it when the time came, and now the diary's disappeared and I can't find it. The Seminar went on for five or six weeks. In the Archive, there's a full report and description of it. Emmanuel Ringelblum (who wasn't a very good lecturer), Yitzhak Schipper,[53] and Lipa

51. Janusz Korczak (Henryk Goldschmidt): Born in Warsaw. Internationally known physician and educator and writer of children's books. Directed an orphanage in the ghetto and, in August 1942, during the Great *Aktsia,* he accompanied the children to Treblinka, although he could have been saved. He was sixty-four years old. (See Gutman 1989: 216–217; Ringelblum 1986; Korczak 1980.)

52. Stefa Wilczyńska: Born in Warsaw. Immigrated to Eretz Israel in 1938 but returned to Poland in 1939. Worked with Korczak in the ghetto orphanage and also accompanied the children to Treblinka in the Great *Aktsia;* she was fifty-six years old.

53. Yitzhak Schipper (1884–1943): Born in Tarnów. Historian, member of the Polish Parliament (Sejm) and of the General Zionists. Social activist in the Warsaw Ghetto; apparently opposed to armed resistance (see Gutman 1989:229). Died in a German concentration camp near Lublin.

Bloch[54] were brought in for specific subjects; Korczak came, but didn't teach many classes. We met with him a few times and with various other people on various subjects. The subjects we discussed in the Seminar concerned the underground movement. From my youth, I have been very fond of memoirs on the anti-Tsarist Russian underground. I was impressed by the ethical position of people who could murder as well as refrain from murder; for example, when a man condemned to be killed went out with his wife, there was a strict order to refrain from carrying out the operation so as not to injure innocent people. Leyzer Levin would tell of his experiences when Po'alei Zion was in the Tsarist underground. That Seminar laid the groundwork for our educational movement throughout the Generalgouvernement[55]—people were shaped in the Seminar, educationally and mentally, and returned full of enthusiasm. Now we had to take care of them, wherever they went. This was when the publication La-Madrikh [For the Counselor] appeared.

Tuvia Borzykowski tells about the library he saved; not everywhere were they saved.[56] In some places, people panicked and the libraries were lost. So we started publishing fragments of things in La-Madrikh. We would type something and the couriers would take the material to the various places. One issue of La-Madrikh on "the national question" was preserved, which included writings of Jabotinsky, Ahad Ha-Am, B. Borokhov, and Nakhman Syrkin.[57] This served as educational material for the counselors (hence the name). Only one issue is left.

We expanded the concept of "Dzielna." In general, when we talked about Dzielna, we meant the commune; but we had many rooms in the same courtyard (it was a house with a closed courtyard) and elsewhere, because, before 1940, everybody with an apartment wanted to make money by renting a room. People in that courtyard were well-to-do—I saw that from the apartments—middle-class folks. It wasn't hard to find rooms in the various floors of the house and in nearby places.

54. Lipa Bloch: Born in Uman, Ukraine. Director of the Jewish National Fund. One of the directors of the Jewish Self-Help Society (YISA) in the Warsaw Ghetto. Caught by the Germans in early 1943 and sent to concentration camps. Details of his death unknown; about fifty-five years old.

55. Generalgouvernement—the part of occupied Poland not annexed to the German Reich, which included four administrative districts: Kraków, Lublin, Warsaw, and Radóm, where there were about 1.4 million Jews. The border dividing the areas annexed to the Reich and the Generalgouvernement was an obstacle in effecting contact between Jewish communities on either side of it.

56. See Borzykowski 1964 (Hebrew):227–229.

57. Vladimir Jabotinsky (1880–1940): Right-wing Zionist leader, founder of the Revisionist movement. Ahad Ha-Am (Asher Hirsch Ginsberg; 1856–1927): Hebrew essayist and influential ideologue of cultural Zionism in Russia, died in Eretz Israel. Nachman Syrkin (1868–1924): Ideologist and leader of Socialist Zionism, active in the U.S.

The Seminar was held at Dzielna. We brought people in and had to feed them. Even back then, Zivia and I would go to the corridors of organizations that might help us. I would bring somebody like Yitzhak Giterman to Dzielna and show him what we were doing.[58] Giterman was one of the directors of the Joint in Poland who obviously was sympathetic to me and gave money. Another man, Henryk Rottenberg, headed the Jewish Self-Help Society (Yidishe soziale aleynhilf—YISA).[59] Zivia used to go there for food. In a conversation with me, he said that the poet Matityahu Shoham had been a childhood friend of his.[60] I started talking with him about Matityahu Shoham's play *Tyre and Jerusalem* and won his heart. Matityahu Shoham, of blessed memory, had no idea of his role in getting food from that Rottenberg.

When I came, I found Yitzhak Katznelson and his family in Warsaw. Yosef Kornianski had brought him there from Łódz. He lectured on the Bible and Hebrew literature and played an important role in our Seminar. The Seminar brought him close to us. A special partnership was created of people who bear responsibility together. I'm sure that that Seminar had a great influence on the party members. It looks simple— you bring forty young people together and make a Seminar; but, in fact, it's not so simple. An aura of underground people was created around us. At that time, the Germans weren't so interested in us. The importance of Dzielna 34 may have been its proximity to Pawiak, which was right next door.[61] Holding a seminar next door to Pawiak held an air of the romantic and that was very important. From morning to night, students stood guard, and we could imagine that what was done at Dzielna 34 was being observed from Pawiak. Our guards were stretched out on the balcony, watching the street, and informed us if Germans passed by—and that also added to the atmosphere. They didn't miss a thing, even if they were absent from the Seminar for an hour. All these things united and shaped a group of young people.

58. Yitzhak Giterman: Born in Homostopol. Sent from the U.S. to direct the Joint in Poland. Active in underground cultural activities in the ghetto, including the Ringelblum Archives; supported defense operations and resistance. Killed January 18, 1943, on the first day of the January Uprising, at the age of fifty-four.

59. Yidishe Sotsiale Aleynhilf: Established in September 1939. After the surrender of Warsaw, it continued as ZYTOS (Zydowskie Towarzystwo Opieki Społecznej) and later became the JHF (Jüdisches Hilfs Kommität), concentrating on Jewish welfare in the Warsaw Ghetto. (See Ringelblum 1986:xliv.)

60. Matityahu Shoham (1893–1937): Born in Warsaw. Hebrew poet and playwright. His play, *Tyre and Jerusalem* (1933), was written during a trip to Eretz Israel. The central theme of the play is the uniqueness of the Hebrew nation.

61. Famous Polish prison on Dzielna Street, since Tsarist times, where political prisoners (among them, Rosa Luxemburg) were held.

That Seminar took place under the shadow of the ghetto. It was the middle of 1940; the idea of annihilation hadn't yet occurred to us. All those who attended the Seminar returned home as planned. They weren't our only source of contact. As news of the establishment of a ghetto in Warsaw approached, we decided to send coordinators chosen from the seminar graduates to the surrounding cities with large Jewish communities so that, if contact with Warsaw was disrupted, these coordinators would be in charge of operations. Thus, David Salzberg, of He-Halutz Ha-Tza'ir in prewar Warsaw, was in Lublin in the early period, and was later in one of the training kibbutzim.[62] The members of the Warsaw branch nicknamed him Dolfus; he was a short redhead. He was replaced by Rivka Glanz, who left Lublin later on.[63] I met her in Lublin during the ghetto period, and afterward, I met her again in Częstochowa, where she worked as a coordinator. In Kielce, the coordinator was Regina Litewska, from an affluent Zionist family of Łódz who came to Warsaw as refugees.[64] (Her brother was Shalom Litewski.) Laban was the coordinator in Kraków. I appointed a few older ones who weren't in the Seminar (graduates of the youth movements) whose job was to coordinate operations. Most of those who attended the Seminar returned home. Kielce, for example, didn't include only the city of Kielce; and the same for Lublin, which comprised the surrounding area and Hrubieszów where seminar participants came from. Thus we built cells in every community and town, and seminar participants were the coordinators in the cities. We tested them before we approved them and collected information about their intellectual, moral, and organizational aptitudes. "Fives" were adapted to underground conditions and began to be organized in all those places.

I already said that Dzielna saved people, saved us as a Movement. Until the end of 1940, we were the only ones who had a movement. The members of Ha-Shomer Ha-Tza'ir worked independently. Neither they nor Gordonia were as lucky as we were, since none of their members came from the west, nor did they take an apartment on Gęsia or Leszno. The last apartment of their commune was on Leszno, but was taken over by refugees. For several months, the members of Ha-Shomer Ha-Tza'ir held

62. David Salzberg: Born in Warsaw. Active in Dror in the Warsaw underground and later in Lublin. Details of his death are unknown; aged about twenty-five.
63. Rivka Glanz: Born in Konin. One of the founders of Dror underground in Warsaw; organizer of operations in Lublin in late 1940. Established a kibbutz in Częstochowa and was one of the leaders of ZOB there. Fought in the uprising in Częstochowa (Yom Kippur 1942) and was killed at the head of a unit of ghetto fighters on June 26, 1943, at the age of twenty-eight.
64. Regina Litewska: Born in Łódz. Active in Dror underground in Warsaw and Kielce. Killed in the Great Aktsia in Warsaw Ghetto in August 1942 at the age of twenty-five.

their assemblies and ideological debates in our apartment at Dzielna 34 and invited us to participate in them. So I know a little bit about those ideological debates. We opened our apartment on Dzielna to them, since they didn't have a proper place of their own. This fact determined the development of that movement. Ha-Shomer Ha-Tza'ir did have people like Tosia Altman, Yosef Kaplan, and Shmuel Braslaw[65]; Mordechai Anielewicz[66] came later, and so did David Nowodworski[67] and others; but at first they were scattered all over the country.

We, on the other hand, had a commune that grew because we were always striving to expand it. And so, the idea of Dzielna as an underground center was born. I think the idea was born even before I came, but it was fostered by Zivia after I arrived. Leah Perlstein and I also maintained a farm in Czerniaków (a Warsaw suburb). Even before that, we renovated our training farm in Grochów, and we generously offered to let other movements share it. The big house in Grochów was destroyed but the outbuildings remained; and, with the help of the Judenrat, we built a hut there. We supported that; we may even have suggested it. Grochów was a symbol of the general Halutz movement, because, henceforth, we and Ha-Shomer Ha-Tza'ir weren't the only ones at Grochów, there was also Ha-No'ar Ha-Tzioni and Ha-Po'el Ha-Mizrakhi. But after a few months, frictions erupted between the movements and lasted a long time. Apparently there was a difference of opinion about what Grochów's

65. Shmuel Braslaw: Born in Moscow. Came to Warsaw in 1940, one of the founders and leaders of the Ha-Shomer Ha-Tza'ir underground in the German zone and one of the founders of the ZOB. Killed on September 3, 1942, at the age of twenty-two. He was described by Peretz Opoczynski as "a talented fellow, a great idealist and a man of action" (Ringelblum 1986:102). According to Chaika Grossman, he "loved classical music, beautiful pictures and poetry. He was a bit of an esthete in his attitude toward both cultural values and people. His thinking was clear and quick, sometimes too much so. He was versed in pure Marxist ideology, most of which had been obtained from books and only a little from life" (Grossman 1987:76).

66. Mordechai Anielewicz: Born in Warsaw. Active in the leadership of Ha-Shomer Ha-Tza'ir, as editor of the underground press and an educator. Was close to the organizers of the Ringelblum Archives. Appointed ZOB commander in September 1942. Led the April Uprising and was killed with his comrades in the bunker at Miła 18 on May 8, 1943 at the age of twenty-four. According to Chaika Grossman, Anielewicz "combined in himself two important necessary traits of a representative of a fighting public: his clear and unequivocal thinking grounded in study, and his decisive, courageous and deliberate proletarian character. Practicality in thinking and thinking put into practice—that was Mordechai" (Grossman 1987:77).

67. David Nowodworski: One of the organizers of Ha-Shomer Ha-Tza'ir in the Warsaw Ghetto; was sent to Treblinka during the Great *Aktsia,* escaped, and returned to the ghetto in August 1942, and reported on events there. Was a leader of a combat unit in the ZOB during the April Uprising. Subsequently escaped through the sewers, joined a partisan group in Wyszków. Captured by the Gestapo and killed at the age of twenty-seven. (See Gutman 1982:222; Lewin 1989:39; 170.)

function was supposed to be. We thought we should open Grochów, build it to hold more people, and wait for better times, the end of the war. Others wanted to "eat" Grochów, to support themselves from it. Our members were responsible for the big commune at Dzielna 34, but others didn't have such a responsibility, since they didn't have training kibbutzim. This was the source of constant friction at Grochów.

At that time, there was free contact with the suburb of Praga, on the east side of the Wisła River (where Grochów was located), but later, after November 15, 1940, there was a ghetto. In this initial period, when Grochów belonged to us, you could ride the tram there with no problem. In those days, there was a ceremony of the first fruits, a Shevuoth holiday attended by Adam Czerniakow, head of the Warsaw Judenrat, in the presence of the Germans.[68] Sak made an impressive appearance at the ceremony. He spoke fluent and eloquent Polish, and, as I recall, he made quite an impression on Czerniakow.[69] I never spoke with the head of the Judenrat, but in my opinion, the Czerniakow of 1940 was not the Czerniakow of 1942. I don't see him as a traitor, God forbid; nor do I necessarily identify the institution of the Judenrat at that time with treason. Professor Feldman Schweren, a great scientist, who for some reason was a member of the Patrons of Grochów, was also at the ceremony. Zivia always took care of "the big shots"; she met with them and brought them to this big celebration. I must also mention the agronomist Israel Sudowicz, who was in charge of "Toporol" (The Federation to Cultivate Agriculture among Jews) and later played an important role in the uprising in Treblinka.[70] It was a great celebration and a lot of people came. It was spring, a really joyous day. Open expanses and fields, as opposed to the narrow Jewish streets in Warsaw. And the Germans were impressed by the fact that Jews were working in agriculture. But we didn't like hearing them scold the Judenrat to give us a cow or a horse. We didn't like their concern for us.

68. Adam Czerniakow (1880–1942): Born in Warsaw. First head of the Warsaw Judenrat. Engineer. During the Great *Aktsia,* when he understood that the Jews were being taken for extermination, he committed suicide (July 23, 1942). He was buried in the Jewish Cemetery on Gęsia Street; aged sixty-two. His diary is an important source of information on the, Warsaw Ghetto (*The Warsaw Diary of Adam Czerniakow*).

69. On May 8, 1940, Czerniakow noted in his diary that "the Halutzim from the Grochów farm brought me a gift of their first crops (rhubarb and asparagus)" (1979:147; see also 148 and 189).

70. Sudowicz helped train Halutzim and assisted in saving every plot of ground to grow vegetables. In the Great *Aktsia,* he was sent to Treblinka and assigned to the work brigade; he took advantage of his position to shape a Jewish fighting force among the workers in the death camp. He was one of the commanders of the uprising of August 3, 1943, in which he fell. [This note was written by Zuckerman himself in Lubetkin 1981:331.] For the Treblinka uprising, see Ainsztein 1974:714–742.

When the couriers came from the trains, they had to have someplace to go. Some came to Grochów, others went to the farm in Czerniaków, where they would sleep and pick up material. Thus we set up a transit point and kept the place until the Germans threw us out of Grochów[71] and we moved the people to Czerniaków. Only later, after the *Aktsia*,[72] did we bring our people back from there.

Let's go back to the Seminar. Marek Folman set up youth circles and Tuvia Borzykowski took care of the more proletarian groups. He could hold his own with the "intellectuals," the high school graduates or even those who had begun the university.

A third area we were involved in was courtyards of houses. By nine o'clock at night, curfew was imposed and you couldn't leave the house; so we came up with the idea of working in the closed courtyards. In one Warsaw courtyard, you could hold five branches of the Movement as big as a branch in Jasinówka or some other place. At night, you could hold meetings and other legitimate activities there. Under the aegis of the "Jewish Self-Help Society" (YISA) you could have lectures on literature (for example about Mendele, and the like[73]); the same was true of our friend the actor Jonas Turkow, who lived with us and got permission for public appearances, and we could take advantage of that.[74]

Where did we get so much strength and ideas and pragmatic ability? The fact is we were in charge, and one thing led to another. That youth then appeared in all its glory. Frequently we tried to surface on the general public stage. Celebrations, like the "Evening for Reb Yehudah Ha-Levi," provided an opportunity.[75] Our Movement undertook such events. All the members would sometimes gather in the cultural center on Tłomackie Street. About a thousand people gathered. That's no exaggeration. I know because we used to count the participants. This wasn't something underground, but a legitimate evening event sponsored by YISA. Members would get tickets through our cells. I remember a census

71. For Grochów, see the testimony of Zivia Lubetkin and Yitzhak (Antek) Zuckerman in the collection *In the Cornfields of Grochów* (Hebrew), 1976.

72. Translator's note re: *Aktsia:* The connotation of this word in the context of the Nazi treatment of the Jews has no English equivalent and I have chosen to leave it in the original (Yiddish, deriving from German *Aktion*). It refers to the (usually brutal) roundup and deportation of the Jews from the ghettoes. In Warsaw, the Great *Aktsia* refers specifically to the events of July-September 1942, when some 265,000 Jews were transported from Warsaw Ghetto to Treblinka, where most of them were gassed.

73. Mendele Mokher-Sforim (Shalom Jacob Abramowitz; 1835–1917): Classical Hebrew and Yiddish writer, presenting a critical view of the Jewish predicament.

74. Jonas Turkow (1904–1988): Actor, in charge of theatrical entertainment in Warsaw Ghetto. He and his wife were the only actors to survive the ghetto. Describes ghetto life in *Azoy iz es geven* (*That's How It Was*), 1948. Settled in Israel in 1966.

75. Yehudah Ha-Levi (1075–1141): Hebrew poet and religious philosopher in Spain.

we took of younger people, using this framework, as well as a program for the older ones. With similar numbers, we put on several of Yitzhak Katznelson's Bible evenings, on subjects he raised. We would count the number of those present since there were various groups of young people. There were about a thousand of us in Warsaw, not counting children in the lower grades, just the middle and adult level—that was a movement!

At the approach of the school year in 1940, the issue of study came up: the Germans forbade schools! Spring was past and summer was gone and there were no lessons. They closed all the Jewish schools. The Poles were allowed to maintain independent schools. But in the Jewish areas, Polish schools didn't exist. Jews were allowed neither *Tarbut* schools nor CYSHO[76] schools nor any other schools. In this period, I started getting involved in cultural enterprises. I participated in the administration of *Tarbut,* along with the "elders," Lipa Bloch, Menakhem Kirshenbaum,[77] and a teacher named Rosenblum. There were debates about whether the Germans would allow us to have schools. I couldn't say to them: "Gentlemen, if you wait for the Germans to allow you, you won't have a school." Over and over, they reported on negotiations of the Judenrat with the Germans. Then came the idea not to wait anymore, but to set up an underground academic Gymnasium; and we did.

Initially, there were three students and eight teachers in that school. In time, the number of students increased. An almost complete list of names was published in *Dappim.*[78] The school needed eight teachers, and we needed money because the teachers needed an income. In 1940 and 1941, we got packages of delicacies from Vilna: sausages, cheese, and so forth. But Dzielna didn't see any of that, since we sold it all and gave the money to the teachers. That was the subject of bitter debate at Dzielna 34. Some argued that the Gymnasium took the food out of the members' mouths and, in fact, that was true.

I can guarantee one thing: not a single one of our leaders in Warsaw had more bread to eat than any other member at Dzielna 34. Sometimes party members wanted to take care of Frumka, Zivia, and me and would invite us to meetings in a restaurant at Dzielna 36. In such cases, we would eat there and not at Dzielna. That happened once a month, or once every two months; I would always "bless" those meetings, not so much because

76. Central Yiddish School Organization, a network of secular schools in Yiddish.

77. Menachem Kirshenbaum: Born in Lublin. Underground activist. Member of the General Zionists and of the ZOB Coordinating Committee. Moved to the Aryan side of Warsaw after January 1943. Taken to Pawiak Prison, where he was murdered at the age of fifty.

78. *Dappim Le-Heker Ha-Shoah,* January-April 1951.

of the topics. They were very simple dishes, but I didn't see such things at Dzielna.

In my opinion, except for Leyzer Levin, Po'alei Zion party activists belonged to the "affluent class" in the ghetto, and their situation was different from ours. We had to worry about maintaining the underground movement, the branches and communications, and Dzielna 34; and we had to provide shoes and clothing to all the members. The families of party activists, however, got whatever the needed; they didn't have the obligation to support the Movement in Kraków and Częstochowa, nor did they have to divide what they got. They got aid from the Joint and an allotment to support the kitchen of the Po'alei-Zion–Z.S. party at Gęsia 12. We, however, had to maintain a Gymnasium, organize seminars, support a movement. In fact, a solitary activist we put in Lublin, for instance, would live alone in a room, cook for himself, travel, and so forth and live better than the members at Dzielna, because we always made sure he had a few thousand Złotys to ransom himself if something happened to him on the way. We could endure those bitter debates about where the money went because we ourselves lived just like everybody else in the commune, and we ate breakfast, lunch, and dinner there. I remember one question we were asked in a meeting of the members: how can you spend money on intellectual things instead of on physical needs? I never regretted that, and I'm proud of the Gymnasium.

The Gymnasium lasted until the beginning of the first *Aktsia* and then expired. The *Aktsia* caught up with it in the summer of 1942, and the Gymnasium wasn't re-opened afterward. At the end, there were 120 students and 13 teachers. Except for the 4 or 5 students who remained alive, all others were killed defending the ghetto or in partisan units. Those four are: Havka Folman, Janka Sak (Yonat Sened), Shoshana Gzęda (Kliger),[79] and Sima Ravitska (Krysinski, the daughter of a Bundist, who now lives in Kfar Saba, Israel; her father sent her to us because there wasn't anywhere else to study). The students organized study groups of five, in various houses—at Dzielna 34, with Havka's family, and so forth. Being scattered in houses made things very hard because the teacher always had to run, remember the places, and teach according to the curriculum. The principal of the Gymnasium was Haim Zelmanowski. First we thought it would be Sak, but he was always busy with public affairs. The person who actually ran the Gymnasium was Marek Folman.

79. Shoshana Gziędza: Born in Warsaw in 1923. Member of Dror underground; active in youth work and distribution of underground literature. Was imprisoned in Pawiak at the beginning of the Great *Aktsia* on July 22, 1942. Identified as a Pole, she was sent to Maidanek and various concentration camps in Germany. Survived the war and immigrated to Israel.

The Gymnasium, called the Dror Gymnasium, held courses and exams in every subject, and maintained all the formalities of a Gymnasium. In addition to the requirements, things were taught there that were never taught in any Hebrew Gymnasium in Poland. We introduced some unique topics, common in the youth movement: mutual May Day celebrations, celebrations of Tel-Hai Day[80] and Hanukah, as well as social discussions. The Gymnasium, in general, was like a youth movement. The senior students were monitors for the younger children. Everyone gave what he could. Yitzhak Katznelson ran dramatic circles; there was a choir and plays were performed. Everything centered on the Gymnasium and the Movement. And that was our semi-legitimate aspect. Naturally, there was no lack of foul-ups. Like this one: Marek Folman tried to get students who could pay tuition. But we also had to support poor students, lower-class students, who didn't have money and couldn't pay. One day, Marek came on the twelve-year-old son of a rich man, Abraham Gancwajch, and was very happy about it. I was still a stranger in the city and I learned that the man paid a lot of money because he wanted his son to study in this Gymnasium. In time, we found out that that Gancwajch was the leader of the *Trzynastka* [The Thirteen], a Judenrat institution whose official function was to fight profiteers, and such.[81] In fact, however, he was simply a Gestapo agent in the ghetto. He was from Radomsk, worked in Częstochowa, and then in Austria. He had been a member of Po'alei Zion–Z.S. but had been expelled from the party for sins he had supposedly committed. He knew Hebrew. By this time, he was already remote from Po'alei Zion. He was intimate with writers, tried to get friendly with Yitzhak Katznelson, Yitzhak Schipper, and others, and demonstrated concern for artists. Once my "musical ear" picked up the name Gancwajch. I began to get interested, and it turned out that the son of the Gestapo man was one of our students, and thus endangered the entire Gymnasium.

When we told Marek what we learned about the "great windfall" he had brought us, he got scared too. We decided that the boy should continue studying a few more weeks or months, and then Marek would go to Gancwajch and tell him that the Gymnasium was being dismantled for lack of money. A few months later, Marek did go to Gancwajch and tell him the story. Gancwajch offered Marek a job as private tutor for his

80. Tel-Hai Day: Tel-Hai, a settlement in the north of Israel. Joseph Trumpeldor and seven comrades were killed defending it in 1920. Tel-Hai Day, 11 Adar, became a Zionist holiday.

81. Abraham Gancwajch (1904–?): A Gestapo agent in the Warsaw Ghetto; submitted bi-weekly reports to the Gestapo on the underground in the ghetto. He also worked for some time in the Aryan quarter against the Polish underground. All traces of him have vanished. See Czerniakow 1979:330 & passim; Gutman 1989:90–94; Ainsztein 1979:7–14.

son; Marek replied that he was very busy but would consider it. When Marek came to discuss it, we told him to take it. So Marek became a tutor in Gancwajch's house. After he became familiar with the place, I asked him to pay attention to the papers and documents there, and he took from the house a kind of report on underground studies in the ghetto and on yeshivas. We were the only ones not mentioned in the report. That is, he denounced everyone except us. At the Bar-Mitzvah of the Gancwajch boy, while Marek was still his tutor, the son showed him a Hebrew book, the *Book of the Shomrim of Ha-Shomer Ha-Tza'ir,* with a dedication in German, a Bar-Mitzvah present from the Gestapo. I don't remember exactly when Marek got out of there with the excuse that he couldn't continue. And so we parted from Gancwajch. I know he didn't denounce Dzielna 34, where groups and discussions took place, or the Dror Gymnasium; he just denounced others.

There were examinations in the Gymnasium. German and Polish were taught along with Hebrew; and there were promotions from grade to grade. One of our students was Hancia (Plotnizka). She had no formal education and we wanted her to study. She studied along with Havka, even though she was much older. Havka's group was an unusual group, which played a key role in the education of the young generation in Warsaw. All its members were killed. The students who later served as couriers played an important role and were killed in various towns. It's not enough to sit "on high" and give orders. They did the work on the ground. I can't imagine how we would have run the Movement without the graduates of the Gymnasium, or what place our Movement would have had in the uprising if not for the Seminars and the Gymnasium. All the links were intertwined and created the Movement web.

After the war, I tried to get details from Zelmanowski; I would remind him of things and try to make him talk. Unfortunately, he didn't remember much; but he did recall some things, especially dramatic events. For example: how we pulled him out of a convoy going to the *Umschlagplatz.*[82] But he didn't remember details about the Gymnasium.

The Gymnasium existed until summer 1942. We finished school in June, the Great German *Aktsia* began on July 22. By that time, I was no longer involved in the Gymnasium. This was after the German operations in Vilna and Chelmno, and other events. I was deep underground at that time, in hiding. This is how the chapter of the Gymnasium ended.

On Yom Kippur 1940, a conference was held, which Zivia has already described,[83] which was attended by many members. Our dining room on

---

82. *Umschlagplatz*—place for transshipment, where Jews were concentrated before being shipped to camps. See map of ghetto.
83. Lubetkin 1981:36ff.

Dzielna was packed; they were sitting on top of one another and on the floor. It went on for a night and a day—a conference of the members of the kibbutzim of Grochów and Czerniaków, and of Movement members and counselors. There were lectures and debates. At this conference, an attempt was made to sum up the work that had been done; there was a lecture on the labor movement, by Tuvia, as usual. I think I spoke about the coming days. But I could hardly envision and guess what was coming—that we faced total destruction; such a thing didn't occur to me. I remember that, in conversations with young people, I would tell them the fable of the Yiddish fable writer Eliezer Steinbarg about the goat.[84] And another parable about the spear and the needle. The needle asks the spear: "What do you do?" And the spear says: "I kill people." "What do you do?" the spear mocks the needle. The needle replies: "I sew here, sew there—make clothing. And you, spear, kill here, kill there, but what comes of it? What is it all for?" I really don't understand the Germans, I said at the time; what do they get out of killing another thousand, ten thousand Jews? What do they want to achieve? It didn't occur to me then that, if the final goal was really the total destruction of the Jews, they were on the "right track." Because all that humiliation and contempt, the oppression and weakening of the mind and body—that was the system they stuck to. I didn't foresee what was in the offing, since I wasn't a prophet. That conference held "for the days to come"[85] was, in my opinion, an historic conference, unifying and very formative; and it was gratifying to see those young people together, listening, debating; that was a profound experience. Frumka came to that conference. She went outside during a break; we didn't have a radio and the loudspeaker in the streets was announcing the establishment of the ghetto. They weren't really setting it up in fact then, just announcing it. The ghetto was established on November 15, 1940. Signs marking its areas had already been put up. A few times previously, they had talked about establishing the ghetto, but it was always postponed; and we thought it would be this time too. It was Frumka who brought that news, which added Tish'a b'Av to Yom Kippur. The conference ended at the end of the holiday, I think, and the people dispersed to their places. A few party members, like Yosef Sak, Leyzer Levin, and Yohanan Morgenstern, who weren't active participants, also attended the conference.

Let me add a superficial review of a few areas of our educational and Movement activity. In the seminars, we had to add another course for the

84. Eliezer Steinbarg (1880–1932): Yiddish educator and poet. His volume of fables, *Mesholim,* published a few months after his death, became a best seller.
85. "For the Days to Come"—the title of a programmatic article by Berl Katznelson in the early 1920s, *Kovetz Akhdut Ha-Avoda* 2, 1932.

girls, to train them as kindergarten teachers. Our schools didn't include all the children, some stayed in the courtyards and didn't study. On Gęsia, there was an orphanage, which was a children's day school. If memory serves me correctly, one of the Plotnitzka sisters was a teacher there, maybe principal of the school. But we also worked in other schools and included only a minority of the children in the courtyards of the many houses. We activated every possible member for educational and social work and, of course, in this respect, Gęsia 12 was of great help since children there got aid from CENTOS[86] and welfare committees not directly supervised by the party.

By now, there were a lot of refugees in Warsaw. Jewish Warsaw was swollen by many uprooted people who were simply dying, even before Treblinka. I spent some evenings in the courtyards of the refugees and stayed overnight because you couldn't move. What could you do in the face of that poverty? Families lived by selling their goods in the market on Gęsia until they ran out of things. Then they died. I saw families, whole tribes, towns that disappeared. When I came back to them some time later, I didn't find a soul. People tried to return to areas annexed by the Germans to the Warthegau-Wartheland area.[87] A family from Konin tried to sneak back there and were expelled. As punishment, the Germans would make bonfires and force the Jews trying to return to go through the fire. They were forced to return to Warsaw. One day, I was called to a girl whom I remembered from before the war. I had been at their house a few times before they tried to sneak back to their hometown from Warsaw, since they didn't have anything to live on. Their town was already *Judenrein,* and they were expelled again, along with the other Jews. Her father contracted typhus and two other members of the family died within two days. I was at the funeral of our student and of her father. I can't describe the sights of those days—the streets, the houses, what was in the houses.

This was at the beginning of the ghetto, before a place was cleared for the refugees who needed a little soup, aside from floors and walls. Mortality was high. According to the numbers, there were about half a million Jews in Warsaw at that time. But if we take an account of the great expulsion, we're not talking about half a million Jews anymore. Many died of disease and hunger—those were the first victims of the Germans. We can be proud of the fact that, except for one case, none of our group died of either typhus or hunger. We were hungry and on the brink of de-

86. Centrala Opieki nad Sierotami (Organization for the Care of Orphans), established in 1936.
87. Poznań region.

struction, and even beyond; but there was only one single case of death by starvation among us, a tragic case of one of our students in the first seminar, who was scolded for not working properly. One day, I took him for a talk and said: "Listen, they're watching you, you've got a function, you're an educator, and there are complaints." He didn't answer. It turned out he was afraid that if it were discovered he had tuberculosis, we would throw him out of the commune. And expulsion from the commune meant death. Of course that was utter nonsense on his part. After we found out about him, we put him in the sanitorium at Otwock, where he died a while later. I don't remember any cases of death among our members, not on Dzielna, or Grochów, or Czerniaków.

We tried to find a solution for many people through seasonal work. We tried "to compete" with the Germans. We contacted many Polish farmers in the villages to get work with them. Since hundreds of thousands of Poles, and not only Poles, were sent to Germany, the farms and estates were left without a sufficient labor force. We took advantage of this situation and got help from Toporol and their organizer Israel Sudowicz. He gave us lists of estates, where we made agreements. Naturally, the agreement, designed to guarantee food and a social life after working hours, could be broken. The work day was long, more than eight or ten hours; but there was always enough food: potatoes and milk. More than in the ghetto, more than at Dzielna 34, and you could spend evenings together after hard work in the fields.

Despite the hard conditions, there were a lot of applicants for that work. We developed it very much and Ha-Shomer Ha-Tza'ir, He-Halutz Ha-Mizrakhi, and Gordonia followed our lead. The Bund, of course, argued with us about it. Their underground paper accused us of doing that "contemptible work" after the Germans took the young Poles from the villages. They forgot that the young people from the Polish villages took all the jobs of the Jews outside the ghetto, without blinking an eyelash, and we were a nation of beggars inside the ghetto. If we hadn't done that work, the Germans would have turned those places into labor camps. And later, I saw what a labor camp was, when I spent a week in one.

In Łódz, the ghetto was closed off on May 1, 1940; in Będzin—later (spring 1943). Of course we knew about that, even though we didn't have contact with the outside then. We knew about the pogroms, and the synagogues that were burned down even in the "good days," before the war with the Soviet Union. We personally experienced the degradation of the Jews. It wasn't epidemics at that time that caused the establishment of the ghetto, as the Head of the Judenrat, Czerniakow, maintained. If memory serves me right, it all began when Czerniakow went to

Kraków with a delegation that included Michael Weichert,[88] Israel Milejkowski,[89] and Yosef Jaszunski;[90] meanwhile I came to Warsaw.[91] A few days later, during Passover week 1940, there was a pogrom. It was carried out by Poles, but organized by Germans. Information about the pogrom reached Czerniakow while he was in Kraków and then he tried to deal with it.[92] One "reason" for establishing the ghetto was "to defend the lives of the Jews from the pogroms and their perpetrators." So, supposedly, Jews had to be separated and a special neighborhood had to be set up for them. Later, the typhus epidemic also appeared as a reason. Supposedly, because of typhus, entrance to the ghetto was forbidden.

Of course, the main cause of the typhus epidemic was the German treatment of the Jews, which produced hunger and diseased sanitary conditions. They denied the Jews whatever could help their lives. Everything was done to increase the typhus. We didn't accept their reasoning, we saw it as another sign of the German scourge; but, even then, the intention of total destruction had by no means occurred to us—until I heard with my own ears, one autumn evening, the information about the slaughter at Ponar and at Chelmno.[93]

In those days, 1940 and early 1941, the western European front was paralyzed; most of Europe was subjugated to Hitler. After Dunkirk, the Germans stood at the English Channel, on the eve of the assault on the Balkans.

The hope that salvation would come from the west had disappeared. There was nothing to believe in; a young person had no confidence about the end of the war.

88. Michael Weichert (1890–1967): Born in Galicia. A Yiddish theatrical producer; he was head of YISA, first in the Warsaw Ghetto, later in the entire Generalgouvernement. Immigrated to Israel and wrote three volumes of memoirs explaining his activities.

89. Israel Milejkowski: Zionist activist, head of the Judenrat Health Department. Did research on health conditions in Warsaw Ghetto for the Ringelblum Archives. See Ringelblum 1986:741–746.

90. Yosef Jaszunski: Chairman of the Judenrat Labor Commission. Engineer, director of ORT (Organization for Promotion of Work among Jews) in prewar Poland; involved with YISA. Deported to Treblinka in 1943, and killed there.

91. For the Kraków meeting, see Kaplan 1973:136; Czerniakow 1979:132–134; Gutman 1989:39.

92. On the pogrom in Warsaw on March 24–26, 1940, see Adam Czerniakow 1979: 71–73, Chaim Kaplan 1973:134ff; Ainsztein 1979:32; Blumenthal and Kermish 1965: 41–42. According to Emmanuel Ringelblum, ". . . 53 persons were murdered in the Jewish quarter. Among them were several excellent and talented people, activists engaged in social work, some youth who were members of organizations, several bakers . . . and some accidental victims" (Ringelblum 1986:705).

93. Ponar: site of mass slaughter outside Vilna. Chelmno: one of six death camps in Poland.

I recalled my parents' stories about World War I, how they would tell about the Germans and their inhuman treatment. But that absolutely could not be compared with what was going on now. I had attended the first Hebrew Gymnasium in Vilna, the leading high school in the Diaspora, which had been established during the German occupation in World War I. The Jewish theater had also been set up then, and great Jewish writers, like Arnold Zweig, had been officers in the German army.[94] That is, things the Tsarist regime didn't permit were allowed by the Germans in World War I. In my naïveté, I thought we'd come out of it now, too, if we just held on in the period of great degradation. But it wasn't like that. In Vilna, they said: *A mensh trakht un got lakht.* (Man does his best and God likes to jest.)

I was amazed: more humiliation and more murder, and those who were killed were laid in front of us. Jews were caught for forced labor and for camps. But the exploitation of the labor force, even in their terms, as it was done, didn't enhance their war effort. Neither in the airfield of Okęcie nor in the camps around Lublin. We read in *Mein Kampf* that Hitler would detroy the Jews; we read his speech in the Reichstag. But we didn't take it seriously. Even today, who would consider every expression of antisemitism? We saw it as rhetoric, not as the expression of something he intended to carry out. The idea was *iberlebn*—we'll get through this. We tried to solve the problems by reinforcing the spirit and education of the youth, and so we cared about schools. It was already a major catastrophe, and we knew that many people would die. By then, we were talking about tens of thousands; but it didn't occur to us that it would be millions!

An incident with a hat is typical of those times. A few days after the Germans put up the ghetto wall, a bottleneck was created in the passage from the big ghetto to the small ghetto; a bridge was set up over Chłodna, a Polish street, and perhaps hundreds of Jews would gather and wait for a chance to pass. The Germans would open the gates in the Polish street for a short time to let the Jews pass. There everyone encountered the Germans face to face, and it was one of the sites of humiliation. One day, I had to pass from the big ghetto to the small one, and I was wearing a hat; the German order was that you had to take off your hat in their presence. Previously, when I came on a German, I would cross the street or slip into an alley or a courtyard so as not to take off my hat. When a Jew met a German on the sidewalk, he had to get off. And it took special senses to devise means not to encounter a German and to "get along" without having to take off your hat. And I didn't take off my hat.

94. Arnold Zweig (1886–1968): German-Jewish writer; lived in Palestine from 1933 to 1948 and then spent the rest of his life in East Germany.

I remember us standing there, in a line, as the Poles were passing by; then the gates were closed, the Jews were given a few minutes to pass, and the shout rang out: "Take off your hats!" In my heart, I made a decision not to take off my hat. I was over six feet tall; I saw the shorter Jews walking along, and I knew the shout was addressed to me. Then they shot, but I wasn't hit. My soul did indeed "drop to my feet," but I didn't take off my hat. From that day on, my decision was firm: I would go out without a hat, even when the temperature was below zero. And most of our members and Ha-Shomer Ha-Tza'ir did the same.

But you did have to wear the Magen-David armband. Korczak was once arrested for walking around without it. Anyone who didn't wear it was sent to prison immediately, but you could also be murdered on the spot, without a trial. I should say that the death sentence for not taking off your hat or not wearing the Magen-David was not "legal." Nevertheless, they could have murdered me just like that, and nothing would have been done to the murderer. It was different if they caught you on a train; in that case, it was the death sentence on the spot. They simply took you off the train and killed you. Obviously, that behavior of the Germans was determined from the top; and yet, I traveled back and forth through the Generalgouvernement. Some places were easier, Hrubieszów, for example, was a pleasure, compared to Warsaw. Of course, it all depended on local authorities, but there was a general order forbidding Jews throughout the Generalgouvernement to ride on trains! In my travels, I saw ghettoes established almost everywhere. In small towns, conditions were more comfortable, they couldn't devote so many forces to guarding the small places. It was like that until they started expelling and concentrating Jews from the small towns in bigger cities.

Acts of resistance took place much later. We knew about murders back in 1941 (in Eretz Israel, people learned about them only at the end of 1942). That was something else altogether. I must say that *Dror* had stopped publication by then. That paper, with articles by Beilinson[95] and Tabenkin,[96] disappeared at that time. And only *Yediyes*, a simple Yiddish informative bulletin, was published. We also published something in Polish, edited by Marek Folman, called *Wolność* (*Freedom*—i.e., *Dror*). He did that in Polish for the circles we worked with, like the former Communists, and the former assimilationists. Some of us came with Polish, and left speaking Yiddish and sometimes even Hebrew.

95. Moshe Beilinson (1889–1936): Hebrew writer and journalist and one of the major spokesmen of the Labor Movement in Eretz Israel.
96. Yitzhak Tabenkin (1887–1971): One of the founders and spiritual leader of Ha-Kibbutz Ha-Meuchad, the kibbutz federation in Israel with which Dror was affiliated.

At Dzielna, there was an ingathering of exiles packed together. All "classes": wretched proletarians and small-town Jews, as well as university students who had had little to do with Jewish life until 1940.

From this point of view, we did something important in many places: an attempt to remember and learn from Jewish history. I remembered An-sky and his work during World War I.[97] While still a boy, I read everything he wrote; and I also knew Dr. Jacob Wygodski's memoirs of that war, as well as those of Dr. Eifuner, our doctor in Warsaw. I remembered the persecutions and welfare operations from then. You always look for a foothold in the past and try to learn something. The important thing we tried to do in 1940 was to publish an anthology, the only book published in the ghetto (except for the play *Job* by Yitzhak Katznelson which we published later): *Payn un gvure*. Some people later wrote that it was edited by Yitzhak Zuckerman. But the truth is that Eliahu Gutkowski edited it with me. In the second edition of M. Neustadt's book (*Destruction and Uprising of the Jews of Warsaw*), he eliminated me and put Eliahu Gutkowski in. Elsewhere, I appear as the only editor. Eliahu Gutkowski was a history teacher and lectured at our Gymnasium. One day, I suggested the book to him, and I remember how we divided the work between us. We found parts of that anthology in the books in my library. I had a library at Dzielna, as in the Soviet zone, with perhaps 2,000 books. How did I amass such a library? Owners of libraries and writers sold their books to stay alive. In Israel Zinberg's monumental *History of Literature by Jews*, we found translated extracts, for example, from the Crusader period.[98] We found the poet S. Tshernikhovsky's "Barukh of Magenza" translated freely into Yiddish by Yehiel Lerer;[99] and we also translated some of Brenner's writings. We found many relevant things. We concluded with Tabenkin's words at the council of Yagur[100] in 1936. As I recall, the subject was self-defense. Tabenkin, as a rule, is very hard to translate; so, we edited his speech a little. That took some nerve but we had to "smooth it out" a bit. The anthology also began with the condition of the soul, in pogroms, and continued with various persecutions: the Crusades, blood libel accusations, well poisonings,[101] and then

97. S. An-sky (Rapoport; 1863–1920): Yiddish writer (author of *The Dybbuk*). During World War I, he devoted himself to aiding Jewish refugees and wrote about their suffering in his books *Hurbn Galicia (The Destruction of Galicia)* and *Ha-Gehenom (Hell)*.

98. Israel Zinberg (1873–1939): Chemist and Jewish scholar in Leningrad; liquidated in the Stalinist purges. His eight-volume history, *Geshikhte fun der literatur bay yidn (History of Literature by Jews)* was published between 1929 and 1937.

99. Yehiel Lerer (1910–1943): Yiddish poet, participated in Warsaw Ghetto literary activities; transported to Treblinka in 1943.

100. Yagur: Kibbutz in northern Israel, near Haifa, founded in 1922.

101. Accusations against Jews during the Middle Ages.

Brenner on the condition of the soul (*He Told Her*), as well as writings about Ha-Shomer and Hagana. That book made an extraordinary impact, and many of those who received the anthology printed in stencil bound it and put it among their books. It was the source of educational inspiration, and it gives an idea of what we could and couldn't learn from previous generations. It was still impossible to learn of Treblinka from history or literature.

I say that in the wake of what we learned about World War I. Nowhere and never had there been pogroms, persecutions, and tribulations everywhere at the same time. Sometimes, Jews fled from east to west as in the days of Chmielnicki;[102] or from west to east, as during the Crusades. But one hand organizing and carrying out total death in all Jewish communities in Europe was unprecedented in Jewish history. So it was hard to learn from the past, from history, and we didn't find the slightest expression of a situation of total annihilation. What we did find was poles apart from the annihilation in the days of Hitler. Nor was there an expression of that in the poet who wrote "The Whole Land Is a Gallows to Me," for that was only an expression, a manner of speaking. When Bialik wrote "On the Slaughter," the whole *country* wasn't a gallows for the Jews. There were, indeed, pogroms, but even regarding Bialik's poem, "In the City of Slaughter," written after the Kishinev pogrom,[103] you couldn't say that pogroms took place on the same day wherever there were Jews. So, there wasn't anything or anyone to learn from; and if I had considered, even for a moment, what we hadn't seen in our worst nightmares, I would have thought: "Yitzhak Zuckerman, go to the madhouse!" Because you had to have a sick imagination to come to such conclusions.

Let's go back to the two farms—one was ours and one belonged to other groups. Ours was the Grochów farm, and the other was the Czerniaków farm. Here are a few details about Grochów:

It had a few stages. The first period included up to November 15, 1940, that is, until the establishment of the ghetto. In this period, Grochów was an independent farm, run only by us. I would also divide this period in two: first, when Grochów was a farm common to the whole Halutz Coordinating Committee, when, along with us, there were also members of Ha-Shomer Ha-Tza'ir, Ha-No'ar Ha-Tzioni, and He-Halutz Ha-Mizrakhi, and second, when we (that is, Dror) were the sole owners of Grochów.

102. Bogdan Chmielnicki (1595–1657): Leader of the Cossack and peasant uprising in the Ukraine in 1648, in which tens of thousands of Jews were killed and hundreds of Jewish communities destroyed.

103. Kishinev, in Moldavia, was the site of a famous pogrom in April 1903, which shocked Jews in Russia and around the world. Forty-three Jews were killed and five hundred wounded in the Kishinev pogrom.

After many meetings, the Halutz Coordinating Committee agreed on the personnel of Grochów. Half of sixty places were allotted to Dror. The other half was divided between Ha-Shomer Ha-Tza'ir, Gordonia, Mizrakhi, and Ha-No'ar Ha-Tzioni. Renovations of the farm began in April 1940.

When we renovated Grochów, we thought there would be continuity, that Jewish youth would find agricultural work honorable. We saw Grochów as a symbol, not only as legitimation. Even the Germans admired it. And I said earlier that we weren't happy about the German intervention with Czerniakow (head of the Judenrat) to give us cows for the farm or to be concerned about us. But the merger didn't go well. As we know, conflicts of interests erupted between us and our partners.

In 1940 (still in November), we didn't know about the impending annihilation, we thought Grochów would survive, just as the Jewish people, we thought, would survive after the war; so we thought we should develop Grochów. And we wanted to invest all income, except for assistance to Dzielna 34 and the Halutzim (in the ghetto), in the development of Grochów. The others thought we should eat better. There were similar conflicts in Dzielna, where there was another division of opinion—some members argued that everything should be invested in Movement work, while others thought the body should be nourished and not the soul. Domestic peace between the movements at Grochów didn't last long; differences of opinion led to friction. And there was another shameful issue that caused many quarrels and endangered the farm: the behavior of one of the girls wasn't consonant with either He-Halutz or Jewish morality; the girl, Anna Milewicz, was suspected of prostitution. Most of the groups at Grochów considered her a shady character and wanted to throw her out. She was in Ha-Shomer Ha-Tza'ir and that movement stood by her and opposed throwing her out, because of the atmosphere of friction and strife that prevailed there. Ultimately, she was sent away. The future proved that that was right. Eventually, she was expelled from her movement and, in early 1943, was executed by a group of Revisionists in the ghetto for collaboration with the Germans. Her presence in Grochów could have brought disaster to the farm.[104]

The situation in Grochów, which collapsed because of internal friction, was solved after an open and frank talk I had with Yosef Kaplan of Ha-Shomer Ha-Tza'ir. Despite conflicts, we enjoyed a mutual admiration, since the friction wasn't personal. In that conversation, I told him that, in this shattered situation, Grochów had no future, and if he thought it should be preserved as a Halutz farm, he had to take his people out of the farm first. After that, it would be easier for us to take the others out.

104. See Zuckerman 1985:45.

Apparently he convinced his members and Ha-Shomer Ha-Tza'ir announced that they were withdrawing from Grochów, even though Ha-
Shomer Ha-Tza'ir didn't yet have the Częstochowa farm and there was
no commune at Nalewki (which was established later, in conjunction with
Gordonia). The members of Ha-No'ar Ha-Tzioni also ceded.

On November 15, 1940, Grochów was dismantled. The Germans and
the Polish police surrounded the farm and took the people there to the
ghetto. Only one, Shmulik Greenberg, escaped, hid in the fields and
remained alone. At Yosef Kornianski's request, I went to the Judenrat
with him, where there was an official named Israel Gzęda from Warsaw,
who had been a member of the training kibbutz in Będzin until the
outbreak of the war. We wanted his help to get to the higher authorities
and save Grochów. I couldn't say we got very far that day. I was only at
the first meeting, then Zivia entered the picture. Several days later, due
to Judenrat contacts with the Germans, the other members were allowed
to return to Grochów.

Shmulik remained alone there and took care of the animals. If not for
him, the gentiles would have plundered the farm; but apparently they
stayed away from the place when they saw someone there. So by staying
there, Shmulik saved Grochów. After the other members came back,
Grochów continued to exist for a time as an independent farm under
our control until one day a trustee appeared on behalf of the Germans, from the Poznań area—I don't know if he was a Pole or one of the
Volksdeutsche—and took over Grochów.[105] From then on, there was a
change in our legal situation vis-à-vis the Germans. The trustee was in
charge of the farm and we got our meager bread from him. This period
is also divided in two: the first period, when the man still didn't fully
understand the lives of our members; and the second period, when he
and his staff persecuted and denounced us.

For us, Grochów wasn't just a farm; it was also a waystation for our
couriers. Couriers returning at night to Warsaw would come to the base
at Grochów and get into the ghetto the following day. Sometimes, they
came to Grochów with underground materials and newspapers, would
hide them there, and then set out. So, Grochów was very important for
the Movement.

Once, one of our couriers, with newspapers and other underground
materials, was followed when she left Grochów. She was captured and
handed over to the Polish police and, from them, to the Germans. I
learned of it only a month later when she returned to Dzielna. After she

105. Trustee: The Nazis appointed Aryan trustees to take control of Jewish businesses
on behalf of the Reich.

told the members and the Central Committee about her mission, she asked to talk with me in private, where, instead of talking, she started crying. Only later did she tell that, before the policeman who arrested her transferred her to the Germans, she had to get rid of the newspapers and the other material so as not to betray Grochów and the Movement. She went through great spiritual torment. She paid a high personal price to reward the policeman, and then she was released. Her act was dictated by the fear of catastrophe for the Movement. The price she paid took a heavy toll on her emotional condition. I told the story to one of our women members who took her to a doctor, but she never recovered.

The situation in Grochów became more difficult by the day. Ultimately, the trustee (apparently a *Volksdeutsche*) simply threw them out of there. That was before the *Aktsia*, that is, before the middle of 1942, if I'm not mistaken.

In Czerniaków, the situation was different, since that was the private estate of a Pole. We met with the owner of the estate only once. At that time, we were on good terms with the agronomist Israel Sudowicz, the leader of Toporol, an organization to develop Jewish agriculture even before the war, and also one of the initiators of Czerniaków; he encouraged that whole operation and made sure that vegetables would be grown in every empty place in the ghetto, flowerpots, as well as ruins; no matter where, just so there would be a few vegetables. With this purpose, work groups arose wherever an agreement could be reached with an estate owner so that the estate wouldn't turn into a labor camp, but rather an autonomous Halutz farm. Sudowicz gave us a list of recommended places, which included Czerniaków, a suburb of Warsaw. This was in the middle of 1940, before we resettled Grochów. At about the same time, Leah Perlstein, who managed the farm, asked me to take care of it, and I went with her to that estate owner. The place was called the "Zatwarnicki Estate." Zatwarnicki was a gray-haired gentile, about sixty-five years old. (Anyone who was a number of years older than me I considered old.) In conversation with him, it turned out that he had heard the name Halutz. He wasn't an antisemite, quite the opposite. The discussion dealt with conditions. We agreed that, in the terms of work, there would be provisions for supervision and oversight. But, after work, we demanded autonomy and complete freedom to dance or study or do whatever we wanted.

We also requested milk, bread, vegetables, potatoes—quantities of food necessary for our subsistence. I must say that he always upheld all the conditions. Housing was concentrated in remote parts of the fields. It was a big estate—I visited there a few times. I remember one visit with Zivia, where we spent one Sunday at an artificial lake without any disturbances. That was in autumn 1941. It was there I heard about the slaughter in Vilna (Ponar).[106] When I left for the east, Grochów still existed; but when I faced the choice of where to go to and where to leave from—Grochów or Czerniaków—I chose Czerniaków.

The steward of the estate, Zatwarnicki's representative, was a *Volksdeutsche*. He didn't oppress us either. He was always shouting, scolding, grumbling; but he didn't raise his hand; our people preserved their autonomy, made a respectable living (by wartime standards), and helped us too. They used to send food to Dzielna, especially when times were hard for us.

There was no fixed number of people at the estate; during the agricultural season, we added people from our reserve, which amounted to as much as eighty people. There was a time when not only Leah Perlstein, but also Frumka would go there. In fact, we set up a Movement waystation there. Zivia would sometimes leave the ghetto, which was closed off by then, and go to Czerniaków, to spend a day with the members. It was an encouraging view—nothing at all like the sight of a labor camp. Relations were correct. I stayed overnight there a few times. I don't remember if there were mud huts or cabins; at any rate, there were a lot of beds and wooden bunks, in tiers. Sometimes many people came and there weren't enough beds, and then they slept in "levels." There was the sense of a pre-war training kibbutz.

At the time of the expulsion of the Jews of Warsaw, our people in Czerniaków stayed there. At that time, we had an ongoing argument about whether to *defend the ghetto* or *join the partisans*. Ultimately, we decided to *defend the ghetto*. Between July and September 1942 the Germans took hundreds of thousands of Jews out of the ghetto; we wanted to save the people who were to launch the uprising, but we didn't know what to do with them in Warsaw. (Nor did we have enough weapons, but I won't get into details now.) We sent them to Czerniaków, where they stayed during the period of expulsion from Warsaw. The first base of the Jewish Fighting Organization (ZOB)[107] was set up in Czerniaków.

Mordechai Tennenbaum was also in Czerniaków, and of course Leah Perlstein, who was there all the time; Berl Broyde was in Czerniaków and so was Frumka. They left from there to make contact with the AK (Armia Krajowa)[108] and the AL (Armia Ludowa).[109] If that Zatwarnicki or even

106. The slaughter in Ponar began in summer 1941.
107. ZOB: Initials of Zydowska Organizacja Bojowa, founded in July 1942; see below.
108. Armia Krajowa: The Polish home army, subordinate to the commander-in-chief in London. By 1944, the AK numbered nearly 400,000 members, making it the largest resistance force in Nazi-occupied Europe.
109. Armia Ludowa: People's Army, subordinate to the Communist (PPR) Party; smaller and weaker than the AK.

the *Volksdeutsche* steward had wanted to hurt us, they had a thousand chances to do it. They must have observed the girls coming at night and leaving at dawn; they must have felt the Movement rustling around there. But there wasn't a single incident either of denunciation or even of antisemitic reprimand.

Moreover, we rescued a few dozen people who weren't members of the Movement there. For example, Gabriel Ze'ev, our friend Eliahu Gutkowski's little boy. One day, during the Great *Aktsia*, Gutkowski came to us in despair: he had one son, who was three years old. We took him out to Czerniaków and he was saved. Later, in the April Uprising, he was killed with Eliahu Gutkowski, trying to flee through the sewers, when the whole family was gassed by the Germans as they tried to get to the Aryan side of Warsaw. As for Zatwarnicki, I don't know if it was for the money he got, or simply out of sympathy, but he brought another Halutz group besides ours to Czerniaków. A few dozen people were assembled there, simple Jews he hid for a time. It's interesting what he told Leah Perlstein during the *Aktsia* in Warsaw. He promised her that if the Germans wanted to harm those at Czerniaków and he knew about it in advance, he would warn them so they could flee to the fields. But nothing did happen, until he was ordered by the Germans, in November or December 1942, as I recall, to send the Jews of Czerniaków to the ghetto. This was a month or two after the Great *Aktsia* in Warsaw. In any case, no disaster happened to us there, not even the sort of thing that happened to our courier, as I mentioned earlier. We hid part of our archive in Czerniaków, we set up a ZOB base and kept weapons there. Mordechai Tennenbaum, Zacharia Artstein, and Tuvia Borzykowski organized self-defense cells there.[110] During the Great *Aktsia*, we kept a few rifles and grenades there; but they weren't used at all because the *Aktsia* bypassed Czerniaków. Czerniaków, unlike Grochów, didn't collapse, but remained an agricultural station until the last day, serving both as a training kibbutz and as a Movement base and helped sustain us physically.

Later on, we lost contact with Zatwarnicki, but we trusted him so much that, during the Uprising, when people burst out of the ghetto at random or through the sewer and were looking for a place to hide, the first thing that occurred to us was to ask Zatwarnicki. And people did indeed run to Czerniaków, where they couldn't have hidden in the fields without him knowing. We never saw him again, at least I didn't; nor did we hear about him even after the war. He wasn't a young man, and he probably died.

110. Zacharia Artstein: Born in Pruszków. Active in Dror; after the January Uprising (1943), he commanded a Dror unit in the Central Ghetto. He fought heroically in the April Uprising; perished in the sewers on May 8 at the age of about twenty. Described by Zivia Lubetkin as "one of the bravest fighters in the Jewish Fighting Organization" (1981:152).

I don't know if he had any sons. I only want to emphasize that our relations with him were correct, and that he didn't abuse the power granted him by the Germans; he kept his promises and didn't harm us. So we stayed in Czerniaków for a long time, until the end of 1942.

After the war, in 1945, one of the first things I did was go to Grochów. But even then I didn't find the trustee; I think he escaped with the other Germans who left Poland before the end of January 1945. I had a strong desire for a "cozy chat" with that gentile.

Now, it's after the establishment of the ghetto. At the time, we've got two farms outside: Grochów and Czerniaków, and later we have seasonal training groups in various places, under harsher conditions than Czerniaków. Nevertheless, even in those places there are no beatings and there is autonomy. All this was only in the agricultural sector. In late 1941, after the establishment of the ghetto, Ha-Shomer Ha-Tza'ir and Gordonia concluded that they couldn't operate without a base like ours at Dzielna, so they set up a joint commune at Nalewki Street 23; they had fewer members in the Nalewki commune than we did on Dzielna, perhaps because our members were typically drawn from the economically poorer classes, who needed more material support, whereas even before the war, their movements were based on the well-to-do and bourgeois assimilated classes who needed less support even in the ghetto. The wealthy were impoverished whereas the poor died—that was the process.

Back in 1940, we were always absorbing more young people at Dzielna, Grochów, Czerniaków, and the seasonal groups; we absorbed not only those from the west, like the kibbutzim of the Borokhov area in Łódz, Będzin, and other places who had done their training in Poland before 1939 and hadn't had time to immigrate to Palestine, as well as those in Warsaw. We had a big reserve of Movement members in Warsaw, living in very straitened circumstances. The joint commune of Ha-Shomer Ha-Tza'ir and Gordonia was smaller, just a few dozen people. The central people of Ha-Shomer Ha-Tza'ir didn't live in that commune, as we did. Yosef Kaplan lived with his girlfriend, Miriam Heinsdorf, in a private apartment.[111] The central man in Gordonia was Israel Zelcer. In mid-1940, we concluded that we had to unify the ranks. Even though there was occasional friction between us and the other movements, there was nevertheless a feeling of mutual responsibility. And when we learned that Israel Zelcer, whom we had known from before the war as one of the leaders of Gordonia, was in Lublin, we sent a messenger to bring him to

111. Miriam Heinsdorf: Born in Warsaw. Member of He-Halutz Ha-Tza'ir and was their representative on the Jewish National Committee and the Jewish Coordinating Committee. Fought in the Többens-Schultz area during the April Uprising. Details of her death unknown; aged about thirty.

Warsaw to assemble the members of Gordonia, who came to us at Dzielna from time to time like sheep without a shepherd. We brought Israel Zelcer and his young wife Hannah (who was from Lublin, which was why they were living there). When they came, we gave them an apartment Dror had on Nowolipki. Zelcer then began gathering the members of Gordonia together. Eliezer Geller joined him later.[112]

We didn't propose to Gordonia to join Dror, nor were we thrilled about the merger. We didn't realize that new circumstances and conditions made it imperative to unify the movements. We had no illusions about promoting our Movement or the kibbutz movement in Eretz Israel. We did discuss unifying the Halutz movement in the Soviet zone, because Gordonia didn't believe you could maintain a separate underground Halutz movement there. We didn't think a separate existence there was justified because of differences of opinion, that those various, delicate variants between movements justified separate movements. However, a unified position vis-à-vis the Communist world was imperative.

In Warsaw, however, vis-à-vis the Germans, there was no need for unification. First of all, at that time, the Germans weren't very interested in us. Why, there were still Halutzim in Germany itself. It was illegal, but it wasn't forbidden. That is, being a "Halutz" didn't yet mean being "anti-German," or "pro-German," simply "pro-Palestine." But wasn't there a Central Committee of He-Halutz in Berlin? In that respect, there was nothing yet to hide and we appeared as Halutzim in the commune at Dzielna 34, for example, and the soup kitchen, and other places. We didn't seek legalization, but they didn't seek us or didn't know about us. We hid the operations of our organization from the Germans. Unification wouldn't have made any difference. And, within He-Halutz, did they care whether we had 1,000 members, Ha-Shomer Ha-Tza'ir 500, and other movements 200, or if there were 1,700 under one umbrella organization? Economically, too, it wouldn't have made any difference if we were unified or separate, because each movement got its share from the Joint through the Halutz federation.

In terms of separate existence, I was referring to our educational movement. The separate existence of the movements didn't cause fragmentation or separation within He-Halutz, and unification wouldn't have added to what existed anyway. The opposite is true. There were, on

112. Eliezer Geller: Born in Opoczno. Fought in the Polish army in 1939 and, on release from German prisoner-of-war camp, he set up the Gordonia movement. Edited the movement publication, *Słowo Młodych* [*The Word of the Young*], with Natan Eck. Fought in ZOB unit in the January and April Uprisings and reached the Aryan side. Was the sole survivor of the celluloid factory fire (see below). Deported to Auschwitz in October 1943 and murdered there at the age of twenty-five. See *Avnon,* Introduction; Gutman 1989: passim.

the one hand, the Central Committee of He-Halutz, which was active, and the umbrella organization of the Halutz Coordinating Committee; and, on the other hand, educational movements were established and operated as they liked. The Central Committee of He-Halutz was established, which brought together Dror, Ha-Shomer Ha-Tza'ir, Gordonia, and Akiba under one umbrella. Later, the *Grossmanites* (members of "The Jewish State" movement, who seceded from the Revisionists) also joined; for a time, they were also on the scene, but there weren't many of them. There was also Ha-No'ar Ha-Tzioni and He-Tzalutz Ha-Mizrakhi, and many operations were undertaken by the Coordinating Committee, not just by He-Halutz, which was constantly active; and, of course, there were special separate educational activities.

Zivia was the secretary of both He-Halutz and the Coordinating Committee. She was an authority in both places. The distribution of money was naturally something we argued about as long as there was a distribution. The argument was whether to distribute according to former relative size or according to new criteria. When I participated in the meetings, I was always in favor of not changing the pre-war status quo in He-Halutz. As I recall, we ("the general bloc") had 67.66 percent, and I don't know if that was fair or not. Any other distribution would have required an agreement on new principles of distribution, a census. We kept telling them: if you want to make a census according to the training kibbutzim in 1940, you had nothing and we had 100 percent, so it's not in your best interest.

The data of the "internal correspondence," internal and privileged material published in *Dappim,* shows that our share in He-Halutz and the training kibbutzim was more than 80 percent. These data are reliable because that was internal material. (The "internal correspondence" contains a report of the meeting of the Central Committee of Dror–He-Halutz Ha-Tza'ir, of May 8–11, 1942, where statistical data about the Movement and its significance were presented. According to that, the ratio between Dror and all others in He-Halutz in 1942, as of the last census, was: 85 percent Dror, 15 percent all the others. In the Coordinating Committee at that date, however, the ratio was: 70 percent Dror, 30 percent, all the others.)

So our proposal to distribute according to the status quo was very decent, since you couldn't take a census. The other movements certainly didn't lose anything with such a distribution. Obviously, every movement had expenses and its representatives wanted to get more; that was quite understandable. We also demanded more. For example, to maintain Dzielna in its existing form and magnitude would require higher annual expenses than the maintenance of Nalewki (the joint commune of Ha-Shomer Ha-Tza'ir and Gordonia); and they didn't show any concern for our distress, considering the larger number of people we had to support. They sought ways to change the status quo.

One day, I got an invitation from Lipa Bloch. He had once been head of the Jewish National Fund in Poland and, at that time, was also active in YISA; his daughter had joined Dror and belonged to a group of young intellectuals in the Movement. He invited me to a meeting with Yosef Kaplan, Israel Zelcer, himself, and me. Initially, they talked about setting up a library for the Halutz movement. I've already said that I was always buying books. I had no reason to oppose the unification of the libraries even though we bought whatever we could with our own money and I didn't know what advantage we would get from a central library when the Germans confiscated libraries. But, when we got to the second item of business, the cat was out of the bag; this was a proposal to set new principles for the distribution of money. Apparently, the other movements were in on that joint proposal because, otherwise, Bloch wouldn't have called the meeting.

I remember Yosef Kaplan and Zelcer at that meeting proposing a new yardstick based on the money collected by the whole movement for the JNF before the war. That was a stroke of genius, since everybody knew that Ha-Shomer Ha-Tza'ir was the clear leader in that field, and that Gordonia, which was smaller than Frayhayt and He-Halutz Ha-Tza'ir, collected several times more than we did. I don't know how such an idea occurred to them. I just burst out laughing. Apparently it was Zelcer's idea, and he had suggested it to Bloch. Naturally, nothing came of it, we didn't give in. You can find notes of that argument in Schwalb's archive (He-Halutz central office in Geneva); the letters written to Eretz Israel include complaints. I can't agree either with what I found in two books that appeared: Dr. Natan Eck's memoirs[113] and David Ron's work.[114] Both of them accuse me of being highhanded with the coffers and not giving them the money they deserved. I accept responsibility for not changing the status quo, along with my friends; but it is not correct that I didn't give money. I simply never held money, I had no connection with the treasury, never in my life, and not then either. Zivia kept the money, not me. Dr. N. Eck considers me the central person, and that's not right either. In He-Halutz, at a certain time, in certain areas, you could have said: "Yitzhak Zuckerman plays a central role" or "almost central"—that more modest formulation is more acceptable to me. The central person in the life of He-Halutz and the Halutz Coordinating Committee was Zivia, who was involved in everything; and I'm not evading responsibility

113. Natan Eck, *Wandering on the Paths of Death*.
114. David Ron, "The Figure of the Commander," *Niv Ha-Kvusta* 9, March 1960; David Ron, "They Shoot," *Tarbut v'Hinukh*, 1960.

for Zivia. But they said they came to me for money and I didn't give them any, and that isn't true. It is true that my friends and I were responsible for the decision not to change the status quo.

When I was asked about it, I explained that this was right and fair. Even now I'd say the same thing. I wouldn't have changed the index of the status quo because our situation was more severe, and we had more people to support and our training farm was bigger. We had a lot of difficulties and needs, and we couldn't accept a change in the status quo. It wasn't the time or place for a census; but if one had been taken, its results would have favored us.

In Ha-Shomer Ha-Tza'ir, the person we accepted and loved was Yosef Kaplan; and I think he felt the same about us.[115] This was, first of all, because of an earlier friendship. I personally didn't know him before the war. He was from Kalisz, as I recall—a proletarian, a carpenter by profession, who spoke fluent Hebrew and Yiddish, and, being from Kalisz, he also knew Polish. Kaplan wasn't a typical *Shomer-Tza'irnik*; he was more like a "simple Halutz" or a member of Dror. He was open and frank, not a typical Warsaw or central Poland character. A very handsome man, popular, down-to-earth. He would often come to us, just to be with us. He was older than Zivia and me, and much older than his colleagues Mordechai Anielewicz and Shmuel Braslaw. So, even in terms of age, he found friendship in our group (I mean Frumka, Yosef Kornianski, Zivia, and me). He would bring along his girlfriend, Miriam Heinsdorf, not because of any issues on the agenda, just for personal relations. He had authority in Ha-Shomer Ha-Tza'ir, but in conversations with him, it was clear that there were divisions of opinions among them. His world view was closer to ours. I once told the members of Ha-Shomer Ha-Tza'ir, and I'll repeat it here, that when I see the development of people against the background of those days, I think Braslaw and Anielewicz were adherents of ideological revisionism whereas Kaplan was a member of Ha-Shomer Ha-Tza'ir zealously devoted to Halutz Zionist values.

Kaplan opposed the world view, professed mainly by young people, that this was an "imperialistic" war, and we shouldn't take sides. We, however, argued from the very first that we identified completely with Poland and the West in the war against the Germans; we sided with everyone who fought against them. Rationally I could understand the failure of the Soviet Union to join the war, as well as the Molotov-Ribbentrop Pact; but this policy repelled me emotionally. Ha-Shomer

---

115. This judgment is confirmed by Chaika Grossman, who says that Kaplan would say: "We would do well to examine both ourselves and others. Perhaps we do not really know the 'Dror' people. Maybe we are exaggerating our criticism, and perhaps in our blindness we are not seeing the real and moral strength of others" (Grossman 1987:84).

Ha-Tza'ir considered this first stage of the war as an "imperialistic war" as long as the Soviet Union didn't join it; and, when that happened, it would "turn into" an "anti-imperialist war." We all thought that when the desired moment came and the Soviet Union moved west, south, and north, and burst into Poland, we would greet them with flowers. Nevertheless, we did argue that that could be the end of the Zionist dream. This was evident in a confrontation in 1940, at the Council of Ha-Shomer Ha-Tza'ir held in our apartment, at Dzielna 34, where they and the members of Gordonia were staying until their apartment at Nalewki 23 was ready. Until then, our apartment on Dzielna was always at their disposal.

This Council was closed, but they invited us to participate, and I would sit through the meeting off to the side and listen. I was no theoretician, but I did think that their conception of the war was too abstract. And it seems to me that we, with our instincts, were much more correct than those other comrades who built themselves an imaginary world on "tomorrow" and the Soviet "world of tomorrow" and the attitude that would prevail toward Zionism.

As I said, Kaplan's thinking was closer to us, and he was involved in internal debate and friction with his comrades. Their movement newspapers were edited by two young intellectuals, Braslaw and Anielewicz. Mordechai Anielewicz was probably three years younger than me and Shmuel Braslaw was my age. Kaplan, as I said, was thorough, spoke somewhat ponderously. Apparently it was hard for him to sit with young people in their twenties, in the movement institutions. Tosia Altman also came with him to visit us. Then and later I sensed that they didn't respect Tosia [in Ha-Shomer Ha-Tza'ir] perhaps because she was attracted to Yosef Kaplan. But she was usually traveling around. Mordechai Anielewicz and Shmuel Braslaw were young men with sharp minds and sharp tongues—young thinkers, both of them students of the Warsaw cell, with a definite ideological conception. Ružka Korczak was then in Vilna; she never came to Warsaw.[116] Chaika Grossman came later and stayed in Warsaw for two or three weeks.[117] We really didn't know Yisrael

116. Ružka Korczak (1921–1988): Born in Bielski. Active in Ha-Shomer Ha-Tza'ir. At the outbreak of the war, she came to Vilna, where she was a member of the Unified Partisan Organization, FPO; fought with the partisans in the forests of Lithuania. Immigrated to Eretz Israel in late 1944. Published a history of the resistance movement in Vilna, *Flames in Ash*, in 1946.

117. Chaika Grossman: Born in Białystok. Active in Ha-Shomer Ha-Tza'ir underground in Vilna; came to Warsaw to tell of mass slaughter in Ponar; active in ZOB in Białystok. Lives in Israel, where she was a member of Parliament. See her memoirs, *The Underground Army* (English edition, 1987).

Gutman.[118] I only heard his name as a young activist, one of the cultural activists, connected with Abraham Gepner.[119] Shmuel Winter, a member of YIVO (YIVO Institute for Jewish Research), who distributed food in the ghetto, adopted the young Yisrael Gutman.[120] Zivia said she remembered him as a boy. Gutman didn't play a central role, he was simply a member of Ha-Shomer Ha-Tza'ir. I met him only in Israel after the war.

When we assess a person's image, we can always relate to it according to the Jewish proverb: "After the death of a saint, you must say: . . ."[121] Privately, we used to call that "Bronze" (a person as solid as a bronze monument). Or you could talk about people as living human beings, with good and bad qualities, and then place yourself in a living argument. To go back to Anielewicz and Braslaw, I don't think I said anything negative or offensive about them; but simply that there was a difference between us, and between them and others.

As for the party and the political development of our Movement, we were supposedly a youth movement of Po'alei Zion–Z.S. and when that party united with Hitahdut, we didn't accept that unification.[122] There were probably very concrete material interests behind that merger; it

118. Professor Yisrael Gutman, currently a prominent historian of the Holocaust, professor at the Hebrew University of Jerusalem, author of *The Jews of Warsaw 1939–1943*, and several other works.

119. Abraham Gepner (1872–1943): Head of the Supply Department in the Judenrat. He was sympathetic to the Jewish, and especially the Halutz, underground. In early 1942, he helped the ZOB a great deal. He was in close touch with Zivia. He was killed in the April Uprising, after the battles of May 3, in the bunker of Franciszkanska Street; aged about 70. (See Lubetkin 1981:213–216; Czerniakow 1979:passim; Gutman 1989:86. For a different view, see Ringleblum 1986:300–301.) According to Dr. Berman, "In the ghetto, Gepner was one of the most popular personalities. He was known as a decent man with clean hands . . . Gepner loved children. He provided food to CENTOS and children's institutions. Personally, he was not an easy man. He sometimes behaved like a capricious and nervous autocrat, but even in the ghetto, people felt that he had a 'Jewish Heart'" (Berman 1977:79).

120. Shmuel Winter: Wealthy corn merchant from Włocławek, board member of the Provisioning Authority, connected with Ringelblum's Archive. According to Berman, aside from being a rich and respected merchant, he was also a "serious and energetic cultural activist, a great fan of Yiddish literature and Jewish folklore . . . In the Warsaw Ghetto, Winter was one of the central activists of the Provisioning Authority and, at the same time, maintained strong ties with Jewish cultural circles and participated both in the underground ghetto archive, *Oneg Shabat*, and with the secret cultural organization YIKOR. He was killed during the Uprising" (Berman 1977:79–80).

121. "Death of a saint [*Mot Kedoshim*]": An expression for a victim killed only because he was Jewish. It is customary to describe him in saintly terms.

122. Hitahdut was to the right of Po'alei Zion and non-Marxist. The unified party was called Po'alei Zion–Z.S. for (Zionist Socialist). People on the left called it "Po'alei Zion Right."

wasn't an ideological unification of two parties. According to the Yiddish proverb, "a pair of corpses goes dancing." That's about how we saw them.

Leyzer Levin opposed that unification all his life. They say that at the Po'alei Zion convention, a sign was hung on the door of one of the rooms (the factions gathered in different rooms) saying: "The leftist faction meets here," or, as they used to call it: "The left wing of Po'alei Zion–Z.S." And when the door was opened, Leyzer Levin was sitting there all alone. Politically, he was a lone wolf to his dying day. In the ghetto, for example, we were the "left" vis-à-vis the Soviet Union. But Levin was "left" vis-à-vis Yiddish (i.e., he preferred Yiddish to Hebrew). Here in Israel, he was "left" vis-à-vis the Soviet Union. At any rate, he never walked on the main road. And if anybody else wanted to walk his path with him, he would find another road for himself. He was a precious man, a wonderful character.

Ha-Shomer Ha-Tza'ir in Poland lived without a party, as a political trustee [for they preached that, at the age of eighteen, each member must immigrate to Eretz Israel]. So now they developed toward being an independent party, although they didn't consider themselves as such. But when they sought ideological and political proximity, they found it in Po'alei Zion Left, where young people were then the determining factor. These were Emmanuel Ringelblum and Shakhne Sagan,[123] who apparently had more influence than Dr. Adolf Berman.[124] Sagan had broad moral authority. Their tendency was leftist, as was that of Ha-Shomer Ha-Tza'ir. Hence, those two groups understandably found a common language in many instances. Moreover, we were Hebraists, even though many of us, including myself, a member of He-Halutz Ha-Tza'ir, felt very positively about Yiddish. The members of Ha-Shomer Ha-Tza'ir were in favor of Hebrew, followed by Polish.

Cultural groups emerged in the ghetto: one of them was the Yidishe kultur organisatsye (Yiddish Culture Organization, YIKOR), whose orig-

123. Shakhne Sagan: Born in Kraków. Po'alei Zion Left; established the first Jewish soup kitchen during the bombing of Warsaw. Was active in the underground in the Warsaw Ghetto, member of the Anti-Fascist Bloc. Was one of the directors of YIKOR (Yiddish Cultural Organization; see below). Berman describes him as being one of the "leading and most popular figures [in the ghetto], both in Jewish Social Self-Help [YISA] and in the public board of the Joint" (Berman 1977:134). On August 5, 1942, during the Great *Aktsia*, he was taken with his wife and two children to Treblinka. (See Ringelblum's admiring tribute to Sagan quoted in Blumenthal and Kermish 1965:82–86.)

124. Adolf Berman (1906–): Born in Warsaw. Member of Po'alei Zion Left, director of CENTOS, and active in the underground. Co-editor of the Anti-Fascist Bloc newspaper, *Der Ruf*. Went to the Aryan side of Warsaw in the summer of 1942; fought in the Polish Uprising; and, after the Liberation, until late 1946, was a member of the Polish Provisional Government. Immigrated to Israel in 1950.

inator and guiding spirit was Menakhem Linder.[125] He was one of Yakov Lestshinski's best students, a fascinating man we brought to all our seminars.[126] I used to read his articles and everything he published. Every one of his lectures was an experience. When I was a student, I attended a YIVO seminar in Vilna; Lestshinski came from Berlin to lecture in that seminar and I "crashed" his lecture. For the first time, I saw how you could turn dry numbers into poetry. That was Lestshinski's genius. However, I also learned how you could turn literature into something boring, as in my Gymnasium. I sat there listening in that seminar, which went on for a few days.

Linder apparently learned to lecture from Lestshinski. I used to sit in on every one of his lectures in our seminars. Notes of his lectures can be found in our underground press. Once or twice he contributed to our newspaper, *Dror*. He had originally been a member of Ha-Shomer Ha-Tza'ir. I think that, at that time, he was close to the Communists, but only close. His position was left of Ha-Shomer Ha-Tza'ir; he was a Yiddishist. His adherents were Bundists and of course members of Po'alei Zion Left; both groups supported Yiddish. Members of Ha-Shomer Ha-Tza'ir also participated, and I'm sure it was because of their political connections with Po'alei Zion Left. I don't mean that the members of Ha-Shomer Ha-Tza'ir didn't continue with their Hebrew activity. I'm talking only about their appearance on the broader social stage. I had no doubt of their loyalty to Hebrew, to Hebrew songs, and to education for Eretz Israel. But there was an external expression on the public stage in the framework of YIKOR, a Yiddishist organization.

The second cultural organization we participated in setting up was called Tekuma (Revival), it was the institution to foster Hebrew culture in the ghetto).[127] The central person in this organization was Dr. Menakhem Stein.[128] He was one of the lecturers in the Institute of Judaic Sciences. At that time, I read his book on Philo of Alexandria, which had

125. Menakhem Linder: Born in Śniatyń, East Galicia in 1911. Jurist and economist; active in social and cultural work in the ghetto, including the Ringelblum Archives. Murdered by the Gestapo on April 18, 1942, at the age of thirty-one. YIKOR organized scientific and scholarly assemblies and literary and artistic events. See Ringelblum 1986:443–446.

126. Yakov Lestshinski [Leszczyński] (1867–1966): Born in Horoditsh, Ukraine. Pioneering scholar of Jewish sociology, economics, and demography.

127. Tekuma: Established in January 1942. See Adolf Berman 1978:145. For a cynical view of the organization, see Chaim Kaplan 1973:292–293. The leaders were Menakhem Stein, Lipa Bloch, Menakhem Kirshenbaum, and Yitzhak Katznelson (Gutman 1989: 129).

128. Edmund Menachem Stein (1895–1943): Born in Dobromil, Galicia. From 1929 on, he was a professor at the Institute of Judaic Sciences (Instytut Nauk Judaistycznychi) in Warsaw. In 1943, he was deported to Trawniki, near Lublin, where he was killed. His book on Philo (*Philo of Alexandria*) was published in 1937.

just been republished. He was an important scholar of the Hellenistic period. To this day, apparently, the man is still respected as an historian.

I learned of the institute at one of the first meetings of Tekuma when I was told that several students were concentrating around former teachers in the Institute of Judaic Sciences and forming a nucleus of a Jewish university within the ghetto. That whole group assembled around Menakhem Stein. Other figures I remember in Tekuma were Yafet (Yehuda Shapiro) of Mizrakhi, Dr. Natan Eck, and Menakhem Kirshenbaum. I was then the representative of all movements in the Halutz Coordinating Committee (not just the representative of Dror) in those institutions. Our meetings were held on Dzielna Street, in Dr. Stein's home.

In comparison with Tekuma, the members of YIKOR were "more ideological," more alert and lively; its members were younger and more lower class, tending to Yiddish; and, of course, YIKOR was very active in lectures, parties, discussions, literary soirées on Mendele and other writers. Tekuma gatherings were conducted in Hebrew (I think that, except for Kirshenbaum, we all knew Hebrew). That was in late 1940 and early 1941. Yitzhak Katznelson, who was in Warsaw by then, wasn't involved in Tekuma.

So, there was cooperation between Ha-Shomer Ha-Tza'ir and the members of YIKOR, and there's something inexplicable here. Yosef Kaplan had an affinity for Yiddish; but young people like Shmuel Braslaw and Mordechai Anielewicz—I can guarantee that neither of them ever read a single book in Yiddish; they never had anything to do with it. As graduates of Polish schools, they spoke Polish with each other and behaved like genuine Poles. They did speak Yiddish, though; Mordechai Anielewicz came from a Jewish home. His mother (who sold fish) certainly didn't speak Polish. And if she did, the Poles would have had a hard time understanding her Polish. But Anielewicz and Braslaw spoke Polish among their friends. Tosia Altman barely spoke Yiddish, and would always speak Polish and Hebrew. As for me, in terms of my position on language, I could also have belonged to YIKOR, but I absolutely refused to give up Tekuma or literature raised on Hebrew culture. But not Ha-Shomer Ha-Tza'ir. That was one of the things that divided us, even though Ha-Shomer Ha-Tza'ir was the movement closest to us intellectually and as Halutzim; nevertheless, if you review their newspapers and ours, you can discern a considerable distinction in views on Judaism and socialism; and we were unique because, despite our Jewish and Zionist enthusiasm, we were definitely not anti-Communist, and that is proved by our Movement literature.

We had correct relations with Gordonia. We were angry about things that Gordonia wasn't guilty of, because of matters between us and the office in Geneva, whose director, Natan Schwalb, discriminated in favor of Gordonia, which was his own movement. This was proved in lists I saw long after the war. It is incomprehensible to me that he didn't recognize our names, while sending money to every person in Gordonia. We knew who got money because you couldn't keep a secret, and because the money was sent by "transfers"; and, even though we didn't know precise amounts, we knew about the transfers. This was an offense in He-Halutz since the money wasn't divided according to the ratio of the youth movements, as required. Nevertheless, Gordonia blamed us for holding onto the "wealth" and not giving up our 66 percent. I smile now as I recall that; and even then I smiled; I really don't know how we could have behaved differently.

The central person of Gordonia in the early period was Zelcer. (Eliezer Geller came somewhat later.) I think he was from Opoczno. Aharon Carmi (member of the ZOB in Warsaw) tells about him. Zelcer was acceptable to us because he was a balanced, thoughtful man, whereas Geller was more impetuous and excitable, even externally: sweat was always pouring from his face. Carmi says he would always put his hand on the shoulder of whomever he was talking to. Carmi was from Geller's hometown and says he remembers him when he was his counselor. Geller wound up in the ghetto after the defeat of Poland, after he had been a soldier in the Polish army.[129]

As I said, we brought Zelcer and his wife Hannah from Lublin, and they began organizing their movement. Later on, Eliezer Geller showed up. We didn't know him from before, and the representative of the movement was Zelcer. During meetings with the two, we understood that there were conflicts between them. Apparently, Geller accused Zelcer of assuming improper authority, of not being dynamic enough, of not building the movement, and there might have been other accusations I don't know about. Dr. Natan Eck, the patron of Gordonia on behalf of Hitahdut Z.S., helped them edit their newspapers and told about that in his book, if I'm not mistaken. In the quarrels between the two, Geller, who was younger than Zelcer, rose and became more acceptable to the young people of the movement. (Zelcer was the oldest of all of us, I think, about thirty; he had been in Eretz Israel during the thirties.) We got along better with Zelcer. We were willing to have disputes in our meetings, but we didn't expect outbursts. It's my impression that Geller had complexes, a sense of inferiority with respect to members of Dror and Ha-Shomer Ha-Tza'ir. I remember he would invite us to his private apartment and welcome us with great joy. We would eat ham and Portuguese canned goods with a bottle of vodka shared by twenty people, all purchased with money from Geneva. The main thing there was

129. Aharon Carmi and Haim Frimmer 1961.

the experience of spending time together. I was impressed that he valued our visits.

Our relations with Zelcer were always very simple and friendly, and on an equal footing; but not with Geller—we never were like that with Geller. They began to restore Gordonia by setting up a commune with Ha-Shomer Ha-Tza'ir. (In the apartment, they put a screen between them.) They did some things in common; for example, they appeared together to get food for the Movement seminar. Their movement was very small; they never had been a big movement in Poland. At any rate, they tried to restore it. I don't know how many of them there were. They began activities, put out newspapers (their newspaper was edited by Dr. N. Eck and written in Polish).[130] I didn't know them well except later on, when I also represented them in Tekuma (formally, I also represented Ha-Shomer Ha-Tza'ir). Aside from the leaflet in Polish, they also put out material in Hebrew and Yiddish.[131] Gordonia had a training place in Warsaw for seasonal training. They didn't have a training kibbutz like Czerniaków or Grochów, nor did Ha-Shomer Ha-Tza'ir. Only later did they set up a training kibbutz.

I had very few written contacts with the outside world or with Eretz Israel. I wrote very little since Zivia or Frumka would write. When we had to write German, I was helped by Benno Rosenberg; I mentioned his name before. He was a member of BAHAD (Brit Halutzim Dati'im), very close to us. He would come and sit down, translate, and write. The fine German in our writings isn't ours, it's Benno's.

Nevertheless, I once wrote to Israel Idelson (Bar-Yehuda) in Eretz Israel, and I used to write occasionally to Vilna. Naturally, I wrote to Vilna in hints: in a code we agreed on. It was a simple code that stood the test and no one succeeded in cracking it. For the areas of the Generalgouvernement, the system was to chose a page from the Bible, which we had previously selected, which would serve as a base to code and de-code. To make it even harder, you could decide on a few pages and use them selectively. We also used a system of first initials of words (the word "we," for example, represented by "w,"). That system didn't "work" when the letter had to go through the censor (i.e., outside the borders of the Generalgouvernement). In correspondence with Vilna, the letters were written according to the code of "Capital Letters": the information we wanted to convey was composed of the capital letters in the letter. This is how we maintained contact with Lwów, for example. Correspondence abroad was done with another system. We were helped by Tamir (Lipski)

---

130. The underground Gordonia Polish journal was called *Słovo Młodych (The Word of the Young)* and was published between 1941–1942. (See *The "Gordonia" Press,* 1966.)

131. The Yiddish publication of Gordonia was called *Oysdoyer (Endurance).*

who we knew was still "wandering around" Carpathian Ruthenia. We wrote a lot of letters, through Switzerland, through Scandinavia. It is no honor to Eretz Israel, the Histadrut, or Ha-Kibbutz Ha-Meuchad that we got practically nothing throughout that difficult period. We didn't think well of them in those days. Our hearts were bitter, very bitter. We simply couldn't understand it.

Later, contact was created with London, the Polish underground, Istanbul, Switzerland; but from Eretz Israel, from our best friends, from Ha-Kibbutz HaMeuchad, from the secretaries and assistant secretaries, from the Shlikhim—nothing. It was the same in Ha-Shomer Ha-Tza'ir; there too, it was incomprehensible. One of the things we needed when we decided to try to work for illegal immigration to Eretz Israel was contact with Eretz Israel. This wasn't the "personal" rescue of some people and others, but an organization committed to getting people out of the cities of Poland and bringing them to safety. The question was where to go. Whom to appeal to? And there was nothing; all the letters we sent remained unanswered. Naturally that led to despair. It was "unrequited love," which always involves heartache.

It was also our people who discovered the Jewish Brigade at the end of the war, and not vice versa. Let me repeat and emphasize: it was incomprehensible to us, that even at the end of the war, no emissary came to us until August 1945, and we didn't get a thing. And I'm not talking here about during the war.

We had to establish contacts between three separate parts of the Movement: the part annexed to the Reich (Warthegau), where contact ended in spring 1940 (except for Łódz); the second part, Vilna, which sent us very valuable packages (I already said we supported the Gymnasium teachers with them); and the third, the underground in the Soviet zone.

In mid-1940, when I came to Warsaw, we started helping the Movement in the Soviet zone. It turned out we could help more than Vilna could. Until the Russians re-entered Vilna in May 1940, that whole zone was one single area. Even then, you could have said of us that it was a case of "two corpses go dancing": neither of us had contact with the outside. Nevertheless, we did achieve something. For example, Oszerowska, Frumka Eshed's sister in Warsaw, had money, and we made a transfer deal with her.[132] That is, we gave her an IOU and we got money in Warsaw. We didn't know if the debts would be paid immediately, but we did guarantee that they would be honored after the war. There was another woman in Warsaw whose husband was in Lwów and had money;

132. Frumka Eshed now lives in Israel.

we arranged a "transfer deal" for him to give money to our people in Lwów and for us to pay her in Warsaw.

In connection with that, there was an interesting episode: we got a telegram from Lwów written in German: *Grüsse Lisobader—Orla 11*. The signature was either Oskar or Edek. What do you do with such a telegram? You sit and try to figure it out. Frumka and Zivia and Yosef Kornianski sat in my room. (When we wanted to be alone, we would sit in my room since I was the only one with a private room.) All day we racked our brains trying to figure it out. In the evening, Yosef Kornianski brought a piece of bread and divided it equally; he sat down and chewed his portion. All of a sudden, he said: I solved the mystery! (He had been a Yeshiva student.) And he said: *Grüsse*—that's obvious: greetings; *Lisobader*—that's the initials of Lithuanian-Soviet rapprochement (dernenterung). *Orla 11*, once was the center of He-Halutz in Warsaw at Orla Street 11. Very nice; we said; fine, but what does rapprochement between the Russians and Lithuanians mean, and what does it have to do with He-Halutz? End of chapter. He couldn't answer. "Let's think about it some more," he said.

The next day, Zivia asked me to go with her to Tłomackie. So, we were walking on Leszno Street near Orla Street. And I said: "Zivia, I've got to go to Orla 11." I asked her not to tell anyone because they would laugh at me. She said: "What will you see there?" I said: "Let's go see together." She went with me, we approached, and there was Orla 11. We climbed the stairs to the third or fourth floor and came to apartment 11. I looked at the door: Lisobader—quite simply. I rang the bell and we entered; I asked: "Mrs. Lisobader?" She said: "Yes." I said: "We got a telegram—*Grüsse Lisobader—Orla 11*. Perhaps you know what it means?" And then the woman started hugging and kissing me, and saying: "Yes, my husband in Lwów gave money to your comrades and you're supposed to give it back to me here."

After we left, I said to Zivia: "Even if they kill me, I won't deliver any more greetings like that." We returned and I told the story to Yosef Kornianski, but he persisted: "I told you right away." He had to be right. Those were the sorts of telegrams that came, and that was the kind of transfer we tried to help and be helped with.

We also sold things. That happened before I came. For example, the last group of illegal immigrants to Eretz Israel just before the war left a shipment of clothing behind and our comrades sold it to the Joint. The bill of sale was dated before the outbreak of the war. The sum guaranteed in exchange was 90,000 Złotys, indexed to the dollar. The rate of the dollar was 5 Złotys, that is, 18,000 dollars. I saw the bill of sale for the last time after the Great *Aktsia*, in Zivia's wallet.

Why do I mention that?

After the war, I had an argument with Dr. Joseph Schwartz of the Joint;[133] I know that he respected and liked me; but though this was a financial debt of the Joint, it also turned out that it wasn't written that the sum was indexed to the dollar. But it was written that the Joint received the merchandise a few months before September 1939, and it specified that the sum was 90,000 Złotys altogether, and also gave the date fixing the rate of the dollar vis-à-vis the Złoty because afterward, in that period, there was inflation, and 90 thousand Złotys wasn't worth much.

Second, during the occupation, we were both scared to hold onto a document from the previous period. But Joseph Schwartz denied that, claiming that, for reasons of caution, the Joint never signed such documents. The issue went on for a long time and I don't know if he believed me or not. In Israel, I pressed him and he came to an agreement with Boria Yudkowski; and we also brought Stefan Grajek and Yosef Sak into it. He agreed with them on the sum, and they got part of the money for the Po'alei Zion party, although they didn't deserve it. I don't know how much it was. In any case, I didn't see any money. I wouldn't have given up a single cent of the 18,000 dollars that was coming to us. I would have insisted on honoring the agreement in full—or not taking anything. The Jewish people wouldn't have collapsed and neither would Ha-Kibbutz Ha-Meuchad if the Joint hadn't paid. But the Joint had a debt and they had to pay it. If we had kept those clothes, we would have sold them.

The comrades in Vilna helped us, and we helped the underground movement in Russia, the Ukraine, and western Byelorussia. They sent us miserable packages from Switzerland. "Miserable" because they contained delicacies. A person needs bread and they sent us chocolate, Portuguese canned goods. We did sell the goods—and the sales did give us real bread. The packages were big and were sent generously—many thanks to the comrades who sent them. In the Soviet period, it was the comrades in Vilna who needed charity themselves. We had transfer contacts like those with Oszerowska—they would pay us and we would give them IOUs and would release money. Most of those who gave money were killed in the Holocaust, and I don't remember their names or the sums. At any rate, there weren't many who appealed to us after the war, which apparently means they were no longer alive. They knew we were in Warsaw after 1945 and would certainly not have refrained from appealing. It has been thirty years since then, and no one has come to demand money, not even in Israel. If anybody did appeal now, it would be a sign that he was an imposter. These were pretty big sums of money, which we used to support the Movement. We didn't use it to buy bread for ourselves, but to do Movement work and help Jews.

133. Yosef Schwartz: Director of the Joint during the war.

I was busy with educational activity until I collapsed when the news came.[134] Before that, I was involved in everything. I attended meetings of the Central Committee of He-Halutz. I traveled a lot; I would go to important centers like Kielce, Lublin, or Katowice; one of our people was stationed in each of those places. How I traveled was dictated by the period. Up to the time of the ghetto, I used the signature of the house committee at Stołowa 13, in Praga. On my trips, I carried a confirmation that the bearer of the photograph was Antoni Wilcyński. If they had caught me, this document would have been completely useless. For example, once, Lonka accompanied me on a very long trip. We got to some station on the Lublin line—maybe even Lublin itself; we were waiting in the depot (naturally we weren't wearing the armband). Suddenly a gentile guy appeared and smiled at us. We were very frightened; we didn't understand the meaning of the smile, which was like a grimace, a warning. We didn't know what sign it was. Did he know me or her? Lonka said she thought the fellow was from Pruszków, her hometown, and that she might know him. It turned out to be a genuine warning. We had fallen into a trap. The Germans surrounded the railroad station and asked for identity documents. Lonka had something to show. I had that picture, and extraordinary luck. I took out the "document" and showed it, with the signature. The German looked at the picture and at me, and said: "*Ja, der selber.* (Yes, that's the same man.) And he let me go. I was one step away from prison. I walked around with that document until I had to get a better one. Until that time, I visited many of our important centers, even the smaller towns, for example, Hrubieszów, but, above all, wherever we fixed as a center of a district, where there were so-called "commissars" of our Movement, responsible for organizing activity in the areas. And from there, I would return to Warsaw.

We were young, we had a lot of energy and a lot of faith; and we also lacked information. You can imagine what would have happened if we had known in 1940 what was waiting for us. It would have changed the situation both for better and for worse. But we didn't foresee the future: we though we would save the young generation, or at any rate the nuclei of the young generation, and protect them as Halutzim, members of the Movement, until the end of the war. We thought we would get through the war, but with a great many casualties. Nevertheless, we believed we would save the main part from the conflagration. In our press, this period is recorded as a time of harsh decrees against Jews. By then, we knew that transporting Jews from small communities to big ones involved endless victims during the transport, on the roads and in Warsaw. It wasn't yet

134. That is, the news from Vilna about the mass extermination of Jews at Ponar in summer and fall 1941.

crowded. There was poverty; people were uprooted; people who had had little stores or workshops didn't bring anything with them. It was a world of beggars. If they had stayed home, they could have eked out a meager living with horrible difficulties. And there were hundreds of thousands of them.

Before the war, there were 380,000 Jews in Warsaw. Let's say that, in the great commotion of September 7, 1939, 50,000 escaped to Białystok, Vilna, and the Soviet zone, or scattered on the roads, and 330,000 people remained in the city. But Warsaw was again filled with refugees from the towns and villages, and her Jewish population grew to half a million. But in the period I'm talking about, it fell again to 300,000. What happened to the rest? They simply died. A few escaped to the towns and villages, maybe 20,000 of them, and I may have made a mistake here and there—but tens of thousands simply died. They died of typhus and other diseases, and from hunger; there were killings of individuals and more than that, and altogether thousands were certainly killed. I'm talking about the first period before the labor camps, and I got a taste of such a camp, a labor camp, not a concentration camp.[135] You have to understand what happened in between those two periods, when the system was to kill by typhus and hunger—they did everything so typhus and hunger would devour us.

The ghetto was established in stages. They took Jews out of the streets in Warsaw where they lived and moved them to special streets; the liquidation was carried out afterward. For example, the Jews of the suburb of Praga were liquidated the day the ghetto was established. I recall pictures of Jews wandering around with their belongings, not knowing were to go. And though everyone knew there would be a ghetto (that was officially announced on Yom Kippur), the ghetto was sealed off on November 15, after the wall surrounding it was finished.

Many families crowded into one apartment, sometimes into one room, and if one person got typhus, that was enought to destroy an entire courtyard. Later, to enforce disinfection, they began closing off courtyards and transferring all inhabitants to the municipal shower. I was there twice. I think I would have done anything to avoid going there again. I thought it was better not to wash; the shower was a center for the spread of disease.

The establishment of the ghetto was a drastic change. The division of the period into chapters will be a schematic necessity. That is, it will be correct, insofar as it determines stages in the liquidation: the dates are correct, but the overlapping isn't distinct; and drastic changes in our way of thinking, in our hearts, may have occurred without any connection to

135. That is, the Kampinos labor camp where Zuckerman was imprisoned for a while. See below, chapter 4.

this. The harsh crisis in our group erupted at the end of 1941, not because of anything the Germans did in Warsaw, but because of the news from Vilna and, later, from Chelmno, which shocked us. I think I was paralyzed when I heard it. In 1942, I was on the brink of madness.

Attempts to get out to Slovakia began before the establishment of the ghetto. Yosef Kornianski was one of the last who left with a group for Slovakia. I accompanied the beginning of the effort to get out. Shlomo Cygielnik kept pressuring for the group to leave; but, before they departed, we tried again to delay them because we were waiting for answers from various places, from neutral countries and from Eretz Israel, and we didn't get any. Ultimately, the die was cast: Shlomo Cygielnik would leave without papers, without a smooth path, really going blind! But before he left, I went to Kraków to examine the roads, to decide how to go. Then we brought Laban into it. Tall and stocky, quiet, smiling, friendly, Laban agreed to organize the whole route. He was supposed to bring them to some point on the border. At the border, they were to be guided further by our people. Laban set the path, but it took a while. He went to Tarnów and we didn't know how long it would be until he signaled. Kraków was the capital of the Generalgouvernement and Generalgovernor Frank was there.[136] In that city, you heard German wherever you turned: it wasn't a place to assemble a lot of people. The route that was finally set was Kraków–Tarnów–Nowy Sącz, where there was an important cell of Ha-Shomer Ha-Tza'ir and a girl, Ida Koral, who was the contact for those sneaking across the border. When we got the word from Laban to come, Shlomo Cygielnik left and went that way, even before we contacted local people; he found smugglers who took him across.

I should say something about the central role of Shlomo Cygielnik, who wasn't satisfied with the mere decision in principle about escaping across the border. He urged us to put the decision into practice and volunteered to go first. He wasn't the only one. He didn't agree to wait for a safe road to the other side, to a neutral country, since it would require accepting responsibility for those who were leaving to lead them to a seashore. At that time, we weren't yet thinking of illegal immigration to Palestine. If we had been, we might have come up with all kinds of devices. We didn't think of illegal immigration when I was in Vilna either; we had thought you might be able to immigrate legally to Eretz Israel from Vilna. Our comrades who were killed on the Romanian border, members of the Halutz movement, weren't seeking rescue or protection for themselves in

136. Hans Frank: Administrator of the Generalgouvernement. Prototype of the Nazi intellectual, well read in law and literature and devoted especially to music. Also devoted to the destruction of the Jews. Was tried at the Nuremberg Trials and executed on October 16, 1946.

Romania. They wanted to pave the way to the Black Sea. We didn't know if we would get people through, we didn't know what we had to do. *Davar* and *Ma'ariv,* the Israeli press, didn't reach us. We read the German papers, and sometimes we picked up an English radio. But they weren't interested in Jews. They couldn't guide us and tell us what to do. We sought a way like blind men.

We didn't get anything either from Eretz Israel, or the Shlikhim, or the neutral countries. Not from Portugal or Sweden, Switzerland, or anyplace else. Then Cygielnik told us it was possible to go. He crossed the border, thanks to Laban, and told us he had set up a base. Of course we agreed on signals because the guides were gentiles; there would be some button the smuggler had to return, as a sign that the person crossed and got to his destination; then, we would pay the money; every group that went had a different sign.

When Cygielnik said he had set up a base and had contacted Bratislava, the comrades of He-Halutz in Bratislava and Slovakia responded and a waystation was immediately set up in Berdejov, beyond the German border, on the Slovak side.

Then we started sending people, a period that lasted from winter 1940 to June 22, 1941, the day of the Nazi invasion of the Soviet Union. As soon as we got the news that there was a passage, we told Yosef Kaplan about it in strict secrecy. At a joint meeting, we decided to turn over the border crossing to the Halutz Coordinating Committee, to include the whole Halutz movement; and we set up machinery. Our couriers were sometimes needed to help with the careful supervision of the roads.

Irena Adamowicz was an escort.[137] First she accompanied Yosef Kornianski's group. At that period, those who were caught didn't face death, but they were liable to suffer serious punishments, to go to jail and to be beaten. We also involved our people in Zagłębie and Silesia in the area of the Reich, and we started moving people: from Silesia, people started coming to Kraków; from Warsaw or the nearby towns, they also tried to get to Kraków. And from there, Laban, with his emissaries, took care of moving them to Nowy Sącz.

I visited Nowy Sącz twice. The first time, to figure out the situation; and the second time to *save* the situation. I don't remember if I was there when Yosef Kornianski's group left for Slovakia. They left on the last day of Passover 1941, the day I was taken to the labor camp. Tuvia Borzykowski tells in his book about the farewell party for Yosef Kor-

137. Irena Adamowicz: A Pole; leader of the Polish Scouts movement before the war. During the war, had close relations with Ha-Shomer Ha-Tza'ir and Dror. Helped make initial contacts with the Polish underground army, AK, in Warsaw and assisted in finding hiding places on the Aryan side. One of the Righteous Gentiles. Died in Poland in 1977.

nianski. Yosef certainly tells about it in his memoirs, too. So, we said goodbye to a big group that set out. A group from Zagłębie also came at that time. They met in Nowy Sącz and crossed the border. When I returned from the labor camp, broken and crushed, beaten and wounded, after I recovered a bit, I set out with Lonka, on my longest trip.

I was a man with many names. Initially, the name on my document was Antek Wilcyński; then, I had another name and another document. My last name was Stanisław Bagniewski; before that, it was Witold Kimstaczas, a Lithuanian name I used later on. Mordechai Tennenbaum brought me a birth certificate. With one thing and another, I had a document in the name of Bagniewski and a forged birth certificate.

So, I left with Lonka and traveled for three weeks, or close to a month. That was just before June 22. I visited Nowy Sącz and Kraków and Tarnów. On the way back, I again visited Biała-Podlaska, Siedlce, Miedzyrzec. In one of those places, I telephoned the Folman family in Warsaw. Since I had previously said I would call, my comrades were on the line.

Papa Folman had been a housing administrator before the war and still had a telephone. Mama Folman's greatness was that she knew all our "*foyle shtik*" (tricks) and all the active "*komplets*" (groups); she was an old-fashioned idealist, who was loyal to us, supported her children, and helped us. The father, on the other hand, was busy with houses, renting, and other deals.

On the phone, Zivia told me clearly that there had been a catastrophe in Nowy Sącz: a group of our people had fallen into the hands of the Germans. I was about to return to Dzielna and I was like a horse who feels his stable nearby. And all of a sudden I got that information and had to turn around and go back, upset and tense, for hundreds of kilometers. We had no choice, left immediately for Kraków where we found Laban. We decided to leave for Nowy Sącz at once. In later times Laban preferred to pass as a German, even though it was hard to hide his Jewish looks. This time, he disguised himself as a Pole, Januszek. We didn't sit together. I sat with Lonka, and he would peep at every station to see if we were still there; thus, we arrived in Nowy Sącz.

Apparently, during the crossing, one of our big groups fell into the hands of the Gestapo, and the people were taken to prison in Kraków. The people in the transit camp in Nowy Sącz were scared. Those from the Reich and members of other movements from Warsaw wanted to go back. I assembled all those in Nowy Sącz and spoke with them. Many years later, one of the women from Ha-Shomer Ha-Tza'ir told me: "I have to thank you for my life." Apparently, she was in Nowy Sącz during the disaster, and she and her comrades were very depressed. I had told them: "Cross! Even if ninety-nine out of a hundred fall into German hands, we have to cross! Don't stay here and don't go back!" She obeyed, crossed, and was saved. That's what she said. When I said that, it didn't occur to me that someday it would mean rescue from destruction. At that time, we meant that we had to go on striving for a safe haven, and we did. They overcame the crisis and went on crossing.

What did we do? I returned to Kraków with Lonka and Laban. Laban had initiative and contacts. He found a Ukrainian lawyer he brought into the case and got all our people out of prison through bribery. This was in 1941, before June. The lawyer took a lot of money from us, but that was nothing compared to the rescue of even one comrade. For example, Shmulik, who save Grochów on November 15, had his teeth broken. It was a pity to look at him. After we got them out, we gave them tickets and instructions to go to the Judenrat in Warsaw, which we made responsible for that group of people; I can't remember how many there were.

They had to return to Warsaw. They were wretched and miserable; every one of them was wounded and crushed. Their documents and everything had been taken; they arrived in Warsaw close to June 22, the day of the German invasion of the Soviet Union. With that, the matter of escape ended, everything changed. The roads to Slovakia, Hungary, and Romania were blocked. Wherever you turned, you came upon Germans.

In terms of quantity, if we take into account all the searching for ways of escape, that whole effort didn't produce great results. Those who crossed the borders can be counted in hundreds, not in thousands. Even if we add those who went straight to Hungary from Zagłębie. However, I strongly reject the contempt for the formulation "nevertheless" ("nevertheless, that was supposedly an important action"), which is like the expression of contempt in the phrase "the uprising of a few hundred people." If that Uprising had any meaning, so did that 1941 trek to the borders, that striving to reach Eretz Israel—because even one comrade from Dzielna going roused a spark of hope, a chance to make contact.

And if I am asked about our Movement, I declare that there never was a finer moment in our Movement than that before its death. It simply flourished, even in human terms. Later on, when everyone in the ghetto was looking for a place to hide and trying to make do, our people waited for instructions and initiative. There was mutual responsibility, we weren't just concerned for ourselves; and if a group of forty or fifty people was on the road, you had to solve its problems, try to save them if need be. If they were doomed to fall, they all fell together; and if they were saved, they were all saved together. The possibility that one person would leave another and look after himself—as happened even within families—didn't exist among us, except for isolated exceptions. I'll say a few words about one such case.

When the Jewish police was established, a few senior officials in the Judenrat were very close to us. One of them was Pinhas Wasserman, a member of Torah Va-Avodah,[138] a traditionalist and ethical Halutz movement. I met Wasserman after I came to Warsaw, when, after a long delay, I had to be put on the list of residents.

Administratively, that was quite problematic. Then someone (I think it was Israel Gzęda) brought me to Wasserman, who, without a word put me on the list, after that I knew him personally and we met several times.

Wasserman was a senior official in the Judenrat, director of the Department of Registration of Citizens. Knowing I was a Halutz, he assumed the risk and responsibility, since by then the Halutzim were known to be carrying out all sorts of things. We knew him as a very decent and fine man, and I'll come back to him later. So we were told that a few fine and decent people, including Wasserman, intended to set up a Jewish police, and we thought that it required men of moral force. We discussed participating in it since we didn't yet know what the police would be, and we shouldn't measure the police of 1941 by what they looked like in 1942. Cautiously, we decided not to involve our people in it, except for one man in order to know what was going on there. It was important for us to have an ear and a voice there. So we assigned Shalom Litewski, a member of Dror, and he would check in from time to time and report things that weren't terribly important. One day, after the establishment of the ghetto, in 1941, he showed up with a swollen cheek. I asked him what had happened. And he said that he was standing at the gate (a German gendarme, a Polish policeman, and a Jewish policeman were always on duty there) and a German hoodlum came by and smacked him in the face. Such things happened every day and a Jewish policeman could be hit by the gendarmes, as had happened several times.

The swelling went down, but the rumor reached us that he hadn't been hit by a German *policeman,* but by a Jewish smuggler. It turns out the smugglers weren't getting along, something to do with bribery. Apparently our honest man, the one we sent to serve us in the police, had turned into a collaborator. If he had at least collaborated with the smugglers! But he collaborated with the police against the smugglers. The smugglers were hardly saints; they were concerned with their profit and their deals. But, *ex post facto,* they did perform a national mission by bringing food into the ghetto, even if the food they smuggled into the ghetto was beyond the means of the poor. Nevertheless, it helped someone who needed it and who could pay for it. Our man demanded his share for standing at

138. Torah Va-Avodah (Hebrew: Torah and Work): Zionist religious pioneering movement, founded in Vienna in 1925, based on labor and a demand for social justice.

the gate, and because he didn't get along with his companions, he took the blows.

We learned of that demoralization in the police from a very reliable source, a party member, who later also fell apart; but at that time, he was still one of the righteous. This man was also a policeman, and he came and told us the tale. The mission of our man in the police ended on the spot: I called him in and asked him how his cheek was. "Feeling better?" He said yes. "But I feel worse," I said. We took him out of the police because he was getting special favors. That was a man we had trusted. I learned that if I assigned people to missions, they had to have a very solid spiritual constitution. But apparently, that doesn't always help, and there are all sorts of perversions. The man suddenly sensed the atmosphere and the possibilities latent in it and collaborated with that corruption. We transferred him to the post office. We had been given a chance to get several workers employed in the post office. For example, Peretz Opoczynski worked as a mailman; the man who had collaborated worked in the post office. But during the expulsions, that man, Litewski, thought he had a better chance without the Movement, and he and his young wife were among the first victims.[139]

In two cases we expelled people from Dzielna. One was a result of a labor camp. When I was with five other people in Kampinos Camp, I gave all my money to our comrade from Germany, Solly, who was the treasurer. He would buy cigarettes at the canteen, which was open during a certain period, and divide them among the comrades at night. Apparently one of the fellows, from Pruszków, took cigarettes out of somebody's pocket, simply stole from one of the comrades. We all knew about this and kept quiet until we returned to Dzielna, and then we said we wouldn't put up with such behavior.

The second instance was when a woman member who played a role in our "hierarchy," not a central role, but a responsible role, made us suspicious. She enjoyed independence and had control over money in some town. It was a lot of money, in terms of our standard of living. On a visit there with Lonka, I saw her doing strange things and discerned various deviations during the few days we spent there. These were only suspicions. Later, she called us with the excuse that she needed more money because the Germans had attacked her and taken what she had. We asked her to return to Warsaw and, talking with her, it came out that she had gotten in trouble and, from then on, we left her at Dzielna. One

139. See Yosef Kornianski, *On a Halutz Mission*, 64, 82. Peretz Opoczynski (1892–1943). Born in Blutomyrsk, near Łódz. Wrote poems and stories. Joined Po'alei Zion in 1927 and was sent to Warsaw by the Movement in 1935 to work in the cultural area. Was active in the ghetto underground and wrote on Movement activities in the ghetto.

day, respectable, well-to-do friends came to Zivia and asked why she didn't return the money in exchange for clothes. What clothes? Apparently, that girl would go to rich people in Zivia's name and pretend we were selling clothes and take a certain percentage. That was too much, so we got rid of her.[140] Her name was Regina Litewska, sister of Shalom Litewski, the Judenrat policeman.[141]

Indeed, now and then, there were hard or easy cases, but these were exceptions. And I don't recall any quarrels either; maybe that was because of a certain distance between me and the comrades when I was at Dzielna. That's not to say I was estranged; on the contrary, I went to parties and even joined in various practical jokes ("*foyle shtik*"); but it was like this: if somebody wanted to confess something, he would go to Zivia; but if people had difficult personal or other problems, they would come to me. Zivia was more open, everybody loved her, and she was an integral part of the group. She sat and talked a lot with the comrades. I, on the other hand, was usually closed up in my room. I traveled a great deal and was busy with various issues. So, I think there was a certain distance between me and the members at that time; it wasn't very serious, just something that resulted from different work. I didn't know exactly what was cooking in the pots in the kitchen, and I can't tell you whether the women members quarreled. But I have no doubt that the Movement in general was on a high moral level.

I'd like to add a few more words about the moral situation of the Movement, the relations within the leadership group and the relations of the Movement toward that group. The Movement had absolute trust in the whole leadership group. It wasn't only full "credit," that they didn't require us to report about money and such. There could have been a debate about how to spend the money, whether to eat better or to invest in educational activity. And I can say that our stomachs weren't at the top of our concerns. I don't have the shadow of a doubt that the members of the Movement believed we were doing important and correct things. They had no basis for doubting or finding fault with our leadership and our judgment. I can say of myself that, even later on, when I had control of millions, I didn't eat any better. Clearly my work obliged me to keep large sums, like walking around with 50,000 Złotys in my pocket. That was sometimes necessary to get rid of a blackmailer, and such things. Only when the work demanded it did we allow ourselves to spend money, even when we had access to big sums; we were careful that our food wasn't as good as what we gave others.

140. Details also in Yosef Kornianski, 57.
141. Ibid.

Zivia was especially strict about that. She was the treasurer; it was her opinion that we had to go hungry—at least a little—out of empathy. I had to devise all kinds of inventions to get money out of her. I could tell interesting tales about that. As for trust, the Movement had complete faith in the leadership group; when we said they were going to Slovakia, they went to Slovakia. They went without the panic typical of most of the "veteran" party members, who would try to elbow their way. With us, there was always the tendency to seek a way to get closer to the shores of Eretz Israel, in an organized manner. Even in the hardest times.

When there were failures and people were captured and murdered, I can't know if those affected saw the fault as our oversight. After all, I can't ask the dead. If a group went by train and fell into the hands of the Germans, I don't know what our comrades thought in the last moments, whether they found fault with one of us or not.

Havka Folman sometimes went with me on trips. She accompanied me on a trip to Kraków. She certainly doesn't blame me for endangering her life. And her mother didn't either. Anyone with eyes in their head understood we were walking a very thin tightrope. The only other choice was to hide, because you could have thought differently: why endanger yourself? Why be among the wolves when I'm only a dog? Why walk around tense all the time? What good will come from this? You don't know what other people are thinking deep down, and that makes it hard for someone who has to make decisions. In the hard times of the *Aktsia,* we took all our people out to Czerniaków, we sent them to Miedzyrzec to Hrubieszów, where we had a major failure—murder on the way to and at the farm.[142] That was just before the German *Aktsia* known as the "Miła Cauldron."

Before September 6, 1942, the day the Great *Aktsia* was renewed, Zivia and I were the only ones left of the Movement leadership; it would have been simpler if we had also gone to Czerniaków, but we stayed in Warsaw. Later, part of the group returned because, by then, the Germans wouldn't allow them to leave, and the group in Warsaw grew again. We did that not because we were good or special people. They all would have done the same—Frumka, Mordechai Tennenbaum, Tuvia Borzykowski, Leah Perlstein, and Yosef Kornianski. But the two of us remained, and we decided to get the people out and take responsibility.

142. In August 1942, during the Great *Aktsia*, thirty members of Dzielna were sent to Kibbutz Dror in Warkowicz (near Hrubieszów) and assigned to begin partisan operations in the area, along with their predecessors. Shortly after, another group of eighteen members was sent. They were caught during a check of documents on the way to Hrubieszów and most of them were murdered by the Germans. The failure of that group also led to the destruction of all the comrades sawing down trees near Hrubieszów.

As for the formal aspect of decision making under those circumstances, there couldn't be any "institution," since part of the people were always on the road. Therefore, we included a few more activists who were involved in youth affairs and He-Halutz: Hancia, Berele Broyde, Munia Reingewirtz.[143] As I said, circumstances didn't suit democratic procedures. If someone had asked me who had appointed me, I wouldn't have had an answer. There was Movement responsibility beyond formal procedures. You might ask who sent Frumka from the Soviet zone to Warsaw. Who asked her and Zivia to do that? And it has nothing to do with whether or not they were formal members of the Central Committee of He-Halutz. Yosef Kornianski wasn't a member of the Central Committee, but he took responsibility. Not in everything and not always did we involve others; sometimes we couldn't. That was how it was in those days.

Regular meetings were no longer held. Gershuni was the secretary of the Dzielna group. He suffered from backaches and was always a bit bent over; until I started suffering from the same thing, I didn't understand it. He had a longing for power, maybe because of his disability. His eyes bulged out of their sockets when he saw the SS marching in a procession. He was a model Movement person, one of the central people at Dzielna, you didn't have to argue with him. He conducted the meetings that still were held, fought the big wars. Finally, he was one of those who was killed. That was the group that made the big decisions: going to the border, removing people, financial affairs, obligations. Sometimes, the group shrank a lot until only two people were left in it—Yitzhak Zuckerman and Zivia Lubetkin; and when I wasn't there—Frumka and Zivia. And sometimes, Yitzhak Zuckerman was left alone. And when I came to places, I had to provide answers, good or bad. I'm sure we made mistakes. Maybe someone complained and blamed us; but I think I would have felt it if there had been complaints. I'm sensitive to such things. If my ear had picked up something, I would have resigned immediately.

I want now to indicate the place of every one of our members, the center of gravity of their actions and the nature of their activities:

Before Zivia came to Warsaw in January 1941, Frumka coordinated all operations. When Zivia came, Frumka became our "itinerant preacher"; she was on the road. For example, when I arrived, just before Passover 1940, she and Leah Perlstein were in Zagłębie, which was had been annexed to the Reich. Later, after the German invasion of the Soviet Union, she wasn't "just a courier," but one of the central people of the Movement. She continued traveling around, and reached the farthest places—Białystok, Grodno, Vilna, Wołyń, and Polesie. She was incomparable. She didn't have proper papers, and even if she had, papers

143. See below.

wouldn't have helped her if she got caught. And her Polish wasn't fluent either.

Zivia Lubetkin was the secretary of He-Halutz and Frumka was the secretary of He-Halutz Coordinating Committee.[144] Her job was internal and external representation—at the Joint or OMA (Organization for Mutual Aid); but, of course, her main work was in the Movement. When the farm was established at Czerniaków, Leah Perlstein was the central person there. She assembled a big group, and was a very popular, beloved, and responsible personality. From time to time, both before and after the establishment of the ghetto, I used to go visit Grochów and Czerniaków with Zivia; after the ghetto was established, it was mainly Zivia who would go to be with the comrades in those places.

Hancia Plotnitzka, Frumka's sister, was at Grochów in the early days, after the farm was set up. When the Gymnasium was established, we decided to enroll her as a student, in the twelfth grade. Hancia was pretty grown up (older than Havka Folman), and she badly needed to study. In my opinion, she didn't fit the time, simply wasn't born for those awful days; she was like a flower bud . . . She should have been in Eretz Israel by then. Blessed with aesthetic taste and in love with poetry, her heart broke at each failure and catastrophe; very fragile. We felt how hard it was for her. If she had gone on the road, to meetings, she would certainly have contributed her share. But she did whatever she could at Dzielna. Because she was older than her classmates at the Gymnasium, she had some authority with them, and her lack of formal education didn't diminish her importance. She learned a great deal in that period, and we were very glad we could integrate her into our lives.

She wasn't the only one. Another example of person who "didn't fit in," in my opinion, even though he was admired and valued, was Zvi Mersik of Białystok. Some people just aren't "made" for such times, which demand a "thicker skin" and a stronger nature. Maybe that's vulgar; I don't think that people who did demonstrate more adaptability had "a thick skin," but they did have a stronger nature and they did what they had to do.

When Tuvia Borzykowski came from Radomsk, he became a counselor for counselors. He would hold circles for counselors in courtyards and seminars, and would lecture in Yiddish; aside from the teachings of Borokhov, his world was Yiddish literature from the beginning to the modern period, that is, the beginning of the century. Proletarian literature—Bovshover, Morris Rosenfeld[145]—were the subjects of his lec-

144. In another place, Yitzhak Zuckerman says that Zivia was also secretary of the He-Halutz Coordinating Committee.

145. Morris Rosenfeld (1862–1923): Pioneer of Yiddish poetry in the United States; he wrote on proletarian, national, and romantic themes.

tures. And that also suited his origins. He was bookish, an autodidact; and every book he read and mastered was a "triumph."

One central person at Dzielna, a Halutz in his soul, who was always involved in councils and meetings was Yosef Kornianski, loved by everyone and a "father" in many ways. He had a special relation to people, to members, and was "solid," a man who could work day and night. He was involved in setting up symposia. He created a sewing shop and a barber shop and other such institutions to support himself and Dzielna with his initiative and participation.

The secretary of Dzielna, whom I've already mentioned, was Gedalia Gershuni, a fine and interesting guy. A physically ill person, but a noble, bookish man who loved poetry. Gedalia Gershuni was always with us and was involved even when I was forced to flee from Dzielna. He was one of the few who knew where I was and maintained contact.

In the past, when we had been a mass movement, no one knew anyone else closely; in the commune, we became close. The evenings were long because of the curfew. We lived at Dzielna, in one courtyard. We got to know people a bit better; circumstances didn't produce a standardization of a certain type. On the contrary, all of a sudden, you saw a broad spectrum of types, one complementing the other.

The younger ones included Berl Broyde, who was devoted to counseling. And Muniek Reingewirtz, who took care of our affairs in YISA—formally, he was the director of our kitchen at Dzielna 34. The people I've talked about belonged mainly to the early Dzielna period (1940–1941).

Zivia and I remained at Dzielna even when there were no longer many Jews in Warsaw. On the last day of the *Aktsia* in Warsaw, September 6, 1942, Zivia and I were the only ones left. There were no more Jews by then, neither at Dzielna nor in the immediate neighborhood. We decided that precisely there, near Pawiak, was the safest place, because all the Jews had been removed. Before that, Ayre Grżybowski, a member of Ha-Shomer Ha-Tza'ir who was a policeman, came to us while it was still dark to tell us that the Jews were ordered to assemble on Miła Street (the whole story is in Y. Katznelson).[146] If not for Grżybowski, we wouldn't have known about that order. The members of Ha-Shomer Ha-Tza'ir took care of that because they knew we were alone on "a desert island." We would sneak from Pawiak Street (not from Dzielna) and meet in the evening. I left Dzielna in January 1942. Later, during the *Aktsia*, I came back when I understood that the Gestapo was no longer looking for individual Jews. But during this period—1940–1941—our whole leadership cadre was concentrated at Dzielna. Aside from Dzielna, we also had communes in Grochów and Czerniaków. I was

146. See Katznelson 1956:337–431.

the only one who had his own room in the courtyard on Dzielna, not because I was a "VIP," but because our "printing press" (a typewriter and a mimeograph machine) was in that room, along with our newspapers. And if I had been caught, I would have fallen as an individual without endangering Dzielna and the other members. Later on, I remember an incident when they came looking for me, and Tuvia Borzykowski was in the room with me.

Let me say something about the women couriers:[147] Aside from me, I don't think anyone traveled as much as the woman couriers.[148] In the early days, when it was still allowed, they would go out from time to time. After the establishment of the ghetto, and even before, I was the only man who was on the road. Indeed one man did come to us now and then, that was Laban; and, of course, Mordechai Tennenbaum came, but he didn't travel much. I would go to Kraków, a long trip, once a month. I was the only man to make long trips to dozens of places.

I already mentioned Frumka, and I must again mention Lonka Kozibrodska, who was a born courier. She had all the natural qualities for it: grace and Aryan looks. She knew many languages—Yiddish and Hebrew, Polish, German, English, French, Byelorussian, Ukrainian; and she knew how to disguise herself. Much of her work was done by means of Germans. She made contact with soldiers, officers, railroad workers, who never knew what they were carrying or what they were doing transporting her suitcases, or doing other favors for her.

Lonka usually accompanied me on my trips. (Later, in 1942, it was Havka Folman who went with me.) Lonka and I had many very difficult experiences together. In the hardest times, when I was on the brink of madness, I would call Lonka, sit down, and read—at that time, reading was a balm for me, like a couple bottles of cognac today; it helped me a lot. Today, much as I would want to, I couldn't stand that and I would certainly give myself away. Externally, it wasn't obvious, but inside, my nerves were stretched to the breaking point. As the poet says, I looked as if "the blood in my face were all the blood I had." And the truth was that I could hide my emotions.

On one of my last trips, I was with Lonka in Lublin, where the Jews were not yet all concentrated in the ghetto and were scattered in various places. There was a Jewish hotel there, and we pretended to be gentiles. Before dawn, they woke us: the Germans had surrounded the homes of the Jews in enclaves and expelled all the Jews. Fortunately, we managed to escape through the back door.

147. The importance of women couriers cannot be overestimated at a time when circumcised Jewish men were in grave danger.
148. See chapter on "The Women Couriers" in Yitzhak Zuckerman 1985:67–70.

When they caught you, you never knew where you would go. Usually, that was the end of the road: a few months of prison and then straight to Auschwitz.

We once had a very difficult experience on a trip from Częstochowa to Piotrków. We had to get into the ghetto at a time when there were still ghettoes in many places. When we rode back in the train, Lonka and I took our armbands off. The train was almost empty. A priest and a Polish woman sat near us. When we heard the conductor asking for tickets, the Polish woman began looking in her bags and saw that her money and her ticket had disappeared. She immediately began accusing me of stealing her money. Apparently someone stole it from her as she got on the train, or perhaps she just lost it. I was very worried. I was sitting next to the window and, first of all, I put my hand in my pocket very slowly, took out the armband, and threw it out the window. She saw me throw something out and started yelling that I threw her wallet out. The priest tried to calm her. Later the Polish conductor came and the priest was my champion, saying that I had been sitting there all the time and that he didn't see me move. When we got to Piotrków, we saw her standing in the station next to the Germans, watching us. We tried to escape through the back door and we made it. We grabbed a taxi and went to the city. You can imagine what would have happened if we hadn't gotten away. Here you've got a story about the stolen wallet, along with everything else! It was a thoroughly dumb experience. Just think, for that, you paid with your life, really with your life! It didn't take much.

On those visits, there was hardly a place where I wasn't shocked—Jewish life, encounters, Jewish existence. It was hardest in the cities. In the small towns, it was more comfortable at that time, relatively speaking, of course. We would allow ourselves to eat better; that was the compensation. I could have drunk vodka, but I wasn't drinking then. Food was cheaper and easier to get in the small towns, and I didn't have to be with the people of Dzielna. At Dzielna, always and without exception, we ate what everybody else ate, which was almost below subsistence level. We were busy and didn't think much about eating, but we were always hungry and I was always willing to get up, even at three in the morning, if they told me there was bread, just bread. And so would everybody else.

Lonka was a very good courier, efficient and responsible. I insisted that someone always accompany me on my trips. And I traveled a lot with Lonka. I wanted someone with me to know if something happened to me, so I wouldn't sink like a stone into the sea. Besides, as a man, if they got suspicious, all they had to do was pull down my pants to prove I was "Yitzhak son of Abraham." That was why the girls played a central role in maintaining contact between the parts of the Jewish organism, which was split into so many cells. I was an exception, so I always had a woman courier with me so she would know what happened. Sometimes we would appear as a couple, sometimes I would go first because of the danger. As a rule, it was important not to go together. In time of danger, I was the candidate to fall first. And if I was captured and taken to forced labor, or if my documents weren't in order, at least the courier would know what happened to me. Frumka's trips were for other matters, and she also traveled a lot; I didn't go outside the Generalgouvernement, but Frumka went to areas annexed to the Reich. Later, we sent another emissary to Łódz. We created contact with the world, with the Halutz youth movements. Two movements that played a central role in creating contact were Ha-Shomer Ha-Tza'ir and us. Gordonia also had a woman courier once, but our women couriers were on the road all the time.

Speaking of Łódz, I must mention Rivka Glanz who was there until spring of 1940. She was secretary to Mordechai Rumkowski, head of the Judenrat in Lodz, and she ran away from there because of him.[149] Our attitude toward the Judenrat was not yet negative in 1940; but then I heard about Rumkowski for the first time from Rivka Glanz; the man was obviously sick or a pervert. And that was known even before the war. Rivka Glanz was the secretary of the Judenrat, and he attached himself to her and wanted to force her to marry him. She realized she couldn't resist his pleas and threats, and she ran away from Łódz to Warsaw. When she came, she told us about Rumkowski. He was a member of the *Al Mishmar* faction of the General Zionists, that is, a follower of Yitzhak Gruenbaum. If the Germans hadn't promoted Rumkowski, he would never have achieved any prominence.

Later, Rivka Glanz was active for a long time in Warsaw; when our kibbutz was established in Częstochowa, she was its moving spirit. She was also one of the founders of the Jewish Fighting Organization there, and she led the comrades in the last battle in the bunkers of Częstochowa.

I should say something about our meetings with social activists, writers, and poets who would come to Dzielna. These weren't formal meetings; we could talk about all sorts of things, as with Yitzhak Katznelson, for instance. He came to Warsaw before I did, and when I came, I found him there. First he escaped from Łodz to Kraków because the Gestapo had established their headquarters in the building of his Gymnasium in Łodz, and they were starting to look for him. His wife and children forced him to flee, whereas they themselves remained in Łodz. He fled to Kraków and, from Kraków, to Warsaw. His family joined him later.

149. Haim Rumkowski (1877–1944): Infamous head of the Łódz Judenrat. Worked closely with the Germans, believing he was thus saving Jewish lives. Was allowed by the Germans to behave as a dictator in Łódz Ghetto. He was killed in Auschwitz. (See Trunk 1977:passim; Reitlinger 1961:63–64; Dobroszycki, ed., xxviff.)

I had known of Yitzhak Katznelson long before. He was one of the young people of Bialik's generation, a brother and companion of the writers of the "Renaissance Generation" of Hebrew literature; from first grade on, I was taught his poem "On the window, on the window, stood a pretty bird," and his other poems. Yitzhak Katznelson was a model for me. The first time I met him in person was in Warsaw, in mid-1940, thanks to Yosef Kornianski, who introduced us; after that, our friendship continued throughout the years we were together. That personal friendship often stood the hardest tests. I loved him and I think he also felt very warm toward me. But one day, that friendship was in danger of disintegrating because of Abraham Gancwajch, after we learned that Gancwajch served the Germans and worked for the Gestapo.

One day, I found out that Gancwajch ate lunch with Schipper and Katznelson. They were seen eating fish in some restaurant. I decided to talk candidly with Yitzhak Katznelson. I asked him if that was true, and he said it was and praised Gancwajch, who "takes care of poets and writers and intellectuals"; he said Gancwajch helped the historian Yitzhak Schipper very much and gave him financial support. Yitzhak Katznelson said Schipper had invited him and that he visited Gancwajch occasionally. He talked about Gancwajch as a cultured man who had respect for Yiddish and Hebrew literati and even knew Hebrew. Then I told Katznelson what I knew about Gancwajch. I gave him the choice: either us or Gancwajch, and he was stunned, crushed, and depressed. But there could be absolutely no compromise here. I put the issue squarely. You have to know what Yitzhak Katznelson meant to me, both in terms of his position and place in literature, and in terms of my own affinity for literature. I should also mention that he was the same generation as Tabenkin and a relative of Berl Katznelson.[150] In terms of our personal relationship, that was extremely hard for me. But the choice was also clear to me. A very long conversation followed but, when it was over, he stood up and shook my hand; he chose us and left Gancwajch, but not Schipper. Ringelblum, I think, tells about that somewhere; that is, he plays a cat-and-mouse game with that drama. He knew they ate together or met, but he doesn't know how Yitzhak Katznelson broke off his relations with Gancwajch.

As for Yitzhak Katznelson, things between us were personally unpleasant for me, but I was willing to tolerate that from him. Katznelson often visited Dzielna and, after the death of Hershele Danielowicz,[151]

---

150. Berl Katznelson (1887–1944): Central figure of the Second Aliya, major ideological and intellectual leader of the Zionist labor movement in Eretz Israel, educator, and writer.

151. Hersh (Hershele) Danielowicz (1882–1941): Popular Yiddish poet, who died of starvation in the ghetto in 1941. He was aided by Katznelson and the Dror underground

Katznelson wrote a poem about the poet who left a thousand poems behind while he himself died of starvation.[152] In that poem, he mentioned and accused important people like Attorney Gustaw Wielikowski[153] and Giterman. Wielikowski was a member of the Judenrat, head of the Department of Social Aid, and also on the central committee of YISA along with Michael Weichert. One day, after the paper with Yitzhak Katznelson's poem appeared,[154] I was summoned to ZYTOS[155] to some "Control Committee." I didn't understand what I had to do with them, I wasn't involved with soup kitchens. I told this to Muniek Reingerwirtz, who was also from Łódz and was active at Dzielna. None of the comrades could explain it. I went there and found myself in a room with two or three people who began interrogating me. Apparently they had gotten hold of Katznelson's poem with its attack on Wielikowski. The interrogation was carried out in the style of the Gestapo. They accused me of publishing an underground newspaper and uttered threats like: "You'll pay for this"— that is, the attack on Wielikowski. I answered that it wasn't any of their business. I asked them if they were Gestapo agents, and said I didn't know who wrote the poem or what I had to do with some paper they read. I said I didn't read the paper and didn't know what they were talking about. I slammed the door and left. Incidentally, the fact that they found me out as editor of *Dror* was brought up before the members, and Schipper and a few others went to Wielikowski. They threatened that, if the interrogations didn't stop, they would suffer unpleasant consequences. Thus, the matter ended. It was almost like a German interrogation.

I can't say if those people really denounced me or if that had anything to do with the fact that they came to look for me later on. But, in 1945, I caught my main interrogator, whose name I won't mention, in the street. He didn't remember me, but I remembered him. By then, I was a member of the Central Committee of the Jews of Poland. I brought him into the office and started interrogating him. I said something to him, and he said he didn't remember. I reminded him of my interrogation and asked him if he had collaborated with the Gestapo. Then he started pleading for his life. I let him go and he never showed up again. I couldn't do anything to him about that interrogation because I didn't have any evidence. He

---

at Dzielna. His archives and poems written in the ghetto were brought by his widow to Dzielna 34 and were all lost, except for two poems printed in the underground paper *Dror*.

152. Y. Katznelson 1951:23–26.

153. Gustaw Wielikowski: Well-known attorney and member of the Judenrat. Was hated by the social forces that set up the soup kitchens because of his bureaucratic behavior.

154. *Dror* (Underground), no. 13 (7–8).

155. ZYTOS: Zydowski Towarzystow Opieki Społecznej (Jewish Organization for Public Welfare).

did what he did either out of stupidity or out of loyalty to Wielikowski. I couldn't blame him, but I did want to scare him a little. And he really did vanish. Since I don't have any evidence, I don't want to mention his name.

Yitzhak Katznelson tried to help us in times of trouble. Once I told him we were struggling with financial support of a Movement seminar, and he told me he had somebody (he told me his name) who helped the Bund and writers. He offered to take me to him. We came to the house, on Nalewki Street, I believe, entered a very big room, and found a man sitting in front of a mirror being shaved by a barber. When he saw people entering in the mirror, he waved hello. Another man was sitting next to him reading Sholem-Aleichem, in Yiddish; when the barber finished his job, the Jew said: "*Ge'endikt mit Sholem-Aleichem.* (We finished with Sholem-Aleichem)"; he closed the book and turned to us. I saw what kind of character we were dealing with, even though I didn't know exactly what he did. I found that out later. At any rate, I decided privately not to take less than 500 Złotys.

Yitzhak Katznelson introduced me as a Halutz. I told the man we needed money for cultural activities and lectures. Naturally, I didn't tell him about the underground seminars. The man clapped his hand, his secretary entered, and he told him: "*Git im finf toyznt (5,000) Złoty.*" And I thought I wouldn't take less than 500—5,000 Złotys! That was quite a sum! I thanked him and we left. When I asked around about the man, it turned out he cooperated economically with the Germans; he was a brushmaker for the Germans. He was a factory owner in Warsaw and Kraków and he traveled a lot. He was close to the Bund and had given them a lot of money back before the war. If I had come on him in 1943, we wouldn't have condemned him to death because I didn't condemn economic collaborators to death; and there were many of them. But we would surely have imposed a fine on him. He made a fortune and escaped to Hungary in 1943; but Jews there who remembered what he had done in the past recognized him and beat him severely. After the war, he escaped to South America. His support for the Bund in the underground was to his credit; and he also supported writers, and he may also have helped Yitzhak Katznelson. But I never asked him about that. After I was told who he was, I didn't go to him anymore.

With the establishment of the ghetto, when we were expelled from Grochów, Yitzhak Katznelson suggested we go to Wielikowski. We went to him and found him very busy; he didn't even invite us to sit down. Yitzhak Katznelson said we had been thrown out of Grochów and something had to be done so the farm wouldn't be stolen from us. Wielikowski replied that he was very busy with general Jewish issues and couldn't get involved in nonsense. To which Yitzhak Katznelson replied: "He who is not concerned with one Jew is not concerned with all Jews," and with that, we left.

We solved the problem of Grochów without Wielikowski. We returned there after Zivia and Yosef Kornianski tended to it. I also tried to take care of that through Gzęda, one of our comrades, who was an official in the Judenrat. Later, Ringelblum asked me to transfer Michael Weichert's archive from Kraków to Warsaw by means of our women couriers. It wasn't a personal archive but the YISA archive. Lonka brought it to me from Kraków. Since it wasn't personal material, I allowed myself to open and read documents I was interested in before I gave it to Ringelblum. Among other things, I wanted to know what Weichert did about our farm in Grochów. Apparently he didn't do anything, even though there was a request there for him to take care of it. After that, I gave all that material to Ringelblum.

I didn't have any contact with Professor Meir Balaban[156] but I used to meet Yitzhak Schipper at various public forums. I also had very good friends at ZYTOS and at Tłomackie.[157] There was, for instance, Melekh Feinkind, one of the central people of Po'alei Zion Left.[158] He had been in Eretz Israel in the 1920s and apparently returned for health reasons. He was a very handsome man, a member of their Central Committee. He was head of administrative personnel at Tłomackie and it was because of him that we got paper for printing; he also helped us with typing and mimeographing. In time, we got a mimeograph machine from Dr. Menakhem Stein, whose wife, Rachel, was a well-known figure at CENTOS. But until we got big jobs to perform, and even after, Feinkind helped me.

The Judenrat and Tlomackie can be distinguished like this: If there were a hundred people in the Judenrat (this is a hypothetical number), I trusted only one of them, whereas at ZYTOS, at Tłomackie 5, out of a hundred people, we were in touch with ninety-nine and only one you had to watch out for. Loyal Jewish public affairs were at Tłomackie, and Schipper was there too. I didn't agree with Schipper, not just because of

156. Meir Bałaban (1877–1942): Historian of Polish Jewry. Died in Warsaw Ghetto, November 1942.

157. Tłomackie Street, where the Jewish social institutions were located: the synagogue, the Jewish Historical Institute, and offices of YISA. See Zuckerman 1985:53–58.

158. Melekh Feinkind: Described by Adolf Berman (1977:179) as "a serious and intelligent activist of Po'alei Zion Left . . ." In his youth, he had been a member of the Polish Social Democratic party but had resigned over their position concerning the assimilation of the Jews and became a dedicated activist in Po'alei Zion Left. In the ghetto, he was a member of the Anti-Fascist Bloc and of YISA. He also assisted in printing the underground Dror press. After the Great *Aktsia*, Feinkind represented his party in the Jewish National Committee and the Coordinating Committee. After the Uprising, he was sent to the concentration camp in Poniatów, near Lublin, where he led an uprising. He was killed there, along with 15,000 Jews, mostly from the Warsaw Ghetto.

his lunches with Gancwajch, but with his whole manner; but there was no doubt about his personal integrity. So Schipper was there, Lipa Bloch, Yonas Turkow, Edek Matwejecki, and David Radunski[159] of Hitahdut; as well as Giterman, Guzik,[160] and Leon Neustadt, directors of the Joint in Warsaw. I could talk with that whole group more or less freely. And we discussed all kinds of things. We had "information," because we had a radio then; they tried to get close to us, and we had something to tell.

Almost every other day, I would go to Tłomackie for some reason. I would go alone or with Zivia who was connected with the place because of her work. We would go during the day because there was a curfew at night, and each of us would tend to his own business. One of the people we talked to was Dr. Yitzhak Schipper, with whom we later had so many arguments; but that was another period, as a result of the problematic nature of the changing times. Schipper was a short, thin man who limped and walked with a cane. He was a well-known historian of Jewish life and economics in the Diaspora.

One day when I came, I saw Schipper near Tłomackie with his daughter, a nice girl. I said hello to him. "Hello, meet my work," he said, and added: "You know, I wrote a lot. All my books are compilations. But this is my real work, perhaps the only one." He did have a sense of humor.

One day, I learned that he was writing a book on the Khazars. I asked him: "Doctor, I heard you're writing on the Khazars. Here in the ghetto— where do you get material, sources?" He looked at me and said: "*Mensh, oyf tsu shraybn geshikhte darf men hobn a kop un nisht keyn tukhes*. (Man, to write history you need a head and not a behind.)" Once, in a conversation with his students, he said that his favorite student was Raphael Mahler,[161] and his least successful student was Dr. Emmanuel Ringelblum. Schipper's knowledge was very extensive; he wrote about theater, economic history, literature, and language. It was a pleasure to talk to him; he was a fascinating, vastly superior man. We would meet now and then and chat.

One of those who came to us was the musician Professor Israel Feibishes, of Łódz, who established the adult and the children's choirs. Dror then turned into a real "empire," and it is enough to mention things

159. David Radunski (1889–1943): Born in Slonim. One of the founders of Hatahdut movement. Member of the Central Committee of Po'alei Zion–Z.S. during the war. Killed during the Uprising.

160. Daniel David Guzik: Born in Warsaw. One of the directors of the Joint in Warsaw. Member of the Public Funding Commission after the establishment of the ZOB. One of the leaders of the Jewish National Committee on the Aryan side. Gave financial support to Brikha. Was killed in an airplane crash near Prague in 1946; aged fifty-six. (See Czerniakow 1979:passim; Ringelblum 1986:344.)

161. Raphael Mahler (1899–): Born in Poland. Historian of the Jews. Immigrated to the United States and later to Israel.

others didn't do, since others also published an underground press. But to establish a Gymnasium, an agricultural farm on the Aryan side of Warsaw, a dramatic troupe directed by Yitzhak Katznelson, an adult and a children's choir—those were all our activities! It was really a pleasure to look now and then at the show put on for the general public. It was very encouraging; although it didn't save anyone from death, it did make the youth and the children hold up their heads as long as we could carry on such activities.

Feibishes often came to us. We arranged for him to eat in our kitchen, but apparently he arranged better food for himself since there was a kitchen on Orla Street for more important people, and our soup was very thin. Israel Feibishes was murdered in Treblinka. Years ago, I got a letter from the Jewish actor, Jonas Turkow, who was then in New York, asking me to receive Feibishes's son who lived in the United States, a talented man, who worked in television, and apparently was attracted to Christianity. He had harsh complaints against his father who allegedly abandoned him. In talking with him, it turned out that in the transport from Warsaw to Treblinka, during the Great *Aktsia,* in an attempt to save his son, Feibishes threw him out of the train as it slowed down for a curve. He was rescued by some peasants and survived. But from childhood on, he had been haunted by that awful memory that his father had thrown him away and deserted him. Interestingly, he was grown up by then and still refused to understand that his father had done it to save him. I didn't want to poke my nose into such a sensitive issue, but I started telling him about his father, what he had done, his greatness, his devotion to his family. I didn't want him to discover that I had been told anything in advance. The thing was buried very deep in him, which was why he was tending toward Christianity (I don't know if he actually converted). He went on living with his great pain and the feeling that his family—his father—had abandoned him.

Someone I often met with in the ghetto was Mordechai Czudner. Like his name, he was an eccentric (*a tshudak*). I remembered him from Vilna. When I was a student, he was a teacher in Charney's seminary and was then the editor of *Galim* (Waves) or *Zramim* (Streams), a Hebrew weekly; later he was the editor of the revived *Ha-Tzfira* in Warsaw. I remembered him because of some episode: the Eretz-Israeli writer Moshe Stawski (Stavi) came to Vilna and Czudner introduced him in Yiddish: "I have the honor of welcoming the great Jewish-Arabic writer Moshe Stawski, the 'writer of the cattle and animals.' "[162] The audience burst out laughing.

162. Moshe Stavi (Stawski; 1884–1964): Yiddish and Hebrew writer, emigrated early to Eretz Israel. One of his well-known books was *The Book of Cattle* (2 vols., 1930).

How did I find Mordechai Czudner? One day I went to Lipa Bloch and found a young woman sitting in his office. I sat to the side and listened. She asked for shoes for her husband who couldn't go out without them. She said they didn't have bread. He answered that he would try to do something for them, and so forth. When she left, he told me she was Czudner's wife. I went home and made a respectable package and came to him. It was a big cold room on Nowolipki Street in a rundown house full of half-naked children. He really didn't have any shoes. I introduced myself and said I was from Vilna and knew who he was, which brought tears to his eyes. (They probably hadn't eaten that day.) And after that, I would drop in on him now and then. I tried to get him to write. He was hesitant and fearful. Later on, he gave me some unpublished material, two short stories set in the Russian Revolution, about the Jews in the Ukrainian revolution. Despite my good will, I didn't see any way to publish them in *Dror*. Every now and then, I would visit him and leave some "secret gift." He had an enormous library of thousands of books he started selling, except for the good books which he kept for himself. I used to buy from him and would bargain, but he didn't want to sell the books that really appealed to me. Naturally, everything was lost. Apparently, he wound up dying in Treblinka.

A few words about Emmanuel Ringelblum. From time to time, some of us, me especially, would meet with him. Ringelblum was a member of Po'alei Zion Left and had a strange attitude toward Ha-Shomer Ha-Tza'ir and us. For members of Po'alei Zion Left we were always Po'alei Zion Right, their opponents, even though we (Dror) saw ourselves as standing on our own feet, as independents. But they transferred their antipathy toward that party to us.

Eliahu Gutkowski was one of the most active members of Ringleblum's Oneg Shabbat,[163] but not as a member of Po'alei Zion. The situation was different with Ha-Shomer Ha-Tza'ir. I knew that Yosef Kaplan and Shmuel Braslaw were close to Oneg Shabbat, whereas I wasn't. I wasn't invited to its meetings—maybe because of what is called "lack of pushiness." But Eliahu Gutkowski kept me informed about what they did.

Quite a bit of what he told me got into our underground press. He himself would get information from our couriers and refugees from the small towns. As I said, Ringelblum's relations to Ha-Shomer Ha-Tza'ir

163. Oneg Shabbat was the code name of Dr. Emmanuel Ringelblum's archive, which was also called the Ghetto Archive, the underground archive staffed by dozens of workers. It was in touch with the Jewish underground organizations and has served as a documentary source for the period of the Holocaust and the history of the destroyed Jewish communities. Aside from Dr. E. Ringelblum himself, Eliahu Gutkowski was also a member of the small directorate of Oneg Shabbat. The workers included Rachel Auerbach, L. Bloch, S. Braslaw, Y. Giterman, S. Sagan, Y. Kaplan, and others.

were very close, even ideologically. But that didn't keep us from inviting Ringelblum to lecture. He was a very boring lecturer. The girls who had known him as a teacher from the *Yehudia* school also thought so. That was the opposite of Menakhem Linder, who was an interesting lecturer in dull subjects like statistics and economics, whereas Ringelblum would take living chapters of history and "kill" them.

But Ringelblum certainly played an important role, not only in the archive, but also in all his activity. His jutting chin indicated an energetic and active man; he filled a central role at Tłomackie, in YISA, and had an outstanding organizational ability. Every now and then, I would see his family.

Of all the members of Oneg Shabbat, Eliahu Gutkowski was closest to me. In times of trouble, he sheltered me. He wasn't afraid to give me a hiding place when I was like a leper, at a time when respectable people were scared to meet me. In those dark days, I slept at his home.

We hid our Movement archive in three places. I wasn't interested and didn't think it was desirable to entrust our material to anyone else. We hid the "internal correspondence" and all kinds of inside things, but it got lost. I could have given it to Gutkowski.

More about the members of Oneg Shabbat: Dr. Natan Eck had less to do with Oneg Shabbat than did Rachel Auerbach.[164] We maintained contact with her at a certain time when I was outside Dzielna. When I came to an assembly, a lunch was arranged for me at a kitchen on our street, where she was director. The meals there were better. I would meet her there in the kitchen. I also met with the teacher Abraham Lewin who was also a member of Oneg Shabbat.[165] I could speak Hebrew with him, and I told him I had read his *Cantonists*.[166] We became friends and he was also one of our lecturers. Rosenblum, the director of *Tarbut*, the Hebrew school network, was also very close to us. The Movement didn't send me to institutions like *Tarbut* as an official representative, but I was requested to participate by esteemed veteran comrades, like Lipa Bloch.

164. Rachel Auerbach: Graduate of Lwów University in philosophy. Came to Warsaw in 1932; published short stories and essays in various journals. In the ghetto, was active in Oneg Shabbat and directed a soup kitchen. She continued her activity on the Aryan side. Later wrote several works on the Holocaust. Immigrated to Israel, where she organized the Department for Collecting Witness Accounts at Yad Vashem. (See Ringelblum 1986.)

165. Abraham Lewin (1893–1943): Born in Warsaw. From a very religious family, studied in yeshiva, but changed to secular studies and became a teacher of Jewish history and Hebrew at a private Gymnasium for girls. In the ghetto, was active in education and in Oneg Shabbat; worked for YISA. Was apparently killed in the *Aktsia* of January 1943. (See Lewin 1989:1–57.)

166. In 1934, Lewin published a work, *The Cantonists*, on the impressment of Jewish boys in Czar Nikolai's army (1827–1856).

Hershele Danieliwicz visited us a lot. He was quite a character, but in a really miserable condition. He was a talented folk poet; as I recall, he lived in Palinicz until the Jews of Palinicz were brought to Warsaw. He came to us through Yitzhak Katznelson. He used to sell us bread he would buy in the bakery and earn a few cents. One day he came to me with his face swollen. I asked him: "What happened to you, Hershele?" And he answered: "A German hit me." "Why?" I asked. And he replied: "I forgot to ask him." When he got married, a delegation of writers came to him and asked: "Hershele, what gift should we buy you—flowers or socks?" He thought a moment and said: "Socks. Flowers wither, but socks last forever." He starved to death in 1941, in the ghetto. After he died, his widow asked us to preserve his literary legacy. She brought a big carton with his writings. There were things that had been published in periodicals or books, as well as unpublished manuscripts. As for his family, Yitzhak Katznelson told us his son was in an orphanage run by his friend David Dombrowski; and, as I recall, Katznelson tells about this in his epic poem "Song of the Slaughtered Jewish People."[167] What happened to his widow, I don't know. The literary estate was kept in a cellar at Dzielna and was lost during the Great *Aktsia*.

Stefa Wilczyńska, who worked with Janusz Korczak, used to visit us now and then. After she had been in Eretz Israel, at Kibbutz Eyn Harod, she transferred her sympathies for Eretz Israel to us.[168] Zivia and I also met her at Korczak's and we became friends. Zivia tells how she and Stefa would meet in the corridors of the Joint and would advise and help one another. I met her at Dzielna. Once, when she stayed overnight in my room, she said to me: "A general with a toothache cannot lead an army." I didn't understand and asked her to explain.

She said: "If leaders of a movement are hungry, their discretion is impaired." She saw how we lived and tried to convince us to take better care of our physical needs so our discretion would remain intact. It was nice to listen to her. But we didn't change our ways.

We had direct contact with Korczak; the affair began with Zivia, who once went to ask him for tools for the restored Grochów, since he also had a farm in Włocławek. But he refused to give tools, and said, "Farmers who leave their land don't deserve help." He was referring to the fact that our

167. David Dombrowski: Prior to the war, he was a teacher in a Hebrew school in Łodz. He was the brother-in-law of Berl Katznelson, Yitzhak Katznelson's cousin. The CENTOS orphanage, on Twarda Street, was directed by the educator David Dombrowski, who was taken to Treblinka with the children of the orphanage. Danielowicz's son's name was Pinhas. For the poem, see Katznelson 1956:418–419.

168. Eyn Harod: Kibbutz at the foot of Mt. Gilboa, founded in 1921; was the headquarters of Ha-Kibbutz Ha-Meuchad, the largest organization of kibbutzim in Eretz Israel, with which Dror was affiliated.

members had abandoned Grochów at the outbreak of the war, in September 1939.

Naturally, Stefa Wilczyńska helped with that. Later, we invited him to lecture at our first seminar. I remember him in the uniform of a Polish officer, wrapped in a civilian topcoat. When he took off the coat, I saw he was wearing a uniform. Our last meeting with Korczak and Stefa was, if I'm not mistaken, on July 20, 1942, on Saturday. At any rate, it was a Saturday, the last one before the *Aktsia*. We still keep Korczak's invitation to Zivia and me, which reads: "You are invited to the performance of the children . . ." And we did indeed go to the performance. It was a special Saturday—the last one before their death.

As for our contacts with the parties, let's start with the more distant ones. The first time we met with the Bund was to negotiate the establishment of the Jewish Fighting Organization (ZOB). Before that, we didn't have any contact with them. We did have contacts with Po'alei Zion Left. We used to meet with Ringelblum and Sagan, and Melekh Feinkind was our dear friend. In the General Zionists, we met with Kirshenbaum, Schipper, and Bloch. Among the General Zionists, we also met with the editors of *Haynt*: Aharon Einhorn[169] and Shaul Stupnicki;[170] there was somebody else whose writings we also published—it seems to me his name was Yitzhak Bronstein—a talented man, an essayist, on the staff of *Der Moment*. I became friendly with him and also asked him for things to publish in our press; but I don't remember exactly what we published. We were cautious with the Revisionists, and we didn't know anything about their underground operations.

As for the poets, I recall Yehiel Lerer, whom I saw a lot and whose writings we published. Zaromb, who was close to He-Halutz, escaped to Russia. You can read about him in Shalom Cholawski's book.[171] He was in Białystok then.

We had contacts later on with members of the religious trends (Rabbi Alexander-Zysze Friedman).[172] There were no Communists around at that time; before January 1942, I didn't meet a single one.

169. Aharon Einhorn: Editor of *Haynt*, the largest Yiddish newspaper in pre-war Poland. He translated French literature into Yiddish. In the ghetto, he was active in YISA. Was shot in his room in Otwock. (See Ringelblum 1986.)

170. Shaul Stupnicki: Journalist, editor of *Lubliner Tagblat* before the war; later was on the editorial staff of *Der Moment*. He poisoned himself at the *Umschlagplatz* before being deported. (See Ringelblum 1986:737–740.)

171. S. Cholawski, *City and Forest Under Siege*. Tel Aviv: Sifriat Po'liam, 1973.

172. Alexander-Zysze Friedman: Secretary-General of Agudath Israel (anti-Zionist Orthodox party) of Poland before the war. In the ghetto, was chairman of the Religious Commission. Was director of the Agudath Israel religious system; a journalist, editor of Orthodox publications and a Hebrew poet. (See Berman 1977:134.) According to Adolf Berman, "he was one of the most popular figures in the Warsaw Ghetto" (Berman 1977:204).

We were in close touch with members of Po'alei Zion, like Stefan Grajek and Yohanan Morgenstern. Morgenstern was formally a member of the ZOB staff and was treasurer of the organization, whereas Stefan, though loyal to ZOB, wasn't a member. To be a member, you had to belong to one of the units or the district or central staff; but I didn't understand why he and his wife didn't join one of the units. Somehow, they were with the fighters in the Többens-Schultz area later on, but that's another story. Morgenstern, however, was formally in ZOB and participated in some of our meetings. Stefan Grajek was very close to us, also because of his youth. He and his wife lived outside Warsaw and came to us a lot, since they felt at home. We attended party meetings (Zivia was a member of the Central Committee of the party) but we weren't invited to all of them. I went to those meetings without being deeply involved in the discussions that went on there. Besides Zivia and me, Frumka also participated when she was in Warsaw. Coming from Frayhayt, she and Zivia were closer to the party than I was. I never was a good party man, and I'm still not.

The central group of the party consisted of Yosef Sak, Leyzer Levin, Yohanan Morgenstern, Stefan Grajek, Israel Lichtenstein,[173] and Abraham Fishelson. This small group would discuss issues and make decisions; from time to time, as I said, they would invite us to a "dinner meeting." I gladly accepted, even though they didn't serve great delicacies there, but it was something. Even an onion in oil as an appetizer, even without an egg, was a great thing; as I recall, a meat course was occasionally on the menu.

When I came to Warsaw from the Soviet zone and got such a nice welcome, I told my comrades about the shots that almost hit me as I boarded the train. "You were very lucky," they told me. And I joked that, when the war broke out, I made an agreement with the Master of the Universe to take me through all the horrors of the war and leave me alive. Later, I regretted that inane joke. But, in fact that's what happened.

I must say that never, in any incident, not even in most difficult moments, in the most difficult emotional distress, not only did I not regret, but I blessed the day I came to Warsaw, even in the days of Treblinka. I didn't regret being where I was because I knew I had to be

---

173. Israel Lichtenstein: An experienced educator; active in underground education; was the administrative director of the Ringelblum Archive and was responsible for burying the Archive. He worked in the soup kitchen at Nowolipki 68. See his last will and testament, Ringelblum 1986:58–59; 696–700. Ringelblum reports that, during the Great *Aktsia,* Lichtenstein proposed a suicide attack on the Germans, and, even though they would all be shot, "we will know why . . . Then we would become immortalized in history like the victims of the Nemirov pogrom" (i.e., in N. N. Hanover's poetic chronicle of 1648; Ringelblum 1986:63).

there. I thought: how could I have lived if I had been in some quiet place?! That is, to this very day, I have never blamed or accused anyone. And I don't blame myself either; no, I wasn't led like Isaac to the sacrifice—absolutely not! Not even at moments when I faced death, I had no regrets or complaints. Maybe that was an expression of vitality: I loved life and that sustained me even when I was really on the verge of madness, of physical or emotional collapse, when the shock of the news from Vilna and Chelmno reached me. Those were the hardest weeks of my life. Weeks of emotional crisis and helplessness, not knowing what to do or how to do it, what to say to our young comrades. It was unlike anything before. In the hardest moments, even when I left the Soviet zone, I went with the clear knowledge of where I was going. Now I saw a gaping abyss in front of me. Indeed, total annihilation didn't occur to me at all, but I went on with my eyes open to everything that was known then—and that was enough not to want to go on—but I went on with a lucid knowledge of where I was going. That doesn't mean I wasn't terrified. I was scared many times. I have met people who said they never knew fear. I did, a lot. I can say I was a good "actor": people didn't know I was scared; but the truth is I was. There were moments when I simply staggered, but I had to overcome it. If I review everything that happened after the outbreak of the war, the first time I was really scared was when I crossed into the German occupation zone. An awful fear descended on me. I had horrible dreams then. That is, the world I saw in my imagination was a world of horrors. But I had to go to Warsaw, and I went.

Life in Warsaw was very hard. I was sick a few days until I got used to Jewish reality and the Jewish street, the humiliation, the German pilots grabbing people for work. That was the first time I had to take to my heels and run away. And there was Jewish solidarity. You can't imagine how the secret "telephone" worked in the street. It was enough for the Germans to come within three streets of us, and signals would already be received. Zivia or Frumka would stay downstairs and I learned to climb quickly to the fourth or fifth floor. But it was hard for me to get used to the humiliation involved in this fleeing. It was against my education and my nature since, from my youth, I always traded blows with any *Sheygetz* who attacked me. That was also the kind of education we received in the Movement and in the Hebrew Gymnasium in Vilna.

Later on, the issue with the hat—to take off your hat to every German! I never took off my hat. Simply because I went without a hat, summer and winter and rain or shine; and I wasn't the only one. In the hardest conditions, even when I faced death, not only in a crowd but also as an individual, even when they set up a gallows for me,[174] I never had any

174. In the Kampinos Camp, see below, chapter 4.

regret or complaint against anyone, not even myself, for the step I took when I crossed to the German occupation zone.

As for that argument with Edek about which of us had to cross to the Germans, it turned out—especially on the Aryan side of Warsaw—that knowing German was less important than an Aryan face. Often, in times of distress, they would look at my face and say: "Your Aryan face is worth its weight in gold, worth a hundred thousand [Złotys]!"

In general, I was at peace with myself. Even about the "question of democracy," which can be stated as "who authorized you." This question didn't bother me very much. In those circumstances, it wasn't so important if you were an elected "representative." Not only did the Jews not elect me, the Movement didn't elect me either or send me to do what I did. There is a moment when you assume the responsibility and the mission of your own free will. If you don't want to, don't accept it. The Movement didn't elect me to play a central role in the underground.

Can you really talk about that in terms of democracy? From the moment I came forward—I or one of my comrades—there was no going back. There's no point repeating every day that it's hard. From that moment on, you've got the responsibility, as if you had been elected. I was two years older than the young members. They believed in me and hung on my words. But there was a time when I didn't know what to say to myself or what to do, where to start. And at first, as I said, that was the time of deep depression that came on me and lasted a few weeks.

That was the period when the problem of the relations and contacts with families of the members grew worse. That was still before the annihilation, but there were already expulsions from small towns. In Łódz there was a ghetto; in Kraków, expulsions. In the small towns there was oppression, hunger, loss of livelihood, ignorance about what would happen. All the members of the Dzielna commune had families throughout Poland. In and around Warsaw and Lublin, the Germans were beginning to snatch people for work. Some of the members had younger sisters and brothers, older brothers, fathers and mothers. And there was a question of whether we could help, rescue.

Of all those, we could talk about helping the families of some of those from Warsaw; we sent some of them to Czerniaków and included them in the councils at Dzielna. For instance, Shaul Dobuchna. I saw the poverty of his home and, every now and then, I made sure he took something for his parents. As for the families of the central group: Frumka's family was in Pinsk, far from Warsaw. Zivia's parents were also on the Soviet side; my parents were in Vilna. For a time, I was calm.

An exception in that whole group, until 1942, was Lonka, whose parents lived in Pruszków. When the Jews of Pruszków were expelled to Warsaw, we gave them an apartment at Dzielna 34 and supported them so that Lonka could travel with peace of mind. They got whatever they needed from our food stores, and we made sure their food ration was guaranteed even when ours was hard to get. That's how it was until 1942. In 1942, Mordechai Tennenbaum came; his mother was in Warsaw and we helped her too. Tuvia Borzykowski's parents were in Radomsk; now and then when I visited there, I would leave them something; and so did Tuvia. He was also exceptional because his parents lived in a nearby town. None of the rest could help their parents because of our limited means, for we were very poor. Only later, during the expulsions from the small towns to Warsaw, did we help absorb them, and, as soon as they came, they were able to find their way to us. Even before the war, we knew all the members of the Movement. If not I, then Frumka; and if not Frumka, then Zivia; and of course we immediately made contact with the refugees, our members, and supplied them with food from Dzielna 34, whose kitchen was open to them. We fought with the Joint and with ZYTOS to increase the soup ration and, aside from soup, there wasn't much, usually only one course you could barely eat.

What haunted me for a long time, in fact, to this very day, was my leaving home. I didn't forgive myself for leaving as I did. Of course, I didn't know it was the last time. I left Vilna, my home, in a few minutes, and I could have stayed another twenty-four hours, to prepare my parents. They didn't deserve such a parting. Later, I was happy when I got letters from friends in Vilna or when they visited there and brought regards from home. Abraham Gewelber once told me he was there and Mordechai Tennenbaum also said he visited my parents. David Kozibrodski said my father visited them. I didn't ask for help for my parents, I didn't ask for anything. In Warsaw I didn't get information directly from my parents, but only in a roundabout way. I knew that they might need help but I didn't have the courage to ask and I never did. Our comrades were sending help to us from Vilna. And I could have written and asked them to help them too, and they would certainly have done it. I have no doubt of that, but I didn't ask. I didn't ask; but it hasn't left me alone since.

With the establishment of the ghetto, a change occurred in our Movement and in the work in it. But, first of all, it had a material influence. Dzielna was a working commune; the girls worked as cleaning women— first of all in the ghetto. One of our friends was a cleaning woman for the family of engineer Yosef Jaszunski, and others worked for other notables; relations were good. Our female members worked in orphanages; one of the male members worked as director of the YISA kitchen. Members worked in Okęcie on the Aryan side.[175] In his poem, "A Jew Went

175. Okęcie—an airport near Warsaw, where Jews were brought for forced labor and abused.

Out," Yitzhak Katznelson talks about Okęcie. Jews went there in groups. Of course, when something bad happened and one of our members was beaten at work, we didn't let him go back there. We had sick people, those who needed special diets; and under the difficult conditions in which we operated, we made sure they had white bread and a minimum of suitable food. It's interesting that those who were considered "dieters" in the training kibbutzim and at Dzielna didn't suffer from ulcers or other illnesses when they got to Auschwitz. I was afraid some of them wouldn't last a week, but they were the ones who managed to stand the suffering. The same is true of a few girls who were sick or weak.

With the establishment of the ghetto, we got less help from the farms of Czerniaków and Grochów because of the difficulties of smuggling food from those places. The members of Czerniaków always took care of us and you could count on Leah Perlstein to reduce their own ration of bread and potatoes for us, but problems arose in transporting food to us. To bring a wagon into the ghetto, you had to get special permission and that required special efforts. You could use the horse and wagon of Grochów, but that was dangerous because the Germans might confiscate the means of transport.

The establishment of the ghetto meant a revolution in our life. Suddenly you saw poverty in a concentrated and harsh form. Every single day, the situation grew worse. Dead bodies rolled in the streets. Your senses did grow blunt in time. You got used to it, you moved a little and passed by. I was used to passing one family: two young people carrying a little girl. I recall the nobility in their stance and their silence. Every time I passed them, I would give them something. One day they disappeared and I knew they were no longer alive.

I would see singers standing in the street and singing. One singer had an extraordinary voice, an opera singer. People would gather around him and give him pennies. There was one clown, Rubenstein, one of whose "tricks" I remember: he would jump onto a coffin being taken through the street and shout: "Stop, just don't turn in the ration card!" Or: *"Shmalts vert biliger, di gvirim lozn zikh oys.* (The price of fat is dropping, the rich are melting [growing poor.])" Afterward, he would claim that only three men would be left alive: Czerniakow, Abraham Gancwajch, and him. He would say: "You think I'm crazy? If I weren't, I would have been dead long ago!"[176] People would gather round him. The streets were full, and all of a sudden, a car full of Germans would appear in Karmelicka

---

176. Haim Frimmer (Carmi and Frimmer 1961:170) says that Rubenstein's words were a "reflection of life in the ghetto": "When Rubenstein saw a wagon of corpses passing by, he would approach, tap the cart and call out to a corpse: 'Hey, fellow! Move over a little and make room, a refugee from the provinces wants to get on!'"

Street, and they'd jump out. I never once got beaten because I fled like a rabbit. People were left killed on the ground from those beatings; Jews went into the street and didn't return home. There were wounded; there was abuse; there was typhus and death. A typhus epidemic also started among us, but we overcame it. One of our comrades at Dzielna got sick and we sent him to Częstochowa; he now lives in Jerusalem. His name is Haim Rosenthal; he was sick with typhus, truly on the brink of death. One chilly day, as winter was coming on, from the top floor I saw him sitting naked. I yelled down at him: "What are you doing?" "He's taking a sunbath," they told me. His temperature was 41 degrees (Celsius). We were afraid he would die, but he overcame it. I already said that none of us died of hunger or disease—except for one, a consumptive, who hid his disease, and I already told about that.

Somehow, we began getting accustomed to the new conditions. The fact that the ghetto was closed by a wall also had advantages. We expanded our activity in the courtyards. There were more residents in one court-yard in Warsaw than in a whole small town. People would go out, and stay overnight in a courtyard. In every such base, we operated through one of the refugees. In the evening, we used to assemble the youth, the children. Of course, if there was someone suspicious, you had to be careful. But we didn't talk about armed uprising in those meetings. We would sing, teach Hebrew songs. Everyone did what he could; sometimes Berl Broyde did it and sometimes Hancia. The members of our "senior class" were required to assemble in the evenings. Leah Perlstein, Havka Folman, and Ruth Shklar[177] also took part.

Hence, the autonomy of the ghetto wasn't only a delusion. It was, of course, an "autonomy of corpses," but there was some development in our enterprise. In mid-1940, we started the Seminar and the Gymnasium, and later it spread. Organized Jewish society was completely incapable of coping with the situation. Only foreign sources could help us and did. As long as the Joint operated (until the United States entered the war), things were easier. Afterward, you couldn't get along anymore. Soup kitchens, the kitchens of the parties, all social welfare activity, ultimately encom-passed only a small percentage of the population; many people just died. Courtyard committees existed but if we read Yitzhak Katznelson's poem, "The Feast,"[178] we see "how they dance" (even the rich) to support the family. I'm not talking about the artistic merit of the poem, but it is a document reflecting the life of the courtyard with rich and poor. And

177. Ruth Shklar: Born in Warsaw. Student in the Dror Gymnasium; active in ZOB. During the Great *Aktsia*, she was in the unit of the arsonists (see below). Was killed with her comrades at the partisan base near Hrubieszów; aged about nineteen.
178. Yitzhak Katznelson 1956:26–31.

people who had died were taken every single day from the same courtyard. There were also lectures and performances, and a little money was
collected for the poor, and people danced a little, drank a little. But even
if those few "rich people" had given all their wealth, you couldn't have
supported the whole courtyard on it, like the Rothschilds' apology that,
if they gave charity to every beggar, they themselves would be ruined.
True, there was a class that made a fortune, there were those who hid their
money. Later on, they sold everything and somehow supported themselves. In time, a class of smugglers emerged along with a police force
where the policemen raked in part of the loot. And there were the wives
of the Judenrat members and the officials of the YISA. It's hard to call
the situation "flourishing," and it's true we shouldn't look at only one side
of the picture. But a lecture on Yehuda Ha-Levy is no substitute for bread.
And death took more and more victims.

Close to half a million Jews were packed into the ghetto. Jewish factories and enterprises remained on the Aryan side; and in the small towns,
shops were taken away from their owners. Individual Jewish laborers who
continued working in all kinds of places were the skilled artisans. In a
short time, most of them populated the cemetery on Gęsia. We saw the
transport of corpses every single day. You got used to it. I went to the
cemetery and saw the graves.

When the ghetto wall went up, fewer Germans came into our streets.
But when they did, they took more license. You can see this in the films
the Germans made: the streets were swarming with people and merchandise for sale. You walk in the street and, all of a sudden, Germans
appear. That happened on Dzielna and on Karmelicka. The Germans
would come to Pawiak, near Dzielna, and it would always end in death.
"The flourishing of autonomy," as it were, was an imaginary flourishing
for the fear of death didn't disappear; the Germans were present. That
was in addition to the Jewish police and the "blue" Polish police. Sometimes I happened to return on a night train and had to stay at the railroad
station because of the curfew, and that was dangerous.

The Jews of Praga were moved to the ghetto. Going into the ghetto
from outside was one of the hardest experiences for me. This was in 1941,
when the full horror of death raged in the ghetto.

How did we manage to get out of the ghetto? Lonka and I had a system:
we usually went into the courthouse on Leszno Street (the courthouse
served both Jews and Poles); you could get to the Aryan side from there
with the help of an official who took bribes. The Germans and the Polish
police stood guard. We would enter with a note, as if we were summoned
to a trial, and leave on the Aryan side. One day, I entered with Lonka and,
since no one was there, we took off our armbands and tried to get to that
official, who would take us through the corridor to the exit. All of a

sudden, a Polish policeman grabbed us because we supposedly wanted to sneak into the ghetto. That was a success, even without bribery; he was sure we were Poles. (Jews who looked Jewish wouldn't have succeeded in that, but Lonka and I did.) We started telling some story about how they owed us money in the ghetto. But he threw us out to the Aryan side.

Sometimes, we snuck out with the help of our police, who organized our exit in advance: I would slip 500 Złotys or some other sum agreed on in advance into my Jewish document and give it to the German. He would pocket the money, give me back my document, and let me through. Our police knew which Germans could be dealt with. We had agents in the Jewish police. One of them, Arye Grżybowski, from Slonim, a member of Ha-Shomer Ha-Tza'ir, later involved a few other policemen who helped us. At different periods, we would contact Grżybowski who would organize a deal. He was a police officer and if a Jewish policeman also needed to be bribed, he would do it himself. Our person would wait a few hundred meters away and, at a given signal, we knew whether we could pass or not. As a rule, they would let us pass when the German patrol changed.

There were other kinds of trips, too. Yosef Kaplan looked Jewish, and it was impossible to mistake his identity. He traveled a few times, to Częstochowa or Kraków, with a forged pass, allowing a Jew to ride the train. Some Germans bought that "tall tale"; we found a person who forged perfect documents; but he also had to slip some money into the identity document not to get beaten up by the Germans as he went through. This was how you traveled as a Jew. I traveled that way only once. Not from Warsaw but back to Warsaw. In the early days, you could cross to the Aryan side through the cemetery, which was outside the ghetto. Funerals were allowed to pass on the street separating it from the ghetto. Later, only the family of the deceased were allowed to cross; but, in the beginning, you could cross over just by joining a funeral. I would go to the Aryan side through the Polish cemetery, next to the Jewish one. But don't forget that when the ghetto was established, the Polish black-mailers, the *Shmaltsovniks*, were already operating, making a living by blackmailing Jews. They worked near the cemetery gates. For instance, if I left as a Jew with a document and an armband, they knew I was leaving with a pass, but they followed me; and if they saw me take off the armband, I could wind up very badly.

On the Aryan side at that time, I didn't usually pay bribes. But once, I traveled with Stefan Grajek and I warned him; but he was careless and couldn't hold out, and paid a lot; we almost paid with our lives. Even after the ghetto was established, we always kept in touch with the outside. Most of my trips were around the time of the establishment of the ghetto. They were important trips because, after the establishment of the ghetto, except for isolated incidents, those who looked Jewish couldn't leave and the entire burden fell on the women who looked "gentile," and me. There was a difference between Frumka and Lonka, which I have already explained. When Frumka stopped traveling, issues of youth and the educational movement fell on me, and later, so did contact with Bratislava and the transfer of people across the borders. I would leave weighed down with fears, even though that was dangerous.

Somehow, we dealt with the threat of getting snatched for work and labor camp. Until Passover 1941, not one of us in Warsaw was taken to a labor camp. But on the road, I would hear about our comrades and young people taken to those camps and brutally killed. They used to tell about one German called Dolfus who was notorious for his brutality. There were labor camps along the River Bug in 1941, when the Germans were preparing for war against the Soviets and would take thousands of young Jews to work on fortifications. (I was also taken for that work then.) They used us to build fortifications and they didn't care how many thousands of Jews paid for them with their lives. Some of our comrades were taken to various places in Zagłębie, in the zone of the Reich, where they worked under conditions that were harsh but somewhat easier than in the Generalgouvernement and in and around Warsaw. Our comrades didn't suffer from that. Those in Grochów and Czerniaków were exempt from that grief, and we took care that people weren't taken from Dzielna. Those who worked in Okęcie had documents, and all the others had documents affirming that they worked in YISA. It was primarily the men we had to protect, since they didn't take girls.

Until the last day of Passover 1941, I would hear dreadful rumors on the road—in Kielce, Lublin, and other cities, as well as Warsaw, until I went to a camp myself. Snatching people for work in 1939 and 1940 was done by the Germans themselves. The Judenrat would intervene and Czerniakow did have influence. Their intention was good: instead of someone going off without knowing where, it would be better if it were orderly and the Judenrat itself gave a quota of people. But the result was that both the Judenrat and the Germans were involved; it was hardest with the Jewish police, who would come at night and take people on their list. The only advantage to this was that you could get out of it with money or by sending someone else instead of a man on the list; and the Judenrat made a fortune from that. You can figure out who was sent, because the rich man would pay and the poor man would go instead of him. A worker who volunteered to go would leave the money he got to his family. Meanwhile, the Jewish man would grow weak physically, since the food in the camp was dreadfully meager, the work was backbreaking, and people died in the camp.[179]

---

179. For an account of the Judenrat and forced labor, see Gutman 1989:22–24; Kaplan 1973:55; Czerniakow 1979:88ff.

On the other hand, those who worked at Okęcie and in *Dienst* (German Work Services) returned to the ghetto after work. They were paraded to and from work by the Germans through the Aryan streets of Warsaw, in the middle of the street. If there was a "good German," you could jump out and buy a kilogram of bread to bring into the ghetto. If you were nimble, you sometimes even succeeded in buying two kilos; and then you would sell one kilo and cover the price of your bread.

We didn't send our people to other places, but there was a time when our men worked in Okęcie, and we were interested in that as long as we could use it to bring food into the ghetto. If the Germans beat them up and gave them only blows and no soup, we wouldn't let them go. Thus, we were part of the work being done in and around Warsaw at that time. They went to work in the morning and came home. I don't remember that our members were beaten at work. The bread they brought when they came back naturally couldn't save Dzielna but, nevertheless, it was an addition. Moreover, those who worked ate better soup and got a half-kilo ration of bread a day. Whereas I, as I recall, ate 180 grams a day. If I ate at all.

When the crowding in the ghetto grew worse and diseases increased, we managed to maintain our standard of life from slipping too far. We did that with the help of money we got. As I said, we got money with a promise to pay it back in Eretz Israel after the war; the debtor was Ha-Kibbutz Ha-Meuchad. The money we got for the Movement, we spent only for the Movement.

The Jewish Social Self-Help Committee (YISA) was sympathetic to the Halutzim. That wasn't expressed in food but in support of the Movement. Later, Giterman and Guzik would come to us and we would protest to them: what you see now in Dzielna, in the Movement, we did that over the years, under starvation conditions. What do you care if you gave the Movement another 100,000 dollars charged to the Joint, and allow us to expand our activities? That's what we told them when we were working in the Jewish Fighting Organization and they "warmed themselves" with the sight of us.

Meanwhile, more and more of those expelled from the surrounding areas were put in the ghetto, and they came with nothing. We worked with the young people among them; there were always members of our Movement. About the time the ghetto was established, an important article appeared on the value of assistance to the needy.[180] That wasn't about theories, but simply about extending help, bread; that each of our members should consider it a mission to give help. Lacking an organization,

180. "Jewish Youth Now," *Dror*, no. 3, July–August 1940. (See Jewish underground newspapers in Warsaw, Yad Vashem, 38.)

in the turmoil that existed, the author of the article called on them to do everything to help, as a step of primary importance.

We tried somehow to operate under those conditions. At the Eichmann trial, Zivia told of the children begging on the streets in winter: "*A shtikele broyt, a shtikele broyt.* (A piece of bread, a piece of bread.)" And, she added: "We didn't have '*a shtikele broyt*'; I would get up in the morning and find the child dead. They were like hunted little animals. You can't imagine the grief and suffering of the Jewish child. How they died like flies! And even if an orphanage was opened, and even if you tried to assemble them and give them shelter—how many could you help? Maybe one one-thousandth!" Some of the children became smugglers, were beaten, and would hide; there were break-ins of houses.

In this situation, the Jewish mind worked, and there were various inventions. For example, how did they get milk into the ghetto? They would pour it into a pipe in a Polish house near the wall, and the milk would flow through to the Jewish side. Or the story of the cart driver who left the ghetto with one horse and came back with two, and the Germans didn't notice. The second horse was slaughtered and sold for meat. The big smugglers would make deals with the Germans; they would smuggle in large quantities of food in automobiles; they didn't do that to feed the masses but, objectively, they filled an important function by bringing food into the hungry ghetto. The more food they brought in, the lower the price. When the Germans stopped it and murdered the smugglers, the price of bread, meat, and potatoes jumped up. There was a big gap in prices between the Aryan side and the Jewish side. A loaf of bread passed through many hands until it got to the ghetto. When more was brought in, the price went down a bit.

At that time, we had our stations on the way to and from the ghetto: Grochów and Czerniaków. In Warsaw itself, we didn't have any places and you couldn't stay overnight. I would usually spend the night at Czerniaków. If I returned at night, I would try to get back in through the breaches in the walls, while impersonating a gentile. Because, if I was caught near the gate, they would have finished me off immediately. Sometimes, I paid the guard at the gate, and he would let me into a dirty bedroom where I slept in a chair until morning.

At that period, the girls were invaluable and their sacrifice was infinite. Without them, it would definitely have been impossible to maintain the Movement throughout the German occupation zone. All of them and every individual according to her ability risked her life and demonstrated unimaginable loyalty. I asked myself (and Zivia) where they drew their strength, what sustained them?

Apparently, what sustained them was a great ideal, as well as the extraordinary friendship within the Movement. I often asked Zivia if she thought I was idealizing the situation. But she too credited the Movement cadre with the friendship and loyalty that prevailed in it. People did have weaknesses, but that was accepted as among lovers, that is, there was no idolatry. Incidentally, idols also had weaknesses. We simply understood that every person has his own weaknesses.

I loved to make jokes about Yosef Kornianski; and he enjoyed that. He would squint and listen as if he were hearing it for the first time. There were few couples and families among us. Later, in Israel, Havka Folman said that when they were students in the Gymnasium, they used to talk about us: wasn't it a "triangle"—Frumka, Zivia, and I? They were very interested and would peep through the keyhole. They didn't have the nerve to talk, but they were very interested in what was going on with us. What was the texture of our relations? When Frumka was there, she lived with us. Lonka was with her parents at that time. As I said, we supported the parents at Dzielna. But the girls were interested in Frumka and wanted to know what would come out of all this, what was the purpose. There were other couples: Muniek Reingewirtz and Hirshke Kutsher and their wives; and there was Shmulik, whom I mentioned a few times whose girl survived. And there was that Shalom Litewski who also had a mate. I think that's all. Everyone would gather in my room, which was natural since that was the conference room. We would spend the evenings together; if members weren't at meetings in the big room in the commune, they were in my room every single evening.

We used to sit and talk and prepare for the next day. There was electricity some of the time. We also used a carbide lantern. And in winter, we would bring newspapers to heat the oven, because the cold was awful. We didn't get an iron stove until late in 1941. You could buy wood, but we wouldn't allow ourselves that indulgence. Later, when I lived in a room with Zivia, we would buy a few kilos of wood. People would dismantle furniture and anything else they could and sell it by the kilo. The Jews in the ghetto made a living from commerce and sold whatever they could.

Food smuggling was a serious element in the ghetto economy. Some lived on that more than on rationed food, which was less than 200 grams of bread a day. Anyone could buy something, not just rich people. A sick child had to get a drop of milk. And if there wasn't smuggling, there wasn't any milk. You couldn't stay alive on what the Germans allotted; however, the Jew couldn't allow himself to buy a half kilo of bread. And not everyone had the right to eat in those miserable kitchens. In such a situation, a Jew would sell his sheets and his suit. In general, the smugglers bought such merchandise and shipped it to the Aryan side of Warsaw, where the gentiles bought it for pennies.

Who in the ghetto knew about our operations? Those who had to know. In terms of the Joint, as far as the Germans were concerned, the house on Dzielna was a soup kitchen. The shows and performances were in the Cultural Department. Biblical evenings were held under the auspices of the Exercise Department of the Jewish Self-Help Organization headed by Jonas Turkow. He, of course, knew of the Movement and even risked his life. We tried not to talk in public about things that were better left in silence.

The Jewish police practically left us alone. They came once, when they took us to the labor camp. But in general, there were high officials in the Judenrat, like Wasserman, who were loyal to us. Nahum Remba,[181] brother of Isaac Remba of the Yiddish daily, *Haynt*, was there. He was a very nice man, a General Zionist, who did many important things. Some members of the Judenrat like Gepner were sympathetic to us and helped us. Sometimes we would get food from the Judenrat, for example, when those who managed to be in the school or kindergarten of *Shulkult* got food, along with their lessons,[182] and they came home, where there was hunger. Those were the children we organized and educated, talked to, sang and danced with.

The people who lived at Dzielna 34 and on Gęsia appeared to the Jewish street as responsible for the stations of refugees who worked under the aegis of YISA, which hadn't yet been banned by the Germans. At a certain period, the He-Halutz center still existed in Berlin. The Halutzim in the commune were connected with the underground press, but no one knew about that except those who had to know. They didn't know about the connection of those Halutzim refugees at Dzielna 34 with the underground Gymnasium and the national organization of the Movement, about the trips throughout Poland. We always had to preserve the legality of young Halutzim, but even the name Halutzim didn't appear in writing. Even if the Germans knew about it, they would have seen it as education for Eretz Israel. At that period, they didn't object to the *Palestina Amt* (The Palestine Office), and we took advantage of that.

There was no lack of denouncers. For example, right after we caught onto Gancwajch, Marek Folman told me about a meeting of the house

181. Nahum Remba: Worked in the ghetto education department. He is described by Stanisław Adler (1982:229) as "Tall and robust, he was brown-haired and of a gay disposition, but an idler—no one knew what he was doing. One could meet him in all the offices, gossiping and joking . . . I understood Remba's real value as a man and a colleague in the hours of supreme test when, after July 22, 1942, he took up assignments in a hospital ambulance at the entrance to the *Umschlagplatz*. His composure and endurance, his great kindness and thoughtfulness, and above all his crystalline honesty and selfless devotion began to shine in all their grandeur." Jonas Turkow also describes his admirable role at the *Umschlagplatz* (Turkow 1969:123).

182. *Skulkult*: Berman describes it as "an educational system connected with Po'alei Zion–Z.S.," which "combined Hebrew and Yiddish in its curriculum." (See Berman 1977: 181.)

committee held in the winter. The people who came to the meeting took off their coats. One of the participants had to leave the meeting and go urgently to his apartment in the same courtyard. When he put on his coat and stuck his hand in the pocket, he suddenly took out a Gestapo document and was terrified. Later, he saw that, by mistake, he had put on his neighbor's coat which looked like his own. It didn't occur to him or his companions that that neighbor was working for the Gestapo. So we had to be careful.

The concierge at Dzielna was one of our people. As soon as the ghetto was closed and the Poles were sent out, we grabbed that "job" and held onto it all the time, until the end. The porter kept the list of residents, so we knew everything.

On the top floor, where I lived, was a bell attached to the concierge's lodge by a concealed string, and a ring for me meant an alarm. We knew the tenants in the courtyard. The first concierge was Abraham Breier, followed by Menakhem Bigelman,[183] both chosen by us. When something happened, he was a representative to the Germans. The concierge had to cooperate with us. It was very important for us to know what was going on; and, if not for this cooperation, I wouldn't be alive. The concierge was in touch with the Judenrat, the Jewish police, and the registration of residents. However, he tried not to endanger himself too much and not to rouse suspicion; when the Gestapo were pursuing or looking for a stranger, he had to show cooperation with them.

In early 1940, during the great snatchings the Germans carried out in Warsaw, the Judenrat, led by Czerniakow, tried to reach an agreement with the Germans so that the Judenrat would supply the people demanded by the Germans, on a daily or weekly quota, as needed. At that time, they weren't snatching Jews for labor camps, but to work outside the ghetto: at the airport (Okęcie), clearing rubble, doing various jobs on the railroad like unloading, things the Germans needed; of course it always involved abuse and murder. After the Germans agreed that the Judenrat would supply the people, things fell into a routine. On the one hand, the Germans didn't give in; and, on the other, the Judenrat was asked and came through and supplied the number of Jews demanded. The Germans weren't satisfied with that and got poor Jews from the Judenrat. The rich ones paid a ransom and the Judenrat sent the poor, most of whom volunteered, in their place. The payment the Jew received for his work on the Aryan side of Warsaw would buy cheap bread. The Judenrat

183. Menakhem Bigelman: Born in Warsaw. Was a member of ZOB in the Warsaw Ghetto; fought in Berl Broyde's unit in the Central Ghetto; one of the few saved from the bunker at Miła 18. Killed in a clash with the Germans on May 10, 1943, when he tried to break through to the Aryan side from the sewers, at the age of twenty-four.

also paid him something and that helped him and his family stay alive. He assumed the danger of beatings, and sometimes even risked his life. This shows you the social aspect of the Judenrat: the rich man saves his skin, while the poor man is a candidate for snatching in exchange for a miserable sum.

Those camps became an unsettling factor in the Movement and in our leadership circles. Some members claimed we were taking a certain, unethical advantage because the number of Jews delivered to the Germans remained the same, whereas our people were spared the snatchings because of documents they got from YISA, which meant that other people were turned over to the Germans who couldn't pay the ransom or get exemptions. I myself, for example, wasn't taken for forced labor and the document I had protected me. This situation caused me many pangs of conscience.

In comparison with Ha-Shomer Ha-Tza'ir, our members were lower on the social scale and, now and then, some of them were snatched for work; even prominent activists were caught on occasion. They worked at Okęcie and other places (post office, railroad).

Ha-Shomer Ha-Tza'ir was against going to forced labor and explained this position in their movement discussions. But that wasn't a rebellious opposition, and those who weren't taken paid ransom or avoided it by escaping or by some other way. This position can't be defined as "passive resistance." They didn't issue an appeal to the Jews not to go or to run away. We didn't do that either, nor did any other movement. And if you ask me if "passive resistance" could have been undertaken, I would say not under the circumstances of those times.

Today we know more about German policy concerning the labor force of the countries they occupied. Fritz Sauckel, in charge of foreign labor in Germany, succeeded in getting command not only of the Jews, but also the Poles, the French, the Belgians, and the Dutch.[184] Millions of those peoples were brought to Germany to work.

Some of our activists expressed the opinion that we shouldn't reconcile ourselves to that reality; they argued that if we could organize for work autonomously, as at Czerniaków, participation of our members in forced labor (labor camps) was preferable to a situation in which only "beggars" were snatched for labor. And there were cases (in Zagłębie, for example), where our members did organize and maintain some framework, even under the harsh conditions of a labor camp.

184. Fritz Sauckel: Plenipotentiary General for the Allocation of Labor, "ordered that foreign workers were to be exploited 'to the highest possible extent at the lowest conceivable degree of expenditure'" (Ferencz 1979:25). He was sentenced to death at Nuremberg and hanged in 1946.

The situation was serious for the Poles, too; but they were taken to Germany, whereas the Jews were kept in the Generalgouvernement. Of course the life of the Jews was harder. Their situation could be compared with that of the Russians (after June 1941), who died en masse in the occupation zones.

The Jewish and the German police performed the snatchings. Initially, the Germans did it. Later, when the Judenrat got into it and had to give the determined quota, the Jewish police carried it out. The snatchings were done in the streets and houses, and at night, with a system of manhunts, both with and without prepared lists. During a certain period, we were protected and some of us were sensitive about that; as I said, the argument was that we were saving ourselves and that didn't show responsibility for the masses.

At one point in time, I supported the idea that our members would go to the labor camp as a group, and I even offered to go with them. It was an operation comprising tens of thousands of young people and I thought I should join it. First of all, to see what it was and how it was run. Later, I discovered that that was naïveté on my part. It turned out you couldn't do anything at all in the institution known as a "labor camp." The conclusion was to try to save at least the few people we had. We couldn't protect the entire Jewish community in Warsaw. We could save our members in Dzielna and protect them from the snatchings. Naturally, the issue might explode, but in fact there weren't any mishaps. We would show our permits, the labor documents, and thus we saved ourselves from the labor camps.

FOUR

A Week in a Labor Camp

On the last day of Passover, 1941, Zivia and I stayed home. We had planned to go to Grajek but, at the last minute, we decided not to. At night, the Jewish police knocked on our gate. There were a lot of them, and they came with their officers. Apparently, they decided to take the Halutzim at Dzielna 34. At that time, I lived in a separate apartment, but I got a warning of what was expected. At first I was sure the members would show their permits and be released. My door was ajar, but they didn't pay attention to me. I heard cries and shouts. They gathered about ten people from our commune and, as I saw them taken away, I decided to join them, thinking I might help with the Judenrat and get them released, although I had never met Czerniakow, and it didn't occur to me that Czerniakow was involved in it. But I thought that if I came with them in a panic at night to the Labor Department of the Judenrat, I could do something. So I joined the group and was led off with them. By the time we got to the office, there was a big crowd of Jews.

Four of our group were released, postal workers, as I recall; the other six, including me, remained. Even before the four were released, I demanded to talk to the director of the Labor Department. If I'm not mistaken, his name was Shneurson[1] a swarthy fellow, with a black moustache. We went in, and I said we had been taken illegally, since all our people were working; he claimed that they had to go too! I said they were

---

1. According to Jonas Turkow, the head of the Labor Department was Leopold Kupczykier (Turkow, *Destruction of Warsaw*). According to Czerniakow (1979:124), Kupczykier was a member of the labor commission, and made a tour of the labor camps (207–208). See Ringelblum 1986:300.

Halutzim and he said it was the role of the Halutz to be first.[2] And with that, he ended the conversation.

I was sure our comrades were making attempts to get us released. Indeed, I learned later that, despite the curfew, Zivia ran to Wielikowski and others and made quite a fuss. One of the Judenrat members she appealed to, Stanisław Szereszewski, husband of Helena Szereszewska who wrote two books, was a decent man.[3] But before dawn, we were led through the streets of Warsaw and the suburb of Praga to the railroad station, accompanied by Polish, Ukrainian, and German police. When they took us to Praga, I had two opportunities to escape, and twice, I wrestled with myself; I was used to this sort of thing, and I thought I could escape at the bends in the road. I was experienced by then and thought I would succeed; but I was in a group and it simply wasn't nice to run away. So we were loaded onto cattle cars and taken to Kampinos Camp.[4]

We traveled for hours, since the train stopped from time to time. We were weak from the night before, exhausted and hungry. I had a few hundred Złotys in my pocket. We weren't dressed properly and it was very cold. The place looked desolate—a lot of sand and nothing around. They led us six or seven kilometers from the railroad station, and everywhere there was only sand, like a desert. We didn't know where we were. Apparently we were the second group that had come to the place. The first group had been brought two or three weeks before to erect the huts, and we were the complement—a few hundred people, only Jews; there was a barbed wire fence there and other signs of a closed camp. In the morning, we were lined up for roll call for the camp commander. It was hard to tell if he was a German or a *Volksdeutsche*; there were also Ukrainians there and people whose nationality I couldn't identify. They spoke Polish and I didn't know exactly what their function was. They held guns and sticks. They lined us up with their sticks and conducted a "formal" review of the beggars. We saw the men of the first group after two or three weeks; they didn't have to tell their tale—their faces were clear testimony.

The camp commander passed along the line once or twice, took me out of the ranks, and asked me if I could write. I don't know why he chose me of all people. I said yes. And he said: "As of today, you're the secretary." That is, I had to make the lists of the men. A clerk! My "secretariat" lasted one day, I think. It was Friday, a day of organizing. On Saturday, we went to work and I passed by and recorded the names of the workers. There were hundreds of people there. The director of

2. Halutz means "vanguard," "pioneer."

3. Helena Szereszewska, *The Last Chapter*, I and II, 1980. Stanisław Szereszewski: Before the war, he was chairman of Toporol. Engineer and member of the Judenrat, associated with YISA. Killed by the Germans in April 1943.

4. A labor camp, near Sochaczów, established in spring 1941.

the construction company that drained swamps and controlled rivers was also there. Apparently it was a Polish-German company that did the work;[5] the supervisor was a Pole. Since I walked around that day and didn't work, I became a "VIP," as it were, and got friendly with the supervisor. I don't know how it happened, but he liked me so much he let me buy food for myself and my five companions.

I must state that the villagers in the area treated us very well, even though it was a very poor area, and that's noteworthy: extremely humane treatment by Polish villagers! They brought us all kinds of food for sale, bread and cheese and eggs and sausage; and the supervisor let me buy it. We parted on friendly terms. The next day—Sunday—I brought all the food to my companions and we were very happy at our first achievements. I gave my money to Solly, one of those captured with me. He was a neat and orderly *Yekke*,[6] and I knew he would do his job faithfully. He became our "Supply Minister." In fact, he could organize our starvation regimen properly. He would divide the bread (200 grams a day) and soup into two equal parts; in the morning, we would eat one slice of bread, and in the evening, after work, the second slice. Some of the camp inmates were furious and demanded he give them some of our bread, but it was the same 200 grams everybody got. He organized things and kept the money and, when we were led after work, one of us was allowed to break off from the group, with the guards' tacit permission, and buy bread or sausage in one of the village houses.

We worked at draining. The water level in the swamps near the camp had to be lowered and controlled, and the flow of water had to be drained off toward the rivers. The whole area was swampland. The men would go into the water and work. The construction company supplied tools. There was a machine there, an instrument with holes to bail out water; the machine would sweep away the sand and enable the water to flow. It was very hard work. On Sunday we didn't work but on Saturday, we did. After standing in the water for hours, the men had to sleep in the same clothes.

On the first working day, when we got through, we tried to wash, to clean off the mud; and the guards, who had been drunk since morning, started beating the inmates. But not our group yet. The supervisor I had made friends with didn't stay in the camp, but came only during working hours, to the area of the swamps. When he came that day, he told me quietly that a girl was asking about me. I asked him what she looked like and, from his description, I concluded it was Lonka disguised as a Pole. That was a few days after we were taken. I was very glad she had come,

5. The Water Control Company.
6. German Jew, stereotypically honest and orderly.

and I waited to be called any minute because my friend told me to be ready for that; but the day went by and nobody called me. I started worrying. According to the camp regimen, everyone had to be in the huts at a certain hour, in bed with lights out. That evening, I couldn't stand it and went to the camp headquarters.

I told the guard a friend had come to me that morning; I hadn't seen her and I wanted to know if I could. He told me to wait, went inside, came out and said: "Go back to your hut. If we need you, we'll call you." I returned, depressed, to the hut; I told my companions what happened, and tried to fall asleep. But soon, I was called to headquarters. I entered the big hut. There were three men there; the commander of the camp police (militia), the camp commander, and another man. They started interrogating me: who came to me? How do I know? And so on. I told them I hadn't had time to get to know the men, that it was one of the guards; I said I didn't think I could identify him and that he had only told me someone was asking about me at the gate. I knew Lonka didn't wear an armband and I claimed it was a Polish classmate. I said she probably heard I was taken to the camp and came to look for me. From what they said, I began to fear that they were holding her. Clearly, I had to keep claiming she was a Pole.

Then they started torturing me. Two of them stood and beat me, first on my head, with rubber clubs. When I felt blood flow, I tried to cover my head with my hands, and then they beat my hands and ears. I put my hands down and saw they were covered with blood. They went on like that, mercilessly, incessently. At that stage, I didn't weep or whine; I took the blows in silence. And the more I got, the less pain I felt. But I sensed I was swelling up and blood kept flowing. They wanted me to admit she was a Jew, but they didn't get that. I kept arguing that she had been my classmate for years and, before that, she had lived in Praga, and I didn't know where she lived now and I had had no contact with her because I was in the ghetto. Meanwhile, I realized they knew her name and something about her, but I didn't know exactly what. Apparently, when she wanted to get in or asked to bring me out, they asked for her documents; but that wasn't the main thing. In time, I learned that if you want to endure an interrogation, choose what is important to you and don't retreat from that. I ordered myself to maintain she was a Pole! I was wounded and very sick, but I kept my composure.

Meanwhile I heard the commander order the guards to execute me. And I heard the police commander tell the camp commander in Polish: "A pity to waste the fellow." So, instead of executing me, they tossed me into a pit in the swampy ground, covered with a wooden structure with a door, and an awning for a roof. I won't tell about the night I spent in that pit, in the water. I was dizzy and in pain and I didn't close my eyes.

I went back and forth between fevers and chills. Before dawn, I heard steps approaching, but I couldn't see who it was because I was on a lower level. Dawn began penetrating through the cracks. All of a sudden, bread was thrown into the pit! My companions threw me their food rations.

I stayed in that pit forever, several hours. When I couldn't bear it anymore, I started shouting. Some time later, someone came and asked: "What do you want?" I said I had heard the commander say yesterday that I was to be executed and I didn't understand why they didn't, why they were keeping me here. Now they didn't beat me; it was apparently after working hours. Suddenly they came and took me out to the camp square. I saw the whole camp standing in rows in front of the gallows. They stood me opposite the men and then the commander made a speech. He didn't tell them what happened, but talked only about the "criminal" in front of them: "This man knows when he was born but he doesn't know when he will die. I can promise you only this: for three days his body will hang here as a warning to the entire camp." Then they took me back to the hole. The sequence of things got mixed up in my head. What I told before, that I demanded they execute me, apparently happened after that roll call. And again they kept me in that pit. I don't know how long, only that it was daylight. I started crying and demanded they carry out the sentence. And the answer was: "They'll let you know!"

I was a hundred percent sure that this wasn't just plain abuse, and that they were about to execute me. I didn't want that abuse, humiliation, or pain; I didn't want to bear them anymore. I thought: if I live another two hours, will it be any better? I wanted them to carry out the sentence. I don't know if someone there supported me. In the interrogation I just heard someone say: "A pity to waste the fellow." But then, they set up the gallows I had seen with my own eyes, along with the roll call. What I mean is that I said farewell. I tried to stand with my head held high. I didn't say anything, just tried to stand tall. After about an hour, the door of the pit opened and the police commander, accompanied by guards, took me out. They said I wasn't going to be executed and that they would release me. They couldn't do that now however, not until night. The commander gave orders to bring me hot soup and to spread straw on the puddles and mud so I could lie down in that dungeon. He repeated that I could be sure they wouldn't kill me. No one ever gave me an explanation.

That night, they took the watch I had gotten for my Bar Mitzvah; except for a few cents, I didn't have anything important, because I didn't have the treasury, Solly did. (I did have a Parker pen on me.) I waited a long time, dozed off, and suddenly I heard voices. I didn't know what the shouts and curses I heard meant, the door opened and Germans in Gestapo uniforms took me out. There were a lot of them, and there was also a woman. A few were riding horses they had apparently commandeered somewhere. There was somebody else who wasn't a Gestapo agent, but an SS man, and there was also a physician. Except for the guard who had taken me out of the pit, all those around were Germans. They asked why I had been thrown into that pit. I had to answer immediately, and I said that I had seen a Pole selling bread at the fence the day before and wanted to buy bread from him and they grabbed me. The officer ordered me to join the roll call. The camp commander was standing there, the one who had beaten me hardest, and the police commander was there too. They were standing and waiting for the Germans to come. I had time to whisper to the camp commander who had beaten me: "The Germans took me out and asked why I was in the pit; I told them I wanted to buy bread. If you want to save me, confirm that." He told me to stand in the line, the Germans passed by, put up a table, and asked if anyone felt sick. I don't know if the man really was a physician or if it was simply more abuse. At any rate, everyone who appeared there was beaten. I decided not to go, not to be sick, not to request to be released; because I didn't want my torments to start again. The roll call ended, I thought I was going to the hut but, all of a sudden I was called to the Germans. They stood around the prison pit with the camp commander. They asked me again the reason why I was in the pit. I repeated my story. I knew I depended on what the camp commander would say, and he said: "That's right! Because of the bread!"

They gave an order to increase the height of the fence and plug up the holes. I was ordered to return to my hut. They didn't torture me anymore after that. For three days in a row, I lay on my bunk. The Germans and the camp staff burst into the hut every morning, always accompanied by beatings; but I must say they didn't touch me during those days. My companions would bring me food on their way to work and soup at night.

When I began to get out of bed, the camp commander told me I would be an official, a clerk. I worked sitting down for a few days, and then I felt guilty vis-à-vis my companions, and I asked to go to work with them even though it was hard work and sleeping in the same clothes you worked in was difficult. Those returning from work would eat their ration in a shed with tables. Everyone had a bowl and a spoon and you had to hold onto them.

Why didn't they beat me? I have only one explanation for that: it was 1941, and the Germans were keeping an eye on the Polish underground; they suspected I had contacts with them, and that this wasn't just some Jew you could execute and get rid of. They were suspicious because right after I was taken to the camp, my Polish friends knew about it and sent a girl to get me released; and that had a serious significance for them. The Poles on the camp staff were careerists who collaborated with the Germans, but were afraid of the vengeance of the Polish underground and didn't want to get in trouble because of a "Yid." As for me, I didn't know if they had Lonka or not. If I had known for sure that she escaped, I could have admitted she was a Jew.

During my few weeks in the camp, the Jewish population there shrank and the cemetery expanded. One morning, we heard shouts, wailing, and pleading, and two shots. Afterward, we buried two strong, young brothers; they had tried to escape and had been caught. Every day, corpses of Jews who had died of starvation were taken out of the camp. In fact, everyone in those transports was destined for a quick death from hunger. These were poor people who didn't have the wherewithal to buy supplemental food. There was a teacher from *Tarbut*, who certainly didn't have a livelihood; and there was a man who claimed he worked for YISA. Most of the people were paupers who died like flies!

One day we learned that a transport of sick people was about to be sent out of the camp, but none of us was included in that group. When I saw that they gave me special treatment and didn't press me to go to work and that I went to work voluntarily, I took heart and asked one of the directors if there was a chance of adding me to the group that was released; and I hinted that I would be willing to pay for it. He mentioned a sum of a few hundred Złotys. I said that I didn't have any money with me but if he gave me a guard to escort me to the nearby telephone, I would contact the ghetto and ask them to prepare the money. A while later, he agreed. Then I informed him that I wasn't the only one, that there were five more men who had been taken along with me, and I offered a bigger sum to release all of them; I got permission for that too. I was given a guard who went with me to the post office in the neighboring village, about four kilometers away, where I called Havka Folman and asked her to raise the money for our release. A few more days passed; one day an order was given to black out the windows of the camp—that was close to the beginning of the war with the Soviet Union; afterward the order was canceled. A few days later, we were told we were leaving at dawn. That was a big group of sick and weak Jews. One of them had gone crazy. He refused to go and claimed he had forgotten his cap. They lined us up and before we started out, the camp commander came to me, took me out of the line, and said: "You're in charge. If someone falls behind, we'll kill him." The first victim was that lunatic, who ran around constantly. Before we left, I called my comrades and told them what the camp commander had told me. I said: "You know they kill people here. Try to be careful and organize the people around you to avoid any mishaps." There was one fellow among us named Armin Laks, of the group of young people. He dragged one of our comrades who had trouble walking. On the way, I saw he had weakened and was leaving him. I slapped him and shouted "Drag him!" Thus we plodded along until we came to the station. I should say that there were Poles who passed by who behaved wonderfully to us. They tossed us bread and bottles of milk. The guards didn't let the prisoners get close and I saw a bottle of milk burst and people ran to lick the milk from the ground. That was the first time I was struck by a severe pain in the back of my neck and in my spine. I really thought my time was up.

On the way to the station, before we boarded the train, people died. They died on the road from hunger. That death comes suddenly—I saw that with my own eyes. You'd be sitting and talking to a person and he seemed fine, and then he'd swell up and drop dead, right in front of your eyes. Behind us came a wagon loaded with corpses. We identified them by documents stuck to their hands. I thought they'd soon put me on the wagon too.

We waited at the station, and it took hours until we got on the train. The camp directors and guards who escorted us to Warsaw loaded us down with suitcases full of food; this was food sent by relatives of the inmates and stolen by the guards. It wasn't bad enough that they had robbed them, they also forced them to carry the loot. There were large quantities of food that relatives brought their families. The operation was well organized, and their contacts came and took the packages from us. When we got to Warsaw, they began distributing us in the ghetto. I was left for last, since I had to pay for myself and my companions who had already been released. I led the camp commander and the commander of the camp police (the one who had saved me) straight to my room at Dzielna 34. When I brought them into the apartment, there was a great turmoil since my companions had already managed to organize a welcoming party; of course they gave us bread but that wasn't meant for our escort; they sat down and waited for their money. Meanwhile, I asked the camp commander: "When you set up the gallows and said you were going to execute me, did you mean that seriously?" He said: "Absolutely! I'm used to a cruel life! I worked at sea for many years, I was an officer on a ship." I didn't ask him: "Why didn't you kill me?"

After he left, I learned that Lonka didn't fall into their hands at all. She got away as soon as she understood the situation. She really did appeal to the supervisor, the one who befriended me and whom I later had contact with. That man's behavior proved he had nothing sadistic toward Jews. Lonka came to him and he gave me the message. The first time I saw him was in the camp that Sunday, since he didn't usually go inside. Apparently, when she came to the guards, they told her to wait; she sensed something fishy and took off. They followed her to the station, but she disappeared; apparently she didn't get on the train at all but slipped out another way; but I was sure all the time that she was in their hands. To my great joy, I learned that Lonka wasn't touched or tortured and they didn't get anything out of her. And I had been terrified all the while.

One thing I can't explain is the beatings on the day they classified the sick. And why they took me out of the pit and asked me why I was there is also vague. The Germans didn't know anything about the gallows. They apparently asked who was in the dungeon and were told a beaten man was there. The guard didn't know German, so they asked me and I told them the story of the bread. Moreover, that was nervy of me to tell the camp commander what I did—that if he wanted to save my life, he had to stick with my story about the bread. As for the change in my treatment, my only explanation is that they were afraid I had contacts with the Polish underground. And, as for the gallows, I think that was only a threat— setting up a gallows, making a roll call, and the pardon in front of the whole camp. Although the camp commander did say he really meant it, I have no other explanation for it. And how can I explain that I was taken out of the line on the first day and appointed camp clerk? Maybe it was because I was tall and young and stood out. Maybe my clothes didn't look so ragged. And I attribute what happened later to Lonka, who escaped from them and made them worry that this case involved Poles who were interested in me. They killed enough other Jews and didn't want to get mixed up in an execution. And though they didn't kill me there, I saw with my own eyes what a "labor camp" was. It was a death camp!

The night I was taken, Zivia ran to the Judenrat members and the next day she went to the Joint and raised a fuss among the social activists. That was the first time a person they knew had been taken. It's true that I wasn't known all over Warsaw, but, in those circles, I was known. They went to Czerniakow, who proposed setting up a public committee to oversee the camp. Some agreed to that and others of course didn't want to participate at all. But I know that my case and Zivia's cries and running around to save me were one of the factors that shocked our small society.[7]

After our release, I changed my mind about the "labor camp." I understood that anyone who went there was truly condemned to death by starvation, typhus, or execution. In sum, Kampinos was one big cemetery! And I am sure that, after our release, the Judenrat sent other people who certainly met their death there. Under those conditions, you

7. For Czerniakow's actions on the labor camps, see Czerniakow 1979:226; 227; 229–231. In his journal, he reports the results of a Judenrat inspection of the Kampinos Camp: "Food is dreadfully inadequate. The workers were to receive 6½ ounces of bread, 2.2–2.9 pounds of potatoes, sugar, marmalade, meat, coffee, etc. There are no potatoes and they receive 4–5½ ounces of bread. There is no fat whatsoever. . . . The camp huts have spoiled straw to sleep on and wind is blowing through the walls. There are no showers or rest rooms. The workers' boots were ruined in wet sand and clay. There are no drugs or bandages. . . . Wages were not paid" (1979:233).

couldn't come out of there alive; you couldn't live and work on 200 grams of bread and one portion of soup a day. Sick people were taken out of there because they were of no use. Some of those sick people died on the way, in the train, and I've already mentioned the wagon of corpses.

For a week, I was the pampered child of Dzielna. They even gave me milk. My head was full of sores, and it took a long time for the scabs to come off; I couldn't touch hot water, I did it slowly and cautiously; my neck was all wounded. I don't know how I remained alive. There were lots of wounds on my body. From my chin to my stomach, there wasn't an intact place, even my ear was sore. I would wake up at night with the sense of a waterfall in my head; as time went on, that passed. Somehow, with the help of good conditions, care, and youth, I overcame it.

For the first time, I had seen with my own eyes what a labor camp was. Before that, we used to distinguish between "labor camps" and "concentration camps," but now I knew it was all the same. At any rate, before the German invasion of the Soviet Union, before the mass slaughter, those camps were one stage of the annihilation. There were tens of thousands of people in them, and everything else paled in comparison to the camps, which in fact were nothing but death camps. There I saw the terrible fear.

German and Polish construction companies were employed there and competed for the work. The camps were established with a dual purpose: to perform various necessary works and to destroy Jews. You could get unlimited numbers of Jews and you didn't have to pity the workers. If the companies had pitied them, they would have given them a bit more bread and improved conditions. The camp guards used the bread for speculation: it wasn't enough that they gave the workers very little, they also stole from the little bit. I saw that when we were carrying their packages. Incidentally, one of the directors there was a Jew, a trustee of the Judenrat. The Judenrat emphasized that. He was from Pruszków, but I don't remember his name; at any rate, he was a shady character. When I arranged our ransom, he was one of those who accompanied me to the phone. When I talked to him about being good to my comrades, he told me he couldn't do anything because the camp guards had threatened him that if he interfered, they would put him in the pit where I had been; and, in fact, he didn't do anything. He was supposedly a representative of the Warsaw Judenrat in the camp. When I returned from Kampinos, I asked Lonka, who was from Pruszków, and her parents who were then living in our courtyard, about that guy. She said he had always been a ne'er-do-well. This was the first time he ever made a "living." For some time, I thought the camp was the most difficult experience I had been through; but it turned out that there was no limit to hardship. Soon after, I returned to my work.

After Kampinos, I learned what happened to the men in the "labor camp." We must remember that tens of thousands of our best young people found their death in the camps. The camps were set up mainly around the River Bug and the eastern regions, where various garrisons and fortifications were built. This was not "secret" work, and they weren't executed to maintain secrecy, but because of hunger and abuse. Tens of thousands of human beings were concentrated there, on the border between Germany and the Soviet Union, a few months before the German invasion of the Soviet Union.

The situation in the "labor camp," including executions, was later described in the underground press.[8]

In the press at that time, there were exhortations not to go to the camps and there were some people who hesitated; they were afraid they would have to do backbreaking toil, but they couldn't imagine what really went on there. We also quarreled about it. For a certain time, I had been in favor of Halutz youth going to work in the camps because a lot of young people were concentrated there. I couldn't imagine what a camp was like. I hoped that, with our organizational ability and that of people involved in education and organization, we could make camp life easier. I thought we should be with the masses. And that opinion was also expressed in the press. I thought we bore a responsibility and that we should be inside. But I found out that it didn't do any good. My opinion was reinforced by Benno Rosenberg of the Alliance of Religious Halutzim, who wrote letters in German for us. One day, he showed up and declared that he wanted to be a supervisor in a camp. Later, we heard he was killed in an *Aktsia* or during the liquidation of the camp. When we got the news, we tried unsuccessfully to find out what camp it could have been. He went there with pure intentions, to help. When he was in Warsaw, even though he was displaced from his movement, he was with us at Dzielna and we helped him. He didn't have any other movement. He thought he could do some good; and that, of course, was absurd, not only on his part, but also on mine when I supported that notion.

There were all sorts of attempts to solve the problems in an acceptable way; for example, not to obey the orders of the Judenrat. But anyone who had pure motives had to know he couldn't change a thing.

8. Zuckerman's article in *Dror* (under the pen name "Wilecz") was mentioned earlier. (Special edition for the 23rd anniversary of He-Halutz, no. 7–8 (13), May–June 1941.) As for the literature on "Labor Camps," see the diary of Rabbi S. Huberband, "Martyrdom," in *Bulletin,* 1940 (of the Bund) and in *Against the Stream* (of Ha-Shomer Ha-Tza'ir), 1941.

FIVE

The Tidings of Job

As I said, after I recovered, I left for an extended tour. (By that time, Yosef Kornianski was over the border; he had no idea I had been taken to the camp.) On this trip, on my way back to Warsaw, we got the news of our comrades who had been arrested on the border. I remember the night of panic I spent with Lonka at the railroad station. We wanted to change direction and go west.

On my return to Warsaw, we managed to get out an expanded issue of *Dror* dedicated to He-Halutz. Marek Folman translated my article on Kampinos, which appeared in a Polish paper (published in Łódz). We also had time to prepare Yitzhak Katznelson's biblical play, *Job,* for publication, and we made a small party for dignitaries in honor of the publication of the play. The news of the German invasion of the Soviet Union on June 22, 1941, became known on the day of the party for Yitzhak Katznelson's book.

We were sure of a quick victory by the Red Army. One of the things that had concerned us in the first days of the war was the fear that "pogroms" would take place as the Red Army advanced. We still lived with the notion of pogroms from World War I that "the Germans would make pogroms, the Poles would make pogroms." We thought we should set up a Jewish defense force for what was expected. Some people are wise in hindsight, but it didn't occur to me in those days that there was anything worse than a pogrom. There are little pogroms and big pogroms and we figured we could expect a big pogrom. Anyone who wants to call us to account on this score should be ashamed. I admit it never occurred to me then that we would be candidates for total annihilation. I never imagined such a thing, even after my sojourn in Kampinos Camp. Neither after the camp nor after the horrors of the ghetto. Apparently there were differences of opinion between us and the party members. Everything novel scared them, a seminar, the publication of an underground newspaper, or any other activity. We had the feeling that we ourselves were in fact a party, although we didn't act like one. And we thought we had to make decisions and we did, independently, without reliance on the party members. And we, in Dror, began organizing for pogroms. We were certainly not the only ones; those same ideas no doubt emerged in others too.

We started setting up "fives," putting into that operation all our members who had hitherto been involved only with leadership and education programs. We started talking with them, explaining to them; but we didn't have to wait very long to understand that things weren't turning out as we had thought. We learned that pogroms might take place, but not exactly in the wake of a quick victory by the Red Army. For the German army was galloping forward and in the first days of the war, they had already occupied Vilna.[1] Hence, some of our momentum waned and, after two or three weeks, our arguments with the party ceased. But I must say that we didn't drop the issue of defense.

Here we come to the story of Irena Adamowicz and Vilna. Even before the war, we had heard of a gentile woman, Irena Adamowicz, of the Polish Scouts, who had contacts with Ha-Shomer Ha-Tza'ir. Afterward, she came to us. When I came to Dzielna in spring 1940, I found her there as a frequent guest. She was a rather frustrated woman, a devout Catholic, who learned Yiddish. (She spoke Yiddish with Yosef Kornianski.) At that time, she didn't distinguish between us and Ha-Shomer Ha-Tza'ir and would come both to them and to us at Dzielna. Later she said specifically that emotionally she felt closer to us. Not just because of our world view, but also because Ha-Shomer Ha-Tza'ir were too intellectual for her, although she herself was a very intelligent woman. She told me about her mother, who had been active in the women's movement and even participated in congresses abroad. I never heard anything about her father; I knew she had a brother. She didn't talk much about her family. When she stayed at Dzielna, she would sleep in our room.

One night, she said some harsh things about Jews, things that had an antisemitic ring. Since she was our guest, I didn't respond. Later, she said harsh things against the Poles—anti-Polish things. I classified her in the "Brenner tribe." She wasn't an antisemite, she spoke frankly and ruthlessly about the weaknesses of nations and of people. I found out that she didn't hate Jews. She took us as we came. Poles too. She spoke of the treason of the Poles and the treason of the youth, which had distanced itself from the new situation. She spoke of the new class of Poles who were getting rich by inheriting Jewish property. After I heard her harsh words

1. Vilna was occupied on June 24, 1941, two days after the war broke out.

about the Polish people, I could overlook the impression of her words about the Jews and judge her by a completely different measuring rod.

I think she had some lung disease. One day, Yosef Kaplan found out it was her birthday and we decided to give her a present. We asked her what she needed, and she said she would like to be our guest at Dzielna for a week, to rest. We understood that she also needed money; we gave her a few hundred Złotys to buy what she wanted. She was supposedly a social worker and would come into the ghetto with an entrance permit. The entrance permit given to Poles had to be renewed from time to time. She came in without any problems and would stay with us.

One day she came to us and suggested that a friend of hers from the Polish Scouts, Heniek Grabowski, should go to Vilna. Since he had all sorts of errands, she suggested adding our mission to Vilna to the others. She had partial funding and asked us to contribute something. He was to contact our members in the eastern zones occupied by the Germans and to bring us news from there.

She brought him into the ghetto and we and Ha-Shomer Ha-Tza'ir met with him. We gave him some money, each movement gave half. I wrote letters to be delivered on his route: Landwarowo—Troki—Vilna. I wrote to Dr. Mark Dworzecki in Vilna and Janetka Bloch in Troki. Grabowski took the letters and left. I didn't send anything to my parents, but I hoped he would go to them on instructions from our members there. I didn't have any other addresses, but I did know it was possible to reach Dr. Dworzecki, a respected and well-known man. Of course, I also gave him a letter for Mordechai Tennenbaum. We told Grabowski what he had to say and how we could help, and we waited for his return. He made the long trip by bicycle since all the trains were loaded with German soldiers. His trip took a long time because he had to travel hundreds of kilometers.

One evening, I was about to leave on one of my trips through the Aryan side of Warsaw. I had to be in Ostrowiec, Częstochowa, and other places. The train was supposed to leave at night and I decided that, this time, I would go alone, without a woman courier. Lonka was to meet me on the Aryan side, but Irena Adamowicz was waiting for me in one of the streets near the ghetto gate. She said Heniek had returned from Vilna and she would come with him to the farm in Czerniaków that night. So I went to Czerniaków with Lonka; and they came too. Heniek said that when he got to Troki, he didn't find any Jews there because the Jews were murdered. I'm telling things as they have remained in my memory since that night.

Troki is an ancient Lithuanian city. There were many islands in the lake of Troki. The Germans dug pits in one of the islands, transported all the Jews of the town there as well as the Jews of Landwarowo, and murdered them. As I recall, the pits were nine meters long and three meters wide. They scattered lime on every layer of corpses. Corpses and lime.

Grabowski couldn't find Janetka Bloch. When he got to Vilna, he met only the members of Ha-Shomer Ha-Tza'ir. We didn't bring it up then, but it made us very angry. The letters to Mark Dworzecki were apparently delivered by members of Ha-Shomer Ha-Tza'ir but it turned out that Heniek was prevented from meeting with Mordechai Tennenbaum. Heniek did hear that there was a group of our comrades in Vilna and he told all he knew about them. At that time, Abba Kovner was on the Aryan side of Vilna, hiding in a convent. All Heniek's meetings were only with members of Ha-Shomer Ha-Tza'ir, and he didn't meet a single one of our people. He was prevented since the address he got from them was the convent where the members of Ha-Shomer Ha-Tza'ir were hiding and the nuns were friends of Irena Adamowicz. When he got to that convent, he was a captive in the hands of Ha-Shomer Ha-Tza'ir, and they did as they liked with him.

The wrong impression was created that Heniek Grabowski was sent by Ha-Shomer Ha-Tza'ir. In fact, he was sent at the suggestion of Irena Adamowicz and was our emissary, too. That offended us very much; in times like those! What interest did they have in preventing a meeting with our members? Every now and then, something happened like that, which indicated that their world was a narrow, sectarian world, lacking breadth and general responsibility. This event left us with a bad taste. I never talked about it with members of Ha-Shomer Ha-Tza'ir. I didn't ask them anything, neither then nor after the war.

Heniek Grabowski told us the story of Ponar, a name synonymous with murder.[2] I knew Ponar; when I was thirteen, we used to go there for outings; twice, we had a family summer cottage there, seven kilometers from Vilna. On the train from Vilna, we would pass through the village of Ponar, with a tunnel close by; there were two huts and we rented one of them as a summer cottage (a dacha). Every evening, Mother would come to us. I stayed there with my two sisters. My brother would stay with our parents, and he would come to us on Saturday. Father would stay on Saturday and Sunday. At that time, I was reading Trivush's translation of Tolstoy's *Anna Karenina;* I would stroll with my sisters in a grove and pick nuts.

At the Eichmann trial, when I told about the nuts, some of the Vilna people claimed there weren't any nuts there, but that's nonsense. I know the area and the high mountain above the tunnel like the back of my hand. During our vacation, we would wander around the woods. I had also been familiar with Troki for many years. I had relatives there and spent

2. According to figures compiled by Arad (1982:210–211), between June 24 and the end of December 1941, the number of Jews executed in Ponar varies from the German figure of 26,881 to 61,898 cited by Dr. Heller in a report to the Alfred Rosenberg Institute.

summers on the lakes. The lakes were leased by my uncle who was one of the notables of that Jewish community. That was the Ponar Grabowski told about. It wasn't a remote place.

I was stunned by the story of Ponar. I didn't know what to do with myself. As for my family, he could only say that they were alive. I had to decide if it made sense to go on with my trip. It was a great blow. This wasn't a pogrom anymore! For the first time, the news that Ponar was death sliced through me like a razor. The thought had often been on the tip of my tongue but, for the first time that night, I realized this was total death. This was November 1941.

That night, I had to decide what I was going to do. I decided not to return to the ghetto, no matter what. I wanted to be alone a while.

So I didn't go back to the ghetto; I just wanted to contact the comrades immediately and give them Heniek's report. Then Heniek went into the ghetto without me and told his tale. But I was the first one who heard it in Czerniaków. After the meeting, I left at night, depressed and stunned. Lonka insisted on accompanying me—she insisted that someone should be with me. I remember that night in the Warsaw railroad station, how the Germans beat the Poles there in the station, really beat them. By chance, I didn't get beaten myself, but I saw the humiliation of the Poles: a matter of luck. In those days, there was no lighting in trains, so my face wasn't seen. I traveled most of the night, it was probably three o'clock in the morning. It was autumn, a cold rainy night, like my soul. It was pouring rain. Thus I came to Ostrowiec. I remember that night. I rode in a cart with gentiles from the railroad station. If you had a train ticket, you could walk around after curfew.

We came to the city square and I got off with everyone else. It kept raining. I had to find a friend's address in the rain and darkness. I had matches and I lit every last one of them but couldn't find the street. All of a sudden, I heard German spoken and dogs barking. I knew that if they caught me, the ticket wouldn't help, even though my forged documents were good.

I entered a narrow street. I remember standing and wondering if there were any Jews there. The night was quiet and then I heard the voices and the dogs barking. I knocked on a door, heard whispers, a light came on, and the door was opened. I asked: Jews? And they took me in. It turned out it was a home restaurant, owned by a man named Zuckerman. So I had fallen on a man named Zuckerman. I told them the Germans were approaching and they turned off the lights and made up a bed. They also gave me something to eat but I spent a sleepless night.

The next day I met Gershon Dichter, a Hebrew teacher in the local *Tarbut* school, who was close to He-Halutz Ha-Tza'ir, and as a result he called a meeting of some of his friends at this house. One of those was the young Hebrew poet Malkiel Lusternik, who directed the Jewish Self-Help Organization in the district and lived in Opatów. Yitzhak Rubenstein, head of the Judenrat in Ostrowiec, also participated in the meeting. He was a tall man, with gray hair, whom Dichter praised to me as a decent and honest man. Other people whose names I don't remember also came to hear what I had to tell. I told them at length what we had learned from the emissary who visited the Vilna area and about the tidings of Job he brought from there. They listened tensely and asked repeatedly if the witness was reliable; they were also amazed at how an entire Jewish community could simply be annihilated.

Someone said: "Very sad, but we must assume it has to do with an awful act of revenge of the Germans on the Jews who were under the Bolshevik regime. We know the Jews welcomed the Red Army enthusiastically and made themselves hated by their neighbors. The Germans had their own account with the Bolshevik regime. The Red Army ran away and who was left? The Jews! So we're the scapegoat."

Rubenstein said it was hard to conclude that the Germans followed a consistent policy in their behavior toward the Jews. We were dependent on the local government everywhere. If you established good relations with the local Germans, you had good chances of getting through the war. Here, for instance, were two cities: Radom and Kielce. In Radom, Jews were beaten for not taking off their hat to the Germans, and in Kielce because they did. For instance, here's Warsaw, a closed ghetto, surrounded by walls and barbed wire, and in the throes of hunger and typhus, whereas Ostrowiec was an open residential quarter with plenty of food. Could one central German hand be directing the Jewish fate?

In Ostrowiec, they said, relations with German authorities were excellent. Naturally, there was no lack of insults and tragic cases. So we shouldn't risk superfluous dangers, nor should a person risk himself or the community. There were enough torments you had to bear. The youth of Ostrowiec and Opatów could tell a lot about what they had suffered while building the German fortifications on the Bug, before the outbreak of the war with the Soviets; they emerged from that safely, too. Now calm prevailed in Ostrowiec. A short time before there had been an evening devoted to the Jewish Self-Help Organization in one of the auditoriums, and the German in charge of the city himself sat in the first row and applauded. In Warsaw, such a thing was simply impossible. You mustn't generalize; no matter how great the grief.

Thus they spoke in Ostrowiec, and thus they thought in Opatów. Rubenstein tried to establish good relations with the authorities and believed that the "good" German would always applaud him. Rubenstein and the other men from Ostrowiec were the first to hear from me about Vilna, about the mass murder. I doubt they drew the necessary conclu-

sions, as was clear from what they said. So when the time came, Rubenstein behaved just like Judenrat members everywhere else.

I spent a few days in Ostrowiec, and walked from there to Opatów to
be alone. I was in great distress and many thoughts were buzzing in my
mind. When the first depression and fear had passed, my vision began
to clear a bit. I knew that the tempest doesn't destroy the seed buried in
the ground. In those days especially, nothing was as important as the
Movement. We had to amass force and turn it into acts that would be
transformed by the meaning of those days. At such times, there is additional meaning and profound substance to the kibbutz, which was a
barrier to the tide rising in the towns and ghettoes and was, perhaps, the
place where the vital forces of youth would be concentrated for the days
to come. I thought about setting up a training kibbutz in Opatów, even
though there wasn't a railroad station there and we would have had to
walk from Ostrowiec.

My conversation about that with Malkiel Lusternik didn't go well. We
had a fairly large group of members there, including Kalman Tshernikhovski; and I thought we could succeed in setting up a kibbutz with
Lusternik's help. But, as I said, Lusternik had reservations and told me
plainly that he couldn't help. He had been close to Gordonia in the past
and was a member of Hitahdut. Later I told this to Yitzhak Katznelson
who was friendly with him and he wrote him a sharp letter. Help came
from a direction we had least expected. Rubenstein, the member of the
Judenrat in Ostrowiec, agreed to provide us with an apartment and
various means of subsistance. So we set up the new center in the worst of
those awful times. Rubenstein helped us get work locally. Aside from the
local people, a group of young refugees was also concentrated there. I
especially remember Franya Beatus, who later played an important role.[3]
I knew some of the people in Opatów and Ostrowiec from the Movement
summer camps.[4]

A week later, I returned to Warsaw. While I was in Ostrowiec, an order
was issued that Jews caught on trains without a permit were condemned
to death. As a result, a young Jew from Ostrowiec, who took a risk, or was
perhaps caught out of ignorance, was killed on the spot, in the station.

Now, as I left Opatów, since my documents weren't especially good,
and because I was very depressed, I decided to try to get a travel permit
from Lusternik and he did give me one. So I traveled to Warsaw under

3. Franya Beatus: Born in Konin. She was driven from her hometown to Ostrowiec. A
member of Dror, she came to Warsaw in late 1942. She was Zuckerman's courier on the
Aryan side of Warsaw and helped bring the fighters out of the sewers after the April
Uprising. She committed suicide on May 12, 1943; aged seventeen.
4. Zuckerman's visit to Ostrowiec, and especially the description of the conversation with
the local people, is also documented in Zuckerman 1985:61–62.

the aegis of a letter of an emissary for the Jewish Self-Help Organization from Opatów and the surrounding area to the center in Warsaw.

At first, I also thought of going to Sandomierz and Częstochowa. But it was hard for me to go on, and I decided to return. I had to put on the armband which was always hidden on me and, when I came to a ghetto, I would put it on. I always kept it somewhere, in my socks, for example.

I rode the train as a Jew, wearing the armband, and reached Warsaw at night. When I came to the railroad station, I took off the armband and became a "gentile" again. I didn't know how to get into the ghetto at night, but staying in the railroad station was one of the most dangerous things. If I had had a girl with me, we could have pretended to be necking. But I was alone and I decided that, no matter what, I would walk through Warsaw and get into the ghetto, but not through the gate; I had to know where there were breaches in the wall. I had never been involved in smuggling; when I left the ghetto, I left through the main gate, with a bribe, or through the courthouse. Now I asked myself: how do I get into the ghetto?

Near one place, I saw three or four people who looked like Jews. I approached and asked them if they were Jews, and if they were going to the ghetto; but they panicked and ran away from me. I had no choice and started walking. Later I saw those Jews walking at some distance and I decided to follow them. Suddenly, out of the darkness behind the trees, detectives jumped on them, and grabbed them, while I passed by unscathed. I didn't know Warsaw well since I hadn't spent much time in the gentile streets of the city. So I walked and looked for the walls.

It was still dark when, after walking a long time, I saw an old man carrying a sack.[5] I asked him if he knew how to get into the ghetto and he said he would take me if I gave him a piece of bread. I told him I didn't have any bread, but I would give him a few Złotys. He led me to a breach in the wall on Krochmalna Street where I entered. I rang the first doorbell; the residents were used to smugglers and opened the door. I paid something and waited in a filthy room until dawn, and then I went to Dzielna 34.

A new chapter began in our lives, one of the most severe. One of its first signs was a sense of the end. My comrades and the members of Ha-Shomer Ha-Tza'ir had already heard the story of Vilna. We took the information to the Movement leadership, to the political activists in Warsaw. The responses were different. The youth absorbed not only the

5. A different description of Zuckerman's entrance into the ghetto is in Zuckerman 1985:64. Instead of "an old man carrying a sack," he tells there of a "man with a child on his shoulder."

information but also accepted the interpretation that this was the beginning of the end. A total death sentence for the Jews.

We didn't accept the interpretation we had also heard in Ostrowiec, that this was all because of Communism. I had heard that interpretation before from Menakhem Kirshenbaum and others. That was the interpretation of the old-timers. Why did I reject it? Because if it had been German revenge against Jewish Communists, it would have been done right after the occupation. But these were planned and organized acts, not immediately after the occupation, but premeditated actions. We heard about Lukiszki Prison[6] and the Jews of Vilna already knew about it, though, for some time, they were kept in the dark about what was going on. It was organized and systematic, not sporadic outbursts. That was even before the news about Chelmno, which came in December-January.

Our internal struggle about what to do began in those days. After Heniek Grabowski came back, we sent Lonka to Vilna. Subsequently, Frumka was also sent. A few weeks later, a delegation of Ha-Shomer Ha-Tza'ir and a group from Ha-No'ar Ha-Tzioni arrived from Vilna. The incident of those emissaries is told in the ZOB report as well as in Chaika Grossman's book.[7] I won't go into details here. None of our people arrived. Chaika Grossman of Ha-Shomer Ha-Tza'ir was also in that delegation. Tema Schneiderman, Mordechai Tennenbaum's girlfriend, whom he sent, came later. Tennenbaum got the letter I sent him, but he didn't see the emissary (Grabowski), and so he sent Tema to us.

I didn't meet with Chaika Grossman when she was in Warsaw and that annoyed me. But she did meet with Zivia. Chaika Grossman asked the Joint for means to set up a leadership cadre of Ha-Shomer Ha-Tza'ir. She didn't tell us about that, but Giterman and Guzik, whom we were close to, reported to us on their discussions with her. The members of the Joint also wanted to know what Zivia and I thought about it. Chaika negotiated on behalf of Ha-Shomer Ha-Tza'ir, not as a representative of He-Halutz.[8]

6. Vilna prison from which Jews were taken to Ponar.

7. The ZOB report was sent in spring 1944 through Polish underground channels to London and reached Eretz Israel (see Zuckerman 1985:99–125; Chaika Grossman 1987: 20–37).

8. See Chaika Grossman 1987:68–84. Grossman came to Warsaw in early 1942 and did meet with various factions and groups (e.g., General Zionists, Bundists). However, she says that ". . . meeting with the members of 'Dror' seemed to us to be superfluous. The latter had gone through the same development as our movement. True, the barriers between us had not yet disappeared, and we still had to find a common language that would leave no room for doubts. At that time every one still feared that his allies were not being completely frank. It seemed to each side that the other was still concealing something, plotting secretly." (79) However, she does add that ". . . Hashomer Hatzair and Dror were the only two large chalutz movements that preserved their integrity, coordinated activity and learned from the experiences of the various geographically isolated parts of their movements." (79)

I didn't participate in those meetings. But, as secretary of He-Halutz, Zivia did, and I got the details "under the table."

When Tema came, she told about the situation of the Dror movement in Vilna. I was very familiar with conditions there, including the training kibbutz on Subocz Street (we had once had property in Wołokumpia). The leaders of our Movement were scattered all over; some of them reached Vilna; but they were refugees there (Mordechai Tennenbaum and Ilya Sheinbaum, for example). This was a big difference between us and Ha-Shomer Ha-Tza'ir who, including leaders and their families, were natives of Vilna, whereas our members were refugees with no social standing or importance in the Jewish community. Since they were refugees and couldn't manage on their own, most of our members couldn't make contact with the Judenrat, and they also lacked permits. At that time, fates were determined: who is to live and who is to die; and permits and contacts were significant.

Mordechai Tennenbaum pondered what to do, how to act. By that time, we knew what had been done in Białystok; we heard about the Germans' entrance there, about the Jews who were burned in the synagogues; but we didn't know that, after the first outbursts, things had calmed down. You might say we learned of the magnitude of the catastrophe from what happened to Białystok, whereas we learned from Vilna that it was a total catastrophe. Tema knew less than what we later heard from Lonka and even later from Mordechai Tennenbaum. In reply to the question of what to do, we sent Lonka and later Frumka, on our own responsibility, to get people out of there, and to leave only a small group, assuming that our Movement wouldn't be very important in Vilna. Anyway, we had a strong group in and around Białystok, as well as in Grodno; we had people in Jasinówka, and even around Vilna; in Troki, the Movement no longer existed. We didn't get to other places. Because it was close by, we decided to set up a base in Białystok. (Ha-Shomer Ha-Tza'ir also set up a base in Białystok at the same time and transferred some of their members there from Vilna.)

Later, Zivia heard things [about the mass murders] from the members of the delegation:[9] Shlomo Entin, a member of Ha-No'ar Ha-Tzioni,[10] Chaika Grossman and the Revisionists; and we had also heard what Mordechai Tennenbaum said (through Tema). It all confirmed what we had already heard and experienced. I repeat: the first time I heard the full horror of those things was that night, in Czerniaków, from Heniek

9. The Zionist Youth delegation that left Vilna in early December 1941 included Shlomo Entin of Ha-No'ar Ha-Tzioni, Edek Buraks of Ha-Shomer Ha-Tza'ir, and Israel Kayfner of Betar.

10. Shlomo Entin: The manager of a Judenrat soup kitchen in Vilna; active in FPO. His office was used as a workshop for forged documents. (See Rużka Korczak 1965:30.)

Grabowski; it was no longer sporadic snatchings, hunger, typhus. It was clear to me that this was organized murder. There was a relatively small Jewish community in Troki; and the entire community was murdered. And in Vilna, there was a murder of tens of thousands. And what the gravedigger from Chelmno brought us later only completed the picture.[11] This was one of the things we tried to explain to our veteran party members, to the Jewish community, to the activists: the annihilation is beginning both in the east and in the west.

The inception of my personal breakdown is inherent here: a personal accounting for what I did during those years. Where does this situation lead, what should be done, and how to do it?

I then received information that my family was still alive. As I recall, it was Mordechai Tennenbaum who told me, when that was still true. After we sent Frumka, in January, Lonka returned. I really don't remember if they left together or if Frumka left after her. Frumka stayed and intended to leave for the cities of Polesie and Wołyń; and Lonka, apparently, came back to us, whereas Frumka and Tema (Wanda Majewska was her Polish alias) went on, to see how things were there. Frumka then called herself the "gravedigger of the Jewish people"—everywhere, she followed the traces of the annihilation.

In January 1942, apparently at the beginning of the month, we got the news about the "gravedigger from Chelmno."

Three of us sat in a room on Dzielna. It was cold and we heated the stove, a regular metal stove with a chimney. There Lonka told her story about Vilna. Among other things, she said, but not explicitly, that she and Frumka had decided to save my sister's only son, but hadn't managed to do it. Then it was clear to me that my family was no longer alive. My family—my father and mother, my sister, her husband, and the child Ben-Zion whom the girls had decided to rescue, only him, because they couldn't save any more and, ultimately, they couldn't save him either. . . . Uncles, aunts, a big tribe of the Kleinstein and Zuckerman families, a big widespread clan, in Vilna.

I remember sitting in silence. Suddenly the alarm bell connected to the gate rang. We immediately took the typewriter and other things to the other side, to Lonka's parents. We stayed there a while until the concierge, Abraham Breier, appeared. He said that a Gestapo agent came and started asking about the commune, the young people walking around; and, incidentally, menacingly, he demanded all the details about "Isaac" Zuckerman, Zivia Lubetkin, Lonka Kozibrodska; the fourth one he asked about was Solly who had been in Kampinos Camp with me. When we were finished, we didn't go back to our room. We waited and asked him to take

11. See below.

all our personal effects out of our apartment; we took out the important things there, including underground newspapers, which were hidden in a secret corner. That was my last night in Dzielna.

That night, Lonka and Zivia went to live with one of the party members and I found shelter with Eliahu Gutkowski. I stayed there a night or two, until I found an apartment, on Wolność or Zegarminstrzów Street; the Polish name meant "freedom" (Wolność), but the Germans were scared of this street name and called it Watchmaker Street. It was a street of poor people, near the ghetto wall. A miserably poor party member lived there, and Zivia and I got a room in his house while Lonka set out on her travels.

Those were the hardest weeks of my life. A depression that went on all day and all night. Thoughts of the end. Isolation. They didn't know about us in the broader community; we didn't have many meetings with members. Tuvia Borzykowski was in Czerniaków then. Gershuni would come, Hirshke Kutsher would come and tell what was going on, individuals came. After a few days, I recovered and reappeared in the corridors, without knowing what awaited me or where danger was lurking. Obviously they were searching for us as members of the underground as a result of a denunciation. Zivia, Lonka, and I weren't suspected of denunciation so, the shadow of suspicion fell on the fourth one they were supposedly searching for. It was a riddle. To this day, it's still shrouded in mystery, and the suspicion hasn't dissipated.

One day, Gutkowski came to me, one of the few who came to my clandestine apartment, and brought the full story of the "gravedigger of Chelmno." This is the story, as it remains in my memory:

The "Gravedigger" was a young man,[12] who was taken by the Germans from one of the towns in the Baltics where there were still Jews. With the members of his community, he was taken to an abandoned castle near the city of Chelmno. Men, women, and children were brought there in one of the transports and gathered together. At that stage, they weren't beaten. That was apparently in December 1941. Then a tall, stocky German appeared; his face was kind, he was smoking a cigar, and he delivered a speech. He said he knew how much the Jews in the ghettoes in the occupied areas were suffering, and now their torments had come to an end. After the advance of the German army and the occupation of the Soviet areas, they were to be settled in villages and other places where their labor was demanded, and schools for their children would be established. He calmed them down, apparently he looked trustworthy. He caressed the children's heads. The people believed him.

12. Yakov Groyanowski of the town of Izbicza. See David Graber's response to the report in Ringelblum 1986:61.

Because the Jews in the ghetto were dirty and typhus was raging, he told them to undress and shower, and he promised them new clothes. He took them to another room (I don't exactly know the plan of that abandoned castle), and then German gendarmes appeared with whips and herded the Jews into an hermetically sealed truck parked outside. The doors were shut, the German driver started the motor, and exhaust gas streamed inside. As I recall, after a trip of about sixteen kilometers, they came to a woods near Kolmdorf, where Germans appeared along with young Jews selected from the previous transports, the gravediggers, who dug the pits, put the bodies in, and covered them. When they finished their work, they were taken back to the jail near the castle or that woods. At night, they were led away in chains.

The "Gravedigger" was one of them. Most of the people they dealt with had suffocated to death in the truck. But there were a few exceptions, including babies who were still alive; this was because mothers held the children in blankets and covered them with their hands so the gas wouldn't get to them. In these cases, the Germans would split the heads of the infants on trees, killing them on the spot.

That man spent a few weeks with the gravediggers and then decided to run away. He got a razor from somewhere and, one day, when their chains were taken off and they were led back to the closed truck, he slit the tarpaulin, jumped out and fled. They chased him but he managed to hide; he went through Jewish communities, places where Jews were still left. He would go to the rabbis of the city and the notables, and tell his story; but they didn't believe him.

He wandered for days until he got to Warsaw, where Eliahu Gutkowski heard his story. Needless to say, it reinforced our assessment that this was the end the Germans intended for all Jews. This was our "ace," as it were, against those who believed the Germans were taking revenge on the Jews of Vilna for being Communists. This was in the west, in the areas annexed by the Germans to the Third Reich, and against people who weren't suspected of Communism. Naturally, that added to our depression.

I stopped eating and paced back and forth like a caged animal. I didn't know what to do with myself; I gave up all educational activity; I didn't want to see people. I was fed up with the arguments on Tłomackie, the stories and the illusions. I would go to Michael Shor, one of the owners of the "Tomor" publishers in Vilna; he and another Jew appealed to me for help one day, since the Germans banned all books and they were in trouble. I was a "generous beggar" and helped them and also started going to them. In those days of distress, I sat and read books. I re-read Balzac. I would come, sit down, and read. Zivia would go to work but I didn't want to.

One evening, before curfew, I went to visit Gutkowski; as I recall, he was living on Nowolipki Street at that time. I climbed the stairs to the upper floor and wanted to ring the bell, but suddenly I fainted. A few minutes later, I came to and found myself lying on the steps, next to the door. I lingered a few minutes—and that was the end of the crisis. When I came to, I knew it was over. I knew I had to pull myself together.

I was always frank with Gutkowski, and he always gave me whatever information he got; and he knew a lot, more than Ringelblum, because Ringelblum didn't meet with many people or gather testimony from them; most of his material came from Gutkowski. He might also have written articles. I know about the work he did and things he wrote; he recorded the words of the "Gravedigger." So I went home with the firm decision: there is no choice but to stop putting out *Dror* and to stop the educational activity. Maybe I shouldn't have shared my hesitations with Zivia. She saw me dropping out. Maybe it was a little easier for her because she was alert, dynamic, excited, active. She was in charge of everyday life, but I was absorbed in other matters, and couldn't get back to that. For me, everyday educational activity couldn't be an answer to what I knew by then. Later, when I balanced things, I realized there was no contradiction between them. Moreover, without the seminar and the educational work, no operations were possible. But in those days, it seemed like a contradiction, it seemed that to go on like that was self-delusion. We were going on, as it were, as if nothing had happened!

The decision was that *Dror* would cease publication and *Yediyes* (*News*) would begin. With *Yediyes* in Yiddish, we would present what information we could about everything that happened. The Jews had to be told what we knew as candidly as we could. I told Gutkowski of my intention and he agreed to help. That is, he would bring me information I couldn't get any other way, from towns, cities, and villages.

What was the difference between *Dror* and *Yediyes*? We started getting involved in everyday reality. No longer an educational newspaper, not ideas, but the naked Jewish reality, as reflected in the information in the paper. With conclusions, and an appeal for a position. Perhaps the information we presented in our newspaper wasn't precise. I wasn't after factual precision. Nevertheless, there is no doubt that the news of death, that they were going to annihilate us, was correct. As I recall, Mordechai Tennenbaum showed up about the time of the third or fourth issue, in February or March 1942, and stayed with us from then on.

This is the story of Mordechai Tennenbaum: he looked Jewish, but he posed as a Tatar named Tamaroff. It took great daring for him to cross the border from Vilna to Białystok and from Białystok, through Malkinia, to Warsaw on the same road I had crossed a few years earlier. Thus he got to Warsaw and entered the ghetto. He decided to ask for a Tatar identification for himself and he took the name Tamaroff from his girlfriend's name, Tamara-Tema. He was the first one to tell us the whole story of Vilna. And about that time, we also heard about a German named Anton Schmidt.[13]

I will tell the story as I remember it. Eliahu Gutkowski subsequently recorded it, as Lonka dictated it. (He arranged a meeting between her and Ringelblum.) The story is in the archive in Warsaw. A distorted version of it was published in *Bleter far geshikhte*, where Anton Schmidt became a Communist or something close. The real story should be checked in the Warsaw archive and compared with the version in *Bleter far geshikhte*, and with what I can remember. Some things are missing there, and the story is connected with me and what happened subsequently.

One day, a woman was walking around crying in the streets of Vilna. A German appeared [Schmidt], looked at the woman, and hugged her. The woman, Mrs. Adler, had once been an opera singer in Vienna. Her former husband was an Austrian named Martinhauer. When hard times came, he separated from his wife and she married an Austrian Jew named Herman Adler. They went to Czechoslovakia and, from there, they somehow reached Vilna.

Herman Adler was caught in one of the "snatchings."[14] Schmidt, a *Feldwebel* (sergeant) in the German army, was a friend of the woman's first husband Martinhauer. His job in the army was to assemble German soldiers who had lost their units. His office was across from the Vilna railroad station. On one of his tours through the streets of Vilna, he ran into his friend Martinhauer's former wife. He started making inquiries about where Herman Adler had been taken and found him in Lukiszki Prison, a waystation on the road to Ponar. Schmidt got him out of Lukiszki. Herman Adler was an Austrian Jew, a former member of Po'alei Zion, but his party loyalty obviously wasn't very strong. He was also known as a poet and supported the Labor Movement of Eretz Israel and the theories of Borokhov. In Vilna, he got in touch with our members.

The connection between Adler and Mordechai Tennenbaum was especially important. After he was saved, Adler put Mordechai Tennenbaum in touch with Anton Schmidt. And here begins the marvelous tale.

Who was that gentile, Anton Schmidt? He wasn't a Communist. He was a democrat. At one meeting—I don't know exactly when—he hinted that he had visited Eretz Israel and was familiar with the country; and both

13. Anton Schmidt (1990–1942): Born in Austria. A sergeant in the German army, assigned to Vilna. Was executed by the Germans for helping Jews. Honored by Yad Vashem as a Righteous Gentile. See Ružka Korczak 1965:44–45; Arad 1982:187.

14. Lithuanian Nazi sympathizers, the *Ipatinga*, brutally "snatched" Jews for forced labor in Vilna. (See Ružka Korczak 1965; Arad 1982.)

Lonka and Mordechai Tennenbaum had this impression. He was also familiar with the Zionist movements and was sympathetic to the Halutzim. When the Vilna people got our information (from Warsaw) that a Movement base was to be established in Białystok and to send people there from Vilna, they didn't want to decide the issue and, at their request, we took responsibility for it. Thus, their accusations of Mordechai Tennenbaum really should be directed at Zivia and me.[15] We said people should be sent from Vilna to establish a base in Białystok, as we had done in Ostrowiec and Częstochowa. We said our forces should be concentrated wherever possible. And, under existing circumstances, we didn't think we could concentrate forces in Vilna.

When our people went to Schmidt, he told them that instead of transferring Jews from one place to another in Poland, they should be sent to Eretz Israel. When we asked him how, he said: "Through the Baltics." He had strange ideas, you might call them lunacies. Since Mordechai Tennenbaum also had lunacies (he was known as a dreamer), the two of them found a common language.

In those days, Anton Schmidt performed a few feats that proved his greatness. Not far from Vilna, in Tortopiszki, Jews were working in peat bogs. One day, Schmidt showed up in a big car to rescue them. And all those who took that opportunity of rescue were indeed saved. However, those who refrained were murdered by the Germans. He had only one assistant, for he couldn't let his German colleagues, who included Nazis, in on the secret. They tell that on the way when they ran out of gas, one remained to watch the truck and he went to get gas, to continue the trip and rescue the Jews.

Mordechai Tennenbaum told me all this. It was on December 31, 1942. In those days, Schmidt took a group of friends, including Tennenbaum, to his apartment. He had a big flat in Vilna, across from the railroad station, where his office was; he hid Mordechai Tennenbaum and his comrades on the top floor. Lonka arrived there at about that time. That evening, he had to invite his fellow officers and soldiers to a cocktail party. During the party, Anton Schmidt would go upstairs from time to time and bring delicacies to the comrades hiding there. One of those times, Tennenbaum told Schmidt he looked like Hitler and Schmidt was very offended. Mordechai Tennenbaum was quite a clown. Later, to appease him, Mordechai Tennenbaum took the Magen David out of his pocket and put it on Schmidt in the name of the Jewish People. After drinking, at night, Anton Schmidt appeared and told Lonka to get dressed. She was terrified. But after she got dressed, he took her with him. They didn't go far. He took her to the railroad station and put her onto a train taking

15. Mordechai Tennenbaum was accused of deserting Vilna and moving to Białystok.

wounded German soldiers from the front. He walked around with her silently for a long time and, after they left, he said to her: "That's your revenge. See how the Nazis end up!"

When there was talk of transferring people from Vilna to Białystok (when Schmidt proposed sending them to Eretz Israel), the issue of money came up, as well as the question of how and where the necessary money would be raised; Schmidt then explained to Mordechai Tennenbaum that he would raise money from rich men to save them, and that he already had some of it. He showed Mordechai where the money was hidden, but said he wouldn't touch it before the time came and, in his words, it should be a joint treasury, a fund for saving Jews. As Mordechai put it, enormous sums devoted to rescue were hidden there. Schmidt's plan was to smuggle Halutzim to the Scandinavian countries by sea. In fact, nothing came of it.

Weeks passed and the danger still loomed large; Schmidt couldn't help. Then he organized the transfer of our members and Ha-Shomer Ha-Tza'ir to Białystok by truck. He did this a few times: he took a group of Halutzim and private people from whom he collected money; he organized their trip and provided food and gasoline. On the back of the truck was a sign: "Caution, high explosives!" On the way, in Warlow, I think, between Grodno and Białystok, there was a border and barriers. One time the guards stopped the truck. One of the Jews panicked and was near hysteria, and a fellow from Ha-Shomer Ha-Tza'ir named Yanci Lebed (he was an actor in a troupe), who was traveling with them, threatened to kill him and shut him up until his rage passed. Naturally, Schmidt didn't let the border guards near, claiming that the car was carrying explosives; thus he conveyed them safely to Białystok. Schmidt's military rank was low, *Feldwebel* (sergeant), but his job was quite high, since he was in charge of concentrating soldiers who had lost their units. His will contained a few instructions: first, to Mordechai Tennenbaum, if Schmidt were arrested (one of his co-workers, a Nazi, hated him), how to take out the money that remained. He left precise instructions how to get into the upper floor of his house and how to get the money out, even if the Germans were downstairs. Moreover, if Mordechai needed help, Schmidt instructed him to appeal in his name to his friend, Martinhauer, director of the airport in Warsaw, and that was guaranteed to help. In sum, you can say Schmidt did a lot, aside from transporting our members and others from Vilna to Białystok.

One day, Anton Schmidt was arrested. Two rumors circulated about his arrest: one was that a Jewish woman was jealous of her girlfriend or neighbor for being saved by Anton Schmidt, and denounced him. According to the other rumor, it was the Nazi in his unit who hated him and turned him in. The fact is that, one day, the man was arrested and taken to Pawiak, and was then stood before a firing squad and executed. Thus we lost a faithful friend. After his death, Tennenbaum tried to get to the hiding place and save the money, but he couldn't because the house was surrounded and guarded. Then he came to Warsaw.

This is a compendium of Lonka's and Tennenbaum's stories of Anton Schmidt. They spoke of him as if he were one of us. Even though I never saw him, he is vivid in my memory. Maybe because Mordechai joked about how he looked like Hitler or the Great Butcher, may his name and memory be erased . . . (Parenthetically, apparently there is a picture of Anton Schmidt, which was discovered a few years ago with his widow in Vienna.)

Mark Dworzecki revealed that after Schmidt was executed, his wife was ostracized by her neighbors, and that has gone on to this very day. Dworzecki, who heard about Anton Schmidt from the stories about him, wanted to meet his wife. She was afraid to invite him to her home and they met in a café. I imagine she has a picture of Schmidt. But she can't know the story of Vilna because he didn't have time to tell her.[16] That Martin-hauer, mentioned in connection with Schmidt, was later to be a key person in a certain mission of mine, which didn't materialize.

In those days, perhaps in our foolishness, we thought that events in the German occupation areas could take place because the outside world didn't know anything about it; so, we started talking about how we had to alarm the world. We talked with Emmanuel Ringelblum, Kirshen-baum, Shakhne Sagan, and Yitzhak Giterman, and we started coming up with all kinds of proposals. But when we analyzed them, we realized that they were futile suggestions which couldn't be put into effect.

For example, on her travels, Lonka made a lot of contacts with Germans. Some of them, who thought she was a gentile, even helped her. One nice German soldier she was in touch with told her he was going home to Germany because of a wound. He said he lived near the Swiss border and was willing to help her if she were in trouble. So, the idea was born: Lonka and I would sneak into Germany, disguised as Poles, of course, and get to the home of that German. Lonka believed he would help and she intended to write and ask him to meet us, and to hint that we were asking for help to cross into Switzerland. The purpose of the plan was to tell the world about what the Germans were doing in Poland. I don't know if the plan would have worked but, because of what happened at that time, it was scrapped. That was around April 18, 1942, when we had started making high-quality forged documents for me and Lonka, with the help of friends, so we could set out by train for that German.

16. On Anton Schmidt, see *Yad Vashem Information*, no. 15–16, 1958; and 19–20, 1959.

The second suggestion had to do with Martinhauer. He was a Viennese gentile, Mrs. Adler's divorced husband. We were trying to take me, in a German officer's uniform, to a safe place over the border. Initially, he promised to help, but later he withdrew. Lonka went to him after Schmidt's death and got those promises. But then he got scared. He really did have something to worry about, because of his Jewish ex-wife and the help he gave her and her husband without reporting it. Ultimately, nothing came of it.

After the war, Herman Adler wrote his memoirs and discussed Schmidt. But he says explicitly that he doesn't know exactly where the border between reality and imagination is in his tale.[17] Herman Adler also published a book of poetry and we translated some into Hebrew. He also translated Yitzhak Katznelson's epic poem, "Song of the Slaughtered Jewish People," into German and published it in Switzerland. Furthermore, he published the book *Ostrobrama,* about that place in Vilna, holy to the Christians. He won prizes for his works. I read his memoirs, in which he tells of meeting me, even though I never met him. He talks about Mordechai Tennenbaum and about two "Zivias," one a real "angel" and the other a real "witch"; and, in fact, he didn't know Zivia at all. But he did know Frumka. He makes up a lot of things, but he himself admits it. When I read his works, I saw that he had indeed lost the distinction between reality and fiction.

In those days, when rumors spread about the beginning of the German acts, or perhaps a bit later, Wasserman came to me. Pinhas Wasserman, whom I mentioned before, helped us many times, for example, when we had to change registration and documents. Or in the case of the concierge who saved me, Breier, whom we had to move out of Warsaw to Częstochowa, and was replaced by another concierge, Menakhem Bigelman, and we had to get different documents. I got the name Adam Breier through a complicated maneuver with the Judenrat: we had to find a person who had died and wasn't yet crossed off the lists and give Breier a new name, in order to get him out of Warsaw; and my picture had to be attached with the name of Adam Breier. Wasserman did all this for us.

One day, Wasserman came to me—by now it was after April—and told me that Abraham Gepner was also convinced we had to tell the world what was going on. That is, at the same time, various people were thinking the same thing: if the world only knew! Up to now, no one took the initiative or said anything. Then we thought that, as soon as the world hears what is going on, things will change. And the truth was that when the world

17. Originally, Zuckerman used the German expression, *Wahrheit und Dichtung,* parallel to Goethe's work of the same name.

did find out, it was silent. At any rate, Gepner said he was willing to give as much money as necessary *to set up an underground radio transmitter.*

Because Wasserman trusted me, he decided to come to me in this matter. At that time, I was attempting to get explosives and weapons. My close friend was Dr. Haim Zelmanowski, whom I trusted implicitly. I knew he had contacts with Jewish academics: biologists, engineers, and chemists in the ghetto. I asked him secretly to put me in touch with people he considered reliable and who knew about the subjects that interested us, since pyrotechnics was not a common Jewish profession. I intended to ask, first of all, for weapons and explosives. I was also looking for Jews who had contacts with the Polish underground to get their help in putting together a radio transmitter. But they all refused. The ones Zelmanowski went to warned him against provocation, and he couldn't tell them who was initiating the project. The name Yitzhak Zuckerman meant as much as Tom, Dick, or Harry to them. Who knew me? What guarantees did he have that he wasn't getting all of them into a trap? That Jews should think at that time of such things as explosives, weapons; a radio transmitter was simply out of the question! That simply wouldn't occur to anyone.

Later, I realized that Zelmanowski really did reach a few places, not exactly specific people, but circles that were in touch with the kind of people I wanted. There were also people there who had contacts with the Polish national underground (AK, Armia Krajowa) and the Communists, although an organized Communist movement wasn't in operation at that period. Twice, they hinted to me that my request had reached those circles. The first time was in the ghetto, after the establishment of the Jewish Fighting Organization (ZOB) and the Jewish National Committee (ZKN[18]). Edward Fondaminski ("Alexander"),[19] the Communist representative on the Jewish Coordinating Committee (ZKK[20]), with whom I became friends, once, while talking in my room, suddenly felt a suspicion and asked me if I was the person who had appealed for weapons a few months earlier. I asked him why he suspected me, and he said that people had talked to him about it. He didn't remember Zelmanowski's name, but that confirmed that Zelmanowski did indeed appeal to someone about it. Edward Fondaminski ("Alexander"), who had then gotten a description of the man who was asking for those forbidden things, now suspected it was me since the signs fit: member of the Halutz movement, loyal, idealist, and so forth. Therefore, he asked me if I was the man.

18. Zydowski Komitet Narodowy.
19. "Alexander"—Ephraim Edward Fondaminski, an engineer, one of the leaders of the Communists in the Warsaw Ghetto at that time. After Yosef Finkelstein-Lewartowski was deported to Treblinka, Fondaminski replaced him as party secretary. Was killed in the bunker at Miła 18 during the April Uprising; aged thirty-three.
20. Zydowska Komisja Koordynacyjna.

The second time it was mentioned was during the Polish Uprising (in 1944), when I ran into a Jewish woman chemist, who had ties to the PPS[21] and the Bund. It also occurred to her to ask me about the same thing. (That was in Żolibórz, when the Polish Uprising was dying out.) This shows me that there was some movement, but everybody who was approached said: Watch out! I don't think a radio transmitter would have helped us; but if we had gotten weapons then, that would certainly have helped the uprising.

But nothing went beyond futile thoughts and groping, and nothing was carried out. March 1942 came and a few issues of *Yediyes* appeared. Mordechai Tennenbaum was in Warsaw and was living with us; Tema Schneiderman was traveling around with Frumka. When I raised the subject of resistance and called the first meeting of the Jewish political groups, to our dismay the Bund said they wouldn't join. Our aim was to get to the Poles, and the Bund's refusal was a very serious setback, since they were the only movement with any contacts with the Polish underground. In fact, the Bund had ties with both the right and left wings of the Polish Socialist Party (PPS).[22]

People like Barlicki and Stanisław Dubois were members of the traditional PPS, familiar figures among the Jews and in the prewar world.[23] They were serious about socialism but Dubois and Mieczysław Niedzielski were executed. We knew Dubois as a moral figure who stood up against rising antisemitism before the war. Maybe he didn't especially love Jews, but he loved mankind.

The Bund had close contacts with both branches of the PPS. The truth is that, in certain places (Kraków, for example), we were also in touch with the PPS; but the Bundists met with PPS leaders from time to time on the Aryan side. (When you could go in and out of the ghetto.)

In those days, we were looking for contact with Poles, and the left wing of the PPS was the faction closest to us. This was before the re-establishment of the Polish Communist Party was declared (in January 1942), but you have to remember that there was a time lag between the declaration and its actual implementation. I should perhaps mention here that,

21. PPS: Polska Partia Socialistyczna, Polish Socialist Party.

22. The right wing of the Socialist Party was WRN (Wolność, Roność, Niepodleglość: Freedom, Equality, Independence). The PPS was against an alliance with Moscow, seeing that as a threat to Poland equal to that of Nazi Germany; hence, the party was allied with antisemitic, pro-German factions. (See Ainsztein 1979:25.)

23. Barlicki and Dubois were members of the left-wing Socialist Party faction. Initially, they regarded the war as imperialist, but after the Nazi invasion of the Soviet Union in June 1941, they accepted an alliance with the USSR and formed the Organization of Polish Socialists in September 1941; chief allies of the Bund. According to Ainsztein (1979:25–27), the complete absence of political realism had "a fatal influence on the actions of the Bund leaders."

back in 1938, Stalin dispersed the Polish Communist Party and executed some of its leaders; but we didn't know that and, as in other matters, we mustn't blur the distinctions between what we know now and what we knew then. We didn't know that the Polish party was liquidated because Stalin and the Comintern claimed it was infiltrated by agents of the Polish government and imperialism. We didn't have any contacts with the bourgeois civilian Polish parties, and we were seeking a way to the Polish left. Therefore, the cooperation of the Bund was vital to us.

I already mentioned one of our mistakes in thinking that as soon as the world knew what was going on here, something important would happen!

The second mistake was the idea that our neighbors on the other side of the wall weren't aware of our fate and that, when they learned of it, things would change. After the war, when I began reading memoirs of members of the Polish government in London, I was stunned by the extent of their alienation from and indifference to the Jewish issue, which was about as important to them as a toothache.

I should mention that there were 3.5 million Jews in Poland, more than 10 percent of the population. We were the biggest ethnic minority in the country. When Poland surrendered, the Polish government disappeared completely as far as we were concerned, all contact ceased. The Poles stopped governing, even the underground government stopped. When the representatives of Poland in London addressed the population, they addressed Poles and we remained in "No Man's Land." I wasn't aware of that until we came to a dead end, to the realization that we were on a one-way road to Treblinka, and there was no way back.

Before that, we didn't feel the nonexistence of the government so much. But now that we were in trouble, any government at all meant weapons, organization, advice, civilian cooperation. But we simply didn't exist; we were "nobody's citizens," citizens only for Treblinka.

For the German authorities, the commissar of the ghetto, Heinz Auerswald, we certainly weren't citizens; that never even occurred to them.[24] But the Poles were also contemptuous of the possibility of exploiting Jewish potential; they didn't believe in it. (Only after the establishment of the State of Israel did this contempt cease. Perhaps the first pause was after the Ghetto Uprising in Warsaw.) We had no authority then, or permission to ask for anything, and no one would give us anything. We thought we should seek partners, allies. There is an analogy between the Polish underground and the Jewish underground. They didn't have any

24. Heinz Auerswald: Appointed Ghetto Commissioner (*Kommissar für den jüdischen Wohnbezirk*) on May 14, 1941. A loyal Nazi functionary, devoted to the Party ideology concerning Jews. He was zealous about the complete isolation of the ghetto. (See Trunk 1977:293–298.)

weapons either in 1942, and they also started with an underground and organized to gather strength. They too did not organize for passive resistance—such as a citizen's tax revolt; they didn't reject laws, there was no such thing.

It's a miserable thing that, sometimes even now, I include the Judenrat and the Jewish police with the enemies of the Jews. The Poles also had a "Judenrat," as it were, and a Polish police, the "blue police," who served the Germans. And they did their job when they had to. They came to guard the gates of the ghetto and carried out assignments against the Poles as well. The Germans thought they should exploit the organized Polish force against the Poles, and they did. If they needed a mayor of a city or village, these collaborated with them. But the Germans didn't take the Polish people to Treblinka; so the Polish police didn't have to do that job. But they did do the job when it concerned Jews. They lent a hand; they cooperated with the Ukrainians, the Latvians, and the Germans. And so did the Jewish police.

So it is strange to read today the memoirs of a Polish mayor who has to defend Czerniakow. The mayor of Warsaw, who did what the Germans wanted, was also killed by them when they wanted him dead.[25] But the Germans never assigned him to execute the Polish people. He didn't have to undergo that trial, and he remained a good man . . .

The Germans did murder the Polish intelligentsia, but they generally did that without the help of the Poles. (In fact, that should be checked: maybe, after all, they did have their help.)

And wasn't there treason among the Poles?!

How did the Germans manage to catch the leader of the Polish underground, Stefan "Grot"?[26] The Germans couldn't have discovered and caught him from Berlin or Hamburg. Obviously, someone close to him must have betrayed him, maybe for money. So there was treason among the Poles. But, unlike us Jews, the Poles don't brood about it very much. And if it's not major political treason, but just "normal treason," "small peripheral traitors," they don't care very much about that. Incidentally, I know of one man among us who had an important function in the Jewish resistance, and I later learned he had collaborated with the Germans. I met with that man in very critical times.

The political parties saw us as a youth movement of Po'alei Zion–Z.S., a party we didn't particularly like. But that didn't reflect the situation. If those had been normal times, we could have split into factions (after all,

25. Stefan Starzyński, the last mayor of Warsaw; see chapter 1.

26. General "Grot" Rowecki (1895–1944): Born in Piotrków. As Commander of the Polish underground army (AK), he was right of center and, at the same time, defended Sikorski's policy of reaching an agreement with Stalin. He was arrested by the Gestapo in 1943, taken to Berlin, and murdered in Sachsenhausen in August 1944.

we're experts in that), since we disagreed with the party on several important issues. Later, it turned out that we were wrong about our relation toward the Soviet Union. But was Po'alei Zion hostile to the Soviet Union because of concentration camps, or because of her betrayal of socialism? They had other reasons for their reservations. They weren't looking for socialism, while we didn't know the truth, and didn't learn it until years later. That was the difference between us. In our innocence, we thought the most advanced regime in the world was realized there. In one of my articles, in those days, I even called the Soviet Union the "stronghold of the laborers." Really! That wasn't just rhetoric, that was what we thought. We thought it was the last island of socialism left in the world. Not everything I saw and knew was nice; but it didn't put me off because I thought that poverty and lack of organization, or lack of efficiency, weren't reasons to negate the value of the great undertaking or the great ideal. We didn't know that thousands were constantly imprisoned and executed. At any rate, at that time in Poland, only the PPS could have been a real force sympathetic to the Jews. And indeed we sought a bridge to that party. I already mentioned our contacts with them in the hinterlands of Poland, in Kraków. But these weren't contacts with the center; in Warsaw, we didn't have any contacts. So, we emphasized contact with the Bund, through which we could get to both the right and the left wings of the Polish Socialist underground.

SIX

The Struggle for the Jewish Fighting Organization

My first appeal didn't turn out well since, without the Bund, He-Halutz meant nothing to the Polish parties. If there had been different leaders of the Bund, they might have been persuaded to join us. So we tried to initiate something through Po'alei Zion–Z.S. and to summon all representatives of political bodies once again. But to know what Po'alei Zion thought of the subject we posed, all you have to do is look at the representatives they sent to the meeting. These were not first echelon representatives; I would be the last to denigrate Shalom Grajek or Leyzer Levin. But Morgenstern and Sak didn't show up and they were always present at every distinguished occasion where the party was to be represented. They sent people they considered second class to the meeting. The same is true of Po'alei Zion Left. They didn't send Ringelblum or Sagan, but Hirsh Berlinski, whom we didn't know well.

The Bund, of all groups, sent two people they respected highly. This was the meeting called by Po'alei Zion. (I must admit that I was a member of the Central Committee of Po'alei Zion–Z.S. and it says something about the Central Committee if I could have been a member of it.) At any rate, the meeting was held on March 23, 1942.[1] I list the participants of the meeting from memory (but it is available in writing): from Po'alei Zion–Z.S., L. Levin and S. Grajek; from the Bund, Abrasha Blum[2] and Maurycy

1. In the soup kitchen on Orla Street.
2. Abrasha Blum: Born in Vilna. An engineer. Bernard Goldstein (1961:51) describes him as "a tall, slim, quiet intellectual. . . . He was a wonderful writer and speaker. . . . Before being co-opted into the underground Central Committee, he had been a leader of the youth movement, *Tzukunft*, and a member of the Warsaw city committee of the Bund. He was one of the most beloved of the underground leaders. . . . He suffered greatly from a stomach ailment which kept him in great pain under the difficult ghetto conditions, but he never

Orzech;[3] from Po'alei Zion Left, Melekh Feinkind and Hirsh Berlinski;[4] myself, for He-Halutz. Ha-Shomer Ha-Tsa'ir didn't participate. Except for Kaplan, they didn't yet know what I was driving at.

There is a protocol of the meeting. I wasn't the only one who wrote anything. Berlinski wrote about it later; I wrote about it briefly in 1944, in the ZOB report.[5] A protocol of what was written in my room remains: when I came back from the meeting, Eliahu Gutkowski wrote down what I said, and that's preserved in his handwriting, which only I could decipher, since he recorded things only in outline form. That was right after I came from the meeting and everything was fresh in my memory. Zivia and Mordechai Tennenbaum and Eliahu Gutkowski were in the room. That was in my underground apartment where I lived after I ran away from Dzielna.

As for the meeting, we had information from the couriers which the parties didn't have, up-to-date information about what was going on all

---

complained. He was more humanist than Marxist. He saw not only the mass but the individual and he was always ready to help."

3. Maurycy Orzech: Editor of the Bund underground publications; was opposed to armed resistance to the Nazis. He left the ghetto during the Great *Aktsia*, was arrested by the Germans, sent to Pawiak prison, and shot; aged about fifty. According to Bernard Goldstein (1961:58–59), he "came from a very wealthy family . . . [and] joined the Bund at the age of sixteen while still attending a Russian high school. . . . An economist and journalist, serving both the Jewish and Polish Socialist press, he was noted for his forthright, forceful articles, his factual knowledge, his common sense, and his gift for rhetoric." Chaika Grossman also met with Orzech during her stay in Warsaw, and was "surprised . . . at [his] declaration, stated with complete confidence, that it would not happen in Warsaw" (Grossman 1987:78).

4. Hirsh Berlinski (1908–1944): Born in Łódź. Was active in the armed resistance movement and represented Po'alei Zion Left on the ZOB command staff. Fought in the April Uprising and escaped through the sewers to the Aryan side. He was killed in the Polish Uprising. According to Adolf Berman, he was distinguished for his "stormy, exciting and revolutionary temperament" (1977:178).

5. In the ZOB report (to London), Zuckerman told of the meeting, including new information from the eastern and western zones. He assessed the situation as the beginning of a planned undertaking to destroy the Jews of Poland completely. He made the following proposals:

1. The establishment of a general Jewish fighting organization.
2. Joint representation of all Jewish political parties and youth organizations vis-à-vis the Polish underground and a ZOB delegation to the command of the Polish underground (AK).
3. The establishment of machinery on the Aryan side of Warsaw to acquire weapons, as well as workshops to manufacture weapons in the ghetto.

Both Po'alei Zion–Z.S. and Po'alei Zion Left supported this proposal, whereas Orzech declared on behalf of the Bund that it was too soon to talk about a general fighting organization (Zuckerman 1985:102).

over Poland. This was after Chelmno, certainly after Vilna, but before we heard of the *Aktsia* in Lublin.[6] As I recall, it was the eve of Passover, 1942. I opened the meeting by presenting the updated information and said it showed the beginning of the total annihilation of the Jews of Poland.

The words of the Bundist Maurycy Orzech were painful.[7] He said that Jews weren't the only ones being killed, so were Poles; and, it was true that shortly before that time the Germans had decided to turn Zamość (the hometown of Y. L. Peretz[8] and Rosa Luxemburg[9]) and the surrounding area into a German colony, and had begun liquidating villages and towns inhabited by Poles. They treated them as they later treated the Jews, and even transported Polish children in trains. Some of them were ransomed in Warsaw, others were sent to death. And we knew about that, too. Orzech also referred to that in his remarks. But I should say that, at that time, Auschwitz and its crematoria already existed and we knew about that, too. I hadn't yet heard the name Treblinka.

The first time I heard about Auschwitz was in other circumstances (after November 15, 1940). The story had to do with the husband of Oszerowska, who had hidden a radio in his office on one of the Aryan streets of Warsaw. Ukrainians, who picked up the sound, denounced the man, and he was taken off. I remember one bitter night—I was there with Zivia—when his wife got the news that her husband had perished and she received his ashes from Auschwitz.

I should say that even in Auschwitz the Jews weren't the first victims. The first ones were communists, socialists, members of professional unions, liberals, and priests; at that time, Jews were only part of a larger whole. We weren't the guinea pigs in the organized murder. But at that time, that is, before the slaughter in Vilna, they weren't yet doing in Auschwitz what they were already doing in Chelmno—that is, using gas.

It was true, as Orzech said, that we weren't the "only ones," that the Poles were also killed. But the difference was that Jews were murdered seven kilometers from Vilna. These weren't specific people who were accused and were supposedly "guilty" of something and sent to a con-

6. The *Aktsia* in Lublin began on March 16, 1942.

7. In Zuckerman 1985, Antek goes into more detail about obstacles to the formation of Jewish self-defense in the ghetto. There, he says of M. Orzech, the Bundist leader: "I think the man represents the oppressors (that is—those who inhibit self-defense) from a general political starting point . . . He was not a man who said: 'Let's not fight,' but rather: 'Let's fight when the Poles do, and meanwhile—not!' . . . The logical conclusion was that we had to adapt to the interests of the non-Jewish underground" (Zuckerman 1985:102).

8. Y. L. Peretz (1852–1915): Classical Yiddish writer.

9. Rosa Luxemburg (1871–1919): Revolutionary theoretician and agitator who played a key role in the founding of the Polish Social Democratic and German Communist parties. She was murdered by rightist forces in Berlin.

centration camp as suspects in some political crime against the regime. The Jews were anonymous and were murdered only because they were Jews. That was the big difference. But Orzech argued: "They're also killing Poles." So when the Poles would decide to revolt against the oppressor, when the Polish proletariat would arise, then the Jewish proletariat would also rebel, shoulder to shoulder with them. Aside from that, he couldn't get rid of his opposition to the notion of "Jewish unity." We didn't even ask him to dismantle the political framework; we asked only for a *joint action*. It didn't occur to me that someone should deny his ideals, his truth. Even his belief in Jewish life in Diaspora, even though we never believed there was a future for Jews in Diaspora. And these were his central points: No Jewish unity! No joint action! Every organization would set up its fighting units separately! You have to remember that this was after the German invasion of Russia and that there was a widely accepted conception, even among the Polish Socialist Party, at any rate accepted by the WRN (the military arm of the rightist PPS underground), which maintained that there were two blocs, the Germans on one side and the communists on the other; an enormous bloody struggle was raging; and one must strive to make the two sides bleed each other dry, while Poland would be in the middle, unaffiliated with either side, and would appear on stage at the historical moment because she would have preserved her forces, and in these circumstances, she would determine her own borders.

Poland had been enslaved by the Austrians, the Prussians, and the Russians for 150 years. The country comprised a million square kilometers, and it took unusual "historical talent" to lose her independence for such a long time. But I must say they certainly knew how to do that. Now they dreamed of greater Poland, stretching from the Black Sea to the Baltic. But even those who didn't dream that historical dream thought of a strong Poland existing between two big neighbors who would be sapped after the mutual bloodletting of World War II. Therefore, from their perspective, you had to wait. But we knew by then that we didn't have time to wait.

Except for the Bund, all the others supported me. Abrasha Blum was there and, ever since, I had a special feeling for him; the first time I met him was in Vilna at his father's funeral. I was six or seven years old when I was taken with the other children in the religious school I attended to the cemetery for a funeral. I knew only slightly who Blum was. I think he was one of the Mizrakhi activists, whereas his son, the engineer Abrasha Blum, "fell into bad company" and became a Bundist and later a Communist.

Abrasha Blum's speech at the meeting came from his heart. Essentially, he said almost the same as Orzech, but he formulated it differently. He refrained from Orzech's obstinacy and harshness. His words had a different tone, they sounded different. At any rate, nothing came of that meeting.

What did I ask at that meeting? It can be summarized like this:

1. To establish a joint Jewish political representation vis-à-vis the outside, the world.
2. To establish contacts with the civilian and military Polish underground and set up our machinery on the Aryan side.
3. To establish a general Jewish fighting force. We didn't call it that, but the idea was an armed force, a Jewish fighting organization. This demand was rejected. And you have to remember that by then, the issue was no longer pogroms, but defending the lives of Jews who were slated for annihilation.

The situation now was completely different from what we had thought it might be after the German attack on the Soviet Union on June 22, 1941. At that time, we had thought there would be a German retreat accompanied by pogroms. Now the issue wasn't about pogroms but about total murder. And lo and behold! Nothing had changed among our public activists in the months since the end of 1941, from the days after Vilna, after Chelmno. At that meeting, I spoke of a Jewish fighting force. In the foreseeable future, this force wasn't supposed to defend Jews against pogroms. For even after the establishment of the ŻOB, we carefully considered under what circumstances to activate the force, what policies to take. But if I had been asked then, I think I would have answered that it should be activated if and when an *Aktsia* began in Warsaw. I demanded the preparation of that force because I realized that the day to give the order was at hand. In any case, not a single one of our members whom I talked with opposed it or thought differently.

I returned to my clandestine apartment, where I found Eliahu Gutkowski who wrote down what I had told Zivia and Mordechai Tennenbaum. I didn't even remember later on that he had recorded my words, but the account is in the Ringelblum Archive and can be deciphered. The episode of the radio transmitter and plans to alarm the world are included in it.

The Socialist-Zionist parties did support me, but I think that if the Bund had supported us, those parties would have had reservations about several things. As is, they could support my position while remaining loyal to their "historical conflict" with the Bund. But we didn't get into details because the Bund opposed the idea itself. The Bund continued to see the Jews as part of the Polish world, "citizens like everybody else," a very strange view at a time like that. I know that some Bundists, including historians, thought I simply wanted to annoy them with my proposal, but that wasn't true; I appreciated certain Bundist values before, during, and after this time; but this position of theirs (as was later confirmed) expressed an anti-Jewish, anti-national interest. Passivity isn't always a crime; sometimes, you can assume passivity without causing harm. But this was a matter of the defense of life itself, not an alliance in both war and peace. This was simply the most elementary thing—defense of life, of Jewish physical existence.

The opposition of the Bund was one of the contributing factors to our mood of great depression. It was also one of our delusions. Just as we believed that when the world learned of what was going on, something would happen, so I believed that when we found a common language with the Poles with the help of the Bund, our salvation would come. But one day we did find a common language with the Poles, and it didn't change the Jewish fate. So today I can't place the historical blame only on the Bund. I am certainly entitled to make an ideological accounting with the Bund and impose a conceptual responsibility on it. But in March 1942, if we had reached both wings of the PPS, I don't think it would have changed much. We might have advanced the date of the Uprising. I'm not sure. But the few weapons we did get didn't come from the PPS or the WRN, even though I know they were sympathetic to us. But they didn't help. Of course, this is said a long time later, in hindsight. But in those days, I was ready to kill my Bundist comrades for their blindness. They really didn't see or understand that the storm was approaching. They didn't learn a lesson; they didn't see any Jewish significance to what was happening. By then, we knew of Vilna and of Auschwitz! This was not a case of taking Yitzhak Zuckerman to some camp because he was a "criminal." They weren't interested in whether they took him there or murdered him. But now it wasn't a case of some individual or other. But of masses, women and children—they didn't do that to Poles, only to Jews. The Bund didn't understand that. But it's hard for me to blame two people—even though they differed in speech and attitude—for the whole movement. But we have to, insofar as they represented their movement. Perhaps, if there had been another representative besides Orzech, things would have been different since his subsequent behavior was hardly a credit to his movement: he ran away, first to the Aryan side, and then tried to flee the country. He was a man who didn't stand the test. That didn't happen in fighting movements. But the Bundists don't like to be reminded of this truth and it's not so nice to say it. But we were raised on the cruel truth.

That was a failure.

There were a few weeks between this meeting on Orla (Orla 14, in the soup kitchen of the dignitaries) and the second meeting with the PPR,[10] in April. After that meeting, we didn't know which Poles to address, but it was important to us to find a way to them and we tried with Irena Adamowicz. We thought that every day was crucial and that we couldn't dally. Meanwhile things happened in Lublin. We learned that the Jews were being taken out of Lublin. This time, things weren't happening in Vilna or Chelmno, not remote, but close by, a few hours away. So, to find out and verify details—what was going on, where were the Jews taken— we decided to send Lonka. She had family in Lublin, she had a place to go, and we also had comrades there; we wanted to know what was happening in Lublin and we needed a little money. So we went to Kirshenbaum. I connect it with Passover because of the bottle of red wine on his table and because the house was clean. Incidentally, all executions were on holidays: Passover, Purim, and Tishva b'Av. I don't remember if I got all the financial help I asked for, but we did send Lonka. She was there a few days and got inside with the help of a German who unwittingly aided her. She claimed that someone owed her money and asked him to help her get in. It was hard to get in because someone was always watching who came in and out. She brought the news that the Jews were taken to Belzec Camp, where they were executed.[11] The tyrant Odilo Globocnik[12] was in charge of the expulsion from Lublin, but I don't know if the seat of his government was in Lublin. He was in charge of the whole operation, named for Reinhard Heydrich, who was murdered by the Czech underground in May 1942.[13] There were special annihilation units there (*Einsatzgruppen*[14]), camped near Lublin, in Trawniki, where there were also SS staff schools.

Apparently, it was Lublin's turn. We weren't surprised, we were prepared for it. After the news from Lublin, one of the Jewish dignitaries of the city came, one of the General Zionists, I think; he claimed we

10. Polska Partia Robotnieza: Polish Workers Party that emerged in the underground in place of the dissolved former Communist Party.

11. Belzec was one of the six Nazi death camps in Poland.

12. Odilo Globocnik (1904–1945): Born in Trieste into an Austro-Croat family. Was active in the Austrian Nazi party; first Gauleiter of Vienna. A dissipated and uneducated loutish man. He committed suicide in 1945. (See Reitlinger 1961:245–246; Levin, 162–163.)

13. Reinhard Heydrich (1904–1942): Born in Halle. Himmler's deputy and chief engineer of the Final Solution; in charge of the Reich Security Main Office (RSHA). Described by some as one of the greatest criminals in history, he was assassinated in Lidice, Czechoslovakia, on May 29, 1942; as punishment, the town of Lidice was destroyed and its population was murdered. The mass deportations of Jews in the summer of 1942 was dubbed "Operation Reinhard" in his memory.

14. *Einsatzgruppen* were mobile advanced SS units used in mass murder operations. (See Höhne 1979:402–418.)

should set up "shops," workshops, since the Germans needed working Jews.

One day, when I was at Tłomackie with Zivia, at the Jewish Self-Help Organization (YISA), there was a great confusion there. They said something was about to begin that night; we met with Henryk Rottenberg. Everyone knew something was about to happen, but they didn't know what. This was April 17, at sundown. Suddenly, I insisted on going to Dzielna because I was worried, and I said we mustn't leave the comrades there without knowing what was happening to them, although I didn't know anything and didn't have anything specific in mind. But someone there wouldn't let me go. Zivia and I argued about that, and so we didn't go and we stopped talking about it. Nevertheless, it was hard not to do something, so we started playing the "intelligence" game, you take a word and make other words out of its letters and the one who makes the most words wins; we played in Hebrew. As a diversion. We were playing and didn't hear a thing. We went to our apartment late and went to bed.

Before dawn, Havka Folman came in a panic, the first time she came so early. She said that during the night (of April 17/18), armed Gestapo agents, including officers, came to Dzielna. Fortunately we had kept the job of concierge. Suddenly, they rang at the gate. Before he opened it, Bigelman ran to alarm our people. Tuvia was in my room and when he came out, they shot and wounded him in the leg; but he ran away and they burst the gate and went upstairs. They had a list of who they were searching for at Dzielna—Lonka and me. Because of Tuvia, the men there had time to get rid of everything suspicious (the concierge had time to warn them). For some reason, all the men ran away, leaving only the women. Hancia was the spokeswoman. As I said, they were looking for "Zuckerman and Kozibrodzka." Hancia explained that only girls lived there, no men; that Yitzhak Zuckerman had been there once, but hadn't lived there for a long time and was in a labor camp. They said Lonka didn't live there. She really wasn't registered in that name and didn't live at that address. They didn't do anything to the women, just went through the rooms and into the next apartment through the kitchen. We had once lived in the next apartment, with the Schultz family, before the war. Mr. Schultz was divorced, and his thirteen-year-old son was a student in our underground Gymnasium. The men were hiding upstairs, so aside from the girls, the Gestapo found only the father and son. The two of them were sitting at the table, the son was doing his homework and the father was rolling cigarettes from cheap tobacco. The Germans took the son and the father downstairs and killed them at the gate, leaving their bodies where they fell.

That is what Havka told.

Later, we learned that fifty-two people were executed that night, according to a list of sixty people, including our friend Menakhem Linder of YIVO, a lecturer in our seminar, an economist, a very active man. Subsequently, when we tried to figure out who was executed and why, it turned out that the newspaper account that only members of the underground were executed was false. Only a few individuals of the underground were killed. They didn't find me, and they killed Linder of all people. The others were from various groups and classes. There were bakery owners, workshop owners, poor people, rich people; and there were also Gancwajch's patrons who killed the staff of Kohn and Heller.[15] It was done by some internal accounting of their own. Very few of the murdered were members of the underground. (That night of April 17/18 was later called the "Night of Blood" or the "Saint Bartholomew's Massacre" of the ghetto.)[16]

The purpose was to instill terror. They killed from a list but the Schultzes, father and son, weren't on the list. They didn't find me and killed them instead. If they had found Lonka and me, they would have killed us. That was the only case of seeking a specific woman according to a list; all the rest were men. Linder and his wife were home that evening; he was reading. The Germans came in, spoke politely, asked a few questions and asked him to come with them; he wanted to take something, but they assured his wife he'd be back soon. They took him a few dozen meters away from the house and killed him. They treated others the same way.

A few days later, they did it again, but this time on a smaller scale. They murdered printshop workers and killed Jews who collaborated with the Gestapo. That murder had a sequel. It didn't happen only in Warsaw, but also in Częstochowa, Radom, and other places. We learned about it later

---

15. Moritz Kohn and Zelig Heller: The owners of the concession of wooden horse-drawn wagons for conveying passengers in Warsaw Ghetto. The Jews of the ghetto thought they were supported by the Gestapo and suspected them. Both of them were killed during the Great *Aktsia* in August 1942.

16. Gutman 1989:176–180; Ringelblum 1975:270–271. Chaim Kaplan describes the random nature of the killing more graphically:

"At 36 Nowolipki Street, a man by the name of Goldberg was killed. He was a barber in peacetime, and when the war broke out he went to work in the quarantine house. His wife worked there, too. When he was killed his wife set up a terrible wailing and would not leave his side. To silence her, they killed her too. Both were left lying by the gate. . . . The baker, David Blajman, on Gesia Street, was murdered in the same way. They came to take the husband but the frantic wife ran after him. To rid themselves of this hindrance, the murderers killed her along with her husband. The morning light revealed both bodies at the gate. At 52 Leszno Street, Linder was killed. At number 27 on the same street a father and son were killed. So it went down to the last victim." (1973:315)

on. The rumor that they were searching for me spread like wildfire, and I became a pariah.

Our landlord heard about it immediately and insisted we leave his apartment; no wonder. I hadn't been in Dzielna since January, though I had wanted to go there that night. But my comrades wouldn't let me. I was angry that night and, ultimately, I didn't go. They saved my life by not letting me go, and I was furious until morning because of it. I still feel guilty about it, since the Germans killed [the Schultz father and son] because they couldn't find me. That's not easy. A father and son, our student, and I wasn't even living in their house; just murdered.

Incidentally, this step was one of the great failures of the Germans. It was always easier for a member of the underground to stay alive than for a normal person; the former was careful, he lived under an assumed name, moved from one apartment to another. The normal person was not as safe. It was the same for the Poles. If there was treachery, nothing helped. If not for my underground activities, I would have been sitting quietly. Schultz was simply rolling a cigarette. All his life, he worried only about his son and his education, he made sure the boy had soup to eat. And he died instead of me. This was added to all the other despair and crises.

Altogether, they practically didn't touch the members of the underground, who apparently weren't on the lists, except for Linder, Zuckerman, and Lonka. Collaborators with the SS and the Gestapo were also killed, each group by the other. They "settled accounts" among themselves. The next day or perhaps two days later, they captured a printing worker, whose connection with the underground isn't clear to me, but he may have been connected with some underground press. They threw him from the fourth floor and killed him, but I don't know what his connection was with the underground. What I do know is that the next day, Czerniakow invited the community leaders, including Yitzhak Schipper if I'm not mistaken, and announced that the Germans had told him that the murders were done because of the underground and the underground press,[17] which he said was conducted by foreign Jews. This was followed by a proclamation signed by Czerniakow warning the members of the underground.

Twenty or thirty copies of *Yediyes* appeared every week or two. On June 9, 1942, there was an article about the impending holocaust titled "In Constant Danger." We should check who wrote it, maybe I did. (Every-

17. Czerniakow records in his diary that he was informed by the Nazis that "it was the underground papers appearing in the ghetto that brought about the repressive measures that night, and that more severe means will be employed if the papers continue to appear." He was told "to inform the public that this was a special action and that the population can return to work without fear" (1979:345).

thing Mordechai Tennenbaum wrote is in his posthumous book *Dappim min ha-dleika*.)[18]

After the April murder, we began to be punctual about publishing an expanded edition of the paper every single week; but we were thrown out of our apartment and we didn't have anywhere to go. As I said, I was a pariah, excommunicated, even by my closest friends. The Jewish community organizations at Tłomackie and CENTOS knew I was a candidate for execution. We moved to Mordechai Tennenbaum's mother's apartment at Leszno 27. In those days, Frumka returned from her travels and joined us. Mordechai's mother naturally didn't know anything about me, but was terrified of the typewriter we used to type the newspapers.

One day, very close to April 18 ("The Night of Blood"), I was told that the Jewish Communists wanted a meeting. Since they also knew I was wanted, they asked that the meeting be held secretly, and two representatives came. Mordechai Tennenbaum and I represented our side; their side was represented by Finkelstein-Lewartowski[19] and another man, Andrzej Schmidt (Pinhas Kartin),[20] whom I met for the first time at that meeting. That was about a month after the failure of the previous meeting with the Bund; they came on behalf of the so-called Communist Polish Workers' party (PPR), and suggested forming a common bloc, an "Anti-Fascist Bloc." We had a long talk. They said that Andrzej Schmidt had supposedly been "parachuted in" from Moscow; in fact, he was the one who restored the Communist Party. (PPR was established in January 1942, and these things happened in April 1942.) The Soviets didn't parachute people in and these men apparently came to Warsaw from Białystok. All kinds of rumors circulated and it was nice to hear that the

18. "In reply to the proclamation of the chairman of the Judenrat, we decided to publish an enlarged edition of *Yediyes* on time in order to reveal German deceptions and destroy any faith of the Jewish population in their promises." See Zuckerman, introduction to Mordechai Tennenbaum 1947.

19. Yosef Finkelstein-Lewartowski (1895–1942): Born in Bielsk Podlaski. He organized the PPR in the ghetto; was one of the founders of the Anti-Fascist Bloc, and one of the editors of its bulletin, *Der Ruf* (*The Call*), which advocated armed resistance. He was captured during the Great *Aktsia* in August 1942 and sent to Treblinka. Adolf Berman describes him as "wise, quiet, restrained, personally warm and friendly, modest and simple . . . He was the recognized leader of the PPR in the ghetto, enjoyed great prestige and was beloved by his comrades" (Berman 1977:230–231).

20. Andrzej Schmidt (1912–1942): Born in Luck. Fought in the International Brigade in the Spanish Civil War. Commander of the military arm of the Anti-Fascist Bloc. Captured by the Gestapo on May 30, 1942. Adolf Berman reports that, from the first, Schmidt "made a strong impression on me. . . . A tall fellow, with a handsome, serious, oval face, and blue, rather sad eyes. He spoke quietly and compactly. Every sentence was weighed and measured, matter-of-fact and substantial. You felt that there was great internal force latent in him, . . . and at the same time the self control of a veteran and experienced revolutionary" (Berman 1977:229).

Soviet Union had sent the man; but there's no truth or historical evidence to support it. Their people were sent by the Polish party to organize, and I think they succeeded in doing that inside the ghetto, more than their comrades outside the ghetto.[21]

We lived in the Tennenbaum family apartment, at Leszno 27 (to make it easy to remember, "three cubed"). The apartment number was 82 ("three to the fourth power plus one"). For me, that apartment was "burned." Later, however, I did live in that courtyard again, this time, as a "gentile."

At the meeting, they told of the re-establishment of the Polish Communist Party. The first party they contacted was Po'alei Zion Left. In the ZOB report I composed and sent abroad, I wrote that Po'alei Zion Left was the initiator of the Anti-Fascist Bloc.[22] I want to explain now that that report was sent abroad through the pro-London [anticommunist] underground, so I couldn't write that the initiator was the Communist party. But I am trying, wherever I can, to correct distortions; the report doesn't deny the Communists' role. It says "professional leftist unions" because we avoided admitting that in the report; and one of the serious charges leveled against us in times of trouble was that we cooperated with the Jewish Communists. But the truth is that they were the ones who called the meeting.

The Communist representative, Yosef Finkelstein-Lewartowski, had been a member of Po'alei Zion in his youth, before the split in Vienna (into "left" and "right"). After the split, he went with Po'alei Zion Left; he knew Sagan well and they were affectionate with one another. Throughout those years he was in Russia, in the annexed areas. He limped, was popular, and had a sense of humor. Later I became friendly with him. He (not Andrzej Schmidt) was the spokesman for the PPR. This was after our great failure to include the Bund, and we grabbed at anything that could shape a force. We were the third group they met with. First they met with Po'alei Zion Left, then with Ha-Shomer Ha-Tza'ir; and I explained earlier that, according to their ideological tendencies at that time, Ha-Shomer Ha-Tza'ir had much in common with Po'alei Zion Left, whereas we were somewhat remote from them. Moreover, we were supposedly a youth movement of Po'alei Zion–Z.S. and they didn't talk to that party. The Communists were informed that we were an independent bloc and they came to us. Subsequently, we persuaded Po'alei Zion–Z.S. to join.

There was dissension at that meeting with the Communists, which was held on Gęsia, in one of the kitchens. They wanted to set up an Anti-

21. Gutman claims that they were parachuted (1989:173).
22. The ZOB report was written in March 1944 and sent on May 24, 1944, via the AK.

Fascist Bloc, whose main purpose would be to help the Soviet Union in the war against the Germans by: (1) helping prisoners and prisoners-of-war; and (2) cooperating with the partisans. (They might also have talked about sabotage.)

We argued with them about the partisans. We said that "our partisan unit is the ghetto." I remember my words clearly. There were only four of us at the meeting: Mordechai Tennenbaum, Yosef Finkelstein, Andrzej Schmidt, and me. The debate lasted for hours. I insisted that the Jewish ghetto was the site of our partisan activity, our front. But since they said they had already talked with Po'alei Zion Left (Sagan) and Ha-Shomer Ha-Tza'ir, I didn't want to assume even one percent of the responsibility for not cooperating in some general activity; so we came up with a joint proposal: to establish a "special committee for the defense of the ghetto," not in contradiction to partisan activity, but with special emphasis on the struggle in the ghetto. They didn't discuss that either with Ha-Shomer Ha-Tza'ir or with Po'alei Zion Left, and they didn't oppose it.

In their opinion, every intelligent person had to understand that from a military point of view, the ghetto was no place for a war, that war could be carried on better in the swamps, the mountains, the forests. And their emphasis was on helping the Soviet Union. That is, the Jewish issue wasn't prominent in this plan. Because there, in the ghetto, all our considerations were one hundred percent Jewish. Not that we were against helping the Soviet Union or promoting the war against the Germans everywhere. And, if not for murder, if not for the clear information about what the Jews faced, we might have put our whole Movement at the disposal of the defense and aid of the Soviet Union; we might have called on our members to go to the partisan units. But we faced something completely different. This was the Jewish issue, and it wasn't our opposition to helping the Soviet Union, but rather what was more important to us than anything else—the need to defend our own lives. For who would defend us if we didn't?!

They accepted that.

At that "four-sided" meeting—I was very young then—I apparently made an impression of an impulsive rebellious youth; Finkelstein wasn't ashamed to tell me that I was endangering the whole organization, since I had been wanted by the Germans since April 18. Hence, what the Communists and others wrote and said wasn't true, that I was active in the Anti-Fascist Bloc. That's not true, because I was warned that I was liable to endanger the organization. Finkelstein was a veteran conspirator and had spent a lot of time in prison, and they simply told me: No! The Bloc was a great responsibility and, apparently, I didn't fit in. I took the hint and we sent another pair as our political representation: Zivia and

Mordechai Tennenbaum. Naturally, there wasn't a thing in the Anti-Fascist Bloc I didn't know. We discussed everything. I identified with the cause, not all of it, but most. I supported everything positive in this matter, but I wasn't a representative on any committee. I was a kind of "leper" and might have endangered the organization.

After that meeting, I fought with the members of our party, Po'alei Zion–Z.S., about cooperating with the Communists and the Bundists. I thought that for the sake of the most important goal we had to cooperate with all sorts of elements, even those we didn't like. That was when we faced a subject of supreme importance, of life and death. It was clear to me that the party members hadn't forgotten anything and hadn't learned anything. Neither Sak nor Morgenstern nor Leyzer Levin nor Stefan Grajek. When the Bund finally consented to join, those characters didn't come. It wasn't until we gave them an ultimatum that we were joining the Bloc, with or without them, that they also joined. Thus the Anti-Fascist Bloc was established, whose leadership included Yosef Lewartowski, Yosef Sak, Shakhne Sagan, Shmuel Braslaw (if I'm not mistaken), and our member Mordechai Tennenbaum, as well as Zivia and Mordechai Anielewicz. The military wing of the Bloc was headed by Yosef Kaplan, Mordechai Tennenbaum, Abraham Fishelson, Hirsh Lent,[23] and Andrzej Schmidt. The expanded Anti-Fascist Bloc was established in late April 1942, with the participation of He-Halutz. A special committee, parallel to this Anti-Fascist Bloc, was established for the defense of the ghetto, headed by Mordechai Tennenbaum.

The staff of *Der Ruf*[24] included Yosef Sak, Yosef Finkelstein-Lewartowski, Szakhne Sagan, Mordechai Tennenbaum, and Shmuel Braslaw, as I recall. Two issues appeared, edited by a different person each time. Mordechai Tennenbaum was supposed to prepare the third issue.

The Anti-Fascist Bloc was short-lived. It was important because it was the first almost general organization; only the Bund and the General Zionists refused to join. I have already said that the Bund rejected any activity of "all Jews," whereas the General Zionists didn't like our ten-

23. Hirsh Lent (1898–1943): Member of Po'alei Zion in Warsaw. Immigrated to Eretz Israel in 1925, but returned to Warsaw because his wife was ill. Member of the underground; worked in CENTOS. Deported to Maidanek in April 1943, and murdered there on November 3, 1943.

24. *The Call*, the Anti-Fascist Bloc journal, published in Yiddish. The first issue appeared on May 15, 1942. According to Dr. Adolf Berman, "The journal summoned the masses to struggle against despair, indifference and seclusion, to an active and united struggle against the Nazi oppressor and those who carried out his orders in the ghetto. It summoned the masses to a 'national liberation front,' to mobilize all 'healthy forces of the Jewish people' for the struggle for 'complete national and social liberation—together with the Red Army and all forces that stood with it in the bloody battle against Fascism'" (1977:239; see excerpt from *Der Ruf* in Blumenthal and Kermish 1965:39–40).

dencies, which were too revolutionary for them. I don't think they refused because of the participation of the Communists, but it's possible. The essential thing was that the ideas of defending life, of a partisan unit, and of the establishment of a Jewish fighting organization (not yet the ZOB) repelled them. And indeed, many cells of "fives" were set up over a six-week period, and then came the collapse.

The cells were organized according to movements, because in this underground work, strangers can't operate together; there has to be some "glue" between them. Thus, the organization structure was initiated not because of conservative loyalty to existing frameworks, but simply because the people in these frameworks knew one another. So the "fives" were established. There were neither weapons nor proper organization. The collapse began in the PPR. Apparently, Andrzej Schmidt was involved in something. I really don't remember. He had to take a typewriter or a mimeograph machine to the Aryan side of Warsaw and there was some treason.[25] They started arresting people on the Aryan side and on our side, too. There was a terrible fear that people would start "singing," which would lead to more arrests. This time, those who initiated the Bloc were the ones who suggested a temporary halt to its operation. The third issue of *Der Ruf* didn't appear. Despite the collapse, the short-lived experiment did succeed simply by virtue of its existence. Fear of denunciation stopped its activity. Once, Lewartowski hadn't wanted to meet with me because of that same fear; now there certainly was a basis for his fears of a total collapse and dismantling of the organization. As for weapons, there are at least ten people who tell about holding a pistol.[26] It was the same pistol. For instance, A. Berman wrote that he held it, and you might think he was holding a cannon; but ultimately, it was a pistol, one pistol.[27] Ber Mark writes that Mordechai Anielewicz received his military training from Schmidt.[28] This is absurd. You don't build an underground movement on one pistol.

At that time, we left Leszno Street (27, Apt. 82) and moved to Nalewki. We didn't live on Leszno for long. It was simply a pity to see Mordechai

25. According to Gutman (1989:174) and Ainsztein (1979:31), Schmidt was arrested on May 30, 1942, denounced by a Gestapo agent who had infiltrated the Polish Communists. Berman (1977:241), apparently by mistake, says that it happened on June 20; but he presents more details of the event. Schmidt was supposed to meet his contacts at a café on the corner of Zamenhof and Gęsia to discuss transferring a printing press to the Aryan side. There he was arrested and sent to Pawiak.

26. Chaika Grossman, for example, relates that "Shmuel [Braslaw] once showed me a pistol. 'This is the only Jewish pistol in the ghetto,' he laughed" (Grossman 1987:84).

27. In fact, Berman does say that the organization had only two pistols (1977:234).

28. Ber Mark published his book in Warsaw during the worst years of Stalinist Poland; he distorted many facts to show that the Communists initiated and organized the Uprising, thus "legitimizing" the Uprising and cleansing it of the stigma of a Jewish national effort.

Tennenbaum's mother standing at the window, to see if anyone was listening to our conversations. The apartment was in an interior court-yard, and she was scared to death. So Zivia, Mordechai Tennenbaum, and I hurried to leave. We moved to Nalewki 33, near the church, where we lived until the first days of the *Aktsia*. In those days, I typed the issues of *Yediyes* on a typewriter and, not to rouse suspicion (we were subletting rooms from two women), I got a permit stating that I worked at YISA. At first I typed with one finger but, in time, my typing skills improved until I was pretty good. Now for the first (and last) time, I had enough time since I was a pariah and unwanted. That doesn't mean I didn't appear. But people everywhere withdrew from me, at the Joint and at YISA, and even friends. Anyone who needed me came to us, but not everyone knew the address.

The whole time I was in the ghetto, I read the *Völkischer Beobachter*[29] and any German journals I could get my hands on. I read Goebbels's articles, since I even had enough time for that. Although I don't speak fluent German, I had read the German classics like Goethe and Schiller in the original back in school. But I didn't speak German freely because I didn't encounter a lot of Germans. I stayed as far away from them as I could, and did everything to avoid them. I read a lot of political com-mentary whose language I understood. I still read German today, almost freely. If there's some word I don't understand, I pick it up from the context.

One day, as I left the house to buy newspapers, I saw a young woman I knew near the house; when I tried to retreat, she said to me in Yiddish: "Don't be scared, I won't hurt you." That was Regina Litewska, whom we had expelled from Grochów because of her immorality. Now when I met her, it flashed into my mind: she's the one who denounced us and gave them our address. Why were the Germans searching for me, how did they get my name? It was a riddle to me, because this time they were searching for me personally at Dzielna, and the list of wanted people wasn't a list of underground members. Lonka and I were the only underground members on that list (except perhaps Linder). Now I suspected that this was her work, an act of revenge. I say that now, for the first time in years. Naturally it can't be checked today, but then, when I suddenly saw her, I wondered what she was doing in that courtyard.

And when she told me she wouldn't hurt me, my suspicion increased. But this was maybe two weeks before the *Aktsia*. I didn't have anywhere to go anyway, and I didn't tell any of my comrades. I may have told Zivia, but only later. This Regina went downhill when the Germans announced they would give bread and jam to anyone who would go to the *Umschlag-*

29. The official newspaper of the German Nazi Party.

platz voluntarily, and she really hit bottom. Apparently, she got something for her services, if indeed she did denounce us.

The dissolution of the Anti-Fascist Bloc was a hard blow. Incidentally, it's easy to find proof of that in the literature. In some Polish publications, I saw something about the collapse of the PPR, and you can determine approximately when the Anti-Fascist Bloc fell apart. The Communists withdrew deliberately; others, because they were stupid; and some, out of a desire to call attention to themselves and their movement. Some see a natural, organic development from the Anti-Fascist Bloc to the Jewish Fighting Organization; but there's no relation. The Jewish Fighting Organization was formed under completely different circumstances. Other forces, other people were operating.

The Bloc simply fell apart around the time of the *Aktsia*, and that was a great catastrophe. I don't know what we could have done. But, in fact, we didn't rescue a single prisoner, or sneak in one bundle of weapons, or train anyone in the use of weapons, or send one partisan to the forests— nothing, except for publishing two issues of *Der Ruf*. It was an experiment, a serious experiment, but we didn't have time. When young people come to us now and ask, Why didn't you do anything?, the answer simply is: our stop watch didn't give us months or years, only days and weeks . . .

Between the collapse of the Anti-Fascist Bloc and the *Aktsia*, I had absolutely nothing to do with educational work. I couldn't do it. But Mordechai Tennenbaum did. He would come to Dzielna and hold meetings of Dror. When we set up the Anti-Fascist Bloc, he actively organized our "fives," and was their commander.[30] He and Zivia had work—I didn't. But I shared their worry.

Of course, with the establishment of the Anti-Fascist Bloc, all the young people showed up to serve, and there was hope that things would be done. So I appreciate that short period of the existence of the Bloc, but we mustn't exaggerate. The Bloc fell apart because it had to. And I repeat: what is written in the history books is not correct. It was not the "prelude" to the Jewish Fighting Organization.[31] Maybe that's how people want to see it, but it's not true. If it hadn't failed, we would probably have begun to argue about where to put the center of gravity, whether to take people

30. Berman (1977:239) emphasizes the central role Tennenbaum played in the Anti-Fascist Bloc.

31. The Communists and some leftists were interested in emphasizing the importance of the Anti-Fascist Bloc because it was Communist-inspired and had the "correct" name. Adolf Berman says that the Anti-Fascist Bloc "crystallized the forces of various trends, mobilized them for armed struggle and created the first broad base for the Jewish Fighting Organization . . ." (Berman 1977:224).

out to the partisan units or leave them in the ghetto.[32] In reality, the situation was different: we who had reservations about the partisans sent people to the forest when we realized we didn't have weapons; and they, the PPR, and others who were for partisan activity, didn't send a single person because of the failures in the partisan units. But the debate ceased because of the major arrests among the PPR, mainly on the Aryan side of Warsaw, but inside the ghetto as well.

And there was one more event at the height of the occurrences, the execution of a hundred prisoners in what was called "Gęsiówka."[33] This happened after the Night of Blood of April 18, 1942. This time the executions were atrocities, no better than street murders. This time, too, it was a terrorist act to impose dread. I remember well the number, 110. Ten Jewish policemen were also included. I wrote a memorial to them in one of the issues of *Dror*.[34] I wrote that this murder was a "medal for the ghetto," that it didn't matter that some of them had been arrested for smuggling and criminal acts. We certainly didn't like the police, for they were the ones who took us to forced labor camp; but that was still before they took part in grabbing Jews and sending them to Treblinka.

One spring day, I went out to buy newspapers and heard an orchestra playing on Nalewki, maybe across from No. 23, near the park set up between the heaps of debris. Adam Czerniakow participated in the ceremony. They were playing [the Zionist anthem] *Ha-Tikva* and I stood at a distance, ashamed for the Jewish "Governor" there. He came in a car and the police stood "at attention" in his honor.

To give you an idea of how we lived in those days, I'll tell a story. Before Passover, Mordechai Tennenbaum and I decided to go to the public Jewish bath, because you couldn't wash well in our apartment, and we thought we should wash decently, at least once a year. But we didn't wash. When we entered and saw the naked Jews, the sight nearly drove me crazy. I said to Mordechai:*"Ikh ze di verem vos esn* (I see the worms eating

32. "The Anti-Fascist Bloc said: help for the Soviet Union, the organization of Jews for the general war, taking Jews out to the partisan units. And we said: Polish partisans were on Polish soil, while Jewish partisans would be outside the walls of the ghetto? Are we authorized to leave the ghetto alone and isolated from its youth, its fighters? . . . After quite a long time of ideological war within the ranks of the Anti-Fascist organization, we decided to set up a parallel organization within the Anti-Fascist organization, led by Mordechai Tennenbaum . . . We said that if we got an order to leave the walls of the ghetto—we wouldn't, we wouldn't obey that order, we would stay in the ghetto" (Zuckerman 1986:135).

33. The ghetto prison on Gęsia Street, where thieves and smugglers were usually imprisoned. The murder in "Gęsiówka" was in June 1942, one month before the beginning of the Great *Aktsia* of July 22, 1942 (Gutman 1989:90). Auerswald announced that it was a retaliatory act (Gutman 1989:174).

34. *Dror*, July 1, 1941.

them)." I experienced such a sharp sense of loss that I fled for my life, and Mordechai ran away with me.[35]

There, on the brink of madness, the only thing that mattered to me was the *defense of life*. From now on, that was the only measuring rod! What we had tried to build wasn't realized, didn't hold, fell apart. And we were galloping to July 22, to the beginning of the *Aktsia* in the ghetto. At that period, June 1942, the Jews of Hrubieszów were taken to their death. Before that, the Jews of Lublin. In one of our newspapers,[36] we published a farewell letter by one Motl (Mordechai Bernstein), a student in our first Seminar, who writes of himself: "*Er geyt mit di idn.* (He goes with the Jews.)" We presented information about the transports of Jews. On Passover, maybe before, a transport of Jews was brought from Berlin to Warsaw and settled outside the walls near the gates of the ghetto, on the side of the Dzielna gate, at Leszno Street 109–111 (across from the *Arbeitsamt*). A few young men and women from that transport were brought into the ghetto. We took them in and they stayed with us a few weeks.

Yitzhak Katznelson and I visited the people at Leszno Street 109–111. We got permission from the Judenrat to visit them. I remember two things from that visit: there was a fellow there from the Central Committee of He-Halutz in Berlin; we tried to persuade him not to believe the German promises to take them to the east to work, but instead to organize all the young people to come to us in the ghetto. We said that even though we didn't have any food, we would share what we had. He said that the Germans were setting up a settlement for the Jews, and he took out a paper that said: *Treblinka*. The truth is that at that time, that name didn't mean a thing to me. But it hurt me very much that he believed the Germans more than he believed me and Yitzhak Katznelson. One more fact: during our visit there, German doctors appeared and said that anyone who had valuables (including fountain pens) were requested to turn them in, and I saw a woman running after the Germans, after they finished their work, because she had a pen she hadn't turned in. That naïve behavior and what the member of the Central Committee of He-Halutz said drove me crazy. Even though I didn't know what Treblinka was, I did know what Ponar was. Not until a few weeks later did I hear about Treblinka for the first time. But that fellow had a paper with the name of a place on it, and he was going "to work" in Treblinka and was one of those who "built" and prepared Treblinka for its mission.[37]

35. Yoske Rabinovitch says that Zivia told him on the day she came to Eretz Israel that when Zuckerman went into the bath and saw the bodies sitting on the benches, he fled in a cloud of steam and came home like a man on the verge of madness.

36. *Dror*, no. 7, July 13, 1942.

37. In his diary, Adam Czerniakow confirms the shipment of Jews from Germany to work in Treblinka. Two thousand nineteen German Jews were sent to Warsaw (Czerniakow

About that time, Zivia upset me: she went to the farm at Czerniaków without telling me. I had enough of my own troubles and fears and didn't need her adding to them. The next day, she showed up as if nothing happened—she had taken a walk to Czerniaków. That's connected with the memory of that camp of German Jews. Foreign Jews had also been living in houses on Tłomackie, but Tłomackie had been taken out of the ghetto. At that time, the ghetto was reduced; it would be shrunk from time to time. And at that time, Tłomackie was only symbolic since it was outside the wall. The *Aktsia* was approaching. A few days, maybe a week, before July 22, rumors circulated that they were moving the ghetto somewhere else—Wola, they said.[38] The rumors came from our leadership. Naturally, the ghetto was electrified by the rumors. At night people listened to every rustling. They said the Jews would be taken in carts and trams and that the whole transportation system would be used for that. Turkow writes about Wasserman (he and Wasserman were from the Residents' Registration of the Judenrat which I've said good things about). He came from City Hall (on the Aryan side) and said he had learned that fifty cattle cars had come to the Danzig Station in Warsaw and were to be used to take out the Jews.[39] Later, before his suicide, Czerniakow wrote in his diary that they asked him for fifty maps of the ghetto, along with a statistical list of all the Jews according to streets and houses. All that boded ill. I am trying to distinguish between the events and the assessments after the fact. A lot of things happened and I've forgotten them or I'm forgetting to tell them.

On the last Saturday before July 22 (the 22nd was Tisva b'Av), Zivia and I were invited by Stefa Wilczyńska and Janusz Korczak to attend a children's performance; all the "big shots" were there, but there weren't many.[40] I remember Giterman, Guzik, and Katznelson. About that time, there were directives about checking scales and weights and an order to

---

1979:340–341). As usual, Chaim Kaplan is more acerbic about this group; he reports that "the Gestapo and the Poles welcomed them at the railroad station with food and flowers. They had been deported in Pullman cars and appeared prosperous and elegantly dressed upon their arrival. In brief, aristocratic exiles" (Kaplan 1973:309–310 [entry of April 6, 1942]).

38. A suburb of Warsaw.

39. Turkow reports that Wasserman got that information in absolute secrecy from a reliable source in the Warsaw City Hall. Turkow delivered the news immediately to the leaders of the Jewish underground, who investigated and confirmed it (Turkow 1969:107).

40. The invitation was dated July 15, 1942: "We are not in the habit of promising unless we are certain. We believe that an hour's recital of an enchanting tale by one who is both a thinker and poet, will provide an experience—'the upper grade in the scale of sensitivity.' Accordingly we have the pleasure of inviting you to come to us on Saturday, July 18, 1942, at 4:30 P.M." (Korczak 1980:235).

bring them to be examined—all of that to calm the public. The rumors and whispers were at their height by then. There was a panic, but it was quite restrained. A great many people were stunned and didn't know what tomorrow would bring.

I remember the atmosphere and the performance of "The Dying Prince" at Korczak's. Suddenly one of the people from Dzielna came to summon us. He said that Laban had been captured by the Germans while trying to enter the ghetto and was imprisoned in Pawiak. He learned that from a guard at Pawiak. Laban had to be rescued as fast as possible. We rushed to contact all kinds of "influential connections" to get to Laban. We made extraordinary efforts and finally got him out, through a Polish police officer, in exchange for a lot of money. We saved him at the last minute, because the first ones taken out of Warsaw were the prisoners (in fact, they were preceded by the beggars). We hurried to get him out of Pawiak, even though we didn't know the *Aktsia* would begin on the 22nd. So he stayed with us during the *Aktsia*. He had come to Warsaw to consult about establishing a Jewish fighting organization in Kraków. He came to ask our opinion because he knew we had an Anti-Fascist Bloc. He didn't know it had fallen apart, and he was willing to risk his life to hear our opinion; as soon as he came, he was put in Pawiak. That was July 21. I was in the YISA offices and, of course, no one knew what was about to happen. On July 22, a few members of the Judenrat were arrested as hostages and taken to Pawiak. The announcement appeared—the first time an announcement wasn't signed by Czerniakow—about the *Übersiedlung* (resettlement). This is well known and there's no point repeating it. We were empty-handed. The issue was presented as the removal of the nonproductive population; and they did indeed take the unemployed, along with their families. People began dashing around in a panic. Jews were warned to save whatever they could, save their families.

I lived at Nalewki 33 only in the first days of the *Aktsia*. Then, we moved to Dzielna. The idea was that when all Jews were in danger, they wouldn't be looking for specific individuals, and thus wouldn't come searching for Yitzhak Zuckerman on Dzielna.[41] So we moved there. On the morning of the second or third day of the *Aktsia*, we went to visit Dzielna. Even before we moved there, we visited there from the first day of the *Aktsia*. We didn't take the young people with us in the first period. We walked as two couples: Zivia and Mordechai Tennenbaum and Frumka and I—one couple after another. Frumka and I were first. Suddenly we saw a manhunt in the streets: only some of the Jewish police were taking part in it. A Jewish police officer said something and stopped us. Frumka

41. Dzielna Street was "out of bounds for Jews" by then.

insulted him; he responded with obscenities, and she slapped his face. Everything was fine until we got to the end of Gęsia and Nalewki Streets, where dozens of police surrounded us, each grabbing some part of Frumka's and my body. Carts and horses were close at hand and Frumka was thrown into one of them. They tried to throw me in too, but I pressed my back against the cart and held onto the steps and they couldn't get me inside. I was a "wild man," and I suspect they caught a lot of blows. I was also swollen, not a limb of my body was left intact, but they couldn't carry out their mission; I simply held on and they couldn't budge me, since I kicked in every direction. I remember seeing a policeman in the distance, a fellow from Ha-No'ar Ha-Tzioni, hiding behind a kiosk. He was ashamed because he couldn't help, but he couldn't participate in the "festivities" either, so he was hiding. Meanwhile a crowd had gathered. Suddenly I saw a member of the Movement who was one of the refugees begin yelling at them: "Bandits! You know who you're taking? The leader of the Halutzim!" That was a bombshell. People started wailing and screaming from all sides, from hundreds of people caught in the blockade. The shouts rose to the skies. I felt strong enough to resist. Suddenly a man I didn't know appeared and said to me: "Let's get this over! Let go and get into the cart. In a few minutes, I'll release you, on my own responsibility!" I didn't know the man and I didn't know who he was; but without thinking much, I let go, got into the cart, and sat next to Frumka whose nose was bleeding from the punches. Suddenly the awareness that I was sitting in a cart flashed through my mind! By then I knew what Treblinka was![42] And here I was being taken to the *Umschlagplatz*.[43] What I didn't know was that Mordechai Tennenbaum had broken through the blockade and run to the Ha-Shomer Ha-Tza'ir commune on Nalewki Street to summon them to help.

Who was that man I believed? That was the first and only time I sat in such a cart. I don't know how long it lasted because every second was like an hour for me; but they did release me and Frumka, too. A Jewish officer came to us, holding gloves in one hand, and a stick in the other (they weren't supplied with anything but rubber truncheons). He was a handsome man, perhaps a few years older than me. (Most of the Jewish officers in the police were intellectuals, several of them lawyers.) He said to me: "They told me who you are, but you behave like a thug." I didn't say anything. If I had said a word, I would have been back in the cart; so I restrained myself and we were released.

42. Treblinka was one of the more notorious Nazi death camps, where masses of Warsaw Jews (among others) were gassed to death upon arrival. The French writer, Jean François Steiner, wrote a famous docu-novel about the camp (*Treblinka;* 1966).

43. Square at the entrance to the ghetto, near the freight station of the railroad, where the Jews were concentrated and taken to the death camps.

I didn't know the man, I said he was good-looking, whereas I "behaved like a thug." Apparently they weren't the thugs, but I, we, were. Of course, there was a danger that the Germans would appear any minute. But the Jews, the Jewish police, did the despicable work of the Germans. Some people try to defend them, others accuse them. What do I think is our great guilt, my guilt (since most of my comrades are no longer alive)? Our guilt was that immediately, from the first day, we didn't begin our harsh war against the Jewish police! Would we have saved the people? No! Absolutely not. But clearly the Germans wouldn't have done the job so easily or so fast, without the Jewish police. Because the Jews would certainly have run away from the Germans, but, when they saw a Jewish policeman, it didn't occur to them that he would lead them to their death. And the Jewish police knew, as I knew, and no later than I did, what Treblinka was, since it was the Jewish police themselves who brought the information about the slaughter taking place there.

You might say they took part in building Treblinka, and there is documented evidence of that. One night in the ghetto, the Germans assigned the Judenrat and the Jewish police to collect Jewish skilled laborers: carpenters, tinsmiths, locksmiths, builders; they ordered the Judenrat to obtain barbed wire, various instruments they needed to set up the camp; it all went to Treblinka. That was Passover 1942, the first time I heard of Treblinka. Later on, it turned out that there were two Treblinkas: the labor camp, where there were few Jews, designed essentially for gentiles; and the other Treblinka, the death camp, near Malkinia, near what had been the border with the Soviet Union before June 22, 1941.

A year had passed since then and we hadn't done anything at all: the Jewish police were armed with rubber truncheons and knives. That is, they didn't have guns. All we had to do was kill them. If a few of them had been killed, others would have been afraid to join the police. They should have been hanged on lamp poles at night, to threaten them; but we didn't. We could even have sent our boys to ambush and scare them; but we didn't do that either. And there's a supposedly "legal" argument that anyone who didn't follow orders was threatened with death. But what danger faced the police force? At most, what happened to all Jews.

I never forgave myself for not doing what we should have. That was the situation up to a certain period. Later, when we did start going that way, it was too late. We should have been selective, since I don't say we should have killed all of them; but it would have been enough to execute a few of them, really execute and scare them. This way, we would have forced the Germans to come into the ghetto and do the job with their own hands.

That was what I demanded in the first meeting of the public committee held in Kirshenbaum's apartment at Leszno 56, on July 22, 1942 (Tisva b'Av). Many people have written about that meeting.[44] There was talk of setting up "shops." One Jew was an expert in those matters. We had a few sewing machines at Dzielna and we also made a "shop," as it were, which didn't really exist. Our firm there was "Leszczinski," which appears in the list of "shops," although the Germans didn't recognize it.

The meeting was held in the first days of the *Aktsia* and, as I recall, it included Kirshenbaum, Sak, Schipper, Giterman, Guzik, Ringelblum, and Berman. I appeared there on behalf of He-Halutz.[45] At first, the Jews had wanted "shops," a tailor with a sewing machine or a carpenter who had tools was a good thing. But that wasn't what the leaders wanted. From the beginning of that discussion, it was clear that there was an abyss between those notions.

First, they talked about the question of what could be done. Should we defend ourselves? Presenting the problem like that required dealing with it. Schipper, for example, said he had information that it concerned taking only 80,000 Jews! He spoke of historical responsibility: it's true, he said, these people might be executed, but can we endanger the lives of all the other Jews? Schipper was a good speaker. He said that there are periods of resignation in the lives of the Jews as well as periods of self-defense. In his opinion, this wasn't a period of defense. We were weak and we had no choice but to accept the sentence.

What in fact did I demand at that meeting? First, demands relating to action. What did I propose? I didn't have much to propose. I proposed that those present and their comrades, the community leaders (we could assemble a few hundred Jews) demonstrate in the streets of the ghetto with the slogan: "Treblinka Is Death!" Let the Germans come and kill us. I wanted the Jews to see blood in the streets of Warsaw, not in Treblinka. Because the day after the *Aktsia* started, July 23, maybe even on that day, we knew what Treblinka was and where it was. The police in the *Umschlagplatz* saw the railroad cars returning from there after a few hours. That showed us how far it was from Warsaw. Moreover, when the doors of the cars were opened to put in more people, they found bloodspots and even corpses. The cars weren't even cleaned properly. Then we began investigating and learned from the Polish locomotive driver that he was taking them to Treblinka, not far from the Malkinia station. This Treblinka now joined the "Treblinka" of the He-Halutz member from Germany, and we knew it meant death. But even before we knew the place exactly, we knew what had happened in Vilna, Chelmno, Lublin, and

44. Some accounts say the meeting was held on July 23. See discussions in Ainsztein 1979:35–37; Gutman 1989:228–229; Berman 1977:265–266; Lubetkin 1981:106–107; and Zuckerman 1986:105.

45. According to the ZOB Report, aside from those mentioned, the participants of the meeting of July 23, 1942, also included L. Bloch, Shmuel Braslaw, Friedman, Lewartowski, Y. Kaplan, A. Landau, Orzech (Zuckerman 1986:105).

Hrubieszów. That was the direction of my thought. I explained it like this: we have no choice. The world doesn't hear, doesn't know; there is no help from the Poles; if we can't save anyone—at least let the Jews know! So they could hide. I also said that we had to attack the Jewish police. If we had worked in this spirit, we might have prolonged the process, made it hard for the Germans to carry it out; because the annihilation would have been a little harder to "manage" with 450,000 Jews then than with 50,000 later on. They would have had to bring military forces and use them day and night to capture all the Jews.

Alexander-Zysze Friedman, one of the leaders of Agudas Yisroel, was weeping as he said words of love and respect to me: "My son, the Lord gives and the Lord takes." Since we couldn't save anyone, perhaps that should have been our answer too, since in the situation the Jews were in, what difference did it make who went to his death first? But we thought we could save some. We thought that if people saw blood, if they knew that going meant death, murder, and if they knew it not from afar, not behind fences, but if they saw it with their own eyes, they wouldn't go willingly. Unfortunately, things weren't done then that should have been done.

I left that meeting, aware that we had sunk deeper into the abyss, but I also knew that there is a limit to how far down you can sink. For months, I had been sunk in that abyss. In fact, we did what others did. I knew they would take every last one of the Jews. But I thought it would go on and on. We should have known all their tactics; we were onto the deception. At least we had to know the inevitable end. I thought they might do it in stages, since that was what had happened in Vilna; but the process went on incessantly.[46]

Czerniakow's suicide made no impression on the Jews.[47] The Jewish family was hounded by anxiety and sunk in fear. They wanted to hide

46. In that *Aktsia*, the "Great *Aktsia*" or the "Great Expulsion," between July 22 and September 12, 1942, with breaks of a few days, about 265,000 Jews were taken out of Warsaw and transported to Treblinka.

47. Adam Czerniakow, head of the Warsaw Judenrat, committed suicide in his office on July 23, 1942, the second day of the *Aktsia* in Warsaw, when he was told by his German masters that the Jews of Warsaw were destined for destruction, and he was called upon to assist. He was sixty-two years old at his death, was buried in the cemetery on Gęsia. There are differing opinions about Czerniakow's suicide. Chaim Kaplan, for example, believed that he thus proved ". . . conclusively that he worked and strove for the good of his people; that he wanted its welfare and continuity even though not everything done in his name was praiseworthy" (Kaplan 1973:384). As for the impression made by his death, Jonas Turkow reports that "Czerniakow's sudden death made a depressing impression on everyone and was a clear sign of the lack of any chance of changing the tragic situation" (Turkow 1969:117). Adolf Berman, like Antek, argues that his suicide didn't absolve him of the guilt of allaying suspicions a few days before the *Aktsia* by "spreading deceptive information and

their little Moyshele from the brutality of the Germans. The Jew didn't think about Adam Czerniakow. Czerniakow was an honest man, but he wasn't a leader. Certainly not a leader of the nation at a time like that. He condemned the underground for its publications. What were those publications?

We published what the Germans were doing to the Jews in Ponar and elsewhere. Shouldn't he have done that, since he had a printing press and paper? But he rejected our people and warned them not to go on publishing. He often pointed an accusing finger at the underground. And at the moment of truth, he decided to die. He could have committed suicide in another way, as a leader of the community warning his people. It was hard for me to forgive him for choosing to die as a private person. A person who is going to be a leader has to know how to finish. At a moment like that, it's not enough to be "aesthetic." He could have won immortality if he had summoned us in the underground and said: I'm putting everything at your disposal! Though he didn't participate in the police actions during the great expulsion, the police did carry it out, and he didn't save anyone and didn't do any good. And they were acting in his name, weren't they?

I used to look enraged at the people closest to me. I asked myself: where is Gutkowski? He was worried about his son Gabriel. Ringelblum was also bothered by personal worries; I think his son was named Uri. They were worried about their children and didn't have a moment to think about Adam Czerniakow. Whereas Jews who didn't have bread or the possibilities of existence or a work permit were candidates for murder, and they certainly weren't thinking about whether Adam Czerniakow died or not. In national and historical terms, Czerniakow's behavior wasn't worthy of his position, it wasn't the behavior of a person who professed to be a leader. I can't accuse him of anything; he was a man with clean hands. But he wasn't the right man for his time. He thought he could go on being part of the age-old Jewish tradition of supplication, when that had become obsolete.

I never met him personally, although I did see him at our agricultural farm in Grochów at that ceremony; but I never spoke with him. Maybe I should have tried, maybe I would have convinced him; maybe I should have done it, but I didn't, I didn't meet with him. It's not a matter of anger. A party can assess a situation and decide not to meet—since we saw where this was leading.

---

delusions. . . ." (Berman 1977:262). And Marek Edelman echoes that: "That wasn't right: one should die with a bang. At that time this bang was most needed—one should die only after having called other people into the struggle. . . . We reproach him [Czerniakow] for having made his death his own private business" (Krall 1986:9).

He committed suicide and left the flock without saying a thing. And if he left a will, it was destroyed and we don't know what it said. He only asked for a glass of water and swallowed the cyanide. Anybody could have pulled that "trick." In fact, emotionally, I was closer to it than he was. But what good would it have done if I had done such a thing?! Who knew us? Who were we, anyway? As far as everyone was concerned, we were on the fringes of Jewish life, although I don't think we really were. I think we were in the heart of Jewish life. But, in terms of our position, what impression would it have made to commit suicide? But Czerniakow is a different matter—by committing suicide as he did, Czerniakow damned himself. He could have called out, sounded the alarm, warned us. We would have held out a hand to him, we wouldn't have settled accounts with him for the past. Nor would we have delved into the social aspect of the Jewish community organization. He could have helped a lot; but he left us, with our wretched typewritten proclamations. Why couldn't he have issued a proclamation: "Jews, don't go!" signed "Czerniakow," and committed suicide before the Germans came to arrest him? We would have gone out and plastered those big posters all over Warsaw.

After that, everything began to fall apart. We called a first meeting, a second meeting. There was no third meeting. The party representatives didn't come. We didn't accept their excuses for not coming: a roadblock here, fear there. These were very personal things. A great fear fell on everyone. I could understand. For example, I can swim, I used to swim across the Viliya.[48] Once, I almost drowned and the scars of that drowning remained on my body. That was enough for me not to go into the water for some time. The trauma that remained with me since I was sent to Kampinos labor camp in the early days was enough for me and it was hard for me to get rid of it. I was young but, nevertheless, I had a terror of the Jewish policeman. At first, they didn't take young people and then, they did, if the daily quota of people wasn't filled. The Jewish policeman was assigned a "quota of skulls."

After two or three days, when we saw they weren't coming to meetings, we tried to assemble the left, proletarian, segments. I don't think the Communists were around anymore. (I did meet Lewartowski later, but under different conditions.) The groups included Po'alei Zion Left, Po'alei Zion–Z.S., Ha-Shomer Ha-Tza'ir, and Dror; Gordonia had vanished. But it all fell apart. They simply didn't come to the meetings. Sagan was taken before the end of the month. He had documents and he was sure they wouldn't get to him. But they took him. Yosef Sak also disappeared. In light of this situation, it's almost shameful to admit what happened—we issued the proclamation with the call: "Jews, don't go;

48. A river near Vilna, Antek's hometown.

Treblinka is death!" And the Jews tore our proclamations off the walls, by force, with blows. The Jews saw it as a German provocation. I heard that from the comrades who were putting up the posters, who told it with tears in their eyes. Yosef Kaplan and Shmuel Braslaw got beaten up. We had a lot of people who were ready and willing. Someplace, Braslaw, as I recall, found switchblades and, lacking any other weapons, they intended to use them and even tried to assassinate a few policemen with them. But that is not what should have been done [at this time].

On July 28, the members of He-Halutz gathered at Dzielna. Aside from myself, this meeting included Zivia, Yosef Kaplan, Shmuel Braslaw. (Mordechai Anielewicz wasn't in Warsaw at that time; he left for Zagłębie.) There was also Israel Kanal of Akiba, who had served as a policeman for us.[49] On that day he "threw his hat away," that is, he resigned. We told him not to do that, since we needed him there and, indeed, when necessary, he would put his hat back on. At that meeting, we decided to establish the "Jewish Fighting Organization." Just us, all by ourselves, without the parties; and we decided to amass our forces and start doing what we could.

During the *Aktsia*, everyone wanted to save his own life. There was no leadership in the ghetto. There was no organization to take care of forging work permits to give or sell to people. The recognized leadership didn't take care of that matter. The offices of YISA were always full. We also went there every day. The Judenrat gave the following document to all the notables: "This man is vital to the war effort." I don't think I got such a document. Maybe I didn't need it. Later on, the members of YISA were taken for Judenrat activities. Some of them participated in blockades. As far as I was concerned, it was a disgrace to have that document.

I participated in all the meetings, since that was when we began to be considered "important," and they took care to invite us to meetings; they would ask us to come and would listen to what we said; but the truth is we didn't have anything to say. These were the meetings held after the first meetings of the political leadership cadres. Then, all of a sudden, our importance started rising, but we didn't have anything to say. We had a political platform, but we didn't have anything to call on the public to do.

We had to make an effort to save at least the remnants of the movements, and we had hundreds of people who had to be saved from the

49. Israel Kanal: Born in Bydgoszcz. Active in Akiba, infiltrated the Jewish police in the ghetto. He was one of the first ZOB fighters and tried to assassinate Jewish Police Chief Szeryński (see below). He fought in the January Uprising, and was commander of the Central Ghetto in the April Uprising. After the Uprising, he escaped to the Aryan side through the sewers. He was deported to Auschwitz in October 1943 and killed; at his death he was about twenty-three years old.

threat of expulsion. First of all, we sent whomever we could to the farm at Czerniaków, to Zatwarnicki, the estate owner, who closed his eyes and pretended not to see. His steward "didn't see" either. This was a lot of people. Ha-Shomer Ha-Tza'ir was based in Landau's shop, which the Germans confiscated and turned over to a commissar—the "Hällman Shop."[50] Afterward, the place turned into the "Ghetto of Shops." The alternative we had debated—forest or ghetto—ceased to be the subject of discussion. We sought a way to get people out because we saw that the danger of death was hovering over their heads. We contacted Poles and sent a delegation to the Aryan side of Warsaw in the early days of the *Aktsia*.

Arye Wilner[51] and Tosia Altman left with the delegation, while a debate erupted among us: Frumka suggested that she stay with Morde-chai Tennenbaum and that Zivia and I go to the Aryan side. Her hidden agenda was to save us, the "couple." It wasn't logical at all, because if anyone knew Aryan Warsaw it wasn't Zivia and me. We had more argu-ments that lasted until we sent the two people out—Frumka and Mor-dechai Tennenbaum. Zivia and I stayed in the ghetto. Our people went to Aryan Warsaw after Wilner and Tosia. We could send them from our base at Czerniaków. Leah Perlstein was there and now we sent them to get weapons we couldn't obtain in the ghetto. They tried and did get something. They operated with the aid of Irena, through her with the Polish Scouts, as well as through PPR, and they also looked for inde-pendent ways to buy weapons.

We had a friend among the people of Zbąszyn, Moshe Rubin, who was a trained graphic artist, a splendid document forger.[52] He made the document in the name of Abraham Breyer as well as many others.

50. Landau's shop was the *Ostdeutsche Bautischlerei Werkstette*, "the most important center of the ghetto underground during the deportation" (Gutman 1989:222). Most of the members of Ha-Shomer Ha-Tza'ir were concentrated there. (Landau's daughter, Margalit, was a member of that group.)

51. Arye Wilner: Born in Warsaw. Was one of the leaders of Ha-Shomer Ha-Tza'ir in Vilna; and, with several other leaders of the movement, he took refuge in the Dominican convent in Kolonia, near Vilna. Marek Edelman says that he was "the favorite of the Mother Superior—blond hair, blue eyes, he reminded her of her own brother" (Krall 1986:98–99). Came to Warsaw on a mission in early 1942 and ran their commune at Nalewki 23. Was the ZOB representative on the Aryan side of Warsaw until he was denounced and captured by the Gestapo. He escaped from the forced labor camp at Rembertów, fought in the April Uprising, and committed suicide at Miła 18; about twenty-six years old. Adolf Berman described him as "an extremely bold, energetic and active underground operator. He looked like a Polish '*Sheygetz*,' spoke good, popular Polish, and sometimes wore a hat with a feather like a well-to-do farmer" (Berman 1977:191).

52. Describing one of the battles in the April Uprising, Borzykowski tells of Moshe Rubin, who "pulled out of his pocket his mouth organ from which he never parted, and played Beethoven and Schubert tunes" (Borzykowski 1972:52).

We set up a shop with a German gentile (Y. Leszczynski). All kinds of (Polish and German) opportunists set up "shops" and wanted to make money with cheap labor, without investing anything. We made our apartment available for the shop. We had gotten most of our people out, so Dzielna was almost empty. We gave them our apartment for the "shop" since we had a lot of sewing machines, left over from a kind of sewing shop we had once had there. Moshe Rubin forged the documents because the SS didn't authorize the establishment of the "shop." Each of us got a document that he worked in the "shop." And the comrades who didn't go to the Aryan side of Warsaw or to the farm at Czerniaków used those documents.

Two places were indicated as partisan bases; another place given us by PPR turned out to be nonexistent. One day we were informed that Havka Folman was to meet the representatives of the PPR partisans near Lublin. A few days later, she returned disappointed: no bears, no forest, no partisans, no nothing. They didn't yet have any partisan units. Then, we sent people to some estate near Hrubieszów, where our people were working. When they talked about partisans, we knew it was the same area. We tried to assemble comrades there. The second place was around Miedzyrzec. We and Ha-Shomer Ha-Tza'ir sent a few joint groups to Miedzyrzec and a big group to Werbkowice, a village near Hrubieszów.[53] One group did get there and, in late August or early September, another group was sent. Almost none of the Dror members were left in the ghetto. We sent the last group out of the ghetto on September 6. So only Zivia and I remained, deliberately to be with our Ha-Shomer Ha-Tza'ir comrades.

On September 3, a Gestapo car came to Landau's shop; they were looking for Yosef Kaplan, who was the shop representative vis-à-vis the *Arbeitsant*[54] and who provided them with whatever documents they wanted. They said they had things to discuss with Kaplan. Landau, who was sure it was shop business, sent a messenger to call Kaplan. By that time, Jews had been evacuated from that area and the "small ghetto" was "purified"; afterward the streets were empty and Dzielna was also empty of Jews.

Kaplan and his comrades lived at Miła 63, a bloc of houses where the people working in the shops were lodged. And here they came from Landau looking for Kaplan and, when he came to the shop, he was arrested and put into the car. A few of the workers, members of Ha-Shomer Ha-Tza'ir, were standing near the car and noticed someone with

53. Most of the members of these groups were killed by the Germans. (See Lubetkin 1981:120; Zuckerman 1986:106–107; Gutman 1989:243.)
54. German Labor Office.

a coat wrapped over his head sitting in the back seat; but they didn't suspect anything. Thus, Yosef Kaplan was taken to Pawiak. I was still at Dzielna that day.

Right after Kaplan's arrest, Shmuel Braslaw came to where I used to live to tell us about it. The apartment was empty because there wasn't a single Jew on Dzielna. We had chosen that place precisely because there was no danger of searches. We entered on the prison side, not from Dzielna. After Braslaw told us the story, we got in touch with one of the members of Ha-No'ar Ha-Tzioni, Mordechai Auerbach, who had contacts with the VIPs with access to the prison; we wanted to know what was going on with Yosef Kaplan. I was assigned to go to the Judenrat, to Giterman or Guzik, to get money to ransom Kaplan. Braslaw took one of his switchblades and hid it in his pocket. (I found out about that from one of the members of Ha-Shomer Ha-Tza'ir after I came back.)

Shmuel Braslaw found Auerbach, and the two of them walked down Gęsia Street. It was a fairly quiet day in the ghetto. Suddenly, they spotted a car filled with Germans in the distance and tried to flee into one of the courtyards. The Germans pursued them, grabbed the two of them, and beat them severely. Because they found the knife in Shmuel Braslaw's pocket, they beat him to death. On the same bitter and cursed day, September 3, they killed Shmuel Braslaw and arrested Yosef Kaplan.[55]

Our radio was hidden in one of the places on Miła Street. By then we had a few weapons—grenades and guns, which had been brought into the ghetto at great risk. Until that September 3, things were "quiet" and we were waiting. The Germans carried out "purges" in Otwock and around Warsaw. We were waiting to resist if the Germans started another *Aktsia* in Warsaw.

I gave orders to bring the weapons to us, on Dzielna, at dusk, when laborers were returning to the ghetto from work; afterward, the streets looked deserted. Dzielna was almost empty. One of our people was supposed to bring the radio and a member of Ha-Shomer Ha-Tza'ir (Regina Justman) was supposed to bring the weapons.[56] We waited anxiously, but the weapons didn't come. Instead a Jew came and told about

55. According to Ainsztein (1974:40), Braslaw "was shot down when, with a knife in his hand, he defended himself against several SS man in Gęsia Street." In Peretz Opoczynski's "Warsaw Ghetto Chronicle" (in Ringelblum 1986:102), "Schmueli . . . was shot in the street yesterday." Gutman (1989:244) states that "he tried to pull a jackknife out of his pocket but was shot on the spot." Berman repeats Antek's account (in Blumenthal and Kermish 1965:62).

56. Regina Schneiderman (Justman): Born in Warsaw. Was a member of Ha-Shomer Ha-Tza'ir and a ZOB courier. She was captured by the Gestapo on September 3, 1942, jailed, and tortured in Pawiak. The details of her death are unknown; about twenty-two years old. Ainsztein (1979:212n), however, says that she escaped from Pawiak and was killed in the April Uprising in the Többens-Schultz factory.

a girl who had been walking in the street and, accidentally (or maybe not), came on some Germans. The man told me he saw Regina walking with a basket and the Germans came to examine the basket and found all our weapons, including the grenades. They put her in a rickshaw and took her with them. Eventually, we met her, after she was released from Pawiak. This, then, was the sum of the day: Kaplan arrested, Braslaw killed, and our weapons captured! Thus we approached September 6. Three days later was to be our historical test.

At that time, the Germans were assisted by the Jewish police. Apparently, by then it was harder for the Jewish police force to get along on its own. The Jews weren't going so easily; they were hiding and that really made things harder for the Germans until they formed the "Cauldron" on Miła Street, where they concentrated and drove the Jews.[57] Then they repeated the operation. But it was really hard to control the big city. The Germans made the "Cauldron," and the Jewish police then played only an auxiliary role.

But first, a few other things:

Before that, we sent a delegation to the Aryan side to get weapons; they got in touch with Irena Adamowicz; but we didn't get anything from the Polish Government-in-Exile in London because they didn't trust us. They said: "The Jews won't defend themselves." They insulted us and said sneeringly that the Jews went "like sheep to the slaughter." But when we asked them for weapons, they said they didn't believe the Jews would defend themselves. So they argued out of both sides of their mouth. And unfortunately, the PPR, who were sympathetic to us, didn't have any weapons. But they did give us addresses and contacts with weapons dealers and, for high prices, we bought a few guns from them, which were good enough only for show. We also acquired grenades. Arye Wilner and Frumka brought the weapons into the ghetto. Frumka brought them in with potatoes since, at that time, Jews were still working outside the city. They would go in and out of the ghetto in a crowd. Later, the Germans took people who had work. On the way back from work, they would deceive them and take them straight to the *Umschlagplatz*.

So Frumka brought those weapons in a basket she carried. The German put his hand in the basket of potatoes, groped around and didn't find anything, and we were thrilled. I'll never forget the drinks in honor of that event. I drank about half a shot glass. But there was genuine joy,

57. During the *Aktsia*, the Germans concentrated the Jews of the ghetto on Miła Street and the surrounding streets and enclosed them there. There are vivid descriptions of the horror of that experience in Lewin 1989:176–179; Seidman 1947:98–111; Berlinski in Blumenthal and Kermish 1965:94–95. The term "Cauldron" comes from the strategy of World War II when part of an enemy army was cut off, surrounded in a small area, and then destroyed.

because we were preparing for the great day when the *Aktsia* would start again and, as I said, that was late August, early September; and, until September 6, there was a respite. The Germans were busy liquidating the towns around Warsaw.

Even before that we carried out some operations that were also connected with the Soviet air raids. There were three operations at about the same time, August 22 or 23. The most reliable source for these things is Yitzhak Zuckerman's report abroad.[58] To this day, nothing written there has been denied. There are things I couldn't tell or that I didn't deal with, but every operation in the report is precise, except for the report on the establishment of the Anti-Fascist Bloc.

One operation I mention there was setting fire to houses. Some of the houses we burned had belonged to Jews who had been expelled, where the Germans had been looting. On Dzielna, for example, we tried to burn down the Folman house so the property wouldn't fall into the hands of the Germans. We did the same with the house at Leszno 27. We started in Mordechai Tennenbaum's apartment. That was done by our gangs. That night, the Russian planes appeared and bombed Warsaw, and some people connected those events. Ber Mark and his comrades, for example, later explained it as the Red Army's assistance to the ghetto residents who were being taken to Treblinka. That was nonsense he repeated often. The fire we started might have attracted attention at night, but the planes didn't come from Moscow to save the ghetto. Maybe they saw fire, came and added their own.

We founded the Jewish Fighting Organization on July 28, 1942. At that stage, the command staff of the Jewish Fighting Organization consisted of Shmuel Braslaw, Yosef Kaplan, Zivia Lubetkin, and Yitzhak Zuckerman.

There was also Mordechai Tennenbaum, but he was sent to the Aryan side; the command staff, that is, the foursome, decided on operations. The staff decided to execute Józef Szeryński, commander of the Jewish police in the ghetto.[59] The most appropriate person for the job, who knew him and could get to him without any difficulty, was Israel Kanal. He put on his uniform, since he had been a policeman; he resigned during the *Aktsia*. On August 20, he came to police headquarters and tried to shoot

58. Sent in spring 1944, through the Polish underground, to London, and from there to Eretz Israel. See Zuckerman 1986:101–25.

59. Józef Szeryński (Shinkman): A Polish police officer before the war and chief of the Jewish Police in the Warsaw Ghetto. A convert to Christianity. He was attacked and wounded by Israel Kanal on August 20, 1942, and subsequently hid from the ZOB. He committed suicide by poisoning himself during the January Uprising. Berman says that "he never had anything in common with the Jews. . . . This commander of the Jewish police Szeryński deserved a bullet in the head" (Kermish and Blumenthal 1965:61).

Szeryński, but his gun jammed for some reason. Then he shot a second time and hit his cheek.[60] He thought he had killed him (we learned only later that the man was only wounded); he jumped on his motorcycle and headed for Nalewki, to the gate of the ghetto, to divert his pursuers, and came to Dzielna. We immediately printed an announcement of the death sentence carried out against Szeryński. Those posters were signed "The Jewish Fighting Organization." I think they were in Polish, but I don't remember for sure. The attack was made in police headquarters. I stood in the street and read our announcement with other Jews. The Jews thought it had been carried out by Polish members of PPS, since witnesses saw a man on a motorcycle fleeing toward the gate—which meant it was a gentile fleeing to the Aryan side.[61] Second, it didn't occur to a Jew that Jews would use weapons, that they had weapons.[62]

So our activities were the attack on Szeryński and our announcement about it, burning down the houses of the expelled Jews and the Soviet air raid that night. All that was still in August, before Kaplan's arrest. Two days in August and what activities! We had weapons and we were on alert. After the attack, Szeryński ceased to function, even though he wasn't killed but only wounded. He was replaced by Lejkin.[63] If we had started

60. Gutman (1989:239) cites a report from the memoirs of a Jewish police officer which describes the attack in more detail. According to that officer, members of the Jewish police "expressed their delight over Szeryński's misfortune."

61. There is evidence of this in David Lewin's diary: "I have heard there was an assassination attempt on the chief of police Szeryński. He was wounded in the cheek. According to rumors he was wounded by a Pole from the Polish Socialist Party disguised as a Jewish policeman. Today leaflets were distributed against the Jewish police, who have helped to send 200,000 Jews to their deaths. The whole police force has been sentenced to death" (Lewin 1989:162).

62. Ainsztein (1979:59) maintains that: "The importance of the attempt on Szeryński's life cannot be overstressed. . . . The resistance organizations in the Warsaw ghetto—both the Jewish Fighting Organization and the Jewish Military Union [the Revisionists]—had no doubt about their priorities: both concentrated on the elimination of Jewish traitors as a first step to the planned battle against the Germans and consequently before the end of 1942 they replaced the Judenrat as the leading authority inside the ghetto."

63. Yakov Lejkin (Leyken): An attorney, assistant to Szeryński, who worked diligently to carry out the Great *Aktsia*. According to Ringelblum, he was "a little man with a small body and small head, was completely corrupted by his power. He became savage, he beat mercilessly policemen and ordinary Jews. Those who saw him during an *Aktion* noticed that there was no sorrow in his face. On the contrary, he looked as though he liked the resettlement operation, as though he enjoyed the whole business" (quoted in Ainsztein 1979:41). Stanisław Adler, however, described him as "ambitious, capable, well-mannered, and indefatigably energetic, but he had not gained the respect of his colleagues. . . . What did contribute to his rejection was his height. I can still recall vividly the caricature-like figure of little Lejkin in his jodhpurs and his canary-yellow cardigan" (Adler 1982:21). Was killed on October 29, 1942, by ZOB members Eliahu Rozanski, Mordechai Growas, and Margalit Landau.

operating against the Jewish police on July 22, as we had wanted, we would have finished them off. We could have done it. I take the blame for the omission—not because I was so important, but simply because my comrades aren't alive. It was the fault of the Jewish Fighting Organization that arose during the *Aktsia*. But who said you had to start operating in the name of the Jewish Fighting Organization? The movements that founded the organization existed before. Does the name decide? We sat in meetings of community representatives where we raised proposals and heard the opposition. Did you need weapons to kill a Jewish policeman? If you wanted to terrorize the Jewish police, wasn't it enough for two strong men to pull a policeman into a courtyard and hang him on a pole and then post announcements explaining the act?

Meanwhile, during the August lull, I was taken to the *Umschlagplatz* a second time. I had decided to go with Zivia to the area of the Többens-Schultz workshops, where I would later be commander, to see what was happening with our comrades; we hadn't heard anything about them, and they seemed to have vanished. We didn't know anything about Yohanan Morgenstern, Leyzer Levin, Yosef Sak, Stefan Grajek, that whole group. By then, they were outside the central ghetto; there were streets in the ghetto where it was forbidden to go. I had a forged document that said I worked in the "J. Leszczynski Company." I knew the document was forged; the Germans and the Jewish police could easily know that, too. That was the document I had or, in other words, I didn't have a document. So I walked with Zivia and I was very glad to meet the comrades, all of them safe, no victims among them. On the way back, a Jewish policeman suddenly appeared before us and demanded documents. I acted like a fool. I treated him seriously and showed him the document. I was taller than he was, certainly as strong. I could have hit him. But I presented the document. He said, "Fake," that is, forged! We started talking, and meanwhile, other policemen appeared. If I had pulled him into a courtyard, I'm sure I could have finished him off. I was quite strong since I worked hard in Landau's shop, even though I wasn't a farmer. Suddenly, some policemen gathered and led us off. They didn't take Zivia, but she wouldn't leave me. Why did they stick to me and leave her alone—they were taking women too! But Zivia went with us. That was right across from the Judenrat building, where Rappoport's monument now stands, on the corner of Zamenhof and Gęsia. Once there was a post office there; it was a Polish castle with a Latin inscription; I don't remember the details. At that time, the Judenrat was there. So they were taking me off and, all of a sudden, a police officer pops up in front of my eyes, one of those who cooperated with us (there were three of them). He saw me and Zivia, came to the policeman leading me off and said: "Let him go." The policeman answered: "But I've got to bring so many skulls."

I won't mention the officer's name here.[64] He's the only one of the three who cooperated with us who remained alive. He came to Israel. The two others were Arye Grzybowski and Yehuda Engelman. I met that officer who remained alive in Poland after the war. When I was in Yagur, in 1947 and early 1948, he would come visit us. One Saturday, as we sat on the lawn, some Jew appeared who knew and remembered him, apparently not exactly kindly. When he served in the Jewish police, he wasn't known for helping the underground, and even if they helped us, those people were still policemen. Aside from Grzybowski, these policemen weren't members of the Movement. I already told about our comrade in the police who went downhill. Everyone we put in that institution went downhill. That officer did good things for us; but not always, it seems, did he behave well. At any rate, I saw that the encounter at Yagur scared him. I saw him once more and invited him when we established the museum.[65] I met at that time with Blumenthal and Dr. Kermish and, at their request, I asked him to write about the Jewish police. Maybe he was scared by the subject. At any rate, he disappeared. I don't know if he's in Israel, if he's even alive. It was a long time ago.

Let's go back to our arrest: that officer said he was willing to sign a receipt for two people, and he would take the responsibility. There was a complicated series of events—a transport of Jews appeared, led by German motorcyclists. The Jews were taken past us in the middle of the street, just as the policeman was about to release us. One of the Germans who saw us approached and added us to the transport, which was on its way to the *Umschlagplatz*. So they took Zivia and me, and in that situation, the officer couldn't help.

But we were lucky. We walked on Gęsia Street, on the way to the *Umschlagplatz*, a five-minute walk from there. I must say we were sure we'd get away and that we wouldn't get to the *Umschlagplatz*. But we didn't yet know how. That was right across from the Judenrat. Fortunately for us, the Germans were riding motorcycles. That is, they couldn't always guard the pedestrians next to them and had to keep moving. At a certain moment, next to an announcement board, Zivia's composure stood her in good stead and saved the two of us. In his slow journey, the motorcyclist made a turn and, at that moment, Zivia pulled me by the sleeve and the two of us began running behind the wide announcement board.

One of the Germans saw something but, before they could do anything, a slight commotion arose, and we were already in the courtyard of

64. According to Hirsh Berlinski (in Blumenthal and Kermish 1965:134), there were three policemen who worked for ZOB: Arye Grzybowski, Yehuda Engelman (whom Antek also mentions), and Luxemburg (possibly the third one referred to here). Jonas Turkow also mentions the three names together (Turkow 1969:212, 217).

65. Beit Katznelson, the museum of the Holocaust at Kibbutz Lohamei Ha-Getaot.

the neighboring house. We hurried up to the top floors of the house. A few members of the Judenrat, including Giterman, witnessed this; they were standing on the other side, near the Judenrat building and saw the transport going by. If the Germans had left the transport and chased us, the people in the transport would certainly have dispersed and escaped. We waited about fifteen minutes. The transport passed and we came down, our hearts pounding. Giterman came to us and shook our hands, since he had witnessed our escape.

Not every Jew could escape from the transport, nor was it always possible. We did succeed, so I didn't get to the *Umschlagplatz*. I had been there once, not as a person who was snatched up, but on a certain mission. But that was later. You could go into the *Umschlagplatz*; only policemen had a function there. You could get people out of the *Umschlagplatz* with a bribe. We got Haim Zelmanowski out twice. I didn't go there but I worked for his release. In the first days of the *Aktsia* and the snatchings, I would go to my friends' houses to see what was happening. One day, I came to Zelmanowski to see how they were. I found him and his wife sitting on packed bags, ready at any moment to be called to come to the *Umschlagplatz*. When I entered, I shouted: "Unpack your bags!" Because that emotional willingness meant they were reconciled to going to death. They simply had no strength left to stand up and couldn't bear the situation anymore without their children with them: they really were like little children and, in their hearts, they had accepted the sentence. After I yelled at them, they put back everything that was in their bags and then hid in the bunker. Both of them had a dose of cyanide so they could commit suicide in case there was no way out.

Later, when the Germans came to their house, Zelmanowski and his wife were in hiding. The mother, who had remained in the house, took the cyanide. The Germans took her and she simply died on them and didn't get to Treblinka. One day Zelmanowski's wife was taken and he remained alone. Twice he was at the *Umschlagplatz*, twice I got notes from the police. It concerned a lot of money for ransom. Of course we collected the sum immediately and saved him. A few days later, they caught him again. (Incidentally, he paid us back. I don't remember where he got the money—maybe he sold some jewelry he had. At any rate, he paid us back, both times.) We succeeded in rescuing him and he remained alive. Later, they caught him again, not for Treblinka, but for a camp near Lublin.

By the way, talking with him here in Israel, I realized that he was missing a big chapter in his memory—the whole episode of the camps. I think I know more about that than he does. That happened to him in 1945, when he returned from there. When I talked with him, I sensed a vacuum in his memory. I must say he wasn't the only one, since I came on such cases of people repressing an episode from their memory.

I, on the other hand, suffer from a "surplus of memory." At a given moment in a conversation, I may not remember what I need to weave into a story, but someplace the memory of events exists, almost the whole picture is preserved. I have an associative memory. Details don't stand alone, isolated from one another. There is always a picture in my head. It is not the individual picture that's decisive. Sometimes, it's like a film— one thing stirs another. In one respect, that's good because I always see everything in the general framework—which explains how things "suddenly" happened. I don't know if this explanation is right. There isn't always an explanation. At any rate, I see things in their framework: why did we behave this way or that way? Why did I go here and how did that happen? Everything in a framework. I don't think there are things that disappeared completely from my memory. Here's an example:

In our archive, there are documents and letters from the Jewish Fighting Organization and the Jewish National Committee, including a letter from Dr. Berman I didn't know about. It might have contained important but not essential things. I once read the letter; I can see it in my mind's eye and I can recite a whole section of it to explain how something happened and when it happened, and so forth. That's what I said about things being in my consciousness, but I had no need to bring them up because I didn't attach any importance to them.

I said before that I had been in the *Umschlagplaz* a few times, but that was in a later period, after September, when we wanted to get permits in order to be in important parts of the ghetto. At this earlier time, I didn't see the *Umschlagplatz*. I didn't see the cars. But I did see the property of the Jews, the clothing, all the things they had packed which was taken by train to Germany.

I was captured by police once more. And what I went through is nothing compared to what other Jews experienced. I mention this in connection with the Jewish police. In two cases, the Jewish policemen did their job. There are attempts to defend them, there are those who say they had no choice, as it were, and so forth. Of course they had no choice— from the moment they decided to be policemen. There were different kinds of policemen, more brutal ones and less brutal ones. There were those who took bribes and those who thought they had to excel. In general, this was a period of human degradation and moral decline, a period of degeneration in every respect. As for us, that was our great failure, our disgrace. Because we could have dealt with the Jewish police and we didn't. We could have threatened them, but that wasn't enough. There were a lot of them—thousands. But they weren't the greatest heroes; they weren't idealists. They served the German occupier, willy-nilly, and thought they could save their lives and their families like that. There was one Jewish policeman named Abraham Wolfowicz (there were two brothers with that name who were known for their cruelty) who was brought to me right after the war. His defense was that he wanted to save his mother. But he didn't.

We shouldn't have executed only Józef Szeryński. We should have executed a few policemen before Szeryński so they would have been scared to go into a courtyard of Jews. When there were hundreds of thousands of Jews in Warsaw, the Germans couldn't have taken the transports to Treblinka without the help of the Jews themselves. It was the Jewish policemen who caught and took out the masses of Jews. They were armed with sticks; we could have used sticks and knives against them; we could have strangled and hanged them. Words or threats wouldn't have helped. You had to be brutal, violent. Unfortunately, we didn't do that, although we did issue moral verdicts on them.

We must remember that, until the Great *Aktsia* (starting July 22, 1942), the Jewish police did not take an active part in leading people to death. But they did snatch people for work, they did take bribes, and they did wicked things, even before the *Aktsia*. At one time, we didn't know exactly how the murders were accomplished in Lublin, what was happening there. We sent an agent there. In Lublin, apparently, the Germans worked by themselves, whereas in Warsaw, for several weeks (until September 6), the Jewish policemen did the job they were given. Of course, the Germans also came—it was enough for one German to show up, ten Germans. But the majority were Jewish police and they did their work faithfully. By that time, we realized that the Jews were being taken to their death. Even those, like me, who were taken to a labor camp had no chance of getting out of there safely. That was the purpose of the *Aktsia,* and we saw it clearly. Hence, our evaluation of the meaning of the acts of the Jewish police.

We didn't operate against the Jewish police because we couldn't decide what to do against them; or, perhaps more correctly, we began operating too late. When we became aware that the war had to start with the police, with collaborators, with the Jews, we encountered harsh criticism from the Poles as well. This was later: when I met with them a few days before the outbreak of the Uprising, one of their charges was that we were spending our bullets on Jews instead of fighting Germans. They didn't understand that it would have been impossible to fight the Germans without ending the internal treason and that would have to continue for a while.

As July 22 approached, we seemed to stand with stopwatches in hand. Every additional day of questioning, of looking for a way, meant ten thousand Jews slaughtered. So we started acting, attacking policemen. We didn't want to slay just any policeman, we wanted to find the policemen who played a special role at the *Umschlagplatz*, organizing the transports.

People like Mieczysław Szmerling or Yakov Lejkin.[66] And don't think it was easy to get to them. Because they were guarded by both Germans and Jews. Therefore, I say that it was our fault; we should have begun those operations sooner. That's more than an oversight; we use that term "oversight" only because of the jargon of our time.

Why the delay? Was it a miscalculation? What was the motivation? The issue wasn't so simple. Today, for example, after all my experience, I'm sure that wherever there is internal treason, war must begin by destroying it. You can fight the enemy facing you, who rises up against you; but not traitors. But then, we hadn't yet come to that awareness about the police. So every day we delayed was lost. I had no doubt about it then, and I have no doubt about it now, and it's been decades since then. I've had many days and nights of thinking. And I've read a lot and tried to rethink what I could have done and didn't do. And I must repeat once more that, even if we had started the war with the Judenrat police on July 22 and done everything possible, we wouldn't have saved the people. That's not what I blame us for. Our blame is that we could have delayed the sentence, we could have made it hard for the Germans, we could have forced them to bring 10,000 Germans to do the work done by 2000 to 3000 Jewish police. In this matter, every German would have been less efficient than a Jewish policeman. He would have been more brutal, because he held a machine-gun and not a stick, and no doubt he would have slaughtered people on the spot.

But our goal was, in fact, to bring Treblinka to Warsaw. If that had happened, the Jews would have done their best to run away and hide, since they wouldn't have believed the Germans; but when a simple Jew saw a Jewish policeman calling him, it was hard for him to imagine that his brother would lead him to death.

In John Hersey's novel, *The Wall,* there's a very sharp incident of one policeman who lacked "skulls" for his quota (that's what they called it), so, having no choice, he took his own father.[67] Such things could happen in those dreary days. *Corruption* is a delicate word to describe where the Jewish police wound up. Such things were incomprehensible and inexplicable. Things got so bad that after the war, in 1945, at a meeting in

66. Mieczysław Szmerling: An assimilated Jew, miraculously saved from a ZOB assassination attempt. Stanisław Adler (1982:74) describes him as a ". . . tall, broad-shouldered fellow with the strength of an athlete who liked to demonstrate his prowess at every opportunity." Ainsztein describes him as a ". . . former boxer, a giant with a little beard and the face of a killer who was in command of the Jewish police in the *Umschlagplatz,* [who] did not hesitate to use his whip and took advantage of his position to extort money and jewels from wealthy victims . . ."

67. *The Wall,* a novel of the Warsaw Ghetto, published in 1950, was based on the Ringelblum Archives that had been unearthed at that time.

London, Yosef Shprintzak didn't want to hear any words from me against the Judenrat and the Jewish policemen. "There are no Jewish traitors," he claimed.[68] Well, on that score, we failed completely. By inaction or delayed action, we failed.

We failed because we weren't ready to start a war yet. Or, we failed because we saw the German as the enemy. Suddenly, surprisingly, an element appears that wasn't taken into account, and this is the most destructive element as far as we're concerned. You have to remember that, in Treblinka itself, there were no Jewish police. And what happened to us was before Treblinka—on the way there; and that was surprising. Until July 22, 1942, the Jewish element wasn't part of our conception. We didn't figure that the Germans would put in the Jewish element, that Jews would lead Jews to death.

Organizing for that change took more time. Moreover, in the first days of the *Aktsia,* it wasn't so obvious. They didn't stand out, since first they emptied the orphanages, the hospitals, the prisons. That encompassed tens of thousands of Jews. But when they started blockades in streets and courtyards, you suddenly saw the Jewish policeman. In many cases, there were mixed forces of Jews and Germans. Here too, the ugliest and most provocative jobs were done by Jewish policemen, as guides and active assistants. True, in many cases, Jews resisted the police. In many cases, they struggled, there were shouts and howls; women attacked the snatchers. But I'm not talking here about that spontaneous phenomenon, but about things done consciously, knowingly. When, as commander, I knew I had to organize our force for war against the enemy, that took time. I'm sorry, that took time.

And I claim over and over that that doesn't have anything to do with the final solution the Germans were preparing for us. No matter what, the people wouldn't have been saved. But at various stages, it was hard for us to swallow emotionally that our war had to begin with the Jewish policemen, since we had our sights constantly trained on the Germans. That idea grew in us during the *Aktsia,* at a rather early stage. During the *Aktsia,* there were occasional intervals; then came a day, August 21, I think, when everything happened in a clump. The first time [that we attacked a Jewish policeman] was in July (July 22), but we committed the act itself in August, knowingly, consciously. Even before that (also in August), we sent Henik (Hanoch) Gutman, a member of Dror, with a group of comrades, to attack Szmerling.[69] Szmerling was a monster figure

68. Yosef Shprintzak (1885–1959): Israeli labor leader and first speaker of the Knesset.

69. Hanoch Gutman: Born in Łódz. Active in Dror and ZOB. Fought in the January and April uprisings; was commander in the Többens-Schultz area until March 1943, and then in the Brushmakers area; wounded on May 2, 1943. The details of his death are unknown; he was twenty-two years old. Kazik, who fought under Gutman's command, says

and it's hard for me to believe that a Jewish woman gave birth to him. And he of all people had the good luck to evade those who were lying in wait for him because he broke his leg that day and was taken out of there. Our comrades returned ashamed. We wanted to start with Szmerling because he was the lord of the *Umschlagplatz*.

We should also remember that our comrades who posted proclamations in the streets saying: "Resist! Don't accept the sentence!" were beaten up by *Jews*.

It's pointless, even ridiculous to explain history with thoughts of "what if . . . ?" What we're doing now is just taking stock. And in this framework, I can state for sure that we had nothing whatever to do with the general delusion! What is delusion! In those days, it meant that, when things were happening in Lublin, people said: "That won't happen in Warsaw." When it did happen in Warsaw, they said: "That happened on Nalewki, but it won't happen on Gęsia." When it did happen on Gęsia, they said it happened at number 32, but it won't happen in my house, number 28! We didn't have any delusions like that. Nevertheless, we didn't figure we would have a war in the rear—with the Jews. If we had been prepared for that, we could have acted, even without being hurt much, with sticks and iron rods. The policemen went into the streets, and we should have been organized, been in the manhunt, in the place where it was set up. But as the *Aktsia* progressed, more and more Germans came in as partners to trap Jews and send them off.

At that time, I was living at Nalewki 33, and I went through several selections. Germans and Ukrainians worked in surprise manhunts during the early days of the *Aktsia*. One day all the tenants were suddenly taken out and ordered down to the street. I was in our room with Zivia and Laban, and there was nowhere to hide. They were searching the apartments and anyone who didn't go down was killed on the spot. So we were forced to go down. We went down at the last minute, when we heard them beginning to break down doors. They didn't yet take us because we were young. Work documents didn't mean much. That is, young people could still maintain the delusion that young people weren't taken.

The whole group—Zivia and I, Lonka, Laban, and Mordechai—went through the selection in the street safely. But members of Ha-No'ar Ha-Tzioni were taken from that same courtyard, where that group had a workshop. Why did they take some and not others? I can't explain it. If they had taken us to Treblinka, I hope we would have jumped off the train and tried to escape. Maybe we wouldn't even have gotten to the

---

that "his speech was terse and sharp—concerning military matters, but his relations with the comrades were generous and understanding" (Kazik 1984:37).

Umschlagplatz, maybe they would have killed us on the spot. Those were the possibilities.

I talked about delusion. But I don't intend to make a historical trial now. As for the "oversight," the best defender can't defend us in this matter. But keep in mind: where and when was our nation ever tested in such a situation?! These weren't snatchings, or cantonists![70] By the way, there too, the "work" was done by leaders of the people and bastards. But this was genocide. There isn't another chapter in Jewish history in which the murderers themselves were basically Jews.

Psychologically, we weren't ready to start our war on the Judenrat police rather than on the main enemy; that was a horrible surprise. Everything we did—like Shmuel Braslaw going out armed with a knife— was the product of confusion and surprise. Was it important? It was my lot to fight with the policemen only when they wanted to capture me. But how many squads did those things? Even when we captured a policeman here and there, it wasn't significant, except symbolically. But to succeed we had to build a force for that purpose, and we weren't prepared for that. We hadn't foreseen the magnitude of the police force working against the Jews. Suddenly a mass of thousands appeared against us, a disciplined force, with commanders, filling a decisive function in the German mission of destroying the ghetto. We didn't know their plans; we didn't know on what day, in what street, danger would erupt. Our policemen couldn't tell us about the plans. Our intelligence people didn't know. Even later, when we did know what to expect, that didn't help us much.

When we sent our man to join the police, we didn't take into account the new situation he confronted. Israel Kanal was a policeman who once "threw in his hat" and resigned. Could we tell him to stay in the Jewish police? He resigned on July 22, 1942. He was a member of Akiba and knew that he was endangering himself. If he had stayed, he could have remained for three or four more months in the delusion that he would survive. But, morally, he couldn't go on. Then he used his policeman's hat again to attack Szeryński. He would put on his uniform when he had to get into the police fortresses. But could we have maintained him and others in the police as informants? In such a case, he had to lend a hand and cooperate in sending Jews to death. There's no point searching and listing what our policemen did besides helping us; their activity in the police can't be described as black-and-white. Things were very hard and very complicated.

---

70. Cantonists—Jewish children snatched by the Russian authorities (1801–1856) to serve in the Tsarist army for twenty-five years.

September 1942 is a special chapter.

On September 6, there was a pause in the German *Aktsia* in the ghetto. The Germans were busy expelling the Jews of the suburbs, and we tried to take stock and reorganize during the lull. Thoughts of "what if" rise and oppress you in such a situation, even if they're not very useful. I don't think it's right that things would have been different if our few weapons hadn't fallen into the hands of the Germans on September 3. You couldn't have made a real uprising with it anyway. Furthermore, in such a case, the revolt of the Jews wouldn't have reached the consciousness of Jews overseas. The weapons taken were a tiny bit—you can imagine the size of our "armory" if a girl could carry it in a basket. But for us, it was everything. We had planned to act with the few grenades and pistols when the *Aktsia* was renewed.

When the *Aktsia* began again on September 6, the Jews of Warsaw were concentrated in a "Cauldron" and held there.[71] It lasted seven days. We succeeded in protecting most of our people during the *Aktsia*, and in getting many of them out of the ghetto. In general, groups of people were caught together. We were lucky, and our whole group got away. Only one big group of Ha-Shomer Ha-Tza'ir didn't get out of Warsaw before September 6. The same is true of Zivia and me, since we had once decided to stay with them no matter what—now we wanted to get them out. We had a good setup for our people outside the ghetto in Czerniaków, whereas Ha-Shomer Ha-Tza'ir's setup at the time was in Landau's "shop." So that force stayed in Warsaw on September 12 and 13, the last days of the *Aktsia*.

I started this section of September with reorganization and stock-taking. To understand the mood of our little group, which saw its mission as fostering and implementing the idea of resistance and regarded the ghetto as its battlefield, you must understand the feeling of the young Jewish Halutz, who saw with his own eyes how the Germans spread their net in the little pool where 150,000 Jews were crowded, and took out their catch. All those who were caught were taken straight to Treblinka. I estimate that after the *Aktsia*, there were no more than 70,000–75,000 Jews left in the ghetto. And we witnessed that, we heard the shouts, the howls; we hid like mice in holes. We didn't have any weapons. We saw Germans, Lithuanians, Latvians, Ukrainians—this time, only them. By now, the Jewish police practically weren't functioning. We didn't know what to do. And that was the source of the crisis. By then, many of us didn't believe we would ever have real weapons. That was our shame and

71. The so-called "Cauldron" was a blockade set up by the Nazis in an area bordered by Gęsia, Smocza, Niska, and Zamenhof streets.

our disgrace. In this mood of crisis and despair, we gathered one night in early September for a discussion. I would now like to devote a few words to that meeting.

Who was there?

Zivia, Arye Wilner, myself, Miriam Heinsdorf, and a few other younger comrades. Mordechai Tennenbaum was then on the Aryan side; Mordechai Anielewicz had returned from Zeglębie during the *Aktsia* but hadn't come into the ghetto. He remained on the Aryan side and came to us after that night. Frumka was also on the Aryan side. The subject of the discussion that night was: "What now?" The comrades were generally thinking of an act of collective suicide. It has been more than twenty-five years since then and I never shared that position. That night, I was the exception among my comrades, isolated. My voice was an isolated exception among my comrades' voices.[72]

72. In Zuckerman 1986:80–81, he writes of that historical meeting:

In gloomy silence, we ate the meager dinner. The young people in the group went into another room. The older ones were left. We were alive. We had to know what to do tomorrow. I don't remember who spoke first, Arye or Zivia. The words were bitter, heavy, determined. There would be no Jewish resistance. We were too late. The people were destroyed. When there were hundreds of thousands in Warsaw, we couldn't organize a Jewish fighting force—will we succeed now, when only a few tens of thousands are left? We didn't win the trust of the masses. We have no weapons and we almost certainly won't have any. There's no strength to start all over. The people are destroyed, honor is trampled. That little group still had the power to restore it. Come on, let's go out to the streets tomorrow, burn down the ghetto and attack the Germans. We'll be liquidated. We are sentenced to be liquidated. But honor will be saved. In days to come, they will remember: youth rose up for that helpless people and saved as much honor as they could.

Other comrades spoke. Everyone in his own way. The meaning was the same. Despair was the dominant feeling. Feelings demanded action.

In an atmosphere of total despair, it was hard to say anything else. Even though one of the comrades [i.e., Zuckerman] grew bold and said, more or less: Those are genuine feelings, but the conclusions are wrong . . . the crisis is great and the shame is great. But the act proposed is an act of despair. It will die with no echo. The damage to the enemy will be small. The youth will perish. So far we have a legacy of countless failures and we shall have a legacy of defeats. We have to start all over. The *Aktsia* has ended for the time being. Perhaps days of relative quiet will come, perhaps weeks, maybe even months. Every day is a gain. Arye must go back to the Aryan side. We have to look for new contacts. We shall raise money in the ghetto, and buy weapons from private dealers. We have to fight the Jewish scoundrels to the bitter end. If not for Jewish treason, the Germans wouldn't have ruled so fast and so easily in the ghetto. Perhaps we shall succeed . . .

First there was general annoyance. They accused the comrade of wanting to prevent the last possible act. If they didn't go into the street immediately, the force wouldn't have time tomorrow to do even that. He was clipping their wings. The discussion was sharp. The atmosphere was charged. But gradually, sober voices of calm were heard. The atmosphere cooled off. Practical suggestions were presented.

We had stocks of gasoline we had acquired over a long time because we had been planning to act with weapons and to set fires. I think it was Zivia who suggested using that gasoline now. To set big fires in the ghetto and to attack the Germans with what we had. The comrades were excited. So were Zivia and I. We were all one family in these fateful hours, a group of activists, burdened by Jewish fate with an unparalleled historical responsibility. (In fact, there was nobody left from Gordonia, the last one was Zelcer, whose fate we learned later.) The discussion didn't go according to movement affiliation. Zivia said one thing. I said something else. All the comrades (with one exception) wanted to finish fast and the discussion revolved around that.

In sum, their suggestion meant public collective suicide. I couldn't stomach that. The concrete proposal was to use our gasoline to burn down whatever we could. We had dozens of liters. We could have made big fires; there were mattresses, furniture. We could have organized within twenty-four hours, made a big fire, and attacked the Germans at the ghetto gate. They were in the area and would certainly have come. That was supposedly a "campaign against Germans"—with bare hands, sticks. An act of struggle, harmless. Most of the discussion was on principle, and concrete proposals would come at the end. We weren't far from making a decision in this spirit: if it had been accepted, I don't know how things would have gone.

I said before that, when the *Aktsia* started, at the end of July, I had proposed that very thing. At the meeting of the Central Committee, I suggested we go out into the city brazenly, with all the public dignitaries, and not let the Germans deceive the Jews about taking them for "resettlement" somewhere. Twenty-four hours after they started capturing the Jews and sending them in trains, perhaps that very evening, we knew the shipments were headed for mass murder. We knew that from the experience of Ponar, we knew it from Chelmno. Within twenty-four hours, we also knew the name of the place where they were taken—Treblinka. But the people didn't know and the people went. The policemen called and the Jews came.

What the comrades were now proposing, I had proposed at the beginning of the *Aktsia*. Then we were looking for something to do to keep the Jews from going, to shock them! I thought blood should be shed in the streets of Warsaw. And it would be better if that happened in a

---

This was the most fateful night for the Jewish Fighting Organization. We decided to take heart and start rebuilding the Jewish fighting force, with all means and forces at our disposal, with superhuman means. On that night, the fate of the January Revolt and of the April 1943 Uprising were sealed.

demonstration of the leaders going out and shouting to the world. Our veteran comrades and the leaders of the people were frightened that the Germans would be spurred into action and, as a result, a lot of blood would be shed. Our argument was: wasn't Jewish blood shed anyway? But the people didn't see it, they were blinded and so they obeyed. Blood had to be spilled, here, and they had to see it! Then I proposed an act to expose and alarm the Jews so they would know where they were being taken.

What the comrades proposed in the discussion *now* wasn't an alarm; this proposal came out of heartbreak, depression, helplessness, lack of faith! If the proposal of the majority at that meeting had been accepted, within forty-eight hours, we would have set fire to parts of the ghetto and waited for the Germans to come. Then we would have attacked them with sticks and stones and would have been killed. For what purpose? So this little group would die an honorable death?! We didn't do that while the *Aktsia* was going on, when there was a point to it. What was left for us now, after everything was over?

It was hard for me to reconcile myself with the general mood. I argued that we still had time to do what they planned, but we had to try to build the force. We might be condemned to die in two weeks. Or we might gain a few months. We didn't know the German plan.

After a long argument, I was deeply wounded; I was most offended by the people closest to me. They saw my position as an expression of weakness, softness. This wasn't a "debate between gentlemen over a cup of coffee." They were the majority, and I was alone; and as the discussion went on, they grew heated and banded together against me and stood like a wall. If the decision they wanted had been made, I would have been one of those leading that desperate act. Perhaps my opposition was because of my emotional constitution; I was motivated by the idea that this was neither the right time nor place for that act. We should have done it on July 22, but we didn't. We didn't alarm, we didn't warn. Now we would be nothing but a rear guard in the parade to death.

When I try to assess my comrades' notion in hindsight, I think it was basically emotional and I certainly don't look down on it. When a person decides to commit suicide, does he decide that in a moment of heroism or of weakness? I don't know. Maybe out of both heroism and weakness. At any rate, when a group of comrades considers such an act, they should know—to use an historical association—that the act they want to perform has no comparison whatever to Masada. If they had taken their action, there would have been no resonance, no influence. I felt that it was a suicide pact to aid the Germans. It was like an announcement to all the Jews who remained alive: commit suicide! As I repeatedly consider the course of my thought, I conclude that it was logical. I think I can praise myself, since I am also willing to take blame. The opinion that we mustn't commit suicide in that way, in that form, was logical. That wasn't the right moment. If the Czech Jan Palach[73] had burned himself on another day and in other circumstances—as Buddhist monks sometimes do—he wouldn't have achieved the desired effect. He achieved his purpose because he did it at the right moment. But we had missed the right moment, even in July. I didn't believe there would be an uprising. In July, the idea of uprising was remote for me, because I didn't know how to build a force. The question then was only how to announce, to alarm. This was the execution of hundreds of thousands of Jews. The question wasn't uprising or Treblinka. There was only Treblinka. The question was how to make the Jews resist going to Treblinka. The first failure was that we didn't fight the Jewish police. The second failure was that we didn't have any instruments: no newspaper, no radio, no other possibility of publicizing what awaited us.

We might have said something to Zelmanowski, Gutkowski; Ringelblum knew about it. We didn't reach the masses and the masses didn't know. For them, being taken to the *Umschlagplatz* wasn't a great tragedy. Here or there, they were hungry. They had certainly heard rumors, but they didn't believe. There was a time when we didn't believe either. And even if our July plan had been done in time, there wouldn't have been an uprising.

And in such a case, the historical accounting was infinitely bitter. If I were convinced that we didn't act on July 22 to 24, 1942, because I envisioned January 1943, I would perhaps console myself with that. But it's not so. Because we could have been captured in July or August and everything would have been over. They could have caught and killed us. After all, we were surely the only group in the ghetto that could launch the uprising. But it seems that at that discussion, we concluded that we couldn't do it, since the essential thing, as far as we were concerned, was to alarm the people. But if the result was that dozens of young people attacked the Germans in the streets, and only a handful knew about it, and the majority didn't know, and in the next street over, they didn't know—I was opposed to such an act.

I never regretted the tough discussion. Later, it gave me a lot of personal strength, when I saw that, nevertheless, there was a beginning.

At a certain moment in the conversation, a crisis occurred and a retreat began. Comrades began to talk more coolly. The meeting didn't end with a majority decision or a vote, but with the determination to try, which was accepted unanimously and wholeheartedly. That is, we would all partic-

73. A young Czech who burned himself publicly as a protest against the Soviet invasion of 1968.

ipate in consideration of what to do tomorrow: "*Vi lebt men?* (How to live?)" That wasn't a matter for one hour. More than one candle flickered out before we decided on something. But the process was rational, and the mood changed.

My first proposal was to send a delegation to the Aryan side, while we who remained behind would do what we had to. We now had to return to the corridors of the institutions, to the leaders who remained alive. Some of them were now waiting for what we would say, and when we appealed to Giterman for money, he didn't turn us down; Guzik also treated us well. Now that they saw there was no saving anchor, they supported us. But they couldn't act instead of us, they could only help. We pulled them behind us and set up a civilian committee which they were eager to join.

We assigned them tasks like providing hideouts for the central group. They saw, as we did, that you couldn't hide on the upper floors anymore and that bunkers had to be built. Shelters also had to be found and prepared on the Aryan side of Warsaw; the Jewish Fighting Organization had to be helped and money had to be obtained—later, we found a way to get a lot more money than the Joint could give us by carrying out "Exes."[74] Now I knew what to do, how to begin. First of all, we had to build ourselves. Second, to try again to contact all possible forces on the Aryan side of Warsaw. As I said, the next day, Arye Wilner and Tosia left; and we began all over again to accumulate weapons. I can't say that weapons streamed in to us because, until January, the Polish underground didn't believe in us at all. Nevertheless, we developed systems to get our hands on weapons. The people on the Aryan side of Warsaw worked like demons and their activity paid off. We were lucky and didn't have any disasters, because a lot of provocateurs would sell weapons and then turn the customers over to the Germans.

One of the decisions we made at the close of that night was to see ourselves as a national movement, since we weren't only in Warsaw but in the entire country. We considered ourselves responsible for Vilna too, even though we didn't know exactly what they were doing in Vilna. There were emissaries, but the connection ceased at a certain stage. When Anton Schmidt was caught and Lonka was arrested, contact with Vilna was broken. We considered ourselves responsible for Białystok and Będzin; we divided our forces, assigned Frumka to Będzin, Mordechai Tennenbaum to Białystok, and Rivka Glanz to Częstochowa. It was a central responsibility, that is, everything was now directed. Laban was with us at

---

74. "Exes"—expropriations, that is, confiscating and requisitioning money from wealthy people for ZOB operations. (Such operations are described in detail in Kazik 1984:39–42 and Carmi and Frimmer 1961:196ff.)

the beginning of that period. It was easier in other cities because they weren't touched yet, they still had a little breathing space left. People began collecting weapons on the Aryan side of Warsaw. We started organizing. Forty-eight hours later, Mordechai Anielewicz entered the ghetto.

When the Jewish Fighting Organization was established on July 28, 1942, it was purely He-Halutz, that is, Ha-Shomer Ha-Tza'ir and us, along with Israel Kanal of Akiba. Nothing was formal; we included in decisions comrades we thought should be included. The "command staff" consisted of Shmuel Braslaw, Yosef Kaplan, Zivia, Mordechai Tennenbaum, and me. Frumka was on the Aryan side by then, Mordechai Anielewicz hadn't arrived yet; we stayed together until everything fell apart on September 3. Then it all had to be reconstructed. Mordechai Anielewicz came in and Arye Wilner went out to the Aryan side. Once again, there were four or five of us. Wilner met with three members of the Polish Scouts. I knew one of them by the name Hajduk, and to this day, I don't know his real name.[75] The second was Hubert Kamiński,[76] who remained alive; and the third was Irena Adamowicz, whose obituary I read in a newspaper six months ago.[77] They knew about the negative attitude of the AK (Armia Krajowa) to us and advised us. The smaller force of the PPR underground, which was understanding and sympathetic to us, had few weapons and, despite its good will, caused us a serious crisis when a group of our fellows who had gone to help them, to join the partisans near Lublin, was captured by the Nazis.[78]

Armia Krajowa (AK), the major force in the Polish underground, not only suspected us but was even hostile to us. Externally, it was disbelief. Instead of saying: "I hate you," it was easier for them to say: "I don't believe you; you don't defend yourself." Later, after the January Uprising, they had another excuse: that is, we were pro-Soviet. After the first Uprising, we heard a lot of praise; then this political pretext of "pro-Soviet" came up. But at this time, it was easy for them to say: "We don't believe you, and we don't have many weapons either; you didn't defend

75. Apparently that was his real last name. He was a member of AK and was killed in the Polish Uprising of 1944.

76. Alexander (Hubert) Kamiński: One of the leaders of the Polish Scouts; was the editor of the major newspaper of the AK, *Biuletyn Informacyjny.* Was sympathetic to ZOB and tried to counter antisemitic tendencies in his own organization. After the war, he was a professor at Łódz University. Died in 1977.

77. This was said in April 1974.

78. This was in August 1942, as Zuckerman describes it in his report to London (Zuckerman 1986:106–107). Mordechai Tennenbaum reported that "the slogans and mottoes of the PPR were meaningless. They weren't waiting, they didn't know, they didn't want to know. All the attempts to dispatch people to groups in the Lublin District—the center of partisan activity—ended in arrest and death." (Quoted in Gutman 1989:241.)

yourselves and went like sheep to the slaughter." The only thing we asked them for was weapons. We told them that, if they gave us weapons, we wouldn't go "like sheep to the slaughter."

Furthermore, Arye Wilner came back to the ghetto and reported to us soon after that his friends in the Scouts had told him that the representatives of the AK wouldn't talk to him because they didn't consider He-Halutz, Dror, and Ha-Shomer Ha-Tza'ir partners for negotiations, but only a youth movement. (His friends in the Scouts could only have been Hubert Kamiński, who later played an important role in the Polish underground and was the editor-in-chief of the AK newspaper, *Information Bulletin*.) If that was how we looked to them, the whole thing could be dead. They pretty much said: You don't really represent the Jews, since you're nothing but "members of a youth movement," and the *Delegatura*, that is, the representatives of the Polish Government-in-Exile, do not talk with youth movements.[79] If they didn't want to give us weapons, they could also use this excuse.

Right after we got this announcement, we sent Wilner back. By then Mordechai Anielewicz was with us. We told Arye Wilner to tell them he represented two institutions: the political institution, the Jewish National Committee (ZKN), which united all forces in the ghetto; and the Jewish Fighting Organization (ZOB), the military arm, which had existed previously but was now reorganized in the ghetto. We agreed to reorganize these institutions so we'd be "covered" in case the Poles began investigating. Wilner went back to the Aryan side and now came to them on behalf of the Jewish National Committee, which in fact didn't yet exist.

We had to appoint another representative, since the Poles weren't likely to accept Wilner. We needed a political representative acceptable to the Polish Delegatura, in touch with underground military blocs, who would deal with acquiring weapons. His operation would have to combine political and social aspects.

We thought Adolf Berman was the right man for that job. He was already outside the ghetto on the Aryan side.[80] So we assigned him the role of representative of the Jewish National Committee. This was opposed by Po'alei Zion Left (his own party). They were mad at him and claimed he didn't ask them when he left the ghetto and didn't get power-of-attorney from them. Sagan wasn't alive by then (he was caught and murdered in a manhunt at the end of August). Berman wasn't the central figure in his party. He had once been one of the directors of CENTOS and now was in hiding, with his wife Batya, on the Aryan side, with the

---

79. The *Delegatura* was the political master of the AK and in virtual control of all Polish underground activity.

80. Berman had left the ghetto on September 5, 1942.

help of Polish friends. His party was mad at him for that, too. In my opinion, that was unfair, since those who didn't leave the ghetto were also in hiding.

In time, I became friendly with him. I didn't accept the criticism leveled at him. He was willing to work and participated in this operation. He had some faults, but he played his part loyally and honorably. He didn't fail us. On the contrary.

Now we had to start organizing the force internally. First, we appealed to all our people in specific districts in the ghetto. It's hard to describe how the ghetto looked now. Many streets were empty and deserted, and it was forbidden to live there. In the Central Ghetto, there were hundreds of empty houses and apartments; it was autumn, at night the windows shifted and banged in the wind, and every word echoed—a real "ghost town." There were the Többens-Schultz shops and there was a labor camp. On the other side, near us, was a wall, and later we found a way through it to the Aryan side. And there was the Brushmakers' Area. That was a time of great activity and meetings with all sorts of political and community groups in the ghetto.

Three problems arose. One concerned the Bund. To this day, I have only a guess, but no documented knowledge about this. The Bund wouldn't appear with us in the same political group and agreed only to coordinate activity with us. In my opinion, that was inherent in the whole Bundist legacy, anchored in their conception of the national problem, which started in 1897. It was all because of the "sins" of Zionism and our "reactionary position," and because of our partnership with "all Jews." The Bund had contacts with only two wings of the PPS. I mention this because of the failure of my own conception which led me to think (even back in March 1942) that we could get to the Poles through the Bund.

As for our position on Jewish representation: we insisted on the Jewish National Committee because it concentrated all the forces (except the Bund). As a result of this situation, we agreed to establish the Jewish Coordinating Committee—ZKK[81] together with the Bund.

The second complication concerned the Jewish Fighting Organization. The Bund agreed to cooperate with the ZOB only in Warsaw and not all over Poland. After we established the Jewish Fighting Organization in July and renewed our outside operations, we saw ourselves as a Jewish fighting organization throughout Poland, whereas they were talking only about Warsaw. To bring them in, two headquarters were created: one for Warsaw, in conjunction with the Bund, and the second headquarters (command staff), hidden and internal, where important decisions were made as well as those concerning all other places (outside of Warsaw); for

81. In Polish: Żydowski Komitet Koordynacyjny—ZKK.

the second part, we had our internal command staff composed only of us and Ha-Shomer Ha-Tza'ir—the staff of He-Halutz. Later, it turned out that this issue of the Coordinating Committee (ZKK) and the Jewish Fighting Organization also solved the problems of cooperation with the PPR [the newly-formed Communist party]; the Jews and the Communists were ready for cooperation, but it was difficult because of their different organizational structure. There wasn't a separate "Jewish PPR" in Poland (nor was there a *Yevsektsiya*, as in the Soviet Union[82]); but there was a Jewish cell of PPR in Warsaw, within the Warsaw branch, and a Jewish cell in Kraków, in the party branch there. But they didn't have a national center for Jewish affairs. When they explained this to us in a friendly way, we understood that they couldn't establish such a national cooperation, but could cooperate only in Warsaw. Therefore, the Coordinating Committee (ZKK) also solved the problem of cooperation with the PPR.

As far as I recall, we didn't hide anything from the PPR and included them in information and issues of the Jewish National Committee (ZKN),[83] since I played a key role in both those organizations. I think they were also candid with us, to a certain extent. We were in touch with Michael Rosenfeld, an engineer, who was in the Jewish Fighting Organization;[84] Edward Fondaminski ("Alexander"), whom I already mentioned, who later asked me if I was the man who was interested in a secret broadcasting transmitter. We developed very good relations. As for our contacts with the Bund, fortunately, the Bund representative was Blum and not Orzech, who wasn't in the ghetto by then. In my estimation, Orzech had been a stumbling block in our relations for a long time.

So, there were two organizations in the ghetto: ZKK, which united the organizations cooperating in the Jewish National Committee plus the Bund and the PPR, as well as ZOB, with two staffs, one for Warsaw and one for all Poland. The Warsaw one was subordinate to the Coordinating Committee, whereas the headquarters of the national ZOB was subordinate to He-Halutz. We didn't report all those arrangements to the Jewish National Committee since there was a time initially when the Revisionists were on the Committee. So were the General Zionists, who were now a body without any power, organization, or outside contacts. We were the only ones involved in decisions concerning parts of Poland outside Warsaw, like Częstochowa, Będzin, and so forth. The members

82. *Yevsektsiya* were the Jewish sections of the propaganda department of the Russian Communist party from 1918 to 1930.

83. Polish—Żydowski Komitet Narodowy—ZKN.

84. Michael Rosenfeld: A graduate of Warsaw University. Active in PPR and a member of the ZOB command staff. He fought in the Central Ghetto in April and escaped through the sewers. He was killed in a clash with the Germans when he was about thirty years old.

of the Warsaw staff didn't know anything about my trip to Kraków, for instance.

I hear that Berlinski's essay says there was a debate about the military network vis-à-vis the political network about which of them had the final authority. He even claims there that we didn't want to give them any of the weapons we got. These accusations are aimed at me since I was in charge of weapons in ZOB. I can say that in no case did I deprive anyone nor did I have a factional attitude in any functions I filled. Those who are still alive, from the Bund to the PPR, can attest to that; I never asked anybody where he came from or what his ideology was, and we didn't have any debates on those matters. I behaved like that later on, too, when I was the only one in charge, whereas here I was the only one of those responsible on the command staff. The sense of deprivation was natural, perhaps, and I too might have felt it, as a unit commander, if I thought that someone got one rifle more than me; but that's absurd, of course. As for the debate about the military network being subordinate to the political network, and the claim that He-Halutz was absolutely opposed to that, I don't understand what that has to do with me.

When Y. L. Peretz Publishers in Tel Aviv issued Berlinski's book,[85] they told me Berlinski talked about me in his memoirs and they asked what to do about it. I told them to print all of it. But when you read it, understand that there are things he didn't know. And there's an explanation for those things. It's easy to check things out in writings of those times. For example, he rejects our claim that the parties didn't do anything. In his opinion, without the parties, ZOB wouldn't have existed, nothing would have existed. And he wrote those things after the fact. Perhaps if we had had to establish an organizational framework in September 1942, I would have been satisfied with the Jewish Fighting Organization. It wasn't we who wanted to set up the inclusive organizational and political framework (ZKN). We were asked to do it by our Polish friends outside. And all the parties, without exception, joined the framework which, as a matter of fact, didn't have any content. But it did exist by then on the Aryan side of Warsaw vis-à-vis the AK and the Delegatura; that is, the Polish civilian authorities knew that a Jewish National Committee existed. It wasn't just a case of persuading the Poles. On the contrary, we had to bring the parties into the ZKN, which didn't exist in fact.

85. Hirsh Berlinski, member of Po'alei Zion Left. His book *Dray* (*Three*), published posthumously by the Ringelblum Institute (Tel Aviv, 1966), was dedicated to three members of Po'alei Zion Left who were killed in the Polish Uprising of 1944 (Paula Elster, Eliahu Ehrlich, and Hirsh Berlinski himself).

By then, Adolf Berman and Arye Wilner were active on the Aryan side, the former on behalf of the Coordinating Committee (ZKK) and the latter on behalf of the military organization. We always attempted to have political issues channeled through the Jewish Coordinating Committee (ZKK) so we and the Bund wouldn't appear separately in general matters. There was no argument on this. Nor did we have an argument with the Poles, since they immediately accepted that. Not that we had much respect for the parties or that we obeyed them blindly. Maybe this dims my own honor, since I was the General Secretary (we didn't have any other rank) of the ZKK and the ZKN, and deputy-commander of the Jewish Fighting Organization. Mordechai Anielewicz was the commander of the Jewish Fighting Organization. This should make it clear that the two institutions were run by two men, the commander of ZOB and the General Secretary of the Jewish National Committee, and there was total cooperation between them.

Maybe Berlinski had arguments with himself or with his party. We weren't involved in such a debate. We were requested by our Polish friends, who wanted to help us, to establish a representative committee. And we called it the Jewish National Committee (ZKN). We established our Jewish National Committee on the model of the National Committee of the *Yishuv* in Eretz Israel.

There was also a middle-stage: a "workers' committee" (*Arbeter-Komitet*), which didn't last. That was in early July. When we despaired of the General Zionist group and the Orthodox community, we tried to set up a joint institution with Po'alei Zion Left, Po'alei Zion–Z.S., and He-Halutz, and that also fell apart. Even Sagan stopped attending meetings a few days before he was caught, because it was too hard for him and the other comrades to come. That was the development that led to the establishment of the Jewish Fighting Organization.

On one of those days, in late September or early October 1942, we collected all the public groups in the Jewish National Committee, the Coordinating Committee, and the Jewish Fighting Organization. All meetings were held either in the pre-dawn darkness or at twilight. Workers in the "shops" also lived there. During working hours, you couldn't move from there. Thousands of laborers worked outside the Central Ghetto, where they lived; they would come and go accompanied by a German guard. Aside from that, it was forbidden to be in the streets of the ghetto. This was September—the Polish autumn and the winter that followed. Before we controlled the streets of the ghetto, Klostermayer[86]

86. Gestapo agent, one of the executioners of the ghetto, who wandered around the streets of the ghetto a great deal terrorizing the inhabitants (Adler 1982:279).

and his buddies would go around in rickshaws in the morning or at dusk, killing whomever they came across.

But let's go back a bit: in the first stages of our activity in the ghetto, we met with various organizations: the Bund, PPR, the General Zionists (their representative was Menakhem Kirshenbaum). Gordonia hadn't yet appeared in Warsaw at that period (we met Geller and his associates for the first time in December 1941 or early January 1942). We also met with the Revisionists, but not in direct negotiations. I went to my first meeting with them through Israel Kanal. One morning, I learned that a few young Betar members were gathered in an apartment; I knew four or five of them. I went to them and said something about us and suggested they join the Jewish Fighting Organization. A few of them were working on the Aryan side of Warsaw. That is, they would go out to various work places on the Aryan side. Negotiations were carried on with Leyb Rodal,[87] an activist in their student groups, and Kagan, who was later the commander of their organization. When we finished negotiations, they joined the Jewish Coordinating Committee (ZKK) and the Jewish Fighting Organization.

A few weeks later, conflicts emerged between them and the other components of the Jewish Fighting Organization. The first source of conflict was that they began carrying on open and separate propaganda in the ghetto and in work places about joining their ranks in the Jewish Fighting Organization. The form of the propaganda and the fact that it was done separately was unacceptable to us. Our problem wasn't a shortage of people, but a shortage of weapons! But that wasn't their problem. It wasn't their fault, but Hitler's, since most of their members were killed, and they were apparently afraid of looking like a small force. The truth was that we all had had casualties and no movement was at full force. The division of who would live and who would die wasn't made on any principle. Some suffered more and some suffered less. We all suffered. By that time, we were no longer a multitude. Many people from the Warsaw branch of our Movement were killed. Even if we count the members of Dzielna and add those from the farm of Czerniaków, who were quite a few—even then, we're not talking about a multitude. I already said that on May Day 1941, in the parade we put on, we had about a thousand able-bodied youths. These were young people who were fifteen years old at the beginning of the war; most of them were killed afterward with their parents. Who remained? Most of the members at

87. Leyb Rodal (1913–1943): Born in Kielce. A devoted adherent of Vladimir Jabotinsky. A Yiddish journalist who contributed to *Moment* in Warsaw and *Der Tog* and *Morgan Journal* in New York. In the ghetto, he was head of the ZZW Information Department. Was killed in the Ghetto Uprising on April 27, 1943.

Dzielna as well as those who were in Czerniaków during the *Aktsia* and came back into the ghetto afterward. Both Ha-Shomer Ha-Tza'ir and the Revisionists, who didn't have any commune at all, suffered many more losses. The religious youth, for example, vanished altogether. That doesn't mean that, somewhere, there weren't five or ten of them; but they weren't seen anymore as an element in the area.

So the Revisionists started conducting open and separate propaganda to join the Jewish Fighting Organization. This terrified us because of the danger that Jewish Gestapo agents would infiltrate the organization; there were such agents left in the ghetto, even after most of the Jewish policemen and collaborators were taken to Treblinka. (That happened on Yom Kippur, September 1942, after *Nie'la*.[88]) We were afraid that all our enemies had to do was track one group of the organization and, instead of our leading the Jews to an uprising, they would lead us to Treblinka. You have to remember that we built the Jewish Fighting Organization on members who were educated in the youth movements or the parties who knew their members and vouched for them. Moreover, we found out that the Revisionists had brought small quantities of weapons into the ghetto and held onto them, not storing them in ZOB warehouses. I should point out that, internally, in the Jewish Fighting Organization, there was no denunciation and no traitors were revealed.

Another source of disagreement between us and the Revisionists was their demand that one of their members be commander of ZOB. They argued that they deserved the position because they had been educated for years in the spirit of Jabotinsky's teachings and were familiar with militarism and were loyal to it. Not one person on our side (including the Bund and the PPR) was willing to agree to this demand, and everyone was united against them.

Because of this, they seceded and set up their own independent organization.[89] I must state here that, except for the Revisionists, the

88. Nie'la is the prayer ending Yom Kippur (which was on September 21 that year).
89. There are, of course, some differences in the accounts of the Revisionists. The Revisionist leader, David Wdowinski, states: "It seemed reasonable to us . . . that in order to have the most effective revolt, the person to head such a united fighting front should be one who was best suited for that command from a military point of view. The other group [ZOB] insisted that it be a political leader, and of course, one of their ranks. In addition, they wanted the Betarim to join the organization as individuals, not as a group" (Wdowinski 1985:79). Apparently, the latter point was the most important source of disagreement. Adam Halperin, deputy-commander of the Betar cell in north Warsaw, writes that the leadership of ZOB "didn't want to accept Betar as a federation within the ranks of the general organization. This right, which all other Jewish federations enjoyed was not granted to Betar. Members of Betar were given the possibility of being accepted into the organization only as isolated individuals but not as an organized, unified bloc" (Blumenthal and Kermish 1965:157). Haim Lazar also cites an ideological difference as fundamental; according to

ghetto was organized militarily and politically in the ZOB and the ZKK. There were few Revisionists, and they enrolled people in their organization who weren't members of their movement, as well as those who hadn't gotten to our ZOB precisely because we were deep underground.

After the January (1943) Uprising, in the period defined by an atmosphere of preparations for war, separate "wildcat groups" of unorganized people who wanted to fight the Germans began surfacing. Some of those wildcat groups wanted to exploit the conditions of "Mexico,"[90] with weapons and violence, in order to get rich at the expense of the Jews. They would attack and rob Jewish houses, representing themselves as the Jewish Fighting Organization and, under this aegis, would perform their robberies. We started a war against the wildcat groups and destroyed them, both by negotiations and force. We brought the good ones, the idealists among them, into the Jewish Fighting Organization. Some members of those groups who later fought in ZOB are here in Israel.

So before January 1943, there were two fighting organizations, characterized by a specific and different mentality in the ghetto: ZOB and the Revisionist group [ZZW]. I conducted negotiations with the Revisionist group after they had set up their own organization. I was with them alone a few times, and with Zivia a few times. Later, after I left the ghetto, Zivia told me she continued meeting with them, along with Mordechai Anielewicz, as I recall. We met them in an empty apartment with no distinguishing features. Our orders forbade keeping weapons out in the open because of expected searches, and we learned that they were openly keeping weapons right in that apartment. This was demonstratively expressed when, in honor of a visit by Emmanuel Ringelblum, they held an armed review of their units.[91] This wasn't the mountains or the forest, but the city, in a movement that was supposed to be underground. Their display was exceptional even among the Poles [who had plenty of weapons]; you couldn't find such a thing.

Our explicit ban on keeping weapons out in the open grew out of some surprise searches made by the Germans in the Brushmakers' area and in

---

him, revolt was "solely for national reasons," while for the ZOB, there was an additional "political and ideological character of their organization which stood for anti-Fascism" (Lazar 1963:197). Of course, there was a larger background to this tension. The Revisionists had seceded from the World Zionist Organization; and, before the war, all socialist movements, including the Zionists, saw them as a Jewish embodiment of Fascism.

90. Nickname of the Central Ghetto, abandoned to acts of plunder and robbery by thugs and profiteers.

91. In Ringelblum's testimony of his visit to Revisionist headquarters, he tells of his impression of the demonstration and the show of various kinds of weapons made in his honor. Ringelblum was not a military man and did not understand weapons (Ringelblum 1986:596–597).

the Többens-Schultz area, apparently on the basis of information they received. After that, eight of our units went underground, whereas the Revisionists openly kept weapons in their apartment. Ringelblum was impressed with the sight of their units coming in and taking weapons. This is not intended to diminish their role or their contribution to the Jewish struggle. Nevertheless, their behavior was arrogant and exhibitionistic, which didn't fit the circumstances.

One of the problems that arose was that of the joint staff. Not the internal (national) staff in the He-Halutz structure; there were no problems there: the heads of Dror and Ha-Shomer Ha-Tza'ir continued to serve on the command staff. I often have been asked why Mordechai Anielewicz was commander of ZOB and not me. The answer is that I could have been the commander without any problem. There were elements in the ghetto who wanted that, for example, my friend Abrasha Blum of the Bund, who was a member of ZKK. (Their first representative in ZOB was Berek Shneidmil, who was much older than us and had nothing in common with us.)[92] Mordechai Anielewicz wanted to be commander of the ZOB and was fit for it in every respect. He believed in his own strength and he was ambitious. He proposed himself for the job at the staff meeting, and I gladly accepted it, even though there had previously been talk about me being commander. As far as we were concerned, it didn't matter whether the commander was Mordechai Anielewicz or me, because no decision was made in ZOB without meetings and discussions. (Incidentally, at that period, Zivia, who wasn't formally a member of the Warsaw command staff, also participated in discussions and her considered opinions carried weight.) Schneidmil resigned, and the Bund replaced him with Marek Edelman.[93] Later, on the Aryan side of Warsaw, we became friends. He was candid with me and told me that the first order he got from Abrasha Blum was to watch me at the command staff meeting, and vote as I did. I had no reason not to be frank with him or not to consult with him and tell him about things, even those that had nothing to do with the Bund. After all, what did we discuss and argue about? All the important issues were general, common Jewish ones.

92. Berek Schneidmil: Born in Łódz. A member of the Bund Central Committee. Was killed in the Central Ghetto during the April Uprising, about forty years old. According to his fellow Bundist Bernard Goldstein, "he did everything with enthusiasm—party work, studying military strategy and tactics, mountain climbing. There was a cynical twist to his witty, carefree, bantering manner, but at the same time he was an incurable romantic. . . . His socialism, too was romantic. He had no interest in weighty Marxist doctrines. . . . You could depend on Berek" (Goldstein 1961:50–51).

93. Marek Edelman: Born in Warsaw. Was active in the Bund from his youth. Was a member of ZOB command staff and commander of the Brushmakers' Ghetto in the April Uprising. Escaped through the sewers to Aryan Warsaw and fought in the Polish Uprising. Is currently a cardiologist in Łódz.

Other issues were exceptional and artificial. Marek Edelman, Bund representative in ZOB, was a noble man.[94] Sometimes, after a meeting, he would look for a chance to stay and talk about other things. We became friends, as I said, and he would sometimes stay overnight with us. When we wound up on the Aryan side, we sought each other out and worked closely together.

Mordechai Anielewicz came into the ghetto a few days after the end of the Great *Aktsia*, between September 13 and 14; when Arye Wilner left for the Aryan side, he met him there. Anyway, the ZOB command staff wasn't an institution like a "shadow cabinet," but a real cabinet of three or four people who met every day and made decisions. Sometimes Miriam Heinsdorf would also sit in; we included her in our meetings because she had been close to Yosef Kaplan. She was a little older than us. Tosia Altman also participated sometimes; but Zivia, Mordechai, and I met almost every day. If Arye Wilner happened to come into the ghetto, he would also join the discussion. At one of these meetings, we decided I would be secretary of the Jewish Coordinating Committee. This was brought up at the meeting of the Jewish National Committee, and it was the only proposal that no one opposed, except the Revisionists. And they would been against anyone who wasn't one of them because they argued that they were closer to militarism and "naturally" deserved the job of commander. The Coordinating Committee was the civilian-political arm, which naturally commanded the military arm. How the man who decided political issues could also be the deputy-commander of the military staff—God only knows!

As commander of ZOB, Mordechai, like me, also sat on the Jewish National Committee and on the Coordinating Committee. There was a collective presidency, and I was General Secretary in both bodies, as I said—I headed them, whereas Mordechai was the commander in ZOB, and my commander, that is, commander of whoever was head of the political arm. According to accepted organizational practice, it should have been the other way around; but under those conditions, there was no particular virtue to the division of roles. It didn't occur to us that something was wrong here. Only after the January Uprising did it assume an ideological aspect.

The Coordinating Committee convened only a few times. *The four days of the January Uprising*[95] were decisive for the pattern of operation and, as for the January 18 Uprising, the principles of the organization forbade starting operations against the Germans without a decision of the Jewish

94. Translator's note: This is a pun—"Edelman" means "noble man."
95. In time, the four days beginning with January 18, 1943, took on the name of the "January Uprising."

Coordinating Committee: as head of the Committee, I would probably have called a meeting of that committee; but it wasn't possible given the circumstances. Now, in hindsight, I think that if a meeting of the Committee had been called, the Uprising wouldn't have happened. Because they would probably have started hesitating. In fact, the force was established back in July, without authorization of the political committee. After the January Uprising, there were actually a few hundred fighters; they began buying and transporting weapons: ten pistols, a few grenades, and other things were acquired somewhere.

In the first period, which was quite long (from the end of September, October, and November), Zivia and I lived with members of Ha-Shomer Ha-Tza'ir at Miła 63; later, we decided to concentrate our people in the area of the *Umschlagplatz,* because, to get there, the Germans leading the Jews to the transport site had to go through a few streets, including Miła Street. So we always wanted to concentrate in the streets on the way to the *Umschlagplatz,* in order to hinder the Germans in carrying out their scheme. If they had taken another route, they would have had to go through the whole city. They went the usual, simplest way. From our position at Zamenhof 56, we could control the *Umschlagplatz.* Our idea was to capture key positions in the streets leading to the transport site. From our quarters on the top floors, we could see what was done in the transport site.

We didn't yet have bunkers. On the contrary, we had an emotional opposition to bunkers. Nevertheless, we encouraged the activists and Jews in general to build bunkers for themselves. There were a few people, one in particular, who wasn't an engineer, but who understood that undertaking very well. There were also Jewish engineers who built bunkers for money. We weren't involved in that. We knew better places than bunkers for hiding weapons, and you didn't have to requisition whole rooms for that. We saw our job as fighting the Germans, which was to end by being killed in battle. We prepared to fight from the roofs. We were afraid that if we had a bunker, someone would panic during the fighting and retreat to the bunker. We made mistakes consciously and deliberately because it never occurred to us that any of us would remain alive after the April Uprising. But when people did remain alive after the Uprising, we faced problems we couldn't solve.

Our first plan was to take up key positions in the Central Ghetto, on streets leading to the transit site. However, until January, in the Brushmakers' area, people were practically not organized. The January Uprising taught us the need for organization. Fighters scattered around an area, not organized in groups, can be caught off guard. Like the lessons of war that generals learn too late, the events of July taught us how to prepare for January. In July, the Germans had put out announcements declaring that nothing would happen; and suddenly, before dawn, the Jews were surrounded by them; prior to January, in September and October 1942, we thought there would be a sign to alert our people. But, in the January Uprising, the people who weren't in designated places ("communes" or kibbutzim) in time didn't even get to the weapons and didn't participate in the Uprising at all.

We thought that the people in the Brushmakers' area and Többens-Schultz should be with us, concentrated in communes; but, in fact, they were scattered. Not many members of Po'alei Zion Left took part in the January Uprising. Ten all in all. Bund members, who numbered a few score altogether, didn't fight in January; not because they didn't want to, but because they couldn't. In fact, I couldn't get in touch with Mordechai Anielewicz then either. The people I sent couldn't get through to him by then. Orders weren't carried out and remained a dead letter. The lesson for April was that we shouldn't rely on a central headquarters to direct the battles.

A long time before the January Uprising, there was development. The Revisionists left the organization. And we started organizing groups. I got up every day at dawn because, until January, the government in the ghetto was in the hands of the Germans, the police, and the Judenrat, and you had to take advantage of the few hours in the morning for meetings and finding and organizing people in ZOB units, not only those at Miła 63 and later at Zamenhof 56, but also other people who had to be found and organized into groups. And we had to set up the skeleton of the ZOB. Mordechai Anielewicz, Zivia, and I were involved in that.

As for financial means, during and after the *Aktsia* in September we went with Zivia to look for Dr. Yitzhak Schipper. We also met with Giterman and Guzik of the Joint. We were hungry. You could buy bread or groats then, through people who went out to work. But our pockets were empty and Giterman and Schipper gave us money. Schipper gave a large sum. Before the January Uprising, in some debate with Schipper and Giterman, Gancwajch's name was mentioned. That terrified me. Gancwajch was on the Aryan side at that time and, at that meeting, Giterman told me he was trying to organize the cadres in the ghetto for an uprising and was willing to get hold of weapons and money. When I heard this, I threatened that that would be my last meeting with them if they continued to maintain contacts with Gancwajch. Schipper responded that we also took money from Gancwajch. I was stunned and asked: "When?" And he said: "When you came with Zivia, I gave you Gancwajch's money." Apparently, he had gotten the money from him.

In those days, we would send people to collect Jewish property left in the empty houses, and we would sell it. Ha-Shomer Ha-Tza'ir members worked in Landau's shop, which had permission to grow vegetables in the

Jewish cemetery. On the way there, they would go into the houses, gather up clothing, sheets, shirts, and such, sell it to Polish smugglers, and put the money in the general treasury. We were hungry, but hunger isn't the main thing that remains in my memory from this time. The hunger of 1941 remains etched in my memory, more than the hunger of this period. In this period, we lived on such exciting things that we forgot about hunger.

So by selling these objects and with the financial aid we got from Giterman and Guzik of the Joint, we got money to purchase weapons. (Later on, when we ruled the ghetto, we disposed of a lot of money, millions of Złotys we got from "Exes."[96] We also took care of other cities.

One day, we got information from our members in Kraków. The dominant force there was Akiba; but there were also members of Dror and Ha-Shomer Ha-Tza'ir. At that time, Laban was still with us; we rescued him from prison at the start of the *Aktsia*. The first chance we got, when we sent a group to Czerniaków, we got him out with them so he could return to Kraków to organize the people there. Now a messenger arrived with an urgent call to come; Arye Wilner went there but came back a few days later. The people of Kraków were mainly members of Akiba and didn't know Arye Wilner or Laban. Dolek Liebeskind[97] and Shimon Drenger[98] asked for me. Arye was a bit offended by his reception in Kraków; he told me that they had suffered a collapse in the ghetto. That was around December 1942. The ghetto in Kraków was small and when the Jewish police and the Judenrat got on the track of our people, Liebeskind and Drenger escaped to the Aryan side of the city.[99] They had prepared a big operation against the Germans, and we had discussed it privately. They had a few weapons, and their system was to attack individual Germans on the street and take their weapons. In our private discussion about this in the Warsaw command staff, we were unanimous that all our fighting forces should not be put on the Aryan side of Kraków without leaving forces for the struggle within the ghetto. Such tactics had to count on at least a 50 percent chance of failure, and afterward, there wouldn't be a force to fight inside the ghetto. With this position, I set out

96. See above.

97. Dolek (Aharon) Liebeskind: Born in Kraków. Was active in the Jewish underground; one of the founders and commanders of ZOB in Kraków. Was killed in a battle with the Gestapo at the age of thirty. Both Zivia Lubetkin and Reuben Ainsztein describe ZOB operations in Kraków in some detail. (See Lubetkin 1981:137–144; Ainsztein 1974: 832–843.)

98. Shimon Drenger: One of the leaders of Akiba and ZOB commander in Kraków. He was the editor of the prewar Akiba journal, *Divrei Akiba,* and of *He-Halutz Ha-Lohem.* He was captured by the Gestapo in January 1943 and escaped on April 24, 1943. He was killed in the autumn of 1943 by the Gestapo at the age of twenty-seven.

99. The entire episode is told in Gusta Davidson, *Justina's Diary,* 1953:83–85.

for Kraków to do everything to make the ZOB members based on the Aryan side go back to the ghetto, after they executed whomever they had to execute, terrified the Judenrat and the police, and gained a lull for themselves in the ghetto. Certain operations on the Aryan side should be done with the participation of Polish forces, since this cooperation could win us trust, weapons, and perhaps cooperation in times of trouble in the future.

What really happened? When I set out, I didn't know the exact dates or plans of the anticipated operation. Wilner didn't bring detailed information when he returned from Kraków, and my knowledge was very general. As for how I got out, as I said, by September, I wound up in the *Umschlagplatz* a few times. One day, I decided that Miriam Heinsdorf and I would join the groups collecting Jewish property in the empty houses in the ghetto. Those groups would leave from Leszno Street, where Jews still lived, pass through the empty streets and "clean" the houses. This operation of collecting property was discussed both in the command staff of ZOB and in the Coordinating Committee, and I was assigned to join. Kirshenbaum said he had a friend in some shop and talked to him about it, and I was given a note to him. So I was sent with one of the groups to collect Jewish property. Hundreds of us left to collect property. The Germans gave us wagons and some other vehicles. They had ordered this operation to send the property to Germany. In general, the Germans would come only to search us, whereas the entire operation was done by Jewish workers and supervisors.

There was a redhead there, an excellent organizer, who tried hard to get everything done safely. Things went on like this for a few days, until I managed to convince a group of young Jews to break whatever they could, and they did indeed destroy a lot. I myself would walk around like a madman, with stones and a stick, breaking furniture, china, and such. I was afraid some bastard among the collectors would denounce me. I joined this group because Kirshenbaum said it was a way to get a pass to walk around freely, like all members of the group. After I got the permit, I left the group. In the group of collectors of property, I worked under the aegis of a Jewish supervisor who seemed consciously to ignore what I was doing. (Incidentally, in one of the empty houses, I found a library. On the bed was the shriveled corpse of a person who had died a natural death, or might have been shot. In that library, I found three volumes of S. Y. Agnon published in Berlin, and I took them.[100] It was the library of an educated person, and I would occasionally take books from there. At night I would read Agnon. I had known Agnon's works,

100. Shmuel Yosef Agnon (1888–1970): Hebrew writer; received the 1966 Nobel Prize for Literature.

but not all of them, from before. I held onto these volumes for a long time.) This time, when I left the ghetto for Kraków, I used the permit I had gotten. I crossed the whole area with it, and, if I came upon a German checkpoint, my permit helped.

Thus I got to the Aryan side where Havka Folman was waiting for me. She was then on a mission for us on the Aryan side and on duty in Warsaw and throughout the Generalgouvernement. Irena Adamowicz was also waiting for me, and we made our way to their apartment. I even remember the borscht I ate there.

Havka's brother's family lived in that apartment in Zolibórz; he himself was in a partisan unit by then. The mother, the brother's wife, and children were there. I left with Havka, who accompanied me in the early evening to the Kraków train. Of course I traveled as an Aryan because, by then, Jews couldn't move around. I had a very bad Aryan document, and if I had been caught, they wouldn't have had to examine it very much to prove it was a forgery. At that time, I didn't yet plan to identify myself permanently as an Aryan. We had contacts on the Aryan side of Kraków, that is, a woman courier who was supposed to tell Laban I was coming; but it turned out that the contact wouldn't take place until afternoon.

We got off the train in Kraków and went into a café for breakfast. Then, we approached the place where we had arranged to meet, and we waited. We decided to go into the cinema, I think that was the first time I went to a German movie. They were showing some bourgeois tragedy we didn't even look at. The important thing was to pass the time until the meeting.

At the meeting with Laban, we realized that activities against the Germans were scheduled for that very night, and everything was ready.[101] If I had known about that in time, I would have come sooner; but I didn't know anything and it was only by chance that I came exactly on the day scheduled for the operations.

I quickly realized that all the operations were supposed to be carried out only on the Aryan side of Kraków. Kraków was the capital of the Generalgouvernement, where Generalgoverneur Frank had his office. The city was full of Germans. The plan of action was: (1) to throw grenades at the Cyganerja Café and at another café frequented by German officers;[102] (2) to set fire to a few garages; (3) to distribute proclamations in the name of the Polish underground; (4) to take weapons from Germans. Along with the ZOB members, a group of PPR pillars in the city, also Jews, were assigned to take part in this operation. That is, it was a purely Jewish action. The entire Jewish fighting force was to participate

101. That was December 22, 1942.
102. There were two other cafés involved, the Esplanada and the Zakopianka.

in those activities, with their base on the Aryan side; everything was to be carried out in one night and not in the name of ZOB, but in the name of the Polish underground. For if they had appeared in their own name, it would have led to acts of retaliation in the ghetto and would have endangered ZOB. My attempts to prevent the activity were in vain. The debate was fiery, and very angry, but nothing helped since I couldn't change a thing by then. I demanded that they send at least one or two of their people back to the ghetto to execute members of the Judenrat and the Jewish police, as they saw fit. One or two of those were among the few survivors of ZOB in Kraków.

When he came to meet me, Laban was wearing a German army uniform and holding a large package of weapons: grenades and pistols to distribute to the fighters; we went by cab from Laban's house, where Germans also lived, and the doorman was a Pole who cooperated with ZOB. Laban lived in the cellar of that house. The doorman, who had a German document, knew that Laban was a Jew and hid him. Our weapons had to be moved from that house to the concentration point of the force waiting to go into action on the Aryan side of Kraków. Since it was early, we decided we would meet at five at a certain place; Havka and I were supposed to go by cab to the concentration point of the main force, on the Aryan side, in a former Jewish hospital on Skawinska 24, which was now empty.

We arrived at that hospital in a cab. We were traveling openly. I looked like a rural Polish nobleman. I wore a three-quarter length coat, a hat, jodphurs stuffed into boots, a moustache. By the way, Germans or collaborators wore boots, and these boots saved me later on. My Aryan identity wasn't in doubt. Havka also looked Aryan. My looks and my clothing, which was like a uniform, were those of a person in a specific military formation in the internal German government in Kraków. However, it was hard to disguise Laban as a gentile. When we approached the alley where the house was, we asked the driver to wait for us. He waited and we first went into the alley, which was empty, and then through a long corridor, to the hospital. We found the fighters in two rooms on the right. Laban explained the missions to the squads and what had to be done, distributed the grenades and pistols, chose the head courier, determined an information center, and told them how to disperse. He ordered them not to stick their nose outside for forty-eight hours after the action. Aside from that group gathered in the hospital, a few other groups were in other places. Only the courier appeared that evening to get information. Havka was assigned to stay in the hospital because I was to meet with Laban and Dolek Liebeskind that night, in the hope that everything would end well. Shimon Drenger wasn't in Kraków then; he was in Bochnia. We were supposed to discuss a change in Kraków, aimed at returning the Jewish fighting force to the ghetto. We went back to the cellar of the German house where Laban lived. It might sound funny but, as soon as I got involved in underground matters, I decided that commanders should know only what they had to know and, for a long time, I wasn't interested and didn't want to know things I didn't need to know directly. I didn't want to know names of people, where they lived, and so forth. So when I entered that house, I didn't notice either the name of the street or the number of the house. I paid dearly for that in the next forty-eight hours, but it saved me later on.

At the appointed time, the courier appeared and told of extraordinary success. But we didn't know then that there were two collaborators in the Kraków ZOB who had joined Akiba. Nor did we know that one of the fellows they denounced, Menakhem Bigelman, had been wounded in the operation and captured by the Germans.

It was some time before we knew exactly what had happened. From the courier's story, we knew only that the operation had succeeded, that the people had returned to their bases. But that same night, after the action, those two provocateurs turned us in. I can't explain why they hadn't turned us in before the action. It would never have occurred to me that two Jewish fellows, members of the movement or of ZOB would do such a thing[103]—even though I have more than a suspicion that I too was once denounced (in April 1942) by a girl from Ha-Shomer Ha-Tza'ir. This time, it was two fellows from Akiba. This was confirmed by the members of Akiba themselves, who knew them and had apparently concluded that these two had turned them in; they had even published their names.

The main action was carried out in the Cyganerja Café. Our fighters threw grenades and killed the Germans sitting there. With my own eyes I saw the Mauser in the hand of the fellow who took it from the dead Gestapo agent. Others did the same. They also set fire to a garage and distributed announcements on behalf of the Polish underground—all according to plan. That night, we got together and drank a toast to the success of the operation.

After the meeting with the courier, Laban came back downstairs with me, along with Dolek Liebeskind who lived with his parents somewhere else, and came to spend the night with us. We had a very sharp conversation. They accepted my demand to do everything necessary to go back to the ghetto. The next day, Laban, as commander of the operation, had to meet with the courier again. I think they set a meeting for 10 o'clock. That morning the Polish doorman, who was a friend of ZOB and who was

---

103. The denouncers who joined Akiba in Kraków were Yulek Appel and Natan Weissman.

keeping Laban hidden, told us there was a great turmoil in Kraków and the curfew had been advanced to six instead of eleven, the normal curfew. The residents of Kraków were also threatened. At the appointed time, the courier didn't appear. Because of the uproar in the city and the instructions to the fighters "not to put their nose outside," we didn't sense anything unusual in the courier's failure to show up. When he came back, Laban told of the great panic in the city, especially among the Germans. The tenants of the house he lived in were Germans. The operations made a strong impression, since Kraków had been a quiet city until then. And now right in Kraków, such a big and well-coordinated operation had been carried out.

I sat with Laban, who had to go to the hospital at 5 o'clock. I joined him to meet with the fighters and congratulate them. We again rode in a carriage; Havka had remained there all night since she wasn't supposed to participate in my meeting with the Kraków command staff. (I might also mention that we had also sent a Warsaw squad to reinforce the ZOB in Kraków.) As we approached the abandoned hospital, we got out of the cab and asked the driver to wait for us. As we proceeded, we noticed a few people at the end of the alley. That didn't mean a thing to me, but Laban remarked that he was suspicious of something. He led me through a big park. Behind the trees, there was a big building where the command staff of the SS or the Gestapo was located. Laban walked ahead. We entered the long corridor of the hospital which, at that time—5 o'clock in the evening—was completely dark.

We took a few steps in the long corridor and suddenly a flashlight beam came toward us: "*Halt, Hände rauf!* (Halt, hands up!)" They could see me but I couldn't see them. It was a terrifying moment. Instead of putting up my hands, I dashed to the door. I saw someone make a futile attempt to open a door handle by pushing it instead of pulling it down. I pulled down the handle, the door opened, and I burst out into the park, and from there to the alley. After five steps, I began to feel warmth and a sharp pain in my leg. I didn't have to grope around too much to prove I was bleeding. I didn't know where I was hit. Nevertheless, everything else was crystal clear. I wish I could be so cool today. I remembered our entrance into the alley, the young men at the end of the alley, and Laban's remark that he felt something wasn't right here. I understood that I had been shot, but I hadn't heard it. I was hit in the back of my leg, the scars are still there. I didn't have anywhere to escape. To hide under the bush in the park was naïve. I understood that the Germans would have to take care of Laban first. Then I took out a cigar (the group had bought cigars in my honor in the evening), lit it, and very slowly walked to the end of the alley. The carriage was waiting. I was afraid to go to it. I tried with all my might to protect my leg, I felt I was losing the strength to drag it.

So I came out of the alley and started walking through the streets of the city.

That was Christmas Eve. Everyone was hurrying and I blended into the passers-by. I stopped a moment to read announcements. I didn't have anywhere to go. I had a good memory but, since I had decided not to look at the name of the street or the number of that cellar we had come from, I didn't know where to return now and I cursed myself for that.

What happened inside, in the corridor, I didn't know then. I don't know if they thought I was one of the underground or didn't suspect me at all. Only after the war did I learn the details. Those were Germans, who continued waiting and watching for twenty-four hours after the encounter with us. They apparently thought more underground members would come. And in fact, a fellow named Poldek did go there in the uniform of a Jewish policeman; he told us what happened there afterward. They didn't shoot him since he was dressed as a Jewish policeman.

So I started walking in the street. I felt very weak. My trousers were soaked with blood. Fortunately, I was wearing boots and the blood flowed into my boot. I didn't know what to do; you could walk in the street only until six at night, and I guessed it was now a few minutes after five, since the whole thing had lasted only a few minutes. I walked without knowing where; there were fewer people in the street. Everyone was hurrying home before curfew. Suddenly, I saw a church and went in. The priest was in his confessional hearing someone say confession. I sat near the entrance and waited. When the person left, I remained alone with the priest. By now it was close to six. I had decided to appeal to him. I approached him and told him I was wounded and asked for first aid and water and, if possible, to spend the night there. He replied that he couldn't take the risk and insisted I leave the church. I left without knowing where to go. Suddenly I saw a doctor's sign in Polish. I decided that this doctor was probably a patriot since, in German Kraków, if a doctor didn't advertise in German also, he probably wasn't interested in German patients. I decided to go in. I rang the bell and, when people came out, they saw at once that I was wounded. I asked for help and was told the doctor wasn't in. I didn't move. It was 6 o'clock. The concierge came out and saw I was wounded, but she didn't ask me a thing and didn't say a word. Meanwhile, two young men came out of the doctor's apartment and told me they were willing to take me to the ghetto in a cab. I don't know what language I spoke, maybe Yiddish; at any rate, I felt dizzy. I said they could take me to the Gestapo in a cab, but I wasn't moving from here. The gate was closed, I sat down on the steps in the corridor; and then the two fellows came back and put a bandage on my wound.

I sat there like that for about an hour. I lost any sense of time. I remember only that I kept having chills and fever. A while later, the concierge came back and put a sack on me. Children appeared and one of them brought me a holiday cookie and all kinds of food. I didn't take anything, except some black bread and milk one child brought me.

As I sat like that, I heard one man say that they had to do something, and a second one answered: "Let him stay till morning. He's lost a lot of blood and isn't getting medical aid. He'll die anyway." Later, everything fell silent and I remained alone in the corridor. It was December, it was cold and dark. I covered up with the sack. Before morning, someone took the sack off me. It was the concierge. Seeing me alive, she burst into tears and asked me not to make any noise. She helped me up and took me into her apartment. I remember she said: "Hard times, we're turning into wolves." She put me in the one bed in the room, took the boot off one leg, but couldn't move the other boot. She gave me something to eat, and I fell asleep. I lay like that until the next evening. She brought me something to eat. Meanwhile, she wept and told me her son was supposed to come for the holiday. She was afraid of him, and had no choice, and she asked me not to be angry at her; the neighbors didn't know I was there, since she had told them all that she had opened the gate before dawn and I was still alive. She brought me a stick and asked me to leave.

I walked away, leaning on the stick, until I came to the Kraków railroad station which was full of Germans. I sat down right across from a cripple on crutches. I dreamed of pulling the crutches away from him. And as I sat meditating, Germans appeared and began snatching people for work. They snatched me, too, but since I didn't have the strength to walk, I lagged behind and remained in back all the time. They didn't pay attention to me, so I stayed behind and hid in the railroad station, waiting for the train to Warsaw. Fortunately, the train was dark and almost empty. I sank onto a bench and, before dawn, I arrived in Warsaw. The driver of the tram I rode from the railroad station pointed to my legs which were covered with blood. One pants leg was completely red. I answered that a piece of iron had fallen on my leg. He wished me a happy new year and I got off the tram and approached the gates of the ghetto.

The area around the gates of the ghetto was unpopulated. There was a hospital only for gentiles and you could go through it to the ghetto. Three people were standing at the gates: a German gendarme and two policemen, one Jewish and one Polish. I decided to start talking with the Polish policeman. I told him that my wife had just had a baby boy and I wanted to go into the hospital to visit her. He hinted that if I gave him some money, he wouldn't turn me in. I asked how much and he mentioned a sum he had to split with the German gendarme and "the Yid, so he won't denounce us." I gave him the money, and told him that, if Germans approached, I would go into some courtyard and, from the distance, no one would see.

The Polish policeman started talking with the German gendarme. Ultimately, they decided to give me one hour in the hospital. Because, they warned me, the guard changed in an hour, and if I didn't come out in an hour, I wouldn't be able to get out at all. They even accompanied me to the entrance. Once inside, I seized my chance, slipped away, and was in the Többens-Schultz area. I saw a traveling cart, sat down on it, and reached Leszno 56.

Until the moment I entered the building, I held up; as soon as I entered—we had an apartment near the entrance of the building—I saw Zivia and Marek Folman. They told me later that, at that moment, I looked like a seventy-year-old man, wrinkled, and covered with blood. I managed to say only, "It's all lost," and then I fainted.

They took off my clothes, but they couldn't move the boot from my wounded leg, which was full of dried blood. Then Marek cut the boot with scissors and wanted to bring a doctor. They brought Berman, Adolf Berman's brother, who was a doctor and a member of Po'alei Zion–Z.S., but he wasn't active in the party. He examined me and stated that whoever had shot me only wanted to wound and not to kill, since apparently he wanted to take me alive. Whoever had shot, he said, was a professional, since the bullet didn't hit the bone; if it had, I wouldn't have remained alive. But I had lost a lot of blood and had a very high fever. He asked me where it happened and I told him on Leszno Street. I said that, coming out of the ghetto, a German had shot me. He asked where I hid and I pointed to a place about 100 meters from the "site of the shooting." He replied that it was hard for him to believe you could walk 100 meters on a leg like that. He didn't know it had been forty-eight hours since the shot. I was very weak until my fever went down.

Zivia said I was saved by the "iron cords" I had for bones. I say that because I don't have "iron cords" anymore. When I reconstruct the event, I realize that I was aware that Laban was captured as soon as we returned to the abandoned hospital since he was ahead of me in the hospital corridor. He didn't try to escape, whereas I was wounded and escaped. He was only one step ahead of me; I saw him put his hands up; and, at that minute, I dashed back to the door. I knew there would always be time to put your hands up. Of course, anyone who plays such games is liable to get a bullet.

All our ZOB members in Kraków who were involved in that attack on German officers in Cyganerja, including Havka Folman, were soon arrested in various places in the city. A few years ago, we got our hands on a Gestapo report from Kraków, sent to Berlin, which mentions Abraham Leibowicz (Laban). According to this report, recorded during his interrogation, it was he who gave his address, where they caught Dolek Liebeskind. I question the truth of those things for several reasons: Laban had lived on the Aryan side of Kraków for a few months. He had Aryan documents, and his name and address were also registered as such in the document. Moreover he couldn't have turned in Dolek Liebeskind because Dolek didn't live in the same place. Dolek simply remained in Laban's apartment, waiting for us, since he didn't know what happened to us. And he was trapped in that apartment whose address was on Laban's documents. So Laban couldn't have added anything to it.

As for me, I learned a lesson: later I had better documents, in the name of Stanisław Bagniewski; and my papers said I lived on Belwederska Street. If they had caught me, it would have been easy to prove I wasn't registered there. But it was different with Laban. Usually, the real address of our couriers and comrades who looked Aryan were registered in their documents. The same was true of Zivia and Marek Edelman, Luba Gewisser[104] and others. I was the exception—I was afraid that others would be caught with me if I was captured. So in my document I registered the former address of the real Stanisław Bagniewski who had passed away.

Havka Folman had Aryan documents. She was held in the women's wing of Montalupych Prison. She kept claiming that she wasn't a Jew, even though she had been captured with Jews. So they didn't execute her but took her to Auschwitz, where she was kept with the Poles, which is what saved her. Like Lonka who was killed, she was often a step away from death, but she held out. We made many futile attempts to get her out.

You can imagine my mood when I returned to Warsaw without Havka, my feeling toward her mother, my comrades, myself. We knew that all the comrades in that building in Kraków were arrested. Havka was arrested ten hours before we fell into the ambush at the hospital; I got there at 5 o'clock and she had been arrested the night before, because of the denunciation of the two fellows who told everything they knew about us.

Our fighters were caught in the hospital and in other places afterward. They were held by the Gestapo and tortured; they included Shimon Drenger, who hadn't been at the meeting, and Gusta Drenger, who left us the diary (*Justina's Diary*). When she was in prison, she dictated chapters of her diary to her fellow prisoners, most of them members of Akiba, but there were also Communist girls. They recorded what she said and hid it under the doorsill, in the oven, and other places. They got one copy out; it was written on toilet paper folded into triangles. This diary reached us after the war. Gusta turned herself in, after her husband, Shimon Drenger, was captured. You could say it was an anticonspiratorial act that

104. Luba Gewisser (b. 1924): Born in Warsaw. Left the ghetto during the Great *Aktsia* in summer 1942. Served as ZOB courier on the Aryan side of Warsaw and in other places. Lives in Tel Aviv.

didn't do any good, but she couldn't get over her love, the solidarity with her husband.

Havka was taken to Auschwitz, the others were apparently taken to Plaszów to be executed. They were forced to lie on the floor of a closed car guarded by Germans. Laban tried to organize an escape as they were taken. He was to signal by whistling. Apparently, they had a razor blade with which they cut the tarpaulin and jumped out. Some were captured, others were killed on the spot, and some also managed to escape. They caught Laban alive, took him to Plaszów, and executed him. According to the testimony received after his death, near the shoulder of his coatsleeve, the Jews found a hidden note with the words: "I'm a Jew." He was afraid that, because of his Aryan documents, he would be buried as a gentile, and he wanted to be buried as a Jew. Those who witnessed his execution in Plaszów read the note. Havka, who was kept in Auschwitz as a gentile, said years later that she had met Lonka Kozibrodska and Bella Hazan there.[105]

Lonka managed to toss a note when she was captured and taken to prison, and a fellow from Korczak's orphanage brought it to the commune on Dzielna. He told us she was arrested and taken to Pawiak, the big prison in Warsaw. From there, she was taken to Auschwitz, where she met Havka who told about her in her letters from there. Lonka died in the camp of typhus and hunger.[106]

I must say something about the Folman family. Havka had two brothers. The older son Wolf (Wocek), the architect, left the ghetto with his wife Rena and their small child Rafi; Wocek was one of the first to go to the partisans and was killed near Kielce. Havka was arrested and taken to Auschwitz. The second son, Marek, was killed in Częstochowa at the railroad station. The mother remained alone, without her sons or daughter. Of course, we supported her all the time, maintained the apartment, and sent packages to Havka. When I met the mother, she told me something like this: because her children who had devoted their lives to the Jewish underground were killed, she wanted to be accepted as an active member of the underground in their place. And she joined. She was over fifty at the time. She went to the Aryan side and was assigned to form aid groups. Through various contacts, we would convey money to the needy. I didn't meet with mother Folman and her contacts very often out of caution; but we always kept in touch.

105. Bella Hazan: Born in Rożyszcze. Active in Dror underground as a courier between Grodno and Białystok. Survived Auschwitz and immigrated to Israel.
106. Lonka Kozibrodska was captured at the station in Malkinia in April 1942 on her way from Białystok to Warsaw. The Germans suspected her papers, searched her, and found four pistols and a newspaper from the Vilna ghetto. She was taken to Pawiak Prison and sent to Auschwitz on November 11, 1942, and died there on March 18, 1943.

As I said, when I arrived from Kraków and got to our apartment, my first and only words were: "It's all lost." A few days later, a man and woman came to the ghetto and asked about me. I won't mention their names. The woman is alive and wasn't part of the plot; but the man she was with was a collaborator and was sent to us by the Gestapo. He came to the residence of Ha-Shomer Ha-Tza'ir but, except for Mordechai Anielewicz, they didn't know what happened to me (my wound, and so forth). Mordechai told them I wasn't in Warsaw, that I hadn't come back at all. So the two of them wandered around Warsaw a few days and went back home. This showed me that the Germans had gotten on my trail in Kraków and had sent the two to follow me. At any rate, in the documents found after the war, my name isn't mentioned, but Liebeskind's name is. If Laban had "turned him in," he would certainly have mentioned my name too, as one of those in his apartment, because he didn't know that I didn't know his address. At a later time, I learned about someone who knew my address and was suspected of denouncing me; but it turned out to be a mistake; the man was innocent. Such suspicions sometimes turned out to be unfounded. We have to be very careful with our suspicions. So I didn't believe Laban turned Liebeskind in, although a person might give information because he can't bear suffering and torture.

Let's talk about what Berlinski writes in his memoirs:

"Sunday, January 17, 1943 . . . At 5 o'clock in the afternoon, a staff meeting is about to take place . . . Agenda: decision on a plan of defense for Warsaw. To my regret, this meeting with Yitzhak wasn't held, since Yitzhak was busy with another meeting of the Po'alei Zion–Z.S. party. Morgenstern told me that the meeting on January 17 had been called to discuss Certificates registering the candidates [for Aliya].[107] The meeting of headquarters was postponed until Tuesday, January 19, at 5 p.m. . . ."

I must say that Berlinski flatters me by saying that the meeting didn't take place because I couldn't attend; but it's not true.

Neither Morgenstern nor Marek Edelman knew about my wound. The only ones who knew were Marek Folman and Mordechai Anielewicz, and Zivia, of course. Yitzhak Katznelson also knew because he came to us on January 17 and stayed overnight.[108] On January 17, I was still very weak and was in bed. Mordechai Anielewicz, who knew I wouldn't attend, apparently postponed the meeting, but I doubt if he postponed it because of me.

And as for Certificates, never in my life did I participate in, tend to, make lists for them, nor was I ever a candidate to leave the country. Nor

107. Certificates—for legal immigration to Palestine.
108. See Yitzhak Katznelson on the Kraków episode and Zuckerman's wound. Yitzhak Katznelson, "Song of the Slaughtered Jewish People," 1950.

was I ever considered fit to be on one of those lists to receive a Certificate. The same is true of Zivia. Even when we did get her on such a list later on, she wasn't at the meeting that discussed it.

I bring up that excerpt from Berlinski only to indicate the depth of the conspiracy, even in the Warsaw command staff. Even in our reports, we didn't talk about the national command staff which included Arye Wilner, myself, and others. This command staff organized operations in other cities, sent Mordechai Tennenbaum to Białystok, and determined all those things. In Vilna, however, things were different, or our instructions didn't reach them. For example, we thought the commander there should have been Abba Kovner, who was known to some of us, and I also knew him before the war. (We didn't know anything at that time about Itsik Wittenberg.)[109]

As for the attack on Szmerling, even before the Great *Aktsia*, we had been keeping an eye on him. We knew when he returned from the *Umschlagplatz* every day. The plan was to attack him with knives. He was just lucky that the day we planned the attack, he dislocated or broke his leg and came home in a rickshaw, surrounded by several policemen—not accompanied by only one or two as on every other day. He was taken straight to the hospital and our comrades returned home without carrying out the attack.

After the *Aktsia*, when the plan of collective suicide was dismissed, we started acting. The moral lesson from our omission and our old sin was that our first operations had to be attacks on Jewish policemen. But there were differences of opinion about this. I may have been too hesitant, even about the operation against the policemen. I was opposed to collective punishment, that is, to attacks simply against policemen, even though there weren't any "decent" policemen because decent men took off the uniform and became simple Jews. The policemen who worked for the Germans were generally from assimilated circles, mostly university graduates, many were lawyers. In our archive, there is a study on this subject by a police officer there. It doesn't get into terrible things the police did, but it does tell how the police force was structured. The policemen generally spoke Polish and only rarely Yiddish. The Judenrat members came from the same class. Szeryński, the police commander, was a converted Jew. After we attacked Szeryński, he was replaced by Yakov Lejkin, a short lawyer who was famous for his cruelty during the Great

109. Itsik Wittenberg (1909–1943): Born in Vilna. He was active in the Communist Party and was appointed commander of the FPO, the United Partisan Organization. He was killed by the Nazis on July 16, 1943, in a famous incident that devasted the Vilna underground movement. See Arad 1982; Dworzecki 1948:440–445; R. Korczak 1965:160–166.

Aktsia. They called him "Little Napoleon." I didn't know him personally but from the things I heard about him and about Szmerling, the two of them clearly deserved a bullet in the head, a few months earlier. Right after the renewal of operations, we decided first to kill Lejkin, since Szmerling had already vanished. Later we also tried again to kill Szeryński since, in August (in the first attack), he was only wounded; but after the January Uprising, he committed suicide. I won't rummage in the secrets of the man's soul, and I don't know why he did that; perhaps out of fear or perhaps because some human spark arose since he saw Jews fighting and contrasted this with himself, the converted Jew, leading Jews to death. He committed suicide after our people penetrated his house, in the bloc of police houses, in an attempt to attack him, since he had eluded us.

On Yom Kippur (September [21,] 1942), with the end of the *Aktsia* called the "Miła Cauldron," the Germans collected hundreds of Jewish policemen, on the pretext that they were supposed to receive medals, and took them and their families to Treblinka. That was their end. When the rumor of that tragedy reached me, I didn't shed a tear. That was the perverse "reward" they got from their German benefactors.

We assigned Mordechai Anielewicz to destroy Lejkin. His job was to organize the attack. He formed a group to follow Lejkin and learn his ways and movements, in order to get to him. That took a long time. The names of the three who carried out the act are known and recorded.[110] Lejkin was shot in broad daylight, on Gęsia Street. Right afterward, we typed out an announcement, which made a strong impression, stating explicitly that he was executed for collaboration with the oppressor.[111]

110. Eliahu Rożanski, Mordechai Growas, and Margalit Landau. Growas was born in Warsaw. He was active in Ha-Shomer Ha-Tza'ir and was a ZOB unit commander in the Central Ghetto in the April Uprising. He escaped through the sewers and commanded a ZOB partisan unit in Wyszków Forest. Murdered by AK with his unit in 1943 at the age of twenty-two. Margalit Landau was the daughter of Alexander Landau. She was active in Ha-Shomer Ha-Tza'ir and was in a combat unit of ZOB. She fought in January and, according to Berman, "she was apparently the Jewish woman who threw grenades at SS men and German gendarmes. She fell in that battle" (Berman 1977:267).

111. The announcement reads:

It is brought to the attention of the public that because the command of the Jewish police of Warsaw, its officers, and policemen are accused as stated in the announcement of August 17, the sentence against Yakov Lejkin, deputy police chief of Warsaw, was carried out on October 29 at 6:10 P.M.

Additional reprisals will be taken with all severity of the law.

Hence, this is to inform the public that the following are accused:

1. *The Judenrat of Warsaw and its chairman* for collaboration with the occupier and signing the order of deportation;
2. *"Shop" supervisors and officials,* who oppress and exploit the workers.

The second one condemned to death was Israel Fürst, and this execution was assigned to me.[112] Fürst was the liaison between the Judenrat and the German authorities—the Gestapo, Karl Brandt, and his staff.[113] I didn't know the Germans personally because I didn't meet with them. At the Eichmann trial, I was asked something about the Germans, and I answered that they weren't close to me. The judge, whose name I don't remember, thought I was "boasting" and trying to say that the Germans were scared of me. He didn't understand that it was I who was afraid of the Germans and didn't get close to them. Fürst had been a Revisionist initially. According to Communist demagoguery, if someone who once belonged to any movement did something, he did it in the name of his movement. But I say: God forbid. The Revisionists were no less loyal to their people than we were. And if one of them did something against the Jews, it was against his Revisionist background. At a certain period, this Fürst was the administrator of the academic house of Jewish students and we knew him from there.

---

3. *The heads of the groups and the officials of the Werkschütz,* for their cruelty to the workers and to the "illegal" Jewish population.

Reprisals will be taken with all severity of the law.

Warsaw, October 30, 1942

Committee of the Jewish Fighting Organization

(Quoted in Blumenthal and Kermish 1965: 116.)

112. Yehiel Gorny recounts this event:

Fürst, the head of the economic department, was shot by an unknown hand. Who is the victim? Director Fürst, . . . 36 years old, carved out a fine career for himself during his lifetime. . . . The son of a small embroidery manufacturer, he broke away, finished high school, finished [the Higher Commerce Academy], fell in love with one of the richest daughters in Kalisz (Reich, the daughter of the owner of one of the largest mills in Poland). . . . Became the director of the Jewish Academic House in Warsaw. After the entry of Germans into Warsaw, he became director of the economic department at the Judenrat and according to information from a Gestapo man, officially the courier between the Judenrat and the Gestapo. In his private life, a terrible person, striving to set himself up above his friends and acquaintances . . . The only pity is that such a man reached such a high position in Jewish life—but this could only have happened in such abnormal times, as we live through now. (Quoted in Ringelblum 1986:91)

113. Brandt was appointed by the SS to oversee the Jews of Warsaw; his rank was *Untersturmführer* (Second Lieutenant). According to Ringelblum's account:

Brandt, an elderly, stout German, his little eyes always smiling, a perfidious, double-dealing murderer who would shoot his Jewish victims personally was for a long time considered an affable and even "liberal" man. He never took off his mask, was always polite, courteous, smiling. Whenever he came, he would cast furtive glances and arrange everything so smoothly that one had the impression one was dealing with a gentleman. Yet he was one of the worst and most contemptible executioners, who had thousands of victims on his conscience. (Ringelblum 1986:140–141)

Fürst's behavior in this period was disgraceful. They said he had a lover on the Aryan side, which made things very hard for us since he spent most of his time on the Aryan side and wasn't in the ghetto much. But at last we learned that in the evening, he sometimes came to the ghetto, where he lived in the same bloc of apartments as our unit; we were on the Zamenhof side and he was at Muranowska 42 or 44, where Judenrat officials lived. Every single hour, three of our people "covered" the path from Gęsia to the approach to Muranowska, watching and following him; we used signals since it was forbidden to be in the street because of the curfew. We followed him home to Muranowska. When the right time came, the signal was given—he was accompanied by a woman we didn't know—and at his house, he got a bullet.[114]

I organized that operation. Berl Broyde led the squad. I don't want to mention the names of the policemen who cooperated with us. They are in Berlinski's book; he tells of our campaign of reprisal against the policemen. Yehuda Engelman, the highest ranking officer of the three policemen who cooperated with us, told me that Fürst once told him that he knew that ZOB understood him. That's absurd, of course. Incidentally, those three policemen helped us a lot, from inside, in setting dates and such. By then the police force was smaller and it was easier to calculate, for instance, when we could expect the arrival of those we wanted (Lejkin and later Fürst), as well as their route. When we killed Fürst, there was a big commotion in the Judenrat. Fürst was the third one. We were gradually taking control of the ghetto. I should also mention Anna Milewicz (the member of Ha-Shomer Ha-Tza'ir, who was executed by the Revisionists).[115]

Before I go on, I have to discuss another document in Berlinski's book. He tells about a meeting in the Ha-Shomer Ha-Tza'ir club, at Miła 61, where the "Shomer Mordechai" was present, along with the "Halutz

114. Lewin discusses these assassinations in his entry for November 30, 1942:

Yesterday a political assassination was carried out in the ghetto: Israel Fürst . . . was killed by two shots in Muranowska Street. . . . Who killed him? I can't give a definite answer. . . . There are two possibilities. Firstly, the Germans disposed of them as they have previously disposed of their assistants who have become superfluous: . . . But there is also a second possibility. He may have been cut down by either a Jew or a Pole, and killed as a traitor, because he had sold his soul to the Germans and assisted them during the 'action.' . . . According to this version he was shot by a Pole from the PPS or a Jew. This event has made a deep impression on the Jews and terrified those who do not have a clear conscience and whose hands are stained with the blood of our martyrs. For myself I incline more to the first possibility. . . . (Lewin 1989: 218–219)

115. Anna Milewicz appears on Ringelblum's list of "People Shot by Order of the Fighting Organization" (i.e., ZOB) as a "Gestapo worker, one of the most dangerous agents of the Gestapo" (Blumenthal and Kermish 1965:146).

Yitzhak" and members of Po'alei Zion Left—Paula,[116] Berlinski, H. Wasser.[117] On the agenda was the defense of Warsaw Ghetto.[118]

"After an exhaustive debate," says Berlinski, "we reached the joint conclusion that the 'Jewish Fighting Organization' was established to prepare the defense of the Warsaw Ghetto and to teach the Jewish police a lesson. An emotional debate arose about the composition of the leadership and whether there could be two kinds of authority: military and political. Ha-Shomer Ha-Tza'ir and He-Halutz vigorously opposed the two authorities, mocking and dismissing the political parties. In their opinion, one military leadership had to be established and get to work. Po'alei Zion Left was strongly opposed to the notion that those present had the right to judge the political party. 'Don't think,' they said, 'that if a person has two broken guns, he has to puff himself up and look down on everybody.' Po'alei Zion thought every armed operation in the ghetto should be carefully considered and measured and 'careless acts' couldn't be allowed. . . . Their party considers the establishment of a political authority to weigh the proper circumstances and time of an armed operation imperative, they said."

Po'alei Zion Left also proposed a delay so they could contact their party institutions and get documented permission for their position. So they got permission and presented acceptance of their position as a condition for establishing the joint bloc. And indeed—as Berlinski says—as soon as two authorities, the military and the political, were agreed upon, the cornerstone of the joint Jewish Fighting Organization was laid.

Berlinski also tells about the debate concerning the division of weapons. This was after we got the first ten pistols, and he accuses us of not wanting to share the stock of weapons. There are additional details in that document.[119] It was sent in those days to London and must be discussed. I want to talk about that document as objectively as possible, that is, to present it in comparison with the ZOB report, which I wrote and sent to London; and I shall attribute the same weight to both documents.

The documents are characterized by the prewar phraseology of our parties. As if nothing had happened! For them, the "nation" stood behind

116. Paula Elster: Director of a large soup kitchen in the ghetto and editor of the Polish language Po'alei Zion Left newspaper. After the Uprising, she was sent to Poniatów camp; was rescued and brought to Warsaw, where she worked in the underground, succeeded Berman in the Polish Underground Revolutionary Parliament. Killed in the Polish Uprising in September 1944.

117. Hirsh Wasser: Economist; member of the Central Committee of Po'alei Zion Left in the ghetto. He worked in the party press and was active in YISA, aiding refugees. Was active in the party on the Aryan side. Immigrated to Israel.

118. Berlinski's account of this meeting is in Blumenthal and Kermish 1965:128–129.

119. Berlinski, 1966:169–170.

the party, whereas in fact, the people hadn't followed them for years. I'm talking about the war years, when the parties didn't really exist. They existed in a soup kitchen, in areas of social help, in distributing money to the Central Committee. But the question is whether that should have been the only activity of a political party during the Holocaust. The Joint could have done that. I would be the last to sneer at giving bread to the hungry. But we had serious criticism of our party [Po'alei Zion–Z.S.] and its position in terms of the times, which was essentially that the party was involved *solely* with welfare activity, and not as only one of its functions; we opposed that as the entire substance of its activity. There was nothing educational in that activity. The parties didn't set up a Hebrew Gymnasium; no seminars; no newspapers, except for the Bund, which put out a lot of newspapers and literature. Our parties, including Po'alei Zion –Z.S. and Left, issued very little journalistic material.

Of course, if someone from Po'alei Zion or the Revisionists did something bad or was even mixed up in treason, we mustn't blame those parties for it. By the same token, the importance of Ringelblum's Oneg Shabbat work is not to be credited to Po'alei Zion Left. Ringelblum did that not as a party member but as an historian. He did what he did out of historical responsibility and very sharp senses.

As for the debate with Berlinski, everyone begins with his own myth of "creation": we have the Book of Genesis. Others begin with the birth of Christ. The Moslems begin with Mohammed. And everyone begins the ZOB from the day he joined it. According to known documents, among Bundists' the ZOB began later, on the date they were asked to join. The fact is that the ZOB was established on July 28, 1942, and it doesn't matter how active it was. For Berlinski, the ZOB begins with their meeting with Mordechai Anielewicz and me; that is, with the first command staff of the ZOB. That wasn't the first meeting and it was, in fact, an unpleasant meeting. I myself didn't have much faith in those political forces, in the parties of those days. But we willingly established this political organization, the Jewish National Committee, because our Polish comrades, who wished us well, pushed us in that direction. Arye Wilner came from the Aryan side, shocked, bringing that demand. We asked him to go back immediately, since he hadn't yet met with the Delegatura or the AK; we told him they couldn't check up on or know what was done in the darkness of the ghetto anyway. We told him to tell them he didn't speak in the name of He-Halutz, Ha-Shomer Ha-Tza'ir, or Dror, but in the name of the Jewish National Committee. If it had been up to us, I don't know if we would have set up the committee so fast, but the Poles pushed us to do it. We had to take their advice. Under those circumstances, you couldn't check initially on who was on the committee, and when they asked Wilner in the early period who was on the committee (before the parties did in fact join), we included them in the group, relying on our confidence that Po'alei Zion–Z.S. and Left were about to join. The same is true of the General Zionists; and we were also certain the Communists would join. We weren't so sure about the Bund. We told Wilner to agree to the framework and we believed we could fill it with substance in time, despite our occasional criticism of the parties.

The Jewish National Committee (ZKN) was established in September 1942. At the first meeting to organize the committee, Po'alei Zion Left disappointed us. We wanted to meet with them and we sought them out; and, one day, in October, we met with their three representatives: Ber-linski, Wasser, and the third, I think, was Melekh Feinkind. They pro-posed we set up an organization to transport members of the movement cadre ("VIPs") from Warsaw to Białystok, where the *Aktsia* hadn't yet taken place and which was still an island of calm, even though harsh things had happened there when the Germans had entered. Afterward, though, there was stability, unlike Vilna, which had already experienced Ponar, or Warsaw, which had experienced Treblinka. The essence of their pro-posal was to save some of the members.

Our criticism didn't center on what already existed formally, but rather on their proposal to start with rescue operations and to save the "VIPs" by sending them to Białystok. We told them we would consider partici-pating in that plan only if their party would conclude that it wouldn't flee. Anyone who wanted to leave would leave later, on his own. We didn't think that any party, as a political organization, should be involved in that. When they agreed, the way was paved for the establishment and expan-sion of the Jewish Fighting Organization.

Let me say something about the organizational structure of operational authorities:

The Jewish National Committee (ZKN) already existed at that time, but only on paper, because the parties hadn't yet joined, and the forces that composed the ZOB and the Jewish National Committee were the same—Ha-Shomer Ha-Tza'ir, Dror, He-Halutz. And they spoke in the name of the Jews on the Jewish National Committee. When we had to decide on a line of activity or to carry out an activity (like killing a policeman), the question would be brought to the ZKN, which would decide, as an or-ganization with political authority. But, in fact, our people were at the head of all three organizations (ZOB, ZKN, ZKK), and I was the coor-dinator (secretary). I called meetings and set the agenda. If I had to write a constitution of jurisdiction for the Jewish National Committee and the ZOB, I would probably have had a hard time; because, on the one hand, there were the two committees (ZKN and ZKK), of which I was secretary, but they formed the political authority of the ZOB. But at the same time, I was Mordechai Anielewicz's deputy in the ZOB and, in that capacity, I was under his authority. The truth is that relations between us weren't typical relations between a commander and his deputy. Perhaps in other circumstances and between other people, in a reality of formal relations, there would have been a difficulty. But not in our situation where we were the actual decision makers; we had force and influence. We (i.e., the Halutz nucleus) were the guiding force, and the parties accepted our authority and obeyed us.

The Bundists couldn't resist us because of the fervor of our devotion, or perhaps because of our age, or our nature. At any rate, Berek Schneidmil (the Bundist) left us and was replaced by the younger Marek Edelman. At our meetings there were always debates about when to begin the uprising. We swore an oath on that September night that our lives and our right to live were given us only on condition that they be devoted to uprising. We tried to instill that in the minds of the party members. That is, when the Germans began taking Jews to the *Umschlagplatz* and to the death camps, we would begin our own *"Aktsia,"* or *"Counter-Aktsia,"* as Mordechai Tennenbaum always called it: "The Germans have an *Aktsia* and we have a *Counter-Aktsia*." That is, an opposing operation; and that, in fact, is what happened.

I don't need to say that our weapons were meager. The only organized groups were ours, Dror and Ha-Shomer Ha-Tza'ir. Party members, including Po'alei Zion–Z.S., lived alone or with their families. Their ZOB members didn't form organized groups or special units. Every one of them lived alone, or with a few other people, whereas we demanded that our members be together, in groups. Later on, in January, that stood the test. The January *Aktsia* and the subsequent uprising came like a shot, by surprise. If there had been time, if there had been signs of the impending *Aktsia*, if we had gotten information one day before, I would have called a meeting of the Coordinating Committee, and they would probably have started arguing. Somebody would have said it was only 10,000 or 20,000 Jews and, if we didn't let them go, we would jeopardize the whole ghetto; and so we had to think and consider and see how things developed, and so forth. They would have warned us that we were assuming an historic responsibility for a fast annihilation and, as a result, there would have been opinions and arguments. But when everything happened suddenly, all possibility of considerations and arguments vanished. When the Germans came into our home, we didn't have a shadow of a doubt that self-defense began there. It started on January 18, 1943, because of the position of the Dror and Ha-Shomer Ha-Tza'ir groups in ZOB.

Two days before January 18, the Germans set up a blockade on the Aryan side of Warsaw as a diversion. As a result, quite a few Polish members of the underground came into the ghetto to hide, not knowing that two days later, on January 18, there would also be a manhunt in the ghetto. We didn't think there could be a blockade both in the ghetto and on the Aryan side at the same time.

The January Uprising erupted spontaneously and I couldn't get in touch with Mordechai Anielewicz, even though I tried to send messengers to him. I didn't know then that the Germans had already caught his group. They came into his house and ordered the people to go with them. He didn't even have time to send someone to tell us.

Concerning the distribution of weapons, Berlinski writes about armories. Of course there were no armories. I was in charge of the few weapons brought into the ghetto, and they were intended first of all for the organized groups. Even if I hadn't belonged to any party, if I had come from outside and was blessed with objectivity—I would still have given the weapons to the organized groups. We know that one Dror group that fell into the hands of the Germans on January 18 wasn't armed. We hadn't had time to arm them because they had set up their base on the night of January 17. Did those comrades later have the right to blame their comrade Yitzhak Zuckerman for abandoning them and not giving them weapons to defend themselves? Po'alei Zion simply didn't yet exist as a group when the self-defense took place. On January 18, there was an event we didn't expect or imagine. If the self-defense had begun on January 20, I would probably have taken a couple of pistols here and a few rifles there to give them. But I absolutely would not give weapons to isolated people, because the weapons were not intended for the self-defense of individuals, but for group action, the only way anything could be done.

While we're talking about weapons, people are occasionally amazed that acquiring weapons involved such great efforts and difficulties. After all, it was wartime, when armies were coming and going, and deserting soldiers were willing to sell weapons; and some say that, after the surrender of the Polish army, the Poles held onto a lot of weapons and there were probably also Germans who could and were interested in selling weapons. So why was it so hard to obtain weapons?

Those who think you could buy weapons from private people are wrong. With the defeat of the Polish army, groups of Poles or individual Polish soldiers tried to hide weapons in woods and hiding places, and only they knew where they were hidden. Sometimes weapons were hidden near some village where the peasants were afraid to give them to the Poles or partisans, because giving weapons to the enemies of the Germans was a death sentence on the whole village since the Germans applied collective responsibility. And there was always somebody who, out of cowardice or obsequiousness, would tell the Germans where the weapons were. The ordinary person didn't keep weapons because that jeopardized himself, his family, and his courtyard. And everyone was afraid his friend or neighbor would denounce him.

With the establishment of the Polish underground organization, after several incarnations, its members began collecting weapons and, if a patriotic officer knew where he had hidden weapons, he first had to go find the place. Sometimes those weapons were rusty and not fit for use. Furthermore, those who did have weapons and were interested in selling them had to bring them in, and those sellers were occasionally Gestapo agents. That was how Arye Wilner fell. He wanted to buy weapons and a Gestapo agent turned him over to the Germans.[120]

It wasn't easy to acquire weapons. The underground armories were controlled by the AK and not by private people. You couldn't buy weapons from Germans before January 1943, when the situation changed; and it was no accident that we also acquired weapons from Germans after January and not before. Because that was the time of their debacle in Stalingrad and after, when demoralization began spreading through the German army. It wasn't yet in the open, but you could negotiate with Germans for weapons.

I don't think our people in Warsaw could have stolen weapons, as they did in Kraków, where they took them by force from Gestapo agents, soldiers, or SS men. There were Hungarians, Italians, and Romanians, military allies of the Germans, who passed through Poland going west, and the Germans themselves returning from the front; on their way home, they carried weapons looted from the Russians and were willing to sell them; but that was widespread only later. They wouldn't sell their personal weapons because, if they had, they would have brought a death sentence down on themselves. If the defeat at Stalingrad had happened in 1941, our systems and means of fighting would have been different. But we're concerned here with the period before January 1943.

There was one other paradox: of all the weapons we bought, the rifle was easier to get and cheaper than other weapons, but we needed it less than the pistol. You didn't know what to do with a rifle, because it was hard to carry. All operations, like attacks on Germans and other actions, were done with pistols and not with rifles. A pistol was easy to hide, but not a rifle. So, a pistol cost more than a rifle. We did need rifles, too, but it was hard to bring them into the ghetto and hard to hide them. And sometimes when we had to stay in a village, the rifle was buried in the ground; and only after the Ghetto Uprising, after Stalingrad, with the start of the German retreat, did people start bringing the rifles out of the ground.

120. See chapter 7 for details.

I don't know how many weapons the Poles of the AK had. I don't think the PPR had many weapons, as I learned in the Polish Uprising. What was our argument? What did we talk about with the AK? Did we ask them to give us thousands of weapons? Altogether we asked for a few score, and they didn't give them to us. That was their crime! After all, they probably had them. They had grenades, too, and they could have given us some. In January, they claimed they didn't trust us, because "Jews didn't defend themselves"; and when we came and said we wanted to defend ourselves, they didn't believe us. Afterward, they claimed that we were nothing but a branch of Moscow. They always saw us as a foreign body.

I'm talking about the AK (Armia Krajowa), the regular, dominant force, which had weapons. Most villagers were members of AK, the priest was a member of AK, the former officer was a member of AK, since there were no Communist officers. You couldn't buy in the black market. We had more than ten pistols (weapons we got from the AK), but in those days, too, what we bought during the Great *Aktsia* wasn't bought from the AK, but in other places I don't know about because I wasn't involved in it. Every pistol, every grenade we got was hidden somewhere, so we couldn't test whether they were in working order. They might have given us defective grenades. At any rate, we only had a few weapons, and all the talk about dissension over the distribution of weapons is absolutely meaningless.

After the Six Day War, when I explained to Israeli soldiers that the quantity and quality of the weapons in one cave near Shekhem was greater than all the weapons of the Jewish Fighting Organization, that sounded incredible. In other circumstances, with different thinking, you don't start an uprising with such weapons. And it's a fact that larger forces than us all over Europe—tens of thousands, hundreds of thousands— surrendered, threw up their hands with weapons in them. They turned them over. We started with crumbs—and that's not rhetoric. If I had had to ask the calm and collected leadership whether to start an uprising with those weapons, they would have seen it as a gamble and no more. What we did in January was done practically without weapons.

To protect our couriers from the blockade on the Aryan side, we ordered them into the ghetto; and thus Tema Schneiderman was in one of the bases that had no weapons. She brought a formula to make fire- bombs: you filled electric lightbulbs with sulfuric acid—because they were thin and shattered easily. We managed to make a rather small stock of them. We had organized groups in the ghetto collecting bulbs from abandoned houses and slowly extracted the copper from them. Then we had to get the acid, and that wasn't easy either, since nothing in the ghetto was easy. It wasn't easy to make Molotov Cocktails either because it was hard to find any bottles since people didn't drink beer in those days.

Incidentally, beer bottles weren't good for that because you had to make sure the glass wasn't too thick to smash when you threw the bottle. That's what we had, along with sticks. In my unit, there were a few score people. Did they all have weapons? No, some had only clubs.

It took a lot of time preparing all those weapons. We fixed what was broken, but making weapons was another story. Even before the Great *Aktsia*, I appealed to experts and technicians, who refused to talk to me. They were warned not to talk with me for fear of provocation, since it didn't occur to a Jew to make weapons, mix explosives, or concoct a radio transmitter. Just having a radio was a mortal danger to an entire court-yard. And we couldn't live without a radio, because we needed news to put out the newspaper.

That was the problem of weapons. The AK gave us only a few dozen pieces, which wasn't enough to equip most of our people in the units that were supposedly ready. The PPR didn't have any weapons. If they had, they would probably have given them to us. The problem of weapons was very hard, really critical. And the problem of transporting them into the ghetto was no easier and involved great danger. You practically couldn't even transport a pistol. And the great quarrel between us and the Re-visionists was, among other things, over weapons. They also bought weapons, kept them in their units, and wouldn't turn them over for general disposition. Their principle was that they had the status of a unit taking care of itself. We might have given them those weapons or some other weapons; but we didn't accept the principle that they were in the Jewish Fighting Organization and, at the same time, would take care of themselves and be their own masters. But even in their case, there were very few weapons. In hindsight, we can say they hardly made an im-pression. They said they killed one German who came into their area, which demonstrates the extent of their operation. I'm not accusing them. Within the ZOB, we and Ha-Shomer Ha-Tza'ir were the only ones or-ganized in groups, each with a commander and a base. But we couldn't train with "live" ammunition, not only because it was dangerous, but also because we had very few bullets.

We tried Molotov Cocktails before we knew what would happen with them when they fell or how to make them. I got the recipe later. In January, we didn't yet have Molotov Cocktails. We didn't even imagine such a thing. I remember the formula to this day. We knew about filling lightbulbs with acid and throwing them, but we didn't know anything about Molotov Cocktails. We had less than twenty pistols, but we made lightbulbs. We didn't yet have any rifles, but there were grenades. We bought some, got others; some of what we had in August fell into German hands, and now we started accumulating again. We started in September and had what we succeeded in amassing by January.

Let's go back to the question of the ZOB command. Anielewicz didn't "take the job"; we gave it to him when he volunteered. As for how this was perceived, you have to distinguish He-Halutz and the party periphery. They thought we had to have a commander, whereas for us, it didn't mean anything. Moreover, Zivia, for example, wasn't a member of the Warsaw command staff, but her considerations were important to us (even to Mordechai), and the formal aspect was simply unimportant. In fact, before the ZOB was established, we didn't have any position of commander; there were command staff members, and they were all equal; I wasn't any more or less important than Yosef Kaplan. As for Mordechai Anielewicz and me, it didn't occur to us that one of us had to be the commander in charge. But because we established a larger, more varied political force, which included the youth movement and the political movements—not only the Zionists, but also the Communists and the Bund—there had to be an "institution" like commander.

The two of us worked together; in fact, I should say, the three of us, because Zivia was a partner. Nevertheless, in a great many things, only the two of us operated. That wasn't a time for meetings; you couldn't always call one. The situation demanded decisions and neither Mordechai nor I would decide alone. So, ostensibly, there was a commander and a deputy-commander, each with his own authority, and all the members knew it. For example, if Mordechai went to the Aryan side for a meeting, I had the power to call a command staff meeting and make a decision. And, after Mordechai Anielewicz's death, there was no argument. Aside from me, the command staff remained (Berlinski and Edelman), and there was continuity. I was the one who brought Edelman, proposed him, and had full confidence in him. As for settling accounts,[121] I can do that, too. I know our members were dissatisfied since they wanted me to be commander. Members of Dror but also others from He-Halutz would have supported me if I had been a candidate, but when he came and volunteered, and I supported him, they wouldn't say no. The Revisionists protested not because he wasn't fit, but because they were pupils of Jabotinsky and always considered themselves members of an army or belonging to paramilitary organizations; so they thought they deserved the job. They didn't fight Mordechai personally; they didn't know him well enough. But the members inside didn't care who did the job. Now, of course, it has historical meaning. Mordechai Anielewicz was a decent man and a talented youth. I just don't accept the Ha-Shomer Ha-Tza'ir glorification of him, which obscures many others who played important roles. Of course, this is not to deny that their movement played an historic role. I'm referring, of

121. In postwar memoirs and party polemics.

course, especially to Kaplan and Braslaw, although they had their own disagreements.

Like Anielewicz, I was also younger than Kaplan, and they saw that as a generation gap. Mordechai Anielewicz was very ambitious and, I imagine, he could have competed for the job of commander with Yosef Kaplan. Yisrael Gutman also tells of friction between them.[122] I myself never fought for the job, certainly not in this case. Nor did it damage my authority in any way. And, at the risk of seeming immodest, I'll say that I was acceptable to all parties. They regarded me as having authority, both as a member of the Jewish Fighting Organization and as a guiding and leading figure. Even people like Menakhem Kirshenbaum, one of the members of the previous leadership, or Abrasha Blum, the leader of a big party (Bund), or Morgenstern—all of them older than me—suddenly saw me at the head and accepted it. Furthermore, they even proposed it; it was Blum who proposed me as commander and, if he hadn't, another one of our members probably would have. Blum correctly assessed the active forces, Ha-Shomer Ha-Tza'ir, Dror, and Po'alei Zion–Z.S. and Left. And perhaps, behind it, was the idea that somebody from the other parties might get the job, God forbid. You have to take such possibilities into account.

Mordechai Anielewicz was three or four years younger than me, and that was a lot, especially at that time.[123]

He was prominent among them throughout the period, but not exactly in inter-Movement forums, where Yosef Kaplan dominated. They had arguments. But after Kaplan and Braslaw were killed, Anielewicz was prominent, and not only in Ha-Shomer Ha-Tza'ir, since he was eloquent both orally and in writing. He was a high school graduate, and it's no secret that there was an intelligentsia in Ha-Shomer Ha-Tza'ir and that most of them were educated. But he also had a non-formal education, which sometimes prevailed over his formal education. Anielewicz knew his way around Socialist and Zionist problematics. We didn't often accept his opinions. His Hebrew wasn't fluent at all; at meetings we'd speak Yiddish, but when we didn't want our "gentiles"[124] to understand, we spoke Hebrew amongst ourselves. He was fit for his job, fit to be commander in all respects. He had leadership ability, the gift of making quick decisions and accepting responsibility. And it doesn't matter that, at a

122. See Gutman 1989. 123ff; 150ff.

123. In 1943, Anielewicz was twenty-four years old; Yitzhak was twenty-eight; Zivia was twenty-nine. Frumka and Arye Wilner were twenty-six; Yosef Kaplan was twenty-nine; Tosia was twenty-five; Lonka was twenty-six. The older ones were Leah Perlstein, who was thirty, and Tuvia Borzykowski, who was thirty-two. Eliezer Geller was twenty-five; Mordechai Tennenbaum was killed at the age of twenty-seven.

124. That is, those who didn't know Hebrew.

certain moment (I'll get to it) he broke down. That was in the big uprising. Zivia was with him in the bunker at Miła 18. That's something I've never talked about, since I heard it from Zivia. He was always near her, leaned on her. He asked her advice because she was a very strong person, and she proved herself in difficult moments. She could hesitate a lot about things I could decide in a few minutes, for better or worse. But when she confronted difficult things, she knew immediately that she had to be active. She doesn't accept, at any rate she didn't then accept, the apathy of inactivity; when I would push her to the wall with "What should I do?" she would always answer: "You don't know what to do? Kick yourself in the behind and yell 'Hooray!'" The fact that Anielewicz broke down doesn't detract from his honor. The burden was extraordinary, the historical responsibility was tremendous, especially since we were cut off. Anielewicz was a leftist, so was Braslaw. If they had remained alive in Poland after the war, they would have gone with Riftin.[125] But not Kaplan! Kaplan's opinions were close to Shalom Cholawski.[126] I always see Kaplan as "one of us." He was a carpenter by trade, a common man, with a sense of humor; he also spoke Polish, but Hebrew and Yiddish were his languages.

When I was commander of the Többens-Schultz area, Mordechai was the commander of the Central Ghetto. I would come to him, taking my life in my hands, or, sometimes, he would come to me; we would hold our command staff meeting in the residential block of the Jewish police on Gęsia Street, at the home of those three policemen who gave us a big apartment and protected us. That was a camouflaged apartment, across from the Judenrat.

We would meet in that apartment and, first of all, take care of food. You have to understand that, in those days, I never ate my fill; I won't say that my life's dream was to eat a piece of white bread—like Bontshe Shvayg[127]—but people always looked for an ideological pretext to taste something good. For example, in honor of me or Zivia, they would bring herring and bread and take out a bottle.

One day, Anielewicz told me about his childhood, his mother, a poor woman who sold fish. He said he remembered always being hungry.[128] Nevertheless, as Jews do, they sent him to high school.

125. Riftin: A leader of Ha-Shomer Ha-Tza'ir in Israel who, in the 1950s, moved in the direction of the Communist Party.

126. Shalom Cholawski: A partisan and scholar; in the mainstream of Ha-Shomer Ha-Tza'ir in Israel.

127. The hero of Y. L. Peretz's story, whose only desire when he wound up in heaven was a fresh roll and butter every day.

128. Marek Edelman also says that Anielewicz was "... constantly hungry. When he first came back to the Ghetto from Silesia and we gave him something to eat, he would shield the plate with his hand, so that nobody could take anything away from him" (Krall 1986:4).

He would spend the days and nights visiting the groups, especially the Ha-Shomer Ha-Tza'ir groups, since he was also the central person of Ha-Shomer Ha-Tza'ir. In the evening, you could go from our headquarters on Zamenhof through all kinds of hidden passages to other groups on Nalewki. He had to spend several hours with those groups. He would sit with them as in the good old days, when he was a leader in the educational movement.

Tosia Altman was older than us, but Miriam Heinsdorf was the oldest of all. We appreciated Tosia, but they [Ha-Shomer Ha-Tza'ir] didn't. I really can't say why, but every now and then, we heard such expressions. Apparently, she was closer to Kaplan, whereas the younger people were closer to Mordechai Anielewicz and Shmuel Braslaw. She was a courier. She didn't have dark skin and hair; she had a "neutral," long face. She was a beautiful person and a devoted courier, who worked a long time. With a face like hers, she needed a lot of courage to be a courier and walk around where she did; but her Polish was fluent.

Miriam Heinsdorf was one of the central people. They [Ha-Shomer Ha-Tza'ir] appreciated her but she wasn't completely accepted by them either. She came to our meetings, and I also remember her singing. I remember a Russian song she sang when we sat together that September night. That was when we learned of Yosef Kaplan's death.[129] She was a little older than me. I think she was Kaplan's age. They met during the war and became a couple. Out of special consideration, they included her in the meetings; otherwise they probably wouldn't have accepted her into the central group. The attitude toward her was very open. They accepted Yosef Kaplan because of his personality, albeit grudgingly. They had differences of opinion with him. Miriam was in the central group and participated in meetings I also came to, until she left the Central Ghetto for Hällman's shop, where she joined one of the groups and remained there until the end.

Anielewicz's girl was Mira Fuchrer.[130] She was always at his side. A wonderful girl, younger than him. She didn't take part in our discussions. She was killed with him in the bunker on Miła.

After the Great *Aktsia*, the Germans destroyed the work places and farms outside Warsaw. In November or December, they destroyed the

129. Zuckerman describes the scene in a previous essay (Zuckerman 1986:80):
She didn't weep. Quietly, in a trembling voice, she sang (in Russian):
The road leads far away,
Lead me, my beloved.
I will part from you at the door,
Perhaps—forever.
130. Mira Fuchrer (1920–1943): Born in Warsaw. Active in Ha-Shomer Ha-Tza'ir and member of ZOB; she was in the bunker at Miła 18 and died with Anielewicz on May 8, 1943.

farm at Czerniaków. The remnants of Jews from the surrounding area were concentrated and put into the ghetto, thus increasing the population by a few thousand. Leah Perlstein and Tuvia Borzykowski were among those coming into the ghetto. During the Great *Aktsia*, Tuvia was in Czerniaków, but he joined my group, whereas most of the girls remained on Muranowska, in one of the apartments. There was no force for self-defense there, but a day before, we re-established the base, headed by Berl Broyde. On the eve of January 18, they all got together for some fun. I was sick and Zivia didn't want to leave me.

Mordechai Tennenbaum was sent out of the ghetto in October. During the *Aktsia,* he was still in Czerniaków. We sent him and Frumka there. Tuvia Borzykowski had been there before. Leah Perlstein was also there. We sent them to organize help for the ghetto. Tuvia didn't get along there very well because he looked distinctly Jewish. Nevertheless, he went from Czerniaków to Kraków on his own. The trip was crammed with adventures and it taught him not to move around. Laban worked hard to release him when he got caught. He was arrested everywhere and blackmailed everywhere, including by policemen in Warsaw and Kraków. Hence he couldn't give us much help by walking around with Aryan identification. Nevertheless, unbeknownst to Zatwarnicki, he organized the self-defense of our members in Czerniaków. They had a few pistols they had purchased. Zatwarnicki, the gentile owner of the farm, promised that if he learned of a plan to take the Jews out, he would tell us. As for Mordechai Tennenbaum, his stormy temperament wasn't yet obvious at that period. This was before he went to Białystok.

We would meet in the Jewish cemetery with Leah, Tosia, and all the members of our group, to give instructions or advice or guidance to the members working on the Aryan side. The people in Landau's shop were given a plot of ground to grow vegetables in the cemetery. On a fixed day, we would take our tools and go there as workers. Entrance to the ghetto from the Aryan side was through the Polish cemetery next door. So we would hold meetings next to the tombstones. Up to that time, Mordechai Anielewicz missed only one meeting. He went to the activists on the Aryan side of Warsaw, left in the morning, for one day. It was arranged by our Jewish policemen.

If the Jews didn't understand the meaning of their transport to Treblinka, you can't blame the Poles of that time who didn't do anything, since this was the early period. But even then, during the *Aktsia*, there were people who escaped from Treblinka. I once told the widow of Yosef Finkelstein-Lewartowski, who was the initiator of the Anti-Fascist Bloc, about her husband. After the Bloc fell apart, he was a very isolated man and, during the *Aktsia*, they arranged something for him in Landau's shop, where there was a big group of Ha-Shomer Ha-Tza'ir and other activists, whom Landau took care of. Landau was close to Ha-Shomer Ha-Tza'ir because of his daughter Margalit, who was a member. Some public figures were gathered there and we were looking for a way to save more people, since we couldn't go on using YISA documents, and we had to get them into one of the shops.

Zivia and I remained alone at Dzielna. We sent our students and comrades to Hrubieszów, near Miedzyrzec, to the forests; we sent others to Czerniaków and one other group remained which we decided to send, whereas the two of us planned to remain in the ghetto. We were on Dzielna, surrounded by empty houses. Every day, I would somehow go from there to the Central Ghetto and would meet Yosef Kaplan and Yosef Lewartowski, who remained alone, without people, without a movement, a tired, aging man. He clung to us a lot. Years later, I told his widow about his death. In August, the Germans stopped the expulsion in Warsaw and concentrated in the small towns nearby. But one day, surprisingly, they surrounded Landau's workshop and captured Yosef Lewartowski and my friend Eliahu Gutkowski, and transported them to Treblinka. Gutkowski jumped off the train and returned to Warsaw. Lewartowski was lame, and couldn't jump off the train. Gutkowski told me about what Lewartowski, the veteran Communist, did on the train. The Jews were crushed and broken, since they knew they were being taken to death; there was hysteria and weeping and bitter shouts. He told them: *"Yidn, farhalt zikh azoy vi yidn, zayt shtolts!"*[131] Eliahu Gutkowski told me that; I told his widow, when I came to Poland in 1948, and she reminded me that he was an active Communist but, before that, he was a member of Po'alei Zion Left. He left the Po'alei Zion party after the schism in Vienna. Later, he turned to Communism. She said that the difference between him and his comrades was that he always remained a "Jewish person (*a yidisher mensh*)," loved Yiddish culture, the Yiddish language, and Jews. So the picture in the train fit her image of him. The man made a strong impression on me, especially in the early period. Later, when he came to me, he was scared. He was a veteran of the [Communist] underground; had spent many years in prisons, where he was almost a regular tenant. When the Germans wanted to destroy me and were looking for me personally, he was afraid to meet me.

That's the story of Lewartowski. And there's another tale of a fellow who escaped from Treblinka, David Nowodworski, a member of Ha-Shomer Ha-Tza'ir, who later was a commander in the ZOB. He was also taken to Treblinka. But any brave fighter was liable to wind up in Treblinka. So the distinction many people make between the fighters and the masses "who went like sheep to the slaughter," was artificial, absurd, and

131. "Jews, behave like Jews, be proud!"

false. In certain situations, it was commanders who fell in battle and, in other situations, the common people who were taken to Treblinka. I myself had been on the way to the *Umschlagplatz* twice. True, I decided not to get to the *Umschlagplatz* no matter what. But not everyone could decide. At any rate, the fact is that many decided to jump—and did. The peasants said that there were places near the track, strewn with the bodies of people shot by the Ukrainians standing guard on the roofs of the railroad cars.

There were very few cases of people who escaped from Treblinka. When the empty railroad cars were returned or when clothes were loaded, someone hid in the bundles. This is where the story of Katznelson's son Zvi comes in. One day we decided to free our prisoners, that is, comrades arrested because of their acts, and he was one. If he hadn't been Yitzhak Katznelson's son and if his father hadn't mobilized all his influence, he would have ended up badly. Yitzhak Katznelson had only one son left, and he wanted his son with him all the time. Yitzhak Katznelson was in the Többens-Schultz area with his son. I was then in the Central Ghetto, at Zamenhof 56; and Yitzhak Katznelson came to me with his son and I suggested he stay. That was on January 17, 1943, and he was working in Landau's shop. He had to work, just to stay alive. At that later time, you couldn't fool around anymore. We were the only ones who didn't work. Kaplan was also registered there and would take care of the *Arbeitsamt* with arrangements connected with Landau's shop. As a rule, no one wanted to work for the Germans, but everyone always had to be at a machine because there was supervision and the Germans would show up for a surprise check. Yitzhak Katznelson really did work. His wife and two young sons were no longer alive and he was left with only his son Zvi. He was very close to us and came to us. It broke my heart to see Yitzhak Katznelson wasting his time at a machine for Schultz. So, I persuaded him that we would arrange a house for him (since there were empty houses all around) or even a room, so he could be with us and not work; and I offered to support him. But he didn't have time to decide because he had to stay with us anyway. He came to us in the evening and found me sick in bed. I didn't tell him about my illness. Early in the morning, we were surrounded. He still tried to leave, but he and his son returned to our base (at Zamenhof 56), because the Germans closed the gates and wouldn't let anyone through. So, he was prevented from going back to his workshop and stayed with us.

SEVEN

The January Uprising and Its Lesson

In January, we didn't have any information or any idea of what to expect. The events of January 18 were a complete surprise to us. We thought we'd have a warning, as on July 22, 1942, when they had talked about the *Aktsia* for days in advance. At that time, people said: Here! Today! Tonight! Some said they had seen railroad cars, and so on. Again it turned out we were fools—we weren't ready. In hindsight, that turned out for the best because if we had had a warning we would probably have called a "cabinet" meeting, even though that was very dangerous, and an argument about the Uprising would certainly have erupted again. I can only hope that this time, despite the hesitations, we would have taken responsibility and done something. But in reality, because we were cut off that morning, everyone decided on his own: Mordechai Anielewicz for his unit and me for mine. Unfortunately, they suffered a disaster—the Germans surprised them in bed.

My estimate is that about 70,000 or 80,000 Jews remained in Warsaw before January 1943, on both sides of the wall. Before the war, there were more than 380,000 Jews in Warsaw. The estimate was that by October 1941 there were only 330,000 Jews, since many had fled. But in this period too, Jews were brought to Warsaw from other places. We can estimate that at the height of the ghetto period, there were about half a million Jews in Warsaw. Before the *Aktsia* began in July 1942, Warsaw had more than 400,000 Jews. By this time, Jews were no longer coming to Warsaw from Western Europe, since they were taken directly to Treblinka, Belzec, or Sobibor. As time went on, many died of hunger and typhus. And figure too that it was common to deceive the authorities and not report deaths, because that meant turning in the ration card of the deceased person. But this wouldn't account for large numbers. The estimate is that about 330,000 were killed in the Great *Aktsia*. This number is reasonable if we take account of the 70,000 or 80,000 Jews who remained. I figure that in the period between the first *Aktsia* of July 1942 and January 1943, many Jews left the ghetto. Somewhat later, we estimated that there were about 20,000 Jews on the Aryan side of Warsaw; so at least 50,000 Jews remained in the ghetto.

Aside from the report sent to London in 1944, we had no contact with the outside world, except Switzerland. Contact with Istanbul began later, through Switzerland. There's a story about a priest who was sent to us with money and a letter; but I didn't meet him. And if he did come, he came to Zagłębie. The main contact of Istanbul was with Zagłębie and not with us. We wrote to Eretz Israel and didn't get an answer. Whether our letters arrived or not can be checked here in Israel. We did send a cable to Dobkin,[1] Tabenkin, and Ya'ari[2] signed Zivia–Yitzhak, dated June 22, 1943. Don't forget that that message went through London.[3] Frumka's letter of June 5, 1942, containing "special regards from *Hashmada Gmura*"[4] who said she felt fine, was sent by a messenger. But we sent regular letters to Eretz Israel through the post office. We sent letters complaining bitterly that they weren't writing to us, that they weren't sending us mail through neutral countries, like Sweden. Moreover, for a long time, you could send mail through Hungary, since in 1940 there was still an emissary of Eretz Israel in Hungary, Shlomo Lipski (Tamir). During the *Aktsia*, we sat with Yosef Kaplan making lists of "who we're going to hang in Eretz Israel," and in what order. Would Ya'ari be first, or Tabenkin?[5] We mentioned various names. We started with the "bigger ones" and classified them by various criteria. We even talked about gallows; this was black humor, but it wasn't only joking; these things were very painful.

I do want to mention a few of our letters that did get to Eretz Israel and were presented to me.[6] A letter sent from Będzin on January 15, 1943, reads: "Your old friend Klalowski [General He-Halutz] is living with Frieda Wolkowyska.[7] The apartment is large. Partinski [i.e., party members] will also move in"; it's apparently signed by Frumka.

1. Eliahu Dobkin (1898–   ): Labor Zionist leader; General Secretary of He-Halutz movement. During World War II, he was head of the Jewish Agency's immigration department, which dealt with rescue operations.
2. Meir Ya'ari (1897–   ): Leader of of Ha-Shomer Ha-Tza'ir and its kibbutz movement in Eretz Israel.
3. The letter left London on August 12, 1943.
4. Translation: "Total Destruction."
5. That is, the leader of Kaplan's or of Zuckerman's movement.
6. The letters were read by Yoske Rabinowicz at the interview.
7. A member of Kibbutz Grochów, killed in May 1935 in an attack of Polish thugs on the kibbutz.

Another letter from January 25, 1943, after the Uprising: "Zivia and her family will certainly move to Ruppin's big house. The house is large and the whole family will be able to live there."[8] That sounds too optimistic. Here's the cable of July 22, 1943, addressed to Dobkin, Tabenkin, and Ya'ari: "The battles in the ghetto are over. Hundreds of our comrades have fallen, scores have chosen suicide. He-Halutz and Ha-Shomer were the backbone of the Jewish Fighting Organization . . . Help save the youth, try to get exit visas, send financial help. Warn the Jews of Holland, Bulgaria, France, that they are going to their death in Poland. Zivia–Yitzhak." I don't know when that cable arrived. It's in my handwriting. As for the memo about Treblinka, it was sent to London and also reached the United States and Eretz Israel.

In her book, Rachel Auerbuch, reflecting her own guilt feelings, classifies the guilty by degrees of guilt:[9] Jewish Gestapo agents and collaborators are at the top of the list, even above the Germans. Then come members of the Judenrat, the Jewish police; then collaborators in the shops; and, finally, at the bottom, all those who survived for, as she says, whoever survived did so at the expense of someone who was lost, since people were taken, expelled, and killed by quotas.

I agree almost completely with Rachel Auerbach about the guilt of those who survive. For we felt guilty, even about the labor camps we generally evaded, and felt even more so about those taken to Treblinka. In a certain sense, she also includes the people of the shops among the collaborators supposedly to absolve everyone of guilt and to say that, in fact, the only guilty one is the German who put us in this situation.

As I speak here, I'm constantly trying to cut myself off from the present; I want to see things with the eyes of 1942. I think that the chapter of the ghetto would have culminated in the January Uprising and, later, in the April Uprising, even if I hadn't remained alive. I can't imagine that one of our comrades wouldn't have drawn the same conclusions.

I've explained a few times that we didn't allow ourselves to seek our own survival; we granted ourselves permission to prepare for battle. No doubt we made mistakes; some of them were justified at the time: we didn't prepare shelters or bunkers for ourselves; we didn't prepare hiding places in or out of the ghetto. We didn't dig exit tunnels, we imagined what awaited us, and we didn't have a rescue plan because we didn't figure that any of us would survive.

And whether I was sent to the Aryan side of Warsaw on April 13 or not doesn't change a thing. That was part of the plan of the Uprising, and

8. Arthur Ruppin (1876–1943): Zionist, economist, and sociologist; "father of Zionist settlement" in Eretz Israel. Hence, "Ruppin's big house" refers to Eretz Israel.

9. Rachel Auerbach 1954.

there's no doubt that the guilt feeling Rachel Auerbach mentions is a guilt we experienced very strongly then; it was also the reason for the demand for collective suicide (of September 1942). We knew we were going to die. The question was only *when* and *how* to finish.

And there was also the strong desire to save someone who would tell about it, to save it for future generations. That explains why Jews in the *Sonderkommando* of Auschwitz, in the crematoria, wanted to write things and bury them in bottles. After all, what did we do and say ultimately? What did we say during the critical times, what did we call on the Jews to do?! We didn't tell them: To the barricades! But rather, we said: "Hide, hide your children, don't believe the temptations of the Germans! Go to the Aryan side! Make shelters!" And we called on the youth to climb the walls. To defend themselves. What did we want to do? To save most of the people. What did we demand from the outside world? To save our people any way they could! We were grown up and mature enough to look things straight in the face and deal with them.

There was an argument in one of my letters about saving the Central Committee or the children.[10] Some in the political cadre thought they were "most important" among the Jewish people. For me, only the children were important! More than the Halutzim, more than anyone!

And I accept what Rachel Auerbach says. Each of us bears his guilt and knows exactly that he remained alive *instead of someone else*. But if it's true that the struggle turned into a struggle for life, it was silly to go up to a German and say: "Kill me, too." Because the struggle continued to the last day, right up until the very last day!

Therefore, we later joined the Polish Uprising; we reorganized right at the outburst of the Polish Uprising; and we didn't surrender, the few of us who were left, and we went on to re-establish the underground; and again, outside of destroyed Warsaw, we re-established the aid network to save Jews. Saving Jews became one of our most important functions. If some former leader came to me and said the most important thing was for him to survive, that was disgusting and repulsive. But I understood that that was also one of the functions the Jewish Fighting Organization had to accept; because it had emissaries, more possibilities, more people emotionally willing to engage in rescue operations. Therefore, we saw that it made sense that rescue operations in Warsaw also be done by the Jewish Fighting Organization (ZOB). We saw that it couldn't be left only to ZEGOTA,[11] the Jewish National Committee, the Jewish

10. Letter of Y. Zuckerman, January 1944.
11. ZEGOTA: Polish Council for Aid to Jews, established in Warsaw in late 1942. Was subsequently joined by factions of the London-based Polish Government-in-Exile and got money from government sources. Helped Jews in hiding. (See Berman 1971:90–98.)

Coordinating Committee, or the Bund. We thought that the function of the Jewish Fighting Organization was henceforth also to encourage rescuing Jews from danger, helping them get forged documents; and these were Jews who couldn't fight. We thought we also had to save young people who, for whatever reason, weren't fit for the ZOB. If a young person wasn't fit, he was looking for a hiding place. We never accused anyone of not being with us or of not fighting. Not only because we had enough people. Our appeal was general, wasn't aimed at any specific individuals. We called on the whole nation to fight. I never looked down on a young person who hid. They too got our help all the time. Such people might have been wounded and destroyed emotionally: maybe the person was the last one in his family and such thoughts and situations impelled him to stay alive. If I wanted to call on him to join the fighters with a clear conscience, I had first of all to provide him with the conditions to fight, and we didn't have weapons for fighting, for we had very little.

I was alone on the Aryan side of Warsaw, where I had great struggles with myself. Zivia and Marek Edelman and Kazik[12] were with me, but it was pointless to share everything with them and constantly bring them the tidings of Job. There were a lot of things I didn't want to discuss with them. There were a lot of things I didn't even tell Zivia. I bore the burden alone, and it was one of the hardest things. We brought the remnants of the fighters out of the ghetto through the sewers and took them to the forest; then I decided to take them from the forest back to Warsaw; but what could I do when the factory where we hid people burned down and I had to take them back to the forest, even though I didn't believe for a single minute that a Jewish partisan unit could exist on Polish soil. A partisan unit demands a hinterland, the sympathy of the surrounding area. This is in my correspondence with Bór-Komorowski,[13] Waclaw (Henryk Wolynski),[14] the Polish army, the Delegatura. For most Poles, if a Pole fought with weapons, he was a fighter; but if a Jew did that, he was a "thug."

12. Kazik (Simha Rotem): Born in Warsaw. A member of Akiba; active in the ZOB. Fought in the April Uprising in the Brushmakers' area and later in the Central Ghetto. Sent to the Aryan side on April 29. The major organizer of the rescue operation of the fighters from the sewers. Considered the main courier on the Aryan side. Fought in the Polish Uprising. Lives in Israel.

13. Tadeusz Bór-Komorowski: Deputy commander of AK; after Grot-Rowecki fell, he took command and led the Polish Uprising of 1944. He died in exile in 1966 at the age of 71.

14. Wacław (Henryk Wołyński): AK liaison with the Jewish underground, who had pro-Jewish sympathies and was a loyal supporter of the ZOB.

Where could we send our people! There is correspondence on the establishment of a Jewish fighting unit in Aryan Warsaw, in a place where the Poles didn't have their own unit. The correspondence was conducted because they didn't want to give weapons or assign necessary functions to that unit. By then we had a foothold on the Aryan side of Warsaw, and you can't say we didn't know what collective responsibility meant; yet, they claimed that "if Jews undertook operations against the Germans, Poles would pay for it." And if the Jews were caught, you can imagine what fate awaited Jews who were hiding with Poles, for there would immediately be accusations of a "Jewish provocation!" We had to take all that into account. Furthermore, even morally, you can call on people to fight, but if you don't let them conduct their struggle in their own name, you can't slander them. So to this day, I don't condemn the Jews. Many came to me as acquaintances and got financial help every single month. And some of them were young and even looked Aryan; but that wasn't enough to call on them to fight. Those who did join the Jewish Fighting Organization did so not because they were called on personally; even if they were in the movements, they could have evaded it. But that wasn't our situation; the opposite was true: people pushed their way into a fighting company. And we also added our civilian population, girls, and sick people to the fighting companies, so they would be together.

Furthermore, we didn't execute economic collaborators in the ghetto. Our attitude, in that period of preparation for the Uprising, was to fine them, and ultimately, that fine was only money. Those people had amassed enormous wealth with the help of the Germans, by collaborating with them. If we had started executing them and their ilk, we would have lost all standards, for there were thousands of them. We made certain distinctions in the Judenrat, too, and considered who the person was. I don't think we would have judged Czerniakow severely, although in the historical trial of him as a public leader, I'm one of the prosecutors. But viewing him just as an ordinary Jew, I've got no complaints against him. However, Marek Lichtenbaum[15] deserved to be killed, and so did Alfred Stoltzman;[16] but the Germans did that them-

15. Marek Lichtenbaum: Engineer. Replaced Adam Czerniakow when the latter committed suicide in July 1942. In a document in Ringelblum's archives, he is described as "a miserable creature, a quarrelsome ruffian, not at all fit for the task" (Ringelblum 1986:40). Berman says he was one of the most hated members of the Judenrat, "alien to the Jewish masses and to Jewish culture" (Berman 1977:80). He was a sworn enemy of the Jewish Fighting Organization. However, Stanisław Adler has a completely different and kinder view of him, describing him as "a good man of high moral standards and good intentions . . . faced with a task far beyond his capacity" (Adler 1982:319).

16. Alfred Stoltzman: Member of the Judenrat from its inception to its demise. A banker before the war and director of the Industry and Trade Division of the Judenrat. He complained to the AK that the ZOB was a separatist group terrorizing the ghetto. He was

selves.[17] However, there were others, like Stanisław Szereszewski (head of YISA in Warsaw), a decent man who was a member of the Judenrat. The institution was flawed, but that doesn't mean that everyone in it didn't try to do some good in his own way. Stanislaw Szereszewski didn't collaborate with the police; he was occupied with some economic function.

As for Gepner, there aren't many figures as fine as he. He held a key economic position, but he helped the ZOB. Pinhas Wasserman of the religious faction came to me in 1942, at Gepner's initiative; he didn't know me but he came to me to set up a radio transmitter for the Jewish underground. Czerniakow didn't think of that but Gepner did!

We need to make distinctions: there were very complex personalities in the Judenrat, like Barasz (head of the Judenrat) in Białystok who, on the one hand, collaborated with the Germans and, on the other, gave money to the underground and put his workshops at Mordechai Tennenbaum's disposal. And there's no point in Chaika Grossman's harsh words about him. Let's not get carried away by rhetoric! We can't make a sharp black-and-white division.[18] I was very restrained about Barasz and I probably wouldn't have demanded his execution. I would have had to have taken into account the fact that at the same time he was collaborating with the Germans, he was helping Mordechai Tennenbaum and sent a big sum of money to us through Tema. He didn't have to send money to Warsaw. He couldn't have known I would live to testify. He didn't even know me or Zivia or Mordechai Anielewicz.

This consideration doesn't apply to the Jewish policemen (there were differences among them, too). For collaborators and Gestapo agents, there's nothing to say! Every last one of them should have been destroyed. For economic collaborators, we had a principle. Some made a fortune by setting up shops, and Landau was one of them! But Landau was a loyal man who took a lot of risks. Some kept a little of their money to prepare an apartment and a shelter on the Aryan side. Our position was not to

---

reported to the ZOB, who planned to retaliate but were prevented by the outbreak of the April Uprising.

17. The execution of the Judenrat members by the SS was done in the courtyard of the Judenrat on April 19, 1942.

18. Ephraim Barasz: Engineer, former member of the General Zionists; like Rumkowski in Łódz Ghetto, he believed in saving Jews through work. However, according to Ainsztein, unlike Rumkowski, he was "neither a crook nor a megalomaniac" (Ainsztein 1974:521). Trunk maintains that he "sympathized with the Białystok underground . . . [and] shared intelligence with [them]" (Trunk 1977:468). Apparently, however, the members of Dror were more willing than those of Ha-Shomer Ha-Tza'ir to believe Barasz's assurances of support (see Chaika Grossman 1987:60–65, 142–155). In the summer of 1943, the Germans sent him to the camps, where he was killed.

delve into the law with them, not to execute them, and even to leave them enough money to escape to the Aryan side, confiscating only the rest for the struggle.

There was one incident in the area I commanded. I ordered the arrest of a man who refused to give money. Our line was not to take all his money, but to leave him enough for the Aryan side, for him and his family. We claimed that we took from him for the nation, the struggle. And who was the nation? Anyone who could participate in the struggle. We argued that the baker, who also had a hard life but who had bread, and was also one of the economic collaborators, had to support his own army, the fighting organization. I don't remember a single case where we executed a person simply because he made money in the ghetto. We did execute those collaborators whose acts were in conflict with the interests of the Jews. The same was true of those who persuaded Jews to go to the camps.

Things certainly aren't simple. I keep on taking stock personally. Sometimes I have all kinds of dreams. My dreams usually touch on the edges of experiences; they're not dreams about the life I've gone through. I'm identified in the dream but the things I went through aren't in it. I seldom dream about what I went through or things I did. I usually dream, not about my life, but about things that are close to the German issue, things I know from literature and not from my own life.

Let's go back to the issue of letters to Istanbul, or letters from Switzerland about Certificates and about the question of saving leaders or children. I personally wasn't involved in all those issues. I wasn't part of the dealings of various political bodies in the ghetto like the Coordinating Committee of the Zionist parties and the Halutz movements. Nor was I involved with Certificates or legal emigration from Poland, that is, from the occupied areas. As far as I know, I was never on any list of "candidates for emigration" and I don't understand that. Perhaps I was unimportant to those who made the lists or not old enough. Or maybe there were other factors. Sometimes the parties proposed their candidates—and I certainly wasn't on their lists. The Halutz Coordinating Committee took care of some cases. Zivia was involved in that and I can't suspect Zivia of not caring about me. But she probably did a movement accounting, too. In that respect, I didn't come up for emigration.

There was correspondence with the outside in 1940, before and after I came to Warsaw, and there were various deals. There was the Eretz Israel office headed by Arye Stein (the husband of Rachel Stein).[19] A

19. Rachel Stein: Directed welfare activities for children in central Poland (CENTOS). Member of Po'alei Zion–Z.S. Also active in the Jewish women's movement. She committed suicide in the *Umschlagplatz* during the Great *Aktsia*.

member of Po'alei Zion, Stein helped us. He gave us a mimeograph machine and, as I recall, a typewriter, too. I know that letters left Warsaw for Istanbul—that was later—to Barlas. But it didn't amount to anything. Once, Zivia wrote a letter to Barlas in code that she was from "Tabenkin's family," and was very worried about the family members in Warsaw or other cities of the Generalgouvernement. She meant, of course, the family of He-Halutz. Barlas answered he was very sorry but he didn't have any family Certificates. Maybe he didn't understand, or pretended not to understand what it was about. At any rate, among the few score who did leave the occupied territories in the first half of 1940, there wasn't a single Halutz. I imagine that if a few dozen more Certificates had come, the leadership remaining in Warsaw would have gone, leaving the simple Jews to fend for themselves.

Zivia and I, as representatives of He-Halutz, once attended a meeting where Grochów was discussed—there was some discrimination in the distribution of money—and the atmosphere was hostile. The people there had one single concern, how to save themselves. Everybody worried about himself and the people close to him. It made a very bad impression on me. There wasn't such a spirit in Ha-Shomer Ha-Tza'ir or in Dror. I can say that confidently about the two movements. I imagine the same is true of Gordonia, about which I know less.

Leah Perlstein and Frumka Plotnitzka attempted to find ways of Aliya in Zagłębie; Munik Merin wasn't yet known as a traitor. We didn't know the nature of the "Judenrat." This was still the early period, and Merin promised to explore the possibilities of Aliya in Berlin; they say he did visit Berlin and met with the Jewish leadership there and with people in the *Palestinaamt* office which still existed in Berlin at that time. But the great change came for us when we saw that there was no point in counting on legal emigration and, even if there was, it would involve only a few individuals. So the idea of finding illegal ways won out. But we didn't get an answer to any of our appeals from anyplace. This was before all the southern countries of Europe were occupied. We appealed to all places with Jewish representation or a Shaliah. We didn't get answers from Istanbul, Switzerland, or from the Shlikhim in Europe. We didn't get any guidance about where to go. And we didn't know the situation in the neighboring countries, since we didn't even have a radio. Then came the initiative of Shlomo Cygielnik and the Slovakian base. All those attempts at legal Aliya were simply an episode involving a few people who got Certificates or who were mandatory subjects and endeavored to get back to Eretz Israel. Others didn't succeed.

An entirely separate story was the hope of getting foreign passports. But that was later and those involved were rounded up by the Germans and transported to special camps. That was a tragic chapter, which began on July 20, 1942. Back in 1940, during the *Aussiedlung* (expulsion) from Warsaw, the Germans rounded up Jews with foreign citizenship. Some of them had genuine documents, some had forged documents. All of them were imprisoned in Pawiak. There were a lot of them, including, for example, Leon Neustadt, one of the directors of the Joint; his wife, Klara Segalowicz, was a famous actress.[20] As far as I know, they were executed in Pawiak. Many others also suffered a bitter fate, although some were saved. Some people had forged passports of South American countries, for example, and those countries could have saved them by confirming that the citizenship was authentic; but most of them helped the Germans and said the documents were forged. There were documents for citizens of Honduras, Argentina, and other countries. I'm amazed at how the Jews got those documents. As for Yitzhak Katznelson, I know how he obtained foreign citizenship, because that was later. But some people acquired such documents in the ghetto. As I recall, there was someone (Attorney Gominowski, if I'm not mistaken) in the Többens-Schultz area, who represented foreign citizens vis-à-vis the German authorities. I think there were a few hundred people in that group. In the early days, people could take advantage of the situation in this respect. For example, Haim Honig, a veteran party member, knew how to do this. He left Warsaw a few days after I came from the Soviet zone. I told him what was going on in the Soviet zone so he would tell of this in Eretz Israel. That was in 1940; but, in 1942, they rounded those people up by surprise, before the *Aktsia*, and put them in Pawiak.

A few people reached Eretz Israel by the end of 1942, through Slovakia. While we're on the subject, after the September *Aktsia*, Zivia was told to appear in the Gestapo offices because she had foreign citizenship. I must admit that I pressed Zivia about that. First, I asked her to check if it was true. Because we had made efforts along that line: we wanted to send out Hancia and Leah Perlstein, someone to go out to the free world, to reach Eretz Israel. But Zivia wouldn't hear of it and it might have been a trap.

I was also called in later, almost before the end, in 1944; I was summoned to the Germans in Warsaw. I made the same calculation: after murdering hundreds of thousands of Jews, it's not reasonable that the Gestapo would concern themselves with Zivia or me personally, since we weren't that important to them. They also knew that Zivia was in their net. But when they summoned Zivia, I thought there might be something to

20. Berman claims that Leon Neustadt did not play a prominent role in the ghetto. Depressed and crushed by the war, he wasn't even interested in child welfare (Berman 1977:89). His second wife, Klara Segalowicz (1896–1942), a famous actress in the Yiddish theater, was politically close to the Communists (Berman 1977:91).

it because, in spite of everything, they did let a few dozen or a hundred Jews leave. However, since Zivia wouldn't hear of leaving, we didn't examine the situation, and I don't know why she got the summons (from the Judenrat) to appear at a certain place because of her foreign citizenship. There was talk of an exchange of prisoners then, but I don't believe it. That was one of the rumors the Germans spread so the Jews would appear.

Between the *Aktsia* and the January Uprising, I figure that between 70,000 and 80,000 Jews were left in Warsaw. That was a time when the Jews of the ghetto recognized only one institution—the Jewish Fighting Organization (ZOB). I'm not sure if the people even knew of the existence of the Jewish National Committee. They certainly didn't know of the Jewish Coordinating Committee because its function was external representation. We appealed to the Jewish public in the name of the Jewish Fighting Organization. And in fact that was the only organized body, since we had never appeared or signed documents or proclamations in the name of the Jewish National Committee or the Jewish Coordinating Committee, but always only in the name of the ZOB.

It would stand to reason that the Jewish Fighting Organization was something anonymous, underground for them, whereas the National Committee was a more general national authority. But that wasn't so. It was the Jewish Fighting Organization that wasn't anonymous but tangible for the public, because they knew it issued death sentences, and they thought that anyone who issued death sentences was really an organization of fighters. Even if we had repeated "Jewish National Committee" a thousand times, the name wouldn't have meant a thing to the people. They wouldn't have identified the Jewish National Committee with the veteran activists—absolutely not! Because, by then, there were other acts, other ways, another operation; not the traditional activities of the previous period. For a new effective force arose, the Jewish Fighting Organization, which revolutionized the lives of the Jews. This new attitude began to take shape after the attack on Szeryński, followed by the executions of Lejkin, Fürst, and Nossig who were well known in the ghetto.[21] The announcements of those acts were signed by the "Jewish Fighting Organization." So this was no longer an anonymous force. The people behind it were anonymous, but the public figured out who they were. I behaved secretly even with Ringelblum and, after the attack on Szerynski, I met him in the street and he asked me all kinds of questions, but I refused to answer, I simply evaded them. I didn't need to tell who

21. Alfred Nossig (1864–1943): Born in Lwów. German journalist and sculptor, a respected figure, who collaborated with the Gestapo in the ghetto. He was assassinated by the ZOB on February 22, 1943.

did what. I think I said that there was a suspicion that someone from the Aryan side of Warsaw did it. Afterward, our announcement was published. But Ringelblum asked me who committed the act even before we had time to print the announcement that we had issued a death sentence against Szerynski. The widespread opinion had been that the executions weren't carried out by a Jew. But it turned out that the anonymous forces were the Jewish National Committee and the Jewish Coordinating Committee.

The Jewish Fighting Organization was known both before and after January and when we came to Zamenhof 56, 58 to set up our unit, the Joint was there or ZYTOS (YISA), and Yosef Gitler-Barski coordinated the operation.[22] (Gitler was his name; Barski was the Polish name he added himself, and still uses to this day.) Gitler would publish articles in the Warsaw *Folksstime*. When I came to him to request an apartment, he didn't ask any questions. In fact, I didn't have to ask him for permission because the houses were empty. But I did because of the proximity of a public institution that we might have jeopardized.

At a later time, when I would pass Leszno and the Többens-Schultz area I commanded, the Jews would take their hats off to me, and that upset me very much. First of all, there was a grain of humiliation in it, and I always remembered who the Jews took their hats off to. Second, I was worried that it would get around that I was a fighter or that I was the commander of the Jewish fighters. I don't know if they took off their hats out of fear. I don't think the Jews were afraid of us then. I imagine it came from admiration and was an expression of a positive attitude, of honor.

I think that the Jews who remained identified us with the Halutz movement. Even General Stroop[23] sometimes mentioned us in his report with a photograph of three Halutz girls. He also wrote in his report that the Jewish Fighting Organization threw into the battle the best of the Halutz fighters. How could Stroop have known that if not from the Jews? So we can guess that the Jews had traced us. The masses called us "*Di partey*" [The Party]. Ber Mark later confused things, claiming that "Di

22. Yosef Gitler-Barski: Was a member of PPR, and had been a member of the revolutionary labor movement from his youth. He served as Adolf Berman's assistant and minister of finances of CENTOS. He fought in the January Uprising. After the war, he served as secretary of the Joint in Poland. (See his account of his escape from the Nazis and Hotel Polski in Shulman 1982:77–80, 156–167, 201.)

23. German General Jürgen Stroop (1895–1951): Born in Detmold, Germany. Joined the Nazi party in June 1932 and the SS in October 1932. He was transferred to Warsaw on April 17, 1943, to destroy the ghetto. His report and the personal photograph album he compiled provide a detailed report of German military operations in the Warsaw Ghetto. He was tried for war crimes in Warsaw in July 1951 and condemned to death.

Partey" meant the Communists. Which is nonsense. "Partey" was the popular nickname for the Jewish Fighting Organization.

How did the Jews react to the execution of Szerynski and the others? I don't know exactly, but I do know that, after Nossig's execution, Germans appeared on the spot, even before we had time to get his archives out. That was after January. Apparently they weren't interested in capturing our members who carried out the action. They only took the report they found in his pocket. Then they took out all the material in Nossig's house—what was there I don't know. We kept an eye on what was going on and watched the Germans who showed up there. They were interested in the archive or in the important documents in it. In any case, our operation made an impression; one single shot sometimes makes a bigger impression than a hundred other shots. That shot was aimed at a specific target. It wasn't accidental. Everyone understood why we killed Lejkin; the significance of his killing was very clear, both to the Jews and to the Germans. The simple Jew saw those operations as acts of revenge. They were pleased with the execution of Fürst, they understood it; the whole ghetto knew that Fürst was the liaison between the Judenrat and the German authorities, the SS and the Gestapo, with the right to go freely to the Aryan side. That single shot made a greater impression than the death of ten unknown policemen. That was one of the things we debated on the command staff of the Jewish Fighting Organization. I was always against collective executions. I didn't think it was right to turn the ghetto into a battlefield of Jews against Jews. The time came when we had to kill, but I wanted us to announce it openly and to justify it, to say why every killing was carried out. I wanted the victim to be known and, furthermore, since there was so much baseness rampant, I wanted his to be exceptionally base.

We also had a similar argument as January approached. Berlinski tells about it in his memoirs and so do other comrades. They wanted us to judge the masses of policemen without any distinction. Mordechai Anielewicz and I were opposed to that.

The Germans didn't respond as they would have to an attack on a Polish policeman, not to mention an attack on the German workshops. In such cases, they acted harshly, took hostages, and punished us. But that was afterward. For killing Jews, like the Jewish policemen, there wouldn't be any consequences. That is, there was no punishment.

Until January 1943, the Germans acted in the ghetto as if the ghetto was still theirs. Gradually, they began to avoid the ghetto, to come less often. Their snipers would pass through hastily and get out. At any rate, they stayed at Zelazna 101–103 all the time, since that was the main base and they patrolled the ghetto from there. Later things reached the point where a lone German policeman, a gendarme or a Gestapo agent, no longer walked around freely in the ghetto. That was a new situation, which hadn't existed from 1940 to January 1943, when the German was lord and master of the Jewish streets. The situation changed. Now the Germans were aware that they were liable to get shot, although we were always careful about acts of provocation; we didn't want to give them an excuse for their acts. And also because we wanted the Jews to understand that we didn't do irresponsible things the Jews would suffer for. We didn't want them to say that a pogrom occurred because we killed Germans. Later, there was one single, exceptional incident when we did something I thought was irresponsible and we later had pangs of conscience about it, since the Germans punished the ghetto harshly for it.

Delusions existed among the Jews until the very last minute, and even then. Even after 300,000 Jews were taken to death. But the delusions were different at that point. I estimate that after the Great *Aktsia*, there were no more than 50,000 or 55,000 Jews left in the ghetto. This was because many Jews stopped believing the Germans and rid themselves of the delusions about staying in the ghetto. Whoever could find a hideout on the Aryan side of Warsaw left. I don't know exactly when the exodus began. About the end of September 1942. Very few found shelter during the Great *Aktsia*. But after September, Jews started leaving in every possible way for the Aryan side of Warsaw; they looked for Polish friends or for apartments. That's not to say it wasn't dangerous, but it was possible to get out, despite the great danger. I myself went out a few times as a worker. Others left by bribing a Pole or a German. The bribe accepted by the Jewish policeman was divided between him and the "gentile" policemen according to rates determined in advance. Quite a few Jews had had previous contacts with Poles. Some had money, others had friends. For example, there were Jewish scientists who had contacts with their colleagues, even before the war. Some of those Poles were humanists who were willing to help. Those with money found a way, since there had always been breaches in the wall, either through houses that abutted it or through ruins on the Aryan side. There were also cellars under the walls and, when they built the wall, the Germans didn't pay attention to those possibilities of getting to the Aryan side.

But there was danger from Polish blackmailers lurking on the other side who were as familiar as we were with all the comings and goings. The blackmailers (the *Shmaltsovniks*) were one of the greatest dangers for a Jew seeking refuge on the Aryan side of Warsaw. Dozens of blackmailers were usually swarming around the exits and gates. They would rob the Jew by threatening to turn him over to the Germans; if they had a hope that this Jew had something left, they would follow him and extort everything from him, down to his last cent. After they extorted everything from him, they would turn him over to the Polish police or the Germans. Many Jews paid with their lives for an attempt to cross to the Aryan side.

As I said, from September on, a certain disillusionment set in which was expressed in the attempts of many people to leave the ghetto. My estimate is that, in time, about 20,000 Jews left the ghetto. About the same time, after September, Jews started building bunkers. That started back during the *Aktsia*, but they didn't set them up in any great numbers because Jews were thrown out of their houses and didn't know where they would be. After September, there was a certain stablization, which continued a few weeks. At that period, Jews did set up hundreds of bunkers. We encouraged this activity. We didn't say: "Prepare bunkers!" We said: "Hide! Let whoever isn't fighting take care of his family!" And we also said: "Provide a hiding place for the women and children and join the rebels!" Our appeal was anonymous. We didn't mention names, but it aroused the fighting spirit of the people.

In the literature about the period beginning in 1941, there are hints of a moral decline in the ghetto. That was a general phenomenon against the background of hunger, epidemics, and oppression. As in the last days of Pompei, there was disintegration; restraints and prohibitions disappeared; families were destroyed. New relationships were formed, not based on love or purity. There were instances of prostitution. You have to remember that a person didn't know if he would be alive from one day to the next, so you can't measure that period by normal standards. I knew about people who were corrupt and I didn't always condemn them because the accepted norm was: "Eat, drink, and be merry, for tomorrow we die." There was a sense of the "last days" and there were various phenomena characteristic of that sort of situation.

There were, however, also instances of moral dignity. People sought a way to us, wanted to help us. Citizens without any political affiliation. Some greeted us with a cry of sympathy: "The party has come! (*Di partey iz gekumen!*)" I remember, affectionately, for example, the sister of Lutka Ottiker from Kibbutz Na'an (her family name was Edelstein—her brother Zvi was a member of the ZOB and was murdered by the Germans). She gave us food and drink for days when I came to her neighborhood with a group of the ZOB. That was when we started setting up our bases, before we made the great "Exes." That woman served soup to dozens of people. The food was important, and so was her attitude.

There were a lot of instances of dignified behavior, an expression of the solidarity of simple people who weren't members of a movement. Later, I remember one day when the whole Jewish Fighting Organization in my area (Többens-Schultz) was in serious danger and, within minutes, we were put in bunkers. You have to remember that the bunkers were "top secret." Every bunker was the secret of its owner. But when we were in danger, we always found people to help us hide. They would appeal to the owner of the bunker with: "You have to rescue," and the owners would let us into the bunker and save us. This story has to do with a provocation followed by the fear that our groups would get into battle against the Germans before the time set for the uprising. For forty-eight hours, until things were clarified, I didn't know the situation well.

There was a class of people in the ghetto who lived the good life all the time. These were the smugglers and the economic collaborators, not the collaborators, the bastards, the Gestapo agents. These smugglers and economic opportunists were another level of collaborator. Perhaps we could say—with grief and bitterness—this group also included the leadership of the political parties: they had plenty of money, which they got from various sources. Their primary concern was supporting the leadership, and that also had an ideological basis. After all, you don't have to look hard for an ideological basis to live a little better. At any rate, they didn't go hungry. That wasn't true of the Halutz movement—some days their members didn't have a crust of bread.

As I said, two days before the January *Aktsia*, there were snatchings on the Aryan side of Warsaw, and the Poles came to us in the ghetto. We didn't foresee what was about to happen and we had one day to prepare for the January Uprising. We were interested in putting it off as long as possible. First, to gain an extension for the life of the Jews. Second, to allow us to improve the deployment of the front. We knew—but not from official Polish circles—that there were breaches in German morale. This was the time of Stalingrad, and the German defeat was beginning to be felt. Second, there was a change in the possibilities of acquiring weapons. That happened with the Poles, too; anyone who had hidden weapons and didn't intend to be a fighter wanted to get rid of them and make some money. Those people were looking for a chance to sell weapons. Despite the disappointments, we were achieving some success. We didn't have many weapons. As January approached, if I'm not mistaken, we had gotten ten pistols. We also bought a few weapons. After the debacle of August 1942, when our meager stock of weapons fell into German hands, our people again tried to buy weapons. They would buy them and put them in the storeroom. The weapons we accumulated were divided essentially between two units that were ready: Mordechai Anielewicz's unit and mine. There were very few weapons. We didn't delude ourselves, nor did we ignore the fact that the great majority of the Jews had already been taken and killed, and only a few score thousand were left. Nor did we think the Germans would be satisfied with that and agree to let the remaining Jews live. Various signs indicated that they intended to take every single one of us. Even more so since most people in the Central

Ghetto weren't working and the Germans knew that very well. They distributed a certain number of ration cards, which weren't enough even for the few Jews of the Central Ghetto. There were two productive ghettoes, as far as the Germans were concerned: Többens-Schultz and the Brushmakers.[24] There were also a few neighborhoods of Jews who went to work outside the ghetto at dawn (to workplaces we called *Placówka*). There were no productive enterprises in the Central Ghetto, but there was a motley crowd; there were a lot of empty houses there where you could hide.

I don't know what those Jews lived on, who stayed in the ghetto without work, without permission to live, without a ration card. Apparently there was a kind of division of labor: they went through the empty houses and gathered rags and junk. Someone who worked outside the ghetto sold the "merchandise" and they would share the proceeds. That man also brought bread into the ghetto.

So we didn't have any illusions about the Germans' intentions. We just didn't know when it would happen and we wanted to be ready somehow for the fateful date.

In terms of battle tactics, we were novices. Of course we had to learn from our own experience. If you look at the map, you see that Miła 63 can be seen from Muranowska, even though it's on the side, farther from Zamenhof. The unit was reorganized. A few weeks earlier, we had been with Ha-Shomer Ha-Tza'ir at Miła 63, and only later did we decide to move to our new base on the way to the *Umschlagplatz*; the idea was that we had to keep the Jews from being taken to the *Umschlagplatz*.

When we formed our second group, we planned it to be on Miła Street, too, without a long-range view, but also on the stretch the Germans had to cross on their way to the *Umschlagplatz*.

It turned out that on January 18, the Germans surprised us again because the signals that had heralded the *Aktsia* in July 1942 didn't exist this time. The opposite was true: we were caught off guard because, for two days, they were wreaking havoc on the Aryan side of Warsaw and we thought they wouldn't be active both there and in the ghetto. But evidently that's what they did. We were calm and a lot of our people gladly

24. After the Great *Aktsia*, in September 1942, the Germans turned the ghetto into a mass labor camp, divided into noncontiguous areas within the former territory of the ghetto:

1. The Central Ghetto comprised several streets in the heart of the former Jewish section of Warsaw. Judenrat employees lived here and several shops were included in this area.
2. The Többens-Schultz area included the large shops, as well as several smaller ones.
3. The Brushmakers' Ghetto contained several small shops and the brush factory.

See Gutman 1989:268–269.

joined in forming a new Dror unit and only a few were left on Miła—
Berl Broyde, Marek Folman, and perhaps one other person. That is,
we weren't prepared.

The literature sometimes mentions that there was some plan to make
a demonstration on Muranowska on January 22, but that's not so. Berlinski makes a big deal out of that. The plan was to commemorate half
a year after the *Aktsia* with a proclamation. As I recall, Berlinski suggested
"beating up" whoever had it coming.

The laborers returning from work, those wretched Jews, were accompanied to the ghetto by German guards and, in the ghetto, by Polish
police. The Germans ordered them to start singing on the Aryan side of
Warsaw. They returned from their backbreaking toil to the unknown, in
order to get up in the morning and go out again to the unknown. The
houses were empty, there were no families by then, everything was dismantled, but they had to sing a song whose words I don't remember
anymore—but I do remember the tune. Today it is sung with different
lyrics. (The song is in Michał Borwicz's book.[25]) The Jews would always
end the song with a familiar Russian curse.

Therefore, now it occurred to Berlinski that we should punish one of
the policemen because you don't sing in a cemetery (the passage from the
Aryan side was through the cemetery). We were against Berlinski's proposal. True, the singing wasn't nice, and it was a cemetery. But to beat
up those policemen on the day they were burying their dead—that wasn't
logical. Moreover, we had the names of Jewish policemen who were
known for abusing their brothers. And we punished them severely, but
we tried to do it so that everyone knew whom we were beating up and why.
We didn't apply collective punishment.

It made sense to commemorate a half-year after the Great *Aktsia* with
a proclamation and by punishing traitors. The Germans didn't come into
the ghetto, and even if they had, I would have opposed any action that
might be seen as provocation just to prove to the Germans that there was
a force in the ghetto, so they would know! The Germans already knew
there was a force because there was always somebody to tell them. (One
of the things we did afterward was punish all those who gave information
to the enemy.) That was no secret; after all, we signed the proclamations.
One proclamation was enough to show there was a Jewish Fighting
Organization. But someone made sure to give additional details. We had
to destroy those stool pigeons. And the policemen who were distinguished
for brutality or for their eagerness to please the Germans also had to be
punished. But we didn't get to that because of the events of January 18.

25. Michał Borwicz, a Polish Jewish writer, one of the organizers of the underground
in Yanov Camp in Lwów.

And I don't know how things would have looked if we had. According to our plan, that was supposed to have happened on January 22; but they surprised us.

Two units were organized and deployed, but couldn't make contact, and that was our first mistake; we later learned from that error. The mistake was in thinking that if something happened, we would manage to maintain contact. By morning, it was clear that we couldn't maintain contact; each unit was left independent. The plan was to surround the Germans in two places, as they were leading the Jews. We thought we could be as mobile as necessary. Mordechai Anielewicz certainly wouldn't have agreed to stay with his group on the side—really on the side—if not for the idea that fighters could be moved from place to place. After all, the houses were empty. So, Mordechai remained with his group on Miła, on the side of the main road. The Germans entered in the morning and didn't surround the whole ghetto, as they had done in July, but rather surrounded each quarter separately.

I remember that morning. First Yitzhak Katznelson and his son, who had left for Többens-Schultz, returned and told us they weren't letting anyone out. That was early, when the laborers began working. You have to remember that in January in Poland, it's still dark at 6:30 A.M. Katznelson left at that hour because he planned to join one of the groups working outside. But they were all sent back. I got dressed when I received the news and sent Hanoch Gutman to Miła to tell Mordechai about the situation. An hour later, we knew we were surrounded and couldn't move. Katznelson had time to get back, but Gutman was caught by the Germans. He got away, leaving his hat behind. Then we knew we were cut off.

Suddenly, in the distance, we saw a Ha-Shomer Ha-Tza'ir unit. It turned out the Germans had surrounded and entered their house on Miła Street, not knowing they had captured a unit of the Jewish Fighting Organization; if they had known, they wouldn't have tried to take them to the *Umschlagplatz* but would have liquidated them on the spot. Since they were still undressed, the Germans gave them a few minutes to put some clothes on and they all succeeded in secretly taking their weapons with them. That is, it didn't occur to the Germans that those Jews had weapons. Later Mordechai Anielewicz told us he was helpless since they hadn't had time to organize for battle against the Germans from the house, and they decided to go to the *Umschagplatz*. Thus I saw them marching in rows in a big group of hundreds of Jews, surrounded by Germans. When I saw that from the fourth floor, I was faced with the question of what to do. If we had thrown a grenade (we all had a few grenades), we would have hit scores of Jews for every German. A great turmoil might have arisen, but Jews would obviously be killed. I must say that there weren't very many Germans.

It happened right before our eyes. A few members of Mordechai Anielewicz's unit were afraid they were approaching the *Umschlagplatz*. (It wasn't far from there.) They begged Mordechai Anielewicz to give the order. When they got to the corner of Zamenhof and Niska he gave the sign, knowing that the hope of being saved was slim. The fighters in the group began throwing their grenades. Most of them were killed. The people scattered. At first we were sure they were all killed; for three days I was sure Mordechai was killed and we didn't know he was still alive. One version of the story says that he took a rifle from a German.[26] Three other members of that group hid in a little house on Niska Street. But the Polish fire brigade, who were in the area because of a fire, turned them over to the Germans who murdered them. Others were killed right on the street itself.

Eliezer Geller and his group made their base in our courtyard. He had returned to Warsaw about a month before, after adventures traveling through Kielce, Częstochowa, and Zagłębie. There was a grudge between us. We were angry at the members of Gordonia for leaving Warsaw. We were opposed to that because that wasn't how we did things. There weren't many of them, and their commune fell apart. Zelcer stayed in Warsaw with his girlfriend Hannah, but she was taken to the *Umschlagplatz* and he was also killed afterward.

Geller suddenly appeared. He knew we had a reason to be angry. Later he would tell me: "You see I've got some sense." He said he wanted to see what we would do. At that stage, we didn't regard his people as a fighting unit. We didn't organize them. It was a kind of moral punishment. But that day, I sent a messenger to Geller to tell him to bring all his people. As I said, we didn't have many weapons—a few pistols, some grenades, and that "lightbulb" invention Mordechai Tennenbaum brought us from Białystok: lightbulbs filled with acid. We gave those to the girls. I was with five or six people in a room when Geller showed up. Prior to that, I had made the rounds, checking the situation. In the house there was a lookout on Zamenhof and, on the other side, on Muranowska. The whole house was empty; we were the only ones in it. We could choose any side we thought fit.

Our assumption that the Germans would search every single house turned out to be true. Later, we learned that they had begun. We assumed they would come to us in the morning. Someone suggested going into the street. I was against it because I saw what had happened to Mordechai

26. That version is in Zuckerman's report to London (Zuckerman 1986:110) and Borzykowski 1972:24.

Anielewicz's unit. I wouldn't have proposed it even before that. What happened to his unit was a catastrophe; he would not willingly have gone into the street either. But for us the reason for the failure was that we weren't able to carry on a face-to-face battle, but only guerilla warfare, taking advantage of the upper floors. We didn't have to wait long until they came into our house. But, that did give us some time. At the Eichmann Trial, when Gideon Hausner[27] asked me if that was when we got into the act, I said no. It wasn't when we saw Anielewicz's group, but a little later, that we went into action.

Now the Germans were clearly starting to go to the houses. Even after what happened in the street, they were sure they could do the normal operation with small forces, as in July, August, and September. Obviously they hadn't learned a lesson either. Apparently everyone makes his own mistakes. That's what saved us.

The first gang of four or five Germans that entered the house scattered on the staircase. They climbed to the top floor of the house at Zamenhof 58; our people were hidden—some behind doors and some elsewhere. I was sitting in a room with my gun cocked. We heard them, we heard the shouts: "*Raus!* (Get out!)" Then, we heard them climbing the stairs. The sound echoed in the empty house. It was very tense.

I'll never forget that picture: Zacharia Artstein was sitting in the first room and, as I recall, he was holding a book by Sholem-Aleichem; he sat and read, facing the door. They came in and there he was, sitting and reading a book. It didn't even occur to them to tell us to put our hands up. After they entered our room, he shot them in the back. Then we shot too and the Germans began running away. After the first shot, they didn't even have time to take out their guns. They were so sure of themselves. One of the fellows threw a grenade at the fleeing Germans. I took the gun from the German who fell in the room. He was still alive, it was a pity to waste a bullet on him. But we did take their guns and grenades. Right after that, we heard a few of them run into street, which was full of Germans. They started shouting and whistling. Regular Prussian shouts, but mixed with pain. We knew that they would soon come up to us, as high as possible. We had checked it out previously and we knew we could go through the attics from Zamenhof Street to Muranowska Street.

Our second gang also ran into the enemy and in this encounter, we had one casualty, Meir Finkelstein.[28] He was badly wounded and we had to get a doctor, but we didn't know where to find one since all the Jews were

27. Gideon Hausner: Chief Prosecutor in the Eichmann trial.
28. Meir Finkelstein: Born in Warsaw. Active in Dror and ZOB. He was wounded in the January Uprising and killed two days later by the Germans at the age of twenty-two.

hiding and no one was to be seen. We knew we mustn't move the wounded man and we couldn't carry him with us all the time over the roofs. So we put him in one of the apartments at Zamenhof 58 and left someone to take care of him. At a certain moment, he asked me to come to him. He was feverish and raving and he said to me: "Yitzhak, Yitzhak, you're so big and you've got such a little gun."

We hid him for twenty-four hours, planning to come back with a doctor. But, in the morning, the Germans came to the house, found him, and killed him. That was their retaliatory operation. That was our only casualty.

First of all, I initiated a reconciliation between Geller and me. My wounded leg hadn't yet healed and was hurting. I took Geller aside and said to him: "Look, I'm wounded." I didn't tell him how I got that wound. "I just now got up. In case of an alarm, I may not be able to run with you. If we need to leave the roofs, you take command." He was embarrassed, but he accepted the fact that I was wounded.

So we took all the people and all the groups and hurried across the snow-covered roofs to Muranowska Street. We got to number 44, far from the previous place, and it didn't occur to the Germans to look for us there. We left the girls there, as well as those who didn't have weapons. We added another rifle and a few pistols as booty, which enabled us to arm a few more people. We left behind those who slowed us down.

We went on. It was hard for me to walk and I limped; as commander, I remained at the end, as the rearguard. Two fighters there noticed it. They didn't know I was wounded, but they saw that it was hard for me to walk. I don't remember who they were. I told them to take Yitzhak Katznelson and his son first, then they came back and helped me climb up. Thus we all got out.

One of us was wounded, but I hadn't previously noticed how badly. He was the first one to burst out after the Germans ran away. The wounded German who was left on the stairs shot and wounded him; we later saw more wounded Germans, but that one was on the stairs right in front of our eyes. We took his gun and got out. It wasn't hard to slip off to Muranowska since the houses were close to one another, as in the Old City. What made it hard to escape was that the houses weren't the same height. It was hard for me every time to cross over, climb, or jump. We didn't have ladders or ropes. Things weren't prepared in advance, but there were always inventive people who didn't lose their composure. People like Zacharia Artstein and Hanoch Gutman would find a box or something like that and would help. At certain times, it was very good to be with such people. By then I knew we couldn't all stay together and that we would have to divide into groups—those who had weapons and those who didn't.

Most of the people in my group didn't have weapons. We had to keep an eye on some of them. There was one fellow from Gordonia who was suddenly confused, really went crazy. He took the safety pin out of the grenade he was holding and wanted all of us to commit suicide, there on Muranowska. I slapped his face and we took the grenade away from him.

Suddenly, the Germans appeared opposite us. But at that time, a psychological change took place in us: our self-confidence increased because of the clash on Zamenhof Street. What did we do? Altogether we killed and wounded a few Germans. But that gave us strength—you can enounter Germans and not die! So when they came up on the roof from the other side (it didn't occur to them that there were Jews organized in a fighting group), our people were so bold that when they came upon the first German, they didn't even bother to shoot him; they simply grabbed him and threw him off the roof from the fourth or fifth floor. Then the Germans started running away and our people began chasing them and shooting them. By then we had looted their weapons.

The Germans didn't come anymore that day. We waited until dark and then decided to move somewhere else. That night, we moved from Muranowska; but we knew the Germans would send a retaliatory unit the next day, and we organized. Once again we used the twilight before total darkness, when the Germans withdrew from the ghetto; that was when we chose to move. At that time, only one fire was blazing; as the result of the fight of Mordechai Anielewicz's group, something caught fire from a grenade. There were no other fires. We organized to go, but I couldn't take Yitzhak Katznelson with us anymore; it was too much of an effort for him at his age, and it was a great responsibility. Someone said he knew of a hiding place in an attic on that street, and Katznelson and his son were taken there. Later, all those who couldn't fight were also taken there—a few men and women. Zivia refused to join them and remained with us.

The next day things were repeated at Muranowska 55 and Miła 61. I don't have to describe again those small episodes that terrorized the Germans. What had happened the day before thwarted their efforts to climb up to the top floors of the houses. Obviously what had happened had surprised them, since a few months before, all a German had to do was yell "*Raus!*" and the Jews would come out. And this time, no Jew came out. This time the Germans came up to us and we killed them.

We weren't familiar with the new place we had reached. We knew all the apartments of the first base (on Zamenhof), and we could cross over the roofs from place to place. But in the dark of night (there was no electricity), we couldn't recognize the new place and didn't know where that house was located on the street. So we looked for a way out. We knew we had to get away from there because the German force would soon return.

Once again we climbed up and went along the roofs and that was fantastic: to see the city from above. Someplace on the path of retreat, in a house at Zamenhof 39, we saw something like a window. We intended to enter through the window, but we sensed that someone was holding onto it by force from inside. It wasn't a bunker, but a hiding place for Jews, built on the roof, carefully camouflaged by a chimney, and it was impossible to detect it except from above the roof itself. It wouldn't have occurred to the Germans to search the roofs. If they had searched the house, they wouldn't have found the entrance to the hiding place. The Jews hiding there had heard the echoes of the previous day's shooting, and we went in there holding our weapons. And what a welcome we got!

These were simple Jews. One of them was a rabbi who blessed us. The barriers between us fell. They fed us and brought the best things they had and cleared a place for us. Their bunker wasn't set up for a short stay, and they had a lot of food. Suddenly, the lookout announced that the Germans had climbed on the roof after us, led by a Jewish policeman. We decided that if the policeman came any closer, we would pull him in by force so that the Germans would approach and we could kill them. And what a change took place in the police: the policeman approached the window, pretended not to see anything, and signaled to the Germans that there wasn't anything important there. Apparently those policemen now preferred not to do their job so loyally. After they took off, we decided to go to Miła 63 that night; we had to leave Muranowska, our second base, and we moved to a new base, which had previously belonged to Ha-Shomer Ha-Tza'ir. It turned out that Ha-Shomer Ha-Tza'ir had one more unit in that place which had a few weapons. We found Arye Wilner, Yehuda Wengrower,[29] and a few others there, who weren't part of that group. We decided to leave from there at night, the night before the third day of our wandering.

That evening, in the Ha-Shomer Ha-Tza'ir base (Miła 63), our unit decided to carry out a few operations. When we arrived and I saw there were Ha-Shomer Ha-Tza'ir people there, I assigned some of them a few missions: to take the uniforms from Polish policemen and commanders (by then, there weren't any German policemen in the ghetto) and from the Jewish police who were there, and to take any weapons the Polish policemen had. The Jewish policemen didn't have weapons.

A few groups left on that mission. Eliezer Geller was in one of them, and the groups carried out their task. We wanted to use the uniforms

29. Yehuda Wengrower: Born in Warsaw. Active in Ha-Shomer Ha-Tza'ir, organized their archives in the ghetto. Escaped through the sewers after the April Uprising but drank poisoned sewer water and died in Łomianki Forest near Warsaw at the age of twenty-three. (See Kazik 1984:63 for an account of his death.)

during the day to bring a doctor to the wounded man. They also brought a gun or two which they took from the Polish policemen, as well as uniforms of Jewish policemen. We were heartened by our success and prepared for the next day. But the next day, the Germans didn't come; they moved into action in the Többens-Schultz area and didn't appear in the big Central Ghetto that day. They didn't appear again until the fourth day. Once again they sent a retaliatory unit, which didn't take risks. They did a lot of shooting in any direction that looked suspicious to them, but they didn't go into the houses. With that, the *Aktsia* ended.

On the third day, the Central Ghetto was quiet and the Germans concentrated in the area of Többens-Schultz, where there was no organized fighting group; there were fighters there, but they weren't organized into groups. Israel Kanal was there. He had weapons and used them.

The series of operations at that stage, concluding as they did, inspired us with pride and confidence. The explanation at the time was that the Germans were scared of our weapons, but of course that was an exaggeration. My explanation is that they were impressed by the fact that the ghetto defended itself with weapons, with the guerilla system of small fighting groups, even though we didn't have many weapons. After all, they didn't know how many groups there were, because the groups kept popping up everywhere. The major point, in my opinion, was that they were afraid that this spark of uprising, of self-defense, would pass to the Aryan side of Warsaw and ignite a Polish uprising. They weren't so scared of us, since they could obviously finish us off easily. But they were afraid that the Poles would be infected with this virus and there would be a general uprising in Warsaw. Given that Warsaw was the most important junction between west and east, they were afraid they would have to devote a great many forces to keep peace there; so they decided to halt their operations for the time being.

Himmler's order of January 1943 states that "as long as the ghetto exists, it constitutes a nest of revolt and anarchy"—so the ghetto had to be finished off.[30] Apparently he was right, but they didn't finish their job.

---

30. Himmler's order is addressed to SS Übergruppenführer Krüger and dated February 16, 1943. It states:

For security reasons I order the destruction of the Warsaw Ghetto . . . Destruction of the ghetto and its transfer to a concentration camp are vital and without them we will never silence Warsaw, nor will we be able to uproot the network of criminals if the ghetto goes on existing.

You are to provide me with a general plan for the liquidation of the ghetto. At any rate, that residential area that has thus far served for 500,000 subhumans and will never be fit for Germans is to disappear from our field of vision. And Warsaw,

In that *Aktsia,* however, they did take about 8,000 Jews from the ghetto to Treblinka. After the war, in the ruins of the ghetto, I found a notebook and recognized Shmuel Winter's handwriting. He wrote about the Uprising and the strong impression it made on him. As I recall, he mentions the number of 8,000 Jews the Germans took out of the ghetto and transported to Treblinka in that *Aktsia.*

The January fighting taught us something.

I had an extraordinary feeling; never in my life had I been so happy. Even before that, I had fired a weapon occasionally. My brother had a pistol, but it wasn't serious. Ultimately, a pistol is a simple weapon. But now we knew that a new period in our lives had begun. Personally, it was beyond all expectations. At least for me personally—and I knew everything that happened—it was so because before we confronted the Germans for the first time, I was sure that "you shoot and you die (*men shist un men shtarbt*)"; you shoot and that's it—a one-time last act. And now it turned out that, in those specific conditions, it wasn't the final act at all. And we behaved like that not because we envisioned what would happen, even though we did a lot of reconnaissance and tried not to get caught in a trap—but you can do reconnaissance and see even without weapons and we always looked for a path of escape if the Germans came. But this time, we appeared actively, holding weapons, and it turned out we had only one casualty and they had many. Furthermore, we gained weapons!

The Germans were routed because their situation was worse than ours. First, they were surprised; they were organized in small platoons. They were always below, and we were always above them. Initially we let them approach, and later they didn't dare come close. The first time they came with the knowledge that these Jews were like all other Jews; after all, they had seen so many Jewish youths that it didn't occur to them now that any Jews were armed. And that was after the incident in the street with Anielewicz and his group. So it was beyond all my expectations and I was very happy. The first time we killed Germans, we felt that this was the final battle. But there was no drama, no heroic outbursts; except for one case of hysteria, there was nothing exceptional. After that, we no longer felt like people going to death, and there was no sentimentality in our behavior. A change occurred in us. The past months had made us mature and sober.

---

a city of millions, which has always constituted a dangerous nest of revolt and anarchy will be reduced. (Blumenthal and Kermish 1965:204)

Himmler visited the Warsaw Ghetto on January 9, 1943. In a letter to Krüger of January 11, 1943, he ordered the deportation of 8,000 Jews. In fact, approximately 5,000 were deported in the January *Aktsia.*

I knew our people. I knew which of them would be the commanders. I had known them at Dzielna; now I knew them as fighters: their behavior, their composure. I had no disappointments; on the contrary, for example, I had known Zacharia Artstein before, but he hadn't impressed me much with the way he talked. That was after the Vilna period, and one night—at the farewell for Frumka, I think—he asked to make a speech. He was from the Frayhayt movement, which had a special style of speaking. He told a few episodes from Pruszków and about how the Jews behaved there. He spoke in a rhetorical and solemn Yiddish I wasn't used to. I wasn't fond of that form of expression; he spoke in a party fashion I didn't like. I remembered that impression when I saw him later, at my side in the Uprising. All of a sudden, I realized that there was no rhetorical flourish in his words. His solemnity was authentic, without any false tone. I saw before me a proud fellow, a person who didn't know fear. There were such people, and they fell quickly. He simply didn't know what fear was. He ran, attacked, threw grenades. And he also proved his intelligence in all kinds of things. He was inventive in difficult moments. I'm not sure, but I think he was the one who discovered the window of the "bunker" on the roof of Zamenhof 39.

Tuvia Borzykowski was with us the first day. Later, he went to the hiding place with Yitzhak Katznelson because he didn't have a weapon. We wanted to spare them suffering for no good reason, and they hid out with the Jews in the attic. We wanted to improve things for them, but conditions in the bunker were harsh. The Germans almost discovered them. Yitzhak Katznelson told me this later. But that was safer than running around all day from roof to roof, emotionally tense and waiting for the Germans.

The second day was a good day. We were very active in the courtyard and took up a lot of positions. When we saw that the Germans didn't come, we weren't yet sure that was the end of the *Aktsia*. And we did learn that they were active in the Többens-Schultz area. But the next day, they came back; this time, as I said, they didn't enter the houses, but only shot in all directions. On the fourth day, there were almost no casualties, because the Jews didn't go out and the Germans were scared to go into the houses; they did whatever they did just to remind us they were there. Then they withdrew from the ghetto and left us alone. On the fourth evening, when we went back to prepare the continuation of the battle, not knowing what the fifth day was liable to bring, Mordechai Anielewicz appeared. We were all sure he was dead. And he suddenly showed up!

Apparently, after that street fight with the Germans in which most of his people were killed, Mordechai (who had a pistol) managed to overpower the German who chased him and took his rifle. He didn't know where to go and hid in one of the ruins. Suddenly, some brave Jew, an underworld character, burst out near him, and pulled him into a bunker. The people in the bunker kept him and wouldn't let him leave for three days. All that time, he didn't know what was going on and thought there were no more Jews left in the ghetto. The people in the bunker were amazed at him (a Jew with a weapon!) and were proud of him, but they didn't let him leave.

We were thrilled when he appeared. Even before that—on the fourth day, I think—Marek Edelman came from the Brushmakers' area with a lot of dollars. The Bund didn't have a fighting group at that time. He brought the money as a mark of respect for the fighters, and he was very excited. We were also excited, even though you couldn't "eat" dollars. Nevertheless, we knew we could do something the next day with the help of the speculators. So there was a different spirit; despite the expulsion of thousands of Jews, and despite the death of the comrades in Mordechai's group and of our comrade, we began organizing for the future.

Our bases were obviously "burned." But it was also obvious that we couldn't remain only in the Central Ghetto and that we also had to "settle" other parts of the ghetto, the Brushmakers' area and the Többens-Schultz and Prosta area. Meanwhile, we were at Miła 63 and so was the Bund, each in the position he had assumed. The first thing we learned was that there are no fighters without a unit. Every member belonged to a unit and was in the unit twenty-four hours a day. You don't go out and you don't leave without permission from the commander.

Henceforth, we were located in four areas: the Central Ghetto, the Brushmakers' area, Többens-Schultz, Prosta. We sent emissaries to the areas to examine and prepare them, since the Germans were guarding the whole territory, and it was very dangerous to go there before the fighting groups had moved in and examined the place. From their base at Zelazna 103, the Germans guarded the entrance to the ghetto, and their patrols circulated all the time. Jews went to work only in groups, escorted by Germans and Jewish police. During the day, primarily in the Central Ghetto, you didn't see a living soul. You couldn't go to the small ghetto; naturally, we knew the territory just as well as the Germans. After we were based there, I was in contact from Többens-Schultz with the Central Ghetto, or vice-versa, every single day. Sometimes I would also get to the Brushmakers' area. I was never in Prosta because, after our emissaries checked out the situation, we discovered that there was no reason to put a unit there. It was also too far away, but the distance wasn't the decisive factor. The important thing was that we didn't have any members of the Movement there or anyone who could take responsibility for a unit. But we did try to build a foundation everywhere else; after all, we did have people. I already said that one of our units, which took part in the defense, was taken to Treblinka at dawn on January 18, and we didn't know what happened to them. We knew that a few were killed and we guessed that the women were taken to Treblinka. It turned out that some of the comrades jumped off the train: Berl Broyde and Wacek (Wolf) Folman returned to the ghetto, and they weren't the only ones. Jews who began to understand where they were being taken started jumping off the train.

We began reorganizing. We learned that the active groups were completely isolated, between one area and another, as well as between two units in the same area. In our organization, we had to allow every unit to have independent initiative. Our one attempt to set up a telephone network didn't work.

A bit later, Eliezer Geller went to the Aryan side of Warsaw, intending to get in touch with a Professor Konopka, whose wife he knew; she was supposed to help him get telephones and other instruments. Geller never got to the professor's house; he fell into the hands of blackmailers who took his clothes and boots and gave him some rags to get back to the ghetto.

After that, everything was built on the absolute independence of every unit, not only every area, because in those circumstances, this independence was imperative. The commanders I knew, like Gutman, Benjamin Wald,[31] and Zacharia Artstein, weren't ideologues, but men who had already proved themselves. Now they had to act independently. They were distinguished for their composure, their aplomb, their initiative—very important qualities for a commander. Thus we began building the foundation.

Later we decided that the command staff should meet every day. Mordechai Anielewicz, Zivia, and I did meet almost every day. We had to because of our responsibility to prepare the base in case of a German attack. Initially, the idea was that I would stay in the Central Ghetto. Then Zivia suggested I move to Többens-Schultz. Mordechai was located in the Central Ghetto, Marek Edelman in the Brushmakers' ghetto, and I in the Többens-Schultz ghetto. I moved there with my unit which later split, since the organization changed completely. We sent people there who first chose the house on Leszno Street, near the church and close to Karmelicka. There was a fence on the street, shaped like a wall, which the Germans had built.

After I was in the Többens-Schultz area a few days, I saw that this base wasn't suitable because it was in a dead end. I thought we should move to a more central and open place and build the base along the central axes of the ghetto entrance. Being on Leszno was logical because, on their way

31. Benjamin Wald: Born in Warsaw. Active in Dror; unit commander in the Többens-Schultz area. He was killed in early May at the sewer entrance on Ogrodowa Street at the age of twenty-three.

to surround the ghetto, the Germans would have to pass there. Nowolipie Street was on the other side, and from there you could look onto our bases, stretching along the roads the Germans would enter.

That was the logic in choosing places. It didn't matter if the windows of the unit's apartment faced the street (Leszno) or the courtyard because all apartments occupied by Jews were emptied anyway during a German attack. First of all, we determined where the bases would be if the *Aktsia* started again. And we decided that the groups had to be in the courtyards so they wouldn't be visible.

We began building units and, at the same time, we controlled parts of the ghetto. Ultimately, by April, nine units were deployed in the Central Ghetto; eight units in the Többens-Schultz area, and five in the Brushmakers' area. We didn't have a single unit in Prosta. Thus we began concentrating people and distributing weapons to them.

Now, after the events of January, the Polish underground could no longer complain that we didn't fight. We got word from the Poles that they "saluted us" and appreciated the fighting spirit of the Jews, and they even sent weapons. Pistols. This was the AK (Armia Krajowa), who were trying to please us with a goodwill gesture. They sent fifty pistols, forty-nine of which arrived; one of the escorting Poles pinched one pistol because it enchanted him. Later they sent us grenades for attack and defense. They also sent us a few kilograms of explosives. And, since we also got the recipe for Molotov Cocktails, we started collecting bottles. They brought the weapons to a place near the wall; in the evening, our unit picked them up and brought them into the ghetto. That is, the Poles risked their lives by going through the streets of Aryan Warsaw to the wall. Aside from that, our people bought whatever came to hand. At first we bought on the Aryan side of Warsaw. That was when Arye Wilner was still there; he went back to the Aryan side after January, and this time he stayed there until he was caught in March, when buying weapons was in full swing.

What happened in the meantime?

The awareness of the end on the one hand, and the fighting on the other, encouraged simple Jews to organize and set up armed units. In January, as far as we know, the Revisionists didn't take part in the fighting.[32] Later, they said they had a battle we didn't know about. I have no basis for disputing their story. It began with the killing of a German who came upon them; we don't have any confirmation of the facts from

32. According to the Revisionist Haim Lazar-Litai (1963:210), reliable Polish sources reported that "the first clash between Jewish fighters and Germans [in the January Uprising] was on the corner of Smocza and Nowolipki, where a ZZW [Revisionist] fighting group caught the German column with heavy fire from Guns and grenades . . . That was the first armed battle between Jews and Germans since the Nazi occupation . . ."

other sources, but it is definitely possible.[33] They weren't yet organized or concentrated on Muranowska. After January, they also began organizing. Aside from the Revisionists, who were an organized ideological group, there were various Jews, some who truly and innocently wanted to fight and didn't know how until they organized into a fighting unit. These Jews weren't "underworld characters." They looked for a way to us; and there were also people with ideological motives, like young members of Po'alei Zion and the Bund, whom we didn't reach and they organized on their own without any connection to us. Later some of them came to us and we integrated them on the basis of ideological affinity. They didn't have any weapons. In addition to them, there were "wildcat" groups who exploited the circumstances and used the name of the Jewish Fighting Organization to rob people and make money. They heard we did "Exes" with rich Jews who collaborated economically with the Germans, and they tried their hand at that too. There was also another kind of person who organized—not for robbery and pillage, and not for fighting—but to buy and sell weapons. Those people had gentile partners. We suddenly realized that they also played a positive role. We had a wise guy who, after we discovered the main base of one of those groups, suggested we attack them and take their weapons. I saw that as total nonsense. I thought they were filling a difficult mission—they bought weapons for the ghetto. We paid them money for the weapons and encouraged them.

In addition to those forty-nine pistols we got, the Communists probably got weapons from their comrades, the Armia Ludowa. And there were also the weapons our comrades bought on the Aryan side, as well as those we bought from Jews in the ghetto. So there was a motley collection of all kinds of weapons, which naturally didn't make it easy for us: there were various bullets, of different caliber, of all kinds: "Kat" and "WIT" made in Radom; PO-38, made in Czechoslovakia; Mausers, the sidearms of German officers; Soviet *Nagans*; Belgian 7.65 and 9 caliber FNs; and others. And there were all kinds of grenades, too: Polish ones and German ones, which looked like bottles with handles.

We faced the question of the use of explosives: we had people who were good with their hands, and we set up some workshops. Although we couldn't manufacture pistols, we could produce two kinds of primitive bombs. We would take a water pipe, which could always be found in the empty houses. We would remove the pipes with a larger than normal diameter, saw out a piece of about 30 to 40 centimeters, solder one side,

33. Lazar also tells of a battle at Muranowska 7–9, where ZZW headquarters was located. It was, he says, "a brief but intense battle with a group of Germans they encountered" (1963:210). Gutman, however, concludes that "we lack any authoritative information on organized resistance action on the part of the Jewish Military Union (ZZW) during the January deportation" (1989:314–315)

and make threads for a screw on the other side. Inside the hard metal
pipe, we would put a thinner tin pipe and load it with explosives. We
would fill the space between the two pipes with pieces of metal, nails, and
such. The effect of the explosion was not only from the pipe but also from
the scraps of metal and nails. We would carve slits in the pipe, as in the
grenades, which scattered the slivers. In the screwed-on top, we would
make a crack to put the wick which went down to the explosives. This
grenade could be ignited only with a box of matches. So we tied a box and
a few matches to it.

Haim Frimmer tells a dramatic story.[34] In April 1943, the Germans
were moving in as he was hurrying to light the wick, taking the risk that
the grenade would blow up in his hand because the wick was short, and
he had to throw the grenade immediately. There were other obstacles:
the wind could keep you from lighting the wick or the box of matches
might be defective.

We had a problem of gasoline for producing Molotov Cocktails. Our
recipe called for gasoline or a mixture of gasoline and kerosene, as need
be. If you want the fire to be bigger and to burn for less time, you have
to put in only gasoline. If you want it to burn longer, you mix the gasoline
with kerosene. You take cyanide potassium and mix it in sugar (at a ratio
of 4 to 1, I think), put in gasoline, wrap it up, (in heavy brown paper) and
light it while throwing it. The contact of the gasoline with the mixture
causes an explosion and a fire. It was better to throw the bottle at a stable
target, the second requirement is that the bottle not be made of glass that's
too thick.

So we had to send special groups to collect bottles. We didn't drink
wine, there was little vodka, and bottles were lacking. Another problem
was that little bottles didn't work. In this situation, every unit had to collect
proper bottles since every unit had a stake in it; that was its responsibility,
since bottles weren't distributed by the center. Nevertheless, some groups
collected a lot of bottles and distributed them to all the units.

Where do you get gasoline? There was one Jew, Moshe Fribes, a
former metal factory owner, from an old and distinguished Warsaw
family that also owned a fuel storage plant—I don't remember if it was
gasoline or kerosene—and they put that plant at our disposal. Moreover,
a big city truck, full of fuel, would come to the Judenrat every day from
the city. We made an agreement with the driver to come into the ghetto
with a full tank, and let us take the gasoline or kerosene from it, leaving

34. Aharon Carmi and Haim Frimmer 1961. Both were fighters and partisans. Frimmer
was born in Gniewoszów, in the Lublin district. He was active in Akiba and was a member
of ZOB; he fought in the Central Ghetto and was one of those who escaped through the
sewers. He joined a group of Soviet partisans. Immigrated to Eretz Israel in October 1945.
Died in 1972 at the age of fifty-two.

him as much as he needed to get back to the Aryan side. Then, he would refill it and return. With the help of his many connections, he managed to mislead the Germans so they wouldn't suspect him. Furthermore, there weren't any cars in the ghetto, and it didn't occur to the Germans that someone was using that fuel for belligerent needs.

So we could prepare many hundreds of bottles and we had enough fuel for that. We could get the cyanide potassium to produce the explosives on the Aryan side of Warsaw. The comrades prepared the bottles themselves; I also knew how to do it. But initially, that recipe was an important discovery for us, and we got it through one of the Bundists on the Aryan side of Warsaw. As I recall it came from the PPS, from somebody who produced weapons for the Poles; for us, it was singularly important. Women could also use the Molotov Cocktail. It was an important addition to our personal weapons since we didn't have so many real grenades. In time, we learned you could aim a Molotov Cocktail at the helmets of German soldiers marching in procession; and you could even throw them on their tanks.

We also used explosives to make primitive mines and planted them in a few places in the ghetto. One was at the entrance of my area (Többens-Schultz). We knew that the Germans had to come through there, but that particular mine didn't explode because of our error. We had invested a lot of work in it. It was a mine operated by electricity. The machines in the shops worked on electricity, and we extended the electric cord and relied on that. But the electricity was cut off just as the Germans arrived in the area and we couldn't explode the mine.

We worked hard in those days. We dug some excavations, including one under the pavement, and were afraid it would collapse if a heavy truck passed by (even though only a few vehicles passed there). We had to reinforce the excavations with beams, which we did with the advice of the builders of bunkers who were experts on that. Moreover, we wanted all the destructive force of the mines to rise and not be dispersed. For that, we got some cement and built a concrete floor so the thrust of the explosion would be directed upward. It didn't work. On the other hand, in the Brushmakers' area, we did succeed. Kazik tells how the mine exploded and the Germans suffered many casualties.[35] The exact num-

35. This is the incident Kazik tells: "One day after the Germans began liquidating the ghetto—on April 20, 1943—as I stood at the observation post near the gate, I suddenly spied an SS unit approaching the gate. With one hand, I pushed the alarm button and, with the other, I grabbed the fuse of the explosives. At that moment, my commander, Hanoch, burst into the post, snatched the fuse out of my hand and, after waiting a few seconds, he exploded the mine: I was nailed to the spot, almost paralyzed—a tremendous explosion! I had a fervent desire to see with my own eyes. And I did see: crushed bodies of soldiers; limbs flying; cobblestones and fences crumbling; complete chaos. I saw and I didn't believe:

ber of Germans killed and wounded isn't important. The fact is that they had several casualties, and were forced to retreat.

There was also a reorganization. If we had two organized units in January, we had twenty-two by April. Henceforth, every commander was in charge of his area. There were as many as five hundred fighters and no single standard of size, some units numbered thirty people. Unfortunately, we didn't have time to complete our preparations.

This may sound amazing, but ostensibly the "head" of the great uprising of April should have been the civilian and political authority, that is, the Jewish National Committee (ZKN), of which I was chairman. However, I was also the deputy commander of the operational body. I've already pointed out the apparent paradox of the situation. But the truth is that the Jewish Fighting Organization was at the center of decisions. Even more so after January, because the others had nothing to say in the new circumstances.

I'm sometimes asked how, in those days, we maintained the "sanctity of the Movement framework?" That shouldn't be surprising. Just imagine what would have happened if we hadn't maintained it, if people were strangers to one another, because there wasn't enough time for them to get to know each other.

However, previous acquaintanceship, Movement contacts quickly developed into what we call "brothers-in-arms." At the time, the Movement framework turned into an essential element. For example, people who knew Zacharia Artstein from before treated him differently from those who didn't know him, and he had been appointed their commander just yesterday. The members of the Movement knew who he was, they knew him in the January Uprising and before, during years of work and life in the Dzielna commune. There was no purpose in dismantling the Movement framework since this affiliation turned into a social glue. Socially, people lived like a close family; it was a good life. I can say that because I was perhaps the only district commander who always lived in one of the units. I would move from one unit to another. I was frequently at Leszno 56. Zivia usually wasn't with me; she was in the Central Ghetto with Mordechai Anielewicz, whose girlfriend Mira was also there. Now and then we met.

Haim Frimmer describes climbing up through the roofs, which, of course, involved mortal danger. Sometimes we would plan to join labor

---

German soldiers screaming in panicky flight, leaving their wounded behind. I pulled out one grenade and then another and tossed them. My comrades were also shooting and firing at them. We weren't marksmen but we did hit some. The Germans took off" (Kazik 1984:44).

groups, but you couldn't always do that because they were escorted by Germans. Once I almost got killed on the spot and was saved by some very old Austrian; by that time I was commander in that area, and Zivia and I joined a labor unit.

I should mention the size of the groups. We didn't have a single standard. A group could consist of fifteen to thirty people. If we had had time before April, we would have formed more groups. Who said there had to be twenty-two fighting units? If we had had time, we would have gotten more weapons. We would have expanded and brought in more young and decent people; after all, we didn't exploit all the Movement and ideological potential that was in the ghetto. If only we had had weapons! For the number of fighters was limited by the quantity of weapons we had. I'm talking about personal weapons. Not other weapons, like rifles, which were really in minute supply. As far as we were concerned, April 19, the first day of the Uprising, was too early. If we had had a few months, we would have formed more units.

This is amazing, but can be explained. The units were organized differently. But one thing was clear: except for the men and women couriers on the Aryan side of Warsaw, every single person either belonged to one of the units or was attached to the general command staff. There weren't command staffs in the areas, but just a commander. Later, there were unit commanders. Mordechai Anielewicz, Marek Edelman, Zivia, and I would hold command staff meetings in the Central Ghetto; there weren't many, but they were held from time to time. I would try to fix meetings at a time when I could be at one of the bases at night, usually at my own base. I would return so as not to leave the area without a commander and not to get stuck until dawn in case something happened. My separation from Zivia was not intentional. The Uprising and not the family was predominant. Zivia said she felt that Mordechai Anielewicz needed her very much. Even in the bunker at Miła 18, Mordechai didn't make a move without consulting her. He was very dependent on her. I know that from many conversations and meetings that were like family gatherings. Mira, Mordechai's girlfriend, was wonderful; she didn't interfere in things, but she was always with them. I came to their place or they came to mine at night. Zivia usually stayed in the Central Ghetto. When the battles erupted, Mordechai joined a fighting unit and Zivia went with Zacharia Artstein. From their base on Zamenhof Street, they could pass behind the houses, thus maintaining contact with Nalewki. Marek Edelman was also nearby. He had to go through some hole in the fence to get there, which he did occasionally and then would join the command staff meeting.

There's something else that also looks strange. Marek Edelman, of the Bund, was a member of the command staff, and so was Hirsh Berlinski, of Po'alei Zion Left. But Marek Edelman was commander of the Brush-makers' area, whereas Hirsh Berlinski was only a unit commander. These facts were strange or accidental, but that's how it was. If we had built everything patiently and planned in advance, we might have organized differently; but with the imperative pressure of time, we did what we could. Arye Wilner was on the Aryan side until he fell into the hands of the Germans. Eliezer Geller of Gordonia was a unit commander in Marek Edelman's area. In March, after Arye Wilner fell into the hands of the Germans, there was a worrisome vacuum on the Aryan side. We started internal discussions (not in the command staff but among the members of He-Halutz) about who would replace Arye; it fell to my lot, and we solved two problems at once. Geller's unit was purely Gordonia. And Geller of Gordonia didn't want to be subordinate to Edelman of the Bund. Edelman also complained that Geller didn't obey him. On the other hand, by then, Geller and I had come to trust each other. (He was older than I.) Geller requested a transfer to my area (Marek Edelman supported the request), and we approved it. We also transferred Hanoch Gutman's group (Dror) to Marek Edelman's Brushmakers' area. The decision re-sulted from two things:

1. Arye Wilner's capture by the Germans and the need to replace him on the Aryan side. It was decided (at the end of March 1943) that I would go.
2. Eliezer Geller's request to be appointed commander and to move to my area.

My move to the Aryan side and our decision to appoint Geller to replace me were kept secret.

Marek Edelman was younger than us. Our relations with him went in stages; relations were always very correct, and in command staff meet-ings, it was hard to know what he thought because he was quiet by nature. Later, when we were on the Aryan side of Warsaw, he told me that Berek (Barukh) Schneidmil, his predecessor, hadn't felt comfortable with us. We were too young, "braggarts," and too bold, and it was hard for him to get used to us.

Marek Edelman was very brave—and I'm not one to pay compli-ments—and very precise about doing his job. But he was a real "slob" in private life. His valor was demonstrated in the great uprising in the Warsaw Ghetto as well as in the Polish Uprising, where I saw him up close. We respected him and became fast friends on the Aryan side of Warsaw. The Bund didn't take care of him; I was the one who took him out of some coal bin in a cellar where he was living, and had to sleep wrapped up like a mouse all the time. I took him to Zivia's and my apartment. We tried not to argue and we avoided discussions about the politics of the Bund.

He was quite cold toward Eretz Israel. He often disagreed with his fellow party members. When the debates were especially harsh, he would tell me about them. I couldn't poke my nose into their internal arguments; we didn't have such arguments. He didn't have much faith in the leadership of his party. Not in Leon Feiner[36] or in Jurek Fiszgrunt.[37] He wasn't alone in his estimate or his attitude. But he had complete trust in me and Zivia and the other members of the ZOB. And it was mutual. To this day, now that he's a well-known cardiologist in Warsaw, we feel the same way, after many years of separation. After those of us who remained moved to Aryan Warsaw, I walked around the city a lot; but the comrades who looked Jewish, like him and Zivia, were forced to hide most of the time. That group spent a lot of time together and grew very close.

I respect Marek Edelman a lot for his courage and his adherence to the goal. His courage was demonstrated not only militarily. In the Polish Uprising, he had to stand alone in battle—I saw that myself. He deserves a lot of respect for his action. But because of the contrast in perspective, I wouldn't assign him political errands.

The Dror unit commanders were Benjamin Wald, Zacharia Artstein, Hanoch Gutman, Yitzhak Blaustein,[38] and Berl Broyde. I've already talked about Zacharia. To understand our relations, you have to remember that I lived at the base, usually with Benjamin Wald's unit. In the past I would visit all the units and sleep at one of them, since most of them had been my students in the Movement. Wald had been trained in Frayhayt and was a good commander, not a shouter; his men loved him and called him "*Tatele* (Daddy)." He took care of the smallest things, and there was order and discipline in his unit. Sometimes it was imperative to establish strict discipline. One day, the situation got so bad that I put our "MPs" in the streets because the fighters were leaving their units without permission. Somebody left a father or a girl at home and would slip off to see them. We wanted to allow such meetings, but with the commander's permission. A comrade would get leave, for at least twenty-four hours, and would then have to return to the base. Sometimes they would take their weapons with them, and that could be catastrophic because we had to be careful of any provocation and of what could result

36. Leon Feiner: Veteran Bundist activist from Kraków. An attorney, who had been the Bundist representative on the Kraków City Council. He cooperated closely with the ZOB. He looked like a Polish aristocrat and escorted Jan Karski (AK representative) on his tour of the Warsaw Ghetto in October 1942. He died after the Liberation, in February 1945, of cancer.

37. Jurek Fiszgrunt: Prewar Bundist activist in Warsaw.

38. Yitzhak Blaustein: Born in Zyradów. Active in Dror; ZOB unit commander in the Central Ghetto. He stayed in the destroyed ghetto after the April Uprising; details of his death are unknown. He was about twenty years old.

if a person were caught with weapons—after all, the weapons were meant for the Germans and we didn't want them to be used ahead of time. If the fighter had to defend himself and if he were fated to be a victim, he had to make sure not to get us caught in a trap too soon.

Incidentally, afterward, on the Aryan side of Warsaw, that was exactly how the underground behaved: only groups on operations were allowed to carry weapons. Important members of the AK underground told me they had also decided not to use weapons ahead of time so as not to bring collective punishment on an entire courtyard. That was a great responsibility. Moreover, they were allowed to commit suicide during the operation. These were, of course, very limited operations, so that an armed person wouldn't go out and kill a German, whose death would be avenged with the murder of fifty people. Obviously that applied to us too. We concluded that even a small provocation was liable to bring the liquidation of the ghetto.

When people ask me why the Uprising erupted so late, I explain that it wasn't us who set the date. It was the Germans who had the power to set it with a provocation. As for us, we couldn't set the date of the beginning of the Uprising when we weren't yet fully prepared. In fact, April 19 wasn't a desirable date either from our point of view.

But let's go back. As I said, there was discipline in Wald's unit. Every unit worked night and day. First, they had to be on the lookout twenty-four hours a day. And various operations had to be carried out, like punishing traitors. There were also death sentences, and every single detail of every person we were about to punish or fine had to be checked carefully. We had so-called prisons, which had to be guarded, in my area and in the Central Ghetto. Wald maintained strict discipline and was also concerned with his people. He was short, plump, with pleasant manners and a sense of humor. I liked to spend evenings with his unit. I had a private room and would read there in the evening, since you couldn't walk around at night. But now and then I would go from one unit to another, even after curfew. Every unit, like Wald's, was located separately. His base was at Leszno 56.

Berl Broyde was different. He was the "intellectual" among our five commanders, a professional educator. He was from Slonim, a swarthy fellow, a member of Frayhayt, but his whole personality was typical of a prewar member of He-Halutz Ha-Tza'ir. A wonderful nature—and I'm not talking about battle conditions now: those are two different things. It might be correct to say that he was a very easy-going, yielding man. I was older than him and I would play all kinds of tricks on him (back in 1940). He was a good counselor, who prepared his guidance classes well. When we set up our base in Ostrowiec, we sent him there as a coordinator. When we set up the Jewish Fighting Organization in Warsaw, he set up the Jewish Fighting Organization in Ostrowiec. Then, we brought the whole group back to Warsaw. He behaved as we expected in the January Uprising. He was to be the commander of the new unit, but he was taken to Treblinka; however, he jumped off the train and came back. It took courage to go through the villages to get to Warsaw. He looked very Jewish: dark, Jewish eyes, Jewish charm. That was Berl Broyde.

I've already talked about Zacharia Artstein. His unit was in the Central Ghetto; but since he was closer to me than to Mordechai Anielewicz, he would call me to come and I would sometimes spend a whole evening smoothing out some rough edges between him and another member of his unit.

Hanoch Gutman was an educator. He was outstanding during the January Uprising. He too was one of the active members at Dzielna 34. He had a girlfriend; as I recall her name was Chaicia. We considered him fit for various roles, not exactly commander, even before we established the Jewish Fighting Organization and set up the units. He participated in the arson back during the Great *Aktsia,* in the days of Russian air raids in August, and later, in the groups of printers. He led the group assigned to murder Szmerling, which failed in its mission. That made him despair, since he saw it as a personal failure, as if he were responsible and had failed. As for his functioning in ZOB on January 18, those two men—Zacharia and Hanoch—were distinguished for their composure and inventiveness. When we formed our units, we saw that he was fit to be commander. He was in my area. Afterward, he moved, in March 1943 I think, to the Brushmakers' area. I was very sorry to part with him and his unit.

Yitzhak Blaustein, like the others, was a youth, I think he was no more than twenty or twenty-two years old. He was also one of those who were distinguished at Dzielna 34, which was our manpower reserve. We saw them up close for years; we lived together, we picked up their strengths and their weaknesses. I can't assess now how he was better or worse than the others. I don't remember seeing him in situations like the others. At any rate, we thought him fit to lead a fighting unit. He operated in the Central Ghetto. I didn't have daily contact with him, so I can't say much about him.

In January, the members of Ha-Shomer Ha-Tza'ir who were in one central and very important unit were killed. The whole unit wasn't killed. Some excellent people didn't live in communes and weren't in the Többens-Schultz area, but in other places. Like Arye Wilner and Yehuda Wengrower, who were in another unit, which didn't fight that day.

The Ha-Shomer Ha-Tza'ir commanders who were killed included David Nowodworski, who had escaped from Treblinka, Mordechai Growas, and Shlomo Winogron,[39] who was in the area of Hällman's shops, as well as Yosef Farber[40]—I knew them all. I knew those who were in my area: as commander, I also knew others from meetings. But we weren't so close. I knew Nowodworski better. I remember a girl, Rivka Saperstein—we called her Tsilke (from Z. Segalovitsh's book, *The Wild Tsilke*); she often came to the commune on Dzielna and to the one on Gęsia. She was David Nowodworski's girlfriend. I knew her from before the war. She was a pretty girl, a little wild, very energetic.

Let me say something about Israel Kanal: the day we decided that I should go to the Aryan side, there was a very serious internal discussion between Mordechai Anielewicz, Zivia, Miriam Heinsdorf, and me. We decided that Geller would replace me. We were aware that replacements weakened us to some extent, and we didn't know how Geller would work out. We said we had to keep an eye on him. But there wasn't enough time because, between the time I left and the onset of the Uprising, there were altogether only six days. Israel Kanal was supposed to replace Anielewicz so he would be free to supervise the units and could get to my area from time to time. Geller took my place and Israel Kanal replaced Mordechai Anielewicz. So Kanal was appointed commander of the Central Ghetto, and Lutek Rotblat was in charge of the Akiba unit.[41] But, in fact, the Akiba unit didn't really crystalize. Most of them were in my area. Po'alei Zion Left, Po'alei Zion–Z.S., Gordonia, and every one of the movements had a unit; Akiba was the only one that didn't. It had good people, and I was very happy to have them in our units; but one day I called Lutek Rotblat and his comrades as well as Israel Kanal and told them it was a sin against their movement not to form their own independent unit. I said I would gladly keep them in other frameworks but, in my opinion, they owed it to their movement. They accepted that, but were a bit afraid they wouldn't have enough strength; but that wasn't so. There weren't many of them, but they were outstanding. Then we started concentrating them in the Central Ghetto. They began organizing and had weapons by then, but they still didn't stand on their own:

39. Shlomo Winogron: Born in Warsaw. Was unit commander in Többens-Schultz area; led the operation to free Jewish prisoners in February 1943. Was badly wounded in the April Uprising and died at the age of twenty.

40. Yosef Farber: Born in Warsaw. Fought in the Central Ghetto during the April Uprising. Died in early May at the age of twenty-two. Details of his death are unknown.

41. Lutek Rotblat: Born in Warsaw. One of the founders and leaders of the Akiba underground. During the Great *Aktsia,* he and his mother hid and supported eighty orphans in a basement. Member of ZOB; acquired weapons. He committed suicide with his mother in the command bunker at Miła 18 on May 8 at the age of twenty-five. Berman describes Rotblat as "a fine fellow; erect and handsome, intelligent and energetic, who looked like a bold soldier. His relation with his mother and her educational institution was touching" (1977:103).

Visit of Yitzhak Zuckerman (*seated center*) to the Vilna branch of He-Halutz
Ha-Za'ir.

Lwów, New Year's Eve, 1939–40. *Left to right*: Oskar Handler, Zivia Lubetkin,
Yudke Helman, Yitzhak Zuckerman.

COURTESY YAD-VASHEM ARCHIVES JERUSALEM

PHOTOGRAPH HEINZ JOEST;
COPYRIGHT GÜNTHER SCHWARBERG

PHOTOGRAPH HEINZ JOEST;
COPYRIGHT GÜNTHER SCHWARBERG

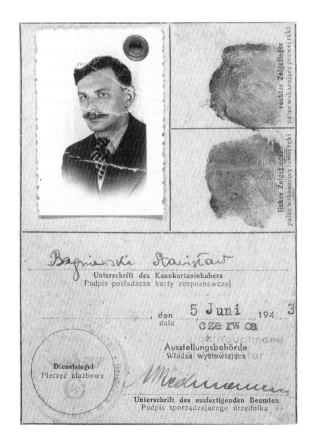

Ostbahn – Kolej Wschodnia

Personenausweis
Dowód tożsamości osoby Nr. *632*

D *em* in nebenstehendem Lichtbild Dargestellte
Na obok zamieszczonej fotografii

Herr *Stanisław Bagniewski*
p. (Vor- und Zuname — *Imię i nazwisko*)

steht als *Schrebaymi*
pozostaje jako (Dienstbezeichnung)
(Oznaczenie stopnia służbowego)

im Dienst der Ostbahn.
w służbie Kolei Wschodniej.

Das Lichtbild ist von d *em* Inhaber
Fotografia jest przez właściciela (tkę)

eigenhändig unterschrieben.
własnoręcznie podpisana.

Warschau, den *10.6.* 19*42*
dnia

(Unterschrift des Inhabers)
(Podpis właściciela)

Bagniewski Stanisław

(Dienststempel)   (Dienststelle)
(Pieczęć służbowa)   *(Miejsce służbowe)*

Czermann

*) Nichtzutreffendes ist durchzustreichen
    Niepotrzebne skreślić

(Unterschrift und Dienstbezeichnung)
(Podpis i stopień służbowy)

ke 3 16 2 (Ostbahn) Personenausweis A6 beigef. Karton Krakau II 43 100000 DrFkV

Antek's Polish ID cards bearing his alias, Stanislaw Bagniewski.

rechter Zeigefinger
palec wskazujący prawej ręki

linker Zeigefinger
palec wskazujący lewej ręki

Bagniewski Stanisław

Unterschrift des Kennkarteninhabers
Podpis posiadacza karty rozpoznawczej

den **5 Juni** 194**3**
dnia   **cze rw ca**

Ausstellungsbehörde
Władza wystawiająca

Dienstsiegel
Pieczęć służbowa

Unterschrift des ausfertigenden Beamten
Podpis sporządzającego urzędnika

Warsaw, May 1943. Kazik (*left*) and Stefan Siewierski, with Antek in
the background.
COURTESY BEIT KATZNELSON, KIBBUTZ LOHAMEI HAGETAOT

Left to right: Shalom Holavski, Abba Kovner, Yitzhak Zuckerman.
COURTESY BEIT KATZNELSON, KIBBUTZ LOHAMEI HAGETAOT

Brikha. Zuckerman is third from the right, Leyb Leviteh left of him.

Zuckerman with Leyb Leviteh.

PHOTOGRAPH HEINZ JOEST; COPYRIGHT GÜNTHER SCHWARBERG

Warsaw, April 19, 1945.

Zionist Conference, London, September 1945. *Left to right*: Itsik Manger, Yitzhak Zuckerman, Aharon Zisling, Israel Bar-Yehuda.

PHOTOGRAPH HEINZ JOEST; COPYRIGHT GÜNTHER SCHWARBERG

Warsaw, May 8, 1946.

Antek with former partisans, probably 1946.

PHOTOGRAPH HEINZ JOEST; COPYRIGHT GÜNTHER SCHWARBERG

PHOTOGRAPH HEINZ JOEST; COPYRIGHT GÜNTHER SCHWARBERG

Dror Conference. Zuckerman is in the center, Yitzhak Tabenkin right of him.
COURTESY BEIT KATZNELSON, KIBBUTZ LOHAMEI HAGETAOT

Conference of Partisans, Tel Aviv 1954.
COURTESY BEIT KATZNELSON, KIBBUTZ LOHAMEI HAGETAOT

PHOTOGRAPH HEINZ JOEST; COPYRIGHT GÜNTHER SCHWARBERG

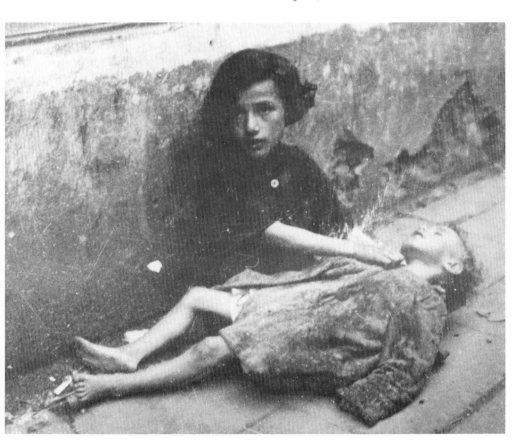

PHOTOGRAPH HEINZ JOEST; COPYRIGHT GÜNTHER SCHWARBERG

Zuckerman with his children,
Shimon and Yael.

COURTESY BEIT KATZNELSON,
KIBBUTZ LOHAMEI HAGETAOT

Zuckerman testifying at the
Eichmann trial, Jerusalem 1961.

COURTESY BEIT KATZNELSON,
KIBBUTZ LOHAMEI HAGETAOT

Zuckerman (*right*) on June 15, 1981, the day before he died, with
Benjamin Meed.

COURTESY BEIT KATZNELSON, KIBBUTZ LOHAMEI HAGETAOT

they were an emerging unit and, the day the Uprising began, they joined Yitzhak Blaustein's unit.

This is the movement breakdown of the ZOB units in Warsaw:

Dror—5 units
Ha-Shomer Ha-Tza'ir—4
Bund—4
Communists—4
Po'alei Zion Left—1
Po'alei Zion–Z.S.—1
Gordonia—1
Ha-No'ar Ha-Tzioni—1
Akiba—1
Total—22 units.

And by areas:

In my area (Többens-Schultz)—8 units
Central Ghetto—9
Brushmakers' area—5.

I might not be very exact now and this can and should be checked. As I said, every member of the ZOB belonged to a unit, was attached to the central staff, or was in communications and didn't belong to a unit. The same goes for those working on the Aryan side of Warsaw, who were all members of the Jewish Fighting Organization.

Some people unjustly claim to have been members of the Jewish Fighting Organization. Stefan Grajek did a lot of work in and out of the underground; but if he claims membership in the ZOB, that's not correct, since he didn't belong to any of its units. I don't mean to detract from the value or honor of Stefan Grajek, who was one of the founders of the Po'alei Zion–Z.S. underground in Warsaw and one of the loyal friends of the ZOB. He provided important help to the fighters by giving them access at a certain stage to the underground passage from Leszno Street to Ogrodowa Street, beyond the wall; though when I was commander of the area, he didn't tell me about it or about hiding places he had on the Aryan side of Warsaw. But it's to his credit that during the Uprising he gave the fighters access to the passage. Later, Grajek participated in the Polish Uprising in 1944; he was saved by a miracle after he was captured by the Germans.

There were more than five hundred people in the organized units, including those who were on staff and a group that had existed on the Aryan side of Warsaw even before I went there, a group sent to carry out special missions. Everybody in that group was a "soloist," each had defined tasks like transporting weapons, welfare, finding apartments, supplying documents, and so forth. All on behalf of the Jewish Fighting Organization in the ghetto, since they were sent by us. For example, Tadek Shayngut of Ha-Shomer Ha-Tza'ir was sent especially to acquire weapons and transport them to the ghetto,[42] so was Tosia Altman, whom we sent to the Aryan side of Warsaw.

She entered the ghetto by chance and was stuck in the bunker of Mila 18, although she was supposed to be on the Aryan side of Warsaw. The fact that she entered the ghetto caused quite a bit of harm, since I was left almost alone on the Aryan side.

The fighters in the units trained as much as we could allow each of them. They trained with Molotov Cocktails. The training was generally "on empty," since we were stingy with bullets.[43] But every fighter had to be able to strip and assemble his weapons in seconds, and to be familiar with the other kinds of weapons, in case he had to use them, since there were all kinds of pistols. And there were also variations and you had to know them all. We didn't get many rifles. I was happy when I could distribute two rifles to every unit. According to my written report sent to London, we had a "machine gun," but we really didn't. That was my error.

From early morning until late at night, the whole unit was busy training. Everyone was busy and everyone knew what he had to do. The unit could be deep in some courtyard or in an alley, but the street, beyond the wall, had to be watched. The lookouts were changed every two hours and if there was some special movement of the Germans, there was an immediate alarm! In my area, too, ZOB patrols frequently walked around. Once I traced some PPR members doing "Exes" on their own.[44] The function of the patrols, of course, was to make sure there were no Germans in the area, to prevent encounters with them; but also to keep the fighters from walking around the streets and carrying weapons and to make sure that those who went out had proper permits, because we were always tense about what might happen.

Some people went on "Exes," others had to provide food every day, go to the bakers, be involved with confiscations, fines, and punishments;

42. Tadek Shayngut [Szejngut]: Liaison with the AL on the Aryan side. Władka Meed describes him as "a sturdy, towheaded young lad, he wore heavy high boots and a farmer's long overcoat and had the looks and ways of a peasant. . . . He was both shrewd and fearless, undeterred by obstacles. He always carried a revolver, and declared that he would never be captured alive" (1979:97). He was indeed shot to death in an operation, described by Kazik (1984:82).

43. Kazik describes this "training": "We couldn't do real target shooting so we aimed at a cardboard target and would indicate the points we presumably hit. At one of our quick draw exercises, my friend's pistol went off—it was only because of his ineptitude that I wasn't hit" (1984:34).

44. "Exes": short for *expropriations*; operations to "raise money" among wealthy Jews still remaining in the ghetto.

for some people in the ghetto were punished with sticks. That was the usual punishment. For example, we used them on people who belonged to "wildcat" units and took advantage of that special climate of licentiousness to plunder in the name of the Jewish Fighting Organization. We would take their weapons and punish them with a number of strokes.

The January Uprising taught us not only that contact between areas was cut off, but also contact between units. So the command staff couldn't always decide on "Exes," but left it to every commander in his own area. However, a general policy was set for some issues, like executions. We would discuss every case in the command staff, except once: I issued a death sentence by myself because Mordechai Anielewicz and Zivia Lubetkin wouldn't make the decision. That was a case when we arrested a person and I had to decide what to do with him within twenty-four hours. I'll tell the story later.[45] I brought the two of them together with him, they heard all the details, and I asked for their opinion. It was hard for all of us because the responsibility wasn't on those who carried out the killing, but those who issued the death sentence. I had to decide because, according to the facts we had, if I didn't make a decision, I put all our units in danger because the accused knew about all the ZOB units.

That was a very special evening. After the sentence was carried out, I was restless. I usually spent the evenings with the units, but that night, I went to Stefan Grajek. I was aware of my responsibility. I didn't tell Stefan a thing. I wanted to drink, and I drank too much; I couldn't get rid of the gnawing worm. It was the sense of responsibility for a human life, which I had accepted because I didn't have a choice.

We met every day. If we had to decide something general, we would decide together. For particular issues in each area, there was no need to meet. When a person was accused of something, there was an investigation. There was no special court; the command staff usually played that role. In fact, the nerve center was not the command staff, but our internal central group, without Edelman. For example, we first decided I would go to Aryan Warsaw and then brought it to the full command staff. "We" means myself, Mordechai, Zivia, and sometimes Miriam.

In the areas, the fighters knew one another personally. There were no meetings between areas, but they did meet on occasion. For example, one day there was an alarm and we took a few units down to a bunker. Yakov Putermilch knows about that from his own experience because he was in the courtyard of Leszno 36, where three or four units were concentrated. The people knew one another since they would meet in various actions. I used to take people from more than one unit for "Exes," because you couldn't take five to eight people out of one unit at the same time; and

45. See below, the episode of "Pilotka."

we would compose action units from a few units, so people met each other.

The password was changed every day and we would inform the unit commanders of it. We were afraid of a provocation, which was one reason why we opposed the Revisionists' behavior. We preserved the secrecy of the weapons and the units. That was also the reason for the sentence I mentioned earlier.

We didn't have a single case of internal provocation in Warsaw and, in my opinion, there couldn't have been. An outside provocateur couldn't have gotten into our organization. All the people were members of movements; we knew them from 1940–1941; we saw them in various circumstances. A new person sent to us brought recommendations from at least one of the movements, either Ha-Shomer Ha-Tza'ir, Dror, Bund, Akiba, or the Communists. Only in a moment of weakness, after he was caught, might one of our people falter, as in one case. But that wasn't a provocation, he simply couldn't stand the tortures, and that's something else altogether.

In general, we had enough people in the movements to establish new units or to reinforce existing ones. But we didn't have enough weapons for them. If the Uprising had begun in May or July or August, that is, if the Germans had decided to finish off the ghetto later, we would have set up another unit or two, because we had a reserve of loyal people. If we caught somebody and locked him up, and later sentenced him to death, it was because he turned someone in or intended to turn someone in, because he was a provocateur.

Of course, we were always in danger even from the Jews themselves who ran into us, saw us going into the bunkers. We did stand guard and we didn't let strangers approach. We only let people from the same courtyard come to us, but there were courtyards of passage from one street to another which couldn't be closed off. But if the courtyard was closed, we knew who the tenants were, and strangers who entered the courtyard were asked where they were going, to whom, and why. But in the passage courtyards, as at Leszno 36, a stranger was suspicious. This doesn't mean there weren't potential provocateurs among the Jews. And there were also weaklings who faltered, but, fortunately for us, we didn't encounter them. On the contrary, after January, we usually found sympathy; I'm sure the people of the courtyard knew about us, they had to know, because we were different; we were young and we didn't work anywhere—a unit couldn't possibly carry out an "Ex" without someone later recognizing them in the street, even though their faces were usually masked during the operation. But the fact is the Jews didn't turn us in, except for those who were forced to, to save their own lives. They didn't volunteer to be provocateurs, but if anybody did that intentionally, we executed him, because they made contact with the Gestapo. I'm not saying we made a bloodbath. There weren't so many of them; but there were dozens. Because of the fear we instilled in them, many ran away and didn't do much damage.

We didn't have any mechanical means of communication except for secret telephone contact with the Aryan side. But we didn't have any instruments for internal communication. For example, in those days, it was practically impossible for me to contact Mordechai Anielewicz by phone. I never used the telephone, although I could call on the office phone of one of the shop supervisors (Schmidt); but I didn't want to. I usually went myself or sent a messenger. We always kept in touch.

At that time, I didn't know anything at all about the Revisionists' bunkers. (The "wildcats' " bunkers is another story.) For example, I didn't know about the Revisionists' tunnel, and I don't think any of us did. By the time the tunnel was discovered, I had been out of the ghetto a few days. It was on Muranowska, near our original base. When I moved to the Többens-Schultz area, I examined that house but I didn't like it because Karmelicka Street was on one side, with no exit; and on the other side, I was far away from the corner of Leszno Street. Subsequently, a Revisionist unit took our place. Just before the Uprising, they got out of there but, before they left, they told our comrades they had dug a tunnel under the street to the other side of the wall. Later, we wanted to use it to save Hancia Plotnitzka. But when I was in the ghetto, I didn't know about it.

I wasn't interested in the bunkers of simple Jews. I knew that the whole ghetto was one extensive bunker since, at night, you heard hammers pounding everywhere. We encouraged Jews to set up bunkers, but I didn't get involved in the details. I realized that if the Germans came, the final battle would take place here. We didn't believe for a minute that we would survive the battle with the Germans. There was food in those bunkers, and in every unit there was someone who knew about them; but the Jewish Fighting Organization wasn't involved in building the bunkers.

Now, five days of war pass and you're still alive! There's no place to go, so you start looking for bunkers, bread. You're alive—and that changes everything. The constant surprise is that you're alive. You wake up in the morning and you're alive.

One day I said to Mordechai Anielewicz, Zivia, and a few other friends: what a paradox—during the *Aktsia*, we thought of how to break through the walls. And now we want to keep the Germans from breaking through the walls. They all agreed that now we had to protect the ghetto and prevent the penetration of the Germans.

To sum up the lessons of the January Uprising: the first and most important lesson was that we could not defend ourselves in hand-to-hand combat, because of the quantity and quality of our weapons. We learned that from the two conspicuous incidents of self-defense: the street battle of Mordechai Anielewicz's unit and the death of most of the unit while my unit watched what was happening from the roofs and the upper floors. That taught us not to go into the street at all, that we must not be caught outside. So we had to carry on a guerilla war from the houses. Later we learned that even in a completely destroyed city, you can carry on a guerilla war. That is, as long as there are walls, as long as you can find a hiding place, you can set ambushes, and then a small force, even small groups, are worth much more than a larger force in open battle.

The second thing we learned immediately, early in the morning of January 18, was that you had to maintain total isolation between the units and to foster their independence. That is, to build on the fact that not only can every area fight independently—there weren't yet areas then, but only a few embryonic units in the Többens-Schultz area, while our main force was concentrated in the Central Ghetto—but also that, in battle, every unit has to stand alone, on its own, on the responsibility of its commander.

And that's what did in fact happen. There was a total isolation between the Central Ghetto and Többens-Schultz. Communication was through me; that is, I knew better what was happening in both places than they knew at Többens-Schultz about the Central Ghetto and vice-versa. This time, we saw the situation in advance. We learned the lesson of surprise—that the Germans surprised Anielewicz's group in its base. I must say that they also surprised us: I sent a messenger—Hanoch Gutman—to find out what was happening; but by then he couldn't get to them and was forced to return because the whole quarter and every house in it were surrounded.

Afterward, we saw the battles in the distance and didn't know how it all happened. Only a few days later did Mordechai Anielewicz tell us. We thought such a thing could happen again, and we took that into account. In the small ghetto, there were fewer Jews, fewer streets, and the Germans didn't need so many forces to surround us and split us. We assumed there could be a cut-off not only between the Central Ghetto and Többens-Schultz and the Brushmakers' area, but also within every one of the areas. In the Central Ghetto, we were divided into eleven groups and we feared that those little groups wouldn't be able to stay in touch either. And that is indeed what happened on April 18.

Indeed, we had to foresee that, because that's what had happened on January 18, too. Not only didn't we have contact between the Central Ghetto and the other parts of the ghetto, but we didn't even have contact within the Central Ghetto, between one unit and another, except at night. We wanted to avoid the mistakes of the Great *Aktsia*, when we thought that, if one quarter was surrounded, another quarter wouldn't be; and we thought that the Germans couldn't surround the entire ghetto at the same time. Which is what they did in January. We had to learn the lesson. By then, there was absolutely no argument about the independence of the units and the responsibility of the commanders. Every unit commander and his deputy received orders about when to open fire.

We were able to convey a lot of information to every unit commander, as well as to perform other operations like setting up new bases for units thanks to the regular observation posts we set up. Lookouts stood on guard in shifts, twenty-four hours a day. We remembered that in January, the Germans entered before dawn, when our people were still asleep; such a thing couldn't happen again in April. The lookouts changed every two hours. All members of the unit were involved in that. From Leszno Street, the lookouts could see what was happening on the Aryan side.

The Germans watched the ghetto from their headquarters at Zelazna 101 or 103. But we also saw what was going on on the other side. From the Central Ghetto, they also watched the gates. It was hard to see the gate of Nalewki and everything on Leszno, but from the Többens-Schultz side, we saw it very well. On the map, you can see that the Germans had to cross in front of us. They could do one of two things—they could come in through the gate where they would be discovered by our lookouts. Or they had to start breaking through the walls because the wall divided Leszno Street. They were seen whatever they did, even if they only crossed the street, because the houses were much higher than the walls. That house overlooked Nowolipki and Nowolipie Streets. They couldn't get in from Többens-Schultz either, and they had no other way, except through the side of the Central Ghetto. And if they came in from the *Umschlagplatz*, they would have been seen from Zamenhof. Plausibly, they would come in this way because their central base was in the *Feldstelle* (Gestapo headquarters at Zelazna 101–103). And this was the way they entered.

The only other possibility would have been to come in through Nalewki, in the "dead" zone.[46] But in that case, they could be seen from the Brushmakers' area. All the units had to set up lookout posts. There were always two people at the lookout post: one watched and the other was to run and inform if they saw anything.

The decision and the instructions about when to start fighting were explicit: at the moment the Germans enter! Their entrance in the April Uprising was known late at night, though I myself didn't know about it, since I was on the Aryan side of Warsaw. Moreover, I had even prepared

46. The zone separating the Central Ghetto from the small ghetto, declared a no-man's-land and not to be crossed.

to go into the ghetto on April 19, for the Passover Seder. Every unit commander knew that order: the moment the Germans enter, open fire; and the units were deployed in accordance with that, along Gęsia and Zamenhof. The order was that if the Germans marched in—and it was likely they would, as they normally did—we were to let them in and then begin the attack. The intention was to let them enter the trap and then start the attack when the head of the German column approached our last position, so they would be trapped in the range between our positions. We would surround them then from all sides, from front and back. And that is what happened, and it began in the Central Ghetto.

Thus, we learned from the January fighting. What more could we do? If we stood guard twenty-four hours a day, if we calculated the total dissociation and isolation of every area and every unit within the area, what other lessons could we have learned? In addition to the quantity and kinds of weapons we had, we learned to make things, like mines. As I said, we didn't prepare hiding places for ourselves.

Nevertheless, I must admit that the Germans surprised us this time too, which we hadn't counted on. It was something they hadn't done during the Great *Aktsia* or in January: after a few days of fighting, when they saw they couldn't conquer us easily, they began setting fires. They burned the passages between our positions and blocked our paths of retreat.

But let's go back, before I left for the Aryan side. I was in almost daily contact with Mordechai Anielewicz and Zivia. From the house at Leszno 56, where I usually lived, I would go through the whole area, from house to house, through the attics, without a single Jew seeing me. The hardest part was on Nowolipki Street, where it always involved mortal danger because there were snipers there who watched and shot at us. The snipers were Klostermayer, Blecher, and one gendarme, Frankstein, along with other Germans whose names we didn't know, who guarded the gates. They were all SS men, based at the *Feldstelle*, and they would also ride down the street on their motorcycles. To cross to somewhere else, you had to go down and watch what was happening in the street and only then set out. The houses were empty and you could pass from house to house. We knew all the houses in the empty area, no longer inhabited by Jews. Everybody could have crossed like that. Sometimes, when we only had to deliver a message, we sent couriers; but for discussing and consulting, it was the commanders who had to cross the road where there was a gate that the Germans didn't guard. Crossing always took hours and was done during the day. The fighters knew all the passages that traversed their area and the entire ghetto. There were experts in that, but I wasn't one of them. I did know my way to the Central Ghetto, for example, but they went to "Exes" and other operations every single day without going through the streets but through the attics. Before every such operation, our scouts would tell us how to get to our destination without being discovered. We didn't have maps, but we knew the area like the back of our hand. Our sights extended almost to the last house on Leszno Street (74, 76), close to the gate.

Once, when we were in touch with the Revisionists, I got information that they went to Leszno 74, 76, to make an "Ex" on a rich Jew. We warned them in advance not to do such operations without telling us or without getting permission (those were death sentences, punishments, and extortions of fines). And all of a sudden, we heard that they were doing an "Ex." They surrounded the home of that rich man, right next to the gate where the Germans were on guard. Because it was dangerous and so close to the Germans, I faced the dilemma of either pretending not to see or doing something. I decided to put an end to this because their success could lead them to make more attempts. So, I called a few units and we made our way through the roofs to that place. We warned them and prevented the act.

I must say this wasn't a group of bandits, but an ideological group; but we saw ourselves as responsible for what was done in the entire ghetto and we couldn't tolerate lawlessness. We sent a warning to their central base on Muranowska Street and threatened to punish them, and we were strong enough to do that. We didn't humiliate or insult them. I can say that they didn't succeed in those acts, and I think that was the last time they tried to do such a thing.

Saving that rich man wasn't important for me; he may have deserved a big fine. But we couldn't let them do such things in the ghetto without telling us about it. Moreover, such acts were always exploited by "wildcat" groups who lined their own pockets. In those circumstances, as the end approached, it was logical to prevent uncontrolled operations by elements acting on their own, to prevent break-ins which would be exploited by Jewish bandits operating in the area.

It reminds me of relations in Eretz Israel between the Hagana and the "Dissidents";[47] except with us, groups of Jewish bandits who took advantage of the situation filled this breach between us and the Revisionists. As for the Revisionists, we never knew what they were liable to do. There was also one case of an "Ex" done by the PPR members of a Jewish Fighting Organization unit, but not on behalf of the organization.

I want to add something else about the bases of the fighters. In some places, we thought we should keep fighting groups in the back of the building rather than in the front. But the lookouts always watched the

47. Hagana: The "official" underground military organization of the Jewish settlement in Eretz Israel from 1920 to 1948. The "Dissidents" were the right-wing underground organizations, ETSEL and LEHI, which violated the established policy of the Jewish Agency.

front from a window or a balcony, usually behind the curtain of a tall window. Sometimes, Jews who worked in the shops still lived in these places and, as long as things were calm, these were their apartments and we were at peace with them. We would use their houses with the clear knowledge that if the Germans attacked, all the houses would be at our disposal and the tenants would flee. So the units didn't need to be at the front of the house.

Furthermore, in case of an attack (not a general *Aktsia,* but a blockade because of a denunciation or something), we wanted to make sure we had a warning. The houses in Warsaw were located around big internal courtyards, and we had to be able to slip away, since we were very wary of provocation. We didn't want to give the Germans a pretext for an operation against us because a single German was killed, which could lead to a catastrophe. We wanted to gain every day of peace in the ghetto to prepare for the future. We assumed that the hour of the final struggle was approaching. We knew what our force was vis-à-vis the Germans and we had no illusions. The fact that our people remained alive in January was a complete surprise to us.

I've already explained why we didn't prepare hiding places and bunkers. We were afraid it would occur to some comrade—why "some comrade?"—that it would occur to me that there are hiding places and tunnels and we could retreat and escape through them. And that could be done even after forty-eight hours of fighting, when some logic whispers: "We've filled our obligation to history, now let's get out of here." We were afraid of the idea that we wouldn't have to fight to the end.

Moreover, in January, it wasn't us but the Germans who stopped the battles on the 21st. Otherwise, we would have gone on to the end even then, as long as we had weapons. Fortunately for us, they stopped. As far as we were concerned, the expected struggle had two aspects: first, not to hide, not to flee, but to fight. Second, not to be taken alive by the Germans.

Although we did know the hiding places of the Jews in the ghetto and used them from time to time (in January), we tried not to leave ourselves an opening for retreat.

The two tunnels we dug were for planting mines. These were deep, like those in the Brushmakers' area: one at the entrance, facing Nalewki, where the Germans had to pass, and the fuses led to the unit bases of the Brushmakers' area; the other was at the entrance of the Germans on Nowolipki Street and its detonation was also prepared from our bases. You could barely crawl through those tunnels; they were only for battle; they didn't lead anywhere. We couldn't count on breaking through the walls as a passage. There was one chance in a hundred for a Jew who got through there not to be identified on the Aryan side. Anyone escaping from there to the Aryan side as good as committed suicide. There was no purpose: you could break through the wall in a few minutes, but what could you do on the Aryan side?

Our whole strategy was built from the first and with the clear awareness that the fighters had no escape. And the command staff explicitly decided to plan everything on battles in the ghetto we wouldn't survive. Furthermore, years later, when I went back to the destroyed ghetto to see how things really happened, and I asked myself why we didn't prepare this or that, the only explanation was that the realm of life we set for ourselves was the space of time between January and April 1943. Even though only a few survived the April Uprising, that was surprising, compared to what we expected in those days. If not for that firm position, we could have prepared hideouts on the Aryan side of Warsaw in advance. To prepare them there, I would have had to go right after Wilner was captured, not on April 13; or Arye Wilner should have been assigned to do it when he was still on the Aryan side. But we were thinking about other things; we planned a battle that would be joined outside the ghetto by Poles in both Armia Ludowa and Armia Krajowa. Aside from acquiring weapons, that was in fact the major reason for my going to the Aryan side of Warsaw.

In that period, just before April, three or four people participated in the command staff meetings: Zivia, Mordechai Anielewicz, and I. As I recall Miriam Heinsdorf was also with us then, since she was in the area of Hällman's shop and, with Yosef Kaplan gone, our contact with her was more tenuous. We would usually meet three times a day and, more seldom, we would also meet with the other commanders. I went to the Brushmakers' area and of course I visited Marek Edelman. But the essential decisions regarding the tactics of our battle had been made back in February.

We had access to warehouses for as much food and medicine as we could amass, and they also served as "hospitals." Later, we distributed individual battle rations. We would dry bread in ovens and make rusks. There were basic things like water, which were prohibited in normal times. Whenever possible, we would renew the stocks, make new food and eat the old food before it got moldy. Water was problematic since we had neither cans nor water flasks, only bottles. Everyone had a special pack of basic first aid supplies prepared by the women. We didn't have a real hospital, but there were "prisons" that could be used for other purposes and people could be hidden there, even though they weren't proper hideouts.

We didn't prepare a defense for many days or weeks; we thought we had to figure only on a battle of a few days. We knew that the next battle that was about to begin wouldn't be like the one in January. For two months, the Germans had been trying to take us out of the ghetto by various means and temptations, and we hadn't responded to them. They used the Germans who ran the Többens-Schultz plants and Jews for propaganda; and, when they saw that it didn't work, they wanted to finish the ghetto off by any means. The possibility that we had the strength to endure for weeks in battles with the Germans didn't occur to anyone. So we didn't prepare for that. Even the food we amassed wasn't enough for more than a short time.

This new policy of the Germans, adopted to deceive the Jews, began right after January. Our first operation was to spread out over the four ghettoes. Our attempt to establish a base in the distant part of the ghetto, Prosta, didn't succeed. So we were concentrated in the other three ghettoes. The initial idea was that I would stay in the Central Ghetto; but after January, in a thorough discussion, we decided for various reasons that Mordechai Anielewicz would remain in the Central Ghetto and I would move to Többens-Schultz. One reason was that some of the comrades, especially from our party (Leyzer Levin, Sak, Morgenstern, Grajek), were in Többens-Schultz and were interested in reinforcement from their own Movement. Later on it turned out that that wasn't very important. I went there with Zivia. We started building the bases, and some time later, we agreed (because of Anielewicz's request) on Zivia's return to the Central Ghetto.

The Germans persisted in their attempts at temptation and deception. You can see that, if not in the first proclamation issued by the Többens people, then in the second or third proclamation to the Jews of the ghetto. The Többens proclamation warns the Jews not to believe us (ZOB), and so forth.[48] Többens had a printing press where Jewish laborers worked. When we learned he was preparing a proclamation, we attacked the printing press and confiscated what we found there. But he had time to

---

48. *To the Jewish Weapons Workers in the Jewish Quarter!*

The Commando of the Fighting Organization posted proclamations on the night of March 14/15. I would like to respond to them:

1. There is absolutely no intention of an evacuation. 2. Neither Mr. Schultz nor I were forced at gunpoint to carry out the *Aktsia*. 3. I state that *the last shipment was not killed——*

In Trawniki and Poniatów, every laborer received his baggage including all the property at his disposal . . . With a clear conscience, I can advise you again: Go to Trawniki; go to Poniatów, for you will have a chance there and you will spend the war there! The Commando of the Fighting Organization is not helping you and its promises are meaningless . . .

Believe only the heads of the German plants who want to transfer the production along with you to Poniatów and Trawniki. Take your wives and children, for they will be cared for too!

Walter Z. Többens
Supervisor of the Evacuation of Firms from the Jewish Quarter of Warsaw
Warsaw, March 20, 1943

For full text, see Gutman 1989:334–335.

post several proclamations on the walls; the fact is that one of them is preserved.

One day, the Jewish shop supervisors came with an announcement in Többens name—the Germans themselves got into that only later—that they were setting up two labor camps near Lublin (Poniatów and Trawniki) because no Jews were to be left in the ghetto; they promised work, education, and such there.[49] We saw that temptation as a great danger and decided to fight it. That was in March—they appealed to the Jews to respond to their invitation and transfer the workers and the workshops; we decided to respond with our own acts. One day we executed one of the supervisors who was most zealous in this issue. We received information that the man was corrupt and was exploiting the Jews. He extorted what little money they had to take them into his shop and thus made a fortune. If it had been only making money and economic collaboration with the Germans, we wouldn't have been so severe; but he was their errand boy and was very eager about moving to Poniatów and Trawniki; and that was too much. Later, we learned that they had already started dismantling the machines in Hällman's wood and furniture shop in order to move them. At night, we set fire to the shop. As long as the workers believed they were being taken with the machines, they were tempted; but when the machines burned down, they understood there was no reason for them to go. What would they do there without machines? We forced them not to respond to the deceitful German proposals. In fact, the plot didn't work, and only a few hundred Jews were seduced by their proposals.

Later, I learned that Többens wanted to meet with the commanders of the Jewish Fighting Organization. The request came through the Judenrat; as I recall, it was Yitzhak Schipper who delivered it to me at some occasion. It also came to us via the directors. Of course Többens promised on his word of honor that no evil would befall us, and that he only wanted to explain; he was concerned only with the good of the Jews and wanted to save his Jewish laborers. Incidentally, he survived the war, was captured, and turned over to the Poles. I don't know how, but he managed to escape before he was sent to Poland.

About the same time, we freed sixty people in jail. This was in my area: the Jewish police and the *Werkschutz*[50] arrested laborers for all kinds of "sins." We checked the situation out carefully and liberated them. They

49. Poniatów and Trawniki: Concentration camps near Lublin, built exclusively for Jews from the Warsaw Ghetto. After the April Uprising, about 15,000 workers from Többens-Schultz were sent to Poniatów. On November 5, 1943, German troops killed 15,000 Jews in Poniatów and 12,000 in Trawniki.

50. *Werkschutz*: Units of Germans, Poles, and Ukrainians who guarded important German factories during the war.

had the police and a jail, and with our simple weapons, we released all those prisoners. All those acts that sometimes involved killing weren't simple murders; they grew out of the conditions of ghetto life and were well understood by the Jews. We didn't hurt anyone for no reason. In time, the Jews began to see us as their saviors.

Another one of our operations was setting fire to the SS warehouses at Nalewki 31. That wasn't in my area, but in the Central Ghetto, near one of our bases.

On March 13 or 14, two Germans were shot in the ghetto. In retaliation for that, 170 Jews from the nearby houses were killed. That enraged people against us. Many of us also regretted it.

We had one friend on the Judenrat, named Mayofis [Ma-Yafit]. [51] That was his real name, so I remember it. He was a little older than us. We knew him as an official of the Judenrat, before the *Aktsia*. A person who was always willing to help us. We met with him right after the *Aktsia*, in July 1942. He had a secret telephone in his home. And we did use that telephone for conversations with the Aryan side of Warsaw: with Arye Wilner and later with Irena Adamowicz. But his telephone, which apparently didn't have a number, could be used only for conversations outside the ghetto; we couldn't use it for internal contact. In our conversations, we used a code understood by both sides. This was how we conveyed information. During the Uprising, the comrades also started using the telephones in the shops.

In time, we realized that Mayofis was an expert in forging documents, for example, documents for workers in the shops. That was very important for us because none of us worked and we couldn't be in the street without a work permit. This was valuable only between *Aktsias*, and not when an *Aktsia* was going on because then the Germans didn't bother with documents and did whatever they pleased. Nevertheless, it helped and added to the self-confidence of our people when you could prove you were working in some shop. Our great forger was Moshe Rubin, one of the Zbąszyn people, who was a graphic artist by profession and inclination.[52] He was a "forger par excellence," as well as a gifted artist. Thanks to the blank forms we got from Mayofis and Moshe Rubin's talents in forging handwriting and stamps, we had various documents we needed.

Mayofis also gave us details about the Jewish bank. That was a bank on Zamenhof Street, guarded by Polish police, where the Judenrat kept

51. Mayofis: In Modern Hebrew, *Ma-Yafit* means "how beautiful," a nickname for a Jew who demeans himself before a gentile. He was a Bund sympathizer, who was killed in the April Uprising.
52. Moshe Rubin: Born in Berlin. Was a member of Grochów, active in Dror underground in Warsaw, and a member of ZOB. He fought in Zacharia Artstein's unit. Details of his death unknown.

money. There was also a steel safe in the Judenrat building. And thanks to Mayofis, we knew who had the keys. The history books say he did what he did because of the 30 percent he got;[53] but I say: No! Absolutely not! I can testify that Mayofis did what he did for the purest and most idealistic motives. He gave us details and we could easily get the keys. Israel Kanal put on his Jewish policeman's uniform and, at dawn, went to the treasurer of the Judenrat and used threats to get the keys from him. We went to the bank and took out the money. We did this twice. The second time was just before the *Aktsia;* but by then I was no longer in the Central Ghetto. Another time, we attacked the treasury of the Judenrat in the middle of the day; to do that, you needed proper documents. Mordechai Anielewicz and I strolled innocently down Nalewki Street to see how it was carried out, how our group was getting along. It was about noon. Two of our people were carrying a vat, the kind they use to transport soup, because there was a kitchen near the bank and carrying a vat was reasonable. The men approached the bank, went inside and took out the money; it was a very successful operation. One of the simplest and most efficient operations.

There's a description of a similar but more complicated operation about the policemen in Haim Frimmer's book.[54] That was after I left the ghetto. He talks about our mistakes in February, but the operation I'm talking about with the bank and the Jewish policemen took place in April 1943. When I was in the Central Ghetto, I was often involved in operations there. Like executing Nossig. Although I was in the Többens-Schultz area by then, I came especially to the Central Ghetto and stayed there a few days to organize that act. That decision was made right after January. I don't remember why I was assigned to it. That was in fact a continuation of my work, the sort of thing I dealt with.

The January Uprising gave us wings, elevated us in the eyes of the Jews, and enhanced our image as fighters, giving us a good name. Every Jew in the ghetto knew about the January Uprising. They "knew" even more than there really was. So many legends were going around that the Polish press, not only in the ghetto, told of our tanks. The January events had extraordinary repercussions even in Armia Krajowa (AK), which had always eschewed us and now agreed to give us fifty pistols immediately (in reality, we got forty-nine). They also supplied us with grenades and the explosives we needed.

After January, we appealed to the bakers for bread. They got flour from the Germans via the Judenrat, in the Central Ghetto, according to the number of people registered. But that was very little and not enough

53. See, for example, Hirsh Berlinski, in Blumenthal and Kermish 1965:186.
54. Carmi and Frimmer 1961:206–209.

for their needs. We didn't have storehouses, but Gepner did. But that wasn't enough either because tens of thousands of Jews had to be fed. As I recall, in the shops, the flour was given by the German owners of the Többens-Schultz shops. Everyone had his own baker, from whom he had to get bread.

There was always collusion between the German employer on the one hand and the Jewish supervisor and the baker on the other. Everybody subtracted a little from the weight of the merchandise he supplied, since none of them was "decent," but such people got rich on that. The bread was given according to documents, the bakers sold the leftovers, and the Germans knew about it. That is, at Többens-Schultz, they knew the bread account exactly. They knew there was enough flour for the fighters because there weren't so many of us in terms of our share of the Jewish population. And there was no problem to supply bread for five to six hundred people. So, we decided not to use "Exes," but to appeal to the bakers to join in supporting the fighters. Even if some baker respected us and wanted to give us white bread, we refused. We had definitely decided to accept only black bread. Most of the bakers we appealed to gave gladly; we set a certain quota for every baker. It was carefully checked; we had "eyes and ears" in every shop, and a few of the shop supervisors also cooperated with us. We had good information about the situation, and we knew how much we could assign every one.

Some bakers gave generously. We would come quietly, when no stranger was expected, and take our share. But others promised and didn't keep their word. Then we would send a retaliatory unit, which would confiscate everything, not just the black bread but also the white bread and the cakes—since sometimes they also baked cakes. That usually helped. If not, we would move to the next stage: a beating. There are all kinds of stories of groups involved in this.[55] I didn't participate in it personally. I didn't think I should take part in it, and I didn't want to be exposed. It wasn't good for me to be too well known.

There were demonstrations of goodwill on the part of craftsmen who came to help us. For example, one of our fellows might have a cobbler friend make a holster for his pistol. The cobbler would express a desire to make holsters for others too, since, without a holster, the fighters would tie their guns on with ropes. Making holsters was a spontaneous demonstration of appreciation for the Jewish Fighting Organization.

And there was a case of "little anchovies." They weren't really anchovies but that's what we called them. A hick like me, this was the first time I heard of such a fish as an anchovy. Before that, they were just the worst kind of little herrings the Germans distributed. It was at this time that the

55. See, for example, Carmi and Frimmer 1961:195–197.

food improved a little, and anchovies were an indication of that. We didn't get food from the Judenrat because as far as they were concerned we didn't exist. But the shop supervisors, or Gepner, would give us something from the storehouses they controlled. If they hadn't given us anything, we would simply have gone hungry. In addition, Lutka's brother (Ottikar Manen), who worked in a kitchen, made us a vat of soup every Sunday, and that was the only kitchen (as I recall, it was at Leszno 36) that helped us.

Meanwhile, we imposed fines and contributions on Jewish economic collaborators. Sometimes someone who was fined took care to spread the information that he had paid up, that is, that he wasn't a candidate for execution. If someone was a candidate for execution, everything he had would first be confiscated. However, the confiscated property wasn't ransom.

In some cases, though, we would issue a death sentence in good conscience against a person we originally planned just to threaten. That, for example, was the case of Herman Katz, commander of the police in the Central Ghetto, whom we ordered to come to some empty house with a lot of money. At that time, we had three men in the police who said that Katz had decided to teach us a lesson. Our note said he was to come alone with the money. Our policemen told us that he assembled a group of Jewish policemen to follow anyone who followed him and find out who those fighting "bandits" were. That man wanted to set a trap for us but because we knew about it in advance, we were prepared and our lookouts saw the policemen he had mobilized. When he came, he wouldn't respond to our demands because he was sure his policemen would come to his aid. As I said, we didn't think of executing him, but we did after we learned about the trap. Until the very last minute, he was sure his police would save him.

In general, all our death sentences were justified. As for that Katz, we realized he meant to cheat us. He wanted to know who the fighters were so as to identify them and turn them over to the Germans, which was reason enough to execute him.

That sentence greatly influenced the hundreds of Jewish police who were still serving. They learned not to "fool around" and that we weren't playing. I must say that in those circumstances, anyone who stayed in the police deserved such a sentence. But we tried to select only those who were "outstanding," distinguished for their cruelty. The truth is, though, that not one of them was clean.

Who were the prominent people we sentenced to death? The first, after January, was Dr. Alfred Nossig. We got information that he collaborated with the Gestapo. In 1940, when he was on the Judenrat in Warsaw, rumors had circulated about all kinds of "good deeds" he did.

We didn't know then if the rumors were gossip or truth. Our attitude about the Judenrat was different then. We didn't yet see it as an embodiment of treason. The Judenrat of 1941 was not the Judenrat of 1940, and that of 1942 certainly wasn't that of 1941. Nossig was on the Judenrat; by then he was an old man, but for me he was a living legend. I didn't know then about the can of worms he was toting around. I heard more details about his life from Yitzhak Gruenbaum when I came to Israel. Gruenbaum wasn't surprised that he had stooped to collaboration. I knew he was Theodor Herzl's cousin and rival; I read his articles and poems; I knew he was a prominent mathematician and one of the first to apply statistics to studies of Jewish life. I knew he was a writer and sculptor and had also tried his hand in politics. They say that after quarreling with Herzl, he became bitter and abandoned Zionism. He had plans for the migration and productivization of Jews—not exactly in Eretz Israel. Nevertheless, when he would appear in some hall or public place, the members of my generation stood up in respect. I saw him only once or twice, by chance, at the Judenrat. But we often discussed him with Bloch, Kirshenbaum, and others. Later, during the *Aktsias*, there were rumors about his relations with the Germans. We didn't know exactly what kind of relations these were. In January, we didn't yet suspect him of direct contacts with the Gestapo on the Aryan side. But, evidently, he would come to the Judenrat and sit with Brandt. At that time, we didn't see the full seriousness of those contacts.

The die was cast after January 18, 1943, after four days of *Aktsia* and battles, when our policemen brought us information that on the morning of January 18, the Germans blocked the gates and didn't let anyone pass (the members of the labor groups, including Yitzhak Katznelson, were returned)—no one went out and no one came in openly, except for one single person—Alfred Nossig. That old man came to the gate, the Germans stopped him and examined his documents. He had an imposing figure. They saluted him and he passed. That immediately attracted our attention, and we asked our policemen to investigate; it turned out that this wasn't the first time. But on January 18, when the streets were empty, it was very conspicuous.

In fact, he wasn't an official member of the Judenrat. The Germans had put him there, and even Czerniakow was annoyed by it.[56] There were others like him who got permits to enter the Judenrat, for example

---

56. From Czerniakow's Diary: "Morning in the SS . . . ordered to give a job in the Community to Dr. Nossig" (Entry of December 9, 1939; Czerniakow 1979:97). "Dr Nossig who was hired two days ago did not show up for work yesterday . . . It appears that he won't be any solace to us" (Entry of December 11, 1939; Czerniakow 1979:98).

Giterman, who wasn't a member of the Judenrat, but of the Joint, and was killed by the Germans on Miła Street.

As for Alfred Nossig, if he had come a day before, we wouldn't have noticed since he was known to be working for the Germans on the Judenrat. But the fact that he was walking openly on that day through the empty streets made us suspicious, and we asked our policemen to ask the Polish guards where he went when he left the ghetto; a few days later, we got reliable information that he went straight to the Gestapo on Sucha Boulevard. Now there could be no doubt about the nature of his contacts with the Germans. And so, I was assigned to carry out the death sentence of Alfred Nossig.

Nossig was the only one who appeared as the authorized representative of the Jews (Czerniakow was dead by then, and we had executed Fürst). But he wasn't even an authorized representative of the Judenrat. So what reason did he have to appear at the Gestapo so freely, when they were killing Jews in the streets of Warsaw?

We began investigating Nossig's moves. I formed a group that studied his comings and goings, and it turned out he didn't go there every day. They said he had a Christian woman, and it was hard to discover where he spent the night and what he did. In the ghetto, he lived on Muranowska, in the courtyard of the Judenrat, that is where all the Judenrat members were living at that time. We sent three people to tail him; Alfred Nossig wasn't anybody special to them. They didn't know his past because they didn't know the history of Zionism and hadn't read books about it. As I recall, it was Zacharia Artstein and two other members.[57] I told them he was a person collaborating with the Gestapo and I emphasized that it was desirable to get a confession out of him. And, in such a case, it was obvious—the death sentence.

I didn't want to be in the group because I didn't want him to know my face, in case he remained alive. The Nossig case was special, and the man was distinguished. I sat nearby and waited. They came back and said they had killed him. They made that decision on the spot. Apparently when they started pressuring and threatening him, he got down on his knees and begged for his life. Then he threatened them with German vengeance, saying that Brandt would avenge his blood. At that moment they shot and killed him. They searched him and found a document in German and gave it to me. I was the first to read it. They also said they saw other documents in his apartment. I immediately went off and started

57. The group that executed Nossig consisted of Zacharia Artstein, Abraham Breier, and Paweł Schwartzstein. Abraham Breier was a member of ZOB who rescued many people from the Gestapo. During the April Uprising, he fought in the Central Ghetto and was killed in the fighting at the age of twenty-seven.

reading. I was stunned. It was a report to the Gestapo about the mood among the Jews after the January *Aktsia;* the report was in German, two or three pages. One thing he wrote was that he thought the Germans didn't act very cleverly by being cruel to the Jews during the *Aktsia* (of January 18/19) in the streets of Warsaw, showing the Jews how their brothers were murdered there. So he recommended using other methods so as not to stir up Jewish resistance.

Nossig was advising them how to behave! After I read that document and after the members of the group reported and waited for an explanation, I said this was extremely important and sent them back to his apartment immediately to take everything he had. But by the time they got there, Brandt and the Germans had already been and had taken it all.

After the war, after we had published the document, a funny thing happened. Alfred Nossig's relatives all over the world maintained that no one had killed Nossig, that he had died of old age. I publicly claimed responsibility for his killing and said I was willing to stand trial for it. Now the event belongs to history and is covered by the statute of limitations; but I wanted to deal with it after the war, in 1945–1946, when I came to Eretz Israel.

He was seventy-nine years old when he died. Herzl died in 1904, at the age of forty-four, and Nossig apparently wanted to be his heir, his replacement. Afterward, I grew increasingly interested in him. Morgenthau says in his memoirs that, when he was U.S. ambassador to Turkey, Alfred Nossig worked in Istanbul for the Austrian government.[58] After the massacre of the Armenians, Nossig offered Morgenthau a bribe to hush up that genocide.[59] That is, even then, the man was crooked. During the great debate among the Jews of Poland about the problem of national minorities and the quarrel with the Polish government, led so courageously by Yitzhak Gruenbaum, Nossig suddenly appeared from Germany as an intermediary between the Jewish minority and the government, without any authority at all, and tried to speak in the name of the three and a half million Jews whose authorized leader was Yitzhak Gruenbaum. Nossig's act led only to failure and contempt. That was when Gruenbaum established the "Kolo" in the Polish Sejm.[60] Apparently, Nossig's quarrel with Herzl unbalanced his mind and, ever

58. *Germany Is Our Problem,* diary of Henry Morgenthau, Senior (1856–1946), a financier and diplomat; he was U.S. ambassador to Turkey 1913–1916.

59. During World War I, possibly a million Armenians in the Ottoman Empire fled, were killed, or deported.

60. In 1921–1922; the "Kolo" ("Club") was a parliamentary caucus of groups of national minorities in the Polish Sejm. Gruenbaum was attempting to form a coalition of Jews and other national minorities in the Polish Sejm; the effort failed because of both Polish pressures and internal divisions among the Jews. See Ezra Mendelsohn (1983:53–56).

since, he had gone in perverse directions, working for the Germans and the Austrians; in Warsaw he deteriorated completely. If it had happened to him in advanced old age, you could say it was senility. But it turns out there were previous, controversial stages in his development. The report we found on him was apparently the typed copy; the original probably got to the Gestapo. The report showed that he regularly sent them reviews of the mood in the ghetto, things he knew and collected, since he was in the Judenrat.

Fürstenberg, one of the "prominent" men who was executed and should be mentioned, was murdered by the Revisionists, and the case also sheds light on their function. He was one of the high-ranking officers of the Jewish police and probably deserved a death sentence for his role.[61] He was afraid for his life at that time and tried to buy it with a "ransom of weapons." He swore to get us weapons, and after all, weapons were what we sought most. Because of that, we hesitated to kill him. Then the Revisionists came along and killed him. I don't think his killing was a great sin. But it shows the lack of cooperation between us. That repulsive Fürstenberg knew what we had done to Szeryński, Lejkin, and Fürst; he knew we weren't fooling around and, in his attempt to be saved, he began getting weapons for us. We had reliable information on that. He was able to get them through the Polish police; moreover, we didn't have to pay for the weapons. And here he is killed by the Revisionists without any contact with us. That was one of the things that clearly proved that, aside from the struggle with the Judenrat, you couldn't also have a struggle between the fighters, even if there were two networks.

One day, when Zivia and Mordechai Anielewicz were with me at Többens-Schultz, a messenger came from Gepner in the Central Ghetto asking that "Miss Zivia come immediately to his department in the ghetto." Gepner deserves a monument to his memory. He was a man who wasn't part of popular Jewish circles, far from Yiddish culture, and was known as a capitalist in Poland, one of the magnates. But in the ghetto he revealed his greatness as a generous person and Jew, helping whomever he could, even the Halutzim. When we appealed to him for our needs, he gave generously.

61. Jurek Fürstenberg: Son of a wealthy manufacturer from Będzin. According to Turkow, "He excelled in satisfying the will of the Germans with 'his accomplishments' in liquidating Warsaw Jewry" (Turkow 1969:54). Stanisław Adler testifies that "there were stories about his extraordinary stamina and endurance when faced with a battery of alcoholic drinks. But this well-built, handsome young man, with his Adolphe Menjou moustache, acted with disgusting servility toward his commander . . ." (Adler 1982:16–17). Haim Lazar describes the assassination: "The fighters came into his house, detailed his sins to him, read him the sentence and shot him on the spot" (Lazar 1963:215). Ringelblum incorrectly credits this assassination to the ZOB (in Blumenthal & Kermish 1965:147).

That day the Revisionists, that is, their fighting unit, besieged the Supply Department and, threatening Gepner with weapons, demanded so many hundred thousand Złotys. He told them: "My boys, you can't threaten me; I'm an old man and I'm not scared of you. Put down the weapons; nothing will help you; I don't know you. If you want something, send Mrs. Zivia to me; she'll come to me without weapons; I'll talk to her but not to you." He told us the story afterward. Gepner was no Fürstenberg they could threaten and kill. That man didn't give in.

Zivia went to Gepner and, after she heard him, she told the Revisionists to get out and they did. Then she and Gepner sat down and talked. He asked her who they were and she explained that they "weren't ours" and that it would never occur to us to do such a thing. He asked what food and money we needed and gave generously; but I don't know if he gave them anything, too.

That was a time when we didn't give anything we got from our "Exes" to anybody else. But they also learned something from Gepner's firm stand. I went to their base on Wartiwoda and told them: what are you doing? Threatening to execute somebody without telling us in advance? True, Fürstenberg deserved to be punished, but we were in touch with him for weapons! They learned a lesson and then we reached some kind of arrangement. This was almost April. In March we divided the areas between us. We agreed that they wouldn't execute anyone without our permission, and that they also had to get our permission to carry out "Exes," or at least had to tell us so there wouldn't be any duplication, because that dishonored us and caused harm. We agreed that they would tell us in advance and we would check it out. After that, we would allow them "Exes." But meanwhile they did a few killings among the Gestapo in the Brushmakers' area; and I must say that all those they executed certainly deserved it. But things were done without our knowledge. Meanwhile, the girl from Ha-Shomer Ha-Tza'ir was executed,[62] and there were episodes such as that of Adam Zurawin, who saved himself; and there was the attack on Lulek (Leon) Skosowski who was wounded.[63] There were all sorts of people, some whose names we knew and some we didn't. The Germans had set up *Zagiew* ("Firebrand"), a quasi-underground group of assimilated Jews which, in 1940 and 1941, put out a few issues of newspapers or bulletins. Then the group vanished and suddenly reappeared in late 1942, early 1943, announced themselves as

62. See above, chapter 3.
63. Adam Zurawin and Leon Skosowski: Official assistants of the SD (*Sicherheitsdienst*). They were mostly on the Aryan side and not in the ghetto. Their job was to denounce Jews on the Aryan side. (See Turkow 1969:67.) The Revisionists claim to have wounded Skosowski (Blumenthal and Kermish 1965:153–154; Lazar 1961: 215). They were also involved in Hotel Polski (Shulman 1982:93; Meed 1979:178).

a fighting organization, and published proclamations. We started investigating who they were and found out that they were in fact a Gestapo-inspired group. We got information about that in the Brushmakers' area, but the Revisionists came to grief by cooperating with them.[64]

I didn't treat the Revisionists as they treated us. I was the one who asked one of the fighting Revisionists who remained alive until the Polish Uprising to write about the deeds of the Revisionists in the ghetto.[65] And he wrote that they killed Lejkin and Fürst. He credited the Revisionists with everything. I gave that material to Berman, adding only a short note for the sake of truth and precision; and I told him I wanted him to send that report as it was, along with my note, to London. Unfortunately, Berman didn't tell me that he didn't send it. I decided privately not to censor that testimony. But, after all, I was also a witness, and I'm allowed to add my own testimony.

Indeed, they claimed that they supposedly carried out the acts in the Brushmakers' area. And there are also a few of us who behaved like them and tried to take credit for their acts, thus perverting the historical truth and the role of the Revisionists as well.

There was one episode that annoyed me very much. Death sentences were issued by the members of the command staff together. (Berlinski wasn't so active, he was a unit commander in Marek Edelman's area.) Three or four people (at any rate, not just one or two) participated in all such decisions. We had one member at Grochów, one of the Zbąszyn people, named Rudolf Samet,[66] whose father was a supervisor of one of the shops. The son didn't join a fighting unit and stayed with his father; but he was a source of information for us about what went on in the shop. He gave us reliable information, which we needed to carry out "Exes." Because his father was friendly with many managers, he knew details. For example, he told us about a Jew who got rich and hid a lot of money in a lampshade; and we arrived there "ready," and they were amazed at how we got to the money. Samet was the source of our information. As I said,

64. According to Gutman, "The exact nature of this organization [Zagiew] is obscure, but it was suspected of being responsible for provocative acts designed to sow confusion and fear within the ghetto" (1989:349). Ainsztein says that the group was formed by Gancwajch, by order of the Gestapo: "The aims of the organization became quite clear when it issued an appeal calling on all the inhabitants of the ghetto to gather outside the Judenrat in Zamenhof Street and there begin an uprising. Had the Jews followed the appeal, it would have been very easy for the Germans to surround them and drive them to the railway yards. Of the sixty members of Zagiew, the ZZW and the ZOB liquidated fifty-nine . . ." (1979:88).

65. The report was published in *Dapim l'heker ha-shoah v'ha-mered*, no. 5, 1987. See chapter 9.

66. Rudolf Samet: Active in Dror underground; devoted to ZOB, provided information about "Exes" in the Többens-Schultz area, helped expose traitors and economic collaborators. Details of his death unknown.

the fellow wasn't in any unit and I didn't care about that either, since his advantage to us was that he was in the field and not connected with the fighting organization—which was why rich economic collaborators weren't wary of him.

One day he told me that a man appeared in the area who was supposedly organizing a Jewish partisan unit in the ghetto for the AK. (That was when Arye Wilner was still on the Aryan side of Warsaw.) That was a surprise to me because the AK didn't operate in the ghetto except through us, the Jewish Fighting Organization. And indeed, it wasn't long before we realized that the AK hadn't sent anyone to get involved in that operation.

A fear of informers arose, but that wasn't all. One day, people started talking about a guy who was hanging around our fighting units, each time near a different unit. Once I passed through the connecting yard between Nowolipki and Leszno, with my courier behind me. And the courier said: "That's the guy." I wanted to see him, but he was standing with his back to me. I jostled him as I passed by; he turned around and I saw him: medium height, unfamiliar face, black moustache, and a leather pilot's hat. I hadn't run into him before. From then on, we always called him "Pilotka" because of his pilot's cap with earflaps.[67] I must add that aside from the information I collected on him, there was a similar case on January 18 in my area, when we lost two men because of an informer, and all our fighters were ordered to get out of the area and go down to the Jews' bunkers. In this case, you couldn't miss him. We saw him going through the Germans' gate alone. A few times, the unit watching the *Befehlstelle* saw him passing SS headquarters and wondered who could be going to that building?!

One day, when I was at that base, they reported to me that the man was in the yard. I ordered him arrested and brought to our prison at Leszno 56. When they started interrogating him about what he was doing at the *Befehlstelle*, he said he had gone to buy a hat. We checked and found it was true. The store was across from our apartment, and he memorized these things in case he got caught. When we beat him, he gave only one name: "Lilka." We knew that a girl of that name had collaborated, that is, a Jewish girl working for the Gestapo; but we didn't know her personally or where she lived. We learned that this "Pilotka" was recruiting people for a Polish partisan unit that didn't really exist, and that he wasn't sent by any authorized element. He was the person who was seen going to the *Befehlstelle*,[68] the person who went through the gate on the day we all hid and it was forbidden to be in the street, the person who hung

67. His real name was Moshe Wald.
68. *Befehlstelle*: Headquarters.

around all our units. And now—after we kept him in prison for twenty-four hours and used all sorts of means against him, including blows—we didn't get anything out of him.

When I met Mordechai Anielewicz and Zivia the next day, I told them the story and that everything indicated that he was connected with the Gestapo. If not, why should he be hanging around our units? And what was he doing at the German *Befehlstelle*? How could he go out through the German gate, where no Jew could? And what was he doing altogether? Why was he organizing a partisan unit? Rudolf Samet, our informant, was sure from the start that this man was working for the Germans, but Samet didn't know how he got to us either. There was nothing in his favor, except for the excuse of buying a hat, which was a dubious pretext that anyone who saw the hat shop could use. What was that man doing at my door where we caught him? I told Mordechai and Zivia that I couldn't hold him any longer, and if he was released or if he got out of the cell somehow, the whole Jewish Fighting Organization of that area was lost since he knew everything. And if he wasn't innocent, I said, the only sentence was death. I added that I didn't think he was innocent, but I wanted a joint decision about him. I can't explain why Zivia and Mordechai Anielewicz didn't join me in that decision. They kept repeating: "You decide." So, I was forced to take that responsibility on myself. I called Benjamin Wald (*Tatele*), one of our wonderful fellows, and said: Listen, you've got to do the cruelest thing! But promise him that if he tells the whole truth, we'll pardon him (even though I'm not sure I meant that). Bring him a shovel and let him dig his grave in the prison yard (on the ground floor). And he did dig the pit, knowing his death was at hand. All he said were things like: "I went here, I went there." How do you make a living? Where do you live? Who are you? Who knows you in the ghetto? He couldn't answer any questions. Since night was coming on, I said we had no choice but to execute him. The sentence was carried out and he was buried there.

That was the first night I didn't spend at the base, the first night I got drunk. I went to Stefan Grajek, who lived at the end of the street. I didn't tell him anything. I just said: "I'm staying here with you. Have you got something to drink?" He did have something and I drank; I drank too much. In such a case, there is naturally always room for doubt, for "perhaps." Although as I pondered the case over and over, before he was executed, I couldn't find a single argument in his favor. After all, he didn't answer even one question. After all, these were Jews—why didn't he answer?! The truth is that he did talk, but he didn't say anything relevant. Nevertheless, it took me a long time to get rid of the worm gnawing at my insides. It was a sense of responsibility for a human life. I was forced to accept it. Maybe he didn't tell because he didn't believe they would release him. He was sure that telling meant certain death; and if he kept quiet, he thought, he might not be executed. But we brought him right up to the grave, which he dug himself, and he didn't reveal a thing. But even after the event, we haven't found out anything more, to this very day. And to this day, I can't help thinking of him as a collaborator, yet we don't know a thing about him.

In many places, the Gestapo infiltrated very deeply. Among the Poles, that was done not only by *Volksdeutsche*, but also by Poles themselves. With us, too, Jews did it. We didn't know where the Germans brought the man from, how they made him do it. It wasn't the only time, but that time, they succeeded in infiltrating deeply!

Every unit had the weapons we distributed, and every member had weapons. For some reason, Geller decided on his own, and without telling anyone, to acquire weapons and consequently fell into a trap, along with two other members of Gordonia, Yehuda Konski and Shimon Leventhal. They made contact with some guy who hung around us, but we didn't know if that was "Pilotka" or somebody else because Geller kept it secret. The two fellows from Gordonia heard about some guy who sold weapons and when they went to pick them up, Gestapo agents were waiting for them and arrested both of them. Those two who were arrested knew all the units, people, and places; when I found out, I realized that anger and shouting about dumb behavior wouldn't help anymore. First, we had to save the organization since it was clear that if they didn't stand up under torture and just told where our bases were, all of us and all our hopes for the Uprising were lost.

So we descended deep underground for a night and a day, hiding in the Jews' bunkers. I stayed with a few couples at Leszno 36, at the apartment of the sister or father of Yakov Putermilch.[69] When I spoke with him later, I learned that it was his sister and brother-in-law, Zalman, both members of the Jewish Fighting Organization. As I said, we knew about the Jews' bunkers and, when we were in trouble, we had to use them to disappear. They accepted us there without questions or worries, even though our existence was supposed to be secret; they fed us and protected us. That was the day that decided the fate of "Pilotka" among other things, since our people working in the shops on the street saw him that day, passing the German patrol at the gate, after showing them documents. That was one of the things that gave him away. We came out of the bunkers after the policemen said they got orders to come take two bodies from the German *Befehlstelle*,[70] the bodies of the two fellows from Gordonia. Since nothing had happened to us, we concluded that they hadn't

69. See Y. Putermilch 1981:44–45.
70. SD headquarters at 103 Zelazna Street.

broken under the horrible torture. Not a single one of our addresses got into the hands of the Germans, so we could come back to the surface. I don't know how they stood it, how they could endure the torture, but they did; and they paid for it with their lives. We waited a little longer, assuming that if they had been executed, they hadn't given anything away because, clearly, if they had told something, the Germans would have raided us *immediately*. They might not have captured all our bases, but they would certainly have captured the base of those two. But there wasn't even a hint, not a sign that the Germans knew anything. After we got the announcement, we stayed in the bunkers a few more hours and, seeing no German activity, we came up.

I should add that none of the unit commanders was authorized to deal with weapons on his own. The center took care of acquiring weapons, and the issue of weapons in general was in the Central Ghetto, not in the areas. The weapons sent from Aryan Warsaw arrived there exclusively. The two fellows clearly fell into a trap. And it was clear to me who had sent them. So I went to Geller, and he admitted his error. He said he had been sure everything was all right and hadn't suspected anything. I don't think he should be convicted for that; but it was a breach of discipline which caused the death of two people, since he should have consulted with me before he sent them. And if Geller had come to me and said that there was a source of weapons and he was about to send two reliable fellows, I might have examined it very very carefully. I should add that Geller was new in the area and didn't know what we knew about "Pilotka."

What was Geller's motive? Did he want his unit to have more weapons? No way to know. I heard that in the Palmakh, one unit "filched" weapons from another. Of course, I did read him off. If such a thing had happened between him and Marek Edelman, he would probably have been insolent to him. He didn't dare talk insolently with me. By that time, I knew that I was about to leave for the Aryan side of Warsaw and that we didn't have any other candidate for area commander except Eliezer Geller. I spoke harshly to him about responsibility. But I could also have made the same mistake, anybody could. If I start counting people who were sent to their death, I could also record things in my own ledger, in terms of conscience. I don't want to hide things; I might conceal the weaknesses of others, but not my own. Maybe private weaknesses, but not my public weaknesses, which had serious significance. Those were extraordinary times. If every commander takes stock, he will find, in hindsight, that this or that person could have survived if he hadn't done what he did.

Concentrating laborers who worked outside in the Central Ghetto was done by the *Werkschutz*. One day when I came to the Central Ghetto for a meeting with Zivia and Mordechai, an incident occurred when the *Werkschutz* assaulted a group of Ha-Shomer Ha-Tza'ir and the latter killed two Germans. This led to a severe retaliation. The day after that event, I was with Mordechai, Zivia, and Tosia Altman in the apartment of a policeman who was loyal to us, Luxemburg, when Germans appeared in the area. They had obviously come because of the operation in which two Germans had been killed. I heard shooting but I didn't want to go down to the bunker. That was a retaliation on Miła Street, as I recall, at the spot where the Germans were killed.

The incident evoked a harsh discussion. I argued that a Jewish Fighting Organization that couldn't protect the lives of the Jews was not authorized to engage in acts that endangered their lives! I felt ashamed in that sharp discussion. There's no trick to killing one or two individual Germans. But if they were caught with weapons, that had serious consequences both for us and for simple Jews. Ever since strict orders had been issued about carrying weapons and possible provocations on our part, we decided absolutely not to walk around with weapons, except when on a specific operation and under orders. We had set similar rules of caution against provocation. I felt that those dead Jews who were killed in a German retaliatory raid were on the conscience of the Jewish Fighting Organization. We couldn't save them, and we weren't set up for that. I must say I didn't encounter any hostile repercussions from the Jews for that incident. There were no accusations of us. But we knew it was our own fault.

There was another incident when the Revisionists killed a few Germans in plainclothes, that is, detectives. We then explained to them that such things weren't to be done in the ghetto because someone would pay a high price for it. I must say that, hard as underground life was, it was relatively much easier than the life of the average citizen; because the organized member of the underground knew he had to be careful, to escape, to hide, that he might be on a German list. But the average Jew and the average Pole went out day after day to make a living and suddenly found himself paying for something he hadn't done, didn't know anything about, and therefore of course couldn't have refrained from. Those Jews might go to lunch in the soup kitchen when the Germans set up a retaliatory blockade in a certain area and all those in those streets or houses were executed.

True, we regarded all Jews as condemned to death by the Germans, and we were firmly determined to attack them the minute they started taking Jews to the *Umschlagplatz*. But that meant refraining from acts of provocation until the time came. After all, the Germans weren't looking for the people who had committed the crime against them. And we thought Jews had to be responsible for one another; and, not only for the Jews, but for the Poles as well.

I would like to add something about the "Exes" and the question of whether there was a connection between the Polish and the Jewish PPR.[71] As long as the connection was a Movement one, I was concerned with it. But after the incident of the two Gordonia members who were tortured and executed, I ordered our patrols and scouts to act with strict caution and not walk around the streets without permission. Needless to say, carrying weapons was strictly forbidden.

One day, the patrol ran into three fellows from the PPR unit and their commander whose name, if I'm not mistaken, was Hirshl (Henryk) Kawe. The three fled but the commander was brought to me. I interrogated him about his actions in the area. He answered me honestly and showed me the pistol he was carrying. I asked him about the three who were with him and if they were also armed. He said he knew about the ban and claimed that he got orders from PPR to do "Exes" in the area for the Polish PPR. I was furious. I upbraided him as commander, for taking orders from civilian political parties, thus jeopardizing the fighting organization. I said that he and everybody else had to know that "Exes" and all military operations had one single authority: the command staff of the Jewish Fighting Organization.

We wanted to investigate immediately whether the Polish Communists had indeed ordered their Jewish comrades in the ghetto to get money like that. (Arye Wilner was still on the Aryan side at the time.) We wanted to tell them that the disobedience of a fighting unit was a serious matter. Moreover, while there was a lot of German money or money from Polish collaborators on the Aryan side of Warsaw, we considered it a serious offense to send Jewish and non-Jewish groups to get money from Jews for their own operations. We told them there were banks on the Aryan side of Warsaw, too.

Their answer was categorical: they had never under any circumstance assigned their PPR cell to get money for them in the ghetto. There's no way to know whether or not that was correct; at any rate, it was the only case of disobedience by the PPR that I came across. There were a few cases of "Exes" ending in death; and to this day, I don't know who was responsible for them. These cases brought neither health nor honor to the ZOB, for they were always attributed to the Jewish Fighting Organization.

In one case, as I recall, a group broke into the home of a rich Jew at Leszno 36. I can't remember who they were, but it wasn't under our command or on our behalf. Maybe it was a "wildcat" group or a Revisionist or PPR group. In that incident, the Jew resisted and fought them and they killed him. In some cases, we guarded the streets and, when we

71. The Communists had one party for Poles and Jews, in and out of the ghetto.

caught the commander and his men in similar acts, they got what was coming to them. We tried to prevent killing in those "Exes"; and we didn't take all the person's money either, just some of it. Murdering a person in an incident like that would be shocking to us. As I said, we couldn't investigate who killed that Jew and took the money.

There were also Polish groups who came into the ghetto to do "Exes" for robbery. There was something even worse than that, after January, on Miła Street, before I moved to Többens-Schultz. A fellow from Ha-Shomer Ha-Tza'ir, Mordechai Growas, as I recall, was ordered to transport some grenades and pistols from one place to another. Suddenly, a group of Poles appeared, attacked him, and stole the weapons. Sometimes Poles would come into the ghetto through the sewers and attack Jews. This ended after January. We posted our own patrols and protected ourselves very well, and I think a few of the villains paid with their lives.

There was an incident in my area when a "wildcat" group did an "Ex" and we found out about it. It seemed that Arye Wilner's uncle Alec (he died two years ago in Israel) was looking for a way to get to the fighters. Our secrecy was so tight that Wilner didn't tell his uncle how to get in touch with the ZOB. By joining one of the "wildcat" groups, the uncle was sure he was joining one of the units of the Jewish Fighting Organization. Afterward, Alec and his group participated in "Exes" that weren't ours and weren't done on our behalf. But we managed to catch all the perpetrators. After an investigation, a quick trial was held, and the guilty were beaten and threatened that, if it happened again, they would be executed! We put Alec in one of our units. And he told us about his comrades who were simply robbers who divided the money they stole. Since he was an honest and ethical man, he gave us all the information. Later, he had another episode: he left the ghetto on his own and the "Cigarette Sellers" found him in the fields of Grochów.[72]

We had our own prisons for those convicted of economic collaboration with the Germans or who had been fined and refused to pay. Others we didn't care to keep in prison, not to mention the special case of "Pilotka," whom we were forced to interrogate and who was imprisoned for that. There were many cases in the central area of people being jailed for a long time. We decided not to execute the head of the Judenrat, M. Lichtenbaum; but we did decide to impose a contribution, a high fine, on the Judenrat. That was a step aimed deliberately at humiliating the Judenrat and making the miserable and evil people among us aware that the only authority in the ghetto was the Jewish Fighting Organization. We assigned

72. The Cigarette Sellers were a group of Jewish children on the Aryan side of Warsaw who supported themselves by selling cigarettes. Their patron was Joseph Ziemian (Zissman). Most of them survive and live in Israel. See Joseph Ziemian 1977.

the social activists to inform Lichtenbaum of the fine, which was an indemnity for the Judenrat's collaboration with the Germans. Marek Lichtenbaum cannot be compared with Adam Czerniakow, who may not have been a great leader, and who didn't understand what he faced and where his path led, but, as soon as he became aware of those things, he drew the conclusion and committed suicide. Whereas Marek Lichtenbaum continued at the Judenrat as if nothing had happened: "The king is dead, long live Marek Lichtenbaum." He had two sons and it was whispered that they were Gestapo agents; but there was no proof.

When the Judenrat didn't reply to our demands, we caught one of Lichtenbaum's sons and kept him in prison; then Lichtenbaum told us he would pay the fine—he had probably consulted with Gustaw Wielikowski and Abraham Stoltzman—on condition that we delete from the indictment the charge that he was collaborating with the Germans. But we couldn't give in on that point.

When we saw that the issue was dragging on, we said explicitly that, if the money wasn't paid soon, the son would be executed. That worked and the money came in. We weren't bloodthirsty; we didn't want to turn killing into an everyday thing because you could easily get used to it. There's no wisdom or ethics in such a policy. The man was released.

There was another case of a Jew named Marian Hendel who made a fortune. He was an economic collaborator with one of the Schultzes, the German owners of the Többens-Schultz workshops, the "big Schultz," who had great respect for him. We knew he had a lot of money and we sent him a letter with demands accompanied by a threat. Instead of replying, the *Werkschutz* began guarding Hendel's courtyard and house to keep us from taking him out of his home. It infuriated us that that Jew, in cooperation with the German manufacturer Schultz, could lead the Jewish Fighting Organization around by the nose. This went on for a while until we got some helpful information. There was a Jew named Gerwinski, as I recall, who represented foreign citizens in the ghetto vis-à-vis German institutions. He wasn't a collaborator, he just handled that issue. And now we found out that Hendel was trying as hard as he could to get a foreign passport. He would occasionally come to Gerwinski about it. We began investigating him and then pressured Gerwinski to get complete information from him. We decided to trap Hendel with cunning. We picked a beautiful, charming girl, Gitta Kwonki, a member of Gordonia, who used all the information we got from the passport man to get through the *Werkschutz* blockade and reach Hendel. She told him that what he had discussed with Gerwinski was arranged, and that he was requested to be in such-and-such a place in an hour. Hendel was very happy, called his wife and said: we should take out a bottle of wine today and eat some cake. He poured wine, they ate the cake; they finished, and

followed her out. They came to the connecting courtyard between Nowolipki Street and Nowolipie Street, where our people were waiting to
take him to the "meeting" and put him in jail. We told him: "There are
no passports, no trips abroad. Give money." He claimed that he didn't
have any. He refused to eat or drink. He refused to eat, he claimed,
because he was religious and wouldn't eat unless we gave him a *tallis* and
tefillin. I didn't appear in his presence except once, at the end of the
incident. We brought him a *tallis* and *tefillin*. A Jew wants to pray—why
not? Then we brought him kosher food: eggs and butter and bread and
milk. Whatever we could get. No meat, of course. He sat in jail one day,
two days, three days. We knew that Schultz and the religious circles were
in an uproar because the man disappeared and didn't come to the person
in charge of foreign passports and didn't return to his family. Nor did he
show up at work. Obviously he wasn't killed since his body wasn't found.

One day, one of the leaders of Aguda, Alexander-Zysze Friedman,
whom I knew from before, came and said he had to talk with me. I
received him. Friedman apparently came to the conclusion that Hendel
was in the hands of the Jewish Fighting Organization. He asked me if we
had Hendel and I said we did. Then he asked if he could meet with
the prisoner. I agreed on condition that he be taken blindfolded to the
prisoner. I also explained that the man wouldn't be released until the
ransom was paid.

We left the two of them alone. Our prison was well guarded. Zysze
Friedman later asked me to join the conversation and I appeared openly
with Hendel. He swore that if we released him, he would return with the
money. After all, there was no point writing letters to his wife. He promised to bring the money in a few days. He also complained about the big
sum imposed on him and argued that if he gave us that much, he wouldn't
have enough money left for an apartment on the Aryan side of Warsaw
and to support his family and certainly not enough to get a document to
go abroad. I managed to persuade him that he had enough money for
both, and I agreed that we would be the last to get the money. We wanted
him to save himself, I said, but he also had to give what the Jewish Fighting
Organization deserved, since the whole city knew he was a millionaire.
That was in mid-April and, meanwhile, I left for the Aryan side of
Warsaw.[73]

When they found out I had released the man, my comrades tormented
me. Mordechai and Zivia assailed me for believing him and said I should
have held onto him. I explained that we were dealing with Zysze Friedman, a public personality, who wasn't a liar, who swore to be responsible

73. There is another version of the Hendel incident in Y. Putermilch's book (1981:
50–57). Putermilch guarded the cell.

for keeping the promise. Of course, the failure was all mine. Only in mid-May, after the remnants had fled the ghetto, did I learn that Hendel had succeeded in saving his money and didn't keep his promise.

This matter ended after the war in the Hotel Polonia at the end of 1945, I think, where the Shlikhim from Eretz Israel were living. I went there almost every day at that time. I was also known in the splendid hotel restaurant. I would drop in there for meetings with Polish government and army men and would also visit the Shlikhim in their rooms. Once, in the room of Dr. Moshe Kurtz, director of the Welfare Ministry, I was sitting with my back to the door. Someone entered and started talking to Dr. Kurtz from the doorway about getting Certificates to Eretz Israel; at a certain moment, I turned my head and there was Hendel. When he saw me, he started trembling, as if he had seen a ghost. Kurtz didn't know about the case and didn't understand why the man turned pale. We brought him into the room and I told him: "Calm down, what you didn't pay then, you won't have to pay now. I just want to know if you saved your family." He said: "Yes, with great difficulty, but not the money. Right after we went to the Aryan side of Warsaw, blackmailers with the help of the landlord took everything I had. Even the money that was for you."

I learned that he later immigrated to Eretz Israel. I was glad he survived, even though he was a contemptible Jew, for whom I have no other name than "bastard," since we're talking about collaborators who were like traitors. I know he made a fortune in Israel, but I don't know if he's still alive. I couldn't care less about him.

Those are two opposite examples: the son of Marek Lichtenbaum, head of the Judenrat, who was an economic collaborator, and when a fine was imposed on the Judenrat, it was paid in full; and the second example—my personal failure—and because of it, a Jew succeeded in shirking payment of the fine.

Imprisonment generally helped. When we wanted to force someone to pay his contribution, we would keep him there.

I should mention the "Ex" made on the Judenrat vault, where our people found a silver candlestick, and the treasurer (Ephroim Malmud) who opened the vault claimed that it was his own private candlestick. Our people took it from him but gave it back to him after checking it out. That shows they didn't hurt just anybody and were even strict about small things.

There were a few prisons. One prison was in the Central Ghetto, on Miła Street; there was a prison in Többens-Schultz, whose entrance was from Leszno Street. Members of the units were used to guard them. We would force people to do this job. We made sure there were always responsible people for it. You had to bring food to the prisoners, but there was always one guard who didn't budge from his post.

Yitzhak Schipper told me about Lichtenbaum who, at a certain moment, said to the Germans above him: "We no longer control the ghetto; there is now a more real authority—the Jewish Fighting Organization." He told the Germans this when they demanded to take Jews to Poniatów and Trawniki. That was when the situation in the ghetto was absolutely unbridled and "wildcat" gangs were running mad there (the situation we called "Mexico"). The proclamations issued in the ghetto were signed by the Jewish Fighting Organization and, in fact, by then the Judenrat had no real authority; it no longer had anything to say and there was no one to listen to it.

Himmler's letter or order for the final destruction of the ghetto was issued in January 1943. We knew about this after his visit to the ghetto.[74] I have some memory of a day when you were forbidden to leave the house. A few days later, we learned that Himmler had visited the ghetto. On January 18, we didn't know anything. After the visit, they did indeed begin to liquidate the ghetto. It was only after the war that I saw the document, including the order itself.[75]

As for the date of the Uprising, I repeat that we didn't decide it, the Germans did, and there's a difference. If I had had to decide, I wouldn't have set the beginning of the Uprising for April 19. I would have waited until some ray of light was revealed, a tiny chance to save someone, in spite of the clear knowledge that all of us were going to die. The possibility of being saved by going to the Aryan side was hard. Some did succeed in going over, but those who remained in the ghetto didn't have many choices. The Jews built themselves an underground city to hide in; but they didn't all have bunkers, not to mention good bunkers, and everybody knew he could hold out in the bunker for only one to three weeks. Because how much food could you hoard? And you also have to remember that the possibilities of bringing water, bread, and fuel into the ghetto were limited. Because of all those things, we waited for the Germans to dictate the time and place of our uprising. We hoped we would be ready in time. As for the method of fighting, it was now obvious that we would try not to fight street battles. We chose the method ourselves. Another advantage was that we knew the ghetto. But we left the choice of the date to them. All we had left in fact was to keep the vow we made in September not to let them take any more Jews to Treblinka!

We thought the situation in the next *Aktsia* would be the opposite of the previous *Aktsia*. At that time we had tried to break through the walls, whereas now, we had to defend the walls so the Germans wouldn't come

74. On January 9, 1943.
75. Himmler's visit to the ghetto was on January 9, 1943, but his order for the final destruction of the ghetto was issued on February 16, 1943.

in. This time it wasn't rescue by breaking through the wall. There was no hope of that. Leaving aside for a moment the fate of the Jews still in the ghetto (and such a "leaving aside" was absolutely unacceptable to me), if we concentrate only on the fighters, obviously, by breaking out of the walls and fleeing to the Aryan side, we couldn't have saved even 10 percent of them. No more than that. We also knew there was no hope for us in street battles.

We always had people on the Aryan side. But when it had to do with vital plans (for example, that the Poles of the underground would join the Uprising and fight at the wall), you had to have a well-known representative of the Jewish National Committee and the ZOB to deal with the Polish military organizations. To understand the circumstances and background of the decision to send me of all people, the central person in the Jewish organizations, to represent them, we have to explain the relations between us and the Poles.

Contact with them was renewed in September 1942. That was contact with the two military organizations: the big, official one, AK (Armia Krajowa), subordinate to the Government-in-Exile in London; and the smaller one, AL (Armia Ludowa, previously Gwardia Ludowa) which tried to reconstruct the ruins of the Communist Party which had been dissolved by the Comintern and renewed after the outbreak of the Soviet-German war. Communist historiography tries to fill the interim, until June 22, 1941, with the existence of pro-Communist, "wildcat" groups supposedly without a center, but which were credited with Communist operations. Polish historians "fill the vacuum" the same way. The Jew Ber Mark also considers the operations of the Halutz youth in the ghetto as miraculous, but he also attributes all that to the pro-Communist left. This is exaggerated, although I can't altogether deny the existence of leftist groups in the ghetto.

The leftist Gwardia Ludowa was formed, as I recall, in January 1942, by the Communist Party (PPR) as its military organization. Later, this developed into a more general national organization (Armia Ludowa—AL). Time passed between the declaration and the real beginning of operations. The fact is that the operations of the PPR in the ghetto didn't begin before January 1942, and they had much greater success there than in Polish Warsaw. It is not correct to deprive them of the initiative in the establishment of the Anti-Fascist Bloc, since they were the ones who initiated it in the ghetto. What I wrote in the Jewish Fighting Organization report sent to London at the end of 1943, that the Bloc was founded by the intiative of Po'alei Zion Left, is nonsense. The truth is that I didn't want to delay sending the report to London by debates with Berman, so I decided to give in. The same holds for the notion that the Anti-Fascist Bloc that collapsed "was the basis for the Jewish Fighting Organization."

That's not correct either, because the Jewish Fighting Organization was established in fact *only by the Halutz movements, after the Bloc fell apart*. And the Arbeter Komitet also collapsed, and the general meetings didn't bear fruit, and people fell into the hands of the Germans and were sent to Treblinka. Yosef Finkelstein-Lewartowski, the Communist, was also captured and sent to Treblinka.

I will briefly review our operations on the Aryan side of Warsaw: ever since the fateful decision in September, we were trying to reconstruct the ruins of the organization, to obtain weapons. We sent Arye Wilner to the Aryan side, and he succeeded in making contacts. The people who helped us were our friends from the Polish Scouts, Irena Adamowicz, Hubert (Kaminski) and the third who always appeared in the name "Hajduk." (*The Hayduks* by the Romanian writer Panait Istrati was popular in the youth Movement and in the Scouts, and I imagine the nickname was taken from there.) [76] He was an educator, a friendly man, very modest. (I'll talk about him more later.) As I said, Arye Wilner made contact with the AK and the AL. In Aryan Warsaw, Tosia Altman and Marek Folman (who went there after January) worked together. And Frumka Plotnitzka and Leah Perlstein were also there (in Czerniaków). Adolf Berman left for the Aryan side on his own, and his activity there was mainly political. I'm talking now, however, about security operations, begun by Arye Wilner, who was captured by the Gestapo on March 6, 1943, when contact with the Polish underground was broken. After he was caught, it was decided to send me to reestablish contact.

After I left, I was in close touch with the Jewish Coordinating Committee, that is, with the Bund, and nothing important was done without joint consultation. After Wilner (whose underground name was Jurek), I was in charge of these contacts. His contacts were made with the help of the the Scouts who had a position in the AK, where they filled important functions. For example, Hubert was the main editor of the *Information Bulletin*, the official organ of the AK. He had influence and standing. Others worked in their spy service and in other, more vital areas of the AK.

The January Uprising resulted in their sending us the almost fifty pistols I've already discussed, as well as explosives and grenades. Moreover, Arye Wilner began buying weapons from arms dealers. At that time, he would come into the ghetto from time to time, and we could also get out. Once, Mordechai Anielewicz went to the Aryan side of Warsaw to

---

76. Apparently Zuckerman was mistaken; Hajduk was his real name. Panait Istrati (1884–1935), of Romanian origin, wrote in French.

meet our activists there (Feiner and Berman); at a certain stage, we informed Arye Wilner that, in fact, there was no need to endanger our network on the Aryan side because there were sharp Jewish dealers who, in partnership with the Poles, would transport weapons through the walls and sewers, and we could get weapons for almost the same price from these ghetto merchants. But of course he couldn't allow himself to give up even one source that came his way. And that was what caused him to fall into the hands of the Gestapo.

That was after he returned to our apartment and we learned, after the fact, exactly how it happened and by whom. Later, I was able to locate the woman who supposedly sold the weapons and who was a Gestapo agent. Wilner lived in the same house as a member of Ha-Shomer Ha-Tza'ir who later left operations and cooperation with us and shifted exclusively to activities in Gwardia Ludowa. This fellow witnessed what happened, since he lived one floor above, and saw the German detectives lying in wait for Arye Wilner; they arrested him when he climbed the stairs. Wilner also told us the story when we rescued him from the camp where he was imprisoned and brought him to the ghetto with his legs badly wounded. He told us that a woman who promised to sell weapons was the one who got him into the trap. That was our first failure on the Aryan side, but not the last. We had other victims because of a deal that looked very safe, but turned out to be a Gestapo trap.

While he was on the Aryan side, Wilner followed our instructions and began negotiations with two elements, the AL and the AK. He also carried on initial discussions about cooperation in case of an uprising in the ghetto. They began working out a joint plan with the AK and a parallel plan with the Gwardia Ludowa, without letting the AK know about our contact with the Communists. The Communists, however, did know about our connections with the AK, didn't reject it, and even encouraged me to stay in touch with them. I shouldn't have told them about it either, but I thought it right to do so because it was hard to hide it and the AK was suspicious of us. The AL, however, did not reject our cooperation with the forces connected with London. The PPR policy strove to form a popular front; they did succeed in that in the ghetto by establishing the Anti-Fascist Bloc, which later fell apart; on the Aryan side, among the gentiles, they had no success. But they understood that our sights were set, first of all, on the good of the ghetto, the Jewish Fighting Organization, and the struggle. And they accepted our priorities. Sometimes, when I gave them information about our operations, they would bless and encourage us. According to our primitive, early plans, at a given signal, the AK was to attack the ghetto from the *Umschlagplatz* and the Brush-makers' area and to connect with our forces as they burst through the walls with explosives. The walls could be easily assaulted since it wasn't a Maginot Line,[77] but a brick wall that the dumbest smugglers opened breaches in every other day.

The plan called for the AL force to attack from Leszno and, for my own reasons, I was very happy about that because I wanted to join forces with the Communists and not the AK. Meanwhile, Arye Wilner, who was highly esteemed by all those who knew him and had good contacts, was caught. I had heard of their respect for him when I was previously on the Aryan side and their sympathy increased after his arrest, when the tortures he underwent didn't lead to the breakdown the Poles feared. They on the Aryan side and we on the other side of the wall also feared a collapse since he had met with many people, and if he hadn't endured the torture and had revealed even meeting places, it's not hard to imagine the magnitude of the catastrophe.

He was indeed tortured severely by the Gestapo; I saw his feet afterward. They hung him up and put white-hot iron on the soles of his feet! When we brought him to the ghetto, he couldn't stand up and was wounded, bruised, and burned all over. But he was tortured primarily on the soles of his feet. After torturing him, they put him in Pawiak Prison, a reservoir where people were executed or taken to Treblinka. Since they discovered he was a Jew—and that was easy—they put him into the Jews' cell, and he expected to die there. But they didn't get anything out of him; he didn't break, didn't tell them a thing, didn't help them in any way. They would probably have taken him to Treblinka, but in March and April, we didn't hear about transports leaving from Pawiak, although many Jews were kept there for various crimes.

The Polish police told us he was in Pawiak. With the help of a bribe, he managed to give us a sign of life. One day, Brandt, appointed to the ghetto by the Gestapo, came to Pawiak to take out several Jews to be sent to death, to a labor camp near Warsaw,[78] where people were employed making bricks. He didn't interrogate or ask much, just pointed to those to be sent. Because Arye Wilner looked relatively young, he pointed to him, and took him with a transport of dozens or hundreds of Jews to that labor camp. When Arye arrived at the camp, he was very weak and wounded. You must know that there were many camps of all sorts in Poland (about eight thousand camps!) and even recently, after so many years, we got information about camps we never heard of. This was one of those camps. In any case, it wasn't far from Warsaw. When he got there,

77. Maginot Line: Supposedly impenetrable elaborate defensive barrier along the French-German border constructed in the 1930s. The Germans literally got around it from the Belgian border in 1940.
78. Rembertów Camp.

Wilner sent word of his whereabouts through one of the guards to a Scout, one of Irena Adamowicz's people, Heniek, a young and ordinary Polish guy who was involved in smuggling, buying and selling, but who was also active in the Polish underground.

So he got word to Heniek who conveyed the information to us. We had a cell of young people who looked Aryan on the Aryan side of Warsaw. These included Tadek, Tuvia Shayngut—and, at some period, Marek Folman was also there. At this time, Folman had left Aryan Warsaw, because of a conflict with Arye Wilner, and had gone to a partisan unit. Tadek was a member of Ha-Shomer Ha-Tza'ir. There were a few more women and two fellows from the Communists in that group. They organized the rescue of Arye Wilner from the labor camp, with bribes, of course. They had to carry him because he couldn't walk. They kept him on the Aryan side of Warsaw a few days, until they arranged with our police to get him into the ghetto. He stayed with us through the Uprising, but he never regained his strength. Miriam Rotblat, Lutek's mother, took care of him in one of the apartments. We tried not to visit him every day so as not to expose his hideout. We were afraid the Gestapo would look for him in the ghetto, since he had really slipped through their hands, from the labor camp. After Arye Wilner was arrested, we were cut off from the Aryan side of Warsaw and the members of the Polish underground we were in touch with. I can't blame them for cutting off all contact with us for a few weeks for fear they would also be discovered in the wake of Arye Wilner's capture; I think I would have done the same. We tried a few times, through our people in the Scouts and Tosia Altman, to get in touch with them, but the answer was: "No, for the time being, no."

Not until early April, I think, did we hear that they were willing to renew the contact, and then we faced the question of who would take Jurek's (Arye Wilner's) place. Maintaining contacts with the Polish underground world, both the Communist and the London people, was an extremely important job. We were firmly opposed to maintaining contact through the PPR members in the ghetto, in the Jewish Fighting Organization. Before I left, there were no contacts with the Jewish Communists, but exclusively with the Polish Communists; and not with the Warsaw Communist cell, which was Jewish, but rather with their main cell on the Aryan side. They did have contacts with the main cell, but that wasn't what we needed. We needed political contacts. They might have had meetings with their main cell behind our back. But we were the only recognized force, and we didn't need them (the Jewish Communists) for negotiations. If the Poles had renewed contact with us earlier, our person could have gone out then, not in April but in February or March. But, the two Polish underground organizations were afraid to renew the contact. As for the AL, the liaison didn't have to be a Jewish member of PPR, he could also be a member of Ha-Shomer Ha-Tza'ir or Dror or the Bund. The question concerned the ZOB as a bloc, one of whose central members had fallen into the hands of the Gestapo and jeopardized them all. Of course, the PPR members absolutely wouldn't meet with the AK, which was reason enough—especially since there were other reasons too—not to need the Jewish members of PPR for negotiations with the underground organizations.

Moreover, the central members of the Jewish Fighting Organization were from the Halutz movement. They were fit for this function. To this day, I can't think of any member of the PPR in the ghetto who could have done the job.

Our forces were meager. When we heard from Aryan Warsaw that they were willing to renew the contact, naturally we were glad. First, we called a private meeting of the usual group of Mordechai, Zivia, Miriam, and me. Two proposals were raised: one was that Mordechai Anielewicz would go to the Aryan side. The second was Mordechai Anielewicz's proposal that I go there. What were the pros and cons of each of the proposals?

Mordechai kept emphasizing that this was a plan of cooperation with Polish forces, if and when battles erupted. Along with the acquisition of weapons, this was one of the most important tasks. Mordechai Anielewicz argued that he was a native of Warsaw and somebody might recognize him, and he would almost certainly run into some *Sheygets* from the suburb where he was born and lived. He was afraid that he ran the danger of being denounced, since he knew a lot of people in Warsaw. Furthermore, he thought he didn't look as Aryan as I did. On the other hand, his advantage was that he was graduated from a Polish school and knew the Polish scene. He looked and talked like a typical Warsaw Pole. He didn't speak like the Jewish intellectuals who, because of their fluency and "literary" speech, would fail and be exposed. It would be as if one of us here in Israel started speaking Biblical Hebrew in the street. The Polish of the Jewish intellectuals would immediately attract attention, though it was quite modern Polish, but à la Mickiewicz.[79] He would have to speak fluent Polish, but the Polish of the marketplace, the street. After all, the Polish intellectual doesn't get his Polish only from the lecture hall or books, but also from shops and friends and street curses. Incidentally, that's how it is to this day. It's their mother tongue, the language of home, courtyard; whereas for the Jewish intellectual, it's an acquired tongue.

79. Adam Mickiewicz (1798–1855): National poet of Poland, advocate of Polish national freedom.

Mordechai Anielewicz's advantage was that he himself was a "street boy." He came from a very poor home and wrestled with the *Shkotsim* as a child. He finished a Polish high school, and his Polish was natural. As for me, my face and the fact that I wasn't known were in my favor. I had never been in a Polish milieu, certainly not in Warsaw. Even before the war, when I had been in Warsaw, I stayed on Gęsia, Dzielna, Nalewki, and Smocza [Jewish streets], and not Marszałkowska and similar Polish streets.

My disadvantage was that I came from eastern Poland, from Vilna. In normal times, Warsaw Poles mocked the Polish of Vilna, which had many "Russianisms." My older sister and my brother had studied in Polish high schools where they were taught in Russian [when still under Russian rule]. I came during the transitional period—that is, I managed to learn only a little bit of Russian. I learned to read Russian when I was six or seven. But then, I switched to Polish and went to a Hebrew school. My whole environment was Hebrew or Yiddish speaking, whereas Polish was a compulsory language, as a school subject. Incidentally, in *Tarbut*, my high school, Latin and general history lessons were conducted in Hebrew. Only Polish and German were taught in the original languages because the German teacher didn't know Hebrew. But mathematics, physics, chemistry, and psychology were all taught in Hebrew. We were so fanatical about Hebrew that, in 1933, we declared a strike when the Polish office of education threatened to take our official matriculation certificates from us if we didn't transfer to general studies in Polish. Teachers and parents tended to obey the instructions and switch to Polish, but we twelfth-grade students called a strike and demanded Hebrew. So we took the examinations and received matriculation certificates as externs. That was my weakness in terms of the spoken language. Later, on the Aryan side of Warsaw, my Polish turned into a certain advantage, because wherever I went, people immediately asked if I was from the east. Apparently a lot of people in Warsaw came from all parts of Poland. It wasn't composed only of the pre-1939 population elements. There were refugees in Warsaw from Poznań and exiles from Łódz. Their Polish was also different and strange and hard to locate, and when people asked me where I was from, I would say I was from Vilna.

Those were the pros and cons. After an exhausting discussion, we brought the issue to a slightly broader forum, which decided that I was to go to Aryan Warsaw. All our unit commanders strongly opposed this decision. I felt as I did when I left Soviet Lwów for German Warsaw. Aryan Warsaw was an alien, hostile world for me, an area I had never worked in, among strangers, among wolves; I had to make an effort to gear myself for this important mission.

The decision was made. I went around to all the groups and explained the situation. Transferring Eliezer Geller from the Brushmakers' area to my area solved the problem of the district commander. Since Mordechai and I both thought Geller didn't completely fit all the demands, we decided that Mordechai had to be free of everyday work in the Central Ghetto as much as he could. So we appointed Israel Kanal commander of the Central Ghetto so Mordechai would have more time for what was happening in the other areas, particularly in mine. I overlapped with Geller for ten days, maybe two weeks. I would probably have stayed a little longer if not for the telephone call I got (which I'll tell about later).

I left the ghetto on April 13, 1943, about a week before the *Aktsia* and the Uprising. I was still in the Többens-Schultz area (the decision about my leaving had been made a few weeks before) when a messenger from the Central Ghetto came to tell me of a telephone call from the Aryan side of Warsaw, from Irena or one of her people, saying: "If you don't want the salt to arrive after the food, you have to come now." That was the signal to leave at once for the Aryan side of Warsaw. The information was from the AK and I had to leave that very day, in a rush. I wasn't ready for it in any respect, not even in terms of clothes. In a few hours, they prepared whatever they could for me.

There was a Bundist named Meir Schwartz, who was a member of the Jewish Fighting Organization and was also in the *Werkschutz*.[80] When the Uprising began, he was sent to accompany Hancia and was wounded. [81] He was later caught in Aryan Warsaw in the fire of the celluloid factory (see below). We took a suit from him for me. I was much bigger than him, so, for a long time, I walked around Warsaw in a nice, clean suit, with "three-quarter length trousers." That stood out so much that, in 1945, the first time I came to visit DPs in the camp in Munich, a gentile came to me and said he had been a German gendarme in Aryan Warsaw and that a Jewish girl he went out with pointed to me and said: "That's the commander of the Jews!" I don't know how he knew I was in Munich. I started asking questions to see if he was telling the truth, and then he gave me indications: that I lived on Marszałkowska Street and wore "three-quarter length trousers."

But that gendarme didn't turn me in and, after the war, he was even proud of that. For a moment, he hesitated, he said, about whether to turn me in, when he saw me in the street on the Aryan side of Warsaw

---

80. Meir Schwartz: Born in Warsaw. A Bundist and ZOB member. Was liaison between the units in the April Uprising. Escaped to the Aryan side and was one of a few who escaped from the fire in the celluloid factory. He ran to a nearby house and was hidden by a Polish woman in a wardrobe, which the Gestapo overlooked when they searched the house. When the woman later opened the closet door, she found him dead of a heart attack at the age of twenty-seven. (For a detailed description of his death, see Meed 1979: 160.)

81. For the attempt to smuggle out Hancia Plotnitzka, see Y. Putermilch 1981:91–93.

"in three-quarter length trousers." He described the suit exactly, the trousers, the color, even the place! Around Marszałkowska 118. (He didn't remember the number but he did give some indications. And that really was where I lived.) Why did he come? Because after the war, he was bragging that he didn't turn in the commander of the Jews to the Gestapo, and thus did a "good deed"—and here the Germans were plotting against him and he was in terrible trouble and didn't have a job. Without thinking much, I gave him money. Later, we corresponded. In time, he came up with arrogant demands and the Jewish community organization asked me about him. I told them that during an emotional meeting (in 1945) I did thus and so and that the case required a more thorough examination. He might have heard things from someone and took advantage of it. After that, I broke off all communication with him.

Let's go back to what I started: they "mobilized" a suit and the basic necessities and I went to the Central Ghetto, where I was to leave for the Aryan side of Warsaw. Our three policemen were to determine the time according to the mood and nature of the German gendarme on duty at the gate; the Polish policeman was less important. I was to leave without the Magen-David armband, as a Pole who had come into the ghetto and was now leaving. If I had left as a Jew, wearing the armband, the blackmailers on the other side, who were swarming in the area, would have finished me off. I had to show a document and we didn't even need a bribe since everything was arranged in advance.

That was April 13, 1943. The day before, I was with Zivia and Mordechai in the Central Ghetto, in that police building across from the Judenrat, in our staff apartment; I didn't know it would be our last conversation. All of a sudden, we got an announcement from one of the policemen: "Go!" I picked up a few shirts, as if I had come into the ghetto to buy them, and I walked down Nalewki Street, through Gęsia Street to the gate. That was an empty area. Inside the gate stood the Jewish policeman with the Polish policeman and the German gendarme. Our policemen stood in the courtyards and signaled to me to pass. Our three policemen accompanied me, protecting me all the way. After I got the final signal from one of them, I approached, took out my worthless document and the German gendarme waved me through, since he had already been "buttered up"; otherwise, my exit wouldn't have been so "elegant": with the shirts in my arms.

About 100 to 150 meters from the gate, I saw Franya Beatus, the courier who always made me smile. She was a member of Dror, maybe sixteen or seventeen years old, blonde, pretty. As I recall, she came from Konin, where there was once a branch of He-Halutz Ha-Tza'ir. I remember their peculiar Yiddish dialect; they had a diction I never heard anywhere else, neither in Warsaw nor in Vilna. I didn't know her before the war, when she was probably thirteen years old.

When the Jews were expelled from Konin, she went to Ostrowiec, where she joined the branch of Dror and continued to be a member of the Movement. When Berl Broyde was in Ostrowiec, he recruited her for the Jewish Fighting Organization. The organization in Ostrowiec existed until late 1942, when they received orders to liquidate the branch, because they didn't have weapons or any chance of defending themselves. Then, Berl brought the whole group to Warsaw. Because Franya looked like a *Shikse*, we sent her to the Aryan side of Warsaw in early 1943. Now she was assigned to greet me and find an apartment for me.

To prove she was grown-up, that girl walked around in high-heeled shoes so she'd look taller and carried a woman's handbag, which she thought added maturity. So I had to smile when I saw her. I was much older than her and felt paternal toward her. I took her by the arm and we walked in the direction she indicated. She said she had a temporary apartment with a Polish engineer, at Marszałkowska 118, where some Jewish woman was also hiding. She told the landlord I was a teacher and he agreed to keep me in the apartment for a few days, as a Jew. I didn't have real documents and couldn't register as a tenant.

That was my beginning, on April 13, on Marszałkowska Street of all places, the elegant Warsaw street. There, on that street, it was business as usual. You didn't feel a thing. I really can't say "as usual," since it was wartime; but relative to war conditions . . . So I walked around as a Pole and, in time, I got used to my Polish identity. It wasn't walking around the street, but the life and the issues awaiting me—that worried and frightened me.

There was a tremendous contrast between the ghetto and that street: cafés were open and so were movie theaters, concerts were performed, the trams ran. Of course, Polish patriots didn't go to the movies, where German films were shown. So I started my new life. Those were ten horrible days, until April 23, 1943. It began that day, April 13. I remember the day because my birthday is December 13, and the number 13 always stays with me. When Franya brought me in and introduced me to the engineer, I realized the apartment was very big—five or six rooms. A luxury apartment. I got a temporary room. At the entrance, on the right, he told me, lived a Polish notary, who arrived at certain times. In another room, he went on, lived a Jewish woman with a little girl. He asked me not to go into that room so as not to frighten her. And of course, he and his wife also lived in the apartment, which also had a big dining room, a bedroom, and my room. No doubt that Pole endangered himself by putting me up, and I can't say the rent was very high—I learned that later, when we paid a lot more. My advantage over the Jewish woman who lived there was that she was locked in, whereas I walked around the city freely, as it were. The landlord saw my documents in the name of Witold Kimstaczas and didn't like them very much. Mordechai Tennenbaum had brought them to me from Vilna and I didn't have any others. Later on, I got better ones, but they weren't terrific either.

EIGHT

The Ghetto Uprising

The first thing I asked Franya Beatus to do was to get in touch immediately with all possible contacts with the AK and the AL, and with Dr.
Adolf Berman. The very next day, I met with Berman and, through
him, I met Wacław, the AK man whose real name, as I learned much
later, was Henryk Wołyński. He's an old man now and lives in Katowice.
His wife is very sick, and in the last year I sent him a little money every
three months. The conversation with him deserves to be mentioned as
one of the war's curiosities. I'm tall and he's short, with eyeglasses and,
in terms of looks, he could be suspected of being a Jew. He was in charge
of Jewish affairs in AK. Of course, he didn't know me before that meeting, but he showed great interest in the fate of Jurek (Arye Wilner). I
said something, and then we got down to business and it's etched in my
memory to this day because he came right to the point. He began by
saying that not everyone—in the ghetto—sympathized with us. The Judenrat, he said, sent information that we were nothing but "simple bandits" who carry out "Exes," steal money from Jews, instead of preparing
for battle. When I told him that didn't surprise me that the information
came from the Judenrat and not from other sources, he smiled. From
these initial things, I understood that he wasn't our enemy. He said that
the messenger who brought that information about us, Leon Tennenbaum, was a member of the Judenrat, whereas the one who initiated the
slander of us to the Polish Delegatura was Alfred Stoltzman, also a
member of the Judenrat.

I registered these things in my memory and a letter went to the ghetto
the next day. Moreover, my interlocutor also told me something more
serious: he said that they had formulated a plan to take the members of
the Jewish Fighting Organization out of the ghetto—to a partisan unit.

I expressed my amazement at that. I told him that when we got the call that we had to hurry lest "the salt come after the food," I was sure it had to do with the updating and developing of our joint plans for the revolt in the ghetto. I told him that, as far as I knew, there was a master plan, based essentially on an AK diversionary attack on the Central Ghetto when the Uprising erupted. I asked if they had contacted us by telephone twenty-four (maybe forty-eight) hours earlier and asked for a meeting because of the partisan unit. He said that in that period of the triumph of forces hostile to the Poles, they were afraid of a revolt that would begin in the ghetto and spread beyond it. Because they didn't have enough weapons to hold out in an aggressive attack—hence their fears.

We knew the essence of their theory, which held that there was a bloody struggle between the two big powers, the *Germans* and the *Russians*, and that they had to wait and see how things would turn out—he didn't say that exactly in those words, but that was the conception that was known to us. That Poland had to wait, amass forces, until her two big neighbors bled each other and were exhausted. Then they (the Poles) would appear on the stage of battles.

I said that I appealed against both the postponement of their intervention in our uprising and the plan to send us to a partisan unit, and that I wanted a meeting with the supreme commander "Grot" (Stefan Rowecki). I didn't know then that his name was Rowecki, but I did know the nickname "Grot," and I said I wanted to meet with him. Waclaw replied that he would give me a reply to that on April 18 or 19.

The second meeting, after more information from Berman, was with the Polish Communists, the AL, which was still called GL (Gwardia Ludowa) at that time. We discussed the help they were to give us during the Uprising. They said they would examine the plans, and they set a meeting with General Witołd, that is Franciszek Jozwiak, AL chief of staff. They also promised to tell us something within a few days. We determined the arrangements of the communication and our contact point, and I had to watch and wait. A few days passed. The first thing I did was to write it all down. The meetings with the representatives of the AK and the AL took place between April 13 and 15; my report went out on the morning of April 16. First of all, I reported the AK proposal, which I found unacceptable, and the reply I suggested was: "We won't leave the ghetto without a battle." By the way, as for their proposal, they promised to find transportation and a temporary place for our people to stay on the way to the partisan unit. I told them their proposal was conceivable only after our struggle in the ghetto. I wrote to Zivia and Mordechai Anielewicz that my opinion of the proposal was absolutely negative, and that the AK proposal really was intended as a substitute for a battle, meaning there wouldn't be an uprising. The AK wanted to take us out of the ghetto, to cut us off from it. I also advised arresting Stoltzman immediately. He had to give an account of his libel against the ZOB, which I regarded as treason. I added that Wacław impressed me as not wanting to take advantage of Stoltzman's denunciation of us, but I had no doubt that others would try to use it and present us as simple thugs.

The letter was sent very simply: every day, a group of workers would leave the Central Ghetto (printers, binders, etc.) for Tłomackie Street, where the Jewish Historical Institute now is. There they set up a printing press where Jews worked printing material for the authorities in German or Polish. It was near the synagogue, which still existed. They were accompanied by policemen, and we always made sure that one of the policemen was ours. Since we had three police officers on our side, it was not hard to make sure that one of our policemen would be in the escort. The courier would wait for the group of workers, either in the morning or after work, on their way back to the ghetto, and give the letter. I got the answer to my letter the day after I sent it. It was an encouraging answer: they agreed that there was no discussion of taking forces out of the ghetto. They thought we had to insist on that and not give in, and to fight for it with all our might.

A few days later I wrote another letter. As I recall, that was on the 17th or 18th. I wrote that Passover was at hand and, since I didn't expect developments or a big turning point in the near future, I intended to return to the ghetto for the Passover Seder with the group of workers. I asked my comrades to wait for me in the Central Ghetto. I got two separate replies: a friendly one from Mordechai Anielewicz, who suggested I not come back because a meeting could be held any day, and if I didn't plan to stay in the ghetto, it would be better if I didn't come, since something unexpected might come up. At that time, it didn't occur to anyone that April 19 would be the "unexpected day." But he meant unexpected developments between us and the Poles.

The other letter was from Zivia. Among other things, she wrote: "You haven't done anything yet and you're already coming back to the ghetto?" In short, a scolding.

On April 18, at nightfall, before the curfew and before I parted from Franya Beatus, I told her to be at the gate of the ghetto at 6 the next morning and tell the policemen I was coming into the ghetto that day. Thus we parted.

I had decided to go to the ghetto despite my comrades' advice. Although I had been gone only six days, I was terribly lonely. I hated being in a strange place on Passover, for the Seder. So I thought I would go in for twenty-four or forty-eight hours; Arye Wilner always did that.

Then came April 19, which came like a bolt out of the blue.

I can't say if I heard or dreamed it, but early in the morning, I woke up drenched with sweat from the thunder of cannons. When I opened my eyes, I saw the sunshine and didn't hear a thing. Everything was quiet. Did I hear cannons or was I dreaming? I don't know.

I washed and dressed and waited for Franya Beatus to come back to know if she had arranged my passage. She did come back to my room but, instead of talking, she began weeping: "They shelled the ghetto, the ghetto is surrounded," she said. Early in the morning, she heard that the army entered the ghetto; the cannons hadn't yet been placed at the ghetto walls, but she heard the Poles saying that you couldn't get into the ghetto because it was completely surrounded by Germans, Lithuanians, and Ukrainians, and the echoes of battles were heard as far away as Marszałkowska Street. Pistol shots weren't heard but, apparently, what I had heard in my sleep were grenades exploding with the thundering opening of the battle.

Frania continued sobbing. She said there was nothing left for her, she couldn't go on living, and was about to commit suicide. She repeated that a few times. Parenthetically, she had a boyfriend named David Shulman and, at that time, she didn't know if he was still alive or if he had been killed. The fellow was also from Ostrowiec and, as I recall, had foreign citizenship, but had burned his documents and joined the Jewish Fighting Organization. He refused to leave the ghetto. But I might be confusing him with someone else. At any rate, Frania's emotional condition wasn't connected only with that.

She went on sobbing and talking about suicide. And I scolded her, told her she was sent here to do a job and she had to carry out my orders! That wasn't the time for tears and desperate acts. Her role was to do whatever had to be done to help the fighters, to send weapons. I wouldn't say that was an "educational" kind of speech, but do I have to explain my own mood?

If I had known on April 18 that the Uprising would erupt on April 19, would I have gone back to the ghetto for Passover? In the final analysis, I *wouldn't have gone back*. True, I was torn and split and isolated. But my job was to stay here, because the recent collapse had essentially been on the Aryan side of Warsaw, where everything had come apart. Arye Wilner wasn't here anymore, Marek Folman had gone off to a partisan unit, Tosia Altman was stuck in the ghetto. A few young people were left, like Frania. There were some I didn't know at all. We didn't have any forces left here. There wasn't anyone to do the simplest things.

What would now happen to negotiations with the AK? Would they help? Who would take care of all that?

That day, a short, dirty guy came to me, a real *Sheygets*. His name was Tadek, Tuvia Shayngut, a member of Ha-Shomer Ha-Tza'ir who got my address from somebody. Irena Adamowicz also came. The next day, Marek Folman showed up: he heard about the Uprising on the radio and came to Warsaw to his family; his sister-in-law also came, with her son Rafi (who is now a physician in Canada). They lived in Zolibórz and he contacted me through Franya Beatus, who also had a telephone. They all appeared.

On April 19, I met with the members of the AL the second time.

I set principles for myself for my meetings with Polish groups. I wouldn't meet with one of them in a place where I had met with the other. I absolutely refused to meet with AK members where I met with the AL. Sometimes one meeting could be in the center of the city and another meeting in Włocławck, beyond Grochów, or in Zolibórz; but usually the meetings were near Gebettner-Wolf, on a corner, where there was a huge bookstore and you could stand a few minutes, looking at new books in the display window; or it could have been a café in Bank Square or even on Marszałkowska or on the banks of the Wisła River. I had a few places I selected. With one officer I would go swimming, meanwhile chatting as if we were on a pleasure jaunt. The place was swarming with people and, after talking, we would leave as after a swim. I used to structure the days so I would hold onto a thread of contact from morning to night. Frania Beatus knew she mustn't join me as a third person in the contacts I maintained. But she knew approximately where I was and that she had to walk around there and wait. We usually made eye contact. She had to get information from me about where my next meeting would be, and I would also make an appointment with her later on—to prevent being cut off.

When Tadek Shayngut came, the secrecy began to crumble, and continued to fall apart after Marek Folman arrived the next day. It began on Marszalkowska. I couldn't always avoid meeting an acquaintance in a café, or walking in the street and such. People started calling and coming over. That went on for twenty-four, maybe forty-eight hours.

One morning, as I was going out, the engineer landlord greeted me with "good morning," saluted, and said: "Hello, commander!" He inferred that from the way the people spoke to me and decided I wasn't a teacher. I didn't have anything to say to him, so I kept quiet. That was the second night, as I recall. He invited me to dinner. There were him, his wife, and me. He put out a bottle of wine and a lot of good food. I felt more like drinking than eating. I wasn't yet used to drinking, but I appearently drank better than he did. And in that conversation I found out how he concluded that I belonged to the fighters and was the "commander," as he called me, and also why he didn't throw me out of the apartment.

While drinking, he told me two things that have stayed in my memory and which he apparently regretted afterward: one was that his wife was a Jew, and the second was that his brother-in-law, his wife's brother, was in the ghetto with the fighters. I didn't ask any questions. I didn't ask the wife's name, and she began crying. Thus, as time passed, every day, as I went out in the morning and came back at night, I would see her with red eyes.

The first thing he did, even before the Uprising began, fearing for the fate of his wife and child, was to arrange another place for them. He gave me her room, which gave me the unpleasant feeling that she had left because of me. But he swore he had moved them to a safer place since the notary also lived there, and because I came and went, and an accident could happen—he said he had arranged a nice quiet place for them, which was fine.

I met him a few times later on. We should have checked up on him and found out who he really was. Because he did a few things I didn't like but, on the other hand, he also did positive things.

But let's go back to April 19, for the unexpected happened. That same day, I met with the political and military leadership—with each separately—of the PPR and the Armia Ludowa. I got as much information from them as I could. They also collected information about what was going on. I met with Witołd and Finder. Paul Finder was the general secretary of the PPR (he was succeeded by Gomułka[1] and Kowalski). The liaison was Leczycki-Brower, whom I met with only once because he was from a lower echelon. Tadek (Tuvia), for example, met with Brower a lot, but not me.

That day, the representatives of the AL (the military organization) told me they had decided to give us twenty-eight rifles with ammunition. That was all they could give. The question was how to sneak them into the ghetto. That was a great thing for us but, ultimately, those rifles didn't get to the ghetto; but they did get to us in Warsaw. In the ghetto, we had only a few rifles we had bought. There was one rifle from January, and we bought a few more. The rifles we got from them were cheaper, but getting them into the ghetto was very difficult, since you couldn't walk around the streets with rifles.

On April 19, the information I had came only from outside sources. And not until the next morning did I get information from the night before. What could I do with the weapons? And even among the Poles, the weapons weren't yet ready for delivery, because they had to bring

1. Władysław Gomułka (1905–1982): Major figure in postwar Polish politics. Was the First Secretary of the Polish Communist Party from 1956–1970.

them from some hideout, and then I had to get in touch with the ghetto to discuss how to send them. Time was pressing and the Poles wanted to know what to do, who would receive the weapons and how would we transport them.

As soon as I got that information—I think it was still on the afternoon of April 19—I got in touch with the Többens-Schultz ghetto by a telephone in a restaurant. I knew the phone number of one of the shop supervisors who was a member of Po'alei Zion–Z.S., named Abraham Schmidt (not to be confused with Andrzej Schmidt of the Communists). I spoke with him personally and told him to tell Geller ("Augeniusz") that the *Aktsia* had started in the Central Ghetto. They had heard something, but they didn't know exactly what was going on. He told me only that they were preparing to send a delegation to the Judenrat. He didn't say "Judenrat," but he mentioned a name from which I understood that the "good Germans" ordered them to send a delegation to the "Committee" and that they had promised them in the shops that nothing would happen to them.

I wanted to tell Eliezer Geller that "there's a wedding at Marjan's today and I want him to participate." Schmidt said he would convey my message.

Militarily, things were very clear. The Germans could come in through Nalewki, in which case the people in Többens-Schultz couldn't do a thing against them, but action could be taken from the Brushmakers' area. But I had no contact with them. At any rate, the Germans chose to come in from the direction of the *Befehlstelle,* which was natural, since that was the center of the Gestapo.

Under these conditions, the fighters in Többens-Schultz could take action against the Germans who would encounter them as they entered the ghetto. They could take action against them along two approaches that bracketed Többens-Schultz: along Leszno Street and Nowolipki Street, the site of the mine we had planted beforehand.

Later, after May 1, when some of the surviving members of the Jewish Fighting Organization came out through the sewers from Leszno to Ogrodowa, to Aryan Warsaw, I met with Eliezer Geller and asked him why he didn't follow my directions, and why they didn't do anything, thus abandoning the Central Ghetto, since they could have attacked the Germans as they entered or left the ghetto. He swore that, on April 19, he got instructions from Schmidt not to act without specific instructions from me. Apparently Schmidt told Geller the opposite of what I had told him. He himself didn't understand my intention either. I say things from a distance of time and place: Wasn't that sentence—"There's a wedding at Marjan's today and I want Augeniusz to participate"—clear? Didn't the man know there was a war there, a battle going on? Hadn't he heard the noise of war for hours? Couldn't he understand who was Marjan, even if he didn't know that was Mordechai Anielewicz's nickname? He did know that "Augeniusz" was Geller!

If Geller was telling me the truth, Schmidt conveyed the opposite to him, consciously, deliberately. That is, if Geller didn't flinch at the last moment, then Schmidt was counting on the promise of his German bosses concerning Poniatów and Trawniki, and believed salvation would come from there; or he believed the Schultzes, who promised that nothing would happen to the "productive Jews." So that was why they didn't join the battle. I had no reason not to believe Geller, but I had no way of checking it with Schmidt because I didn't see him again. So, the Central Ghetto acted alone, without help, for a few days, since the fighters from the Brushmakers' area didn't come to their aid either because the Germans entered that area a day or two later. Hence, the Central Ghetto was isolated when the battles erupted.

On April 19, I didn't expect a phone call. We looked for some way to get in touch with the ghetto, since people weren't going to work anymore. Until April 19, my only contact was through the work groups and the policemen who came out of the ghetto to Tłomackie. But on the night of April 19, Tosia Altman called Franya Beatus from Brauer's shop on Nalewki; one of the first things my landlord did the next day was disconnect his telephone. But even if he hadn't, it wouldn't have helped because I didn't have time to tell my comrades his number. And if the telephone had rung, my landlord would probably have appeared, since he dogged my steps. If it had been possible to get in touch during the day, I would have gone into some restaurant with a phone and I could have said important things we knew with hints. But it was impossible to get in touch at all during the day, only late at night, because no one was at the phone during the daytime. And in Franya Beatus's house, you could call only at night when the Germans had left the ghetto. Tosia did call and tell what was going on there, but she didn't know much either, since every unit was cut off from the others, unless they encountered each other in one way or another. And she didn't call during the battles but at night, when the Germans had retreated. After she called, Franya would come in the morning and tell me what Tosia had said. The comrades in the ghetto had no information about the plans of the operation. I told them only that the AK was urging us to leave the ghetto and promised to give us a partisan base, temporary apartments in Warsaw, and transport.

I didn't tell them about the rifles they had decided to give us because I didn't know if I could ship them. Nor did Franya know if it was twenty-four or twenty-eight rifles; and I didn't tell Schmidt about it either. I didn't intend to ship the weapons to Többens-Schultz, but to the

Central Ghetto. One of the first things we wanted to do on April 19 was check all possibilities of contact—I didn't know if telephone contact was still possible and I assigned Tuvia Shayngut to check the connection from the Polish cemetery. The Jewish cemetery was now outside the borders of the reduced ghetto, and the Polish cemetery was next to it and there was a passage between them. I knew that because, when I was in the ghetto, we would hold meetings with comrades from the Aryan side at the grave of Y. L. Peretz. We had to find out if they still brought corpses from the ghetto to the Jewish cemetery, and if we could make contact there. On April 19, nothing was yet clear. Not until the next day did Tadek bring the information that there was contact since he saw the Pinkert men going by (Pinkert was the head of the burial society). So this was how I sent my letter about developments on our side. Zivia tells of how my letter produced arguments, dreams, and fantasies. I wrote in Hebrew about the Communists and Eretz Israel.

Afterward, on the night of April 20, Franya Beatus was ready to receive a telephone call. I taught her to say things which would tell Tosia about a shipment from the Polish cemetery to the Jewish cemetery, and they should contact the burial society and organize the transport of the shipment. She was to ask if that could be done. Tosia got the call and understood it perfectly. That was just before April 21. She confirmed that they had received my letter of April 20. The Pinkert men delivered the letter and brought things for me on April 23, including Mordechai Anielewicz's famous letter to me. The Hebrew original of that letter was lost; what remains is a Yiddish translation I made for Berman, who extracted tidbits from it for the Poles, who heard it on their underground radio station, *Swit.*

There is a considerable difference between the three documents. My translation, which was found in Berman's archive, was almost precise. And what is the truth—what was omitted and what remained?

Among other things, he writes: "Know that the pistol has no value," and that Yehiel fell "at a machine gun." The truth is we didn't have a machine gun. The original says "automatic rifle" and I translated it that way because that's how Berman wanted it, for the effect. It isn't exactly the original letter, but it's the closest text to it (except for the "machine gun"). And that's the authentic version. Other versions exist—like the one broadcast over the Polish underground station and others, which are further from the original and the formulation presented in it.

[The following is Mordechai Anielewicz's letter, as published by Yitzhak Zuckerman in *Book of Ghetto Wars* (p. 158), from the Yiddish translation preserved in the archive of A. Berman. The Hebrew original was burned with the rest of the ZOB documents at Leszno 18, during the Polish Uprising.]

April 23, 1943
Dear Yitzhak,

I don't know what to write you. Let's dispense with personal details this time. I have only one expression to describe my feelings and the feelings of my comrades: things have surpassed our boldest dreams: the Germans ran away from the ghetto twice. One of our units held out for forty minutes, and the other one for more than six hours. The mine planted in the Brushmakers' area exploded. So far, we have had only one casualty: Yehiel, who fell as a hero at the machine gun.

Yesterday, when we got information[2] that the PPR attacked the Germans and that the radio station *Swit* broadcast a wonderful bulletin about our self-defense, I had a feeling of fulfillment. Even though there's still a lot of work ahead of us, whatever has been done so far has been done perfectly.

From this evening, we are switching to a system of guerilla action. At night, three of our units go out on two missions: an armed reconnaissance patrol and the acquisition of weapons. Know that the pistol has no value, we practically don't use it. We need grenades, rifles, machine guns, and explosives.

I can't describe to you the conditions in which the Jews are living. Only a few individuals will hold out. All the rest will be killed sooner or later. The die is cast. In all the bunkers where our comrades are hiding, you can't light a candle at night for lack of oxygen . . .

Of all the units in the ghetto, only one man is missing: Yehiel. That too is a victory. I don't know what else to write you. I imagine you have many questions. But for now, be content with this.

The general situation: all the workshops in the ghetto[3] and outside it were closed, except for *Werterfassung, Transavia*, and *Daring*. I don't have any information about the situation in Schultz and Többens. Contact is cut off. The Brushmakers' workshop has been in flames for three days. I have no contact with the units. There are many fires in the ghetto. Yesterday, the hospital[4] burned. Blocks of buildings are in flames. The police force was dismantled, except for the *Werterfassung*. Szmerling has surfaced again. Lichtenbaum has been released from the *Umschlag*. Not many people have been taken out of the ghetto. But that is different in the shops. I don't have the details. During the day, we sit in hiding places. Be well, my friend. Perhaps we shall meet again. The main thing is the dream of my life has come true. I've lived to see a Jewish defense in the ghetto in all its greatness and glory.

Mordechai

Moreover, I know there is another version of a letter Mordechai Anielewicz sent me in the archives. But I must state categorically that

2. At the beginning of the Uprising, there was telephone contact with the Aryan side.
3. That is, the Central Ghetto.
4. At Gęsia 6.

there was no letter from Mordechai Anielewicz after the April 23 letter. The other letter published in a collection of documents at Yad Vashem is from March 1943. It is quite conceivable that, for propaganda purposes, Berman made up a few things here and there, and I don't condemn him for that. Others would have done the same without considering historical truth under the special conditions that prevailed. Those were the needs of the hour.

As for me, I didn't know the letter was to be broadcast on radio *Swit*. We found the version that was published in the Lohamei Ha-Getaot book in Berman's archive with indications of parts he omitted. As I said, there is a problem with scholars—Dr. Kermish, for example, would kill me if I didn't agree with him on some detail or other. If, for example, I say there were fifty pistols, while he found that there were forty-nine; or if I say there wasn't a machine gun, he finds a piece of paper and argues: "Here it's written!" Well, let him argue; but I state, with all due respect, that the "second letter" isn't real; that's a letter from March 1943, and not April.[5]

I know that certain historians have reservations about the testimony of a living person. One day, Zivia and I sat with some historian and told him what happened and what was said. But if testimony comes from a living person, apparently it's no good!

As for the argument that Mordechai Anielewicz didn't sign the letter, of course he didn't! It wouldn't have been acceptable to sign his real name. He never signed any letter or document Mordechai Anielewicz. He used aliases like "Marjan" or "Aniol." And as for the fighters' appeal to the Poles, it was composed by Berman on the Aryan side of Warsaw![6] I didn't have time to go into all those things then, because it wasn't my central concern; but I always kept in touch with Berman. Sometimes I would meet with him twice a day because there were things that required civilian care, and that was his domain. The AK didn't decide on those things, but the Polish civilian authorities did, the Delegatura.

As I said, the AL gave us twenty-eight rifles; now transporting them was supposedly up to me, and I didn't know what to do with them; but I did know that our fighters had to get them. Moreover, the AK representatives said frankly that they were caught off guard by events in the ghetto and didn't have forces ready to burst into the Többens-Schultz area. What they could promise was that they would carry out as many guerilla operations near the walls as they could.

5. Two letters were published in Blumenthal and Kermish 1965:219–221. The second letter, whose authenticity Zuckerman questions, is dated April 26, 1943, with no addressee and no signature.
6. The Declaration appears in Blumenthal and Kermish 1965:221.

I got a reply to my appeal to "Grot" Rowecki, signed "Konar," as I recall.[7] (I saw the letter many years ago but I remember it by heart and have quoted it on various occasions.) The letter began: "The Polish army salutes the Jewish fighters!" He feels positive about the cooperation between us which has been going on for a long time and writes admiringly of Jurek (Arye Wilner). He writes: "Please tell Antek that now is not the proper time for this meeting; this is the time to act." But the meaning of the letter was clear: if there is no reason for a meeting, there is no joint plan, no help, no Polish operation by the AK.

The day after I got their answer (it reached me quite quickly by means of my new couriers), on April 20 it seems to me, Irena Adamowicz came to me and said she wanted me to meet with Hajduk (whom I've already mentioned). As I recall, the meeting was set for Śliska Street, in some school. At any rate, it looked like a school to me, since it had benches. It was certainly a neutral place, since he wouldn't have invited me to meet him where he worked or lived. He impressed me as a man who felt warmly about us. I told him about the ZOB and he already knew a lot. Later, I found out he was a member of the Scouts. He told me he would tell me of a meeting with a certain person who had authority and that Irena would let me know where and when the meeting would be held. He himself would also attend.

I think it was held the next day. That was only one of the discussions, and I can't remember how many there were. They started in the morning at various times and went on till night, without lunch, since I wouldn't go into restaurants. I would leave in the morning and come back at night absolutely exhausted, not physically—it was the issues that wore me out. One day I was taken to a private home in some street near the ghetto which had been a Jewish house before the liquidation. I came with Hajduk to a big apartment. It was noon; a family was sitting in the dining room eating lunch. I was taken to a big room where a man was waiting for me, standing at a desk. He didn't live in that house, it was only a meeting place. He was a tall gentile, broad and fleshy, with a very big bald head. He and I were the only ones who talked. Hajduk didn't utter a word—apparently he was subordinate to that man, who shook my hand and called himself "Grenadier Karol." He began by explaining his desire to meet me. I told him what I knew about events in the ghetto, about the battles there and the gravity of the situation in terms of the precarious material conditions, and I estimated that they couldn't hold out very long. I wanted to abide by the plan for military cooperation

7. "Konar" was the alias of Major General Antoni Chrusciel, AK commander in the Warsaw area.

between their forces and ours, which had been discussed before and which I raised again when I went to the Aryan side of Warsaw. I also said that I was encouraged by the information I got about the stand of our people in the battles, since we had thought we couldn't hold the Germans off for more than twenty-four to forty-eight hours. I said I wanted to set up temporary shelters for the people, if necessary, and I asked for a plan of the sewers in order to maintain contact with the ghetto. I didn't tell him about the weapons we had, since they hadn't given them to us.

He replied that they knew what was going on in the ghetto, and they also knew it was a Communist uprising and that the Communist organization (AL) was designed to serve the interests of Moscow. I told him that his information was wrong. This was the Jewish Fighting Organization and, just as in the AK, they didn't ask everyone who and what he was, but rather whether he was a patriot and if he wanted to fight, and then they certified he wasn't a traitor, so did we. And I added that from personal acquaintance, I could assure him that most of the fighters were Halutzim. The others were Zionists and Bundists, who were represented on the committee of the Polish Government-in-Exile in London, the political arm of the Polish government. Furthermore, I told him that I myself was a Halutz, that the commander of the organization was a Halutz, and most of the commanders whom I knew personally were Halutzim, and there was no basis for his accusations. He repeated his proposal to stop fighting and get the people out of the ghetto to a partisan unit. They didn't have a plan of the sewers. But they would find a way to bring out the fighters. They would give us apartments and send us to the forest. I replied that, even if I agreed to his proposal, the fighters absolutely would not and that the war in the ghetto would continue as long as there was one bullet in the hands of the fighters.

He stood up and told me that if the ghetto proved to be a Moscow base and continued to fight, not only would they not help us, but they would fight against us. That was how things stood.

In his book on the Uprising, Ber Mark says, ostensibly on the basis of a shorthand account of something I said in 1948, that the man ("Grenadier Karol") used the words *Zydo-komuna* [Judeo-Communist]. That's Mark's own addition; in 1948, he asked me for permission to publish the statement and I refused. If the man had said the words *Zydo-komuna*, I would surely have gotten up and gone, because I would have immediately recognized his antisemitic aspect. But even without antisemitic expressions, I saw whom I was dealing with. He didn't insult us as Jews, but simply gave an ideological basis for the notions of the extreme right wing of the AK. He spoke of the "Moscow base." Mark added the *Zydo-komuna* for his own needs. I guarantee that these words weren't in the shorthand account.[8] Although I didn't get a copy of the shorthand account of my lecture during a visit to Warsaw (April 1948), and though I'm quoting from memory, what I said above reflects reality and that's an end to that episode. I saw that man once more, some time later, in 1943, when I was standing near a Gewetner-Wolf bookstore one Sunday waiting for a meeting that had been scheduled. I saw him pass by. I was standing there waiting for someone and, meanwhile, looking at books. In those days (1943–1944), the only purpose of display windows was to reflect passers-by. To this day, I still have something of that side-vision. When he was still far away, his approaching figure was reflected in the display window; I turned my head, he smiled at me and passed by. I had no interest in approaching him.

Years passed. In 1945, the first time I met Irena Adamowicz after the war, she told me about Hajduk, who had brought me to that "Grenadier Karol," whose real name, she told me, was Major Janiszowski. At the time of our conversation, in April 1943, Hajduk sat humiliated and ashamed of Janiszowski's attitude toward us. Even though he didn't offend me personally, the attitude he expressed made Hajduk mad—Hajduk, who was one of those who started the Polish Uprising in central Warsaw. At the beginning of the Uprising, he heard on the radio about a proclamation I issued to the Jews, calling on them to join the Polish Uprising, and concluded from that that I was still alive. He asked Irena Adamowicz to tell me, if he didn't get out of the Uprising alive, that they had come to realize that Janiszowski ("Grenadier Karol") was a double agent for the Gestapo. He had stooped to that after he had fallen into the hands of the Gestapo and was released. His comrades were amazed at his release and began following him. They learned that he was hiding with his mistress after he found out they suspected him. Hajduk led the group that carried out the death sentence against him by the Polish underground.

Although those facts, which I later learned from Irena Adamowicz, didn't resolve the situation I'm talking about, they do illuminate the character of the person who influenced our fate. However, another AK representative might have given the same answer because Janiszowski's position wasn't unusual, but was widespread in the AK and we were aware of it; the fact is that Grot didn't want to meet me either personally or through an envoy. The AK attitude toward us was also reflected in Wołyński's report, which discusses it explicitly and reveals that they were unfair toward us, distrusted us, and had no sympathy for us; and that squares with what we knew. But I want to add something about Wołyński. Less than a year ago, I got a letter from him; I know his personal warmth

8. Zuckerman refers to the notes of a lecture he delivered at the Jewish Historical Institute in Warsaw, May 1948. Archive of Beit Lohamei Ha-Getaot.

for me, and I know he suffered from that AK attitude toward us—that's an episode in itself which has all kinds of implications. Despite that, one of the Poles arranged additional meetings to try to reach an agreement with the AK. In our meetings with the AL, their representatives said they would carry on a struggle near the walls, as much as they could; that they would carry on a guerilla struggle, with small groups. They were sorry they couldn't abide by the big plan since they didn't have enough weapons or forces to carry it out.

On the other hand, even today, 1974, after all the historical accounts we have with the Soviet and the Polish Communists, in those days, the Armia Ludowa (AL) was willing to give us all possible help. They were willing to do that because of their attitude toward us; they were probably willing to do that because of their political position which was to help the Soviet Union under any conditions, to fight the Germans any place, any time. Keep in mind that this was early 1943, after Stalingrad, when Moscow called on all peoples occupied and oppressed by the Germans to revolt.

Later, talking to people I trusted (Hubert Kaminski and others), I heard not about attempts to burst into the ghetto or revolt—they hadn't even used such terms—but about feints, attacks of isolated AK groups on the concentration of cannons on Muranowska, Kraszinski Square, and other places. A report by some group commander was even published, which says they brought explosives to blow up the wall, but they didn't do anything since they were fired on; the explosives blew up and a few of them were killed. I have no reason to doubt that, since the AK included not only the rightist prewar Senatorial bloc, but also Socialists, peasants, and liberals. After all, there were Polish leftists, who, as in any war, united for joint struggle for a joint purpose. They didn't get instructions to help the Jews from Grot Rowecki or from "Chirurg,"[9] their commanders; but, on their own initiative, they came to our aid. I don't doubt that. If I had had time on April 25, 1943, and if I had been an historian, I would have tried to document those things. At any rate, I have no reason to doubt that among the Poles, in the AK, there were people who suffered from the hostile attitude toward us and were ashamed of it. And they tried to do something.

What I said about Hajduk indicates that. After all, he didn't expect to get killed in the Polish Uprising. So what motivated him to send me the story of "Grenadier Karol" via Irena Adamowicz? He did it only because it tortured him and it mattered to him. The same goes for Hubert. Many of them opposed the unfair and humiliating attitude of the AK toward us. They saw the Jews fighting and even if they didn't join the war, they

9. Alias of Stanisław Weber, AK chief of staff of the Warsaw district.

could help with weapons, by saving people; but the AK itself didn't. I know for sure that they had a map of the Warsaw sewers, whereas the AL didn't, even in 1944, during the Polish Uprising. That was considered a military secret. The sewers of a big city have many uses. Things can be done in the dark, underground, right under the noses of the enemy. We know those uses from World War II, for example in Odessa, and you can find many other examples. Sewer workers were municipal employees, the whole department, including the engineers, was staffed by AK people. They must have had the maps. If only one of them had been in AL, we would certainly have gotten the maps. But, unfortunately for us, AL wasn't part of it.

During the Polish Uprising, when the AL joined the fighters in the Old City, one of my assignments from the AL command staff was to look for ways out of the Old City through the sewers. That was when the fighters there were about to surrender, but they didn't have maps of the sewers. They gave me all possible help, they gave me armed groups; but all the maps were in the hands of the AK. And you can't imagine what a tremendous city was under the ground, a city where you could go astray and never get out. Quite a few people lost their way and died there. We knew about people eaten by rats and people who went into places with no exit, people who were stuck and swept away by torrents.

On May 8, 1943, I appealed to the AK for help to take the remnants of the fighters out of the ghetto; but they wanted to finish off not only the Uprising but also the rebels. As far as the AK was concerned, as fighters we weren't wanted anywhere on Polish soil. I'm not saying there weren't some who considered the human aspect. But their organization wasn't built for that. They weren't an aid society but a military organization. As a military organization, we were superfluous for them both in the fighting ghetto, and as fighting groups on the Aryan side of Warsaw. We were also superfluous in a partisan unit—as Jews, at any rate, we were superfluous. They had offered to take us out to a partisan unit, but afterward they killed us.[10] And in a partisan unit, too, the partisans killed us. And you didn't need much imagination and sense to understand from the first meeting, even before the Uprising, that they would do everything to make sure there would be absolutely no uprising in the Warsaw Ghetto. That was because of both their general and their Polish world view. For them, we were dung. Even if I don't attribute that to clear antisemitic intentions, even if I don't accuse them of this Nazi sin, of wanting to annihilate us—it's clear that as a fighting bloc, we were like thorns in their

10. Zuckerman is referring to a group of comrades who were sent to a partisan unit near Hrubieszów, guided by the AK, and fell into a trap. See below.

flesh, they didn't need us. They wanted peace in Poland, in Warsaw, to amass forces, until they found the right moment. History paid them back.

Their anti-Communist argument in this case was obviously only a pretext. Those people who sentenced the Jews to death must have known who Mordechai Anielewicz or Yitzhak Zuckerman was. After all, they included Irena Adamowicz, who used to stay overnight with us, talk with us, knew us, and sympathized with us. Didn't they know who the Zionists were and who their leaders were in Poland? Didn't they know about the Halutz movement? Of course, they knew all that and it was a pretext, like any other. Just as Moscow says that Israel is an American Imperialist-Fascist bastion. It's the same thing, since they also know the truth. And, there I was on the Aryan side, with just a few girls, without a Jewish fighting force, and I made a desperate attempt to do something with a few people, including some Poles, who began joining, lending a hand. Heniek, a member of AK, didn't show up; but there were people who helped out the Jewish Fighting Organization in their hour of need. After communications were cut off on May 1, or maybe May 2, the first to appear were the survivors from the Többens-Schultz Uprising, and I was told that they were on Ogrodowa. The uprising at Többens-Schultz ended on April 29; they came out through a tunnel to Ogrodowa Street on the Aryan side, where there was a factory owned by the same Schultz who owned the shops, along with a "little Schultz." Until the day I left for the Aryan side, I didn't know about that tunnel, which had been dug by Stefan Grajek and his comrades. Nor did I know that there was a shelter for them on Ogrodowa, on the Aryan side of Warsaw. And all of a sudden, I heard of people who came out of the ghetto and were on Ogrodowa.

Meanwhile, the AL sent me their man, who went by the name of Krzaczek.[11] He told me he definitely wasn't a Communist, but a member of the leftist branch of the PPS, who joined the military organization of the Communists, the Gwardia Ludowa. A short man, with a brush-like moustache, trustworthy eyes, a brother and friend to the underworld. Brave, ingenious, nimble, active. What I shall tell of him, I have never told anywhere else for reasons that will become clear later on. He was sent to us as a liaison by the AL. I would meet with him as with one of our own couriers. He was at my disposal when I got word at my apartment on Marszałkowska that people from the ghetto had moved to Ogrodowa. But, as I said, I had troubles with the landlord and I had to leave the apartment not because I wanted to, but because the landlord didn't want

---

11. Krzaczek (Władysław Gajek): Member of AL. He helped bring the fighters out of the sewers and transfer them to Lomianki. He was exposed as a collaborator with the Polish police; was responsible for the deaths of many Jews. This discovery led the AL to sentence him to death. He disappeared under mysterious circumstances. (See below, chapter 9.)

me there. So the information didn't come directly to me but to one of the couriers—Tuvia Shayngut or Franya Beatus. When I heard about it, I immediately went to consult with that Pole, Krzaczek. He was the one who arranged to take the fighters out to Łomianki Woods, seven kilometers from Warsaw. To get there, you had to go through central Warsaw and cross the bridges of the Wisła.

Eliezer Geller was one of those who escaped to Ogrodowa Street and he himself came to me. With the help of my engineer landlord, we found a temporary apartment for him on Albertynska Street, not far from Teatralny Square. I thought of using him for our purpose, but I was always afraid he would fall into the hands of blackmailers. Right after the people were moved there, with Krzaczek's help, two more men showed up who had gone through the Revisionists' tunnel: Zygmunt Fryderych[12] and Kazik, who were sent to ask for help to rescue those left in the burning ghetto. Zygmunt Fryderych, a Bundist, really wasn't sent to Aryan Warsaw, since he had been there before me. He had always been on the Aryan side of Warsaw and went into the ghetto, even though he didn't have to be there. The same goes for Michael Klepfisz, another Bundist.[13] Those people helped Arye Wilner politically, and all of them were in the ghetto on April 19. I could have been there too, since I also wanted to go in. What happened to us on January 18 with our courier also happened here. It was simply a catastrophe—we fell into a trap. And on that day of all days, when every one of our people was precious to us, they weren't where they were needed. Klepfisz returned to the ghetto and was killed there. Kazik (Simha Rotem) was first in the Többens-Schultz area, and then moved to the Central Ghetto; and all of a sudden, he showed up with Zygmunt Fryderych.

I heard about this from the Bundists; maybe from Władka[14] who said they had arrived at the Sawicka sisters' apartment.[15] Of course I went

12. Zygmunt Fryderych: Born in Warsaw. Was a Bundist liaison on the Aryan side; he returned to the ghetto and fought in the April Uprising. Afterward, he helped rescue the surviving fighters. In May 1943, he was killed by Polish police while leading a group of fighters to shelter. He was thirty-two years old at his death. See Meed (1979:157–158) for details of his life.

13. Michal Klepfisz: Born in Warsaw. An engineer. An active Bundist and member of ZOB. On the Aryan side, he assisted Arye Wilner and obtained weapons and the formula for Molotov Cocktails. He fought in the April Uprising and was killed in a clash with the Germans at the age of thirty.

14. Feygl Peltel, a Bund courier, who lived in Aryan Warsaw under an assumed name.

15. The sisters were Marysia Sawicka and Anna Wachalska. Kazik describes the warm reception they were given by the two women: "They suggested we first wash and change our clothes. This was my first shower since April 18 and an opportunity not only to wash my body but also to restore my soul. When I went into the bright bathroom, covered with white tiles, and was given soap and a fragrant towel—it was like a dream . . . We shaved and

there at once, but "at once" in the big city took a few hours. When I arrived, they were still looking for shirts and trousers for them. That was May, fine spring weather. They fed them and gave them showers and shaves. The apartment wasn't big, and, aside from them, a Jewish girl was also hiding with those two gentile sisters. There I got the information: the ghetto was dying. They didn't know how those coming out could even avoid the blackmailers and gendarmes. Nor were they the first to leave, since others had come out before them and were rescued. The question was how to get out through the sewers. Each one of them set off somewhere and wandered around not knowing where to turn. If they were lucky, they came to some opening in the sewer. And if it was at night, they would raise the manhole cover, and see whether they were in or out of the ghetto.

Those two came out through the Revisionists' tunnel and found shelter because they looked like Poles. This was in the early morning. Zygmunt Fryderych knew the address of those two women, one of whom was a widow. You didn't need to go far to pass under the walls, but you had to know the direction. They were very lucky that they succeeded. As soon as they came, they sent word and I met with them.

With their coming, I got reinforcements and, henceforth, joint work began. The apartment they went to wasn't ours but belonged to the two Polish sisters. The deceased husband of one of them, a railroad worker, had been a member of PPS, the old revolutionary party, which had been organized into fighting groups. The widow's younger sister, Marysia Sawicka, lived with her. Their nephew Stefan Sawicki also lived in their apartment, and so did a Jewish woman with children, named Zimra. When I arrived, I found the two of them: Zygmunt, who was older than me, and the seventeen-year-old Kazik. Zygmunt was a Bundist; Kazik was a member of Akiba. The two of them, especially Kazik, looked Aryan. He was young and energetic. We immediately began reconnoitering the areas around the ghetto, including the sewers, and Krzaczek occasionally joined us. We spent a lot of time looking for ways out of the sewers.

What takes minutes to tell lasted days. In early May, I met with two AK officers whose names I never knew, although they always knew who I was—they had only one "Antek," but I met with a lot of people. No doubt they received complete information about me from their security services.

---

washed and put on the clothes we were given, . . . We were invited to the dining room, to a table covered with a white cloth, loaded with food: an abundance of bread, sausages and vodka too. . . . The welcome of the two women, whom I had just met, dazzled me. . . ." (Kazik 1984:51).

From time to time, someone would come from the ghetto. Hela Schüpper arrived;[16] Tuvia Borzykowski was sent but didn't come. Others tried to cross and didn't make it, and there were casualties. But those who did come told us that everyone in the ghetto was dying and we had to act fast to get the remnants out. So I started working along the lines of the plan once suggested to me by "Grenadier Karol"—even before April 19—to get the people out of the ghetto.

I met with two people, one of whom turned out to be Stanisław Weber, in Praga, in a garden. I gave them a concrete description of the burning ghetto: no weapons, no food; I described the urgent need to organize the exodus. They said they would give me an answer. I also asked for transportation and temporary apartments in and around Warsaw. They promised an answer to that, too. On May 6 or 7, I gathered all the comrades, including Zygmunt and Kazik, and told them: "If we don't find a way to get into the ghetto in twenty-four hours, I tell you that, on the night of May 8, I myself will go into the sewers to find a way to the ghetto, since there's nobody to count on." (Kazik tells of that dramatic meeting somewhere.)[17]

They did try to get into the sewers a few times—both Kazik and Zygmunt and Krzaczek too; but they couldn't find a way. They could barely get out again. But since they looked Polish, they managed to get along wherever they came out.

In hindsight, I think if I had carried out my desperate ultimatum and gone to look for a way to the ghetto in the sewers, I wouldn't have arrived, and I wouldn't have gotten out. I would have put an end to my own life and to all the rescue attempts I was involved in. I reached these conclu-

16. Hela Rufeisen-Schüpper: Born in Kraków. Attended Polish Catholic school, which later came in handy for her underground work. Member of Akiba. Member of ZOB in Warsaw. Sent to Kraków in August 1942, where she served as a ZOB courier, smuggling weapons, people, and information. After the uprising in Kraków in December 1942, she was arrested by the Germans trying to enter the Warsaw Ghetto; she escaped but was wounded and remained in the ghetto until the April Uprising. On May 8, she was sent to the Aryan side to contact Zuckerman. In the summer of 1943, she went to Hotel Polski and was shipped to Bergen-Belsen, where she remained until the Liberation in April 1945. Currently lives in Israel. See Hela Rufeisen-Schüpper 1990:115ff.

17. Kazik's account is somewhat different: "I met with Antek and we had a very difficult conversation. We estimated the situation and concluded that we might be too late. Antek even issued an ultimatum: 'If things don't work out, I'm going back to the ghetto tomorrow.' I replied: 'If you're thinking of going to the ghetto through the wall, that's crazy, and you won't do anyone any good; our comrades there are waiting and counting on us; I would go only if I thought we had a way to rescue them. But if you want to do it anyway—you can do it whenever you want.' It turned into a kind of shouting match. I remained firm and so did Antek. We separated before curfew. Antek went back to his house on Marszalkowska Street. Apparently he accepted my opinion and gave up the attempt to return to the ghetto" (Kazik 1984:54).

sions from the stories of the group that was accompanied to the ghetto by two sewer workers—which sounds like a fairy tale—how they walked in water up to their neck, the dramatic encounter with the group of survivors looking for their way in the labyrinth of the sewers, and so forth.[18]

As for me, I said what I did because I felt I had come to the end and I thought that, in those conditions, a person should know when to quit. What prevented me was Krzaczek who said he wanted to carry out one last attempt, and that he had a man (a friend of a friend) who was a sewer worker. He didn't have maps, but he did know that underground labyrinth.

The Uprising went on for more than a month—until the middle, even the end of May. But the active Uprising was on those first five days, from April 19 to 23, perhaps to the 24th. Five days when the groups still functioned as groups, attacking during the day and regrouping at night. The whole time I had a picture of what was going on in the ghetto, with a twenty-four hour delay. Franya Beatus got reports every night from Tosia on the telephone in Brauer's shop. Although no one in the ghetto, including Mordechai Anielewicz, knew exactly what was happening on all fronts, the members of the fighting groups would sometimes meet in the evening. It couldn't be during the day because then there were operations. If a house was burned, one group would go look for the other group and didn't always find it. The fighters were no longer fixed in their places, they became mobile. You can read stories about that in the accounts of the comrades. Zivia and Tuvia Borzykowski tell of night searches in the ruins.[19] I got a general picture; this wasn't the time for long reports, and it was dangerous. So they would always tell the most important things I needed to know by telephone.

Every day I would tell Franya the essential things I wanted and needed to know—not details or episodes, but the essence. However I got a general and detailed picture only in Łomianki Woods, where the people of

18. Tuvia Borzykowski tells this amazing story of a miraculous chance encounter between a group of fighters escaping the ghetto and the rescue party: when the situation in the ghetto was desperate, a group of some eight or ten men undertook to get to the Aryan side through the sewers. For hours they trudged and crawled through the sewers, not sure they were going in the right direction. "We had been walking for several hours when we received a jolt. A bright light, as if from a powerful electric torch, appeared in the distance. . . . With the glare in our eyes we could not see who was carrying it, . . . Then came the great surprise: in front of us stood Symha Rateizer (Kazik) . . . We fell into each others arms, . . . They offered us hard candy and lemons. I shall never forget how we started to devour the lemons without bothering to peel them. It was the first fresh food we had tasted in months" (Borzykowski 1972:102). Kazik also tells the dramatic tale (Kazik 1984:55–58).

19. Lubetkin 1981:178ff; Borzykowski 1972:90–91.

Többens-Schultz gathered after the first fighters were taken out through the sewers.

To this day, when I hear stories about the comrades, I clearly sense the difference between eyewitness accounts and hearsay. Everybody is strong in his own domain. Over the years, things have undergone a special process. Some things the witness heard with his own ears are absorbed inside him, and he also became identified with things that happened somewhere else. This is even true of central people like Zivia—what she tells about other groups is nothing but hearsay, even from that very night, or from stories she heard at later meetings.

Some units were wiped out completely, but we knew about them when they were still functioning. For example, on the night of May 8, Zacharia Artstein's unit was lost and, as for other comrades, we know about their end only "approximately," but not exactly.

Some information came to us later, in autumn 1943. In this period, ZOB fighters who had been active in the ghetto tried to get to us through Poles. At this late period of the Uprising, we organized to send bread to the ghetto through the walls. When the ghetto was destroyed, the Germans used Jews to work in the ruins. On Gesiówka (where the prison had been), they set up a labor camp for Jews from Greece and Bulgaria, as well as some Warsaw Jews. Another group employed there were Poles, who came to work there and would leave. This group included members of the underground. They came upon feeble Jewish fighters trying to contact us. We tried to get sacks of bread into the ghetto by means of these Poles, but we never got confirmation that the bread had reached its destination. This operation went on for weeks. A special group was concerned with it.

In fact, the Uprising didn't end on May 16, as General Stroop stated in his report. The major German units left the ghetto on the night of May 8. What did the survivors live on? The leftovers they found in the bunkers? Did they find other Jews? Did they find the bread and other things we tried to send them? Did they get the information from us? There was no way to get an answer to these questions. We made several attempts to get to them. Zivia was furious; she wanted to go back to the ghetto, but I wouldn't let her because I didn't think she'd get there and that the attempt was suicidal. Even after she got to Warsaw from Łomianki, she couldn't get the lost fighters out of her mind; we tried to do whatever we could. I wouldn't have hesitated for a minute to go back if there was a chance or a purpose. Kazik did go back to the ghetto on May 8, looked for people, and didn't find anybody or any of the previous bases. The addresses he had were useless because all the fighters had retreated from their bases, the houses were burned down and in ruins, and the Germans had discovered the bunkers. Our people looked in vain. They knew what had happened at Miła 18 and went there too, but Miła no longer existed.

That was the great tragedy. If we had taken the fighters out through the sewers one day earlier, maybe even a few hours earlier, we would have saved a lot more people. However, I don't know what we would have done with them on the Aryan side of Warsaw, because on the Aryan side too, we had a lot of victims on May 10.

I have a general picture of the first five days, when the initiative was in the hands of the fighting groups, which were still more crystalized and deployed. I would picture the situation to myself from hints and letters— the comrades constantly attempted to tell us what was happening. I knew the situation, I knew about the successes, and I always had to subtract something from the stories I heard, even from information supplied by members of the Polish underground whose policemen reported to their superiors.

The rifles we obtained were ready for delivery. I didn't have them, the Poles did; but they were on hand the day the Uprising erupted. But the Uprising developed quite differently from what we had planned. The original plan wasn't carried out, except for Zamenhof Street and the Brushmakers' area.

I knew about the situation in the ghetto from the nightly telephone calls, which I didn't receive directly. From these telephone calls, I didn't know the number of Germans who fell in battle. Anielewicz writes in his letter only what he knew about his own unit. Apparently, what they told was generally correct. And even before the fighters gathered at Miła 18, in the bunker, battles went on and many Germans were killed. That is also confirmed in other sources. We can say it was a great, extraordinary victory. Although our information wasn't precise, we did have the general picture. The information that came through the Polish underground, from the Polish policemen, was partially based on what they heard from German gendarmes. In the whole area surrounding the ghetto, we always noticed a "duet": on one side the thundering shooting of the Germans and, on the other, the weak replies of our people. All that time, the residents of the area were witnesses to the resistance put up by the Jewish fighters. Later on, legends were created. Some of those things were published.

For example, there is the story of the waving of flags. That was something the Revisionists did on Muranowska. I don't know if they had two flags there. There was a blue-and-white flag. Maybe they also hung out the Polish flag. There certainly wasn't a red flag there. We had other plans: once, when I was still in the ghetto, we made slogans on cloth which could be hung across streets. Not flags, but banners; but that wasn't done. In my mind's eye, I see the slogans: Moshe Rubin painted them on sheets spread all the way across the street. They were written in German and addressed to the German soldiers: "Don't Shed Blood!" "Don't Aid the Murderers!" Such things, which weren't worth much. It wouldn't persuade a single German. They were obeying orders.

From the January Uprising on, we learned that things happen suddenly. Just before the January Uprising, there was still an early warning. By the night of April 18–19, the comrades knew what to expect, but I didn't, since they didn't have time to tell me; and I don't know if that would have made any difference. At any rate, on the morning of April 19, I didn't know anything, except for my nightmare. Then Franya came and brought back the letter I had written to our policemen telling them to wait for me.

Afterward, almost every day, we issued propaganda communiqués in which *Dichtung und Wahrheit*[20] (truth and fiction) were intermingled.[21] Historians tend to think that everything written in a document is the truth; but I can prove it isn't so. Sometimes, we "fabricated" things, and they weren't precise; and I would add that this wasn't so important to me in that period. For example, it didn't occur to me then to treat the names I wrote there as if they were real names, as Kermish, Blumenthal, Trunk, Friedman, and Mark do; because that wasn't the function of the documents we were issuing. At that moment, I wasn't thinking of historical precision. It was an appeal to the Poles designed to stir their feelings of sympathy for our struggle; and it didn't matter how that battle occurred, or how we were defending our lives. It was not an official bulletin of the Israeli Ministry of Defense. And sometimes the Ministry of Defense isn't so precise either. We didn't have newspapers then, we didn't have radio, and we wanted to create a sympathetic public opinion. We conveyed things to the Polish underground and they took care of publishing them. They were typed up in Polish (Berman did that). Things were collected from all kinds of sources and I always knew they weren't terribly precise. And if I had it to do all over again, I would probably shape the material again in the same form.[22]

The information on the situation was sometimes called a report, sometimes an "appraisal of the situation." Even though the name "report" suggests a precise document, the information in it wasn't all precise. That became clear later, when we could check things more thoroughly. "Estimate of the situation" means an attempt to describe a general picture of the situation. There were various sources for that: first, the Polish

20. The title of Goethe's book.
21. See "Announcements of the Jewish Underground," Zuckerman, *Book of Ghetto Wars,* 178–185.
22. The bulletins referred to here are in Blumenthal and Kermish 1965:211–219.

underground, that is, the Polish policemen. Then, the telephone calls I received. This is after April 23, when we still had contact through the gravediggers. We based our estimate of the situation on that. Furthermore, there were Polish observers. Not the simple Pole, whose house was close by, but members of the Polish underground who would view the ghetto, beyond the walls, and of course, also from tall buildings near the walls, where they saw what was happening in the ghetto; they saw German ambulances entering and leaving the ghetto.

Our basic weakness was inside the ghetto: a lack of weapons. All the talk about whether there were ten guns more or less is unimportant. That's not what would have made a difference. I can't say anything about the Revisionists because so many incorrect and untrue things have been published on the subject and legends have been created. I assume they fought just as well as any unit of the Jewish Fighting Organization. But their war was shorter. That early business about the tunnels and the sewers was, I think, what destroyed their war. All of a sudden, they vanished, and then they reappeared in a house near the ghetto wall, on the other side. Muranowska Street was where they fought and where they crossed, through a tunnel they dug, to the Aryan side. If not for that tunnel, they probably wouldn't have gotten out. On the Aryan side, there was a concierge who prepared a shelter for them in an attic and helped them hide there. They fought brief battles of perhaps only one day because, by the next day, they were on the Aryan side. Then they disappear from Stroop's report for a while, and later, he mentions them again.[23]

They were bold fighters and knew what they wanted. The fact that they were capable of leaving the ghetto after a day of fighting is characteristic of them.[24] Ultimately, our wars, even in Israel, except for the War of Independence, are short—six days, seventeen days. But in the ghetto, even a war of one day was sometimes the limit of human ability: not to mention a week or two; and certainly not three weeks.

A day of war in the ghetto was a day of mortal danger, without hope of any force coming to your aid. Aside from that, the fires were destroying everything! It never occurred to us that they would use that weapon.[25] And I must say that arson was the most effective weapon.

23. They suffered a bitter end. As a result of a denunciation, the Germans discovered the house where they were hiding. The house was besieged and all the fighters fell in a battle without surrendering (see Lubetkin 1981:239–240). Stroop refers to them as "the main Jewish fighting unit," and says that "the Jewish and Polish flags were hoisted on top of a concrete building in a call to battle against us" (Stroop 1979:5).

24. The ZZW account of their activities in the April Uprising is obviously different. See Wdowinski 1985:167–206; Lazar 1963:242–261, 170–290.

25. Marek Edelman has a different memory: "Antek, I remember, was the first one to predict during a meeting of the Command Group that the Germans would set the Ghetto

These were enormous areas. To burn a large quarter of Warsaw is not simple! I calculated that the ghetto covered four square kilometers. They went with flamethrowers, burning one building after another. The flames didn't always destroy the whole building, the bunkers underneath it sometimes remained; when the fire was burning, you had to get out of the bunker because of the stifling smoke and the flames; but, two days later, you could go back to the same bunker, under the burned building. In guerilla warfare, the burned building and the bunker below it were sometimes more important than a whole building, since you couldn't burn it down twice.

Nor did we figure the Germans would use cannons and we certainly didn't think of tanks. Every day I walked around the ghetto for hours and saw their artillery outside the wall shelling the ghetto. It was hard to pass by there because of the thick smoke that covered Warsaw. The smoke was not only in the ghetto; I could see the fire at night from my apartment on Marszałkowska. Later I learned that the fire was seen for dozens of kilometers away.

No one would help those fighters, neither the Poles nor anyone else. I'm not one to dismiss stories of help of certain groups of Poles. But it wasn't effective and had nothing to do with the problems that came up during the fight in the ghetto.

There is one story about a group of Poles from the AL who attacked a battery of cannons, and they say they silenced one; but that was outside the ghetto. I didn't investigate it. Even if they did silence one cannon, within fifteen minutes, another one was moved to the front. At any rate, the fighters didn't know about it in the ghetto. If they had, they would have told me. Even if the Poles had attacked somewhere else, it wouldn't have made any difference, because it didn't influence the operations of the fighters and wasn't planned in conjunction with them, and they had no connection with it. So it didn't help. If there had been cooperation, even with one group, in a coordinated operation on both sides, it could have shaken the German positions for a while. But such a thing wasn't planned together in time. It's conceivable that Polish patriots and liberals with pangs of conscience organized and did something. But that wasn't according to plan, since the intention was only to work out a joint plan with AK and AL. But, unfortunately, one underground group wouldn't and the other couldn't.

---

on fire. When we were still pondering what to do, what kind of death to choose—whether to hurl ourselves at the walls, or to let ourselves be killed on the Citadel, or to set the Ghetto on fire and all of us burn together—Antek said, 'What if they set the fire themselves?' We all said, 'Don't talk nonsense. They wouldn't want to burn the whole town down'" (Krall 1986:66).

Any operations that were done were simply humanistic gestures. They didn't change the struggle in the ghetto one iota; it didn't create an opening for rescue. They couldn't even help me with what we could do by telephone, by coordinating between us—like shipping twenty-eight rifles into the ghetto. So even if something was done, it was only symbolic, an expression of the brotherhood of Polish people, and not an act by an organized Polish force coordinated with the Jewish fighters.

We can say that the Polish street in those days was pro-Jewish. I'm not talking about fringe groups, who were thrilled that the *Zhids* were burned in the ghetto. Even though the simple Pole tended to be antisemitic, what was happening in the ghetto roused extraordinary respect for the Jewish fighters. The Polish press was full of excitement and wonder, not just some leftist or liberal leaders, but the simple sympathy of the masses. You had to be a real bastard to enjoy what was happening to the Jews at that time. Although some people were happy that the Germans were burning and liquidating us, the general sympathetic atmosphere in the street did help us a little; I felt it especially because I didn't have documents and, all that time, I walked around, usually near the ghetto walls or at the manhole covers, along with a few people I had with me. Nevertheless, even in the generally sympathetic atmosphere, we sensed the suspicion hovering over our little group that was constantly looking for something and wandering around the edges of the ghetto.

As I said, the Polish street was sympathetic; and that was also expressed in the AK's "*Information Bulletin.*" Obviously, Alexander Kaminski (Hubert) had a hand in this; for me, he was one of the Righteous Gentiles, even though he couldn't give concrete help. But he gave good advice and he himself tried to find ways to help. Those good Poles were as miserable as we were—they wanted to help and couldn't. They saw who had influence in the AK, since the AK had the means and probably could have done something. Their behavior was deliberate and conscious. I don't include them in the "Polish street," which was spontaneous and could go either way. But, by the AK, I mean the big social and military force, the leadership, the people who decided in cold blood not to help.

Let's be objective about this. I'm not talking either about antisemites or about those who sympathized with us. The AK always made its own, Polish, accounting, which told them that, if our uprising spread beyond the wall, Polish Warsaw would be prematurely inflamed by an uprising doomed to failure because the Germans would easily put it down.

In general, aside from "Karol" Janiszowski and people like him, who spoke in that spirit, all those I talked with were full of admiration and goodwill; but nothing came of it. History requires facts, and even good intentions don't leave traces. The intention was expressed but not carried out—that's the sum of all my meetings with Wacław and Hubert, Hajduk, Irena Adamowicz, and others.

From our perspective, the act of Stefan Sawicki, the young gentile, who simply went and joined the Jewish Fighting Organization, was infinitely more important than all the good wishes that accomplished nothing. When I talk about the sympathetic Polish street, I mean the simple man, the head of a household, who walks in the street and sees the fire, the smoke; he's a human being, and he expresses that—sometimes with a tear, sometimes with a good word, an expression of identification. But that doesn't obligate him to anything. Organizational force is something else. Another example of sympathy, as it were, which didn't result in anything was the position of the Red Army on the Wisła at the gates of Warsaw, during the Polish Uprising (in 1944).

Nevertheless, if there were expressions of help, groups that did something, that was because the AK wasn't homogeneous: it included members of PPS, socialists of the left and the right, democrats as well as fascists. I imagine that in this perspective, their fighting units were constructed like ours by previous ideological links. Thus, for example, ten former members of PPS constituted one unit. And if, by chance, the unit had a diligent and humanistic commander, he and his comrades expressed their difference in some act. Antisemites wouldn't have done that. Those who performed those good deeds were ashamed of the situation, and their actions were not the result of orders from the top. That is, it was the initiative of a low-ranking commander. Nowadays, Poland takes credit for those acts, but in fact, it was a human, though extraordinary, expression of a few specific groups within the AK.

On the other hand, in terms of its position and sympathy, the AL could have given instructions for action and assistance; but unfortunately, they didn't have anyone to give instructions to, since their forces were then very meager and badly armed. They told me this frankly. You have to understand that the Polish Communists of 1943–1944 weren't the same Communists of 1963 and our own day [1974]. At that time, our relations with them were candid and open. Sometimes they would say things that were identical with my own Jewish nationalist views. And they told me regretfully that they didn't have any power. If they had had twenty-nine rifles, they would have given us every last one. After all, they told me they'd give me the twenty-eight rifles in their armory. And I saw how sparse their weapons were during the Polish Uprising; I can swear they didn't have maps of the sewers. I was aware of that during the Polish Uprising too. I believed them since they gave us people and advice. In April, they tried to help and would run around the streets like us, doing what could be done for the ghetto. But that wasn't what the AK did.

As for the Uprising, I must say that the reality was way beyond our expectations, and that has nothing to do with the details. I was satisfied to get telephone reports every single night about the fighting units, even though they couldn't tell me exactly what was going on. Even if I had spoken on the telephone myself, I probably wouldn't have asked for details about any specific unit. I was interested in basic issues: rescue, sending weapons, the lack of food, how to get to them, how to get them out. Messengers came from the ghetto both before and after Kazik and each told his own tale. For the most part, I didn't meet with them at all. They were in some hideout, because the first thing we did was to hide them. Afterward, I would send the courier to find the comrades but, at that moment, I was neither a politician nor a historian. It wasn't my job to record their testimony but rather to know how they got out and what were the most urgent things to do. Hearing about what happened was postponed till later. I began to be concerned with that when I went to visit them in Łomianki Woods.

I emphasize: the Uprising was way beyond our expectations. I didn't believe the fighters would hold out even for three days; and that's not taking the fires into account. But we must know that since the Germans couldn't conquer the whole ghetto, they had to devote a lot of forces to conquering every individual building. And when they did conquer a building, they had to leave a German force in it. In such a case, you could attack them in the courtyard, which is just what our fighters did, even though the Germans kept units and patrols at concentration points. When we switched to guerilla warfare, they didn't know who they were fighting against or where to look for the enemy; and then the Germans began setting fire to the ghetto.

NINE

Underground in "Aryan" Warsaw

In those fervent and bitter days, a group of people who had previously been strangers began to take shape in Aryan Warsaw. I hadn't known Zygmunt Fryderych before at all; Kazik had been in the ghetto and came out later. And there were two Communist fellows I knew only by their aliases (their names were Jurek Złotów and Ryszek Musselman).[1] There were a few women couriers for the Bund who began to form a group.

There were other people: Tuvia Shayngut (Tadek of Ha-Shomer Ha-Tza'ir), and Marek Folman who came from the city. I met Władka on about May 8; she tried to arrange a meeting for me with Abrasha Blum, at his request, but it didn't take place. I would meet with Dr. Leon Feiner at one of the restaurants in Theater Square.[2] I used many restaurants, but I wouldn't meet people of different ideological groups in the same restaurant. When making my appointments, I always had to calculate the time it took to walk, because I was afraid to ride the tram. All I had to do was imagine that the tram was suddenly stopped and blocked at both ends, with a gendarme on every side; but when you walk in the street, you sense the panic sooner and have enough time to hide, to slip into an alley. I had been used to walking for years and it wasn't a problem for me. My legs are long and I was wary of the tram. My limp disappeared, but I sometimes had rheumatism, which practically didn't bother me then; I was strong and healthy and I had never been sick. I never had fever, dysentery, typhus, or any other disease.

1. Ryszek Musselman: Born in Warsaw. Was a liaison between the PPR on the Aryan side and in the ghetto, participated in rescue attempts. He was killed in Aryan Warsaw on May 10, 1943, as the result of treason by Władysław Gajek (Krzaczek), at the age of eighteen. For details of his death, see Kazik 1984:60–61.
2. Feiner was Mikołaj, a Bundist leader. See above.

Our lack of money was felt immediately and seriously. As I recall, when I left the ghetto, I took $100. We had a lot of jewelry in the ghetto, and there were millions of Złotys from "Exes," as well as dollars and British pounds. But I took very little out of the ghetto so as not to rouse suspicion in case I was caught. We decided to transfer our whole treasury to the Aryan side of Warsaw, but the comrades didn't have time to do that. I had no money, which produced a sharp discussion between Berman and me (on May 8–9). I had enough money to support myself, but when more people came—even before May 10—the question of money became crucial. It came up when the first fighters from the Többens-Schultz area came out. I hadn't needed money for the rifles since we got them for free. Franya didn't have much money either. But now we needed a lot of money, and I didn't have it. Only after the fire in the celluloid factory (see below) did Eliezer Geller tell me he had gold rings on his fingers and in his pocket, and I felt like a grave robber. He was severely burned and his head and hands were bandaged; there wasn't an intact place on his body.

The members of one of the fighting units in the ghetto who didn't come out had once brought me jewelry. But now the question of money was crucial. I appealed to Dr. Berman, who told me he didn't have any. One day there was a three-way meeting of Berman, Guzik of the Joint, and me. I believed that Berman didn't have money but, at the meeting, I heard them discussing certain sums, and I said to him: "But you said you don't have any money!" He answered: "Right. But I have a responsibility to many Jews in the city and I have to keep this money." That infuriated me; we were in a restaurant, but I couldn't control my temper. I banged on the table and exploded: "I'll kill you like a dog!" And he responded: "Why kill me like a dog? Turn me over to the Gestapo." Guzik intervened and the result was that I got money; it was stupid of Berman and a disregard of the fate of the dozens of fighters in Łomianki, whom we needed to support and feed; I really was penniless! Ultimately, he gave me quite a big sum.

As long as I was alone, I had enough money for myself and Franya. But it wasn't enough to support dozens of people. Blackmailers didn't get any money from me, even though I was a victim of blackmail twice. The issue of blackmail appeared mainly later. Keep in mind that, in fact, I didn't have documents and my situation could have been very bad if I had run into a German. And Aryan looks didn't always help, since the Germans would block streets even for gentiles.

After May 1, I wandered around the streets of Warsaw, looking for sewer openings. There were places where underworld characters were always hanging around, looking for prey. However, I was careful not to walk alone, and we always went in pairs. Kazik, Tadek, or Krzaczek went with me. If they had caught me at that time, I wouldn't have been able to ransom myself because I didn't have any money. At that time, I didn't eat in restaurants; I would eat at my landlord's at night, as long as I was living on Marszałkowska.

Finding apartments for the people who came out of the ghetto on Ogrodowa Street was harder. We started looking for apartments around Grochów and Czerniaków. We also thought of finding shelter for the people who left those farms and might have been hiding in the area, without apartments. And we did indeed find people in that condition. Every day, we sent our people to wander around the area, and we got results from that operation. One of those we got out was Sara Biderman, a native of Warsaw, whom we found wandering in the fields of Czerniaków.[3] I didn't have a single apartment for those people except my place, which I had to leave. And that was before May 10. One day, early in the morning, the engineer opened the door, saluted as usual, and addressed me as "commander." I have already told that one evening he invited me to a good dinner, that was during Passover and close to Easter. Then we started talking and he told me the story about his wife and his brother-in-law, who was fighting in the ghetto. He was terrified of the whole thing. They treated me extremely well, but they concluded that it was dangerous for me to be in their apartment, which was indeed true, since people were beginning to come to me and the house was becoming more and more obvious.

Franya came there and so did Irena Adamowicz, Tadek, Marek Folman; and, when Kazik and Tosia Altman got out of the ghetto, they also came. Serious danger was indeed imminent for that family since they didn't have anything to do with any of our operations. At that time, I had $100 for expenses, which I had hidden in the bedroom, under the rug. For my own needs, I used the few Złotys I had—my expenses weren't much. One day, when I came home, the engineer told me that the police had been asking about me. I suspected he was lying to me. Nevertheless, it was quite decent of him to tell me he had found another place for me.

That day, I left the house. He sent me to an apartment on Polaska Street, telling me that the landlady was Armenian and ran a restaurant in her house; nobody lived there except her grandson. He added that because of the interest the police had shown in his apartment, he was also leaving the house; separating from his wife wasn't pleasant or easy, and was accompanied by tears.[4]

3. Sara Biderman (Krysia): ZOB courier on the Aryan side of Warsaw; she lived at Miodowa 24.

4. In a previous chapter, Zuckerman says that the woman left and the husband stayed in the apartment.

That wasn't my last encounter with that man, since I met him again later. I didn't have any baggage when I left the apartment, because I didn't have any clothes or anything else. I realized that only Germans were living in the house I was about to move into. A German gendarme always stood at the gate. I was told that Gestapo agents lived in the yard. That was the apartment he put me in, but I had no choice. The landlady, the "Armenian widow," greeted me very warmly.

One night, I woke up with a hand stroking me. It turns out I had been crying, talking and shouting in Yiddish in my sleep. And here was that "Armenian" woman sitting next to me and weeping. That was strange, since up to then, no one had told me I talked in my sleep. I had a vague memory of some nightmare, but I couldn't reconstruct anything. Apparently, I had yelled aloud. And the woman was simply sitting next to me, stroking me and weeping.

The next day she told me that the children tormented her grandson at school, saying he was a Jew, because, as an Armenian, he looked Jewish. I would have been satisfied with that story except for what was involved with it. Every day, after school, that child would run along the ghetto wall, and he would come home late. I began to suspect that the child really was a Jew. I asked myself if the "Armenian" woman really was Armenian, since she cried like a *Yidishe mama*. I didn't ask because there was no need to ask.

The apartment was quite big, with a restaurant, a rather small dining room, always neat with nice things and pleasant service. But twice a day, I had to pass through the gate with a German guard. And things reached such a point that he began saluting me. One day I noticed I was being watched. I didn't say anything to the woman. That was May 13 or 14. In the morning, I said goodbye and didn't return. I knew that if I came once more, they would take me. By then, our people were in the Łomianki Woods, so I spent the nights there with the rescued fighters; in the morning, I would go to the city on my business, only to return to Łomianki at night. This went on until I found a place. In less than a month, I lived in three or four places.

Let's go back to the sewers. Finally, we found two Polish fellows; one of them was a sewer worker, whose address Krzaczek gave us. That was after my ultimatum of May 7, and after their other unsuccessful attempts to get the fighters out. On May 8, I wasn't sure we would succeed, but we made one more attempt to get into the ghetto. Fryderych was no longer in this delegation; there was only Kazik, one of the Jewish Communists, and that sewer worker.[5] They entered on Franciszkanska Street. The

---

5. For a detailed account of the rescue from the ghetto, see Kazik 1984:55–61. According to Kazik, those who participated in the rescue mission through the sewers were

sewer worker went because of money and, knowing that, they tempted him with promises to show him where gold was hidden in the ghetto. At a certain stage, when the guide refused to go on, the two comrades took out their guns and forced him to lead them. Thus they walked single file. The man was very familiar with the maze of the sewers. In the evening, they emerged from the sewers at some street near the small ghetto, which still existed at that time. They came to a place on Franciszkanska Street and began wandering around looking for a living soul, but didn't find anyone.[6] The ghetto was completely burned. Kazik knew the places, since he had left there after the battles, looking for a way to save the remnants of the fighters. He knew where the bunkers were, but he didn't find a single person, not a trace of the fighters; he didn't know about the fall of the bunker at Miła 18[7] and went there, too, but didn't see any entrance or exit. (There were perhaps five entrances there he didn't know about.) He saw that something had happened there, but he didn't find a living soul anywhere. After wandering around, Kazik and his companion had to return to the sewer. And here the "miracle" happened, the dramatic encounter Zivia describes.[8]

After nothing was left in the ghetto and all hope was gone, a group of our fighters came to the bunker at Franciszkanska 22, found an opening to the sewers, entered and got lost in them. Suddenly they heard footsteps in the sewers, and voices swallowed up in the noise of the flowing turgid water. They heard steps from two sides, but they didn't know who was coming toward them. As I recall, Tuvia was also in that lost group; he was making that trip for the second time. Kazik and his escorts left on May 8, after the fall of the bunker on Miła 18, depressed, with the slim hope of saving someone else. And suddenly they heard these voices in the sewer. Then they heard Yiddish and it turned out that those coming toward them were the group that had been sent a second time to try to find a way to the Aryan side. Kazik and his companion forced the gentile to go back to the ghetto with them because the fighters knew the situation a few hours before, and knew where the fighting groups were. So they all went back to the ghetto. Meanwhile, they had to keep the gentile from

---

Kazik, Ryszek, and two sewer workers. (Tadek and Kostek remained on guard at the manhole cover on Prosta Street.)

6. According to Kazik, they came on two men and a woman with a broken leg, who were so weak they couldn't move.

7. Miła 18 was the central command bunker, which was captured on May 8, 1943. One hundred forty fighters were killed (including Mordechai Anielewicz) and sixty were captured.

8. Lubetkin 1981:243; Borzykowski 1972: 102–104; Kazik 1984:57. See above, chapter 8.

running away so that he would lead them out afterward. By then, the gentile knew they weren't looking for hidden gold but for Jews, fighters. They got to the manhole cover the next day, on the morning of May 9, after they gathered all the remnants of the groups they could collect in and around the place where Zivia, Marek Edelman, and the nearby groups were. They couldn't get to all the groups, nor did they know where they were by then. Time was pressing because it was almost dawn, when the Germans would return to the ghetto.

Then they went back to the sewers, with everyone they gathered right up to the last minute. More than eighty people were collected there, trudging through the mazes of the sewers and coming to the manhole on Prosta Street in the early morning. They all stayed inside, close to the manhole, except for Kazik and the gentile, who went out to the street. We had agreed in advance with Kazik that he was to return in the morning, no matter what. We fixed the schedule and the places where he could find me. Kazik knew I was in Bank Square, in a little bistro. Krzaczek also got instructions to come and the Jewish fellow who worked for Gwardia Ludowa was also summoned there at a certain time. That is, communication was well organized.

Kazik came there after he had shaved and washed off the filth of the sewers in the apartment of the two Polish sisters where he lived. My first thought was of the great danger that they would be turned in, since they had let that sewer worker go. They had attracted him to the ghetto by fraud, even though they paid him afterward. I was afraid he might bring the Germans into Prosta Street. Everything depended on one gentile, who was neither an idealist nor a member of AL; we didn't know who he was. Then we all started running around and found that we couldn't bring the people out of the sewer because we didn't have a vehicle to take them away from there. They were hungry and thirsty and there was no way to save them. We decided that, as soon as it got dark, we would tell them we were working on getting them out, that they should wait patiently and know they weren't abandoned. We wrote them a note and slipped it into the manhole.

The second thing was to look for transportation. Krzaczek once again showed his inventiveness and his ability to improvise. He brought up the idea of contacting a big moving company and ordering two trucks. He suggested that he order the trucks for a shoe factory near the place, which made shoes with wooden soles, and used big trucks for shipments.

The people in the sewer crowded together at the manhole. It was wet, they all held onto wooden boards and leaned them against the walls of the sewer so they could sit and rest. At first, we told them to wait; then, at dusk, we told them we couldn't rescue them that day (May 9); meanwhile we sent soup, lemons, sausage, bread and drinks down to them. We bought a lot that day and sent everything down, with the regretful announcement that we wouldn't be able to get them out until the next morning. Since they were all gathered together and had time, they decided to leave the manhole area, which was flooded, and go to a drier place for the night. At least they had food and drink.

It wasn't yet certain the truck would come. That morning, I had made an appointment with AK members in Praga.[9] I didn't yet know if we could get our comrades out. So I went to the meeting, since nothing was sure. It was clear we couldn't get them out on May 9, but it wasn't certain that we could the next day either. I was in continuous contact with members of the AK. One of the people I met that time was General (or Lieutenant-General) Weber (he himself revealed his identity to me), accompanied by some other person. I intimated to them that I didn't have any transport to take the people out of the sewer; nevertheless, I didn't say where they were assembled. I just said that our people were in the sewer and we had to take them to safety. They said they would give me an answer that afternoon. I pressed them and said that every hour we delayed endangered the people who had been there since May 8. They didn't ask me where and, if they had, I wouldn't have told them the exact location.

When I returned to Bank Square, where we had agreed to meet again, someone was waiting for me and told me that the people had been taken out. At the time, I didn't know that only one truck had come to take them out. I learned later that, when the truck approached, Kazik, another fellow, and Krzaczek were waiting for it. It was a big truck. One of them (Stanisław Arczyński) sat down next to the driver and ordered him to drive up to the manhole; when the driver expressed his amazement, the fellow took out a gun and forced him to obey. They had to open the manhole cover immediately and bring the people up. The truck was filled with fighters, but a few of them who were far from the manhole didn't hear the shouts addressed to them and remained in the sewer. That was one of the things that has bothered Zivia to this very day.[10] She tried to keep the truck from leaving Prosta, but she couldn't. Nevertheless, when the truck moved out, she was sure the second truck would come.

The story that Zivia wanted to go back to the ghetto to look for the comrades who were left isn't part of the episode of the truck. True, not all the surviving fighters went into the sewers, and when Zivia realized there was a delay of a day (from May 8 to May 9), she may well have wanted to go back to the ghetto and try to bring them to the manhole on

9. A Warsaw suburb on the eastern side of the Wisła River.
10. For a dramatic account of these events, see Kazik 1984:58–61. Edelman claims that it was he who told that group to go off to a wider sewer for the night (Krall 1986:76).

Prosta Street. And Shlomo Shuster[11] and one other fellow[12] did try to return to the ghetto, but found the way blocked by the barbed wire and gas the Germans had put in the sewer. But that's another story. Like her, we all were sure the second truck was on its way. And to this day, I don't know if it did come or was late or perhaps ran away. At any rate, two trucks were involved.

After the fighters were loaded on the truck, Krzaczek arranged for them to be taken to a small woods near the village of Łomianki, seven kilometers from Warsaw. You had to cross a bridge over the Wisła where there were major checkpoints, which were common at bridges and important strategic places in Warsaw. Unfortunately, the second truck didn't arrive and about forty people were left in the sewer.

Some time later, two Communists, Jurek and Ryszek, as well as Krzaczek and Kazik, came to the restaurant in Bank Square, as we had agreed, where I heard for the first time that only some of the people were taken out and others remained in the sewer. I told them to try the "exercise" with the truck again to save the ones who were left. I instructed the people to wait at the manhole and I went to meet again with the members of AK (the meeting had been arranged before) to see what could be done. I realized that we might not be able to get them out during the day. At the meeting with the AK, they told me they had neither transportation nor apartments. So I came back empty-handed. Apparently, it was reasonable to assume that if Krzaczek had managed to arrange the truck on his own, the AK could have done the same.

When I returned, I didn't find anyone at the restaurant. I had a drink, went outside, and saw a lot of people milling around the square about 50 meters from the restaurant. I approached and saw Jurek and Ryszek lying dead. Their trousers had been removed, so I understood that the Nazis had checked to see if they were Jews and killed them on the spot. As I stood there looking at the catastrophe, I saw Kazik in the distance. He winked at me, and I understood that he hadn't found the people at the manhole and had also seen the gathering and the murdered men. Krzaczek, who was supposed to come, hadn't shown up.

When I returned to the restaurant, I heard rumors that two men in a cab were stopped by the Polish police and a German had immediately appeared on the scene. They took the two out and killed them. It wasn't clear what had happened to Krzaczek—had he escaped? Here, suspicion

11. Shlomo Shuster: Born in Pruszków. Member of Dror; ZOB liaison in Többens-Schultz area. He was killed in a clash with the Germans while trying to break through from the sewers; aged seventeen.

12. According to Tuvia Borzykowski (1972:107), this "other fellow" was Adolf Hochberg, who fought in the April Uprising. Like Shuster, he too was killed in the street battle; aged twenty-one.

began to creep into my heart, which later turned into certainty. In those days, I didn't reveal that suspicion of Krzaczek either to the Poles or to the Jews.

So two men were killed. The truck didn't come. Krzaczek didn't show up. Kazik and I hurried back to Prosta Street where we got the full information: Stroop had ordered the entire area surrounded. He didn't know exactly where the people were hiding. Those who remained in the sewer waited endlessly, sure we would come get them out; and when we were late, they concluded that they were abandoned, opened the manhole cover and emerged into the street. Not far away was a building that had been destroyed by the bombings of 1939, and they rushed to hide there. But a Polish woman denounced them to the Germans in the area, and they were discovered. A pitched battle began in the street and every last one of them was killed. These things took place on May 10.

That very same day, I was supposed to meet someplace with my main courier, Franya Beatus; but she didn't show up. The next day, I sent someone to the address I had for her, and they didn't find her there; but they did find a letter and some money wrapped up with a detailed report of expenses. The letter was addressed to me. As you remember, Franya had talked about suicide back on April 19; I scolded her and she understood she mustn't do that, that her job was to help with the rescue. I treated her like a daughter. Now she wrote me that since the people were brought out and she had done her job, she was going to commit suicide. How did she do it? Where? Did she turn herself over to the Germans? I don't think so. Did she jump into the Wisła? I don't know. Her body wasn't found and we don't know a thing except for what was in her letter. Thus ended the story of Franya Beatus.[13]

All that happened on May 10, everything on the same day. It seems to me that the experiences of that day were enough to fill many days, even years, for a person. You grow hard and you don't know what tomorrow will bring. How did I know that gentile truck driver didn't tell the Germans where he had to pick up the people? But the fact is they did come out of the sewer. The gendarmes might well have stayed there for forty-eight hours, and, one way or another, we might not have succeeded in repeating the rescue. Or on the other hand, we might have managed to get them out one at a time and hide them somewhere. However, they were exhausted after all those weeks and didn't have the strength to wait; they decided to try and fell victim to a denunciation.

As for Krzaczek, quite a few facts accumulated over time which reinforced my suspicion. Naturally, after the murder of the two Communists, I asked him to explain it, since I went on meeting with him for a long time.

13. See Kazik 1984:52.

He told me he had left them and they made an appointment for later. I asked him why he hadn't gone to keep the appointment, and he answered that when he arrived, he found them killed. According to him, the three left the restaurant together, but only the two got into the cab. At that moment, I didn't suspect him; but even then, I thought it strange that those two fellows, who had worked for a long time in Warsaw for the AL and had gotten along well without anything happening to them (apparently their Jewish heart made them aid the Jewish Fighting Organization), should suddenly be identified as Jews! It smells of denunciation. The restaurant owner didn't explicitly confirm that the three of them got into the cab; he only said that the three of them had left. Nor was it clear what the restaurant owner saw himself and what he knew from hearsay. Thus ended the episode of the sewers. Some were killed, others were taken to Łomianki Woods, where they joined the group from Többens-Schultz that had come out earlier.

The contemporary literature says that the fighters were joined in the sewers by people who weren't in the ZOB. In fact, there was only one such Jew who joined when our people were going into the sewers. This is the story I heard in Łomianki from that Jew: since getting out of the ghetto involved many dangers, they told him to get away; but he stayed; one of the fighters said he would kill him, and he said: "Even if you kill me, I'm not moving." They told him: "A bullet costs 70 Złotys." And he said: "No! Only 30." So they took him along. When I came to Łomianki a few days later, that Jew came to me, saluted, and asked permission to go to Warsaw. He claimed he had friends in the city and he wanted to arrange something there. I called Israel Kanal and told him to guard the man and not let him leave under any circumstances as long as there was one fighter there. If he fell into the hands of the Germans, that could lead to a catastrophe. And they did indeed guard him day and night.

Aside from that, all eighty people who came out were fighters. Later, in the forest, others also joined. These were a few of Pinkert's gravediggers who found another route of escape, probably through the cemetery.

Stroop's journal shows that initially he didn't understand where the ghetto fighters had disappeared; and only later did he realize that they were on the Aryan side, near Prosta Street. And perhaps that's why it ended as it did.[14]

14. On May 10, 1943, Stroop wrote to Krüger that ". . . a large number of Jews were unexpectedly pulled from the bunkers . . . Today at 0900 hours, a truck drove up to a manhole in the so-called Prosta. A passenger of this truck exploded 2 hand grenades, the signal for the bandits who were waiting to climb out of the manhole. The Jews and bandits . . . were armed with carbines, small arms, and 1 machine gun. They climbed into the truck and drove off in an unknown direction. The last man of this gang, who stood sentry

At sundown that day, I met Kazik and Krzaczek at Łomianki, where Kazik told me the general outlines of the event.

Łomianki Woods was about seven kilometers from the Warsaw suburb of Praga. I asked a lot of questions, but I refrained from asking if Zivia was alive, because I was afraid of knowing the truth. As soon the survivors reached Łomianki, I knew that the headquarters bunker was destroyed. I knew about Israel Kanal and a few of the survivors, and I didn't ask about Zivia. Rather casually, Kazik remarked that Zivia looked good and held up well. I knew Mordechai wasn't alive, that there had been a great catastrophe; the one encouraging thing was that Zivia survived. I didn't learn of the death of forty people on Prosta Street until the next day, May 11, which can be deduced from the fact that, on the 10th, we continued sending food into the sewers until we learned they had been killed.

Neighborhood gentiles witnessed that battle of the forty on Prosta Street. The next day, we started investigating what happened; we asked if they had seen the bodies. When asked by interviewers who were apparently gentile, they said they saw the refugees from the Uprising coming out of the sewer. At that time, the Uprising and the tale of the forty was on everybody's lips. The event on Prosta Street took place in a populated area, and people saw it, and said that a Polish woman told the police there were people wandering around in the ruins.

Now our central problem was what to do with the fighters in the woods, out in the open. One of them, Yehuda Wengrower, had died. He had drunk sewer water and perhaps was also poisoned by gas. He was buried in Łomianki.

I got to the forest about three days after they arrived. They were perplexed, not understanding that the woods wasn't a solution. But it was clear to me. It was a woods, not a forest, not far from the road. Even though it was a rather large woods, it couldn't serve as a permanent hiding place. When the Poles learned of the place, I got instructions from the AK commander in the Warsaw area to take the fighters out of Łomianki Woods to the partisan forests in Wołyń, and they took responsibility for their safety. I had already received a similar proposal in the past, but not for Wołyń. When Wacław gave me the proposal, I answered no—for two reasons: first, none of them would get to Wołyń since they were Jews and had to go through hundreds of kilometers in enemy territory to get there. Second, Wołyń was a battlefield between Poles, Ukrainians, and Germans and there was no room there for Jewish partisans. I said this after I had

in the sewer and was charged with closing the sewer lid, was caught. He provided the information" (Stroop 1979).

won Wacław's confidence and had become friendly with him. The issue
of the partisan unit in Wołyń was something unusual in our relations.

We usually met in his apartment and the things he told me weren't in
writing since he was ordered to read commands and various instructions
to me, but not to give me anything in writing. He would read from a
paper, but he would let me write down every word. My records of what
he said are still in my archive. I would give a copy of especially important
things to Berman, which is how they were preserved.

So my answer was that the plan to go to Wołyń was tantamount to
murder and was unacceptable because the fighters wouldn't get there
and, if they did, they would be a small, untenable Jewish force that would
be crushed between the Poles, Ukrainians, and Germans. And if they
didn't move to Wołyń, they had to stay around here. I was firmly resolved
not to put our people's fate into the hands of Armia Krajowa. At that time,
the Armia Ludowa had a weak partisan unit, and contacts had not yet
been created between them and the Soviet partisans. In truth, I must
admit that another reason why I didn't want to send them to the distant
forests was that I wanted time to get a better sense of the situation.

They couldn't stay in the woods, there were no apartments, and, if
there were, the tenants were in danger of being murdered; we had to do
something. After May 10, perhaps from the 13th, I started staying overnight in Łomianki. I would get there at sundown, either with Marek
Folman, who was involved in all those rescue operations, or with Kazik.
I realized then that I had a bad sense of orientation in the forest. Apparently it takes a special talent. Maybe I wasn't experienced enough. The
first time I went to Łomianki with Kazik and stayed there. The next day,
I got there at sundown with Marek Folman who hadn't been there before.
I, who had been there, couldn't find the way; I didn't even know what
direction to go in. From the last station, you had to walk a few kilometers;
we rode in a farmer's wagon. We got off somewhere nearby. Then you
had to walk a bit to the village, go around it, and get to the woods. And
it was Marek Folman, who hadn't come to Łomianki Woods with me the
time before, who led me this time. He would bend over the lawn, trace
the grass that had been trod on, look at the sky, check the moss on the
trees, and from that, he was able to find the right direction. It took a while,
perhaps two hours, but he finally did bring me to the fighters. If not for
that, I wouldn't have found the way on my own; I would probably have
spent the night under a tree and gone back. I admitted that he was gifted
with that talent. Maybe he learned it during his months with the partisans
near Kielce.

For a few days, Łomianki Woods became my "home," which I left in
the morning for Warsaw. We would sleep in the open in the woods. That
was May, and it was still quite chilly. I couldn't return to the "Armenian"

woman in the house guarded by Germans. And I had been thrown out of the house on Marszałkowska. I didn't have time after work to look for other houses because I had to get out to the woods before curfew. So, I would go to the woods and stay there; in the morning, I would return to Warsaw and go on looking for shelter for the fighters. One day I decided to go back to my engineer. I told him about the fighters we had saved and asked if he had any suggestions. He lived in his previous house, which he returned to right after he grew accustomed to the fact that I was far away and he wasn't afraid of the police and the Gestapo anymore. He said that he had an idea and would give me an answer later. And he did give me the address of an apartment on Albertynska Street where I put Eliezer Geller. He also said that he had two Polish partners in a celluloid factory in Praga; if we could pay a reasonable sum, it would be worthwhile for him to lay off the workers and give us the building. He had to vacate the factory, which was an isolated building in a courtyard. Only the janitor and the partners knew about it. As I recall, we settled on 60 Złotys per person. The first one we had to house was Tuvia, who had come down with typhus in Łomianki. I found a temporary place for him in Irka's apartment (Luba Gewisser's friend).[15] Irka stayed in Poland until 1967; I think she's married to some Italian marquis and lives in Italy. We cleared a place for Tuvia there (Komitetowa Street 4, not far from Pańska Street), and he was the first one in that apartment. Two of us brought him—Kazik and I, I think—one of us walked ahead of him and one behind. We pretended to be drunk, and we were laughing, and thus we brought him to the apartment. His temperature was over 104 degrees.

Marek Edelman decided to stay in Warsaw. Marek Folman was supposed to go to the partisan unit. The PPR offered us a place near the River Bug (about fifty kilometers from Warsaw). We couldn't stay in Łomianki any longer. The people hiding in the woods were saved by a simple gentile, a member of AK, whom we called *Hlop* (Polish for peasant), and whose real name was Kajszczak.[16] One day, one of the fighters left the woods to look for something to eat and came upon that gentile, a born

15. Irka was Irena Gelblum, a ZOB courier.
16. Bronisław Kajszczak: A Polish peasant who chanced upon the fighters, protected them, warned them of danger, and fed them. He hid Leyzer Levin and his relatives in his home. He was denounced to the Germans who burned down his cottage. The fighters helped him reach Warsaw. Kazik describes him as a "a good, warmhearted peasant. The man agreed to supply food for the comrades. We would give him money and he would arrange his purchases in various places so as not to make the storekeepers suspicious. In the evening, he would hitch his horse to his wagon and bring them food. On his own initiative, he would always add something to drink, sometimes it was hot soup he cooked in his own home; he would bring the food and hot soup to the forest with the help of his children" (Kazik 1984:62–63).

and bred peasant who owned a flour mill. Later, we learned he was a
member of AK, a sergeant or something in the underground. This man
truly risked his life for us. We gave him money and he brought food and
water. He also kept our people from getting hit. As I recall, his brother
was mayor of the village; he didn't tell his brother anything, but he always
got information from him about what the Germans were planning to do.
One day he came to warn us that people in the village were starting to
complain about the Jews hiding in the woods. Once when I was there,
there was an alarm; but it turned out to be nothing but peasants going
out to gather branches. It was very dangerous there. You could be discovered and captured even by accident. We had to liquidate the hideout.
That gentile managed to arrange a hideout in the village for Leyzer Levin,
his son, and brother-in-law. I didn't see Stefan Grajek, but I knew he was
hiding somewhere. He might have come out of hiding a few times, once
when the house he was hiding in was "burned." He didn't come out much.

I liked the Polish engineer's offer of his factory. We agreed on the sum.
We hoped to get the money from Berman and Guzik. But it turned out
that Guzik didn't have any money. The fighters, however, had brought
a little money with them, and we got some help from the jewelry we sold;
so we rented the building. The factory shut down and the laborers were
laid off since there was no work.

In time, it turned out that other fighters had come out of the ghetto
on their own. There were, for example, groups wandering around the
fields of Grochów and Czerniaków. We took them into the factory, too.
Stefan Grajek found himself a new shelter, but his wife lived in the
factory. Tosia had an apartment, but came to the factory occasionally. On
the day of the fire, they were waiting for me there because I was supposed
to visit.[17] I was late; if I had come earlier, I would have been burned with
them. Tosia was badly burned and was caught by the Germans. The place
was ideal, but we weren't there very long. Meanwhile, we had to take the
fighters out of Łomianki.[18]

First I brought Tuvia out of Łomianki, but it wasn't until the next day
that I took Zivia out. I insisted she stay with me, and if anyone blames me
for taking care of my wife, so be it. I was alone and isolated, and I had
to consult with someone. I did the same thing later with Marek Edelman,
who came out of the ghetto with Zivia and decided to stay in Aryan
Warsaw for a time. Earlier, the Bundists had found a place for him, but
I took him out of there; I learned he was miserable, cramped in some coal

17. See Lubetkin 1981:256–7 and Borzykowski 1972: 123–124. The fire was on May
24, 1943.
18. For details about the fire in the celluloid factory, see below.

cellar, with no room to move and had to lie down all day long. It was an awful place. And when he was there, we couldn't meet. I needed another person to help and I also needed him politically, because one day the Bundists would probably accuse me of grandstanding and not giving them any credit. Tosia remained from Ha-Shomer Ha-Tza'ir. She didn't live in that factory, but she came to meet me. She left for the Aryan side with a delegation we had sent in September and arranged an apartment for herself. She also had proper documents. Later, during the Uprising, she was in the ghetto; when she left, she returned to her apartment, explaining that she had been traveling. I was the only one who didn't have an apartment. Later, I joined Tuvia and we also added Zivia. That was the home of a Jewish woman and her daughter. She introduced herself as Mrs. Kopik and spread the rumor that her husband was a Polish officer in London. But she and her daughter looked Christian. In fact, her husband had been killed in the Great *Aktsia* and she went to the Aryan side with her daughter. I don't know where their money came from. They took Tuvia into their apartment. I got the place for him through Jurek, Luba Gewisser's boyfriend; and Luba was a friend of the landlady's daughter; and they gave her the apartment.[19] They also agreed initially to take me in too, and then Zivia. I added Marek Edelman later.

Those are only a few examples of the problem of apartments. It's hard for me to remember how many apartments we moved into on the Aryan side of Warsaw and how many of them were "burned." The fighters were taken out of Łomianki and sent to the Bug. I got the factory after I took the fighters out of Łomianki, as I said, after we got information from Kajszczak that the villagers were beginning to whisper about us. The base in the woods had to be liquidated urgently. I had only one apartment until I arranged for the factory and that wasn't done in a day either. Meanwhile, they pressed us to destroy the base in the woods. Taking them out and shipping them was organized by the AL, who thought our participation important. Their partisan unit was indeed weak, but a few Polish or Byelorussian villages were nevertheless under Communist influence, and although they didn't love us, they didn't regard us as enemies. Every one of my requests to the AL for a meeting was granted, and I met with the chief of staff of the AL, General Witold.[20] (Gomułka's authority was

19. Jurek Grossberg. According to Kazik, he was "one of the leaders of the Polish Scouts, a student who had good connections with Polish patriotic circles (the Scouts were known as lovers of their homeland and language); but the hitch was that the man looked extremely semitic, which would have given him away" (Kazik 1984:75).

20. General Witold (Franciszek Józwiak): A veteran Polish Communist. He was commander of the Polish Police after the Liberation. As a result of the Kielce Pogrom in 1946 (see chapter 15), he ordered Jewish youth armed for self-defense against Polish rioters. He died in 1966.

in the political realm.) Unlike my contacts with the AK, my main contact in AL was with the chief of staff, who gladly met with me. Our meetings usually took place in Guczisławak, the last station after Grochów. He was a short, nearsighted man who wore eyeglasses. I never felt a trace of antisemitism in my meetings with him and his colleagues. I could even discuss our relations with the AK with him.

He knew almost everything. My principle was to tell the whole truth except for the most important thing I couldn't reveal. As for the rest—tell the truth, or you're liable to get in trouble.

I didn't act like that with the AK, and I concealed my contacts with the AL from them. From the first, I could consult with Witold, from the moment they decided to give us what they had—twenty-eight rifles, even though they had neither fighting units nor plans of the sewers. Krzaczek brought us the sewer worker. That whole operation was not done by a single person. There was also "Black Antek" and Sanek Molecki who proved himself a great friend of the Jews even after 1967 (when everyone, including Moczar, was against us).[21] I met with them a lot and never once felt a trace of hostility. Witold never forgot me and later remembered me favorably, when he was in power, when Gomulka was arrested, and even before.[22] Witold's attitude was revealed many times, for example, after the pogroms in Kielce (1946), when the Communists went to Witold and said that a Jewish self-defense had to be set up. He said: "Set up a defense but on one condition: the commander is Antek!" Then they came to me and said: "Józwiak wants you to be the commander of the defense!" I said: "Amazing, you've got your own colonel, a good Communist." And they said: "That's what we said, but he insists on you. If you take it, you'll get whatever you want." I went to meet him, and it turned out that was true. Another time I heard of his attitude from Attorney M. Y. Landau, who died two years ago in Israel. He was in the delegation to Poland. That was about a year before Gomułka's fall, when he was still in power.[23]

Keep in mind the nature of relations that were created then and continued later with the aides and secretaries of those figures. They would protect me in 1945 from the "great Berman," Jakob Berman.[24]

21. General Mieczysław Moczar was in charge of security services in Poland in 1959; launched an antisemitic campaign in 1967 after the Six Day War.

22. Władysław Gomułka, Polish Communist leader, was arrested in September 1948 and was returned to power as First Secretary of the Party, 1956–1970.

23. Gomułka was forced to resign as Premier on December 20, 1970.

24. Jakob Berman (1901–): Born in Warsaw; the brother of Adolf Berman. He joined the Polish Communist Party in 1928 and spent the war in the Soviet Union. He returned to Poland after the war, was rumored to have a direct line to Stalin, and was all-powerful in Poland until 1956, when he was accused of Stalinism and removed from all government positions.

Our relations were such that I could consult with them without any hesitation. And sometimes that was enough and I didn't need help from higher powers. For example, in the issue of organizing small defense groups of Jews. If they could assist, they didn't refuse. Even though they had limitations, they also had many possibilities to help.

The moment suspicion is born, it develops. Krzaczek was the loyal man of the AL; and I've already said that it seemed strange to me how two of our fellows were suddenly identified as Jews and shot in Bank Square. They looked to me like hundred-percent Aryans. That left question marks. If I had been asked about Krzaczek then, I would have been very cautious about suspecting him. But various details converged. When Krzaczek ordered taking the people out of Łomianki Woods to the Bug, it didn't occur to me not to believe him. Otherwise, I would have shared my suspicions with those who sent him. I knew he was very sharp, that he had contacts with the underworld and with policemen. The underground uses such people. His ideological background was Left PPS (led by Barlicki and Dubois). He dissociated himself from the AK and contacted the Communist organization. He didn't seem to have a family; he wasn't young, a few years older than me, I think; a very bold and agile man. How he managed to get along even under difficult conditions was admirable. Even though he didn't have to worry about being caught as a Jew, he could have been hit by blackmailers even as a non-Jew. But he wasn't afraid of blackmailers. He himself could curse and abuse and trade blows. He could talk their language. There's no comparing his situation and mine if I had been caught at the sewer—even if only because I was suspected of being a Jew. And apparently he could be a blackmailer himself and extort money. But we'll get to that later.

As I said, I didn't believe a Jewish partisan unit could exist on Polish soil. Objectively, the place was unsuitable, too. The Bug area wasn't the eastern region with its forests and swamps. There wasn't any room there for a big partisan unit. The Bug is only a medium-sized river. Farther away, near Białystok, there were virgin forests but not near the Bug. When I got the hiding place in the factory at 10 Listopadowa Street,[25] I decided to dismantle the partisan unit and gradually bring the people back to Warsaw.

We had to get them out of Łomianki Woods without delay. Some people had taken off on their own and, if not for the fire in the factory, I would have taken all the fighters there, because that would have given me time to look for apartments. Our couriers helped us, and so did those

25. The ZOB hideout in the celluloid factory. On May 24, 1943, there was a fire in which eight comrades lost their lives. The only ones who managed to escape were Eliezer Geller and Meir Schwartz. (See below.)

from the Bund and the unaffiliated ones, like Inka Szwajger[26] (daughter of the late educator and writer Yitzhak Szwajger-Damiel). Her mother was the director of *Yehudia*.[27] Her parents separated, her father immigrated to Israel, and Inka remained with her mother and completed her medical studies in Poland. She wasn't a member of the Bund, but was active in its group. After I came to the Aryan side, a few girls gradually came to work with me; apparently it was more convenient and maybe even nicer to work with me than with the party "bosses," and they were at my disposal. I didn't check people's political credentials. I didn't care about that then and I still don't. The important thing for me was that they were totally devoted to their job.

So we started looking for apartments aside from the factory. On that bitter and violent day, there were more than ten people there, some who hadn't gone to the Bug and some we had found wandering around the fields of Czerniaków. Sometimes our people literally ran into them on the street; often they were sleeping outdoors. We collected them all, including people who came out of the ghetto by all kinds of ways and didn't know where to go. Ultimately, each person went his own way. Most of them were citizens of Warsaw, who knew the city, searched for shelter, and sometimes found it. I'm not saying we got to everybody, but we gathered the ones we did find and lodged them in the factory. For better or worse, finding that apartment had quite an impact on the fate of the partisan unit.

The story of the factory is in Tuvia Borzykowski's book.[28] It was a celluloid factory. I visited there only once, before we took possession of it. I saw the place and the surrounding area. It was on a quiet side street in Praga, a factory with an enclosed courtyard. The laborers who worked there were dismissed, the only one left was the janitor who brought food. We took care of all the needs of the people. During the day, they didn't have anything to do. There are a few variants of the description of what happened. Geller told me some things, whereas other people had a different version. But the essence of the story is this:

The people were sitting on sacks of celluloid in the attic; some fellow lit a cigarette and tossed the match away. The building was full of celluloid and was all ablaze in a minute.

We never got a place as good as that.

We managed to get a hideout here and there for one or two persons; but not a big building like the factory. It wouldn't have occurred to

26. Physician and author of *I Remember Nothing More: The Warsaw Children's Hospital and the Jewish Resistance* 1990. Currently lives in Poland.
27. A Jewish girls' school in Warsaw.
28. Borzykowski 1972:123–124.

anyone to abandon such a base, even though we would probably have dismantled it later. But as a temporary base, the place was very important to us.

When I wanted to meet with the fighters, I didn't have to fix a time because they were always in the building, and I came when I could. I set a meeting with Tosia and Geller there (Geller had an apartment at Albertynska Street 4). When I had to visit, I asked them to wait for me. Maybe I also set the time. There was no telephone there, and when I had to see them, I would come. I came right during the fire and I saw a lot of people, the fire department, Germans, police, and the building burning down. Since I knew that Geller was also supposed to be there (I didn't know Tosia's address), I went to his apartment and found him covered with burns. His face was scorched and only his eyes looked out through the burns; he could barely speak. His landlords knew his secret, gave him first aid, and even called in a trustworthy doctor.

He said that everybody was together, waiting for me. Then the fire burst out. He was the only one who wasn't caught. Tosia Altman tried to escape but was captured. Some ran away over the roofs; one of them was Schwartz of the Bund (the one who gave me the suit); he escaped and found shelter in a nearby courtyard with a gentile woman who hid him—not everybody in the world is evil—in a wardrobe. The Germans combed all the buildings around and went into that house too, but it didn't occur to them to look in the wardrobe. After they left, she opened the wardrobe and the man fell dead at her feet from a heart attack. We heard that Tosia and another comrade had been taken alive. We had to find out where they were taken, and that took some time. All the rest were burned to death. After I heard the details from Geller, he told me to take the jewelry he had.

I'll never forget that day. I walked home from Albertynska Street, to our apartment on Komitetowa. Tuvia was in bed with typhus, Zivia was waiting for me on pins and needles. On one of the nearby streets, I ran into Kazik, who also knew about the catastrophe.

I remember coming in and sitting down next to Tuvia who had a high fever. Although Kazik knew about the fire, he didn't yet know the details I had learned from Geller. It was sundown. Tuvia was feverish and didn't understand anything. I told him all kinds of stories. But Zivia felt that I looked strange. I was silent a while, but then I told her. I couldn't keep it inside. I usually didn't tell everything, since every day all sorts of things happened to Jews, and I didn't think I should tell everything I knew. But I had to tell this. In our apartment, they would make food and keep my lunch for me, and I would eat it later, after work. I would leave at a regular time in the morning and come back late, which looked better for the courtyard and the neighbors. But I never went out in the middle of the day so that I could keep up my appearance as a working man. I had a document the Sawicka sisters made for me. The late husband of one of them had been a railroad worker and my document stated that I also worked on the Polish railroad. Every month, they would paste a stamp on the document. The document was obtained with the help of a German and with the assistance of Polish elements, through underground contacts. The German made good money on it and I had a good document. I could say everywhere that I worked on the railroad; but, as a railroad worker, I had to work normal hours. I could come home late, but I couldn't be at home in the middle of the day. So I would always run around until sunset, even if I didn't have any work.

That was perhaps the first time Zivia encouraged me to drink. I didn't drink in those days, but that time, I finished a bottle and she gave me more. I told her about the fire, quietly, so Tuvia wouldn't hear. The world was spinning and I couldn't tell the ceiling from the floor. I barely made it to bed, fell on it, and slept in my clothes until morning. Whenever I awoke, I felt pain. The next day, I went to work.

That's the emotional aspect of the case, which determined the fate of many acts. I had counted a lot on that foundation, the factory, which would give us time to arrange things and disperse people whenever we could, since it wasn't healthy to keep a lot of people together.

Within the next day or two, we learned where Tosia had been taken. We were told that she and another woman had been taken to some hospital and were being held under guard in a corridor and weren't given any medical attention—they were simply killing them. We didn't know if Tosia died of her burns, but they probably didn't even give the girls a drink of water. They were constantly interrogated in that corridor. We planned to try a rescue operation, but we were told it was too late. Right after the tragedy, we contacted the AL because it was easier for them to find out. They could even ask the nearby police but, by the time we learned the details, it was all over.

After the fire in the celluloid factory in Praga, two questions arose, one personal and one general. I'll start with the general question: that fire sealed the fate of our partisans who had to be moved to the Bug. I realized that, because of the hostile attitude of the population, there was no chance for Jewish partisans to remain alive without any backup. On the contrary, the environment was inimical. Keep in mind that there was a Polish fascist movement in Poland which didn't fight the Germans but even collaborated with them; and they had a common goal—the murder of the Jews. Moreover, the underground AK fought the Germans, but didn't accept Jews in its ranks and was composed of all sorts of elements, including antisemites as well as philosemites, socialists, democrats, and liberals; it also included a large bloc of Sanacja,[29] most of them antisemites, and we had to be careful of them; and there practically wasn't a single village that was sympathetic to the Jews. Under such conditions, a Jewish partisan unit simply couldn't exist.

Furthermore, we cooperated with the weakest Polish element, the Communists, who were also persecuted, and suffered, both from the AK and probably also from the Polish phalangists (ONR[30]). The exodus of our people to the Bug originated because of the arousal of suspicion about the Łomianki Woods. We had to get them out fast, anywhere we could. We didn't have time to find enough apartments but, nevertheless, we did find a few apartments, even when they were still in Łomianki. Four or five of our people were brought to the Bund apartment in the village of Płodyz, not far from Warsaw. But as soon as they got there, the police were lying in wait for them and killed them. It turned out the owner of the hut turned in our people.

Now we faced the question of what to do with our people at the Bug. I told them not to rely on us and to try to get to Warsaw any way they could because our forces in Warsaw were slim at that time.

We got the factory after they were removed from Łomianki to the Bug. Otherwise, we would have taken them all out of Łomianki straight to the factory, where there was ample room. In the factory, we also gathered people who had come out on their own or who lived in apartments that were "burned." (Not set on fire, simply suspected.) Or who had been attacked by blackmailers, or were being followed by the Polish police or the Germans.

My plan was to bring them to the factory and wait until we could make other arrangements for them; but that plan collapsed. Dozens of people remained at the Bug; Marek Folman joined them. Israel Kanal was prominent among them. Eliezer Geller remained in Warsaw. Havka Folman was in Auschwitz by then; she had been arrested in Kraków the night before I was wounded, on December 23, 1942. On April 19, Marek Folman was in the forests with the members of the Gwardia Ludowa, near Kielce. He heard about the Uprising on the underground radio and reported for duty the next day. Naturally, that was a great help. As I said, he had left Warsaw earlier because of conflicts with Arye Wilner. Apparently, even in the hardest times, there are conflicts; Marek was a very easy-going, good-natured person. And I don't know what exactly was between them because I didn't have time to check it out. He then asked

29. Sanacja (Polish for sanitation): A right-wing antisemitic party which took control of the Polish government under Pilsudski in 1930.
30. ONR: National radical camp, a prewar fascist organization.

for permission to leave Aryan Warsaw, and there was no point bringing him back to the ghetto. So we agreed to let him go to a partisan unit. That was a "casting your bread upon the waters."

On April 20, he returned to Warsaw, immediately found my apartment on Marszałkowska, and reported for duty. When our people left Łomianki, he went with them (at my request). Israel Kanal and he were put in charge of the group.

How did our people live at the Bug? There were a few villages whose population I imagine was Byelorussian. The minorities in Poland tended to Communism more than the Poles, and we did have trustworthy people in those villages. The fact is that there was sympathy for our people in those villages, even though they weren't in the village, but in the forests. But in the forest itself, without help, people can't exist, and there was also a problem of information and intelligence since you can't live without that. First of all, they got the twenty-eight rifles the Gwardia Ludowa was keeping for us, and they formed a unit that was supposed to be mixed but the AL didn't have Polish Communists to integrate into such a unit. But there was a sympathetic village (even if not the whole village), and there were people in the village who gave our people the necessary help; I supplied them with money; there was no question of money then. One of the things customary with our people was not to take money or property from sympathetic villages, not to steal or use weapons to acquire things, but to pay good money. But if they came on unsympathetic villages or on collaborators with the Germans (and there were plenty of those) or on Germans themselves, they behaved differently. It was summertime, but they also lived in the forest in the winter and would dig trenches in the ground. Krzaczek, whom we knew, went with them to the forest and to the Bug; since he knew the area and the Polish villagers, he held all the threads of contact to the Communist activists.

Soon after he arrived, Krzaczek prepared an attack on the Polish police. The point of starting an operation on the Polish police wasn't clear to me. I was in Warsaw and, a few days later, Marek Folman came to me and told me this story, which worried me a lot.

Our people were well armed; in addition to the personal weapons they had brought out of the ghetto, they got the AL rifles and also had grenades. But the Polish police were informed in advance and were ready for that attack, which was led by Krzaczek himself. Before the attack, he was drinking a lot. While the people were attacking, he stood up straight and gave orders. The attack ended badly. He gave orders to retreat. We had people killed in that operation.

When I got that information, there was something in it I didn't like, and my suspicion was again aroused. I remembered the meeting in Bank Square and the two Jewish men who were killed there. At that time, I still couldn't put the details together; I had interrogated Krzaczek then and he told me that he left them after making an appointment with them. They were hit right near the café. I hadn't yet become suspicious, but the incident left a bitter taste for the man. Now the combination of his drunkenness with the attack, when he stood up and issued orders, and the police being prepared for the attack—and I have no doubt of that— were obvious facts.

I rushed to the AL chief of staff, Witołd, and told him the story. While he was considering how to explain it, I got more information: the Pinkert men, the ghetto gravediggers, arrived in the forest. They had not been a negative element in the ghetto. Gravedigging may not have been a highly esteemed occupation, but it was vital since the dead had to be buried. At the same time, they were also involved in smuggling through the cemetery, in empty coffins which were returned to the ghetto. They would bring food into the ghetto. People knew how the things were brought in, but nevertheless they ate the "funeral meats." The gravediggers also made money by roaming around the streets and abandoned buildings. They did that even during the first days of the Uprising. They probably also found valuables in the empty buildings. So they had a lot of money. They also filled a national function by serving as a means of communication, since they could leave from Gęsia through no-man's-land, and cross the Polish street that separated the former ghetto from the cemetery. The fact is that they delivered the letters I sent, and the two letters I got from Mordechai Anielewicz. They risked their lives as the only link between the ghetto and us (on the Aryan side) at a certain period.

Now the gravediggers also got instructions to go to the forests. When they came, Krzaczek put them in the ranks of our partisans and, in the name of Gwardia Ludowa, ordered everyone with money to turn it over to the party treasury. The people were scared, turned in their money. In this way, he collected a lot of money from them—hundreds of thousands of Złotys, some of it in dollars. I was furious when I heard this from a Polish girl student who was a courier for the Gwardia Ludowa. There was once a Communist group carrying out "Exes" in the ghetto, and the commander maintained that he was acting on orders from above. We then investigated the matter and the Polish Communists responded sharply that they had never asked their members to collect money in the ghetto. And here was the same thing in the forest. Krzaczek referred to orders he had supposedly received from the Gwardia Ludowa.

Witołd told me explicitly that Krzaczek had never been asked and had not received authority to collect money from the Jews in the forests. He asked me to come to another meeting with him the following week, where he told me that a death sentence had been issued against Krzaczek and an order to return to Warsaw had been sent to him. At that opportunity,

I told him about the incident in Bank Square and about the attack on the police; he didn't know all the details about that. It turned out that the robbery now was the third incident, so there was no longer any doubt and a death sentence was issued against him.

This was very serious. The man came to Warsaw and I ran into him a few times, not far from my new clandestine apartment. When he came to Warsaw, Krzaczek apparently smelled that his comrades were panicky about all the things he had done on his own. Apparently, he was a very complicated personality. On the one hand, he demonstrated great talent and innovation. Without him, we wouldn't have succeeded in rescuing the people from the ghetto and bringing them through the sewers to Łomianki Woods. He also led our people from Łomianki Woods to the Bug. But on the other hand, he was collaborating with the Polish police, if not worse; that is, he was a traitor, a collaborator. Apparently, he was a double agent.

When he got an order to return to Warsaw, he returned. By then I knew we had to watch out for him. The sentence against him wasn't carried out since they apparently couldn't catch him. Later, I met him. I remember the place exactly, I was going from Marszałkowska to Swieta Krzyska Street. I was walking toward my new apartment on Komitetowa Street and suddenly he popped up in front of me and asked me for a loan. I knew it wasn't a loan but blackmail. If he was wandering around in this neighborhood, it meant he knew things he shouldn't have known; and I also knew that if I gave him one loan, I would have to give him many, endlessly—if he didn't turn me over to the Germans. I told him I didn't have any money, but I immediately informed the AL about it.

He lay in wait for me a few more times, but he didn't denounce me. The end of the story was in January 1944. It was the result of a defeat, and I don't know if he was one of the factors in it. At any rate, it ended with the death of the partisans who were removed from the forest and he apparently ran to the Gestapo or the Kripo[31] to ask about the fate of the people—who had survived, who was killed, and so forth. After that, traces of him disappeared. Did his German or Polish partners kill him? At any rate, after January 1944 he disappeared and we didn't know anything about him until the end of the war. We don't know where he disappeared or what happened to him. In the end, he walked around with a death sentence hanging over his head.

He hadn't ever joined the PPR but only the Gwardia Ludowa or the Armia Ludowa, the military organization, not the party. They didn't tell me that, and I didn't know exactly how to behave with him because he didn't stand trial and the death sentence was issued *in absentia*. To this day,

31. Criminal Police.

we haven't investigated the matter and the incident isn't mentioned anywhere. But I know for sure that a death sentence was issued by the AL,
and I didn't talk about it. There were rumors that the man was awarded
a medal for "heroism" after the war. Those who gave him the medal might
not have known about his other deeds. You have to check when he
received the citations—if it was during Witołd's time or after his death.
Witołd might not have been very interested in things like whom to award
medals to. At any rate, in my few meetings with Witołd after the war, we
never talked about Krzaczek. As I said, that wasn't his real name, but an
alias for camouflage.

After the failure of the attack on the police station, our fighters stayed
where they were and reorganized. We didn't attribute much value to
those operations. The Uprising overshadowed the activity of the few
groups who continued partisan operations. When I compared our partisan activities to the Uprising, I realized that the partisan activity didn't
constitute an advance, but rather the opposite, a tragic fall.

Nevertheless, some of our people were slowly brought to Warsaw.
After the disgraceful case of the police station, Israel Kanal was broken
and got away from that activity; Marek Folman also returned to Warsaw.
At the time, our contacts with Częstochowa and Będzin were in trouble,
and we decided to send Marek there. We didn't have enough female
couriers; there were a few girls from Ha-Shomer Ha-Tza'ir, Dror, and the
Bund, but before we shaped them into an operational unit, we had to go
through all kinds of operations to contact the other cities and our comrades there.

I hadn't seen Israel Kanal since Łomianki. I learned that he had gone
from the forest to Hotel Polski and that's a story in itself. Hotel Polski was
a hotel where genuine and phony foreign citizens were gathered.[32] Israel
Kanal was broken and depressed when he returned from the forest.
When I found out he had gone to that hotel, we found a shelter for him
in Warsaw; but by then he was no longer in the hotel. He had been taken
with one of the transports from Hotel Polski to Bergen-Belsen. From the
people who met with him, I know he had weapons—a pistol and grenades—when he was at Hotel Polski; that is, he was worried when he went
there. I heard this from Attorney Alexander Landau.[33]

We succeeded in returning a few dozen partisans. The AL couldn't
increase the partisan unit with their own Polish comrades. The core of the

32. Hela Rufeisen-Schüpper 1990:125ff.; and Shulman 1982.
33. Hela Rufeisen-Schüpper confirms this in her account of Kanal in Hotel Polski:
"Israel was depressed, often feverish. He said he had returned to Warsaw to meet with
Yitzhak and Zivia and to discuss the future of the struggle and, in Warsaw, he realized
he could stay only in Hotel Polski. His face was so semitic, it was a miracle he got to the hotel . . . Israel went everywhere with a pistol" (Rufeisen-Schüpper 1990:127–128).

partisan unit was composed of Jewish fighters of the ZOB, who were joined by individual Jews who weren't members of the Jewish Fighting Organization. But in time, it evaporated. We kept in touch with the partisans almost constantly through couriers (Kazik also visited them) and our Christian women couriers as well as through Yakov Celeminski and Władka. We sent them money. The Bund also sent people and especially food.

The AK was aware that we had our own partisans who were cooperating with the Gwardia Ludowa (later the Armia Ludowa). I was told that a group of AK partisans appeared there one day and suggested joint operations, unification. We had to decide what to do. We sent one Polish woman courier, a devoted Communist who had been a student before the war, to the AL; and she returned the same day with a definite answer warning us against that partnership. There was great danger lurking for that group.

Meanwhile our partisan unit split up. Mardek's (Mordechai Growas's) group met with the AK; other individuals joined the mixed partisan unit of Poles and soldiers of the Red Army escaping from German prisoner-of-war camps. Some of them survived the war.

Some of the members of the unit continued on to Warsaw. Others, as I said, joined the mixed group and went farther east. Mardek's group waited for an answer from the AK partisans, which they apparently received, but we don't know exactly what happened afterward. We inquired about them in the villages that were friendly to us and learned that the Polish partisans set up a joint meeting with them in the forest, which was supposed to be a kind of party. When they arrived, they put their weapons aside, as usual among the partisans, and sat together to plan the cooperation. Mardek, who had begun to suspect something, tried to draw out the conversation, to gain time. As they sat there like that, they were suddenly attacked by Polish partisans from that unit. That's all we know. We imagine that they were all murdered on the spot.

When I found out what happened, I reported to Wacław and he said he would check, but he didn't have any more information. I asked to meet with Hubert Kaminski an old friend who wasn't involved with Jewish matters at that time. We met at Pańska 5, an apartment that belonged to a Jew of the Polish Scouts. I told Hubert the whole story, which grieved him. To find out if our people were in one of the AK partisan units (the hope was slim), he offered to give camouflaged information in his bulletin, and whoever it was addressed to would catch on. He said the newspaper reached all their partisan units.

Indeed, in the AK bulletin of the end of 1943, there is information addressed to Mardek, a name that doesn't sound Jewish: "Mardek, contact your friends at once." Signed: "Celina." At Hubert's suggestion, we decided not to sign my name so the AK wouldn't know it had anything to do with me. They had quite a well-developed intelligence service and they knew who "Antek" was. "Celina" was Zivia's underground name and Mardek knew it. Since I didn't get an answer, we had no doubt that that group had indeed been murdered by members of AK.[34]

Carmi and Frimmer (each individually) joined the mixed partisan unit, which included Red Army soldiers, and they are among the few who survived. If we counted up all those who were removed from the ghetto—people we took out of Többens-Schultz and the Central Ghetto, plus our groups on the Aryan side of Warsaw and those who came out on their own—I estimate that about a hundred people remained from that large population. And I'm not talking now about those who were killed in the counterattacks of the Polish police and the Germans. Even in Aryan Warsaw, Jews were murdered whose apartments were "burned" and who fell into the hands of the Germans and were executed, or who were killed on the way to the forest, or later on in the Polish Uprising. One of our groups of five or six, most of them Ha-Shomer Ha-Tza'ir, suffered such a fate.

Throughout this whole time, there was no shelter for Jews anywhere. Whoever survived was lucky, like those in the mixed unit with the gentiles. A few who hid in the ruins of Warsaw until after the failure of the Polish Uprising also survived. Our group was involved in those battles from the first day to the last and hid for six weeks in ruined Warsaw in a bunker near the Wisła. We spent the rest of the time until the Liberation in Grodzisk near Warsaw.[35]

A few survived from the partisan unit—Haim Frimmer, Aharon Carmi, Yakov and Mashka Putermilch—who were brought to Warsaw and hidden there, where they remained there until after the war. Everyone has his own story, there is no common denominator. Every last one of Mardek's big unit was murdered, and not a single one of them survived. In the United States, there was Hanna Fryszdorf, whose husband Gabriel (Gabusz) was killed in the forest. She was pregnant and was taken to Warsaw; she has a grown son and works at YIVO in New York.[36] I think

34. See the letter of Bór-Komorowski in reply to Yitzhak Zuckerman's complaint of early 1944. The correspondence with the AK was published in *Yediot Bet Lohemei Ha-getaot* (nos. 9–10), April 1955. There are also details about the murder of the group in Wyszków Forest.

35. See below.

36. Gabriel and Hannah Fryszdorf: Veteran Bundists, members of ZOB; they fought in the April Uprising. According to Meed, "Every mission [Gabriel] had carried out had shown the same planning and attention to detail and the same valor and heroism. The partisans in the woods had come to admire and respect him . . . I could still see his tall figure, his handsome face, his eyes mirroring deep concern. He radiated calm and fortitude, and nothing escaped his clever eye. He knew almost all there was to be known about life in the

it's no exaggeration to say that perhaps ten members of the original Jewish Fighting Organization are still alive today [1974]. A few died a natural death after the war. In 1945, a small group remained; if we add the couriers, a few dozen survived.

In those days, May 1943, right after the Uprising was crushed, we first had to support the people and provide housing for them, in or out of Warsaw. It was hard to get an apartment and that was a continuous preoccupation which took up all our time, especially since our team was very small.

The Jewish National Committee couldn't help at all. At that time, I had only one demand for both the Jewish National Committee and the Co-ordinating Committee: money! I didn't have any money because we didn't have time to transfer sums we had hidden in the ghetto. I was left with a few pieces of jewelry I couldn't do anything with, and I didn't even have those at that time. I literally had to support the fighters in Łomianki, even get them black bread. Right after the Uprising was crushed, Rivka Glanz came to me. That was when the ghetto in Częstochowa still existed, and that's a story in itself, but there are people more qualified than I to tell it. For example, the book by Liber Brenner, the Bundist, is worth reading, as well as Adam Brand's works on that subject.[37]

Rivka Glanz came to us from Częstochowa asking for help. She came with a young man, a member of the Jewish Fighting Organization. I asked her if, given the position of the ZOB in Warsaw, it wasn't desirable (after what had happened to us when the Uprising was over) to remove the fighters from the ghetto and try to set up a partisan base around Częstochowa and give up the war in the ghetto. For me, the question was rhetorical. But I had to hear what she said about it. Her answer was clear: absolutely not! Against joining the partisans, and for war in the ghetto. They stuck to that, even after they realized that the Jewish Fighting Organization in Warsaw was bigger and stronger than their own organization. Moreover, the fact that the Uprising ended as it did gave them strength and encouragement. They would fight, she said.

When I heard that, I helped them a little with money and promised to do everything to get weapons for them. She went back the same day. I accompanied her to the Częstochowa train. In Częstochowa, before the war, there had been a strong training kibbutz of Ha-Shomer Ha-Tza'ir

---

woods, and his advice and decisions were usually considered authoritative" (Meed 1979: 221, 224). Hannah Fryszdorf (1920–1989) immigrated to the United States in 1949.

37. Liber Brenner, *Resistance and Murder in Częstochowa Ghetto* (Yiddish). Warsaw: Jewish Historical Institute, 1950. Adam Brand, *Man in the Ghettoes* (Hebrew). Merhavia Sifriat Po'alim, 1954.

and a large cell of that movement; we [He-Halutz Ha-Tza'ir] were quite weak there. But during the war, we got into circles of young intellectuals; we set up a Dror kibbutz there and, in autumn 1941, we sent people. One of them was Rivka Glanz, another was Moshe Wilnitzki, a student in our Seminar.

Ha-Shomer Ha-Tza'ir had a farm in Szarki (near Częstochowa). They had an important group of people there, and there were also people from Gordonia, the Communists, and a politically unaffiliated group. All together, they constituted the Jewish Fighting Organization in Częstochowa, similar to the composition of that of Warsaw. The central person in Ha-Shomer Ha-Tza'ir was Yehuda Glikstein,[38] and Rivka Glanz, of Dror, was on the command staff of ZOB there. There were also the Bund, Po'alei Zion Left, and Communists. All sorts of stories are told, which I take with a grain of salt.

We had to renew contacts with Będzin and seek ways to Białystok. Marek Folman returned from the forest with dreadful stories. We had few people and we decided to send Marek to Częstochowa and Będzin. He got there after Rivka had left and before she was killed at the head of a group of ghetto fighters. In Częstochowa, there were two attempts to engage the Germans in battle. (That has already been told, and I won't go into it.) Marek participated in one of those battles. From Częstochowa, he went to Będzin. I think he was in Czestochowa two or three times, and in Będzin twice. Frumka Plotnitzka and Hirshl Szpringer[39] were in Będzin. Dror no longer existed in Będzin but there was still contact between Będzin and Sosnowiec. There was a joint ghetto of the two cities. Marek met with our people and tried to set up a partisan base in Zagłębie. That was May 1943. He was there again, in June or later, just before the final days of Będzin, shortly before the struggle and resistance of the inhabitants of the bunkers there.

One day in late 1943 we got the bitter news that Marek was killed. I didn't know the details until early 1944; we had a few screw-ups then. In early 1944, the Germans were on my trail and almost caught me. In late 1943, we and Armia Ludowa both screwed up. Even though I managed to warn the AL in time, both of us suffered casualties. I managed to warn Witold and all those I was in touch with, including Yosef Molecki (Sanek),

38. Yehuda Glikstein: Born in Warsaw. Active in Ha-Shomer Ha-Tza'ir; sent to Częstochowa in late 1940 to set up a training kibbutz. He helped establish the ZOB there in September 1942. In 1943, he set up a partisan base near Koniecpol. Killed by Polish Fascist NSZ (Narodowe Siły Zbrojne, National Armed Forces) at the age of twenty-two.

39. Hirshl Szpringer: Born in Wolbrom. Prominent in the He-Halutz underground in Upper Silesia; one of the leaders of Dror, and one of the founders of the ZOB in Będzin. In June 1943, he jumped from a train transporting him to Auschwitz. He was killed on August 10, 1943.

one of the commanders of Warsaw, who was ordered to leave Warsaw in time.

I already said that riding the tram was traumatic for me because of the fear of being trapped in a closed place. Nevertheless, I did it a lot, feeling that the Germans would stop the car at any time with me locked inside it as in a cage. One day I was riding the tram when I suddenly saw someone familiar next to me. He was so well disguised that I barely recognized him. That was Sanek Molecki. He also saw me, came close, and nudged me with his elbow as a signal. I got off the tram with him right behind me.

And here's the story he told me: at the Częstochowa railroad station, he saw a man he remembered seeing with me a few times. The man was obviously nervous, which looked suspicious; Germans came up and arrested him. They checked and killed him on the spot. That was Marek Folman. All the indications he gave me testified to that.

The information we got later was that Marek came to Będzin; through the AL and the PPR, he got in touch with some Pole whose job was to help set up a partisan base in the territory of the Reich, not far from Będzin and Sosnowiec. They planned to prepare the base in coordination with Frumka and take people out there in time. We were experienced by then and knew you needed a small core to absorb newcomers. The first group was sent to one of the forests in the area and was annihilated by the Germans; it turned out that the Pole recommended by the AL, who had given us his address, was a Gestapo agent. They said the man, who was supposedly a member of AL assigned to help Jews, was a double agent and turned our group over to the Germans.

Apparently Marek was depressed and in despair. He was a conscientious man, who couldn't forgive himself for the failure. Meanwhile he decided to return to Warsaw, and on the way, he changed trains in Częstochowa. He was killed at the railroad station where his nervousness and his depression looked suspicious. That was what Sanek Molecki told me.

We didn't know anything about Białystok. Będzin is a separate chapter in the documents. After the Folman episode, we had no more contact with Będzin. Although we sent messengers there later, that was the last contact with Będzin and Częstochowa, too. Before Marek's death and after Rivka Glanz, we still had gotten messengers from there.

One day, Wacław, the AK man for Jewish affairs, told me the AK had gotten a letter signed Tamaroff (Mordechai Tennenbaum).[40] He was ordered not to give me the letter, but he read it to me. The letter asked for help from the AK in Białystok. From there, it reached the AK in

40. ZOB commander in Białystok.

Warsaw, that is, the main headquarters, and thus came to Wacław's attention. He brought the letter to me as head of the Jewish Fighting Organization. Thirty years later, when the letter was examined, it turned out that months had gone by from the day he wrote it until it reached its destination and was brought to our attention. Moreover, when we published the book in memory of Tennenbaum, *Dapim min ha-dlika (Pages From the Blaze)*, we had a version of that letter—I don't remember how it got to us—which was missing things. I remembered that there were things in the letter Wacław read me that weren't in the letter we got after the war. In the original letter, Tamaroff explained the anti-Communist position of the Halutz movement or of the Jewish Fighting Organization. In my introduction to *Dapim min ha-dlika*, I remarked that the spirit didn't fit Mordechai's views, but that apparently it responded to the immediate needs of the Jewish Fighting Organization.[41]

After hearing the contents of the letter in May, we tried to organize somehow; we looked for someone to send to Białystok. Not everyone could do that job. It had to be someone who could transmit our message and discuss things with them. At last, we sent someone there, but, unfortunately, it was too late. I didn't know him well. I met with him just before he set out for Białystok and Vilna. He got to both places, after August 16, 1943,[42] but by then, he couldn't find anyone and came back. This shows that we made efforts to communicate with Częstochowa and Będzin; and the same goes for Białystok and Vilna.[43]

We got information later about Białystok and Vilna. As I recall, we got the wrong date for the uprising in Białystok. At any rate, the man we sent didn't find a trace of our people. There were rumors that Mordechai Tennenbaum (Tamaroff) was taken to the Lublin area after the uprising. We learned about the uprising in Białystok later, but not the precise details. Nor did we know who survived. We knew that Mordechai was taken to Poniatów or Trawniki or to one of the Lublin camps, and we searched for him in vain. Keep in mind that, before the Uprising in Warsaw, the Germans did all they could to get the Jews out of Warsaw to those two labor camps, and we resisted that with all our might.

With the Uprising, some of our people and the civilian population with their factories and machines were taken to all those concentration camps run by the SS, including Lublin, Mayden-Tatarski, and Budzyń. We followed the Jews and searched, we made contact with Poniatów and Trawniki. Emmanual Ringelblum was in one of those camps, and so was

41. The complete letter was published in the last edition of Mordechai Tennenbaum 1947:111–114.

42. The revolt in Białystok took place on August 16, 1943.

43. See Zuckerman's introduction to Tennenbaum's book for a discussion of the messenger to Białystok (Tennenbaum 1947:20).

Dr. Yitzhak Schipper. We got to the AK in Lublin; and we also made contact with Budzyń, when we learned that Dr. Haim Zelmanowski was detained there. I managed to get some letters to him. We also picked up the trail of Lipa Bloch. Neither the Jewish National Committee nor the Jewish Coordinating Committee could take care of these things. Only the Jewish Fighting Organization could do that.

We formed cells of the Jewish Fighting Organization in Poniatów and Trawniki, which weren't open labor camps, but could be infiltrated. We developed activities around the camps and started investigating and watching what went on there. In a letter of February 1944, there is a report of Skrzysko Camp and Strachowiec Camp; as soon as the ghetto in Częstochowa was liquidated, we contacted Hasag Pelzerei, a camp the Germans set up in Częstochowa. We got to dozens of other camps. We sent people to Plaszów and tried to create contacts there. Our operations became more extensive. We had to take care of the members of the Jewish Fighting Organization who survived, both those in the forest and those in Warsaw. We had to contact cities where there were still Jews. Sometimes we succeeded and sometimes not. We sent people to make contact with the camps where Warsaw Jews were held and with other Jews we could reach.

We were concerned with foreign contact. We all wrote letters, some of which were published by Neustadt.[44] Other letters were also written in the name of the Jewish National Committee. In general, we would sign them, both Berman and I, sometimes Guzik, sometimes other people. Since Berman and I were in full cooperation every day, I would usually sign letters with him. Contact was through the post office, not as with Switzerland, and through the underground of the Polish Delegatura connected with London.

Another area of operations which wasn't planned in advance was the rescue operation of Jews, and their support within Aryan Warsaw. Our couriers were usually occupied with other matters. But, by chance, they would come upon Jews hiding here and there and would have to take care of getting apartments, identity documents (*Kennkarte*), and financial support for many Jews. I couldn't say that was none of our business because we were well known. The Jewish National Committee also had aid groups and so did the Bund; there were joint operations of the Bund and the Jewish National Committee. The Joint no longer existed and Guzik didn't have any money. Guzik himself was one of my links of communication. And there was the aid organization, ZEGOTA,[45] established in cooper-

44. Melekh Neustadt 1947.

45. Council for Aid to Jews, established in Warsaw by liberal elements, supporters of the Polish Government-in-Exile in London.

ation with the Polish political parties connected with London, including the PPS Left, except for the Communists. Berman worked for the Jewish National Committee. And the Bund was represented by Leon Feiner ("Mikołaj").

Small sums of money began arriving from two sources. One from abroad—money would sometimes come to the Jewish National Committee from Zionist organizations in the United States or Eretz Israel, through London—and some money was sent directly to the Bund. Now and then sums sent to the various parties would also arrive. For example, to Po'alei Zion Left, Po'alei Zion–Z.S., and so forth. He-Halutz didn't get money sent directly to it.[46]

When we set up the general Jewish Fighting Organization, we faced several problems. The first concerned the Bund; the second problem was the Communists. The common denominator of all groups was the Jewish Fighting Organization in Warsaw. The Jewish National Committee and the Jewish Coordinating Committee existed until after the destruction of the Warsaw Ghetto. I always supported operations in all of prewar Poland, without considering the German administrative division, in order to involve all active forces. That was important in terms of social and political operations too. We solved the organizational problem by putting the new staff in charge of Warsaw. We took responsibility for all of Poland along with Ha-Shomer Ha-Tza'ir. On the Aryan side of Warsaw, other forces also confronted the fact that there were Jews not only in Warsaw, but also in other places like Częstochowa, Będzin, and so forth.

I suggested forming a joint treasury for all the money we got in case one of the groups, like the Bund or one of the blocs under the aegis of the Jewish National Committee, happened to be without financial means. Although I was supposedly "neutral," I didn't lack means; I was like someone who is covered by a blanket with one person on his right and someone else on his left. Sometimes, the blanket is pulled to the right and sometimes to the left, but I was always covered. About 3,000 Jews cared for by the ZOB suffered less than others when money was short. But my suggestion to set up a joint treasury wasn't accepted and things were managed somehow by loans one group would give another. Even though the Bund and the Jewish National Committee got on well together, they didn't go so far as a joint treasury.

I know that there was dissatisfaction in the Bund with their historical leadership. There were accusations and attempts to form an anti-establishment Bundist organization against the comrades who ran things. Their top man was Dr. Feiner; his second-in-command was Salo Fiszgrunt

46. Apparently in Będzin, Frumka got letters and money from Venya Pomerants (Hadari) in Istanbul.

(Henryk), who escaped from Poland after 1967 and died in Israel. The third was Ignac Simsonowicz, who died after the war. The absence of Abrasha Blum and his Jewish soul was tangible. Blum probably couldn't have been very active because he looked too Jewish, which would have forced him to hide; but the members of the Bund would certainly have considered his opinion. He was missed, and the Bund factionalism existed right up to the end. However, I must say I was on good terms with the members of the Bund.

Gradually people who had never belonged to any movement were drawn to us, and so were members of the Polish Scouts, and the few members of Dror and Ha-Shomer Ha-Tza'ir. The Jewish members of PPR were active as long as they were on the Aryan side. I usually lost track of those who looked Aryan. They were active in general Communist operations, although a few of them were active in our sector, like Nestek Matywiecki, a member of the general staff of the Armia Ludowa, who was killed in the Polish Uprising.

The situation with the Revisionists was different: according to Stroop's data and the information I had from sources in the ghetto, they disappeared after the first two days of the Uprising and were discovered a week later, again on Muranowska Street, but on the other side of the ghetto wall. A very gloomy and foggy episode is added to that. We accused the Revisionists of being in contact with the extreme Polish right, who promised them money and weapons and finally deceived them. We accused them because they always claimed that they maintained contact only with the AK. Arye Wilner once checked on it and the AK told him categorically that they maintained contact only with one single Jewish organization, the Jewish Fighting Organization. They certainly were not in contact with the AL; and, if they weren't in contact with the AK, whom could they be in contact with?

After the war, a group of Poles appeared who were part of the AK and claimed they had been in touch with them. The first one to construct a whole theory on that, right after the war, was Ber Mark, who was a gifted journalist, but a lousy historian, if for no other reason than in writing the history of the Jews in that period, he adjusted his writing to where he was living at the time. If he wrote in Moscow during the time of the Jewish Anti-Fascist Committee, he would show up with the blue-and-white flag. But when he got to Poland, another wind was blowing in his sails, and the history was also different; and so on until his last book. I think there are four such variations in his writings. When he calculated the Communist share in the Jewish Fighting Organization, he couldn't deny that of the twenty-two fighting groups, only four were Communist. How could he come to terms with that? He constructed a whole concept about two branches, one was the ZOB we know about, and there was another organized by the Revisionists. And, like other branches, not many Revisionists survived since Hitler didn't distinguish between Jews. And you can't accuse them or anybody else that few of their people were left until the Uprising, since that was pure chance. The same is true of He-Halutz Ha-Mizrakhi, which had a training kibbutz, but their members disappeared completely. I am sure that if they had remained, they would have participated in the Uprising. But they disappeared during the *Aktsia*. They certainly had youth as good as ours, no less idealistic, but they vanished. The same thing happened with the Ha-No'ar Ha-Tzioni, which once had hundreds of members in Warsaw. But they had only a single fighting group and they are not to blame. It wasn't because they were scared and didn't report for duty when orders were given.

When the Revisionists saw that very few remained, they began making noisier propaganda, which we opposed because we were afraid it would give us away to the Germans and lead us to Treblinka. We were opposed to it also because they brought people into the organization without sufficient examination. Out of that, Ber Mark built a theory that the Revisionist organization was a "General Organization," supposedly with a lot of Communists in it. That is, the Communists were not only in the Jewish Fighting Organization, but also in the second, Revisionist, organization.

We knew that the Revisionists constituted the base of their organization, but others also joined them, usually unknown persons. We were also aware that there were all sorts of groups in the bunkers, including young people with weapons whom we called "wildcat groups." I don't mean bandits who took advantage of the situation, but people who sincerely wanted to fight but couldn't get to the fighting organizations, or people who thought their job was to defend the bunker as their home. Mark also counts those as a "voluntary Communist organization." And he builds his conception on that.

We know for sure that there was a Revisionist group whose core numbered about sixty to eighty fighters, and it expanded into an organization of hundreds. We know where their bases were. Later, Poles also appeared, including one Henryk Iwenski, who might have been a man of some stature.[47] When I was in Poland in 1948, I didn't meet him, but he wrote me a few letters. According to him and others, there was a large faction in the AK that gave money and weapons, including machine guns, to the Jews. Every now and then, increasing numbers of Poles are dis-

47. Haim Lazar characterizes Iwenski as "One of the Righteous Gentiles, who did much to help Jews in general and the ZZW in particular" (Lazar 1963:87).

covered who supposedly helped Jews but, since they can't prove their claims with the Jewish Fighting Organization, they "prove" them with the Revisionist organization.

What did we know about the Revisionists' fight? We knew about the day of heroic battles and how they left for the Aryan side of Warsaw the next day through the tunnel, which in hindsight justifies our notion: we thought that preparing a tunnel in advance to get out to the Aryan side wouldn't help the struggle, but rather the opposite.

Today we can say that a few hundred fighters in big Warsaw against a big army was a drop in the bucket! And yet those few, those isolated groups—what a commotion they made! Even though the Germans later found a reply: they burned down the ghetto. If they had had to conquer every building, to search for and not find every single group, it would have been much harder for them. For we knew well all the exits, all the entrances, and all the passages over the roofs. They would have had to keep a big army to protect what was conquered, to prevent the fighters from coming back and recapturing it. According to Stroop, thousands of German soldiers participated in the ghetto war, aside from the SS, the Ukrainians, Latvians, Polish police, and others. If the war had been carried on by "human" means (although there isn't such a war), without flame-throwers, they would have had to put tens of thousands of Germans into the battle to triumph over us.

What did the ZOB fighters do?

When the exit was blocked, they went from base to base, from building to building, and continued to fight! What did the Revisionist fighters do? They fought a very important battle, with flags flying, a battle that made a strong impression (and anyone who tries to attribute the flags to the ZOB is distorting them and history), but they abandoned the ghetto through their tunnel, after a brief war.

On the Aryan side of Warsaw, they prepared bases. They were supposed to go to the forests; the Poles were supposed to guide them. Later, we learned that one group, which included Pawel,[48] reached Grzybowska Square. Another of their groups, operating as partisans near Otwock, was liquidated, as far as we know. In the *Book of Ghetto Wars*, there is a German announcement, if I'm not mistaken, of April 23, telling that they came upon "Jewish bandits" near Otwock. The German announcement shows that the Revisionists included Jewish fighters and partisans who were all killed.

Even then there was a suspicion that the Polish guide who led them was the one who turned them in. He told them to rest and, meanwhile, he

48. Pawel Frenkel, the military commander of the ZZW. See Wdowinski 1985:131–132;208.

called the Germans. That information reinforced our opinion that the Revisionists had maintained contact with the Endeks.[49] After the war, very "humanistic," "liberal" forces, as it were, began to appear, which had been latent in the AK. To this day, I can't determine the truth of the matter.

There was also a Revisionist group in Warsaw on Grzybowska Street, which got help from me. One of them was called "Pawel the Red" (Pinia Beshtimt), a redheaded fellow who spoke good German and apparently came out of the ghetto two days after the Uprising and found shelter with a Bundist, David Klein. In time, David Klein's apartment turned into one of our bases.[50] The first time I went there, I encountered Pawel, who told me he was the treasurer of the Revisionist organization. He also told me about the group of Revisionist fighters who found shelter in Warsaw and had nothing to live on. He was the patron of that group until the day it was discovered. They defended themselves and fell in battle on the Aryan side of Warsaw, he told me. I asked Pawel to write a report on the Revisionist war against the Germans in Warsaw. He drew from two sources, two documents I read. One was a summary written in Hotel Polski by one of the Revisionist fighters who reached the Aryan side of Warsaw and then Hotel Polski. This man wrote the document and delivered it at the request of Lolek Skosowski and Adam Zurawin, two Gestapo agents who took care of the Jews at the Hotel Polski.[51] Eliezer Geller brought me a copy of that document which recounts Revisionist operations, including a few done in fact by the Jewish Fighting Organization! For example, the execution of Lejkin and Fürst, or the burning of the abandoned buildings. Later, at the end of the document, Lopata, whom I knew, the son of a baker, accused the Revisionist organization of bringing destruction onto the Jews with those operations. I saw that as lip service to the Gestapo. It wasn't a personal denunciation, there were only general things in it, things the Germans probably knew. What interested and angered me was that they took credit for the operations of the Jewish Fighting Organization.

49. N.D.—Narodowa Demokracia, National Democrats, the rightist, Fascist wing in the Polish parliament. This is mainly the extremist faction of the Endeks, the NSZ, which collaborated with the Gestapo in hunting Jews.

50. According to Władka Meed, Klein had been "supervisor of food supplies for Jewish self-help in the days of the ghetto." His apartment "was on the fourth floor and belonged to a gentile official in the municipal gas works. Two small nailheads protruding unobtrusively near the doorbell were, in fact, electrical contact points; if one placed a coin across them a bell inside the apartment was activated. In this way a caller could signal that he was one of our comrades." (Meed 1979:189).

51. See chapter 7.

The second document was written by Pawel himself, at my request; this was a report I wanted to send abroad. I don't think that Pawel was one of the top figures of the Revisionists, or he wouldn't have written what he did. In that document, he again lists several operations of the Jewish Fighting Organization and credits them to the Revisionists. I told him the truth but I didn't erase what was written since he gave me the document; but I did add a page to the report with a few of my own notes. I wrote that I didn't see myself as a censor for things written by a member of the underground, but I added a list of the operations we carried out. I gave Pawel's report to Dr. Berman, along with my comments, accompanied by a request to send it abroad.

Unfortunately, that report was never published abroad, and apparently wasn't even sent. But recently, when we acquired Dr. Berman's archive, I saw that report in it. Before examining it carefully, I saw that the page I added was missing. That is, Berman wanted to censor those things and decided on his own to delay it and not to send it. That's not Berman's whole archive; apparently part of it got lost. I heard that there were forty letters of mine in it; but my paper attached to the report isn't there.

As for Revisionist literature on their participation in the Uprising, a first pamphlet appeared by one of their people, Adam Halperin, who served in the Jewish Brigade. He met me for a conversation, which wasn't taped or recorded, and later, he published a pamphlet entitled *The Truth on the Warsaw Ghetto Uprising*,[52] he supposedly refers to what I said and attacks me. Moreover, irresponsible journalistic work was done by Haim Lazar, who came to Poland with his wife and collected testimony, including from that Iwenski I mentioned and others. That's a book in which truth and myth are mixed up.[53]

There are also many things in that report that added to what we knew, as well as things that are simply wrong. Evidently, rumors circulated among them, which might have been put out by their commanders, about operations they didn't perform but which they took credit for. If their people had survived, they might have told what they did do and about the war they did fight. The truth itself would have been sufficient.

And as for the Uprising, I am sure they fought as well as any of our fighting groups. In the months before the Uprising, they took credit for all kinds of operations to prove that they were the major force in the ghetto. But you don't need much math to know the truth. One camp included all variants of the Halutz movements, plus the Bund, the Com-

52. Published by Government Information Department, Betar, in Israel.
53. Haim Lazar 1963.

munists, and all Jewish parties, whereas the other camp was only the
Revisionists. Even someone who is unfamiliar with party relations has to
understand that the one united camp was the large force in the ghetto,
whereas the Revisionists were a small minority.

Haim Lazar was one of the Revisionist fighters in the FPO[54] in Vilna
(he comes from Lithuania), an admirer of the Revisionist Glazman, who
had been in the police and resigned, and led his comrades and others
toward the Uprising.[55] Lazar wrote a very harsh pamphlet against Abba
Kovner, a pamphlet that can be called not only unfriendly but really
swinish, accusing Abba of very serious offenses. He practically turns Abba
Kovner into a traitor, a coward. Even if he did think that, he should have
explained it and proved it in another way. No doubt there were mistakes.
All our acts in that period are one big mistake. But to accuse Abba Kovner
of Glazman's death, to accuse him of sending Glazman on a mission out
of malice and of abandoning comrades! When Abba Kovner's own
brother was one of those who was killed![56] The accusation that there was
no uprising in Vilna can be understood; but I don't think that that was
just Abba Kovner's fault. And as for the Wittenberg affair, if anyone is
to blame, it's the entire fighting leadership there.[57] To write about Abba
Kovner like that is a malicious personal attack.

That Lazar, who wrote a book a few years ago, came to me at the time
and I sat with him pleasantly and told him what I knew. But he didn't
consider my testimony; it wasn't enough for him. Apparently he got
"better" testimony from the Poles who tried arrogantly to prove their
"great help." And he bought that. He wanted to glorify and exalt his
organization and went to the Poles in Poland; not Communists, of course.
In general, after the suffering and torments the men of the AK went
through, they received credit. Now the history of the period 1939–1945
is a Polish national history and even the Uprising of the Jews in the
ghetto is part of that Polish national history, as written by Communist
historiography.

The Revisionists on the Aryan side had no political framework or
public relations. They didn't appoint people to that. My only contact with

54. Fareinigte Partisaner Organisatsie—the United Partisan Organization in Vilna, led
initially by Itsik Wittenberg (and subsequently by Abba Kovner), which included all political
groups, from Betar to the Communists.
55. Yosef Glazman was a popular member of the FPO, who led a group of partisans to
Narocz Forest, where they were all killed on October 8, 1943, in a battle with the Germans.
56. Michael Kovner.
57. Itsik Wittenberg, commander of the FPO in Vilna, was denounced to the Gestapo,
and was turned over to the Nazis in July 1943. This created a major crisis for the resistance
forces in Vilna Ghetto. (See Arad 1982:387–395; Dworzecki 1948:440–445; R. Korczak
1965:160–166.)

the group hiding on Grzybowska Street was through Pawel, from whom they got help. Other than that, there was no organized Revisionist political structure. As for Mizrakhi, there might have been members of Mizrakhi, but they didn't have "representative figures," whereas the General Zionists did.

One day, Pawel's report should be published, the story of their actions should be accompanied by background notes that for some reason weren't sent abroad at the time.[58] I am not telling the story of a certain Lopata at this time either. I couldn't speak about a fighter who presented a report to the Gestapo and debased himself and his fighting comrades. I haven't told about such things. I don't think the Revisionists mention him in their books.[59] Maybe they don't know anything. I had no interest in publishing that incident—it was something extraordinary. Up until less than a year ago, I was sure the document had been sent abroad. Pawel was the only source for that information. His comrades were no longer alive. He was the only one left. There was no copy of it either. One day, I went to meet with David Klein, the Bundist, and I told Pawel: "You have to tell the story and I promise you to send it abroad. You owe that to your comrades." And what I gave Berman remains the only source. Naturally I also made a copy of it for my archive, but it got lost in the Polish Uprising, along with everything else.

I don't know the source of the information that reached Israel that Tosia and Zivia were killed. The two of them were alive at the time. The cable about their death came from Będzin. You should know that Zivia's name was a common code word in foreign correspondence, which stood for He-Halutz in Poland or our movement, Dror. Tosia Altman was a member of Ha-Shomer Ha-Tza'ir. The cable might have been meant to say that Jewish Warsaw no longer existed. The announcement came through Slovakia and we should examine how it was sent. Maybe that's not what they meant; but if it were they would probably have chosen people who were known to be dead.

Our expectations from the AK were bitterly disappointed. And there is a question: if the AK didn't give us weapons (except for the fifty pistols, a few grenades, and explosives); if the AK began a joint plan with us for the defense of the ghetto and didn't do anything; if the AK didn't give us people to remove the fighters through the sewers or a base on the Aryan side of Warsaw, but simply wanted to send us to Wołyń and

58. Pawel's report was published in full in *Dappim: Research on the Holocaust*, no. 5, 1987.

59. Actually he is mentioned in their works, but as a hero of the Uprising, not as a traitor (see Lazar 1963). However, in their introduction to the collection of documents on the Warsaw Ghetto Uprising, Blumenthal and Kermish regret the absence of a document written by Lopata in May 1943, which reached the Jewish Fighting Organization in clandestine ways. It may be this document that Zuckerman is referring to.

abandon us (because, even if our people had gotten there, they would have been murdered there by the Poles or the Ukrainians); and, if the AK kept a letter calling for help from Mordechai Tennenbaum and didn't deliver it until few months later—why did we have to maintain contact at all with the AK?!

Henceforth, our contacts with them waned. One day I sent a letter to General Bór-Komorowski,[60] which included a pointed accounting of the AK, including the case of our partisans murdered by their people near Częstochowa. My letter also contained a summary of our cooperation and a dramatic appeal to the Poles and Bór-Komorowski. The letter said: "We appealed about the camps, and we were not answered; we asked for weapons to die with honor, we, the last Jews on Polish soil, in our struggle with the Germans, and were not answered in that either . . ."[61]

I received an oral reply to that letter, from Wacław, at his home. I wrote down what he said, but my notes were lost with my whole archive; but I remember it well and I can vouch for its accuracy. It said: "Please tell the commander of the Jewish Fighting Organization, Antek, that the Jews are like a man drowning in the sea and we (i.e., the AK) are like a man on the shore who can't swim. Nevertheless, we will do everything to help."

That was the answer to my long letter. Later, as I recall, Irena Adamowicz or Hubert Kaminski told me that my letter did get to Bór-Komorowski who was amazed at the "Jewish gall." Hubert delicately advised me to be careful because there were plotters who were intriguing to settle accounts with me. I was sure of Kaminski's good intentions; he was an honest man, loyal to the Polish homeland in his own way, a democrat, an adherent of the Polish government in London, a responsible man with no antisemitic tendency. He is still alive, but I haven't

60. General Tadeusz Bór-Komorowski, one of the leaders of the Armed Polish National Organization, Armia Krajowa (AK). From 1943, he was the commander of the AK and leader of the Polish Uprising of August 1944. In his memoirs, *The Secret Army*, he says he knew that the expulsion of the Jews to the concentration camps was the beginning of the final destruction; but he claimed that if the western powers, with their modern weapons, weren't able to stop the crime, what could the Polish underground do? He also claims that the failure of their attempt to assist the Jews might have stimulated the Germans to accelerate the destruction. He also argues that Wacław (Henryk Wołyński), head of the special department to assist Jews, received instructions to go into the ghetto and contact the Jewish leaders and was supposedly ordered to tell them that the AK would assist them by supplying weapons and coordinating the timing of attacks outside the ghetto with the resistance operations of the Jews inside; he says the Jewish leaders rejected the proposal, arguing that if the Jews behaved quietly, the Germans wouldn't destroy them all. Therefore, the AK decided to sabotage the railroad lines, to postpone the expulsions. This would appear to be a somewhat fictional account; Bór-Komorowski doesn't cite any documentary evidence in support of it, and it is also clearly refuted by Antek's book.

61. Zuckerman's letter to Bór-Komorowski is published in *Yediot Lohemei Hagetaot*, April 1955.

contacted him, and I won't because that might harm him. As I recall, he was exiled for years in the Polish version of "Siberia," and then was professor at the university of Łódz. I inquired about him a few times; by now he's no longer young. If he is alive, he's retired.

So I was warned that they would liquidate me. That was one of two times I got such a warning. The second time was during the Polish Uprising in Zolibórz. As a matter of fact, we had no choice; all contact with the outside world went through the Delegatura, the representatives in London. Berman attempted to send information through Moscow, but I don't know if it got out of the country. Even if he did succeed, we still would have had to maintain contacts with the AK, with the Delegatura, because the money from abroad was sent to us through London. And that was help for about 12,000 Jews who got assistance on the Aryan side of Warsaw. We also had to stay in touch with the camps. It was a lot of money and I haven't even mentioned weapons, which they didn't give us and we acquired on our own. After all, we couldn't abandon the Jews hiding on the Aryan side, which was why I had to meet with them (the AK) from time to time. I must repeat that personally, Wacław treated us extremely well. I could come to him any time. I knew his address and could come to his home whenever I wanted.

Only after the war did I learn the real names of the people I met with directly. Every one of them says he would have met with me and some even blame me for not going to meetings because I looked Jewish. There's an excuse for you! Look at me and judge for yourself! Wacław would tell me: "I, Gentile Wacław, wish I had your face!" In fact, he did look Jewish and he suffered from the blackmailers and would even pay them now and then. He told me they would latch onto him and he was scared, because he had a Jewish wife, and because he was involved in important underground matters and thought it better to pay the blackmailers than to risk troubles. He didn't want to be turned over to the Germans for fear they would start prying into his affairs. He was an attorney and had worked in the prosecutor's office before the war. He was an important person who couldn't hide his identity for long. He was afraid to pass by the Polish police station. Interestingly, in their memoirs, some of them tell the same story, that my face was supposedly Jewish, so I refrained from meeting with them. I swear on my word of honor that there wasn't a single instance when I didn't appear, not a single instance when I wasn't careful to arrive on time. But after the liquidation of the ghetto, after what happened, I didn't have any special reason to meet with them; especially when I was busy (until September 1943) with other matters, since we were trying to construct a joint plan to rescue young people from the Poniatów and Trawniki camps, where we formed groups of the Jewish Fighting Organization. They promised help but didn't keep their promise.

In Berman's archive are Wacław's complaints about the AK after the meetings with me, for not keeping their promises to set up bases near Lublin to rescue the people in those camps. As for us, I was willing to supply weapons myself and we asked them only to give us a base so our people could hide there after escaping from the camp.

You could escape from the camps, but you had to know where to go, you needed some base, some assistance, some friendly village, hut, forest. Where could a Jew escape? What happened to the Jews who escaped from Treblinka? After all, hundreds did escape and only a few dozen arrived in Warsaw seventy kilometers away, because they were killed on the way from Treblinka! Sometimes there are such naïve and absurd questions. You can't convey the "climate," and the "geography" of Poland in those days. You simply can't describe the relations between Jews and non-Jews, everything that threatened the Jew in that period! As an individual, a Jew might still have a chance to escape from Poniatów or Trawniki; but when there were dozens or hundreds of people, someone had to prepare the escape. We were very weak; Jewish Lublin no longer existed. There had been Jewish partisans in the forests of Lublin, but they were murdered— and not only by the AK, but also by Polish Communists or pseudo-Communists.

There are serious charges against Moczar, the strong man in Poland after the war, and his comrades.[62] But we sought any grain of help, and they promised help. It is paradoxical that the AK, the Delegatura, and Bór-Komorowski accuse us of getting money from abroad and using it to buy weapons for the Jews instead of rescuing and supporting them; and so, they said, they shut off the faucet. For weeks, they would hold onto the money sent to us from London. Not to mention how they cheated us by getting the money in pounds sterling or dollars, selling it on the black market, and giving us only a small fraction in dollars or sterling; they would give us the rest according to the official German rate, which was perhaps 10 percent of the black market rate. Thus they discounted the sums sent for us a great deal. Those were the conditions we had to operate under in underground Poland.

The Communists, on the other hand, were weak; they had neither weapons nor money nor important bases. If I have to reconstruct my relations with the Communists in the 1940s, I would have to say that they listened to us sympathetically; but they didn't have anything to give and they couldn't help us much. That is, it wasn't that they wouldn't, but

---

62. I.e., the commanders of the AL. In 1964, after power struggles within the Polish United Workers' Party (PZPR—formed from the union of the PPR and the PPS), General Mieczysław Moczar, minister of the interior, emerged as leader of the strongest faction. Moczar and his supporters, who adopted an anti-Zionist policy in 1968, remained in power until 1971.

simply that they couldn't. Under those conditions, we had no choice but to continue our relations with representatives of the AK.

I don't think there were any Jews on the Aryan side who could help us with money; at any rate, I didn't know about any. Every Jew had to take care of himself, even a Jew who had collaborated economically with the Germans. As long as he was in the ghetto, he made money; but when he went to the Aryan side of Warsaw, not only did he squander his money, he also had to pay blackmail and he had to figure that his apartment could be "burned" any day, or he would fall into the hands of the Polish police. I wouldn't even have asked a Jew with a million Złotys for money because I knew he needed his money for hard times and you could never know when that would be.

I think I've told about the note I sent to Jonas Turkow, who was active after the war in the Jewish Committee. I was in touch with him during the ghetto period, when he was in charge of cultural activities for the Yidishe Sozial Aleynhilf (YISA). At that time, he took some risks in the ghetto by giving us permission to commemorate the birthday of Yehuda Ha-Levi or Bialik. He knew the content of our activities. At this time, he was one of the people brought from Poniatów or Trawniki to the Aryan side of Warsaw, where he found shelter. Later I took care of him. One day I got a call for help through a courier that the blackmailers had gotten onto Turkow's trail and if I didn't send—I think it was 20,000 or 40,000 Złotys—that would be the end of him. Keep in mind that the average Jew got about 500 Złotys a month from us. This was a lot of money. The blackmailer threatened to turn him over to the Germans if he didn't get the money immediately. I had to decide in five minutes whether it was only blackmail, to get money out of me, or whether his life really was in danger and if I didn't pay, I was abandoning him. I decided on the spot to send the entire sum all at once, with a few lines in Polish: "Here is the sum; please let me know the situation at once," signed "Antek." I got an acknowledgment from him with warm thanks, because it did save his life.[63] After the war, Turkow lived in New York. On one of his trips to Israel, he said he had a gift for me and gave me that note I had sent him.

Many of the Jewish intelligentsia found shelter on the Aryan side of Warsaw, for example, Professor Mieczysław Centnerszwer, an internationally known chemist, who was remote from Jews but got close to them in the ghetto. I wouldn't say he deliberately assimilated, but he assimilated "naturally," without an ideology of assimilation. His whole life was concentrated in the scientific world of chemistry and Polish interests. I don't

63. Turkow was in Grochów Camp (Turkow 1969:206ff). The sum he requested was 40,000 Złotys (Turkow 1969:342). The entire incident is described at length in Turkow 1969:338–345.

know how Zivia tracked him down in the ghetto and made him a member of the political committee we set up for Grochów. He survived the liquidation of the ghetto because he was a scientist and the Poles he was in contact with took care of him. He was under my protection for a certain period. Then he was denounced and the Germans executed him.

One of the famous Jewish economists of Poland, Ludwig Landau, was hiding on the Aryan side. He was active in the Delegatura and worked for them. He kept a diary that was published in Poland, in three volumes, I think.[64] He was also denounced and executed; I didn't have any contact with him.

Who found shelter on the Aryan side? On the one hand, Jews with money, rich Jews who could pay; and, on the other hand, intellectuals who had contacts with the good Polish intelligentsia. You can't generalize about the Poles. There were decent and pure people among them as among other nations, people who risked their lives and sacrificed their safety fully conscious of why they were doing that. Although there were also Poles whose motive was money and who took large sums for sheltering Jews, there were also people who knew that their job was to rescue, that that was their human obligation. Some of them were simple folk who were content to receive pennies and saved Jews simply out of human kindness; and even when the Jews ran out of money, they went on supporting them. And there were others who kept Jews as long as they could pay, extorted their last cent, and then turned them over to the Germans. Some were in cahoots with the Polish police, others were blackmailers who sucked the marrow of the Jews. There were all kinds of Poles. The Polish Catholic clergy cannot be singled out for merit. My personal encounter with them wasn't encouraging: in Kraków, when I was wounded, the priest wouldn't even give me a drink of water. The clergy did assist in rescuing children but that was done only to save souls.

And I must say that even Irena Adamowicz, that mystical, romantic figure, also coaxed Jews to convert later on. It was Irena who put me in touch with Hubert, who was also from the Polish Scouts. He was a central person in the Polish underground, whereas she was more connected with Catholic circles. Hubert was a person who hung out in the circles close to Bór-Komorowski. I don't know if he met him personally in the underground, but I am sure he influenced those circles and was our advocate, even though that wasn't his job. Personally he was favorable to us.

Years passed. A year ago, I got a long personal letter from him, very sympathetic and affectionate, and I realized he was in great distress. He wrote that Dr. Marek Edelman had saved his wife's life. We wrote and asked how we could help him and decided to send financial aid. We were

64. L. Landau 1963.

able to send a rather small sum of money every three months. Right after the war, I was popular in Poland and had good contacts. But as far as I remember, I didn't meet him on my visit to Poland in 1948. Except for Warsaw and Łódz, I didn't go anywhere. One of the things I did later on was to look for him and I found him in Silesia, where he was apparently hiding. I helped him. I knew he was in big trouble in Communist Poland as a former member of the AK. I assume he knew about my visit because it was published in the Polish press, and they would occasionally publish something about me. I wanted to do something for him and I did the elementary things I could.

As for Wacław, I don't know if he wrote his memoirs; I think they took testimony from him, since some people base their stories on conversations with him. If he did write, I don't think that under the circumstances [of Communist rule], he could have written everything. But among Berman's things, in the archive of the Jewish National Committee which we received, we found Wacław's evaluations, which express friendship and support for us, as well as criticism. Therefore, it must have been very hard for him sometimes, in meetings with me, when he had to tell me their decision and listen to my protests. Because he couldn't be stammering anything or say he agreed with me. Later, we found his personal signature, his responses. He would respond to what I said in our conversations. Most of the time, he would meet me and Dr. Berman. He would respond sympathetically, but couldn't change the basic attitude of the Poles.

I would like to add a few words about my letter to Bór-Komorowski, which was an attempt to sum up our cooperation with the Armia Krajowa, without praising or encouraging that cooperation. There were arguments in the Jewish Coordinating Committee about whether to write at all; ultimately, I decided to write the letter. The first draft was very sharp. I decided to consult with Hubert Kaminski, who suggested softening the style in a few places because there were sharp things and obvious accusations, and he feared it might do some harm. He didn't see it as an "historical summation," since he wanted to achieve everything possible in the circumstances.

The concrete question dealt with the establishment of a Jewish fighting unit in and around the Aryan side of Warsaw. There were fighters and partisans, and we thought a special Jewish unit should be formed; and, so they wouldn't be treated as bandits, we wanted it to be recognized, because it could also be wiped out, which the AK would gladly have done, as they have done with the Communists.

In the underground, everyone is a "soloist" and operates as he likes; but a group would be used for specific goals. After a long conversation, Wacław suggested I appeal in writing, and I received approval for the establishment of the unit from the proper authorities. We also appointed a Jewish commander for the unit who would operate under AK guidance. I don't remember his name anymore, but I do remember that he was a former officer in the Polish army, an assimilated Jew; I got good recommendations about him and he was supposed to organize the unit. The instructor was to be a member of AK.

Anyway, just as they didn't keep their other promises, they didn't keep this one either. And the people who were supposed to perform specific activities, like destroying blackmailers, for example, were neither called nor organized. I must add that in those days, there was already talk of the Polish Uprising, although that possibility seemed remote. Our plan was to assemble the Jewish youth who looked Aryan and prepare them for specified operations. But the Poles gave us neither weapons nor a trainer nor a base. So that was another promise that wasn't kept.

The AL knew we had contacts with the AK, but they didn't hold it against us, whereas the AK was suspicious of our group at the Bug. They suspected that we were in contact with the AL, but they couldn't prove it, since the group was independent. They stopped talking about it, but they did investigate us.

I don't know why they didn't kill me after my letter to Bór-Komorowski. It was no "big deal" and they could have finished me off easily in some alley. At any rate, it was a very hard time since I had to be careful not only of the Germans, the blackmailers, and Poles in general, but also of our allies in the AK. I am sure the AK was quite capable of arming a small Jewish unit of a few dozen fighters; but they didn't. They didn't want us. They didn't want to see armed Jews.

TEN

On the Edge of the Abyss

In spite of everything, this was a time when we acquired weapons. We got nine pistols for Zaglębie and fourteen pistols for Częstochowa. But there was a different climate then, with the onset of demoralization in the German army. After Stalingrad and the other great defeats they suffered, cracks appeared in German "morale," and you could buy weapons. Bear in mind, too, that the loyalty of many German partners—the Romanians, Hungarians, and Italians—was shaken; and because they needed money, they would sell us weapons, even though we also had bitter failures because of provocations.

While we're on the subject, I remember a story about a provocateur named Czarny (Black), who apparently lives in Sweden now; they say he got a medal. This Czarny wrote to a friend of his from Poland who was working in a steel factory here in Israel complaining that in Poland he was being accused and persecuted. The name Czarny jogged my memory and curiosity and, after I investigated, I concluded he was a Jewish professor we knew from back then. Since Czarny was asking his friend to help him immigrate to Israel, I told the friend to suggest to Czarny that he send a picture and the history of his life. When the photo arrived, I sent it to Kazik, who had met him in those days and knew him well, without hinting who it was. Kazik indeed replied that he was sure it was the same Czarny.

The story of the provocation is in Kazik's book.[1] I was interested in him because of an incident involving a member of the AL who was friendly with us, Stefan Pokrupek, one of the Righteous Gentiles who hid Jews in

1. Where the details of the incident are somewhat different than those reported here. (See Kazik 1984:80–83.)

424

his house.[2] Czarny also found shelter there and claimed that he wanted to join the partisans. Stefan asked me to handle this situation and I promised to check into it.

I met with one of the AL commanders, Sanek Molecki. Kazik watched our meeting from afar. But he made a mistake by letting Czarny, standing next to him, see us. He shouldn't have brought him along. Later Czarny said that weapons might be obtained. They made an appointment to meet in Stefan Pokrupek's house to close the deal. Tadek Shayngut came by for no good reason, and when they reached the house, they fell into a Gestapo ambush. Czarny disappeared altogether, while Kazik jumped out the window; but Tadek was shot and killed and so was Stefan Pokrupek and his family. It was an open provocation that ended in a major catastrophe. This was supposed to be a big joint weapons deal between us and the AL, and the weapons were supposed to be divided between us. But the whole thing was a provocation, with Czarny at the center of it.

After the identity of the provocateur was definitely established, I didn't want to write to Poland to request that he be arrested immediately. If Poland had been different, I would have appealed to my Polish friends about it; but the atmosphere was antisemitic by then. Molecki was alive and I think he still is. He was one of the victims of that case and was forced to escape. (He was the one who told me about the death of Marek Folman.)

Incidentally, in those days, a few commanders of the Armia Ludowa were killed. One of them was "Black Antek," who was also involved in acquiring weapons. As I said, it was a big and extensive provocation. I managed to inform everybody who was in contact with me to break relations with Czarny, and Sanek Molecki escaped from Warsaw. I also informed General Witołd about it and asked him to warn anyone who was in touch with Czarny. Afterward, the man vanished; we knew only that he was active and was a German agent.

What I mentioned earlier about the latest encounter with Czarny occurred in the sixties, about the time of the Six Day War. Relations were different—there was antisemitism in Poland and I was afraid that the Czarny case, a case against a traitor, would turn into a trial against a Jew. So, I turned to the "06" group, which took care of the Eichmann case in Israel;[3] I told the story and, without going into details, I also brought

2. His apartment in Warsaw, Washington Street 80, served as a base for the ZOB members on the Aryan side of Warsaw.

3. Bureau 06 was established in Israel "a few days after the official announcement that Eichmann was in Israel and would be tried here." It was "a special police investigation bureau . . . headed by Commander Abraham Selinger and a corps of German-speaking officers and policemen." (See Ben-Gurion 1971:581.)

Kazik to them as well as the Israeli friend who had come to me on behalf of Czarny. The Israeli and Czarny came from the same city and they had been good friends and neighbors; the Israeli didn't suspect a thing. When I brought him to "06," he didn't know where he was going. The members of "06" started interrogating him to clarify the details. In sum, we decided to bring the provocateur to Israel and put him on trial. We made his friend write him that he was sending him a ticket and travel expenses. But at the last moment "06" backed out after consulting with somebody. I couldn't bring Czarny to Israel on my own; what would I have done with him—could I have executed him? I assume that if I had turned him over to the Poles, they would have killed him without any fuss. The Poles themselves didn't trace him. Apparently they did have some suspicions, but they didn't put things together and draw conclusions. Czarny most likely didn't imagine I was still alive. Otherwise he wouldn't have appealed to his friend for help. Nor did he necessarily know that this "Antek" was the same "Antek" he saw from afar in Warsaw, talking with Sanek Molecki. He may not have heard about me at all in connection with the command of the ZOB, and it's also quite likely that he didn't know Sanek Molecki's role either, since he hadn't met us personally and only saw us from a distance. But he certainly did know Kazik and Tadek.

The Jewish Coordinating Committee (ZKK) in Warsaw consisted of A. Berman, Leon Feiner, David Guzik, and me. We would meet every week or ten days. Normally I would meet with Berman every day or every other day, and we also had constant contact through the couriers. In early 1944, Berman fell into the hands of blackmailers, and I was being pursued by the Gestapo, which had formed a special team to catch me. I would come to Berman on Sunday in Zoliborz. Berman was in hiding, and I altered my appearance so I could walk around and hold meetings. I changed my hair style, shaved my moustache, dressed differently, and wore glasses. Changing documents wouldn't help because nobody knew my Polish name anyway; and nobody was looking for me in my Jewish name. They didn't even know I was a Jew. If they had caught me then, they wouldn't have suspected I was a Jew. I was known as "Major Antek," a Pole helping Jews.

In those days, we learned of the special Gestapo team that was apparently on our trail. Its members prowled around various places in the city, primarily specific streets or a specific section they suspected.

I'm talking now about December 1943. I remember December 13, since that was my birthday and it was a few days after one of our serious failures concerning apartments (the first apartment was "burned"). Zivia and I moved to the apartment of Luba ("Green" Marysia) on Pańska Street 5, in a building that had been partially destroyed back in the bombing of September 1939. It wasn't an orderly building, but it had a concierge and two cellars. The concierge had an apartment where he lodged and hid a group of people, including someone named Kutsher (not the one from Grochów, who produced weapons with Hillel Schwartz). He was a builder who helped Jews build bunkers and helped us put up an underground "prison" and such things. He was skilled in those crafts.

Kutsher was supposed to make improvements there and build a shelter, but since he didn't have the necessary materials, we asked Felek Rajszczak who was an expert in such things to come help. Rajszczak was a veteran Communist, a friend of the Jews. We sent him and he did excellent work.[4]

The gentile concierge had a son in the AK. One day the Gestapo got on his trail, and he and his gentile girlfriend hid in the cellar along with the Jews. Kutsher, who knew me from the ghetto, thought that if he introduced me to the concierge and his son as a Polish officer it would help improve the attitude toward those who were hiding—the gentiles might take better care of them and not extort so much money. That evening I decided to go there with Kazik, and that was the only time I was there. I visited and brought them weapons, as they [the Jews in hiding] had requested, and gave them to Kutsher. The concierge's son saw me then. That was December 13, 1943.

We don't know the exact details but it is almost certain that the concierge's son was an informer. Or maybe his gentile girlfriend wanted to get even with him. Or else he got fed up with sitting in the bunker all the time and decided to go out for some fresh air. Whatever it was, one day, he went out for a walk before curfew and ran into some German gendarmes who arrested him. Such arrests usually lasted a day or two; then they realized who he was, and he began to "sing." The Germans immediately attacked that building; people were arrested and killed. There was a big group of Jews there. From that moment, we knew that that gentile guy was collaborating with the Gestapo. Then something else happened—another failure, which cost a lot of people, and because of it, we had to move out of the apartment on Pańska Street within twenty-four hours. So we had no safe houses at all. We moved Zivia in with Stefan Grajek and Leyzer Levin, whose landlord was Felix (Felek) Rajszczak. Kazik and I found temporary shelter someplace. Kazik was always with me. The girls (Luba and the others) also took off. We removed all the people from the apartment and scattered them throughout the city.

4. According to Kazik, Rajszczak was a "first-class builder, a dedicated Communist from his youth, and a man you could trust from the very first moment" (Kazik 1984:98).

That was a Sunday. In honor of Zivia, Felek Rajszczak invited us to a "big feast." As I recall, it was on Twarda Street; Kazik and I went there in the afternoon, and they told us that Felek Rajszczak had disappeared on Friday and no one knew where he was. He had obviously been arrested, but since contact with Zivia was broken (I sometimes wouldn't see her for weeks) and we hadn't met, we didn't learn that Felek had disappeared until we arrived that day.

We were worried that some catastrophe had befallen him. We were still wondering when the doorbell suddenly rang. All the women went into the shelter behind the wall; only Kazik, Felek's daughter, and I remained in the room. A Polish policeman came in with a letter from Felek to me, from prison. The policeman was from the Kripo (*Kriminalpolizei*).

The letter said: "*Antek uciek!* (Antek, escape!)" The Polish policeman was apparently a trustworthy patriot. Felek's letter said that one day he was walking home on Zelazna Street when German agents suddenly jumped out of a cab, accompanied by the concierge's son; they arrested and tortured Felek, but he didn't give them anything. I took the letter from the policeman who didn't know I was Antek. We gave the policeman a generous reward and asked him to keep in touch and tell us everything he knew. He did indeed tell us details about where Felek was, and we told him we would do all we could to rescue him. And we did rescue him. As I said, he didn't give away a thing, despite the tortures he suffered. He kept claiming he had no contact with Jews or non-Jews, that he made a living building ovens. He was arrested by agents of the German *Kriminalpolizei*, but the concierge's son apparently couldn't have told the Kripo anything about him—neither that he was a Communist nor that he was hiding Jews—because he didn't know any of this.

We were forced to leave the excellent apartment on Twarda immediately. We moved the women to various places. Tuvia went to live with Stefan Grajek. We moved Leyzer Levin back to Łomianki to Kajszczak; Zivia went to Leszno 27, where Mordechai Tennenbaum's mother had lived. Afterward we got an apartment at Leszno 18 and Zivia and I moved to Leszno 27. I moved there from my temporary housing, since I couldn't leave her alone. As I recall, life at Leszno 18 was the hardest time for Zivia. She was as hard as nails (even if I did see her cry a few times), but she couldn't stand the pressure. I'll never forget, for example, the meeting of the Jewish Coordinating Committee in Fiszgrunt's apartment. Fiszgrunt wasn't a high-ranking Bundist, but the meeting was in his apartment and he entertained us well, served refreshments, and even put out a bottle of vodka. My rule was not to drink liquor during the day but only at night, with friends. But when he put the bottle on the table, I had a shotglass and stayed there longer than planned.

It was autumn and, on the way home, I saw that it was five minutes to nine and the gates had to be closed at nine because of the curfew. I went from Marszałkowska to Święta Krzyska Street—pitch black! By the time I got used to the darkness, I heard: "*Halt, Hände hoch.*" I put up my hands, the gendarmes lit a flashlight: "Documents!" I took out the document; the situation looked very grave. I did have a first name and a last name; but the document said I lived on Belwederska Street. So what was I doing here on this corner, far from home?! I was really scared. They started asking questions. Naturally, I understood everything, but I answered in Polish, and in pidgin German: "*Schnapps getrunken!*" At that moment, I got a slap in the face and one of the gendarmes sniffed and said to him companion: "*Ja, dieser Kerl hat Schnapps getrunken.* (Yes, this guy really has drunk schnapps.)"

Incidentally, during the war they encouraged drunkards because if you're busy drinking and such, you don't think much about underground matters. At any rate, after the slap, they gave me back my document and didn't ask me anything else. Meanwhile, my eyes grew accustomed to the dark, and I saw hundreds of Poles standing with their faces to the walls, their hands up and a heavy patrol of Germans next to them. Thus I passed the first patrol, with my hat on my head and my documents in my hand; I was five minutes away from my apartment and I managed to get there safely. I was upset and my blood ran cold. I rang the bell; the concierge was scared. When I went upstairs and entered the apartment, I felt as if we were all in mourning and I saw tears in Zivia's eyes. They thought it was all over. Two days later I learned that all the people who were stopped and lined up with their faces to the wall were sent to Auschwitz. They were all Poles. What saved me was the business about "*Schnapps getrunken*" and the little bit I had drunk, which smelled. For some reason, that convinced them I was a "decent person."

The second time I saw Zivia cry when friends were around was when she and I were living at Leszno Street 27, with a young family of Poles. One day the Germans hanged fifty Poles on street lamps, something they often did. This time it was on Leszno Street, in retaliation for harassing Germans. In such a case, they would take fifty Poles from their "stock" in Pawiak, publish their names, add the crime for which they were being murdered, and hang them in the city on electric poles. In this case, they also strung people up on the outside walls of the ghetto, where there was still a wall, even though there was no longer a ghetto. Zivia knew about it; and, because I was wary of trams in those days and walked for kilometers, I was late coming home and arrived after curfew. When I entered, I never saw a person as miserable as Zivia. Nothing could stop her tears. She was sure everything was over and that I was dead. The street really was empty and my footsteps echoed in the distance. Then she broke down and couldn't restrain herself.

That time I was late because of a meeting in Praga, and it took me a long time to get home. I was usually very punctual. For me, that period was a "university" in punctuality. And I did acquire an extraordinary punctuality. I would always plan distances to get someplace a few minutes ahead of time. I wouldn't come to the meeting early, but I would "sniff" the area and come precisely on the minute agreed upon. But this was my own apartment and I could be late. That did happen a few times, not many.

In general, in the evening, when I came home, I wouldn't tell what happened to me all day. I would act jolly, try to hide the tragic events, since people were being killed every single day. Here an apartment was "burned," there blackmailers got onto someone, and so forth. There was one case in which about forty people were killed because one man fell into the hands of the Germans. Such a situation hurt us a lot.

At that time, in late 1943, early 1944, our center was not in one place. One of the first apartments I knew was on Pańska Street, but I didn't live there. Luba and her husband Jurek did. He was a Jew, but was a member of the Polish Scouts and dealt with the Poles. Because he looked very Jewish, Luba and Irena would "cover" the apartment. Back during the Uprising, I would sometimes make appointments there with the Polish Scouts; Jurek belonged to that organization and knew Hubert Kaminski. From time to time, when I passed by the neighborhood and had a "hole" in my schedule, or when I couldn't go back to my own apartment, I would drop in on them. The apartment was at Pańska Street 5, where I later lived with Zivia. That was my third apartment; Zivia's first apartment was at Komitetowa Street 4, which we got from Luba.

In that place, on a small street on the fourth floor, a Jewish woman was living as an Aryan. She called herself Stasia, but her last name was Kopik. That "gentile woman" had a daughter, Zosia, who knew she was a Jew and was a friend of Luba. As I said, Luba lived at Pańska 5. The first one we brought to that apartment was Tuvia Borzykowski, who was sick; when we abandoned Łomianki as a hiding place for our people, I also brought Zivia there. Later I joined them and, for appearances, I was supposed to be the bridegroom of the daughter, Zosia. There was a concierge and a house committee there. Komitetowa was a side street, not far from Pańska. I was accepted there. We knew the woman was a Jew, and she knew who we were.

In every Polish courtyard it was customary to set up a little platform with a picture of the Madonna, and the tenants would pray together. There was a "courtyard committee" whose function was to preserve morality. The only Jews there were Zosia and Stasia. Not everyone went down to pray. The committee collected contributions and I always gave generously. Somebody there always climbed onto the platform and I gave him money. I was supposedly working as an railroad official; I had good documents and everything was fine; but my documents said I lived on Belwederska, so I might be asked what I was doing on Komitetowa. I would have to explain that I was Zosia's bridegroom, which was a very good cover. One day, Stasia Kopik's brother or brother-in-law showed up. The man heard from Stasia, who had heard from Zosia, who had heard from Luba, that I had done something to help the needy; therefore Stasia appealed to me for help for her brother-in-law. I agreed. Some time later, that brother-in-law reappeared and said that a Jew was hiding in or around Otwock Forests and he had no money or any way to support himself. I said I would find out what could be done.

I didn't want to answer on the spot lest he think me a millionaire; I said I had to investigate the matter. I wanted them to think I would get the money from someone. Meanwhile the man began coming to me from time to time. When the doorbell rang, I would tell Zivia and Tuvia to hide and I would stay "in the field" with Stasia and Zosia. As I recall, by that time Tuvia had moved to Twarda Street. In our room, there was a double wall and a movable shelf with a hiding place behind it. It wasn't the best arrangement, the walls were wood covered with wallpaper. In this case, Zivia and Marek Edelman went into the hiding place and I remained. Through the half-open door, I heard the voices of a man and a woman. The man was supposed to be the "brother-in-law," and there was a gentile woman with him. I heard them order Stasia to demand thousands of Złotys from us or else they would turn us over to the Gestapo. Stasia begged for a delay until evening, when she would give them her answer. I realized that it wasn't the brother-in-law, but a stranger who spoke in his name. The pretext was that the brother-in-law was arrested and had to be ransomed. And in fact, the whole thing was made up. They told her that if she didn't get the money, the brother-in-law would turn her and the whole household in to the Gestapo.

I heard this from behind the door, and I also heard her going out with the blackmailers. After they left, I called the comrades and told them to hide. I got dressed, took our bags with the archive I had, and all the weapons. Because if they entered that room, they would find everything. We had to find a hideout immediately for the Kopiks, the weapons, and the archive.

I went to Pańska 5 where I fortunately found Luba and Irka.[5] I told them to run immediately and dismantle the apartment on Komitetowa

---

5. Irka Gelblum: Member of the ZOB, worked as a liaison between cities.

and bring everything to their apartment. We had a few hours to find an apartment for Stasia Kopik and her daughter. I realized that the apartment on Komitetowa had to be dismantled immediately without a trace, no matter what other apartment we found.

I should add that when I left the apartment, I saw the man and woman, but they didn't know who I was; when they saw a man with a moustache and bags, wearing a hat, and dressed plainly, it didn't occur to them that I was the man in question. They were waiting downstairs, probably guarding the house in case someone ran away. I wanted to summon Kazik at once, and I told the girls to take everything suspicious out of the apartment and to bring Zivia; I stayed to wait for them. I also ordered the girls to make an appointment with that woman at a certain time, at a nearby restaurant.

That woman was a blackmailer.[6] I called Kazik and two more armed men to kill her. Kazik told me later that he did kill her; but it turned out she was only wounded. That night the Germans searched Komitetowa 4, but by then there wasn't anybody there. Thus the tenants of the courtyard learned that the "landladies" and the "daughter's bridegroom" were Jews, and that apartment near Pańska Street was "burned." I was in big trouble. I had to be careful in the street; fortunately, it was autumn and the days began growing short. I would go out in the dark and come back in the dark.

That was how the apartment at Komitetowa 4 was "burned." The apartment at Pańska 5 was "burned" in another way. In one of my groups, there was a courier named Juziek. I didn't know his real name. A member of the Scouts, Jurek, brought him to us. He was the courier for a rescue network, and for us, too. He was connected with Hubert Kaminski and the other activists who worked with us. He knew them and they knew him. This Juziek had been coming to Pańska even before I knew the apartment or the people. Before that, Jurek and Luba had lived on Pańska. I first met Hubert Kaminski during the Ghetto Uprising. Juziek was at least as loyal to me as the other Polish Scouts. Why shouldn't a Jewish Polish Scout who worked for an underground network be loyal to me?

The first time I came to Pańska 5, I found two women there. I got to Pańska through one of the couriers who arranged a meeting with Hubert Kaminski there. Only then did I learn that the swarthy Jurek who lived in that apartment was a Jew and a member of the Scouts. I didn't want to use Marysia herself as a courier, because the apartment was listed in her name and for a long time she wouldn't forgive me for not using her.

6. Kazik says she was one of the tenants of the house, who suspected them and wanted to extort money from blackmail. (See Kazik 1984:74.)

Irka, who lived with her, was used more, especially on errands inside Warsaw.

One day we got information about Grzybowski Square, where a group of fighters was hiding, after being brought back from the forest. The information was that the Germans had surrounded the place where they were hiding and a battle had taken place in which the group was killed. I knew the concierge of the building on Grzybowski Square; he was a sergeant in the AK (naturally in the underground). It was five minutes away from us, but we didn't know how or whence the evil came. The next day, I heard that Juziek had been arrested. So things were connected. That was early 1944.

So we decided to move out of the apartment on Pańska because many of Juziek's group had been killed or were caught. Many of the Jews who received aid, including a doctor, were also seized. Whole families were captured. All the comrades thought Juziek had broken under torture or had turned traitor and had given away the comrades after he was arrested. I was the only one who didn't think so; it didn't seem right to me. I agreed that we had to move out of the apartment at Pańska 5 at once; but I would swear that Juziek wasn't a traitor. To buttress my opinion, I said that if Juziek were a traitor, he would first have brought them to us. How did they get to those places? They probably found lists on him. Pańska 5 wasn't on the list since he knew that address better than I did; but the others were caught from the lists they found on him. That was my explanation of why the Gestapo didn't find our address on Pańska Street.

Later my position was confirmed. On a nearby street was a Polish shop where once or twice a month, Juziek would distribute aid to his group. The gentile owners of the shop knew him and knew who he was. They thought he was one of the Righteous Gentiles and knew that he used their shop to help the Jews. A few days after his arrest, he came there with his German guards and pretended not to know the owners. They were terrified, thinking he had brought the Germans down on them. He asked if he could use the telephone. He got the telephone; maybe he wanted to prove something about his situation and his fate. He picked up the receiver and started to dial; seeing that his escorts weren't paying attention to him, he suddenly dashed out of the shop and started running away; they chased him and shot and killed him. He didn't reveal the Polish people who helped him. The fact is that he didn't reveal our apartment either. Other apartments did fall, since there were probably lists in his address book. That "burned" the apartment on Pańska for us for a few months, until we went back to it. Meanwhile, we moved Zivia to Twarda Street; the people who lived there dispersed, and we started looking for them to find new housing for them. We put them all on their feet. Every day we sent one of our people to Pańska Street to walk around the neighborhood. You could never know if the beggar wandering around there was a Gestapo agent or a member of the underground. The same goes for the organ grinder or the cigarette seller. The nearby cigarette vendor saw the traffic around Pańska 5, and it was important for us to know what was going on there, not just because of the apartment. We did learn that no one came to Pańska, and there was no suspicious movement there. One night, I decided to put an end to our wandering. Luba remembers the evening well. I told her and Irka that I was going back to Pańska, and we returned there at night and lived there until we found a new apartment at Leszno 27.

At that time, a new generation of women couriers had formed: Marysia Feinmesser,[7] Inka Szwajger, Rivka (Zosia) Moszkowicz,[8] Irka Gelblum, Mirka the *Shiksa* (Felek Rajszczak's daughter).

Marek Edelman, the Bundist, was one of our young men; in the ghetto, he activated his Bundist youth organizations, SKIF and Tsukunft;[9] he was an orphan who had been educated since childhood in the Bund. He worked in the Jewish hospital on Czyste with Inka Szwajger. Inka wasn't a member of the Bund, but was close to Marek; she was older than both him and me, and she also reported for duty. I went looking for her because of Marek. I said that he was suffering because he was living in a coal cellar. I don't understand why they couldn't have found a human apartment for him. We took him and his girlfriend to our apartment on Komitetowa. We moved Tuvia out of Komitetowa to Twarda because the place wasn't big enough for all of us. Along with Inka Szwajger came Marysia Feinmesser, a girl who didn't have anything to do with Jewish life, a bit assimilated, but a good courier.

7. Marysia (Bronka) Feinmesser: She had worked as a telephone operator in the children's hospital in the ghetto with Inka Szwajger and the two of them shared an apartment at 24 Miodowa Street from 1943–1944, which Kazik describes: "It was good to come there—it was like an oasis in the desert, you could relax a bit there. Marysia, who was optimistic and quiet by nature, would create a good mood. Her easy nature would even calm me and, I assume, the others who came to the house . . . It's hard to say what was nicer in that apartment—the quiet or the feeling that here you could get rid of all the cares of the day." (See Kazik 1984:104.)

8. Rivka Moszkowicz (1921–1944): Born in Będzin. Was an active member of Frayhayt in her hometown, where she remained until summer 1943, when she was sent to Warsaw because of poor health. In Warsaw, she was active in ZOB; she worked with Antek on the Aryan side. Was cited in the Jewish National Committee report of May 24, 1944, for her devotion to helping Jews hiding on the Aryan side of Warsaw. She was killed on August 1, 1944, by a German shooting at random on the streets of Warsaw.

9. Tsukunft was the Bundist youth organization in Poland, which numbered 15,000 members on the eve of the war; SKIF (Sotsyalistisher Kinder Farband; Socialist Children's Union) was the Bundist children's organization.

So we began gathering people through acquaintanceship. I looked for people who could be relied on, and we checked everyone very carefully.

Berman had a card file of people he took care of. I also had three thousand names of Jews, just their Jewish names and not their addresses. I didn't want to have their gentile names and their addresses because if such a list had fallen into the hands of the Gestapo, I would have brought down thousands of people.

The ZOB had a command staff of Zivia, Marek Edelman, and me. By that time, nobody from Ha-Shomer Ha-Tza'ir was on the command staff. Tadek Shayngut may have been with us, but he wasn't suitable. And I must say that in those days it didn't matter if someone was a Bundist or something else. The Bund was satisfied with Marek as a representative. We discussed important things that demanded consultation, even if they weren't directly connected with the Jewish Fighting Organization.

Zivia stayed home and went out only rarely, if she had to. One day we decided to take a risk for a festive luncheon across town, at the home of Bundist David Klein. It involved an escort front and back. Zivia had forged documents just in case, but she usually stayed home as I said, as did all the members of that group: Tuvia, Stefan Grajek, Leyzer Levin, Yosef Sak—people who couldn't go out because they looked Jewish. Berlinski and Wasser of Po'alei Zion Left hid. Wanda, who was also in Po'alei Zion, was an active courier who carried messages between Berman and me.[10] Genia Levy was in hiding and wasn't active. The Bundist Władka was an active courier; when operations were united in the Jewish Fighting Organization, she joined our activity and was also assigned to deal with other matters and other dangers. Marek Edelman was in hiding because he looked very Jewish. When we had to move him from one place to another, we did that carefully. When we brought him to Komitetowa, we bandaged his face. Kazik guarded one end of the street and I watched the other end. He walked alone but we stayed near him and winked to signal if the coast was clear or if the concierge or a neighbor was around. There were a lot of problems with every Jew like that. Tuvia did look like a gentile but he had another weakness: his Polish wasn't Polish.

A single picture of me on the Aryan side has remained. The young Pole, Stefan, also appears in the picture, so I know it was taken before he was killed; Kazik and Stefan are next to one another and I'm in the background. That is, they were my escort. In our neighborhood, there were street photographers and Stefan told one of them to take our

10. Bella (Wanda) Elster: According to Berman, she was "one of the boldest couriers of the secret Jewish National Committee and of the party. She was the right hand of my wife Batya in the great rescue and aid operation. An energetic, responsible and careful girl—a model underground activist. Today she lives in Israel" (Berman 1977:176).

picture.[11] I avoided being photographed at that time. That reminds me
that I saw the story of a fighter from Kovno in an historical journal
published in Munich; in the picture, a young man is jumping over a fence
and the caption says (in Yiddish): *"Der doziger held beys antloyfn fun der
gestapo.* (This hero during his escape from the Gestapo.)" Just imagine.

At any rate, I knew it would be better to have few pictures of me and
I didn't even know about the existence of that picture. Apparently it was
near Stefan's apartment. He still had time to get the picture and leave it
with his family. A young Jewish girl also found shelter with that family;
she's now a mother in Kfar Saba; Stefan gave her the picture and she kept
it. A few years ago, she suddenly remembered the picture and sent it to
me. In the picture, I look like a tall young man with a moustache accompanied by two fellows, one of whom is Kazik. He didn't know about
the picture either, and I sent it to him as a gift.

We found Rivka, a member of the Movement from Będzin, and Sara
Biderman hiding in the fields of Czerniaków. We found a room for Sara
Biderman at once; as I recall, she lived with Hela Schüpper. One day,
when Hela was out, someone told the police that Jewesses were hiding in
a room and two gendarmes came. Sara Biderman tried to escape but the
policeman shot her and thought he had killed her. It turned out, however,
that she was only badly wounded and, with the last of her strength, she
went to a Polish friend, from the Communist Youth Movement, Hela
Bilecka, whose father was an engineer. The father put her into the
hospital and took care of her. The doctors who treated her knew she was
Jewish but Bilecki took responsibility for what might happen. We had
gotten word that she had been killed. We didn't know the details, just that
the gendarmes had caught her and taken her off. We were sure at that
time that she was dead.[12]

Kazik, who was very young, was curious about gypsy fortune tellers.
One day he met a gypsy fortune teller who told him a girlfriend of his,
whom he thought was dead, was in the hospital. He was stunned and when

11. Kazik's version is a bit different: "And since we're on the subject of photographs,
in a few places a photo was published showing Antek walking on a Warsaw street, in May
1943, with Tadek Sawicki and me walking in front of him like bodyguards. These are the
circumstances of that picture:

We were walking in the street and a street-photographer came on us. I told him: 'Shoot!'
In spite of the danger, I wanted to be photographed, perhaps out of mischievousness. I got
a note from the photographer and, a few days later, I went and got the picture. Comrades
were mad at me: 'You're careless, you don't know who the photographer is.' I told them
he photographed a lot of people in the street and it wasn't so bad. All the photographs got
lost except for one that remained with Marysia Sawicka. This is the only authentic photo
we have left from that period" (Kazik 1984:88–89).

12. The full story of Sara Biderman is in *Testimonies,* journal of Beit Lohamei Ha-Getaot
(Hebrew).

he came to the apartment, he told us about it. We laughed and didn't believe any of it. But we did start searching and tracked her down. It turned out that Sara Biderman really was alive.

This should also be recorded: when we had to get her out of the hospital and arrange a *Kennkarte* (ID card) for her, that Polish engineer, Bilecki, her friend's father, took care of it and even got a birth certificate for her. One day we took her out of the hospital. She had been wounded in the stomach and had lost a lot of blood. But they had saved her life and the engineer kept her in his apartment until we took her to our house and found an apartment for her.

As for the fate of Bilecki: once when he was walking in the street, next to a trolley stop, gendarmes suddenly appeared across from him, ordered him to put his hands up, as usual, and when they searched him, they found the card in Sara Biderman's name. He said he didn't know who she was and that he had accidentally gotten hold of the card. They took him straight to Auschwitz, where he stayed until the end of the war. We often met the daughter, Hela Bilecka, especially during the Polish Uprising. After the war, that Bilecki was deputy minister of transportation in Poland. I met with him several times; he was one of the "good Communists," a Communist even before the occupation. When I went to Poland in 1948 with a delegation from Israel, he held a reception for me in his home, attended by ministers and generals. He did that privately, not on behalf of the Polish government. The guests were very interested in us and expressed much sympathy for us. I had never heard a word of complaint from Bilecki, who had spent years in Auschwitz because of that Jewish girl. He died a few years after the war. Some Poles are humanitarians, with a special nobility—those were the ones who saved Jews during the war. They are people of genuine honor and nobility. I should point out that even some of the Endeks (the Polish Fascists) saved Jews during the war. Even though they wanted to see the Jews out of Poland, they couldn't imagine the horrors of the "German solution." Their slogan was: "Jews to Palestine!" They may even have been willing to beat up Jews, but in their wildest dreams, they couldn't imagine Treblinka. But nevertheless, there were also a great many people who collaborated with the Germans.

On the first anniversary of the Uprising in the Warsaw Ghetto, we published a proclamation addressed to the Polish people and the Poles took note of it. I don't know if it was mentioned on the radio station but it was marked in various ways; I don't know if you can talk about the whole nation in this respect, but, as the underground press put it, the Polish people saluted the last of the Jews, the surviving fighters. On the anniversary of the Uprising, a Polish proclamation in the same spirit was also issued.

The Hotel Polski episode had started on Długa Street in mid-1943.[13] When those events began, I was very busy and very tired. Even though I had great physical and emotional force, it was sometimes hard for me to stand up at the end of the day because I had been running around so much. And add to that the tension, the need to keep your eyes open all the time and hold on from morning to night in the face of failure and despair, helplessness, lack of money, and disappointing negotiations with the Poles. It was so hard, and my life was full of disappointment and tension.

I heard about the Hotel Polski, and when I began to get interested in it, I realized that one of the people involved was Guzik. At first I didn't suspect anything. I talked to Guzik and even considered whether it was worthwhile to take advantage of the opportunity and send one or two ZOB people to look for a way of rescue.

Hela Schüpper-Rufeisen, a member of Akiba in Warsaw, asked me in 1944 about Hotel Polski and I didn't know what to tell her because at the time I didn't know anything about it. If she had asked me a week later, I would have told her: No! But when she asked me I didn't know. She survived the Hotel Polski incident on her own and she never mentioned it to me. I see her sometimes, I have great respect for her, and we are friends. I think that, to this day, she still feels loyal to me. But at that time I really didn't know what to answer her because I was beginning to wonder if there was some crack in the system. And then suddenly I began to understand what was going on all around. But I must admit that for some time I didn't understand the trap.

When did I become suspicious? During a conversation, when I realized that it wasn't hard to get to Hotel Polski, that is, it wasn't hard to get forged documents, and it was easy to get foreign passports of distant countries. This ease seemed suspicious and dangerous to me.

When I began to deal with it, it turned out that more people were involved: one Kenigel, Lolek Skosowski, and Adam Zurawin, all three of them Jews working for the Gestapo. But earlier I simply didn't know any details and, for a moment, I had even thought of sending Zivia to Hotel Polski. I have already said that after the Great *Aktsia* we got word from the Judenrat that there were documents for her like the ones the customers at Hotel Polski had. But she absolutely refused. That was before we became suspicious. Some situations demand the consideration of

13. Hotel Polski was at 29 Długa Street in Warsaw; in 1943 it became a trap for thousands of Jews, who were lured out of hiding on the promise that they could get passage out of Nazi-occupied Europe. At the Polski, the Germans collected Jews who had documents or promises from foreign governments in order to exchange them for German POWs. Zuckerman goes on to explain the fate of the Jews. See Schüpper-Rufeisen 1990:124ff.; Shulman 1982.; Meed 1979:219–226.

various suggestions. I don't know if it was logical or not; for example, two days before the outbreak of the Polish Uprising, I got word that an emissary was coming from abroad and wanted to meet me in a German residential neighborhood, near the Gestapo. People warned me not to go but I figured differently. I saw the Germans retreating from the fronts and I considered whether or not that would be a good time for the Gestapo to set a trap for "Antek," when they didn't even know who he was. I said to myself: "Maybe there's something in it. I'll go see." In another situation I would probably have been more cautious. But I went and it turned out it wasn't a trap; somebody really did come to propose ways of rescue, an agent from the rescue center in Switzerland. Another time an emissary came from Hungary who suggested possibilities of rescue to Zivia and me.

The question here was, after they had killed hundreds of thousands, was it conceivable that they would tell the Judenrat they had documents for Zivia. I tried to talk with her but she refused categorically. That was also acceptable. Now, living on the Aryan side, I was ready to agree to get documents for Zivia for "Polski," not to save her, but to get her out so she could let the world know what was happening! I had tried to do the same thing before with Hancia! At one time we would have given everything for that. For, in our ignorance, we thought the world didn't know!

When I saw how easy it was to get documents, I changed my position: I told myself that it was very dangerous. I now told Hela Schüpper not to try it. If I had known then what I knew later, I would have been more forceful: by no means, no! But at that time I couldn't say that to people who had decided to go there. I didn't see Israel Kanal at all before he went to Hotel Polski, since he went on his own. People broke down and fell into a trap, like Israel Kanal when he came out of the forest. It wasn't hard to break down. I also peeked in there once and it cost me a lot.

I told Eliezer Geller not to go through Hotel Polski but he he decided to do so no matter what. I got information from him about the people hanging out there, Adam Zurawin and Skosowski. Geller didn't know they were Gestapo agents.

I've already mentioned the letter of the Revisionist Lopata—who wrote to the Hotel Polski—which Eliezer Geller brought me.[14] And, one day I heard that Attorney Landau and his wife were in Hotel Polski. Landau survived and his wife remembers our meetings (he himself died two years ago). Anyway, I got word that they didn't have any money or anything

14. This was a letter by a group of Revisionists led by Haim Lopata (commander of a ZZW fighting unit in the April Uprising) confessing that they regretted becoming partisans. They surrendered their weapons, for which they were later condemned to be boycotted by a board of their fellow inmates in Bergen-Belsen. (Testimony of Henryk Zamoszkowski, in Shulman 1982:81–82.)

else. At that time Geller also was at Hotel Polski, and I decided to go there to see what it was and to reply to those who had friends or relatives there and were asking for advice and information. I realized that for all those people, the Polski was a "last straw" to cling to. Many were broken and tempted to believe there was a trace of hope. I met the people there and asked them if they were sure there really was something to it.

Yitzhak Katznelson also figures into the story. When I went to the Aryan side of Warsaw, we decided to take three people: Katznelson, his son, and Tuvia Borzykowski. I agreed with Zivia on that. They weren't needed for the struggle, the Uprising. Meanwhile, Katznelson had been in Többens-Schultz. As you recall, I went to the Aryan side not knowing where I would spend the night, but we decided that moving them would be one of the first things as soon as I got an apartment. As long as I was commander of Többens-Schultz, I took care of Yitzhak Katznelson. He would come to me and pour out his heart. There wasn't always time, but every now and then I would drop in on him and his son Zvi. So we decided to get them out, if I could find a place. Meanwhile April 19 came and all traces of him vanished. Subsequently we learned that Katznelson and a few other good Jews had made their way to Hotel Polski and were shipped to Vittel,[15] a transit camp in France; from there, Yitzhak Katznelson and his son were taken to Auschwitz. We have a German document confirming their arrival in Auschwitz.

There's something vague about the whole Hotel Polski episode. When I went there I met a few people, including the Landau family, and gave them money. I questioned them and examined what I could. After a long time, I left there with Irka and was immediately surrounded by a group of blackmailers.

Sometimes you have to decide things in a flash. The crucial factor was that I didn't yet have documents for Belwederska Street, or Pańska Street either. If they caught me, it would have been the end of me; if they caught Irka, it would have been the end of the apartment at Pańska Street 5 and the whole group there because she was registered on Pańska. For many years after, she remembered what I told her: "Look happy! We're coming to the intersection; there's a market there. I'm turning left and they'll all run after me. You turn right. Remember: you're responsible for the people in the apartment!"

That's what happened. I don't know how many people were following us or how old they were. They ranged in size from small to big. Suddenly the tram passed and I jumped in it. But they were also nimble. I rode inside the tram and they stood on the platform constantly chanting: "Jew,

15. Vittel is a spa in the Vosges in eastern France, site of a transit camp under Nazi occupation.

Jew, Jew!" They stuck to me only because I came out of Hotel Polski. After an eternity, I led them to Targowa Street in Praga because it was quieter there. I thought that in such a place I might reach a compromise with them.

When I got off the tram, they surrounded me, but they didn't hit me. I asked them: "What do you want?" And they said: "Why did you run away?" I asked: "What do you want?" They answered: "What you've got." I didn't have a lot of money; I had a watch and I was wearing Marek Folman's coat. I said: "If you kill me, you won't have anything. If you call the Germans, you won't get anything either; they'll kill me and take everything for themselves. But you really don't want to kill me. I'll give you what I've got on one condition: after you get it, you won't leave this courtyard with me."

They gave me the "blackmailers' word." I didn't have anything to lose. I asked them to leave me a little money so I could ride back on the tram, and they gave me some small change and took the big money.

I think I traveled for hours after that. I changed trams, I got off, and walked through quiet streets where I could see if they were following me or not. On Marszałkowska, which was crowded, it was hard to tell. I came home broken, ashamed. Irka didn't reveal a thing. She had come home before me. She was very tense, almost hysterical.

It was hard to rationalize that while some Jews were being caught in the street, other Jews were sitting comfortably in Hotel Polski. I realized it was a trap, a way to get a few thousand Jews out of hiding without any effort. And after all that, those Jews were sent to the camp at Vittel. The world didn't help them either, but just wrote them off.

When the issue of apartments was settled, I was able to get involved in the Hotel Polski situation and meet with the activists. Meanwhile, I met with Guzik. One day I learned that Lolek Skosowski was cooperating with the AK; that is, the AK was using Lolek Skosowski and Adam Zurawin for its own needs. Instead of collaborating directly with the Gestapo and giving them the names and addresses of Communists and active Jews, they used Lolek Skosowski to do it. I learned this from the Polish Communists, at the time of Hotel Polski. One day, I told Guzik some hard facts, that I saw Hotel Polski as a trap to finish off a few thousand more Jews. He replied that he was sure of the good intentions of the initiators. He was in touch with Zurawin and Skosowski. Guzik knew something about the episode, but he was killed right after the war and I didn't have a frank conversation with him. He told me at that time: *"Oyb ikh vel vissn az ikh vel rateven ayn yid, vel ikh kushn Lolek Skosowskis un Adam Zurawins tukhis.* (If I knew I could save even one Jew, I would kiss Lolek Skosowoski's and Adam Zurawin's ass.)" That was his profound conviction. In a certain sense, he was naïve. I have letters from Guzik complaining that I didn't give him enough money. By that time, the Joint didn't have a lot of money, and he didn't have anyplace to get any; but he got money, according to the number of Jews on the list he submitted. I couldn't check those things, but Guzik had a team that helped him keep track of the needy.

I started looking for Lolek Skosowski. I knew he hung out in some café where he met people. But I didn't know where it was. I started investigating and, after Guzik said something to me and then interrogated me about my intentions, it occurred to me that his questions weren't innocent. He started to warn me that if I got involved and did something about it, it could cause trouble for the Jews. I didn't answer him at all.

A few days later, I told the Armia Ludowa where Lolek Skosowski was and they executed him. That was when Hotel Polski was still functioning.

Adam Zurawin apparently also believed in that "rescue," since he himself was taken along with all the other Jews. Later, about mid-1944, the Bundist David Klein told me that Adam Zurawin came to Warsaw from Bergen-Belsen or from Vittel. Apparently one day they put the Jews on trains and brought them to Auschwitz. Zurawin jumped off the train and came back, without money or documents. He knew that the Jewish Fighting Organization had issued a death sentence against him and said he was ready to stand trial at a court martial. He requested help until his trial was carried out, because he didn't have anything to live on. This time I didn't want to be naïve and honest; I told David Klein to tell him, first of all, to bring a photograph and his data. I didn't intend to try him but rather to execute him, by authority of the ZOB sentence against him. He took advantage of the Polish Uprising. I did get his photographs and I gave them to some people for identification; they told me David Klein refused to pass them on. Klein was loyal to us; and we located Zurawin through him. Ultimately, Zurawin got through the war safely.

Zurawin came from a good family in Łódz. He was going with a girl from the Bund and was apparently involved in smuggling. One day on his way between Łódz and Warsaw, the Germans arrested him and gave him a choice: either collaborate with the Gestapo or be executed. He chose life and started working with the Gestapo, along with Lolek Skosowski's group; but he didn't touch the Bundists.

One day I tried to get Guzik to talk about Skosowski and Zurawin because I heard from General Witold, AL chief of staff, that the AK was using Skosowski (especially) to turn Polish Communists over to the Germans. According to my information, the AK didn't give the names to the Germans, but gave them to that Skosowski to give to them, which he did. The names were always those of Communists or leftist democrats.

Zurawin also disgraced himself by claiming to be one of the leaders of the Uprising and a member of the underground. I was aware that if he left the country, he would deny his Gestapo connections, slander collaborators, and pretend to be a saint. From our point of view, all those were good reasons to issue a death sentence against him.

Guzik told me that Zurawin (or maybe Skosowski) had tried to deny all those acts and accuse others (for example, someone named Kalerstein, who had been active in the Judenrat).

Despite everything that was written, there's one thing I don't understand: if Adam Zurawin had known, at least in this case, that he was a full partner in a great deception, he didn't have to join one of the transports and go with the rest of the Jews; because in fact he went. (In April or May, Yitzhak Katznelson's transport was taken; as I recall, he arrived in Auschwitz on May 2.[16]) I don't have to explain how I feel about that great deception of Hotel Polski, but Zurawin's going to Auschwitz is still strange, even if we're talking about a traitor, and the riddle of Zurawin's joining the death journey remains unsolved.

The Polish Uprising began on August 12, 1944. David Klein came to me about a month and a half before that—at any rate, after May. He was an active Bundist and worked in the Jewish Social Self-Help (YISA), where I had met him. He lived on the Aryan side of Warsaw. He had left the ghetto early and got an apartment for himself and his wife. After the Uprising, one of the Revisionist activists, Pawel ("Pawel the Redhead"), lived in Klein's apartment. Klein had a radio there.

David Klein died a few months ago in Paris. In his younger days, he was a bon vivant who wouldn't turn down a drink. Now and then, maybe once every week or two, I would come to him to get information, to hear what was going on in the world. Once I even took Zivia there, dangerous as it was, just to get her out of her closed room. I think it was on Saint Anthony's or Saint Stanisław Day, but I don't remember any more.[17] My real birthday is December 13, but I celebrated other dates, to fit whatever alias I was using.

The Polish Uprising saved Zurawin. Today he's a millionaire in the United States and he summoned a rabbinical court to acquit him. Incidentally, Yakov Celeminski (Celek) was an admirer of Adam Zurawin and argued with many Bundists in the United States because of it. Strangely, when I visited there, the Bundists held two receptions for me, one on behalf of the whole group and one on behalf of Celeminski. We never talked about that. But someday, I'll ask him to explain why he supported Adam Zurawin in the United States.

16. On April 30 and May 1, transports from France arrived in Auschwitz. The April 30 group included French intellectuals, dignitaries and members of the Resistance, as well as a small group of Polish emigrés (Czech 1990:617).

17. The feast day of Saint Anthony is June 13; that of Saint Stanisław is May 8.

Some more about Hotel Polski:

M. Kirshenbaum, who also came to Hotel Polski, was murdered even before he was sent from Warsaw. And that's strange: why did the Germans execute him separately? People say he boasted of belonging to the underground; but the Germans could have known the truth. I didn't meet with Kanal because I simply didn't have time. But Eliezer Geller met those members of the Gestapo (Zurawin and Skosowski) and they certainly knew the truth. In the Hotel Polski, there was also that Revisionist who wrote the report. I don't know why they executed Kirshenbaum of all people. The fact that a man boasts isn't enough. There were enough "experts" there to understand the situation in the ghetto correctly and to know that Kirshenbaum wasn't a dangerous member of the underground, but just a normal social activist. Why didn't they execute others? Other people were murdered, both Geller and Kanal; but not in Warsaw; at any rate, it's incomprehensible. It isn't likely that Gestapo agents, at least the Jews among them, wouldn't know Kirshenbaum's position, for example, as opposed to Geller's; but in fact, that's what happened.

When the transport left Hotel Polski for Vittel or Bergen-Belsen, Kirshenbaum, his wife, and, I think, his daughter were taken to the forest and killed—simply murdered. Guzik swore to me that one day he was in the home of Zurawin or Skosowski when the telephone rang—there was a telephone extension in Skosowski's house—and he gestured to Guzik to listen in on the conversation. Judel Kalikstein was on the line. I mentioned that he had once helped me get a document, and I didn't think I would ever come across that name again. Anyway, Guzik said he listened in and heard Judel Kalikstein talking on the phone with one of the two. (It's hard for me to remember if it was Skosowski or Zurawin.) After that conversation, the Gestapo agent (Skosowski or Zurawin) told Guzik: "You think we're doing these things? You see who's doing it—it's Kalikstein!" Guzik wanted to convince me that those people were acting innocently.

After the war, when I was in New York, the Bundists were split over Zurawin. Some didn't talk to others because they defended Zurawin. Adam Zurawin came to the United States with his girlfriend. Fortunately for him, he fell into a family of millionaires and he also got rich. To purify himself, he summoned a rabbinical court to judge him. A few years ago, I got a letter from that rabbinical court asking for my testimony. I didn't answer because I'm afraid that such courts in the United States can be bought for money. I knew that the plaintiffs were very rich. Then I got a second telegram asking for my testimony. I replied: "On such and such a date the ZOB issued a death sentence for the Gestapo agent Adam Zurawin. To this day, the sentence hasn't changed and is still in effect." Signed: "Former Commander of the Jewish Fighting Organization."

Since then they haven't asked me for anything else. Adam Zurawin is alive and well—and very rich.

Despite all that, how did people get out of Hotel Polski and go abroad? Apparently there was some deception here. The Germans apparently had various plans—either to exchange prisoners or something else. The fact is that a few people did survive. The invitation [to those with foreign documents] came from the Germans and was deceitful. When people asked the Germans (through various channels) whether they would be sent out, the Germans would say it was true; but since those (South American) countries said the Jews' documents were forged, that gave the Germans authorization to execute the people. Nevertheless, they didn't execute people who had (Mandatory) Palestinian citizenship, as in the case of Ruth Adler and others.

How were people transported to Vittel, a transit point in France where foreign citizens really were kept? There were English and Americans there, as well as people from other countries. You can read about that camp in Yitzhak Katznelson's *Vittel Diary* and in other testimonies (for example, Miriam Nowicz).[18] Natan Eck and Yitzhak Katznelson were brought there. And Katznelson was taken from there to Auschwitz. Natan Eck jumped off the train and got to Paris, but his wife was taken to Auschwitz.

Miriam Nowicz was sent to Vittel from France, where she had contacts. I never asked her the details. She was connected with the French underground *Maquis*, in the Vittel episode. Hela Schüpper, who was also in Vittel, survived, as did Landau and his wife. But most were killed. At any rate, it was an awful trap for many Jews. Some Jews gave most of their money to get the necessary documents and then it turned out you could get the documents easily, which was what first made me suspicious. However, initially, I thought we could also send out one or two people through Hotel Polski, so they could tell our story to the world.

I saw Eliezer Geller at Hotel Polski. I also met with him before the Hotel Polski episode came up. Incidentally, for a long time, packages continued to be sent to Eliezer Geller at Albertynska Street 12, even after he was dead. And "Eliezer Geller acknowledged receipt . . . ," that is, the tenants of Albertynska Street learned the "craft" or perhaps there was a Jew who helped them write replies and would also send "regards from Celina." We found the letters in the Istanbul archive, a correspondence with Eliezer Geller after he was dead. Apparently, the packages were pretty good.

18. Miriam Nowicz (1908–1990): Born in Juratyshki, Byelorussia. Emigrated to France before the war, where she was active in left wing circles. She was arrested and sent to Vittel. There she befriended Yitzhak Katznelson and smuggled his poetry out of the camp. She immigrated to Eretz Israel in 1946 and was a member of Kibbutz Lohamei Ha-Getaot. Her testimony is in Tzvika Dror, *Testimonies of Survival*, 1984:499–518.

At that period, we also had some contacts with the outside world. I stopped writing to Istanbul or Switzerland. We sent letters through the Delegatura to London and got letters and money from there. One of the most painful episodes was the case of contact or lack of it with Eretz Israel. Apparently Venya Pomerants (Hadari) had contact with Frumka in Zagłębie. There was an emissary who came to Warsaw, but I didn't meet him. There were also emissaries who collaborated with the Gestapo. There's a story about a letter from Frumka, a copy of which was found in the hands of the Germans. Barlas[19] told me that those who delivered the letters weren't always reliable. They carried letters and money, but they photographed every letter and gave it to Canaris's people.[20] I met twice with the woman emissary from Switzerland but that was just before the beginning of the Polish Uprising, in July 1944. She spoke some Polish but my German was enough for her. She said she wasn't a German, but a Swiss. She brought me a letter and some silver and gold and was on her way to Kraków; she intended to go to addresses she had gotten from Schwalb, or other comrades working in Switzerland. She gave me most of the things but, because the Russian cannons were already heard around Mińsk-Mazowiecki, we decided she would try to meet me again. She found me from the address of Rivka Moskowicz, who was known in Switzerland, and came to me in a few hours.

We agreed that if she couldn't find the addresses I gave her, she would come back and leave me everything, including things for the people of Kraków. And that's what happened. As I recall, she got out of Warsaw one day before the Polish Uprising began, before August 1, 1944. We didn't have direct contact with Kastner.[21] I didn't know that name at all; I knew only that in Hungary and Bratislava there were "synagogue treasurers" who were ordered to help but I didn't know by whom.

The emissary I talked about earlier didn't mention the name of Kastner or Hungary or Budapest. He came on behalf of the "Rescue Committee" in Slovakia. From what he said, I understood there was a group there who got instructions to rescue Zivia and me (without any payment). The instructions were specifically by name. Only us. That is, the man was ready to take other people with him or to send them through the border, but for these others, it would cost money. He also explained to me that

19. Barlas: Representative of the Jewish Agency in Istanbul during the war.
20. Wilhelm Canaris (1887–1945): Commander of German military intelligence.
21. Rudolf Kastner (1906–1957): Born in Cluj, Transylvania. Moved to Budapest in 1942 where he was a leader of the Jewish community and negotiated with Adolf Eichmann about trading Jews for goods. After the war, he moved to Israel and was active in the Mapai Party [Social Democrats]. He was accused of collaborating with the Nazis but was cleared by the Israeli courts. However, before he was legally exonerated, he was assassinated on March 3, 1957.

Zivia's and my leaving was a condition for rescuing other people. I referred to the people who gave him the instructions as "synagogue treasurers" since I didn't know their names. Maybe he mentioned names but they didn't mean anything to me.

That emissary was a Pole and I don't know how he intended to get across the border. I didn't check out all those things because we weren't at all inclined to agree to the demand to move to Slovakia. I certainly didn't concede and neither did Zivia. I could understand how she felt although, at that time, she wasn't active in Movement work.

I'm not objective about these things, but in that group of activists who survived the Ghetto Uprising, her opinion had more weight with me than any other. That is, she was simply needed from time to time for consideration of important issues. As I said, there were a thousand things I wouldn't tell her; but, nevertheless, there were essential things that had to be discussed with her; for the most part, I was alone and her presence was important. Nevertheless, I urged her to leave Poland, but she wouldn't.

To preserve contact with Slovakia, however, I sent a letter with that emissary leaving the door open. That letter was kept by one of the activists who is still alive. A photostat of the letter found in the Istanbul archive during the Kastner trial is preserved in the United States. I saw the original. That man who had the letter visited us; he's from Slovakia, but I don't remember his name. He showed me the letter and allowed me to hold it—the letter and my answer to whoever wrote it in my own handwriting. There were a few paragraphs: the first paragraph was that I wouldn't consider going. The second paragraph concerned Zivia, leaving an opening for some kind of "maybe," even though I knew it was hopeless; but I wanted to force that committee to send the man back to us so the contact wouldn't be lost. A third point was concern for the children and public figures who weren't active and who only burdened us with an extraordinary responsibility to supply apartments, provide for their support, and such. And as I recall, I wrote that if we had survived so far, something should be done to save *all of us* and to rescue the children. But there was also a point about the payment of money: we couldn't meet the smuggler's demands for payment for every child; that would be at the expense of what little money we had to support Jews in hiding.

I didn't get an answer to my letter, nor did I get any money. I met the man at least once more, maybe twice. And the old demand for me and Zivia to escape was repeated. In my mind, I even planned a double-plated armored car to ship children or those who didn't look Aryan. This emissary was the only real outside contact. We didn't get any help or anything else from there. That messenger didn't rescue other prominent figures, for example, party leaders; nothing. He knew only our two names. You can probably find my letter in our archive and my answer indicates what they wanted to do. I don't know if they could have sent us on (from Slovakia)—I imagine they could have, because other comrades, like Yosef Kornianski did get to Eretz Israel in 1944.

Those were all the contacts and, except for the messenger from Switzerland whom I mentioned, I didn't meet with anybody. And I decided not to write—there was no point in correspondence with Istanbul. Incidentally, people who had been sent from Istanbul didn't reach us. One of them might have reached Warsaw but I didn't run into them. They usually came to Zaglębie and they might have contacted Frumka. A few people got packages. Irena Adamowicz told me she got shipments from Switzerland at her address, but that didn't interest me. It didn't matter if she got Swiss cheese or canned goods. What was important was millions of Złotys we got from abroad, money collected by a big fund composed of several sources, which came through London. That was why we kept in touch with the AK until the last moment. The money was collected by the Histadrut, the World Jewish Congress, the Bund, and the parties. It was public money for a specific purpose.

As for whether there was Polish money involved, there were liberal elements in Warsaw who supported the Polish Government-in-Exile in London. They set up something called ZEGOTA, an acronym for the "Committee to Rescue Jews." They got money for rescue, not big sums; it was a gesture. They didn't get aid on a per capita basis, but in a global amount. This committee got money and ran an independent support operation with a few departments: one for medical assistance, one for renting apartments, and one for supplying forged documents. Of course, the money given by ZEGOTA was really nothing in comparison to what we got from abroad. But I must add that what we got from abroad was a tiny sum in relation to our needs, a few tens of thousands of dollars. It's hard to comprehend how Jews in Eretz Israel and in the Western world didn't understand what ransom meant. We didn't have any other sources.

We helped support many Jews. As I recall, we generally distributed 500 Złotys per person a month (there may have been a few exceptions), which was very little. Nevertheless, it was something. There were two or three kinds of people who received aid: the Jewish intelligentsia, who were certainly not rich and were helped by the good, liberal, democratic, Communist, and perhaps also Catholic Polish intelligentsia. And there were simple Jews who certainly didn't have money. There was also a very small group of wealthy people who didn't need our 500 Złotys a month. Not to mention thousands of Jews in and around Warsaw and, later, in other parts of Poland, who had nothing to live on and whose only support came from us.

We estimated that there were about 20,000 Jews hiding in and around Warsaw and that 12,000 Jews received that aid. That is, we can assume there were Jews who looked Aryan and found a way to make a living. There were also Jews who didn't want anything to do with us, who were afraid to reveal themselves as Jews, and somehow lived as Poles. I don't think the number of those we helped went over 12,000.

About 3,000 names were in my card file. Within the Jewish Fighting Organization, we insisted on the need to deal not only with weapons and fighting, but also with welfare. We couldn't avoid that elementary need to help Jews. In the wake of the Gestapo infiltration into the group of Jewish women in Kraków and the fear that they would also infiltrate our network, I always required group leaders to demand a "life history" of any new candidate for assistance. I wasn't interested in the real name and was satisfied with the current, phony name; but I wanted to know the name in case it didn't exist; I wanted to know where the person had lived in order to investigate if he belonged to Zurawin's and Skosowski's circles or such. And I must say that, internally, we didn't find any acts of treason.

We did make a definite dinstinction between aid to members of the Jewish Fighting Organization and to other Jews. For ZOB members, we assumed total responsibility: for the apartment and as much support as necessary. The ZOB, ultimately, numbered no more than a few dozen, never more than that. Now and then we found more people and added them to the list. People also came to us on their own, and we had to take care of them because they didn't have anything. When others (I wouldn't say all Jews) were "hoarding money," these were people who maintained their movement ties; sometimes they arrived not even from Warsaw but also from the forest. We knew that the forest wasn't an ideal solution to the problems of the people, except for isolated individuals who survived in the forests; many of them were murdered, too, or fell in battle.

We were responsible for these people because, unlike other Jews who left the ghetto in September 1942 or in early 1943 and somehow managed to find a place to live or a hideout and take care of minimum needs, these ZOB members had nothing.

There was a special problem of the children, which involved help in finding a hideout, medical aid, giving birth—after all, people did give birth. One of the group leaders told me of the father of a newborn Jewish child who wanted to circumcise the baby without considering either the danger of doing it or the danger he exposed the child to. They did indeed bring in a doctor and circumcised the boy. That, of course, was exceptional. Call that heroism or martyrdom, but there was something honorable in it. But in general, people were lonely, and couples couldn't always live together in the same apartment. Life was hard and brutal;

sometimes life forced relatives to separate; sometimes fate chose one member of a couple to be killed while the other survived.

It's hard to describe and appreciate the dedicated work of the couriers. They would visit regularly, through circuitous routes, because danger was always lurking. All kinds of things would happen in a month: their house was "burned"; or they sensed they were being followed by the Gestapo; or the blackmailers "jumped" them. The couriers dealt with that every day, and every single day I heard of people murdered or caught by the blackmailers which ultimately ended in death: when a Jew didn't have any money or when the blackmailers couldn't extort any more from him, they would turn him over and get paid by the Germans for that. And we're talking about a lot of people from all groups.

All the time I've been telling this history, I have deliberately refrained from reading anything because I wanted to be more authentic. Now I think maybe that's wrong. I've been examining my memory. If I had checked documents, I really could have been more authentic. If I had read about things thirty years after they happened, things I'm telling might have been told a little differently. I would have refreshed my memory. Maybe I'll start doing that, just leafing through writings.

Now the episode of Michael Weichert.[22] He was one of the greatest theatrical talents of Polish Jewry. Professionally he was a lawyer. As I recall, he cooperated with the Germans during World War I; but that was a totally different and positive cooperation. In any case, he had close contacts with them. He was a devoté of German culture, the representative of the Jewish Social Self-Help (YISA), and later the Yidisher hilfs komitet (YHK, whose initials were also YSS, but the Germans ordered the name changed because of the "SS"). That was an umbrella organization of welfare operations. I never heard anything good about Weichert, but that's not to censure him. I heard that he wasn't an easy or a friendly person; but that doesn't say anything against Weichert either.

The Weichert incident began after we picked up on the intensive social activity he was carrying out in 1943, after the Uprising. We realized that just when the Germans were taking the Jews of Warsaw, the Jews of Poland, even the Jews of Kraków to death, Weichert, following orders from the Germans, formed JUS (Jüdische Unterstützungstelle) to replace the YHK. At the same time that the Germans were executing Jews, they assigned him to summon the Jewish world abroad to send material aid: medicine, food, and so forth. And the simple question arose of what was the purpose of these letters of appeal sent by a well-known figure of

22. See above, chapter 3. Weichert's memoirs present his version of events. (See Weichert 1963 and 1970.)

the prewar era, and during the war as well, a man who led welfare operations and represented the Jews vis-à-vis the German institutions?

His letters abroad, sent in those very months of bloodshed and mass murder, created the impression abroad that this money was needed for the hungry. True, Jews were dying of starvation, in 1941–1942 and in 1943; but in 1944, that was no longer the problem. The difference between him and Ringelblum, and even between him and Kirshenbaum, was that those Jews did everything to alarm the world to the fact that the Germans were killing us—simple murder! Whereas Weichert requested material aid in his letters; and, if material aid was requested, it was requested for live Jews! So we suspected this activity as a first class deceit. This assessment didn't come only from Jewish sources, we heard it from Polish sources too, for example, the Polish Committee for Welfare in Warsaw (RGO), a few of whose members cooperated with us in ZEGOTA; one of these was Marek Arczyński, the democrats' representative. (He was in Israel a few years ago and we entertained him.) Everyone felt that Weichert was a traitor, that he was doing the work of the Germans.

Weichert was the only Jew who didn't wear the Magen-David armband. He lived in his own house on the Aryan side, when there were no more Jews in Kraków. The remnants of Kraków Jewry were gathered in the Plaszów concentration camp, whereas he lived in Kraków under German protection and ran their errands. He received several shipments of food from abroad. When we learned that, we did two things: we wrote to London condemning the letters published in his name—in order to expose Weichert and proclaim that he was not the representative of the Jews; the second thing was to send Marek Arczyński to Weichert to persuade him to give up that disgraceful work and to suggest he go underground. We were willing to accept responsibility for his safety under the circumstances. At that time it didn't occur to us to issue a death sentence against him. We thought we would hide him in Kraków or someplace else and support him, although I'm sure he didn't need our money. We said we would provide an Aryan document for him; but he rejected our proposals. (We had a branch of self-help in Kraków led by Marianska, who is now head of Yad Vashem in Tel Aviv.)

When changes occurred in the status of the Plaszów concentration camp, Weichert announced he was willing to accept our offer; but when he realized that his position with the Germans was as firm as it had been, he again avoided accepting our judgment. He had two "forced" assistants, Dr. Eliahu Tish[23] and Dr. Haim Hilfstein,[24] in the Plaszów camp. Wei-

23. Dr. Eliahu Tish: An attorney, journalist, and, according to Weichert, "an outstanding speaker." A democratic Zionist, who immigrated to Israel after the Liberation (Weichert 1963:78; Weichert 1970:23).

chert, as I said, was the only person in Kraków who operated freely. Those two were well-known public figures, honest men, members of *Et Livnot* (the right-wing faction of the General Zionists). But we couldn't say anything to Tish and Hilfstein since they were both prisoners in the camp. Not Weichert. Ultimately, he disappeared.

There were meetings and discussions that resulted in a death sentence against him. He survived only because of our weakness. At that time, in 1944, we didn't have a force in Kraków to carry out the sentence; I would have had to send at least one armed man on the train to Kraków to carry out the sentence, which meant abandoning the agent to his fate. That wasn't simple. If there had been a branch of the Jewish Fighting Organization in Kraków, the situation would have been different. But that was after December, after events in Kraków, and the collapse in Bochnia, when there was only a remnant of ZOB left.[25] I couldn't figure out a way to do it; I would have thought it impossible to send an armed man 400 kilometers to search for his victim for days. So the traitor survived.

Later on, we learned that during August and September 1944, during the Polish Uprising, Weichert nevertheless did appeal to our organization for help. By then it was the Jewish-Polish combined organization (Marianska of Yad Vashem was one of its leaders). The members of the organization did indeed hide him. If they had asked us, we would have said: absolutely not! Don't give him any help! But they didn't ask. Afterward, for two months, I was involved in the Polish Uprising. And for a month and a half, I was hiding on the Aryan side of Warsaw, along the Wisła. Then we started looking for the survivors and began reorganizing. It was almost January when we learned that our people, members of the Jewish and Polish underground, were hiding Weichert.

In the book Weichert wrote in the United States, he attacks me. I haven't read the book; I only leafed through it. His trial in Poland was widely known. To his dying day, he didn't know that I was against the trial, since I was opposed to trials against Jews in Poland after the war. Not for opportunistic reasons, but because the Poles murdered us there morning and night and antisemitism flourished. True, the members of the Polish government weren't antisemites; but the trial raised all kinds of episodes which didn't have to be brought up. So I didn't assist in the initiatives to try Weichert after he came to Israel, because it wasn't a trial against an

24. Dr. Haim Hilfstein: According to Weichert, he was a "distinguished Zionist activist," who participated in Jewish educational activities for more than forty years. A physician in the Austrian army during World War I. He survived World War II and immigrated to Israel after the Liberation. (See Weichert 1963:78; Weichert 1970:23.)

25. In September 1943, 3,000 Jews of the liquidated ghetto of Bochnia were sent to Auschwitz. (See Ainsztein 1974:828.)

individual. In addition, there were all kinds of intrigues and dirt I despised.

As for the trial in Poland, I didn't appear in court until I got an official warning about contempt of court. Then I showed up. Aside from a temporary document I had, I obtained a semidiplomatic document for the flight to London in 1945; I didn't have real documents. I continued to obtain documents in the name of Stanisław Bagniewski and I lived in a splendid apartment I got from Minister Spychalski in ruined Warsaw—an expression of honor and appreciation. There was only one reason for my remaining in Poland after March 1945: to look for Jews!

I appeared at the trial in the name of Stanisław Bagniewski, which I used in the underground. The trial occurred at a period in Poland when Jews were taken off trains and killed. There were emissaries who witnessed that and could tell what they saw with their own eyes. Anyway, Stanisław Bagniewski was supoenaed and appeared. To this day, I don't know who summoned me to testify. The trial took place in Kraków. It wasn't a military court but a court for war criminals or collaborators. I had been in Kraków many times, but that day I stayed there only as long as I had to be in court. I hadn't been in the court before or after, and I left there immediately.

At the trial, Weichert tried to make me into a hero. When I appeared in court, Weichert asked permission to speak. Even before I opened my mouth, he stood up (we should find the record), and said: "I don't know if your honor knows who this witness is or if your honor knows that not since the days of Bar-Kokhba has such a hero arisen, and so forth." When I heard that, I smelled flattery. I ignored what he said; I was amazed that he knew who Stanisław Bagniewski was—"a descendant of Bar-Kokhba?" I ignored all that rhetoric; it was simply lip service he offered me, and I didn't buy it. I explained simply that what Weichert had done was definitely opposed to our policy since we were shouting, "They're murdering us," and we wanted to alarm the world. Whereas he wrote letters requesting aid. Witnesses from RGO and other organizations also testified that the Germans were interested in him for two reasons: first, to calm and tell the world they weren't murdering anybody, just asking for material aid; and second, simply to take the medicines, the good coffee, the canned goods for themselves. In his posthumously published book, he made his own accounting. I asked Mordechai Sonnschein[26] why he published that book; he apologized and said that the publisher's name, *Menora*, wasn't printed on it and that he had done it reluctantly. I told him I had seen the book, which looked like all the other books from the same

26. The publisher of *Menora* in Israel who put out Weichert's book.

press. He had probably gotten a bribe. This is a book "from the grave," which appeared after Weichert's death.[27]

The one thing I wanted was to prevent Weichert from filling any public function in Israel. One day, Shprintzak invited me to the Knesset (he was then chairman of the public committee of Beit Lohamei Ha-Getaot) to talk about Weichert; he didn't know anything about him. Back in 1945, in London, after I had given a speech there about the function of the Judenrat in the destruction of the Jews and about Jewish treason, Shprintzak said to me: "Jews aren't traitors." I knew that he couldn't imagine the phenomenon symbolized by the Judenrat; but we knew very well that there could be Jewish treason, even deliberate treason. Nevertheless, he sent for me. Shprintzak wanted to form a national theatrical network in Israel directed by Weichert, and he wanted my opinion. I mentioned our conversation in 1945 and told him: "You said there are no traitors. That's your right. I say: according to the facts I have, Weichert is a traitor. I don't want trials, but I warn you that the day Weichert's name appears as a public figure, as head of any network or institution, there will be a trial! But I'll oppose all trials if he lives quietly!"

At the Kraków trial, Weichert was found innocent. It turned out that the trial judge in the case was murdered because of some other case, and the trial was adjourned. The assistant minister of justice in those days was a Jew named Haim who invited a few Jewish public dignitaries and consulted with them about not renewing the trial because of dirty episodes involved in it and because of the fear that it would lead to outbursts of antisemitism. He proposed a public trial for Weichert, which did indeed take place; but that was after I had left Poland. A public trial can't send anybody to prison, but Weichert was banned from public life. This time, if I had been asked to appear, I would have come; but I wasn't asked and I didn't take part in any of it. In his book, Weichert tells only about the Kraków trial but doesn't say a thing about the public trial. I didn't read the book, but I think he attacks the judges, attacks everything and everyone. Ultimately, he was allowed to leave Poland. When he was still in Poland and in jail, the manuscript with his memoirs was taken from him and the memoirs are in our archive. The memoirs he published with Sonnschein at *Menora* don't coincide with things in our archive written during the German occupation, in 1944, in Polish. First the copy of those memoirs reached the "historical committee" in Kraków, where I had friends (Michał Borwicz and Yosef Wolf); I got the material from them and brought it to Israel. To the end of his days, Weichert didn't know that that material was in my hands. If he had tried to climb onto the public

27. Weichert's account of this trial is in Weichert 1970.

platform, I would have published chapters of the diary he wrote in those days. But now there's no reason for any of that.

At the trial in Poland, there were also people (from the Plaszów camp) who testified in his favor, since he paid a lot of bribes. There's no case of collaboration, even the most famous, that doesn't help someone. Our rage at the Kastner affair can be seen in this light. I wasn't in favor of making a trial; but in his case, too, there were people he helped, including Halutzim like Zvi Goldfarb.[28] We once had a conversation at Efal, the Kibbutz Research Institute, during the Kastner trial; it was hard for me to hear Goldfarb's defense of Kastner, because he saw the case from a narrow, not an inclusive, angle.

I don't know any other public figures like Weichert who were involved in that kind of dirt. That is, if I overlook Tish and Hilfstein, who were "forced"—I didn't meet either of them, even after the war. As I recall, one or both of them survived.

There were collaborators in Łódz Ghetto, but that's a story in itself. If we're talking about my personal experience, I don't know any other collaborators like these, not including Kalikstein, whom I really didn't know and didn't associate with this group. I had never even heard that name until I needed a permit to be in the ghetto, and I must say that I really didn't trust the cleanliness of his hands because Guzik's story about Kalikstein raises questions. I didn't have time to discuss that with Guzik after the war because he was killed in an airplane crash over Prague (in August 1945, as I recall), when I was in London. You might say that Guzik was also involved somehow, quite peripherally, in that mishap. He was a man with no political savvy. I'm sure he was a good Jew. Giterman, for example, wouldn't have gotten into such a situation, even though Giterman did meet with that bastard Gancwajch, who was head of the *Trzynastka*.[29]

Weichert was never a Zionist. He was once close to the Communists, a kind of "salon Communist." He was a man who no doubt had great merit in the Jewish theater, but that has nothing to do with his behavior. For example, the Judenrat in Piotrków and Lublin were Bundists, but that doesn't mean they were Bundist agents in the Judenrat. It's important to emphasize that it was harder for leftists to gain the trust of the Germans. They were absolutely prohibited. A former Communist couldn't have

28. Member of the Halutz underground in Hungary during the Holocaust. His activity is told in his book *Up to the End*, 1981 (Hebrew).

29. *Trzynastka*, the origin of the name is the Polish word for "13." Nickname for the Gestapo office set up in the ghetto in January 1941, at Leszno Street 13 (hence the name). The office was disguised as a "Control Office for Combatting the Black Market and Profiteering." The office was set up by Abraham Gancwajch and operated as an independent unit, employing 300 policemen.

been in the Judenrat. The Germans would probably have killed him, just because of his politics. Keep in mind that, until 1941 or 1942, an Eretz Israeli office still existed in Berlin, even though Zionism wasn't recognized. And at the same time, the Germans were putting Communists into concentration camps; only later did they start putting Jews in. I don't remember a single distinguished or well-known Zionist in the Warsaw Judenrat. Stoltzman was a Zionist from Włocławek, as I recall. As for Czerniakow—by the way, an apologia about him is now developing in Poland on a big scale. His diary was published and praised.[30] Even the Polish mayor of Warsaw wrote that Czerniakow was a "distinguished personality." Czerniakow had once been a member of the expanded Jewish Agency, on the non-Zionist side. Can you say he was a Zionist? Was Wielikowski a Zionist? Or Rumkowski (head of the Łódz Judenrat)? They weren't Zionists. Rumkowski, as I recall from my conversations with Gruenbaum, was on the fringes of Gruenbaum's group Al Ha-Mishmar [left-wing General Zionists].

Those who joined the Judenrat didn't do so as Zionist representatives. I can state that there were many kinds of Judenrats; I don't support the total rejection of people in the Judenrat. I'm against the Judenrat as an institution, but I distinguish between the people in it, because they weren't all the same. Some people believed fully that their job was to lead and help; and some were careerists; some were traitors; and some—not many—used the Judenrat to help the underground. But the institution itself was a tool in the hands of the Germans, a tool designed to assist in the liquidation of the Jews.

The deceit of the Communists, both Jewish and non-Jewish, is expressed by the fact that they took someone like Gancwajch, a very perverse man, who had been a member of Po'alei Zion in the twenties, and turned him into a Zionist. That's as if I said that General Vlassov represented the Soviet Union. Vlassov organized hundreds of thousands of soldiers to fight against his homeland; that was treason! And he doesn't represent Communism. I have a lot of accusations against Communism, but the Communists did make war against Hitler to save Russia. At any rate, I reject the argument that collaborators had rightist tendencies or were Zionists. I reject both arguments.

But I don't think there was a single case of collaboration in the major Socialist-Zionist parties. Nor were there people who were tempted and went downhill, even out of naïveté. For example, in the first Judenrat of Vilna, as I recall, there were two former members of Po'alei Zion–Z.S. who both later moved to the General Zionists. One was Barantshuk and the other was one of the great experts on Borochov, Shabtai

30. Czerniakow's diary was published in English in 1979.

Milkonovicki.[31] Both of them were murdered by the Germans because that Judenrat didn't suit them.

My appraisal of the Judenrat in 1941 was not the same as my appraisal of it in 1942, since there was a gradual deterioration; they ceased to be advocates of the people and became executors of German orders. That was felt every day.

In the period we're talking about, 1944, after the historical experience of those people, there was no longer any delusion. By that time, there was no longer a Judenrat or any Jewish quarters. And, after 1942, that whole group, operating among the Jews on behalf of the Germans, were Gestapo agents in every respect. These were people like Zurawin, Skosowski, Kenigel, and others. The exception among the Jewish public figures was Weichert.

Forgive me for returning to the episode of Hotel Polski. The Jews were naïve to think there was really something to it. After the meeting with Guzik, when I realized that any Jew could get in, I was on alert. I had been around long enough and had enough training in the "German universities" to figure out that that was a fraud. I think that Jews like Geller and Kanal went there because they were broken and worn out. After the fire, Geller was down and out. Those were hard times. If he had listened to me, he wouldn't have done it. The same goes for Israel Kanal, who also went there because he had collapsed. He was a strong, handsome man, an idealist, a member of Akiba, one of the few who resigned from the police, "threw away the hat." He "used his hat" only to attack Szerynski. But he also broke down. At the time, I didn't know he had come out of the forest, and all of a sudden, I learned he was at Hotel Polski. I tried to save him, to get in touch with him. I was in Hotel Polski only once. Some things are hard to explain. We can't appreciate fully what it means for a soldier to go home, to have support and be able to rest, if only for twenty-four hours. I really don't know where we got the strength. Where did I rest? When? Even in Kibbutz Yagur, I used to wake up at night when a car passed by on the road. I couldn't sleep quietly.

People broke down under that great tension. Even when they were hiding, even when they weren't doing anything. Even those who lived in huts in the forests, threatened by every slight rustle day and night, day after day, hour after hour, for months and years! It's no wonder people broke down; it's harder to understand how there were some who didn't. My breakdown came after the war, in January 1945, and then I started drinking. Until January, I lived in a constant fever of activity. At that time, until the Liberation, I didn't sense the passage of time, I didn't feel how

31. Shabtai Milkonovicki: An attorney, the last chairman of the prewar Jewish Community Council in Vilna. Head of the Health Department in the Judenrat.

the days went by. There were fears and terror, but I never reached the breaking point. Not that. And I think that at the end of that period I broke down twice: the first time was right after the war. After all, I knew everything, but there's a difference between knowing and seeing with your own eyes. You can read all the books and know everything. I think I knew what was happening to the Jews better than anyone else in Poland. Nevertheless, in light of what I saw "after the deluge"—that there were no Jews, that Poland was without Jews—I broke down. The second time was when I was in France, in early 1947, when Tabenkin and some other comrades decided that the most important thing was for me to go to Germany to stir up the Jews in the camps, and then to the United States. I didn't have the strength for it. Maybe I should have done it, but I knew I had to get to some haven. Nobody forced me to do it. It was the kind of appeal I was used to accepting, certainly in 1944; but in 1947, I was in Paris and was an "immigrant." At that time, I didn't have the strength to agree to do it. I'm not surprised that people broke down.

In that period, we expected changes at the fronts. The second front was opened in June (1944), with the invasion of Europe. Tuvia Borzykowski tells in his book that he came to Leszno and I regaled him with a drink in honor of the event.[32] We cavorted and drank. Our constant hope was to live until the Liberation! I was aware of two things at that time: one was that I was liable to die any day! When I went out, I didn't know if I'd come back. And the second was that I set my sights on life. But that doesn't mean I wanted to live at any price. Nevertheless, when the Allies invaded Italy or Europe, or when the Russians won great victories, we went off into all kinds of speculations, most of them wrong, because everything lasted much longer than we thought.

When we heard of the invasion of Europe, I was with some gentiles from the underground, and we drank a toast in the middle of the day, something we didn't usually do. But there was genuine joy in the street and we went into a tavern freely to drink a toast. Afterward, we cavorted at home. That was one more delusion.

The thread of relations with the AK in June and July 1944 was almost cut off because even the minimal help they gave us ceased. We maintained good relations with the AL to the very end, through the Polish Uprising. That was after Bór-Komorowski's letter,[33] after the answer I got from him, after the warning that the AK would kill me because I constituted a stumbling block to them. In fact, they didn't do anything. According to the letter, the sum total of cooperation was very paltry. And there was

32. Borzykowski 1972:152–153.
33. See above.

more to it later on. It was only the political issue that forced me to stay in touch with Wacław; not Wacław the person, but Wacław the AK representative—and he was aware of that. Wacław's writings, in Berman's archive, show him in a good light, fighting our war. But I didn't care about those contacts, except for the political issue of having a pipeline to the world. If not for that, I would have broken off relations with them. The AL wasn't strong, but they did what they could, and I don't care what Gomułka and his comrades did afterward.

His actions can't detract from their treatment of us in hard times. Sometimes we were richer than they were, and we helped them. In the AL, I met with Witold. I met with many of their people, but I saw Witold regularly, once a week. I could see him within twenty-four hours, if need be. But we usually met on Sunday at the station beyond Włocławek. He would stand at the station—not a young man, much older than me, myopic. He would hold a piece of paper and write. I couldn't understand how he could write so small. He didn't see well and would put lenses on top of his eyeglasses. We always had amiable and frank conversations. He was aware of our mutual helplessness. He knew everything. I would tell him about the texture of relations between us and the AK, and he would always justify and encourage us. He understood that we faced the problem of saving Jews or of fighting the Jewish war with whatever we could muster.

In those days, the AL were genuine patriots. After all, they suffered all the torments: their leaders were killed; they were hated by the Polish people; they were hated by the AK; they were a minority in distress. Anyone who chose to be a Communist at that time was a Communist idealist, not a careerist. And they were simply fine people! I would meet with that veteran group—they included middle-aged workers and some even older, maybe fifty or sixty. I told Tabenkin that they reminded me of the Second Aliya.[34] Fine people, aware, firm in their opinion; and they helped us with whatever little bit they could.

While we're on the subject, let me say something about the aid we got from the Polish people in general, and especially from the women. Why was the proportion of women helping us especially large? It was easier for women to help. Those gentile men who were sympathetic to the Jews or who "just" didn't hate Jews, who were members of the underground, had other work—like me, since our main activity wasn't welfare operations but organization, weapons, partisan units, and so forth. The job of women in the underground was more limited, and they carried out their underground activity by helping Jews. This group included women of

34. Second Aliya: The immigration of idealistic socialist Zionists to Eretz Israel from 1904 to 1914.

various classes, simple women and educated women. The initial contacts were made by our women couriers. Thus, a circle of educated women was formed from the entire political spectrum—Communists, PPS, Catholics.

One day I tried to make a list of these "Righteous Gentile Women," but couldn't. I got mixed up with the names and dropped it. In Władka's and Batya Berman's books, you can find the names of many women, most of them Poles, like those who helped us, at a significant risk to themselves.[35]

While we're on the subject, I would like to mention a few names of women couriers who worked with us: Miki Kossower, Emilia, Franya, Bella Elster, Ita Wanchotska, Irka Ravitska, Janina Buchholtz, Marysia Wachman, Zofia L., Yisia Golomb, Andzia, Ella, Inka Szwajger—I could and should tell a lot about every one of them. And there also is much to

---

35. Here is a list of names of women (and a few men), with a few words of explanation. Zuckerman collected some of the names and mentioned them in his remarks; but didn't complete it. Other names are taken from additional sources, such as the books of Władka Meed and Batya Berman (Batya Tabenkin Berman 1956).

Antonia Bogowska was director of the municipal office for women. She saved many Jewish women by finding suitable work for them.

Zuckerman mentions the "three Graces" of Krasiński Street whose apartment was one of the centers of the Communist underground and of help for Jews. These were: (1) Dr. Nina "Asoreh-Dibraye" [= "Ten Commandments," nickname], a sociologist, active in saving Jews for the Jewish National Committee; (2) Dr. Zofia Podkobińska, an archeologist, active in the PPR underground; assisted the Jewish underground on the Aryan side; (3) Irena Sawicka, PPR member, active in the anti-Nazi underground who helped many Jews.

Some of those who were killed were:

Dora Ackerman, a laborer, active in saving Jews. Zofia Rudziewicz, librarian, who helped many Jews. Stanisław Osowski and his wife Maria—professors of ethics and aesthetics at Warsaw University. Irena Soleska, one of the great actors of the Polish theater, was active in helping Jews at great risk and was a warm and humane attitude toward those she helped. Irena Korowska, Maria Osowska's sister, was a teacher who helped many Jews.

Janina Laktowicz, initially helped the underground, and later it turned out that she collaborated with a Polish Fascist organization, ONR, and was a Gestapo agent. Theodor Pajewski, a Pole, maintained contact between the Jewish National Committee and the underground in the camps. It was he who took E. Ringelblum and Paula Elster out of Trawniki Camp and hid the Jewish actor Jonas Turkow in his house. (See Turkow 1969.) Maria Grzegorzewska, a professor, director of the teachers' pedagogical institute, who ran a vocational school during the occupation and saved many Jews. Dr. Felicia Pelhorska, a psychologist, helped by hiding Jews. Helena Meanholz (her underground name was Stasia Królikowska), a Jew who later worked in the Jewish Central Committee. Mania Laska, a Polish librarian worked in the municipal registration office and helped save Jews. Krystyna Kowalska (Isolde Greifel), a Jew, wife of Richard the Pole, AL commander in the Old City during the Polish Uprising; on errands for the AL, she crossed the Wisła and came to Lublin during the Polish Uprising. Maria Parnowska, a psychologist, helped save Jews.

Keep in mind that the list is not complete.

be told about Luba Gewisser and Marysia Sawicka—and Marysia's nephew, Stefan Sawicki, who was killed as a member of the Jewish Fighting Organization, trained by the PPS, from a Socialist family.

I've mentioned a few names, mainly of women, but remember: these weren't people who performed one single act, but people who did their work every single day. We gave a meager subsistence to the two Sawicka sisters because neither of them worked and both were devoted to the Jewish cause. Marysia, in whose name our last apartment at Leszno 18 was registered, constantly risked her life. A few years ago, we brought her to Israel for Holocaust Memorial Day, to the assembly at Lohamei Ha-Getaot (I was in Argentina at the time). When they welcomed her with flowers, she got excited and wept.

When the Six Day War broke out, she was in Paris, doing something in the Polish embassy, probably washing floors there. Later David Klein told me she sat and wept for days. She couldn't show her sympathy for us since the Poles had broken relations with us. How can we explain that? Where is the self-interest here?

Anyone who fosters total hatred for the Polish people is committing a sin! We must do the opposite. Against the background of antisemitism and general apathy, these people are glorious. There was great danger in helping us, mortal danger, not only for them but also for their families, sometimes for the entire courtyard they lived in. In 1945, I was restrained at an international press conference when all kinds of questions were asked. I said honestly and I repeat it today: to cause the death of one hundred Jews, all you needed was one Polish denouncer; to save one Jew, it sometimes took the help of ten decent Poles, the help of an entire Polish family; even if they did it for money. Some gave their apartment, and others made identity cards. Even passive help deserves appreciation. The baker who didn't denounce, for instance. It was a problem for a Polish family of four who suddenly had to start buying double quantities of rolls or meat. And what a bother it was to go far away to buy in order to support the family hiding with them.

I didn't visit many places because I couldn't; but now and then I would visit the fighters and I met Poles who were the glory of mankind. And I argue that it doesn't matter if they took money; life wasn't easy for Poles either, and there wasn't any way to make a living. There were widows and officials who earned their few Złotys by helping. And there were all kinds of people who helped. But you have to admire the group of AL activists who weren't all intellectuals.

There were people we ruined, really destroyed their lives because their houses were burned down and their property destroyed. For example, Krzaczek and Rajszczak, two simple people, but what devotion! The glory of mankind. Not only did they not receive medals, but some Poles appealed to us, even in 1945, not to publicize their names because of the antisemitism of their neighbors.

Which Jewish social activists survived?

Some of them were in camps and survived. Some lived outside Poland. You have to distinguish between various kinds of people. There's a difference between Antoni Buksbaum[36] and Leon Feiner ("Mikołaj"), one of the Bundist leaders, who came to Warsaw from Galicia and wasn't in the ghetto at all. His major activity was on the Aryan side of Warsaw. He was a representative of the Bund and worked with Dr. Adolf Berman for the Jewish Coordinating Committee (ZKK), and in ZEGOTA. Ignac Simsonowicz and Leon Feiner would attend meetings on behalf of the Bund. Abrasha Blum's absence was sorely felt, not only by the Bund but also by me, since we were very close. Salo Fiszgrunt was one of the social activists of the Bund who survived the war. He was a member of the Jewish Central Committee. After the Six Day War, he moved to Israel, where his wife lives now. Not all Bundists, in the ghetto and later, stuck to their Bundist positions, as, for example, Władka Peltel and Celek Celeminski. I published the Hebrew edition of Władka's book (*On Both Sides of the Wall*), written in 1947–1948 in the United States, from a Bundist perspective. When we were about to publish the book in Hebrew, she asked me to put some changes in it. I wanted to know what changes. She had had a Bundist education and was now "pro-Eretz Israel." I saw that she wanted to change her perspective and I couldn't agree. I had to convince her that the basic value of the book was her authentic view of the 1940s, when she was still a Bundist. I told her she could write about the changes in her world view, but that was another book, since now she was an active Zionist. During the Yom Kippur War, she wanted to come to Israel and help in hospitals or something.

Celek, on the other hand, has remained an orthodox Bundist to this day. I see him, since he has been in Israel for some months now. He's a tailor by profession; an uneducated man but with a native intelligence, he had a position in the Bund. Władka was very close to the Jewish Fighting Organization; I used her much more than I used Celek. She was younger and, as a woman, demonstrated supreme devotion. He was always a Bundist, but he also did several errands for the Jewish Fighting Organization. As far as I know, Celek wasn't active in the ghetto, but only on the Aryan side of Warsaw. He had a son in Eretz Israel, a pilot, I think, who was killed in the War of Independence when Celek was in the United States. And even this didn't change him. I met him only yesterday, when

36. Antoni (Natan) Buksbaum: Active in Po'alei Zion Left. One of those who went to Hotel Polski.

he told me he wanted me to publish his book in Hebrew.[37] The book reflects a Bundist point of view, and should. It wouldn't occur to Celek to change his perspective, and I wouldn't agree to do it. He remains an orthodox Bundist to this day.

There are changes in the Bund today; there are two factions in it: one remains as it was in the 1930s, and another part is pro-Israel, like, for instance, Dr. Jacob Pat, who died a few years ago.[38] However, there is also a diehard remnant that has remained loyal to the Bund as it was. (Incidentally, I appeared with them in the United States in honor of Władka's book.) I was very careful not to get into an ideological argument with those people who ranged from assimilationists to Halutzim. I wanted to see them crystalized for a joint purpose and not in conflict with each other. I was remote from all debate, all factional perspectives. Therefore I couldn't accept the fact that the Bund, Po'alei Zion Left, and our groups couldn't work together—and it didn't matter to me if everyone brought his own world view from some other framework. But there were people who couldn't get rid of that burden. As a rule, the ZOB didn't operate by orders from the movements, especially on the Aryan side of Warsaw. My concern was who the person was. What was he worth? How strong was his position? That is, I wanted to examine his character. Naturally, members of the movements were closer to one another, but I can't say that I felt alien with Bundists. Absolutely not! I felt myself to be their comrade. And they didn't constantly remind themselves that I was from He-Halutz. And it didn't matter if I was younger than them. Because of my role, I had a different status.

As for Po'alei Zion Left, I would meet with the Berman brothers, Jakub and Adolf. There was one more brother, Samuel, a member of Po'alei Zion–Z.S., who was murdered in the ghetto or taken to the camps.[39] I would also meet with Wanda Elster (Rotenberg). Today I'm much closer to her personally than I was then. She was a courier. I didn't meet her socially, as I did others. There were rooms of women couriers where I would sometimes come for lunch or dinner, to settle matters. I tried not to eat in streetcorner restaurants very much. I never argued with the couriers in these meetings.

37. Celeminski's book is titled *Tsusamen mit dem folk* (*With the People*).

38. Jacob Pat (1890–1966): Born in Białystok. He joined the Bund in 1920. He went to the United States from Warsaw in 1939 as a member of a Bund delegation and stayed there, subsequently leading the pro-Zionist trend in the Bund.

39. Dr. Samuel Berman: A surgeon; the older brother of Adolf. In 1939, served in the Polish army as a doctor; after the defeat he was stranded in eastern Poland and returned to Warsaw. He worked in the ghetto hospital. Samuel Berman treated Antek in Warsaw Ghetto for the wound he received in Kraków in December 1942. He was caught by the Nazis in January 1943 and killed in Treblinka (Berman 1977:12–13).

Almost never in Jewish life in Poland did the Bundists and the Zionists work together so closely and enjoy friendships and personal trust as during the Holocaust. To this day, we keep in touch. I think that all those people have complete trust in us; that's not just arrogance. I know from talking with Bundists, even from my meeting with Celek yesterday, that they still feel we didn't cheat, exploit, or disappoint them. That was a time when blocs crystalized into general frameworks with goals that super-seded everything and overshadowed all frictions and conflicts that I didn't care about.

In political terms, that is, in terms of political activism, I was always on the fringes; in other words, I was a typical alumnus of He-Halutz Ha-Tza'ir. If they hadn't made me join, I wouldn't have been a member of Po'alei Zion–Z.S.; that side of political activism remains my "weak side" to this day. I wasn't an "ardent" (*farbrenter*) member of Po'alei Zion; in my presence and on my visits to the groups, there were no argu-ments. When I was with the Bund, I heard or read that on May Day they met in some house on Miodowa Street and sang "The Oath."[40] I wasn't involved in that, even though it was permitted. But in my presence, these topics didn't come up. The topics were the concentration camps, the partisan unit, daily activity, plans and dreams which mostly weren't realized.

But aside from loyalty to the Jewish Fighting Organization, aside from general loyalty, there were also secondary loyalties. I know, for example, that the primary loyalty of at least some Bundists was to their movement. That is, they waited for what Feiner would say. But they weren't all like that. I think that Marek Edelman's first loyalty was to the Jewish Fighting Organization. I would sometimes hear Adolf Berman say: *"Haynt iz gezesn der tsentral komitet fun po'alei zion.* (Today the central committee of Po'alei Zion met.)" There weren't any Jews, but *der tsentral komitet fun po'alei zion* existed!

There weren't many from Po'alei Zion Left, except for Wanda Elster and the two Bermans (Adolf and Batya), who were very active. I don't think there were any other prominent activists among the members of Po'alei Zion Left. Berlinski was in hiding; I hadn't seen him since the ghetto and knew only that he was alive. Paula Elster and Eliahu Ehrlich[41] were murdered by Vlassov's soldiers during the Polish Uprising.[42] Hirsh Wasser and his wife Bluma survived.

40. The Bundist anthem, written by S. An-sky.
41. Eliahu Ehrlich: Born in Wyszków; member of Po'alei Zion and ZOB. He fought in the April Uprising in the Central Ghetto and the Brushmakers' Ghetto. Escaped through the sewers and joined a partisan unit near Warsaw. Was killed in the Polish Uprising.
42. André Andreivitch Vlassov (1900–1946): Soviet general. After fighting in the Red Army, he was taken prisoner by the Germans and went over to their side in 1942. He raised

Lipa Bloch was former director of the office of *Keren Kayemet*; I would meet with him occasionally. He had suffered a great catastrophe. His daughter, a wonderful girl, became active in our youth circle in 1940 and was murdered on a train with a youth group on her way to our partisan base in Werbkowice. Up to late 1942, I would meet with Bloch who played a key role in the Jewish Self-Help Organization (YISA).

In late 1942, after the Great *Aktsia*, when everything was topsy-turvy, we still didn't know what was going on. But for Giterman, Bloch, and Guzik, we suddenly became the major force. And prior to September 1942, Bloch requested a meeting with us and asked what to do. Giterman did the same. The leadership was asking what to do! I avoided meeting Bloch, after September 1942, after I learned about the tragedy of his daughter.

Dr. Shimon Gottesman wasn't born in Warsaw, but in Galicia.[43] He was active to some extent on the Aryan side of Warsaw. At a certain period we added him to the Jewish National Committee. He also signed a few letters. He visited Israel twice. The first time was many years ago; he came to visit me when I was still living in a hut. The second time he visited was a few months ago, but I didn't see him. I heard from Berman that he had gotten very old. Even then, he wasn't a young man. He must be over eighty by now.

Unfortunately, after the disaster of the bunker on Miła, very few members of Ha-Shomer Ha-Tza'ir were left. In Warsaw, aside from Tosia Altman, there was Esther Fuchs and Abraham Warman,[44] who was murdered by the Germans. Julcia (Esther) came to Israel and went mad. She was the woman courier I've talked about who hid her little sister. She died a few years ago in an insane asylum. Lodzia (Leah Ziberstein) was Tuvia Borzykowski's girlfriend after the war. When they came to Israel, as soon as they got off the plane, they separated. She got married and studied library science; as I recall, she worked in the National Library in Jerusalem.

I heard that she left Israel two or three years ago or went on some government mission; at any rate, she's not in Israel now. There was also David Nowodworski who had been a partisan. He was murdered on the

---

an army for them for the so-called "liberation of Russia." He was captured by the Americans in 1946 and returned to the Soviets, who hanged him in 1946.

43. Shimon Gottesman: Attorney from Kraków, representative of the General Zionists on the Jewish National Committee. Survived the war and migrated to Brazil.

44. Abraham Warman: Active in Ha-Shomer Ha-Tza'ir in Lwów, where he was rescued from a death convoy and placed in a concentration camp. He escaped from there and reached Warsaw in September 1943. He lived underground until he was caught by the Germans and shot on May 24, 1944.

way when a whole group tried to get to Hungary. Only a very few of them survived.

As for the letter we sent to Tabenkin and Ya'ari, they had no obligation to write to us, except as a matter of conscience.[45] We signed the letter

45. This is the text of the letter written to Tabenkin, Ya'ari, and Dobkin, dated November 14, 1943:

As we write these words, we do not believe we shall ever see each other again. Of three and a half million Jews, about 200,000 now remain. When this letter is received, it is almost certain that no more than half of them will still be alive. Just last week, the camps in Trawniki, Poniatów, and Lublin were destroyed. About 40,000 Jews were murdered.

You will not understand or believe our torments, for thus is the situation. For someone from London or Tel Aviv to understand it, he would have to have a sick imagination. All Jewish centers of life have been wiped off the face of the earth. Their inhabitants met their death in the slaughter houses of Treblinka, Sobibor, Belzec, and Auschwitz.

So that a trace shall remain of those who fought the enemy with weapons, we write to you of the final days of the Polish Halutz and its youth federation—Dror (Frayhayt–He-Halutz Ha-Tza'ir), Ha-Shomer Ha-Tza'ir, Akiba, Gordonia. The history of He-Halutz in this period is to a large extent also the history of the Jewish Fighting Organization. At the beginning of the liquidation operation, hundreds of our cells existed in places of Jewish settlement.

In Warsaw, there were five kibbutzim—two of them on the Aryan side—in Grochów and Czerniaków; in Częstochowa—three; in Białystok—two. There were also kibbutzim in Vilna, Zarki, Ostrowiec, Hrubieszów, and Będzin. In addition, we had a great many places for seasonal agricultural training.

Our kibbutzim later became cells of active resistance in all the cities. If armed resistance at the beginning of the liquidation of the ghetto—in July to September 1942—was so small, that is not our fault. Various factors, both external and internal, had an influence here. And if the second expulsion in January 1943, and especially the final liquidation in Warsaw in April 1943, and afterward the liquidation in Białystok, Vilna, and Częstochowa, became legends of our war of liberation—they were based on the heroic war of the Jewish Fighting Organization, which arose in our movement in the blood of almost all our people—both commanders and soldiers.

We organized the branches of the Jewish Fighting Organization in other cities from Warsaw. Our emissaries organized the youth for battle everywhere and they themselves participated in those battles and were killed in them. The list we send includes only the names of the central activists who were killed in the war against the occupier . . . [A list of those killed is included.]

This list is not complete. May their memory be preserved in your heart.

We are still cooperating with the Jewish National Committee and with the Coordinating Committee of the Jewish National Committee and the Bund.

In 1942, fifty to sixty of our comrades went to Slovakia, where they encountered the liquidation operation. Some of them escaped to Hungary. Did any of them reach Eretz Israel? We are trying to send a group of Jews to Hungary. Dr. Schwartzbart wrote us about a contact with Budapest. Can we expect tangible help from there?

When you read this letter, please don't think that our spirit is broken or that we are desperate. We are simply looking soberly at the inevitable fate. We know that you would have done everything to save us. And we also know that you are power-

"Zivia and Yitzhak." We who survived considered ourselves responsible for our brothers in Ha-Shomer Ha-Tza'ir in Warsaw.

One of those who survived was Yakov Putermilch who was young and free then. His sister was an active member of Ha-Shomer Ha-Tza'ir. Not many of us were left either. We had five units of fighters and a few of us survived: Zivia, Tuvia, me. Who else? Havka Folman wound up in Auschwitz and survived, as we know.

The members of Ha-Shomer Ha-Tza'ir who were in the Warsaw Ghetto and survived include Julcia, Lodzia, Yakowak. It turns out they had members left who did important jobs after the war. They were no different from us—not many of us survived either. Yanka (Yonat Sened) was still a child in the ghetto. Yisrael Gutman, the historian, was also one of the young people. Ha-Shomer Ha-Tza'ir seemed to have been wiped out in the Uprising. Their central members were killed. Even fewer members of Gordonia survived. But a few did, like Soyke Erlichman; Yakov Feigenblat[46] of Gordonia was killed in Aryan Warsaw, as I recall, in January 1944, in our great collapse, along with Gitta Kwonki,[47] who was hiding with him. It seems to me that five people—a whole group—fell at one time, after defending themselves. Another of our members, Sara Biderman, survived and came to Israel. And there was also Zvi Edelstein, Lutka Ottikar's (Manen) brother, who was burned in the celluloid factory.[48]

---

less. It will be easier for us to die knowing that a free world will arise and with the faith that Eretz Israel will rise as a homeland for the Hebrew people.

Yours,

Zivia (Lubetkin)

Yitzhak (Zuckerman)

P.S. Eliezer Geller left for a camp for foreign citizens in Bergen (Bergen-Belsen) near Hanover. We have no information from there. Tell Ahuva Lubetkin in Ben-Shemen and Sara Zuckerman in Ramat Ha-Kovesh that we are alive. (Reprinted in Neustadt 1947:151–153)

46. Yakov Feigenblat (1919–1944): Born in Warsaw. Active in the Ghetto underground and commanded a Gordonia unit in the Többens-Schultz area. Got to the Aryan side on April 29 and, a few weeks later, went with a large group of partisans to Wysków Forest. He was one of the few who returned to Warsaw in early 1944. Was caught by the Gestapo along with two comrades in their hiding place and killed in an armed conflict.

47. Gitta Kwonki: Born in Łódz. Came to Warsaw in 1940. Served in the ZOB as a spy and fought in the Gordonia unit. Was the treasurer of the ZOB and was entrusted with money and valuables confiscated by the organization. Escaped to the Aryan side and was sent with a group of partisans to Wyszków Forest, but was forced to return to Warsaw (accompanied by Yakov Feigenblat) because of illness. Apparently they were denounced and caught by the Gestapo in their hiding place. They defended themselves and were killed in the battle. She was about twenty-four years old.

48. Zvi Edelstein (1922–1943): Born in Warsaw. Served in Hanoch Gutman's Dror unit in the Brushmakers' area; but a day before the Uprising, he went to visit his sister in the

Apparently he was one of the Többens-Schultz people who came out through the sewers to Ogrodowa Street.

And there were others like Rivka Moszkowicz (Zosia of Dror), who was killed on August 1, 1944, in the street when the Germans opened fire in all directions. She took off a ring and asked someone to deliver it to me. But I never got it. She was Tuvia's girlfriend at the time.

Dr. Inka Szwajger was active on the Aryan side of Warsaw. She was a physician, one of the group in the hospital on Czyste. I don't know if she finished her doctor's degree at that time. At any rate, she was working in the hospital. She married a gentile in Poland who was a very sick man. As I recall, she was about to immigrate to the United States.[49]

Of the members of Po'alei Zion–Z.S., Leyzer Levin and his little boy were with us, and so were Stefan Grajek and Yohanan Morgenstern, who came out through the sewer. The latter remained with a few other people on Ogrodowa. They didn't join the group that went to Łomianki Woods and called me to find a place for them. Even before our people got out of the Central Ghetto through the sewers, another group had come out to Ogrodowa Street. I don't know if it was because of a denunciation or some other reason, but they were discovered and killed on the spot.

As I recall, Sara, Abraham Granach's girlfriend, was with him at Ogrodowa. The women weren't killed there, just the men. I don't know exactly how things happened. One of those who was there, if I'm not mistaken, was Kozinski, a member of Po'alei Zion from Łódz. And I don't know how he got out of there. I met him a few times and I got documents for him. That was before the Polish Uprising. I learned that he broke down after the war and decided to stop being a Jew. He didn't convert to Christianity but he did cut himself off. I looked for him because I knew he and his wife had survived. But he told me he didn't want any contact. Incidentally, that's not an isolated incident. For example, I had a teacher of German and Polish in Vilna who lived in Łódz after the war, Katzowna (i.e., Miss Katz), and old spinster. One day, in 1945, I learned that she had survived, but I didn't know any other details. I sent word to Katzowna (I imagined she remembered me) that I would help her (by then I was able to help), and that I wanted her to let me know if she needed anything. She replied that she didn't want anything to do with Jews.

Yosef Sak was in hiding, and so was his wife Hela, who was the active one in the family, and their only daughter Janka (Yonat Sened). I would come to them every week or two, just to be sociable. He was no longer

---

Többens-Schultz area and remained there, fighting in Benjamin Wald's unit. Got to the Aryan side, but was killed by the Germans on May 6, 1943.

49. See Adina Szwajger 1990.

young (he was one of the veteran activists of Po'alei Zion–Z.S.) and I
didn't want to use him. I was younger and had the patience to listen to
his advice. I would come to him and tell him things I thought I could tell
him, mostly general things. With the outbreak of the Polish Uprising, he
came to us at Leszno 18, to the apartment that had turned into a public
place; when we joined the Uprising in the Old City, Leszno was still in the
hands of the rebels. When we joined the rebels, Sak joined too and formed
the Jewish fighting group in the Old City. He stayed with us only a short
time; Janka remained with her mother and he lived alone.

The Polish Uprising began in August 1944. During the Uprising, when
the Poles freed the prisoners in the Gesiówka jail in Warsaw (hundreds
of Jews from Hungary and Czechoslovakia were freed there in an attack
by the AK), the Poles didn't know what to do with them and those Jews
had a very hard time. They were saved by the AK, who would send them
to the barricades as cannon fodder against the German tanks. I got
interested in their fate and asked Sak to deal with civilian matters, including their case. He contacted the AK and the AL; most of the Jews
were under the AK command but for a very short time. The AL offered
us generous help.

I would sometimes participate in staff meetings of the AL and since I
didn't believe in the success of the Uprising, I would dare express my
skepticism to them. We—that is, the rebels—still held our apartment at
Leszno 18, which housed the archive and our armory, and where there
was also an excellent bunker. It occurred to me to set up bases in a few
places. I told them of our extraordinary bunker on Leszno Street and I
suggested moving a few Polish and Jewish women there and making our
base in that house. I thought we could retreat from there and leave
Warsaw if necessary, since surrender was out of the question for us.
According to our information, that area was no longer populated, but it
wasn't yet conquered by the Germans. I thought it was a good holding
position.

The decision was made to establish an AL rebel base at Leszno 18. We
sent a group of our comrades there, including Kazik, Stefan Grajek, and
Irka Gelblum, as well as Yosef Sak, Tuvia Borzykowski, Felek Rajszczak's
daughter, and Marysia. The idea was to move people who weren't vital
to the war to hold the base at Leszno, which we would use for retreat if
necessary, and, meanwhile, for preserving the archive and the armory.

I left with Nestek Matywiecki (an AL escort) and an armed escort to
accompany the group to the place where they could go to Leszno; I left
them and returned to my own base. I must note that Kazik was a fighter
and was very vital to us, but he knew the bunker and the way to it, and
we relied on him to lead the group and organize it on the spot. When we
left, I promised to visit them that night. We didn't imagine we would be

cut off. That was in the thick of the fight and that very night we were cut off. What happened to that group is a fascinating tale.[50]

I have already told about the Folman family. The oldest son, Wolf Folman, was one of our first partisans. He was killed in a partisan unit near Kielce. The story of that family is like the feat of "Hannah and her Seven Sons."[51] Havka is the only one left. The mother died in Israel. It was a splendid family and deserves an epic! The children and the mother—a fighting family!

Wedek's (Wolf's) wife and child, who was born in the ghetto, lived in Zolibórz. Wedek went off to fight and left his wife and son and mother. He went off to a partisan unit and there he fell. His son, Rafi, is a doctor. Now in Canada.

Hela Rufeisen-Schüpper is related to Shmuel Rufeisen, a Jew who came from Vilna; originally a member of Akiba, he later became a priest.[52] I heard about him after the war, when he was in a monastery in Kraków. I knew him in Poland; we wrote to each other and we were friendly. He answered my questions. He took the initiative, writing me from the monastery in Kraków. We became closer in the early 1950s, when he was still in the monastery in Poland and I had moved to Israel, when I was working on the *Book of the Ghetto Wars*.[53] We got a few letters from him, and I thought they were very interesting. Later, I realized he was Hela Rufeisen-Schüpper's brother-in-law and his life story intersected somewhere with ours. The story has many variations. There's the story written by Hillel Zeidel, who knew him in Vilna.[54] And there's the story by Yudke Helman from Shlomo Harhas.[55]

Rufeisen himself didn't write about the Jewish part of his life; others did. At any rate, to know how the Jews felt about him, you should know that the Jews who lived in the house before he warned them to escape from the ghetto (in Mir, Byelorussia), gave him a model of the house with a dedication as a gift. It's not a big model. When he was in the monastery (in Haifa), I asked him to give it to us or let us make a copy of it for the Ghetto Fighter's Museum and we had the original for a few years. Then

50. See Kazik's description of this episode in Kazik 1984:118.

51. Hannah and her Seven Sons: A story in Maccabbees II, chapter 7, of seven brothers and their mother seized by Antiochus IV Epiphanes, and commanded to eat pork as proof of their loyalty to the king. Encouraged by their mother in their refusal, each was put to death before her eyes. Famous story in Jewish martyrology.

52. Samuel Rufeisen (Father Daniel): Born in Zivietz. He came to Vilna after the German occupation and worked in the Jewish resistance and partisan movements there. Sheltered in a monastery, he converted to Christianity and currently lives in a monastery near Haifa. (See Yuri Suhl 1975:246–252.)

53. Yitzhak Zuckerman and Moshe Basok 1947.

54. Hillel Zeidel 1973.

55. Shlomo Harhas on S. Rufeisen in Zuckerman and Basok 1947:480.

the priests, monks, and nuns concluded it would be a great honor for them if the model were in the monastery. We made a copy of it and he couldn't tell the original from the copy. But I let him choose and he took the original and left the copy for our exhibit. As far as I'm concerned, in his feeling for the Jews, he's more Jewish than many rabbis. When I get together with him, we don't talk about religion or faith, and he's like one of us. I count him among the victims of the Holocaust.

Rufeisen's crisis originated in the Holocaust, like Kosinski of Łódz, who ran away and held out until after the war, and only then did his crisis occur. The same with me—if not for Eretz Israel, I would probably have sunk into an abyss or turned into a chronic drunk or committed suicide. I think I would have chosen drunkenness. Israel saved me.

Up until the Polish Uprising, there were countless episodes, day after day. It's enough to browse through Berman's archive, even though I haven't gone over all of it. Every sentence is a dramatic episode, and I haven't even touched on those things. Memory is choosy by nature. I think I have a good memory, and yet, after reading some of the letters I realized that memory has a natural selection. Even the most dramatic things remained on the fringes of memory if I didn't experience them personally or if they were extremely general. As soon as I pick up a piece of paper, the incident immediately appears in my mind's eye. Jews are murdered— that was a daily event. But suddenly in my mind's eye I see Germans wanting to kill me. My life must have been very hard.

In my mind's eye, I see fascinating incidents. You could list them by areas of operation. I divided the material in Berman's archive into eight areas of operation: (1) operations of material assistance, helping people to live; (2) apartments for hiding; (3) preparing forged documents; (4) saving and helping children, including health and medical aid; (5) contact with Jewish partisans; (6) contact with and help of Jews in the camps; (7) contact with the outside world; (8) contact with the Polish underground (with the two Polish undergrounds).

There was also the episode of contact with the ghettoes. By 1943, there were camps. But there was a period, even in 1943, when there were still ghettoes: Będzin, Częstochowa. I intended to search for remnants in the cities where uprisings took place or where there was still some Jewish life, saving people who fell into the hands of the Gestapo. For example, there was even the case of Felek (Rajszczak) who asked and begged us to save him (in a letter in Berman's archive)—and we did. And we also have to include in the list the war against the blackmailers and the acquisition of weapons for the camps—and not only for self-defense. We foresaw the Polish Uprising that ultimately erupted, and I collected quite an arsenal for it. Sometimes we acquired weapons in conjunction with the AL. I had an extraordinary hiding place at Leszno 18, which burned down one day;

and I also slowly built an important archive. Berman wasn't the only one who did archival work; the Jewish Fighting Organization also had an archive—I took care of that, moving the archive with me from one apartment to another. In terms of quantity, my archive was much bigger than Berman's. Mine had all the contacts with the cities and camps. In the ghetto, I also had contact with Ringelblum (he also spent time on the Aryan side), who was executed in March 1944, after he was found in the bunker on Grójecka Street. Berman met with him on the Aryan side.

The stories of Tuvia Borzykowski, Adolf Berman, Wladka, and Jonas Turkow are on the Aryan side; Turkow's book is especially interesting.[56] He underwent the hardest experiences on the Aryan side. There's also an interesting literature in Polish on these subjects.

As for Shoshana Gzęda, who was later the wife of Moshe Kliger in Israel, we didn't know what happened to her until after the war. She was one of the intelligentsia, a student of our Gymnasium in the ghetto. In 1946, when I was in Warsaw, I suddenly got a telegram from Paris, and one day she showed up. The meeting was replete with both kisses and blows; she really slugged me—kissing and slugging went together with her. In subsequent conversations with her, I realized that a chapter of her life was completely erased from her memory. What happened to her? How? Because of what crisis or experience did that happen? I can't explain it. This is what we knew.

The Great *Aktsia* began on July 22, 1942. The last issue of *Yediyes* also appeared at that time. Shoshana, a student of sixteen or seventeen, was one of those who distributed the newspaper in the Warsaw Ghetto. Her father was a concierge in one of the buildings. I still remember my lead article in *Yediyes*; I keep the issue with me. She took the papers to distribute, according to a list of names she had. She went past her father's building, found out he had been taken to the *Umschlagplatz*, and rushed there. The German gendarme started asking who she was (they weren't yet taking young people). When she put her hand in her pocket to take out her document, a copy of the newspaper slipped out. He picked up the newspaper and started investigating: he took two Jewish policemen and demanded from each one separately to translate for him what was written, so they couldn't fool him. After they translated, she was taken to Pawiak. The wife of Yosef Jaszunski was also arrested the same day and she told me details she remembered about Pawiak. They identified Shoshana as a Pole and took her to Maidanek. We wanted to keep track of her, but she disappeared. She was shuttled back and forth to many camps and, after she was liberated, a lot of things vanished from her memory. She didn't return to Warsaw. She went to Paris from Germany in early 1947.

56. Turkow 1969.

A whole chapter of what she had gone through sank into oblivion and was lost to her and to us.

Food was one of the hardest problems on our agenda, even for people like the tenants of our apartment on Komitetowa, later on Pańska, and afterward on Leszno. Because if the landlady began buying large quantities of food from a baker or a shopkeeper, people began suspecting her, that something wasn't right. And after all, some food always had to be bought in the stores. The Polish landlord had to continue buying the normal quantities in his store, and the rest of the things somewhere else every time, or in the market, so as not to arouse suspicion. Even two additional rolls indicated another person in the house and was sometimes a cause of denunciation or a mishap. Bernard Goldstein gives a detailed description of the apartment at Leszno 18; he tells of one blocked wall at the entrance, which included a big hiding place that could accomodate ten people.[57] There was also an archive there and an arsenal. And Goldstein tells of Marysia Feinmesser (whose Jewish name was Bracha), who married Zygmunt Warman.

Dr. Inka Szwajger and Marysia Feinmesser lived in the apartment at Miodowa 24. The apartment at Leszno 18 was registered in the name of Marysia Sawicka, the gentile, one of the two sisters, who moved to Leszno as a seamstress. The wall of the hiding place was built by Haim Ellenbogen and the Pole Władek Swietochowski. I was there when they put up that wall. The device was built on our initiative, not by the Bundists, but for the ZOB. One of those who knew about the building was Benjamin Miedzyrzecki (Meed), who walked around the house during the construction. It was hard to bring in materials and take out dirt; and, every evening, Marysia would go down to church, as if to pray, and buy food in the nearby store. When we went to the city in the morning, we would distribute the tasks and everyone would have to bring various foods. Goldstein tells about a store at Leszno 13, but I remember that the address was Leszno 18. We wouldn't buy all the food we needed in one store, but would always divide the purchases among various stores. Kazik and I were both responsible for making purchases.

The entrance to the hiding place wasn't from the wall but from the eastern side, through the oven. The oven went along the eastern wall, and you entered the hideout through it. It was a good hideout covered by the

57. According to Bernard Goldstein 1961:219: "It was a cheery, spacious apartment of three rooms, with a blind wall facing the Evangelical church. Parallel to this wall we built a second solid wall, providing a hiding place large enough to accomodate as many as ten people. Such a major construction operation required large quantities of building material, as well as a great deal of hammering and the removal of debris; it was difficult to do secretly. The work was carried on under the pretext that Marisha was putting in a bathroom in honor of her marriage and her new position in life."

wall. It wasn't that way on Komitetowa, where the hideout was made of wood, and if anyone had knocked on the wall, he would have noticed that it wasn't natural and was newly built in an old house. At Leszno, however, the wall was made of bricks. On the outer, blocked side of the house, it faced the church. This was a "blind" wall, without windows.

Apartments and hiding places were one of the hardest problems. There never were enough apartments, and some apartments were "burned" from time to time and had to be evacuated; all the apartments our members inhabited on the Aryan side had to have what was called a *Malina* (that is, a camouflaged hideout). In general, wherever Jews hid, either with Poles or anywhere else, there was some kind of camouflaged hideout. If the person didn't look Polish, he needed some kind of *Malina* because neighbors and strangers would come into the apartment. (Incidentally, no one knows for sure the origin of the word *Malina*. Some think it comes from thieves' slang. The antisemite Pritze published a dictionary of underworld slang to prove that thieves used Hebrew words, and the word *Malina* apparently comes from the Hebrew word, *M'luna*, a place to stay overnight; a shack.) The Jew would have to pay the gentile whose house he was living in for building the hideout; in some cases, the apartment was in the basement; you couldn't build a *Malina* in every apartment. When the Polish landlords would go to work, the Jews couldn't be in the apartment, since the pipes in the house carried voices to the floors above and below. A conversation next to a water pipe, for example, could reveal the inhabitants of the apartment. Some couldn't build because they didn't have money, and sometimes they couldn't build because the apartment wasn't suitable. Some apartments had niches, where two or three people could hide for a while. The difference between the small *Malina* at Komitetowa 4 and the *Malina* at Leszno 18 was like day and night. At Leszno 18, people could even sit down. I don't think our comrades had to go into the hiding place a lot. Only when a stranger rang the bell would they all go into the *Malina*; but that doesn't mean there were a lot of strangers visiting. Sometimes, someone would come from city hall or would come about the electricity, but no more than that. Unlike other places (Pańska, for example), we tried to keep that apartment "clean." Close friends who walked around outside used two nails stuck in the entry, which rang by connecting them with a coin. Each of us kept a metal coin; the bell only rang inside and didn't make any noise outside. The door would be opened and the people would come in.

The apartment on Leszno was safer than the others and was built for safety. The landlady generally didn't entertain guests because she herself had moved there not long before and didn't know anybody in the neighborhood. She was a Pole, our friend. Until 1940, this apartment had been in the ghetto. The people weren't generally neighborly and the residents didn't think they were obliged to do anything more than say hello to their neighbors. I walked around more freely at Leszno 18 than anywhere else because it was a new apartment. I lived there, even though the address wasn't on my documents. I was always registered at Belwederska; only the local people recognized me.

We had contacts with the craftsmen who built *Malinas*. I said that putting all the Poles into one "pot" not only does them an injustice, but also violates the truth. For there were different kinds of people among the Poles; for example, that Polish woman who had the apartment on Leszno and many others. There were many gentiles who were loyal to us. Most of them weren't paid for their work. Some people could be counted on just as much as the most loyal Jew. None of them hinted even delicately at his very difficult situation, or asked for help. The construction required the assistance of skilled electricians, builders, carpenters, and other experts; and there weren't many Jewish builders. And if I mention Jews like Benjamin (Meed) or other Jews who built, they were "auxiliaries." The experts were always Poles—except for that Kutsher I mentioned who was himself a builder. Construction wasn't a Jewish profession in the city, and most of the builders were loyal Poles. Our landlady, Marysia, was a member of PPS; I think she was close to the right wing, WRN (the PPS faction that cooperated with the rightist Polish underground); but she ceased all Polish conspiratorial activity so as not to endanger her Jewish friends. Her older sister, Anna Wachalska, did the same.

We met them through the Bund. The first time I met the two women was that morning when Kazik and Zygmunt Fryderych came to Aryan Warsaw through the sewers. They informed me immediately of their arrival and I went to the apartment and found them washing; and there I saw those two women and Zimra (Zosia), the daughter of a Bundist and a former student in our school who was hiding in their apartment. The Bund had contacts with groups of laborers on the Aryan side. Celek Celeminski writes that there were traitors in PPS circles among the people he was in hiding with.[58] I read that book a long time ago, but I remember what he said. I think such cases were exceptions. In general, the people who devoted themselves to helping and saving Jews were fine people. What was decisive with Marysia and Anna was personal acquaintance, since they couldn't have cared if I was a Bundist or not. In time, during and after the war, we became close personal friends. We brought Marysia to Israel and entertained her here. But our contacts began through the Bund and the PPS.

I said that we thought that almost none of the members of Ha-Shomer Ha-Tza'ir were left on the Aryan side, since most of them were killed in

58. Yakov Celeminski 1965.

the ghetto and on the way out. What existed at that time on the Aryan side was Dror, Po'alei Zion–Z.S., Po'alei Zion Left, and the Bund. Some Ha-Shomer Ha-Tza'ir and Dror groups went to the forests even from the ghetto and some were on the Aryan side from before; but only a few of them survived. But the Bund had a lot more people on the Aryan side since they had made arrangements for them before the Ghetto Uprising. Some Bundists had never even gone into the ghetto, like Leon Feiner or Salo Fiszgrunt. They may have come to visit once or twice, but that's all. Władka tells about discovering an apartment we had prepared in advance. When we came to the Łomianki Woods, the Bundists took their fighters out and settled them in apartments. But we couldn't put all our fighters in apartments at that time.

We brought some members of Ha-Shomer Ha-Tza'ir from the forest and hid them near Okęcie. We took out whomever we could, but we couldn't take many. The closest groups of partisans were those near Częstochowa and at the Bug, in Wyszków. After the war, we found out that the Jewish partisans, with whom we had no contact, were even murdered by members of the Gwardia Ludowa. One of the most serious charges against Moczar, one of the postwar Communist leaders in Poland, was that he was mixed up in the murder of Jews in his partisan groups; but it must be emphasized that, in general, the Armia Ludowa treated Jews very well, although there were aberrations. We have to distinguish between the leadership of the Armia Ludowa, who treated us—both as Jews and as fighters—splendidly, and the men in the field, all kinds of Poles, whose attitude toward Jews wasn't monolithic. I should add that the PPR, a group of idealists, wasn't the same as the total military arm, which had all kinds of people. There weren't only Communists in the Armia Ludowa; it was a popular organization. They enlisted in the underground not only those with party cards, but every man who wanted to fight in their ranks. Initially the organization was called the Gwardia Ludowa; then they changed the name to Armia Ludowa, which indicates the expansion of the ranks. One of the fighters in the forest who survived, Yakov, a member of Ha-Shomer Ha-Tza'ir, comes to mind.[59]

There was one fellow from Ha-Shomer Ha-Tza'ir, Yardiv, and the word was that he was killed. I think he chose to get out of Jewish activity for personal reasons. One day, I was on Marszałkowska Street on business and I met him. We went to drink some ersatz coffee and then left the place. Suddenly I saw gendarmes approaching (it was a routine

59. [Zivia adds: Only a few people participated in operations on the Aryan side, only those who looked Aryan were fit for operations, like Yitzhak (Zuckerman) and others, not members of Ha-Shomer Ha-Tza'ir, except for Tuvia (Tadek) Shayngut, who was killed on Washington Street.]

sweep) and we separated. I decided to go toward the gendarmes and he went in the opposite direction. I did that because they were very close by and I didn't want to look as if I was running away. They checked my document, saw that I worked on the railroad, and let me go. I never saw him again.

There was also Yakov Feigenblat of Gordonia, a partisan who fought in the Wyszków Forests, but later returned to Warsaw and lived in the home of the Pole Jablonski. In general, the partisans continued to function until the Liberation. And they were liberated before us by the Red Army. The whole story of the partisans hasn't yet been written, except for Haim Frimmer's book. It was only after the war that he told of their liberation and rescue; we stayed under German occupation until January 1945, and the partisans were liberated in the great Red Army offensive, even before August 1944. By August 1, the Red Army was at the gates of Warsaw. That is, their liberation was half a year before ours.

When they returned from the forest, Haim Frimmer told me what they had gone through, how they had stayed alive: they joined the Soviet partisans and worked with them. One day, after August 1944, they were joined by a group of Ukrainians who had escaped from Treblinka after the Polish Uprising. Our people knew who these newcomers were, but they were afraid to say a word for fear of the Ukrainians who were involved in the murder of Jews at Treblinka.

As the Red Army approached, the liberated partisans became happier and then Haim Frimmer (or Aharon Carmi) saw that one of the Soviet commanders in the liberation army was a Jew. They told him about the composition of that unit and the identity of the Ukrainians in it. The officer said: "That can be checked." He assembled the Ukrainians and "checked"—without a trial, he executed them! That story should be verified; it's too bad we didn't continue to hear what happened to those people from the Ghetto Uprising to their liberation because we don't have details about that group—things happened during the liberation of the areas they were hiding in.[60]

Aharon Carmi's story of how he was integrated into the militia after the Liberation is also interesting. (I still remember him in the uniform of the UB, the Polish Security Service.) That's the story of our fighters in the partisan unit. And that's not the whole story of Jews in partisan units. We're talking only about the partisans connected with us. Some of them, for example, those in Koniecpol, hid because they could have been murdered, and ceased partisan activity because of the Polish hostility. Apparently, the murderers weren't members of NSZ, but of AK who were

60. Yakov Putermilch affirms this story in his book *In Fire and Snow*, 157–158. Putermilch was in the group of partisans who fought in the Wyszków Forests.

wandering around Wyszków.[61] The only ones who survived were those in contact with the Soviet partisans. But these were only a few individuals. And that was probably not a solution for hundreds or thousands.

Even though I didn't believe in it, we made many efforts to join the partisans. I had to construct a scale of priorities: if I had the choice between staying in Poniatów and Trawniki or going to the forest, which I didn't believe in, I would certainly have chosen the forest. In this context, I should mention that the AK promised to set up contact points for us and didn't keep their promise. After the war, it turned out that the AL partisan units couldn't have incorporated many people either. I'm not saying that dozens or hundreds of Jews didn't join, but it wasn't a solution for escapees from the camps. Not even for those who escaped from Treblinka, most of whom were killed not only by the Germans, but also by Polish villagers.

As for contact with the camps, as I recall, we wrote in one of our letters about a number of camps we had contact with: Skrzysko, two camps in Częstochowa, Hasag,[62] Poniatów, Trawniki, Będzin, Majden-Tatarski near Lublin, Płaszów. Committees were set up in all these camps. In Poniatów and Trawniki, there were core groups and head-quarters of the Jewish Fighting Organization. We also sent a few weapons there, but it wasn't enough, and things didn't happen exactly as we had foreseen. You couldn't defend yourself in the huts because the Germans would set fire to them and their inhabitants. As for the possibilities of rescue and escape, that was always only for individuals, like the incident of the messenger from Slovakia who came to rescue only Zivia and me. After all, there were thousands of Jews! All those responses were only for individuals. I didn't have an answer for the masses; the same goes for arrangements on the Aryan side—and that was the best we could obtain, even though there were casualties every single day. There was no place for Jews in the Polish forest. Yet a few Jews who fought did stay there. Crossing the border was only for individuals. As I said, there was no solution for the masses.

Before the Polish Uprising, we estimated that there were 20,000 Jews altogether hiding in and around Warsaw. We knew 12,000 addresses, although a Jew may well have gotten assistance from two sources at the same time. In the underground, you couldn't clarify the necessary details with any certainty. Berman writes about 6,000 people he knew about directly. There were also Bundists and the groups of ZEGOTA

61. NSZ–Narodowe Siły Zbrojne, the armed national forces, a Polish Fascist organization, joined the AK in March 1944.

62. Hasag (Hugo Schneider Aktiengesellschaft): A forced labor camp at Skrzysko-Kamiennas for the manufacture of munitions, where several thousand Jews were employed and died. (See Ainsztein 1974:818–822, for details.)

and the various forms of help people got, from 250 Złotys (usually up to 500 Złotys). In addition, there was a small group that needed apartments. But we know there was contact with 12,000 Jews who got help from us. Everything was topsy turvy during the Polish Uprising. We tried twice—before and after the Polish Uprising—to reorganize our welfare operation. But we didn't get to the people; we don't even know how many survived the Polish Uprising. After that, everyone lived on his own. When the Poles left Warsaw, the Germans stayed and searched for Jews. Many Jews, like many Poles, were killed in bombings. But many Jews were also murdered by AK soldiers; even in our own neighborhood.

That's the story of Jurek Grossberg, Luba Gewisser's boyfriend, who was killed by the AK at the start of the Polish Uprising, when many Jews thought salvation had come and left their hideouts. Jurek had a gun, he shot out the door of his hideout, and was immediately picked up by AK members on Komitetowa. He tried to call on Hubert Kaminski, but his captors ignored his explanations and killed him.

As for contact with the ghettoes: we sent a messenger to Łódz in 1944. By that year, there were no longer ghettoes. In 1943, when the Warsaw Ghetto no longer existed, there were still ghettoes in Częstochowa; Jewish Będzin no longer existed. A joint ghetto was established from the two cities of Będzin and Sosnowiec, in between the two places.

We didn't have contact with Łódz either. Only in 1944 did we send a messenger to Łódz, who contacted his Polish comrades. The only one who had contact with the Aryan side in Łódz was Rumkowski. We sent money and letters, but we didn't know who survived. Near Kraków was the Plaszów Ghetto, which was subsequently a camp shifting back and forth from a concentration camp to a labor camp. After the Uprising, we kept in touch with the ghettoes in Częstochowa and Będzin-Sosnowiec. In Sosnowiec, there was an arm of the Jewish Fighting Organization, and we removed fighters from there in late 1942 and brought them to Warsaw (Berl Broyde, for example); these included members of Ha-Shomer Ha-Tza'ir, whom I managed to see one day before the Polish Uprising began. These were partisans who returned to Warsaw. We got them a place and I provided them with dollars because we sensed the coming of the Polish Uprising and didn't know what tomorrow would bring. We heard cannons and I remember riding in a rickshaw to Okęcie Airport, and I even remember the apartment I visited. I gave them money and left them. Later that area wasn't taken by the rebels at all, and as a result, the Germans discovered them and killed them in the bunker. Undoubtedly there were more comrades there, but not one of the people we knew survived. As far as we know, the people there couldn't have been active in the Uprising. They were hiding. But there was one person from Łódz who was active.[63] When all is said and done, Ha-Shomer Ha-Tza'ir had just as many activists as we did.

One of the last of the members of Ha-Shomer Ha-Tza'ir to arrive was Abraham Warman who came from Lwów and, because he looked so puny, I didn't use him as a courier. His Polish was excellent, but I wouldn't risk him or myself.

We didn't know details about Białystok, but we learned from the Poles that there was an uprising there. I knew our comrades were in big trouble from Mordechai Tennenbaum's letter.

As for the search for survivors hiding in and around Warsaw, some people came to Warsaw in time, but we didn't know about them. Some of them were fighters or members of the movements. As for the search for Jews in general, I remember one incident: I was riding on the tram. Next to me on the platform stood a woman. I looked at her and was sure she was a Jew and was very miserable and depressed. I went on riding, since I wanted to see where she got off so I could talk to her. When she got off the trolley, I followed her. She hastened her step, thinking I was a blackmailer. I started talking to her in Yiddish, but when I saw she was terrified, I left her alone. I simply wanted to help. And we could have offered first aid at least. But she ran away. That was a chance encounter, right after the Polish Uprising. We knew that people had come out of their hiding places. Afterward, we learned that even during the Ghetto Uprising, people were sent to the Aryan side through the sewers.

In a burned-out abandoned bunker, refugees from the ghetto found a pile of potatoes scorched from the fire. Every potato was like a lump of coal. I kept one of them to show at the meeting of the Jewish Coordinating Committee. It was a rainy autumn Sunday, and we were still living at Komitetowa 4. I usually went out without a hat or coat, but because it was raining and it was Sunday, I put on my coat and my formal hat. So as not to get wet, I turned up the collar of my coat. Suddenly I heard footsteps behind me and a man appeared opposite me and started talking to me. I asked him with whom I had the honor to be speaking and, instead of answering, he took out a gun and gestured to me to go in the gate. I entered and found a group of four or five armed men waiting for me. They took me into the staircase, searched me, and found money, which I always carried with me, and the scorched potato.

I should add only that I wasn't accompanied by anyone that time. I usually felt safe when I was accompanied by someone. When walking around was dangerous, Kazik and Stefan Sawicki accompanied me. That was also the case when we searched for sewer openings. The blackmailers gave me back the burned potato and even left me a little bit for travel.

63. Leah Zilberstein.

Ultimately I got to the meeting after a long trip and after I confirmed that I didn't have a "tail."

Those blackmailers searched my clothes and, aside from money, they also found letters from one of the camps, that I was bringing to the meeting. I didn't usually carry such material on me. They examined the letters and found that I was a Jew, but they pulled off my pants to be absolutely sure. I didn't know what kind of blackmailers they were since they were armed. They might have "worked on me" or it could have been a denunciation. At any rate, I didn't have anything to lose. I told them: "Yes, I'm a Jew. Take my money. But if you intend to turn me over to the Gestapo, I'm telling you that I'm not alone in the street and you'll come to a bitter end in twenty-four hours." And they didn't hurt me. They gave me back my trousers and the potato. They told me to wait a few minutes and they disappeared. It wasn't the money, but the humiliation and the insult! I got to the meeting late, but I got there.

This happened close to the house on Komitetowa and I was afraid that the apartment and its inhabitants would be turned in. The next day, I stayed home. That was an isolated misfortune. I was miserably depressed and said I didn't feel well. I told Kazik what happened and told him to go get Netek of the Scouts (who later was killed); I said I was afraid the apartment was exposed and we should walk around and keep our eyes open, at least for a few days; otherwise, we would have to evacuate the apartment. I wanted to see if the blackmailers were still lurking in the area. I walked first, wearing a hat, and they (Kazik and Netek) followed a few steps behind. We agreed that if I approached one of those blackmailers, I would take off my hat as a signal. We walked around the neighborhood like that for hours, but the gang had vanished. I walked around like that until the last minute before curfew. I swear to God I lived in mortal tension until we left Komitetowa, as long as the danger hovered over the whole house. I don't know who those blackmailers were or what they would have done if they had known in advance that I was a Jew. That was one of two incidents.

The second incident happened before that, when I left Hotel Polski and I've already told about that. This time, I recall, we worried about being discovered until December 13, when we moved from Komitetowa to Pańska 5, which, incidentally, was in the same quarter.

But we didn't move from Komitetowa because of what happened to me but because of the blackmail attempt on us through one of the residents of the house, which I described before.

I'll never forget those days, filled with emotional tension. I would go out in the morning; we would eat some bread with margarine or jam and I would go out for the whole day. In the courtyard, a gentile from the house committee would sometimes meet me, and if I could, I would buy him a drink. Kazik would also join us. We didn't join the morning prayers in the courtyard, but I would contribute to the charity fund of the house, and the people knew me. I was always afraid of those blackmailers, but I didn't see them again. Maybe they were scared off by my threats. I didn't have anything to lose in the game with them—they could have finished me off without a witness. But when they saw the material on me, the letters, they apparently were impressed that it wouldn't be a simple robbery. Evidently that was why they left the area. My explanation for the attack was that since I was walking on an autumn day, with my collar turned up, hiding my face, they thought I was a Jew taking advantage of a rainy day to take a walk. But I don't know. Poles didn't walk around in the streets much on Sunday. Some went to church, others stayed home.

There were various kinds of blackmailers, and they can be divided into a few groups. One group worked for the Gestapo. They weren't simple blackmailers; their job was to spy. Apparently they had an agreement with the Gestapo to take part of the loot of their victims or all the property— clothing, money, and so forth. Some blackmailers worked on their own and didn't turn Jews over to the Gestapo. Others would blackmail Jews, extort the very last cent, and then, even if they weren't regular Gestapo agents, they would turn the Jews over to the Gestapo, thus blurring their traces and preventing retaliation. They simply finished off the Jew. There were blackmailers who would "land on" a Jew from time to time, and live off him as long as they could. Some Polish "landlords" took Jews in, from the beginning, to turn them in, and kept them for money. When the Jew's money ran out, if the Pole was decent, he tried to help the Jew. If not, he would throw him out in the street. And, if he was a real bastard, he would turn him over to the Germans.

I don't know of an organization concerned with that. I know the blackmailers worked in gangs, because it was hard for an individual blackmailer to make do. A few groups would come to the same place and poach on each other's territory. You had to be quite an expert to succeed in that trade. And some blackmailers were careful to get the ransom and not the person himself. They saw a Jew as a lemon to be squeezed, and if he didn't have anything, they left him alone. Others turned the Jew over to the Gestapo directly. That was a fresh blow. We tried to work through the Polish underground to end the blackmail. And in fact, they would occasionally issue a death sentence in the most serious cases or when important people were involved. That happened in January 1944, when blackmailers attacked Batya and Adolf Berman and paralyzed their activity. Ultimately, as I recall, the AK executed those blackmailers. But in other cases, no matter how much we appealed to the Polish underground about blackmailers, it didn't help. Once an announcement of a death sentence appeared in the Polish underground press which declared that the sentence had been carried out. It's not correct, that the underground was satisfied with warnings, as Goldstein writes[64]—they also settled accounts with collaborators, who started with Jews and reached another kind of collaboration. There's a difference between saying they didn't fight hard enough against the blackmailers and saying that they didn't carry out any death sentences at all. I am sure some sentences were executed; but that was a drop in the bucket. That is, if they had really wanted to fight them, they could have done more. It was easier to fight the blackmailers than the Germans; but when it came to Jews who fell victim to blackmail, the Polish underground didn't "fly off the handle." For example, Ludwig Landau, the chronicler who published his diary, worked for the AK and was killed by the blackmailers. And other prominent Jews, scientists, who had nothing to do with Jewish life, were murdered by blackmailers or turned over by them to the Gestapo.

In the case of the blackmailers, you have to understand that we had weapons, and we should have pursued them with a special platoon of Jews who looked Aryan; but it wasn't simple. Moreover, when you carry out an armed operation, you have to figure they'll catch you and discover you're a Jew. You can imagine what would happen if they had discovered that Jews killed a Pole. In such a case, the blackmailer isn't a blackmailer anymore, but a Pole; and the Jew isn't just a fighter, but a Jew. We were always aware of that. Moreover, we didn't have a way of retreat. The Polish underground, however, had many possibilities. We didn't have intelligence services, and they did, even though, now and then, we did know something. But they had their people in the police and fire departments, City Hall, and even the Gestapo, whereas we didn't have any connections.

We had male and female couriers. We didn't have many men; I didn't think we should use men as couriers. It was always more convenient to use women. But we decided not to move against the blackmailers.

On Komitetowa, I would see the picture of the Madonna, but I never participated in prayer. I did contribute money. Conceivably, other people in the courtyard weren't strict about observing the ritual either. Our landlady would go out to the yard to pray. We were afraid that one person there suspected us. And in fact, one day the Germans came to that house. That was the only time that, for some reason, my heart told me to go into the hideout. Normally, when someone knocked on the door, I would stay on the scene. Our landlady was ironing at that time and her daughter was with her. For some reason, I thought there had

64. "Several times it [the Polish underground press] printed warnings against the schmaltzovniks [blackmailers], but I did not hear of a single trial or of any punishment being meted out to them" (Goldstein 1961:199).

been a denunciation and that our house on Komitetowa Street was suspect. Instinctively, I went into the hideout. And in fact the Germans did
come in and we heard their voices. There were two rooms, and they also
went into the second room which was ours, and into the kitchen. They
didn't find anyone and they left. It turned out it really was a denunciation. Conditions in the hideout were very hard because, occasionally,
when someone rang the doorbell, we would have to hide and the room
that served as a hiding place was full of fleas. It was arranged behind a
wooden wall, with a bookcase at the opening. (Now and then, I would
buy books and put them on the shelves.) We reinforced the bookcase so
that it wouldn't move, God forbid. At that time, Polish society was given
to religious moods; people went to church a lot. And the Jews who were
disguised as Christians had to play that game too, since all of Polish
society was caught up in it. It would be an exaggeration to say there was
a picture of the Madonna in every courtyard, but people prayed in every
courtyard. I think there was another reason for that: in times of distress,
people seek God; and the Polish people had always been devout Catholics. Moreover, everybody knew that the Germans didn't respect the
church, but the simple people were religious. To go to church on Sunday
was dangerous because the Germans would sometimes trap them there
and take them to Germany or to Auschwitz. Congregating in church
endangered anyone who participated. So people prayed in courtyards—
naturally, not the Jews in hiding, but the Jews who were disguised as
Poles.

After a while in that room, your hands were full of stings; you couldn't
cough or make any noise. You could sit there a few minutes, a quarter
of an hour; but you couldn't hold out longer than that. The story of the
apartment is special, because the landlady was a Jew disguised as a Pole.
She wanted to be like all the other Poles, so she was friendly with the
neighbors. They would come into her apartment sometimes just to chat,
and we would have to sit in the hiding place. I would usually remain on
the scene, ostensibly as the daughter's bridegroom, because the daughter
also lived there. The woman's husband had stayed in the ghetto, where
he was killed.

When we brought Zivia to the apartment, relations in the family were
already shaky. In the early period, the tenants were Tuvia, Zivia, myself,
the landlady's son, and his wife. Tuvia was very sick and the woman's
daughter, son, and daughter-in-law were living in the house and things
were explosive. Afterward, they went to Hotel Polski, and by then, I knew
what that meant. I told them I didn't recommend it. Later, obstacles arose
with the Paraguayan and Uraguayan visas and some people figured out
it that was nothing but a fraud; then the Germans killed everyone who
seemed to know the truth.

There were two kinds of documents: documents of dead people (which were half real) and forged documents. There was a considerable difference between them. For instance, between my documents and Zivia's documents. I had the real birth certificate of a person who was thought to be dead, but later it turned out he was alive. The man simply sold his birth certificate and later came and said he had lost his documents and took out new ones. In this matter, I almost fell into a trap once. But my birth certificate was a real document and was properly registered, as that of a living person. When I went to take out a *Kennkarte*, as I stood at the counter, I realized that there was suddenly some confusion among the clerks. Kazik sat next to me all the time, and I saw a clerk show my document to another clerk. I understood that the document was making them suspicious. They went to clarify something. You must know that in all such places, there were Gestapo agents. At the last minute, I decided to leave. I signaled to Kazik to follow me; I left my hat with the doorkeeper and asked him to keep it for me since I wanted to go out to buy cigarettes. I left and Kazik followed. I lost my hat but I saved my life.

I told Wacław the whole story, and he investigated it through his contacts and discovered that Bagniewski, who sold his documents, lived in the same neighborhood, on Belwederska; and when he needed a *Kennkarte*, he came to the same place to get it. Apparently there were two documents with exactly the same data, except for the photograph. So one of them had to be false. Through Wacław's contacts, the documents of that original Bagniewski were removed from there and destroyed. Some time later, the real Stanisław Bagniewski had been able to take out another birth certificate. At any rate, there were two holders of an identical document in Warsaw.

As for me, they brought me the *Kennkarte* with my real fingerprints. That is, only if they had caught me and done a thorough investigation and interrogation could they have discovered the forgery; and since the AK had people everywhere, such things could be taken care of. At any rate, I walked around with that document until the end of the war and it is in our archive. It wasn't changed because it wasn't necessary. I had to keep from being caught at any price, since all they had to do was pull down my pants to prove I was a Jew and the document was forged. So another document wouldn't have helped me; I was sentenced to death in any case. That wasn't true of a suspected Pole, who could have been sent to Auschwitz after an interrogation. I had to have false addresses on every document so as not to give away all the people who lived with me. I had to be registered in a place where I wasn't known at all, because I couldn't endanger helpless people. So I wasn't registered at Komitetowa with Mrs. Kopik and her daughter Zosia; but I came there as the daughter's bridegroom, and the neighbors didn't know if I stayed overnight or if I left. When they began to suspect, they sent the Germans, as I told before.

I wasn't registered at Pańska either. The apartment was registered in the names of Irena Gelblum (Irka) and Marysia. As I said, I was registered on Belwederska. Even in the first stage of an interrogation, I couldn't allow myself to be registered in one of those apartments on Pańska or Komitetowa. But I had to be registered somewhere. On the other hand, if I lived as a Pole and resided somewhere else, I would have been completely cut off from the comrades. I would have to come at night and leave for work in the morning. For if I didn't stay overnight, the landlord would get suspicious. Even if he was an honest man, he wouldn't want to risk his life for a suspicious tenant, who came one night but not the next. There's no middle way in this situation, no middle between life and death. That is, a Gestapo interrogation would lead only to death. And I was prepared; I knew exactly how I would die.

Unlike my document, Zivia's birth certificate was really forged. She was given a Polish name, Celina, on the *Kennkarte*. Under all conditions, she had to carry a document in case she was captured. We did that with all the women in the group. They didn't walk around outside and she wasn't registered anywhere. On my *Kennkarte*, everything was true, except that it wasn't me. With her, everything was false. The same goes for Stefan Grajek and Tuvia—every one of them got a forged document. At a certain stage, we were forging the documents ourselves, in cooperation with the AK cell that was willing to help us with that. So, with help from AL, as much as they could give, and ZEGOTA, which did a lot in that area, we made our own stamps in 1944: we got forms from Wacław for forged documents and we also made documents in the name of dead people or those who had sold their documents.

We would get documents from the Polish underground. I got my document, for example, from the AK; my close call was in fact their fault, since they knew the document was bought and the man was alive. They had contact with patriotic priests who would tell them of the death of a Pole and would arrange things in City Hall so the dead person's name wouldn't be taken off the rolls. The people were buried but the "name lived on"; and their birth certificates would be taken. This was how the Polish underground also got documents for their members. My case was special, and I'm sure they didn't intend to get me into trouble. That is, that man sold the document and didn't take himself off the rolls; since he wasn't dead, he could have caused my death.

Those documents we got from the Polish underground, ZEGOTA, AK, or AL, were made in special cells for forgery, in a mass production process. For example, a document like mine would have been good enough for a member of the Polish underground. His risk depended on denunciation or underground operations; whereas my risk was greater, because in the very first stage of the investigation or the examination, I would be exposed as a Jew.

When I said before that I knew how I would die, I didn't mean cyanide. I distributed doses of the poison among the comrades; and I also had a dose. I distributed it to people who moved around outside, to those who had nothing to lose if they were caught by the Gestapo. Later, I concluded that a person could also use that poison when his nerves grew weak or if he suffered a deep depression. We did have such a case, which had nothing to do with underground conditions. We saved that man from death at the last minute because he didn't take enough or his cyanide evaporated and wasn't strong enough.

Because of these and other considerations, I became aware of such failed attempts, and then I threw away my dose of cyanide. Instead, I constructed another plan for myself: in all my walking around in the city, I became familiar with a multistory building on Leszno Street. At the top of the stairs, a hole had been blown out of the wall in the bombings of September 1939. It had been a Jewish house, which was later inhabited by Poles. I went there on a reconnaisance tour for my couriers, and I made up a plan for myself: if they did catch me and torture me, and I felt close to breaking, I would take them to this house which was supposedly my contact point. I tried to investigate how the Germans behaved when they led their captives to some place. I knew that the one who leads (that is, me) walks in front, followed by the escort of Gestapo agents, in uniform or in plainclothes. I planned to tell them I didn't remember the exact address of the place, but I would lead them to that house on Leszno. I would walk in front, climb up a few stories to the hole in the wall, and jump. That was the ideal place to jump to your death—a very high story with a whole wall broken out; and until you got there, you didn't know a thing. It was truly mortal fear to go up one more flight. But no one took pains to fill in the hole in the wall. That was the right place to carry out my own death sentence. After that, I didn't keep cyanide. I must say that even though I knew my nerves were strong, there were times when I feared a nervous breakdown. At a certain stage, I took the cyanide from all those I had given it to. I really took it away from them by force; I told them I was scared they would break down before the last minute. It was generally a little easier for the women. If they had documents, they were taken to Pawiak or Auschwitz either as Jews or as Poles. The serious threat was for the men—death on the spot; and if the captive was a member of the underground, it was also death by torture; you had to take that into account. My plan was in case they wanted me to lead them [to my "contact point"]. Otherwise they would either kill me or take me to prison and interrogation. I took torture into account, when you never know how you'll respond. But usually in interrogations, they demanded that you show them the places they were interested in.

Our Scout, Juziek, also led his interrogators to his contact point. At a certain moment, after he brought them into the store and they took their eyes off him, he began running and they shot and killed him. They could also have killed me as a Jew, going by the ancient proof. And they might have done that without hesitation, but if they caught me as a member of the underground and had me lead them to my contact point—since I knew what the tortures were and there was no point ignoring them—then the possibility I described would look good to me. I also had to consider behavior during torture. My decision was firm, and I knew that if I wanted to keep an important secret, I had to acknowledge that I was incapable of lying in all matters along the way. A person has to know what are the important things he wants to hide at any cost. You have to tell other things, fully and truthfully. For example, I could reveal that my name is Yitzhak Zuckerman and that I was born in Vilna. I could tell everything, except for the basic truth I decided to hide. Then they start interrogating: what, who, where? And I could tell them the truth about someone I know. I could say I don't know his name, I know it's Anatol or something else; and if they demand that I tell where the contact point is, I could then say I don't remember the exact address, but I do remember the place and I can take them. That's what you need to do.

We stopped using cyanide after the man collapsed. I saw strong people behaving oddly in certain cases; they were on the verge of collapse and couldn't stand it anymore. That's how it was when someone very close to you wanted to depart from the world. That same person, who was next to me, collapsed and asked me for cyanide. But after a while, he recovered and worked as usual up to the end.

I've already told about various situations. I told what I felt when I left Zivia alone until late, and I know what she felt. You can learn something from the case at Leszno I mentioned—when I came home after curfew. We kept weapons in the apartment on Leszno because we had to, even though we strictly forbade carrying weapons. The ban started in late 1943, when the Polish underground forbade all its members to carry weapons, even for self-defense because the Germans imposed collective responsibility. One day when we were about to set up a fighting group, I asked the AK for weapons for the Jews in hiding who knew how to use them—for instance, members of the Jewish Fighting Organization who were hiding because they looked Jewish. I wanted to give them weapons; but in a very friendly way, Wacław told me their decision on this issue. He said that even if the Germans came to take him, he wouldn't have defended himself because the whole courtyard could pay a high price for it, and he knew it was a heavy responsibility. They decided not to defend themselves so as not to cause the death of innocent people who got in the way. Only in exceptional cases of self-defense were weapons given from the armory, for a specific operation. Hence, I didn't walk around armed with weapons except after the blackmailers grabbed me in the street and we tried to find them. At that time, my two escorts were armed, but I didn't carry a weapon even then; I kept eye contact with them.

[Zivia adds here: I don't know if we would have kept to that rule if the Germans had come to us.]

Right, we would have defended ourselves, even though the weapons weren't intended only for our use. We also collected weapons to send them where they were needed, but we did keep something for ourselves. No doubt we would have defended ourselves with weapons and the Germans wouldn't have taken us alive. Even in the ghetto, when Jews were being taken to the *Umschlagplatz*, we swore that none of us would willingly fall into the hands of the Gestapo. At that time we didn't have weapons, and each of us knew he would try to escape. If the Germans had come to Komitetowa, for example, and taken us out of the bunker, we would have used weapons. We all dreamed of having weapons to be able to shoot our oppressors if we were caught and not to be taken alive. We had light weapons, grenades, and revolvers, our major weapons, which we had also used in the Uprising. Everyone had somehow managed to take his pistol out with him through the sewers. Later, in the Polish Uprising, we had better weapons, including machine guns—something like Stens. In the apartments on both Leszno and Pańska, we kept the weapons in the hideout and we thought that if the Gestapo rang the doorbell, we would go into the hideout and take the weapons.

Leyzer Levin and his son moved to Łomianki, to Kajszczak, that loyal villager, and Kazik and I found an apartment with a Polish woman. It was winter. Zivia was also with us, until the two of us moved to Leszno 27. I would go out in the morning and come back at dark. The owners of the apartment were Poles, strangers, who let us stay in the apartment for money. The attorney Leyb Katz rented the apartment for us.[65] That was also Grajek's apartment and Sak always stayed there too. His wife Hela, Yanka's mother, was a courier. Apparently Sak bragged about me to his landlords as some high-ranking personage. They thought I was a Pole, and would greet me like a Polish officer in the underground. I would go into Sak's room and tell him the news, and, in exchange, he would give me good advice. I must say that among the older people in

65. Leyb Katz: Born in Łomźa in central Poland. Studied at the university in Vilna. A member of Po'alei Zion–Z.S., who was devoted to the party and generously supplied professional services. He was the legal advisor to the party in Warsaw. Was director of *Shulkult* in the underground and worked in the financial department of CENTOS. He committed suicide after the suppression of the Ghetto Uprising in spring 1943.

the group, Sak was one of the bravest, as he demonstrated in the Polish Uprising—he didn't work in the Jewish Fighting Organization; but he fought on the Aryan side and later, in the Polish Uprising, he proved his courage.

There was a radio with earphones in David Klein's apartment at Chlodna 17. I would come to listen but I couldn't stay for long. Pawel (the Redhead) was also there, and so was Klein's friend who could type and who typed my London reports. She was hiding there with Zimra Kaminski (who lives in Kfar Saba). It was a big apartment, and in one of the rooms was a secret bell. Kazik, Anna, and Władka also would come there, and I would get all sorts of information. I could go there without making prior arrangements through couriers; and I would come and get information. I didn't know about the informational bulletin that Klein issued; but that is conceivable. He was an adventurer sort of guy. He kept a radio despite the strict ban and the death sentence for violators, even Poles. David Klein tells about a few meeting places: at Kawiarnia, a café at Chlodna 20, as well as a pastry shop in Bank Square.[66] I stopped going there after two members of AL were killed near the place (on May 10, 1943). As I recall, there was a dairy restaurant close by and there were cafés on Marszał-kowska and in Praga, where I would meet people. There were probably more than twenty cafés like that. When a café didn't look very nice and was beginning to make us suspicious, we would move somewhere else. I never ate expensive things; I was always strict about staying below the accepted norm. My main meal was at home, in the evening, with Zivia. That was a very meager meal, but a cooked meal.

Curfew for Poles began at 9 in the evening. (There were various periods; there was a time when curfew began at 7.) At the beginning of the occupation, the Germans started destroying the Polish intelligentsia, and they continued that to the end. What happened to the university of Kraków was typical: at the start of the academic year, after the Germans gave permission to open, when all the professors were assembled (except for those who were sick and those who had stopped coming), they took all of them to the camp at Sachsenhausen.[67] Only a handful survived; and, afterward too, it wasn't hard to find them, even in the telephone book, by the description attached to each one: Atty, Dr., Prof., Eng., and so forth. Only some of the Polish intelligentsia was active in the underground, because the underground couldn't absorb them all.

I recall the day of the murder of Igosin, a famous Polish actor, executed by the underground. At that time, I was with Lonka at the railroad station; we had to get to Warsaw and wound up there right after the

66. David Klein 1968.
67. A concentration camp near Berlin.

murder of Igosin, which led to the arrest of many of the best Polish intellectuals. That was at the time when the ghetto still existed.

I would like to mention another case of "ransom" involving Felek Rajszczak, the landlord of the apartment where Stefan Grajek and his friends lived.[68] This man fell into the hands of the criminal police (*Kripo*). And here in front of me, by chance, is my letter to Berman, of February 19, 1944:

> Dear friend, the situation is quite sad. We got a letter today from Grajek's landlord from the *Kripo*; they beat him hard to make him turn over Antek and Kazik. The landlord claims he doesn't know any Antek and that he saw Kazik only once. He asks us to rescue him. We contacted our influential connections, but unsuccessfully. Can you possibly [help]? His name is Felix Rajszczak (born in 1901). He is still at the *Kripo*, arrested on February 11, on a charge of building bunkers for Jews and Communists. Clearly we'll have to pay some money.

That's my letter to Berman with everything in it—even the date of Felek's arrest.

Because of incidents of "ransom" like that and Turkow's, there always had to be money in the treasury; nothing was visible, but there was a certain sum. I must say that, financially, my situation wasn't bad, relatively, since I worked in the Jewish Fighting Organization and was a kind of *Kestkind* (dependent) of everyone. In these terms, it was better for the Jews we took care of—there was always something for them. The Bund, which had foreign sources, had a lot of money. Maybe no more than we did. But they didn't have the problem of changing dollars through the Polish Delegatura, which made a profit at our expense.

At a party in Israel, when A. Berman's archive was placed in Beit Lohamei Ha-Getaot, it was mentioned that money earmarked for us wasn't delivered or was only partially delivered. As a result, Z. Shner got a letter from Wacław Zagorski, a former member of the AK and one of the Righteous Gentiles, complaining that that description of the distribution of money during the war had an anti-Polish character. But the whole issue is documented on the Polish side as well, and there's no doubt that it's correct.

Financially, there were many days of great trouble. The assistance we gave the Jews wasn't enough. It was about 500 Złotys a month per person; but some got more, those who were totally helpless, or who didn't have any other contacts, or who needed to pay a lot to the landlords. We examined every case. Some even got a few thousand, all according to possibilities and conditions. Things were better in the Jewish Fighting

68. See above.

Organization. We had a little jewelry we had taken out of the ghetto, and we didn't know what to do with it. Some of it was with Geller, and I took it from him after the fire. I didn't know how to turn it into money, and it got lost during the Polish Uprising. The same goes for a gold box I got just before the Uprising in a shipment from the activists in Switzerland. A lot of dollars I got a few days before the Polish Uprising were also lost. I argued with the comrades that the money would be safer at home, since the building and the bunker at Leszno 18 would probably remain. I didn't want to carry the cash on me; I loathed the thought that if I fell dead, the dollars would be found on the body of a Jew. So we left it at home on Leszno Street. When the house was blown up, the money was all lost. At the very last minute, I managed to supply our comrades in hiding with some of that money. We expected something to happen soon, but we didn't know exactly when. So we divided the money: we also gave simple Jews an advance of a few months, so they would have something no matter what happened. The hardships in the Polish Uprising came not from a lack of money, but from the bombings.

Children of various ages stayed with mothers or were given to Polish families, like the children in the monasteries. Some families had little children; other families hid their children in villages while they remained in the ghetto. They risked their lives because every Pole who was caught helping a Jew was executed. (There were even posters in the streets: "Anyone who hides Jews will be punished.") And many people were afraid. We don't have numbers on those righteous Poles, but even if we take into account Polish people who did good exclusively for humanitarian reasons, we had to compensate them. For they also had to struggle to survive.

Let's make an accounting: if 20,000 Jews were hiding on the Aryan side of Warsaw (we knew specifically about approximately 12,000), an average of 2 Jews were hiding in every house that sheltered Jews. That is, about 10,000 Polish families were involved in hiding Jews; and if there were about 4 people in each family who participated in this help, at least 40,000 Poles in Warsaw helped in some way to ease the fate of the Jews. It's not right to condemn all the Poles out of hand. From this perspective, the French were no better than the Poles, and were perhaps even worse. And keep in mind that this stood out against a strong and deep-rooted antisemitism in the Polish people.

A great many of those in hiding changed apartments at least twice, and some of their landlords arranged hideouts for them somewhere else when their apartment was "burned." And don't forget the activists of ZEGOTA, which included the Polish intelligentsia, among them many doctors, psychologists, actors, historians, as well as laborers, simple people. (Batya Berman writes about this in her book.) We never knew who the people were; and that was at a time when the mood on the street was incredibly antisemitic. Those people would walk around and hear the masses talking about Jews.

As the ghetto was burning, I would mix with the crowd assembled to watch the ghetto walls. At that time, there was a lot of sympathy and admiration for the Jews, because everyone understood that the struggle was against the Germans. They admired the Jews' courage and strength. But there were also some, mostly underworld characters, who looked upon us as bugs jumping out of burning houses. But you shouldn't generalize from that. With my own eyes, I saw Poles crying, just standing and crying. Some days I would go to Zolibórz. One day the ghetto was shrouded in smoke and I saw masses of Poles, without a trace of spiteful malice. And if I consider the treason carried out against me by individuals, there were just as many Jews among them as Poles. For example, when I was condemned to be executed on April 18, 1942, it was because of a Jewish denunciation. You can say there was also treason by Poles, but there was rescue by Poles, too. These phenomena stand out even more distinctly against the background of German terror.

If I gauge the phenomenon by one of the finest figures I knew, Irena Adamowicz, who helped Jews deliberately and consciously, as a devout Christian, who assisted as much as she could, I nevertheless cannot ignore the fact that she also saw another mission for herself: to convert Jews, since there is no greater commandment than to convert Jews to Christianity, accompanied by the faith that will save the world.

I'm not saying she would have abandoned someone even if she hadn't kept her sights fixed on the Christian purpose; but let's look at this from the other side: for example, if a rabbi chanced to save a gentile. He wouldn't see anything bad if, at this opportunity, he began telling him about the religion of Moses and the various practices of Judaism. Is there anything wrong in that? Irena also filled such "missions." I know of at least four or five such cases. One of them concerns a woman who is now in Israel, who was hidden somewhere and whom we took care of. We wanted to move her to Warsaw, but her rescuers wouldn't tell us where she was; they claimed they couldn't tell—and it was Irena Adamowicz who was hiding her. Only after the war did we learn that she was hiding her—our comrade was working there under difficult conditions. (That was Mira, who was later at Kibbutz Dafna, whose brother works in the Foreign Ministry, and was in the Gdansk unit and came to London when the war broke out.) And they arranged a trip for a fellow from Germany, disguised him as a *Volksdeutche*, and all traces of him disappeared. There was another case of one of our comrades ("the girl with long hands"): I was riding on the tram with Kazik and, all of a sudden, on Miodowa Street, I saw the girl in the street. Kazik didn't know her. We both jumped off the tram. She told me she was working as a maid someplace and was taken care of; she gave us her address. We said we would come take her the next day. By the time we got there, she was gone. Irena Adamowicz did that; she said so herself. They took her out of the apartment immediately, moved her somewhere, and she vanished.

I don't know if the priests saved many children like that; I don't think they saved many Jews. They may not have saved any. At any rate, it was easier for them to save children. But we can't deny they were intent upon their missionary goal. After the war, it was hard to find and ransom the children. This was well known. They might not have saved any children at all without this motive; if not, they should have returned them gladly to the Jewish people. There were many children who were treated well, and some didn't want to leave their rescuers. After the war, children would continue genuflecting even after we had liberated them. It's worthwhile, for example, to read *Adam's Father's Diary*, about this episode.[69]

Some children were taken to gentile families who treated them well, and they stayed with the families. Sometimes their rescuers weren't even told that they were Jews. There were all kinds of phenomena of antisemitism. Sometimes the child suddenly learned he was a Jew and broke down. The issue surfaced with the rise of the wave of antisemitism after the war. In many cases, adoptive parents didn't tell a boy the truth, and he was sure he was their son. Moczar discovered these things.

There was also a problem of children hiding with their own families, which was dangerous since the children could become a hindrance; we know of many cases like that. Both Władka and Batya Berman tell about that. The "Cigarette Sellers" were something else, a group of street urchins.[70]

Let me say something about diseases and epidemics in this period:

People often had a high fever; there was no medicine, and they recovered in spite of physical weakness. In the ghetto, we had no cases of death from typhus, a contagious disease with a temperature of 104 degrees, which was widespread in the ghetto. A surprising fact—without medicine, without proper food, people overcame disease. It's hard to know what internal forces a person musters in trying situations, both emotional and physical forces. I saw weak people, on the verge of death, who triumphed over the disease, even physically, which is extraordinary. Once we believed that emotional or psychological tension causes infirmity. But we witnessed the opposite—that it generated the will to overcome disease. There weren't any medical means, there was no special

69. Arye and Malwina Klonitski 1970.
70. See Ziemian 1977.

food, and dozens of comrades were sick with typhus. There was no medicine, but no one died in our group.

During the Great *Aktsia*, I had typhus of the stomach, accompanied by great weakness and a rather bad cough. It passed, even though such cases usually resulted in death. That was when we set up the fictive "shop" on Dzielna. I got sick at the height of the *Aktsia*, and the landlords came and found me in bed. I remember drinking spirits at night. In the evening, the Germans would stop the *Aktsia*. It was like being in jail.

You couldn't prevent diseases and, in such cases, we had gentile doctors on the Aryan side. There may also have been doctors disguised as gentiles. But you could generally ask for a doctor from ZEGOTA. I'm sure that if I had called on someone, he would have come. In Tuvia Borzykowski's case, he probably had typhus with a very high fever, and we feared for his life. The miracle is that he didn't infect us. For Jews who were seriously ill, there was a cell of loyal doctors who would be informed and they would appear. But that was when ZEGOTA existed. I don't know if or how simple Jews got to a doctor.

In cases of natural death—and there were some—it was very hard to bury the body. There was a person, who now lives in Israel, whose wife went mad and had to be poisoned and there was a question of how to bury her; apparently the man himself didn't know how that issue was solved.

Keeping an archive was a very dangerous thing but no more dangerous than the life and support of people. It's doubtful if there was anything in it to compromise us. Let's say the files of the Jewish Fighting Organization were there—three thousand appeals for help. A Jew's name and place of birth were written there. How could that give a person away? The other question—if the archive had been seized, would it have endangered the people even more by indicating that there was a center and a junction of the underground movement? I'm sure this archive couldn't have given other people away, it could only have supplied curious Germans with information about underground areas of operations. To the best of my recollection, there were whole sections in the archive. In one, for example, there were a few thousand letters, Jewish appeals for help.

Incidentally, I've already told of one encounter, in 1943 or maybe 1944, when we learned of the existence and activity of the Committee to Aid Jews operated by women from Kraków who worked for the Gestapo. The Germans poured lots of money into this committee, tens of thousands of Złotys a month, as much as necessary. The women expanded the circle of those receiving support and turned the names over to the Germans. That was very serious, but we couldn't track them down. The women were aware of the significance of it, but we didn't even know what group they were from. Later we ran into them. (This has nothing to do with Weichert; I never accused Weichert of turning Jews in.) In this case, it was a wholesale denunciation. A lot of women collaborated with the Germans, maybe to save their own lives, in exchange for promises. I don't know how they came to do that, just as I don't know how other people came to collaboration with the Germans. Everybody's got his own weakness.

We learned of it when we suddenly came on the fact that a whole group of Jews was captured, and we started looking for the common denominator of those who had been caught. We learned what had happened from Poles who served as intermediaries in this episode. They told us that those families who fell into the trap had been receiving help from a group of women. After it was discovered, the women vanished. The operation took place in Warsaw, but the women were from Kraków, so I don't know exactly who they were, or their real names, or how the operation was stopped.

We began to fear that our ranks had also been infiltrated. The women themselves or other Jews in big trouble might have been blackmailed by promises to save their lives if they did what they were told to. And so I asked the Jews we took care of to take cautionary measures apparently not required by other groups—and I didn't want to know their names or addresses, but only what their names and addresses had been in the ghetto—and that couldn't give anybody away. I also wanted to know whom they knew and what groups they were in. That occasionally allowed us to check up. I figured it would take months before a Jew would get the answer when something was suspicious. I must say that, in fact, we didn't encounter suspicious cases. There were all sorts of Jews. One made his case on half a page, another would write a whole notebook because he had an emotional need to tell. And our unit coordinators were instructed absolutely not to write the current Polish names and present addresses of the people. Our list, as I said, couldn't have given anyone away. For example, if I said I was Stanisław Bagniewski, that didn't say a thing. Even if I wrote that I was locked up, in trouble, and gave details about my birth, what I did in the war, and so forth, even that couldn't give anyone away because there were several thousand people like that. I used to read their autobiographies with great interest, first of all to know about them, and sometimes such testimony, the stories of thousands of Jews, would make me extraordinarily curious. I kept the material. I wouldn't make copies; I didn't transfer it to anyplace. So it was all destroyed in the Polish Uprising.

The second big section in the archive was correspondence with the Polish authorities, the AK, and the civilian authorities in London. I had microfilms of letters—material transferred to us. It wasn't a big section, but it was valuable, and was partially preserved by Berman, who mainly preserved material about contacts with civilian institutions. Now and then

I would send him copies of my correspondence with (underground) military institutions. Anything I didn't send out was lost, and I didn't have time to transfer it all. Sometimes I moved the archive from one apartment to another; other times I didn't have access to a typewriter. At one time the typewriter was attached to the house we were living in; somebody there could type, so I gave him the material. That was Jurek, of the Polish Scouts, who looked Jewish; he was Luba Gewisser's boyfriend, who was killed in the early days of the Polish Uprising by the AK.

And there was a file of correspondence with our partisans and with our contacts in the concentration camps; we maintained contact with a lot of camps. A letter I once read aloud also tells about concentration camps in Częstochowa and other places; messengers would come and go. I used to leave copies of my letters and the answers I got. It was like that with many places. Trawniki, Poniatów, Częstochowa, Skrzysko, and Płaszów and with the aid council in Kraków.

I kept it all because I intended to keep some memento of that period. All of it couldn't have been shipped out of the country. If we had to decide whether to send a child or the archive, I would have sent a child. I didn't have an idea of even one loyal person I could entrust the archive to. During these years, two people came to me from abroad: one was a Pole who lived in Slovakia and the other was the Swiss woman who came to me two days before the Polish Uprising; and I certainly wouldn't have endangered her for the archive. It didn't even occur to me to give her the archive. I was sure that Polish Warsaw wouldn't suffer the same fate as the ghetto. But it turned out that Polish Warsaw was also destroyed.

Later, we realized that the Germans were searching for me. A special squad in the Gestapo was tracking down "Captain Antek." they didn't know my real name and thought I was a Pole. I learned of it from the Poles and from our own couriers. Why they made me a "captain" I don't know. But they did. The name "Antek" had to do with a visit I made to a guy named Kutsher (not Hirshke Kutsher of Grochów), who worked in a weapons workship for the Hagana in Eretz Israel, and later with us in the ghetto. He was the one who built our underground prison in the ghetto. He was a loyal man who did all sorts of things for us gratis, even though he wasn't a member of the Movement. Now he was hiding in a bunker on the Aryan side. Apparently, wanting to praise me, he said I was a Pole called "Captain Antek." But I was called Antek back in Grochów; it was a popular and common Polish name, like Ivan among the Russians. I adopted it and used it when I went to the Aryan side. I couldn't use Stanisław Bagniewski then since the Poles would quickly expose the forgery by means of a registry of residents. But Bagniewski was what was registered in the documents. Antek was my underground name—even before I was Stanisław Bagniewski. I also had documents in the name of

Witold Kimstaczas, but no one knew I was called that. In the underground, I was "Antek," "Commander Antek," "Captain Antek." That wouldn't give me away; nor would the name Stanisław Bagniewski, which wasn't on the registry of residents, but only in my identity documents.

The search for "Captain Antek" originated with the concierge's son, who was caught and began "singing" and caused many catastrophes. Among other things, he told about "Captain Antek," as he had heard from Kutsher. Then the Germans started searching; but the concierge's son didn't know many details, just the name and the appearance. Kutsher also wanted to show the Germans he had relations with the Polish underground. So they searched for "Captain Antek." For the Germans, Captain Antek was one man, and Stanisław Bagniewski was another. Yitzhak Zuckerman was a third person.

If I had fallen into their hands by chance, as a Pole, they wouldn't have investigated whether I was a member of the underground; they would normally have put me in prison and, from there, would probably have sent me to Auschwitz. My address was registered on Belwederska, and they couldn't possibly have found my real apartment. However, if they had caught me in the apartment, the documents wouldn't have mattered. I was a Jew and that was enough. It's not likely they could have captured the archive. If they had gotten onto the trail of the house or had come to it by chance, they wouldn't have captured the people; they might have captured me because I usually didn't hide. The other people hid behind the wall, which wasn't wood, but was a real, massive brick wall; you entered the hideout through the furnace—the front of it was raised by pressing a button. They went inside, and the door was lowered. All you saw on the outside was kindling and ashes. We were the only ones who knew about the hiding place.

If the builders of the hideout had told, we would have suffered a bitter fate. But they were as loyal to us as our closest friends and would not have told. Along with the archive, there were weapons in the hideout. I kept explosives, pistols, and grenades there. When the house burned down in the Polish Uprising, that was a supplement that "helped" destroy it completely, along with the hideout and all it contained. We were very careful about that archive, but we didn't assume that Warsaw would be destroyed and that house would be burned and blown up. The loss of the archive was a great national and historical loss. A genuine catastrophe because, without it, an important link lacked testimony. What is left is only from memory. And since not many people were active, there were things only I knew, but not Berman, for example. Later I talked with him (when he was writing his book) and learned that he simply didn't know a lot of things. I wouldn't have told him everything, not, for instance, things that had no public significance, or things I didn't depend on others for, or issues that didn't require any cooperation, except between me and the liaison. As for the briefings with Polish commanders, with the people in London, and with the Communists—there's nobody anymore except me who knows about them. I didn't even tell Zivia about many failures that happened. I would hide it inside myself and come home happy and goodhearted. There was no place to unwind. It was horrible that I didn't allow myself to share them with even one person. Apparently that was because of youth, of my age; and, because of loyalty to the idea of conspiracy, I thought the less a person knew the better it was for him. I myself also did everything not to know things I didn't have to know. That's hard to maintain, but it's true. For example, the first time Marek Edelman told me that Wacław's real name was Henryk Wołyński, I couldn't forgive him. Because I used to go to Wacław's apartment, and it was most unusual for one member of the underground to invite another conspirator to his apartment. Especially since he was a Pole and I was a Jew, and he was an important person, in charge of Jewish affairs in the AK, and I earned his trust and went to his apartment; his real name was written on the door: Henryk Wołyński. But I tried not to see it; I would really close my eyes not to see it, would ring the bell and not know.

Sometimes I seemed to pay for that, but it turned out that it also saved me, as in the story of my flight from Kraków which I've already told. Why didn't I look at the name of the street and the number of the house in Kraków? I might get caught; I still had a long way to go. Both in Kraków and afterward, I would have to return to Warsaw and get into the ghetto. I could have been caught and tortured. I thought it was better not to have anything to tell. If I told only that I had a friend named Laban, I didn't do anything bad; not as far as his address was concerned. I would have done something bad if I hadn't held out under torture and had revealed something. You have to figure that. I didn't think I would break under interrogation. But I always figured on the line of least resistance, the other possibility; so there were things I didn't want to know.

It's hard to answer the question of how a person living with the tension of danger and responsibility every day doesn't allow himself to relax in the evening. At any rate, I didn't let myself relax in any case of danger. There were two big failures I didn't want to bother the people in my house with. No one could have helped me and I would only have brought them dejection, and it probably wouldn't have done me any good. But it was different if it made sense to discuss something, not the problems of live people, but relations with the AK or the AL, or some camp or what was going on in the camps, and the remaining ghettos. But those weren't secrets a person could tell the next day. If I say we're in touch with Płaszów, am I telling names? Addresses? Am I telling the names of couriers? It's nothing. But I worried that general things, like those I just mentioned, would be known beyond the circle of the comrades I lived with, like Stefan Grajek, Leyzer Levin and others.

I used to go talk to Sak. I was very careful to have contact with him at least once a week. I could imagine how a public figure would feel who had to sit closed up and withdrawn. He and his family waited for me because I was their only contact with the outside world. What could they hear from the gentiles they lived with? I could tell them about what was going on, information from abroad and from home, general matters, details of the death camps, attempts to help, messengers that had been sent. Not names, but where they were sent—Białystok, Vilna, Częstochowa. I also put out a bulletin for the comrades. I would make copies with carbon paper and send them out, keeping one copy in the archive. I would report on whatever I could; for example, on problems concerning the AK, pressures from London. There were frequent problems about our money, which they delayed.

Berman also preserved some things. There was an episode of the desertion of the soldiers from Anders's Army, after it moved to the Middle East and even came to Eretz Israel.[71] The desertions had to do with antisemitism, and there were several deserters in Eretz Israel who hid in kibbutzim. (When I came to Yagur, I met one or two deserters from Anders's Army.) At that time, the AK demanded I write a letter of condemnation and even threatened to cut off relations with us. I didn't do it and said I had to investigate the issue. I said: "It's not enough that you say so; I have to hear the other side." I wasn't convinced. They also tried to persuade Berman and the Bund to attack the deserters. I used to tell the comrades about the pressures, discussions, threats. And I know that was important. In general, I would come and talk to them, but when I was upset, I would make sure that Kazik, who knew the places, brought them the bulletin. There was always danger that someone distributing an underground newspaper would take risks and be caught. And there was no limit to the dangers.

I usually followed the principle of not having anything in my pocket except money and an identity document. So, in sum, the archive couldn't have given anything away, even if it had been found. It would have revealed issues, but not people. That is, it wouldn't have endangered anyone's life. And issues can't be endangered since they can't be caught.

Kazik was always "at hand"; he knew where I was, even though he didn't attend all those meetings with the gentiles. I didn't ask him to

71. Anders's Army: General Władysław Anders (1892–1970), commander of the Polish forces in the Middle East and Italy in World War II; a leading anti-Communist who refused to return to Poland after the war and died in exile in London. Anders's Army was formed in the USSR of former Polish POWs and deportees and went through Iran to Palestine in 1942; then fought in Italy. It numbered 80,000.

accompany me all the time, but he had to check whether I "was alive or not," by examining the places where I was supposed to be. If I didn't show up, it meant something had happened to me. I was punctual and would appear on the dot, even if it was at the other end of the city—I simply had to leave earlier; the people I met also knew that that was the principle, and that someone couldn't walk around waiting outside a few minutes, unless he had made an appointment with a girl. Otherwise it was very dangerous. I never knew if the violinist or the beggar, the newspaper vendor or the cigarette seller, standing or innocently strolling, was really a violinist or a cigarette seller—or a Gestapo agent. In my apartments, I could check that. If, for example, on Pańska, which wasn't a busy street, a violinist or cigarette seller had suddenly appeared, it would have been obvious that he wasn't there to make a living. Otherwise, why wouldn't he take another couple hundred steps and stand on a bustling street, like Marszalkowska? That made us suspect that he was watching someone. We often talked about a new face that suddenly appeared in the street, a beggar, for example, who was walking around collecting charity.

Another detail. In the early days, Zivia and I agreed to hang a towel on the windowsill all the time, even in summer. If the towel wasn't there, it meant: "Don't come in." That was easy enough to do. If someone knocked on the door, she would take down the towel; there was a door-bell, and she wouldn't know if the person ringing was a neighbor or someone from outside. When a neighbor lady or a stranger would come in, Zivia would take down the towel before she went into hiding. When I approached the house, I would look to see if the towel was in its place. If not, I would wait, walk around and come back later; but the towel was usually in its place.

In the evening, I would play cards with the landladies, even though I was never very good at it; or I would tell jokes. I would read detective stories. One day, I was waiting near Gebetner Wolf, a big publishing house, a corner building with a lot of display windows, and I had a little time. I bought and read the correspondence of Eliza Orzeszkowa[72] and Maria Konopnicka.[73] I would sometimes buy classical literature, but I usually bought detective novels for Zivia and the other people in the house, to help them pass the time. At that time, I also became familiar with the "distinguished writer" Baxter. Once I told Tabenkin and he didn't know who he was either. I asked him: "Shakespeare you do know, but the

72. Eliza Orzeszkowa (1841–1910): One of the most popular novelists in Poland of her day. A champion of better treatment of Jews and peasants and of an education to prepare women for independence.

73. Maria Konopnicka (1842–1910): Author of short stories and important poet of Positivist period in Polish literature. She sympathized with the Polish peasants and was a philosemite.

distinguished author of westerns you don't?!" He didn't know who Baxter was; and I didn't know him either before I read him in those days.

I used to read a lot of newspapers. I read Goebbels's weekly, *Das Reich*, the *Völkischer Beobachter*, and I would bring home the miserable paper the Germans published for the Poles. I wouldn't buy the German newspapers in one store or kiosk, but in various places because I didn't want people to suspect that I knew and read German. But I would buy it every day. I would get all the Polish underground papers. We had a special box for underground newspapers. Not a mailbox, but a secret box, where they would put the newspapers of the AK, the PPR, and so forth. The box was in the house of one of our women couriers, who would get the papers on a regular basis and keep them for me. Of course that was fascinating material: a lot of information, what was going on in various places, leading articles; the newspapers weren't big and every line was significant. I knew that the editor of their official bulletin, the *Information Bulletin* was Hubert Kaminski, our friend from the Polish Scouts, who also made sure the newspaper always got to us. The AL also printed a few newspapers and so did both parts of the PPS and the peasants' party. This press naturally has archives in Poland. A few issues are here in our archives.

I had contacts at various levels with the AL, beginning with the supreme commander, the chief of staff of the Armia Ludowa, General Witold, who was no longer young—he was one of the oldtimers, older than Gomułka. Until they were corrupted by authority and even more so by Stalin, those people demonstrated exceptional personal and movement integrity. Their lives were hard all those years; they spent a lot of time in Polish prisons. They were friendly with Jews; after all, the Jews had played a central role in the Communist Party in Poland, even though they didn't reveal their Judaism because they were in the party leadership. There was antisemitism even in the Polish Communist Party; but I personally can't complain. Never did they make me feel I was beneath them or different from them—not once! I would tell them about relations with AK and they would give me good advice. They knew the situation; they understood and encouraged me. They didn't see my contacts with the AK as a violation of the pact with the Communists. They knew that the essential, the most important thing was to save Jews, to prepare them to defend themselves.

They knew that the AK and the Delegatura were the main force and that we had to stay in communication with them. Not only did that not matter to them, they even encouraged it; that was true of the leadership, including the commanders of Warsaw and the area. Meetings with the AL were arranged through the couriers; that is, a woman courier would bring word of where the meeting would be held. For example, I would meet one of the people in a suburb of the city, not in a house. And I would meet younger commanders in cafés, parks, sometimes on the shores of the Wisła; we would fix a time to swim together; we would undress, go into the water, and talk. There were a lot of people there and it didn't look suspicious.

There were military ranks and political ranks and there was probably a difference between them. For the most part, Berman met with the political ranks. But there was nothing concrete in meetings with them because the money didn't come through them. And information from Moscow wasn't in their bag either. That is, there was nothing practical in meetings with them; Berman considered himself close to the Communists. I can't say what Ringelblum was in these terms. As for Berman, his development was leftist within Po'alei Zion Left. A similar development also occurred in Ha-Shomer Ha-Tza'ir. After the war, Berman claimed that Ringelblum was also like that. I don't know, but Berman was obviously very close to them. He didn't cross the final, thin barrier only because of Eretz Israel.

By the end, even before the Polish Uprising, Berman and I knew our ways were parting because of the Jewish issue. That is, the Jewish issue really didn't interest Berman very much since his attitude toward Eretz Israel didn't reflect his attitude toward the Jewish issue. There was a period, in the 1950s, for example, when he was in Israel, when we yelled and shouted about the Jewish fate in the Soviet Union; but Berman and Sneh didn't yell with us.

At that time, this development led Moshe Sneh to an anti-Zionist, pro-Soviet position. He would say "yes" to whatever was said in Moscow. Indeed, for Berman, that orientation came later on, during the Prague trials or afterward.[74] At any rate, Sneh's leftist orientation began just before the establishment of the State of Israel and developed over time, whereas with Berman and many members of Ha-Shomer Ha-Tza'ir, it began back in the ghetto.

Apparently, there is a combination of two things here: the ideal and the force, the liberating force, that is, the fighting force plus the ideal. Before the Soviet Union entered the war, I heard, even from Mordechai Anielewicz, that this was an imperialist war, whereas I saw myself as a participant, on the fighting side, in this war because of the Jewish issue. And I'm not denigrating Shmuel Braslaw and Mordechai Anielewicz. That was their notion; until June 22, 1941, they said that the imperialists should kill each other off. I, however, knew that one of the sides which

74. Prague Trials: In November 1951, Rudolf Slansky, a Czech Communist leader of Jewish origins, was tried for espionage with thirteen others and sentenced to death. Ten of the condemned were Jews and there were antisemitic accusations during the trial. This later proved an embarrassment to the regime, which absolved Slansky posthumously in 1963.

was, willy-nilly, our partner couldn't be killed off; I knew it that was also a Jewish war. You can find in Ringelblum that when the Germans invaded the Soviet Union, Ha-Shomer Ha-Tza'ir removed its members who were working at the airport in Okęcie. And Ringelblum praises that; that is, suddenly the war assumed a different meaning for them. No doubt it added meaning to it, but they thought the situation required an ideological upheaval; for me, it was the continuation of the war.

A similar development took place with Berman. In this respect, the opinions of Ha-Shomer Ha-Tza'ir (except for Yosef Kaplan) were very close to a part of Po'alei Zion Left. I don't know the exact position of Sagan, but that was so at least with Berman. I started meeting with him only when I came to the Aryan side, because he was active in CENTOS and was busy helping children. The argument with him wasn't easy for me. I also used to meet with Ringelblum occasionally, but I didn't know his position.

It's quite obvious why a youth movement like Ha-Shomer Ha-Tza'ir crystalized almost as a party. Every one of us had a party where we argued internally; but externally, one position was presented. Ha-Shomer Ha-Tza'ir didn't have a party and they had to relate to and fix a position on various subjects. They could no longer be occupied only with educational matters, and so a development occurred. A development occurred with us, too. If the war had gone on some more, I think we would have split from Po'alei Zion–Z.S., because we were completely different from them. We were sympathetic toward the Soviet Union—it's not nice to say this in 1974, but it's a fact. On one issue we expressed our disagreement with that country: we didn't yield on the Jewish issue.

For example, Mordechai Anielewicz—he was a brilliant lecturer—said that if the Red Army (this was back in 1940) went into the Middle East and occupied Eretz Israel, we would welcome them with open arms. They would occasionally invite me to attend the sort of conferences we attend today in Israel. I said then that the entrance of the Red Army into Eretz Israel could be the end of Zionism, so I wouldn't welcome them gladly; naturally, I said, we might not have the strength to resist them. That was the big difference in conception. Moreover, in a history workshop held just last week, I told about our underground movement and, for the first time, I also dealt with the underground movement in the Soviet Union. I concluded that if our Dror underground had survived for long even in the Soviet zone, it would not have been like the Dror that took shape in the German zone; there we wouldn't have imparted an anti-Soviet nature to it, by any means! But we would have tried to preserve the ember of Hebrew, the connection with Eretz Israel, whereas in the German zone, where we were faced with Nazism, our world view was generally pro-Soviet. However, on the Jewish issue we didn't agree with their position and acted in opposition to the form of socialism practiced in the Soviet Union—but that was the Russians' business, not ours.

I wouldn't have recognized the young people who were fourteen years old when I left them in the Russian zone if I had met them when they were twenty. The Zionist movement would probably have taken on a more general nature if it had been allowed to function in the Soviet Union. Even in the ghetto and afterward, a process of ideological crystalization took place. Po'alei Zion Left and Ha-Shomer Ha-Tza'ir moved toward a pro-Soviet formulation, even with additional concessions on the Jewish issue, and didn't fight hard against the Soviet policy toward the Jews. That doesn't really have anything to do with Eretz Israel because you could be for Eretz Israel and think that the Soviet Union had solved the problem of its Jews. But we denied that, and formed an underground in the Soviet zone. These differences in views had consequences at the end of the war when we started talking with Adolf Berman about what to expect in the near future; and that's in fact what led to the split between us. Before that, we had a common language; but when we started talking about the future, I emphasized that the most important thing was the Jewish issue and that if those who came to power in Poland didn't support our Movement, they wouldn't allow it to exist and we would set up the Movement underground. And I told Berman then, I think for the first time, that I had already been in the underground in the Soviet zone. And he said absolutely not! No to illegal activity in the area under Soviet rule. He did believe that legalization would come for Zionism but, if not, he wouldn't support an underground; and he really didn't. I never appealed to him in these matters. And it's also true that they did give us legalization; but at first we functioned illegally, at least, I mean, for Brikha.[75] That doesn't mean Berman didn't know about these things.

After the Soviets conquered Poland, I was a member of the Central Committee of the Jews in Poland.[76] The Communists knew I was involved in Brikha. So did Berman. I never thought Berman would hurt me, but I also knew that he was absolutely not to be told about those things. I talked about them with Sak, even though he wasn't active in Brikha. But Sak didn't share Berman's conception and we thought he was with us in this (even if it wasn't legal); from our perspective it was legal. But not

75. Brikha (Hebrew for "Flight"): The organized underground operation to move Jews out of Central and Eastern Europe to Palestine, 1945–1948. About 200,000 Jews were estimated to have been transported by the organization. See below, chapter 13.

76. Central Committee of the Jews in Poland: Formed in October 1944 in Lublin of representatives of various Jewish parties, led by Dr. Emil Sommerstein (see below). It was initially concerned with material aid to the survivors, but later expanded to social and cultural activities.

Berman—up until the pogroms in Kielce (in 1946).[77] In those days, I went to Berman and told him about my meeting with an agent of the Polish secret police; I suggested we go together to Marian Spychalski,[78] and he accepted that because that was legal.[79] So he re-established cooperation between us. The question of Berman's Zionism was solved the day he came to Israel.

Our political contacts with the Polish Communists were very general, except for Berman, who thought Po'alei Zion Left should cooperate in every Communist public issue. For example, if they set up the KRN (the National Council for the Homeland, a kind of underground parliament),[80] he tried hard to have a representative of the "Jewish masses" on it, and I think Berman was right about some things. In one of the annual publications, a participant of the first session of the KRN says there was a Jewish woman, Paula Elster, a ZOB courier; Berman always claimed she was a representative of Po'alei Zion Left. I think Berman is right, but I think they thus denigrate Po'alei Zion Left. I wasn't interested in that representation, just as I wasn't interested in being in the underground Polish Sejm of the London people, which was what the Bund was dying for. In point of fact, I wasn't interested at all in belonging to any Polish political group. I didn't see it as a last resort, or an element advancing the Jewish cause. It was only an expression of being part of a general world view. We have to distinguish between the reality of three and a half million Jews in Poland and a situation in which only a remnant was left. Many things then turned into empty rhetoric: whose representative was it? The representative of the graveyard? I always treated the political party quite contemptuously. But in point of fact, moreover, if I had thought it added something, if I had known I could have saved a single Jew like that, I would have weighed it differently. But my Jewish interest didn't tell me I should worry about that—absolutely not!

What was the purpose of those declarations supposedly "in the name of the Jewish masses"? I must say that the first time I saw that expression, "in the name of the Jewish masses," I was ashamed and offended. That's how Po'alei Zion Left always was—a small party speaking in the name of

77. Pogroms against Jewish survivors by Polish nationalists on July 4, 1946. (See chapter 15.)

78. That is, the delegation appointed after the pogroms in Kielce which came to Spychalski and requested granting free passage to Jews through the Polish borders. Details below, in chapter 15.

79. Marian Spychalski (b. 1906): Architect. Member of the GL and AL staffs. First Deputy Minister of Defense, 1945–1949; arrested and imprisoned 1950–1956. Later, Minister of Defense and President of Poland, until 1970.

80. KRN (Krajowa Rada Narodowa): An underground parliament established by PPR on January 1, 1944. After the war, it continued to function as Poland's legislature until the elections of January 1947.

the masses. But we weren't adherents of rhetoric. When Berman told me that a meeting of the "Central Committee" had taken place, I would conceal a smile and ask who attended. "Batya and I," he would answer. That was the "Central Committee." Absurd! At any rate, I never convened the "Central Committee" of He-Halutz. I consulted with many people, together and separately. Once we especially brought Tuvia to discuss issues of world view. I think he told about that in his book.[81] But that wasn't the Central Committee of He-Halutz.

As for relations, you have to understand that there was a difference between "us vis-à-vis London" and "us vis-à-vis PPR" and "Armia Ludowa vis-à-vis London." We were a tiny, inconsiderable force, "cowardly" Jews, as far as London was concerned. We were also part of world Jewry; but in respect to our importance for them, they could tell whatever they wanted about us to the world; they always maintained their superiority, because we were dependent on them. The Government-in-Exile in London brought us money; if they wanted to, they gave it to us; and when they didn't want to, they would "hold us by the neck," since we were dependent on them for a thousand other things. Although American Jewry pressured them, in the dark you can also murder (and they did); and I'm always amazed when they're presented as Righteous Gentiles.

As for the Communists, the situation was different. They themselves were weak. In comparison to them and from their point of view (AL and PPR), we were a force, even an important and dominant force sometimes. Our active participation with them during the Polish Uprising was a very valuable encouragement to them. Although my appeal to the Jewish fighters to join the Polish Uprising was very general, the Communists accepted it because they understood that I couldn't write it any other way. The physical participation of a group of the last Jewish fighters in their fighting ranks was very significant. After the Polish Uprising, we played a very important role in the activities of the Armia Ludowa, since they were completely crushed in the Uprising and hadn't yet recovered, whereas we somehow maintained ourselves.

There were some Jews in their underground. For example, the wife of the AL commander in the Old City was a Jew; and one of the most active women in the Warsaw center of AL was also Jewish. Jakub Berman (the "Great Berman") and Hilary Minc, the Communist economist, spent the war in the Soviet Union—they were members of the Soviet faction of the Polish Communists.[82] The Jews were very important in the Polish

81. Borzkowski 1972:153

82. Hilary Minc (1905–1974): Minister for Industry and Trade after the war (1944–1949). Spent the war in the USSR, where he was one of the organizers of ZPP (Związek Patriotow Polskich; Union of Polish Patriots) in March 1943. Member of the Polish Politburo (1944–1956); Deputy Prime Minister (1954–1956). Forced to retire in 1956.

underground, but most of them were killed in the ghetto. They shared the fate of the orthodox Zionists. Some who looked Aryan were saved. One of the Communist activist women who was always thought to be a gentile came to Israel after 1967 and published her memoirs in *Moreshet*; I recommend it.[83] She tells about antisemitism in the underground, and not only in the ranks. In fact, I didn't sense that; I can say that I had very close friends among the underground. Ultimately, I helped them more than they helped me. But they were always willing to help, they were open to all my appeals, and they were limited only in their ability. They knew exactly who I was, since I never hid my identity from them. They probably knew I was a Jew; but they also knew my other identity, that I was a Halutz, a Zionist, a supporter of Eretz Israel. I used to talk with them, present our case. Sometimes there were also social meetings. I would tell a little about the Jewish solution, about Eretz Israel. I was sure that if another Poland arose, less tied to Moscow, we would have friends there. And they were indeed friends. But we didn't carry out the death sentences against collaborators with their help and, in the early period, we didn't want their help at all, not for Lolek Skosowski, since we didn't get him. If we had caught him, we would have carried out the sentence against him without their help, even in Warsaw. It was my considered opinion that when you go on an operation with weapons in hand, you have to figure only 50 percent success, even with the best preparation. Because a person could fall into the hands of the Poles, or the Germans. If a Jew who killed a Pole had fallen into their hands, even if the Jew wasn't in the underground, it would have been used against the Jews. They would say the Jews were killing Poles.

There were also cases of provocation. For example, an AK member made an appeal to me; he said he suspected that his neighbor was collaborating with the Germans, and he asked me to send people to kill her. The man who made the request was a friend of Irena Adamowicz, and I saw it as a provocation. I asked him why he, who belonged to such a strong group as the AK, asked a handful of Jews to do this for him. He couldn't answer, and I wanted to know if he was an instrument for someone who wanted to destroy us or to accuse us of killing Poles or of wanting to kill Poles. It might not even have come to killing, but rather that they wanted a pretext to accuse, to get even with me. The man who talked to me might not have been aware of all that because he was a simple person, a member of the Scouts, who was willing to help us at that time; but he came to me with such a suggestion.

Let's go back now to the AL, a small force, whose members were pursued both by the Germans and by the AK, who killed them in the

83. Anna Doracz 1972.

forests, too. Elements like the NSZ, the Fascist organization, the Polish phalangists, wrought havoc on them.[84] In the villages they not only killed leftists from the city, but also peasants who showed a leftist tendency, as well as democrats. Their life wasn't easy. Some of them had been imprisoned during Piłsudski's time,[85] some were condemned to death by Stalin; but when they appeared after the war, in the ruins of Poland, they were recognized as genuine patriots, who stood for an independent, Polish way to socialism and who weren't simply a tool of Moscow. But afterward, Moscow "kept them on a short leash." In those years, Gomułka was the embodiment of the independent Polish way to socialism. That brought them closer to the people: they talked to the Poles, and not in the language of pressure. But later, they were scattered and crushed until not even a trace of them was left. They were fools, like us. Maybe they didn't know Moscow very well. They were denounced and brought down only on orders from Moscow, since the Komintern no longer existed then. Our relations were friendly, based on mutual admiration between equals. Incidentally, that holds to this day. I never read any incitement by them against us. In the military, I met with commanders, even the supreme commander, the chief of staff, whenever I needed, and in any matter.

I've already told about that commander, Witołd. After the war, I learned he married a Jewish girl who later left him. He became Gomułka's opponent during the Stalinist period after the war. Witołd died a natural death. Before 1956, there was a Communist delegation from Israel in Poland, which included Attorney Michael Landau, a former member of Po'alei Zion Right, who had been in Hotel Polski. He was a pleasant man, noble (I went to Hotel Polski for him, too). In Israel, he became a follower of Sneh. One day, in 1956, Landau called and told me he had been in Poland and had met with Witołd. This was before Gomułka came out of prison and Witołd was playing a central role. He said that Witołd asked a lot about me and that he wanted to meet with me; Landau advised me to write a letter to Witołd, for the good of the country, since it was important and could be advantageous. But I hesitated. After 1956, the Israeli government asked me to go to Poland. At first I refused, then I agreed. But by then it turned out the Poles wouldn't let me in. I learned the reason later: because of the Sinai Campaign of 1956, after Gomułka

84. NSZ (Narodowe Siły Zbrojne): The National Armed Forces, a Polish Fascist military organization. Established in 1942. Its commander Kordiusz was connected with the Gestapo and took part in the murder of Jews. At the end of the war, some of their units helped the German army.

85. Jósef Piłsudski (1867–1935): Leader of the Polish struggle of independence and the re-establishment of the Polish state in 1918; led the Polish army in the Russo-Polish war of 1919–1920; Chief of State from 1918–1922 and Minister of War, 1926–1935; Prime Minister, October 1926–June 1928; August–December 1930.

came to power, there were attempts at pogroms and riots against Jews. They thought I was coming to organize the self-defense of the Jews. It didn't occur to them that I was coming to explain our policy in the Sinai Campaign, our connection with the French and the English; I sat in a seminar in Jerusalem for several days on this issue. That only proves Witołd's attitude toward me, after so many years.

Someone else who was very close to us was Alexander (Olek) Kowalski, one of the younger people I also met with after the war.[86] He helped me a lot. He was the secretary of the party in Warsaw and a member of the Central Committee. He died shortly after I left Poland. During the underground period, I met with people whom I knew only by their underground names. One of them was then called Sanek, and I learned only later that that his name was Molecki. We would meet in dark corners he would propose, where he drank a lot of vodka; but I didn't drink much. After the 1967 war, he hurt me by joining the anti-Israeli campaign. It was hard for me to believe. But Gomułka did too, that is, the whole leading Polish *Garnitura* I knew. I didn't know those who had been in Moscow in 1944, who began to be "important" when they returned to Poland. Once, when I told the Armia Ludowa about messengers I was sending, they would give us their contact point in those places. It's hard for me to estimate their power, but always and everywhere, there was someone loyal to them or a courier. It wasn't a large force, but it was a dynamic one.

There's a story about D. Klein who helped on the German side, the Aryan side of Warsaw. Incidentally, Klein tells of a course in the use of weapons organized by the PPS militia which he attended. Anyway, Klein says that a German SA man named Paul Handelmann, whom he knew from the Jewish Social Self-Help (YISA) and who worked in the commissariat of the ghetto (he was in charge of giving permission to bring food into the ghetto), once stopped him in the street. This Handelmann told Klein he was working in the tax office of the municipality, and had lost two sons on the front, his house in a Berlin suburb had been destroyed by bombs, and he hadn't gotten a letter from his wife for a long time. He said that Hitler was also doomed to defeat and that he was "fed up with all that *Scheisserei* [shit]." He asked Klein if he could help him in some way and Klein requested written confirmation that he (Klein) worked in Handelmann's department. There were negotiations later. Handelmann asked for a picture and an address, but Klein didn't want to give him his address and asked for a "blank" confirmation. Klein was very suspicious, but finally gave Handelmann the real facts. Rudi Paul

---

86. Alexander Kowalski (1908–1951): During the war, he was initially in the USSR; returned to Poland in May 1942. Warsaw Secretary of PPR. Chairman of the Young Fighters' Union, 1945–1948. Removed from power along with Gomułka in 1948.

(the Revisionist "Pawel the Redhead") was protecting him throughout that time.

The German gave Klein his telephone number in case he was captured and encountered difficulties. The next time they met, Handelmann gave Klein the confirmation that he worked in the tax office; he also brought one to Rudi Paul. After two meetings, the German put a package on the table and told Klein to open it later. It contained a gun and bullets.

David Klein died a year ago in Paris. He had very strange connections in Warsaw. When he came to me, I received him with open arms. But then he wasn't the same David Klein who loved to eat and drink and have fun. It was sad to see such a dynamic person deteriorate. I never knew exactly what his limit was. I think he said that I gave him a radio he had in his house on the Aryan side. I went there occasionally. I could go there without telling them in advance since we had signals for that. You could relax in his house in the middle of the day because he was living legitimately. Aside from Pawel, there was a girl there named Zosia, Zimra Kaminski, who now lives in Kfar Saba, who found shelter with him. I'm not sure he told about that in his book; he deliberately created an image of himself as a collaborator with the Germans so they wouldn't touch him. I don't know whom he got a car from, perhaps one of the Germans, because, as far as I know, the Poles didn't have cars. At any rate, he was taken in the car to the barber with a honking of the horn so people would see. And he would get out and the car waited for him, and the barber treated him with respect and obsequiousness; then, the car took him off. He himself told me that he created his own image and wanted to be talked about. In his book, he tells about some café where he met friends. Once the waiter began to suspect that he wasn't the character he was trying to present. So he asked the waiter if there was a telephone in the place, picked up the receiver, asked for some number, and started speaking German. Something like: "You caught that Jew?" And he issued all kinds of orders over the phone. That impressed everyone.

Klein could do that. Pawel was also an adventurer and created an image of himself as a *Volksdeutsche* or something like that. One day, that "Redhead" who spoke fluent German bet a Pole that he could stop a tram in the middle of the street. He stood in the street and raised his hands and the tram stopped. The driver thought he was dealing with a German. Apparently he had German documents and he got on the tram, naturally in the car reserved for Germans. At the next stop he got off and collected his bet. Those two were an "odd couple." Pawel may well have been some kind of bodyguard, constantly protecting David Klein.

The story of Klein and the German from city hall is typical of the period when the Germans began to suffer defeats on the front and some of them wanted to guarantee their "afterlife." I didn't come across many such phenomena on the Aryan side. There was the case of Rudolf, but that's another story: he was a German who had lived in Poland for many years and was even a member of the Polish Scouts. When the war broke out, he didn't know whether to desert or go into the army, and the Poles in the Scouts' movement advised him to go to the army. He was a physician by profession and served on the Leningrad front. One day he came to us in the ghetto. He looked decidedly anti-Nazi; he told us about the murder of Jews, especially in Estonia and the Baltic states in general. This Rudolf survived and lives in Germany, in Hamburg; he wasn't forced to hide. I don't think he was one of those who wanted to "redeem himself." Irena Adamowicz asked me one day if I could help him when the time came. That was back in the ghetto and Irena Adamowicz apparently believed I could help; she believed that the Jewish people would survive, and I would play some role; and she asked if I would support Rudolf if I were asked. I said yes and I would have kept my promise to him if Rudolf had appealed to me after the war. If he had asked, I would have helped him as much as I could.

But apparently, we don't have many German Righteous Gentiles, aside from Anton Schmidt and Rudolf, who also risked his life and gave us information. Even then, in 1941, he prophesied the German defeat and spoke of that. There are German Righteous Gentiles listed at Yad Vashem, but in my experience, there were almost none. Neither in the ghetto nor on the Aryan side. I also know about Martinhauer who helped Herman Adler; but he didn't help me. In that period of the German collapse, I didn't come across any Germans seeking contact with us to create an "alibi" for themselves. I'm sure the Poles ran into people like that, but they could help Poles as they were killing Jews, and didn't see any contradiction in that.

As for Aryan Warsaw, the urban Polish underground was preparing for something. They didn't yet say "uprising" at that time, they didn't say "uprising now," but they did say: the day will come and it is at hand. As for the Communists, it's not correct that they were waiting for the Red Army. They were willing to revolt immediately, but the London people saw that as a provocative idea. Their position was that as long as the struggle between the Russians and the Germans continued, as long as blood was shed, the better off Poland would be. But the Communists said they had to fight immediately, everywhere. That was also their position when the Uprising began in the ghetto. If the Communists had had any power, they would have put it into the Uprising. But they didn't have any. As for the people in London, even if we assume they weren't antisemites, in terms of their cold-blooded calculations, they didn't want the Uprising.

And as for what was outside the ghetto, there were still concentration camps and we encouraged the spirit of uprising in them. I don't have any letters but there are a few responses. We encouraged them and formed cells of the Jewish Fighting Organization in Skrzysko, Częstochowa, Lublin. Why? The Poles lied; they didn't set up contact stations as they promised. We didn't have the power to set them up. The stations were needed for shelter and passage in case inmates escaped from the concentration camps before they were executed.

Every concentration camp could in fact also be a death camp. The difference was only that not all the camps—Trawniki and Poniatów, for instance—started out as death camps; they began as labor camps and concentration camps; but in September 1944, they turned into death camps. One day, on the third or fifth of the month, murders took place there.

We also formed the Jewish Fighting Organization in the camps. But that wasn't enough; we also had to give our people some transit point, where a Jew could escape to, since the first gentile he met might turn him in. So the Polish underground promised to set up contact stations of loyal Poles where Jews could try to reach and, from there, they would be transported to a safe place and to the war against Germany.

Rescue was a mission of the highest importance, which took first place in the Jewish National Committee, the Bund, the Coordinating Committee. I couldn't ignore the issue of rescue either. But for me, it didn't have top priority. Sending weapons and organizing Jews for struggle came first. When we set up the organization, Częstochowa still existed. There were still Jews; not many, but a remnant. It doesn't matter if there were ghettoes or not. In Częstochowa, there was still a ghetto and we sent a person who didn't get there. In Aryan Warsaw, the Polish underground didn't fight Germans. It only carried out specific operations because the Poles were always aware of "collective responsibility." Fifty Poles were hanged on lamp posts—that can turn you off. And those were mostly innocent people taken out of Pawiak from a list; they always kept a reservoir of people. The Polish underground tried to perform kidnappings and assaults on high-ranking Germans. For example, one who was considered the most brutal man in Pawiak. They tried to carry out a death sentence, but the Poles didn't go into the streets and kill Germans. You can't call this policy a "war against the Germans." It wasn't a continuous war. They didn't simply attack the Wehrmacht. It's true there was a personal terror against a notorious German, but the Polish underground couldn't accept fifty Poles executed for the death of some anonymous soldier.

By its nature, war is total and such a war didn't exist. We weren't strong enough. We had no reason not to kill the German Karl Brandt, who was instrumental in the death of hundreds of thousands of Jews. But we simply didn't have the power. We knew the war would come and that, when it did erupt, we would join it. And that's just what happened.

We invested a lot of effort in supporting and saving Jews in hiding. That was a big job and we had important instruments for it, like the Jewish Fighting Organization. But if we called ourselves by that name, it was because war and uprising were uppermost; otherwise, we could have called it the Organization for Aid and Rescue. However, I could have transferred those Jews to the care of the Bund, the Jewish Coordinating Committee, and such institutions. But we didn't have to be convinced that one of the essential things for us was to rescue Jews; we all knew that. However, the essential function of the Jewish Fighting Organization was to organize Jews for war wherever possible. In Warsaw, there was no room for a continuous Jewish war, but there were Jewish remnants in various places. What did we want to do with those Jews? We couldn't bring them to Warsaw because we didn't have any place to hide them. So we wanted to move them to partisan units in the forest, and that required help. Very few were brought to Warsaw; and each one of them is known by name, like Ringelblum and Turkow. Every person was important, but it was symbolic and you could count them on your fingers, there were so few of them. Nevertheless, there were some tens of thousands more Jews, even in the two camps of Poniatów and Trawniki. Assisted by my contacts with Częstochowa and Hasag, the camps around Częstochowa, I could save two or three people and I'm not denigrating the importance of that; but the major activity was forming and organizing the forces that were left in Częstochowa, the political Halutz forces, organizing them for the future. Letters and various instructions were sent. First of all, we organized help for them, and we sent money. After the war, there were charges against the committee that handled that and all kinds of rumors reached me about the man who was generally seen as the central figure there. At any rate, he didn't show up after the war to shake hands with me or meet me personally. It's very hard to know the truth in such situations.

Afterward, we formed the Jewish Fighting Organization there. Some of the people, the young ones who survived, are still with us. At a certain stage, they received instructions of how to behave in case they were transferred; that was when the German retreat was at hand, and they had to organize for escape. And people did escape. At such a time, you can't imagine how important it is for imprisoned people when someone comes to them and encourages them to do that.

They ran away when they were taken west. They weren't given any means of transportation, and they were driven on the roads in caravans, by foot, and they needed any kind of encouragement. We knew that every such transport was tantamount to murder. I can produce testimonies of people I met after the war who got the announcement to escape and did; we were in touch. We used to tell them what was happening in the world, and we also sent them weapons. You can accuse Yitzhak Zuckerman of not making rescue a priority, but not the Jewish Fighting Organization. As a matter of fact, there's no excuse for accusations against me either; so don't accuse the organization of not putting rescue at the top of its list. For, with one thing and another, it was concerned with rescue; but its first priority was fighting the Germans. Nevertheless, we also looked for Jews. We were continually occupied with that, as with everything else that was important. We sent messengers, even when we knew we couldn't rescue anybody. I know I made a thousand mistakes during that period, but they were all technical errors. Maybe I could have done things differently, and I certainly know now, with hindsight, how to do things better. But I don't have an answer, not even a theoretical one, about the basic issue—how to save the nation! I can't blame myself and, to this day, I don't know the answer. And it's now 1974, and I've had many years to think about it. I don't even have a partial answer: move them out of the country? Hide them? Even today, I don't know. We did all we could. For instance, Turkow got ransom money not because of his pull with me. I would have done the same in any case like that, when there was a need to rescue someone in my group. And I don't know what was done in other groups. There were several hundred Jews, a few thousand. If we knew of a "burned" apartment, we immediately sent couriers to hide people, get them out, move them.

A year ago, Yad Vashem published a collection[87] which includes my report, as well as an essay by Yakov Robinson about this. In that essay, Robinson talks about "sanctification of the Name" [*Kiddush ha-shem*], and calls the Uprising a "sanctification of the Name," in the sense of dying for the Jewish faith and Jewish pride. On the other hand, there's something he calls "sanctification of life." We, the remaining branch of the Jewish people, of Polish Jewry, were saved by rescue. "*Lebn un iberlebn* (To live and survive)" was the greatest revenge, according to Robinson, because Hitler wanted to destroy the Jews, so that not even a trace of them would remain.

In my opinion, that's an artificial division. We thought that uprising and rescue went together. We thought so all along the way, from the time of the Jewish Fighting Organization in the ghetto. We always said that those two things didn't contradict each other, and we told the Jews that. At a certain stage, but too late, the Jews understood the situation. From the beginning of the ghetto, we called on them: "Jews, save your wives and

87. Yisrael Gutman and Livia Rothkirchen 1976.

children, hide them!" And on the other hand, we called: "Stand up and fight!" Those two things weren't contradictory. I never said we had to give up the lives of Jews. I said we had to save as many as we could; but nevertheless, we called for armed fighters to report for duty.

The same thing was also true on the Aryan side of Warsaw, where the situation was more serious because we had to figure not only the quality of a person's soul, the strength of his position and courage, but also the way he looked! It was very hard for a Jew to meet all the demands: to be both ready for war and also to look Aryan. He could have been a warrior in his soul, but he could have endangered the entire operation with his appearance. So, first of all, we searched for those who looked Aryan. Sometimes we didn't know how a person would stand up in time of trial; we didn't know where he came from, how he would hold out. How many candidates, after all, could we assemble on the Aryan side? We estimated that there were about 20,000 Jews on the Aryan side, and keep in mind that about 90 percent of them were hiding because they looked Jewish. What could they do? Only hide. So we helped them hide.

We searched high and low for anyone we could use. But only a few dozen Jews could be considered. Yet, where Jews were concentrated in a camp, imprisoned as Jews, we called on them to resist the enemy.

So I don't see that we presented one goal in the ghetto and another goal on the Aryan side. We wanted to save Jews in every period. I never had the nerve to say to a person: "You have to fight." Anyone who felt he had to fight made his way to us by himself. I never accused anyone who could have been a fighter and didn't fight, to this day. It matters to me only when, after the war, those people became fighters, commanders, as it were. A person may save his own life, act as he likes. I don't look down on anybody for that. But some people shamelessly assume the glory without any right. Those people are mostly lying deliberately. What are they counting on? The sensitivity of their friends? I won't expose the truth or give names. But it's indecent. They should blush with shame! Interestingly, their names don't appear in testimony or documents; they're not quoted or presented by any source; and all of a sudden, they turn into a "commander." There's a list of commanders, of the command staff. Where did this one come from?! I once witnessed something that appalled me. I can tell it because many people heard it.

There was once an argument about Israel's contacts with Germany. After Ben-Gurion's appearance on that subject, the partisans assembled. (At that time, I was still trying to be active; since then, I've stopped.) There was one man there who appeared next to Ben-Gurion at the *Mapai* center and expressed support for contacts with the Germans, Eliezer Lidovski. The partisan fighter, Barukh Levin, also attended the partisan meeting. He was a typical Jewish fighter. (He reminded me a little of Benny

Marshak, perhaps without all the ideological baggage.) He was like a volcano, a person whose wife and children were murdered, whose weapons, as with Benny Marshak, were something holy and clean, who never plundered a single thing for himself. A "ragamuffin," *sans-culotte*, as the gentiles called it, a legend. He was famous all over. Who hasn't heard of Barukh Levin?! We became friends the first time we met. When they came out of the forests, he wrote the "oath" of the Partisans, Soldiers, Halutzim. I edited it a bit and it appeared at the end of the *Sefer Milhamot ha-Gettaot* (*Book of Ghetto Wars*). He was a Communist, both in his youth and in the forest. Later, he "became a Jew." In Moscow, he was glorified and exalted after the war, but he left everything, went to Israel, and started a new family.

At that conference, we all attacked the idea of ties with Germany. We complained and rebelled against Leyzer Lidovski. If he hadn't appeared in public, nothing would have happened. We told him: "You have to be more sensitive to your comrades who aren't members of *Mapai*, but who were fighters and partisans. The decisions would have been made even without your speeches." Barukh Levin was sharper than anyone else. He got up and said: "When did you become a leader of fighting partisans?" There were some people who appointed themselves political leaders after the war because they were supposedly "partisan leaders." Since that episode, you don't hear much about Lidovski.

Barukh Levin was different. I salute him. He wasn't a commander but a person with the qualities of a fighter, and I love him dearly. Yosef Kaplan was the same.

In this context, I don't care if Barukh Levin was a Communist and Yosef Kaplan a Revisionist, while Leyzer Lidovski was a member of Po'alei Zion–Z.S. Taking that arbitrary credit is at the expense of others and, in my opinion, is loathsome.

Many books say that those who went to the forest did so from a desire to survive, thinking that their chances of surviving were greater in the forest than in the ghettoes, or on the Aryan side of Warsaw. There's a grain of truth in that assessment, but what was the "Aryan side"? The Aryan side of Warsaw wasn't like the "Aryan side" in a small town, where there is no "Aryan side" at all. In a big city, you can hide somehow. There was no "Aryan side" in Vilna either, and only very few people hid there. Vilna was a city of a quarter-million inhabitants, including Jews. Many of them came to Warsaw and hid there, where no one knew them.

But that's not the whole truth. For example, I can't imagine among the members of the youth movements that the decisive factor was to survive. Most of the partisans weren't from the youth movements, a great majority were "simple people." But the Vilna partisans were idealistic. They were young and they sought refuge in the forest. The family camps were also created like that. Engelstern's book on Vilna and its surrounding area shows the Jewish experience in that period.[88] Her book is an authentic diary. She isn't a writer but a woman who is very credible. She hides, loses her husband in the Vilna Ghetto, goes into hiding on the Aryan side. When she can no longer remain on the Aryan side, she is moved to a village.

Of course, there were also underground groups, for example in Baranowicz, young people organized for war in the forest. For them, that organization was a goal. But in a great many places, the Jews escaped to the forest, as in the case of Mir. Many Jews escaped to the forest, thanks to Oswald (Rufeisen), including Jews who were looking for a way to be saved. They knew they were going to a war zone, but they also probably took account of the hope of living. And there's nothing wrong with that! You can say that, unlike the ghetto uprisings, which were carried out only by members of movements, crystalized and aimed at their goal, and had an idealistic and organizational framework, the forest absorbed anyone who strove to survive, along with those who sought a channel to the war.

Another decisive factor was family ties, which were often a stumbling block for the Jews in Nazi times. Yakov Robinson says that breaking up the family could give a better chance for rescue, and that's true. But a loss in the family often paralyzed the rest of its members or undermined the spiritual and emotional ability to endure of those who survived. That happened in a great many cases, even in my own family in Vilna; and I know that certainly with Frumka and Mordechai Tennenbaum too. I had a big family, a big tribe, in Vilna. Not only the Zuckermans, also the Feldsteins—it's an extensive family. But the situation of my immediate family—father, mother, my oldest sister, her husband, and their little son Ben-Zion—was this: my father had a *Lebensschein* (work permit) he could use to protect Mother. My brother-in-law didn't have one, which meant that my sister and their child didn't have one either. I already said that Frumka tried to bring the child to me, but it was too late and didn't help.

What happened? One day, they seized my sister and brother-in-law and the child. My father, who had a *Lebensschein*, took Mother and reported along with my sister; that is, he supposedly had some "document that guaranteed life" and he reported for his fate in order to be with the family and not to distinguish between life and death; by then, they knew it was death. Afterward, I heard from someone who came out of prison, that they were in separate cells in Lukiszki.[89] He went with them, because of his daughter, my sister Lena; but there, men and women were separated. In the morning, my father would "keep up morale." He would

88. Ruth Engelstern (Laymenson) 1973.
89. The prison in Vilna.

wash the floor in Lukiszki Prison; Mordechai Tennenbaum, who met with him, told me that. He also said that if they had put buckets of water on Father's head, not a drop would have spilled—he was tall and erect and walked straight. Later they were taken. They didn't die together.

Those are facts about family ties and their outcome. It would be right to say their daughter Lena was worth it to them. We other brothers and sisters were like "birds of passage"; my older brother left for the Soviet Union; one sister (older than me) left for Eretz Israel; I was a kind of "ragtag" character. Lena had taken care of the family for years. When Father and Mother grew old in their apartment, out of Honor thy Father and Mother, Lena took them to her apartment, and they treated each other with mutual admiration. I don't have enough words to appreciate her deed; in comparison with her, you can say I behaved like a bum toward my parents.

That often bothered me. But can you imagine me, who was supposedly so "important," telling Frumka to bring them to Warsaw. That didn't seem ethical to me. I don't think it's right to discriminate in their favor and endanger people for them. That didn't look good to me. Furthermore, I knew Warsaw eventually wouldn't exist either.

So there is some basis for that statement that family ties were sometimes a stumbling block. It was also true in Warsaw. Many people had a shred of hope of surviving, but were lost because part of their family was killed. Husbands often reported to the *Umschlagplatz* on their own, after their wives were taken. But, family ties were also an ancient source of Jewish strength; it was a sign of moral superiority; but it is also true that it physically injured some families in terms of surviving. We must also say that those who cut themselves off from their families to survive degenerated morally since they later imagined that anything was permitted in order to survive. I don't know if we Jews are exceptional in this, but maintaining family ties is a very characteristic Jewish trait.

ELEVEN

The Polish Uprising

Did the German retreat on the Russian front and the rumors about that, which spread among both the Polish and the Jewish population, change the behavior of the Germans and the Poles toward the Jews? And did this increase the possibilities of rescue and assistance operations?

All information from the front had an emotional influence on the Jews, and probably the Poles, too. You can find signs of that among the chroniclers. The Jews were divided as usual between the optimists and the pessimists. I can mention names of people whose hopes were roused by every German plane that was brought down. For example, back in the ghetto, during the Great *Aktsia*, there were Russian bombings of Warsaw (on August 20, 1942), the day we attacked Szerynski and set buildings on fire. Meanwhile, bombs also fell in the ghetto and some people said the Soviets were coming to help the ghetto; naturally that was absurd. Some say the fire drew the Russian pilots, which is more conceivable because the bombing didn't hit any defined target, and probably not any strategic targets. They hit the civilian population. The ghetto was empty and a few buildings were hit. What help could that have been?

All that information, even absurd information, encouraged many people throughout the war; but, in this period on the Aryan side, there was a difference. In 1941, there was delusion or encouragement for 2 million Jews. In 1944, only for a few tens of thousands. None of us was completely free of the influence of changes on the fronts, especially since, in December 1942 and January 1943, there was a great turning point on the war fronts: first Stalingrad; and second the battle of

El-Alamein.[1] Of course, that was encouraging. But I won't be the public spokesman on this because I lived without delusions. That is, despite the encouraging rumors, I had to understand that, in another five minutes, I might not be alive. I was devoted to a specific work, a specific situation, which had nothing whatever to do with the front at Stalingrad or the defeat or victory of some other front. In my personal case, some group that didn't know all the details about me was searching for "Captain Antek," and they thought he was a gentile. I lived in emotional tension twenty-four hours a day. I could overcome that externally and even Zivia didn't always feel it. I know that people hide their fear with artificial gaiety and macabre jokes. And I was always jolly. At any rate, I was less nervous than in 1944. But we felt the change even before April 1943, before our Uprising. We sensed that a change was taking place in the ethics of the German soldier, signaled by the fact that he began to sell weapons. Some of the weapons of our fighters were German weapons sold by them, as well as plundered weapons. Today I don't have to explain; we all know there are weapons for sale, even here in Israel. Maybe the Germans didn't know they sold their weapons to Jews; they sold them to Poles, to speculators. But the weapons also got to us and we sensed their declining morale, since the acquisition of weapons became freer. In any case, we sensed a certain change by August 1944, when you heard the sound of cannons from the front, thirty kilometers from Warsaw, from Mińsk-Mazowiecki. When we saw the German civilian population, the families of the German administration, maybe tens of thousands, those who governed the occupied territories—when we saw them crossing Warsaw, we sensed that a change was taking place.

I already said that an envoy from Switzerland came just before the Uprising. If that had happened three months before the Uprising began, I probably wouldn't have gone to the German quarter to meet a strange woman. I had an argument with our little commune. I said I was going because I didn't believe that the Gestapo squad looking for "Captain Antek" would try to catch me so stupidly with that bait. I went. And it turned out she really was an envoy. I went despite the danger, because a change had taken place. I may not be representing public opinion. I don't know what other Jews thought. At any rate, I, who always walked around the streets, sensed the real change only about the time of the Polish Uprising, with the approach of the Russian front.

1. The battle of Stalingrad took place from the summer of 1942 to February 2, 1943, when the encircled German army surrendered. The battle of El-Alamein was fought in February 1942, and from October 23, 1942, to November 4, 1942.

It's hard for me to say whether German operations in Warsaw grew weak, just as I can't say that one day was like another. But when you look at it over time, it was one long period of terror. And if I talk about the Poles, they also had an unbearable and inconceivable situation. Bodies hung in the street, on telegraph poles, there were murders, up to the final day. People were seized and sent to concentration camps, death camps. In sum, I don't think the defeats on the front changed the Germans' plans for the places they ruled. The terror may even have gotten worse, it's quite possible; but I can't say that for sure, because who can record and weigh those things? A person in hiding hears only rumors. But a member of the Polish underground, who was active as a politician, was in danger every single day. In terms of tension and risk, what difference does it make to him if the front is distant or close? The person as an individual was in mortal danger up to the very last minute. He saw himself in a trap. There were all kinds of weaknesses, all kinds of fears. For example, even a tram ride could have been a trap; I felt that personally, and it turned into a fear of going into a small place that can always be blocked on two sides; they posted two German soldiers and you were in a trap. I trusted my feet and would walk kilometers. At the time, there was a kind of "vibration" in the air that told you Germans were around. When I walked, I knew that here is an alley, there is a yard, a building you can climb up to. But not in a tram, where I couldn't flee. Sometimes, I had no choice, I had to run from one meeting to the next and from one part of the city to the other. There weren't any taxis or buses. There were only trams and rickshaws. I used rickshaws, but not much, only a few times. Incidentally, the Polish underground also put rickshaws to use. Quite a few of the rickshaw drivers were members of the underground who transported newspapers, information, and other things this way; and it also served as a familiar means of transportation. For there weren't any cars, except for the Germans or exceptional cases like the mayor. Czerniakow also had a car in the ghetto.

Even before the Uprising began, we sensed that something was taking shape, but we learned the real date only when the Uprising started. Fortunately for me, on the day the Uprising began I was in the quarter where I lived; that is, the part of the city controlled by the rebels. When the Uprising started, the Germans may have been surprised but they immediately took up arms to subdue it. The Uprising didn't encompass all Warsaw. In Praga, for example, there was no uprising. I often had meetings in Praga and, if I had chanced to go there at the start of the Uprising, I would have gotten stuck outside the Uprising, and I don't think I would have felt comfortable in that case. But we were on a nearby street when the Uprising started, and I could get to my apartment at Leszno 18. Before that, I didn't know a thing. Later I learned that the

Communists (the PPR) and the AL didn't know a thing in advance either. They were surprised and didn't know what to do at the first moment. But they decided—correctly, I think—to join since there was an uprising, a war against the Germans. I'm talking now about the Communists of 1944. And I emphasize that thirty years have passed and, to this day, I can't forget how lucky I was to have been put with that group of Communists in those days—idealists, loyal to the socialist idea, genuine Polish Communists. What happened later when the government was in their hands is another story—when they turned to instructions from the east. Frankly, if I weren't a Jew and the Eretz-Israeli solution weren't in my bones, I would have joined their ranks. Moreover, I would have brought their ideals to Eretz Israel. It took a very long time until I began to have reservations, because I didn't know what went on behind the scenes, since things were known in dribs and drabs. In fact, everything that took place there, in the USSR, the labor camps, all the inhuman suffering of masses of people there was shrouded in fog; and we defended them because we really thought there was a genuine idea behind it. We gave them an extraordinarily, uniquely large amount of credit. We saw something historic in "October."[2] I can't deny that appreciation. I myself called on the Jews to join the fighters in the Polish Uprising. I say specifically that I called on the Jews to support the Polish fighters. I composed a declaration on the third day of the Uprising and signed it: "Commander Antek." It was published by the Communists and later by the AK in all the underground press that appeared at the start of the Uprising. When I wrote it, I knew I would fight in the ranks of the Communist Armia Ludowa. But my public responsibility told me that the declaration had to be general and had to call on the Jews to join the fighters for democratic, free Poland without mentioning which side.

Although I knew my place was in the ranks of the AL, I also carried on negotiations with the AK and I emphasize *I carried on*, because in the *Folksshtime* I got yesterday[3] (I think I'm the only member of Lohamei Ha-Getaot who reads that newspaper as well as the *Sovietish Heymland* from Moscow), they quote a fragment of that proclamation in the thirty-year commemoration of the Polish Uprising. And that group is proud of the Jewish Fighting Organization and the survivors who joined the rebels and fought in the ranks of the fighting organization, as Jews. And it's all well and good even without mentioning "Commander Antek," especially since the Poles don't refrain from mentioning him in various contexts.

2. That is, the October Revolution of October 24–25, 1917, with which the Bolsheviks seized power in Russia.
3. August 31, 1974, no. 35.

But the truth is that the *Folksshtime* published the proclamation without the signature. It was apparently written by some anonymous person. That borders on forgery, since the proclamation is signed. What would have happened to them if they had printed the author's name?! Incidentally, the Poles don't treat me like that. I saw a few official Polish collections of documents that mentioned me. It's not important if those Jews in the *Folksshtime* attack me as a Zionist, but let them tell the truth!

In the last issue of *Sovietish Heymland* I received, they write, among other things, that the Zionists did participate in the uprisings and were in the anti-German underground; but they weren't sent by the underground or the movements. That is, they fought as individuals. That was written in 1974! There's no limit to the falsification! I think I was very close to them but this horrible falsification—who is it for? Who's forcing them to write this article? Let them write about literature, fiction. I must say that they behave like whores.

They say the *Yevsektsia* was once the height of degeneration and humiliation, but I don't think so.[4] I think the Jewish Communists in Poland in 1946 were much worse than that. The *Yevsektsia* operated at a time when there were millions of Jews in the Soviet Union and they saw their operations as a way. They saw a solution in integration into Socialism; they learned from general Bolshevik theory. But today they know the truth and they lie deliberately; they lie not only about what has been proven to exist in Israel as truth. Doesn't the editor, Vergilis, know? He knows, but he just doesn't care. He lies, and that's humiliating. As a Jew, as Antek— that matters to me, that whole subject of the "participation of the Zionists in the uprisings." The greatness of Zionism, of the Halutz movement, was expressed in the ghetto uprisings, in the Warsaw Ghetto Uprising, both in places where there were Communists and in places where there weren't any Communists. After all, Hitler annihilated them and Stalin annihilated them even before that; that's loathsome. I threw out the *Sovietish Heymland* because I couldn't read it, although I usually do read that paper, as a person interested in Jewish life everywhere.

In my meetings with the AL and the AK, did the possibility of an uprising come up? Was there a sense that such a moment was approaching? Did they think there would be an active operation of the Polish underground before the Soviets entered Warsaw? I must say that in my conversations with the Poles, the AK and the AL, I never heard any concrete plan. But it was in the air.

The AK and most of the unorganized Aryan Polish population, not to mention the organized population—that is, the part that was loyal to

---

4. The *Yevsektsia* was the Jewish department in the propaganda wing of the Soviet Communist Party. It was set up in 1918 and closed in 1930.

the Government-in-Exile in London, which was most of the Polish people—saw the AL as phraseologists or as aliens. But the AL was close to
my heart from the very first day, because they called for revolt and
resistance everywhere, at every hour and at every opportunity. True,
their call was more thunder than acts performed, but there's sometimes
value in the spoken and written word, too; and they did call for war all
the time. So preaching revolt wasn't concrete for them, since they had
appealed for an uprising before, without making it operative. I was very
close to the command staff of the AL and was invited to discussions with
its members, and I didn't sense any special preparation; and I know they
were surprised, too. Nevertheless, they were willing to join in an orderly
way and prepared for that in the underground. They counted on the
approaching Soviet cannons. I can only repeat what I said in the council
of Kibbutz Ha-Meuchad at Na'an[5] in 1947, that the Polish Uprising was
an armed uprising against the Germans; but, politically and more clearly,
it was an uprising against the Russians. Every educated person understood that immediately. After all, we heard the Russian cannons every
single day. And you could expect that their battle for Warsaw would be
fought within forty-eight hours. That's what the Poles needed and, from
their perspective, they were right. That's what De Gaulle did in Paris. He
didn't need the Allies at all, but he thwarted their plans. He simply
confronted the Allies with a fact. He had pretensions, a characteristic "De
Gaullist majesty." Here, there was no majesty. Here, there was a carefully
calculated political course. De Gaulle certainly wasn't afraid the English
or Americans would take Paris for themselves. But here, a great danger
threatened that the liberation of Warsaw would be done by the Red Army.
And that meant a Red Warsaw. They wanted to create a fait accompli. I
understood that, but I didn't accept it. My opinions were very close to the
AL and, like them, I didn't praise that act. Not because I didn't want to
fight the Germans, but because I was against that political course. But, in
general, I think the Poles were right. They didn't succeed, so they were
abandoned by the Russians and forced to pay the price.

This week, I saw in one of the newspapers the figure of 150,000
Poles killed in Warsaw during the two months of the Uprising. All
the years, I knew about 250,000 Poles who were killed in the Polish
Uprising, and that doesn't only include fighters, but also the civilian
population, including Jews. There are a few books on this, but not much
has been written about it. If I changed the Polish names in those books,
it would sound like a Jewish story. The Germans used the same methods
against the Poles. They would take them out, have them dig their own
graves, and shoot them; that's what they did in Warsaw, in the suburb of

5. Na'an: A kibbutz in central Israel, affiliated with Ha-Kibbutz Ha-Meuchad.

Wola. The gravediggers were young people who burned the bodies on the spot. Polish soldiers taken from the barricades or who became prisoners burned the bodies.

I don't know if the gravediggers were promised their lives in exchange, but that is what they hoped for, at least. The Germans killed them just like they killed the Jews. When I talk with young people who visit our museum,[6] I explain to them that you can turn people of any nation, any race, or religion into "Jews"—make them behave just like Jews. My comrades and I were lucky that we were always on the other side of the barricades. But those who fell into the hands of the Germans—and this time it was Poles—behaved just like the Jews had. In a short time, in weeks, the Germans turned them into loathsome, humiliated, fearful people; and keep in mind, the Poles weren't starved for years like the Jews in the ghettoes, but were led away with their hands up, and they saw their nation, their families, their neighbors falling into the pits and dying. Tens of thousands of people.

The AK leaders probably prepared the timing of the Uprising, and there was a sense that something had to happen. As for me, even then I didn't accept their perspective. I didn't care if Warsaw was "Red." So I couldn't accept that act. But I think they were right in terms of their perspective. If you opposed "Red Warsaw," you had to try to make the Uprising at that date. They also counted on the sympathy of the outside Western world. But the Red Army behaved as it did, according to its accounting; and on the other hand, the West abandoned Poland. Their act wasn't in tune with my perspective; I didn't think they should anticipate the Red Army with a political act of Polish participation in the liberation of Warsaw. Such an operation didn't suit the Polish Communists either. Their newspaper did indeed call for an uprising in May 1944. They attributed importance to the activism of the Polish people in their war against the Germans. But that date, when the approaching Soviet cannons were echoing, that is, near August 1944, didn't seem suitable to them.

I cannot know if the Polish Communists had pretensions to an uprising of their own. The PPR was built on the ruins of the Communist party, which was destroyed by the Komintern and Stalin some time before the war, and re-established in 1942, with the permission of Moscow. So I can't know what pretensions Gomułka or Witold, the AL chief of staff, had; but in fact they didn't do anything, although they were Polish patriots—I have no doubt of that—because they couldn't do anything in Warsaw without instructions from Moscow. I think that the "sages" in Warsaw were the same kind of "Kremlin sages." The Soviets definitely didn't want an

6. Beit Katznelson, the Holocaust museum at Kibbutz Lohamei Ha-Getaot.

independent uprising in Warsaw. They were interested in the conquest of Warsaw without a Polish Uprising; so they stayed on the other side of the Wisła. They have their own explanations of why they didn't offer the help needed. They explain that their army suffered a defeat near Deblin, seventy kilometers from Warsaw. It's dubious if this explanation is correct because, at the end of the final month of the Uprising, their army reached Praga on the outskirts of Warsaw. They gave only symbolic help to the Polish people. I have no reason to feel sympathy for the AK; but I must say, simply from a human angle, people were simply killed and murdered en masse in Warsaw. And those were futile sacrifices. But you also have to remember that the Uprising was done in coordination with London.

I said that even without knowing an exact date you could feel the Uprising in the air; and as for considerations and thoughts about what we would do if the Uprising started, I didn't have a single minute of doubt. After all, we had constantly tried to construct a fighting unit on the Aryan side of Warsaw. In my correspondence with AK, there are letters from Wacław authorizing the establishment of a Jewish unit that would join their fighters. My ideas and their ideas—that's not important. I wanted to organize a Jewish unit and you couldn't establish a Jewish force without help from the Poles. Although 20,000 Jews in Warsaw is an impressive number, that doesn't mean there were so many young people who had gentile faces; and if I had succeeded before the Uprising in forming a unit of even fifty people, I would have regarded that as an achievement. We brought that idea up constantly: wherever there is a war against the Germans, we're there! And every war against the Germans is our war! It was clear immediately, from the start. So we weren't surprised by the Uprising. We expected it. It was the day we had wished for.

When the Polish Uprising started, I didn't know what our real force was. How many people did we have? Because there is a difference between an established unit when the Nazi government was still at its height and every fighter had to look Aryan, on the one hand, and a time of uprising, when fighters appear openly as Jews, on the other. At that time, I didn't know the bitter truth I learned only after the Uprising, that in those days, AK members murdered many Jews, including our people. When the Uprising began, I was in the area of Pańska Street 5. If I hadn't been, I would have been cut off from the people who were close to me. At the start of the Uprising, when the Polish flag waved in the sky, I called on all those who could to join, even those who looked Jewish. (Didn't Zivia and Marek Edelman look Jewish?) The Jews were scattered throughout Warsaw; we were in the Old City, a separate quarter, where our battle was fought. The same is true of Zolibórz, a suburb of Warsaw near the Wisła, where I had spent several days in January and February 1944, when I knew they were looking for me. I would go out early in the morning, leave Zivia and all the comrades. Kazik was the only one with me. Zolibórz was about eight kilometers from the center of the city, and because of my "tram trauma," I would walk.

Who reported for duty in the Polish Uprising? In our area, the remaining members of the ghetto fighting group joined, including people who were later murdered by the Germans as well as those who were murdered by the AK. There were also some who joined not as Jews, but simply as fighters. Polish publications tell of many Jews who joined the Polish units as individuals, registered in their Polish aliases. Many Jews who were killed in the Uprising were buried as Poles.

We have to take account of the fact that the desire to fight the Germans, expressed in the Polish Uprising, wasn't exclusive to the members of the Jewish Fighting Organization. That was a day of revenge that many people looked forward to and when it came, they joined the ranks. We counted on all those we could reach. Our group wasn't important in terms of quantity, but symbolically, it made an extraordinary impression. To this very day, the Poles mention that. There was something strange in it and, perhaps, in fact, not so strange. Between 1.4 and 1.5 million Jews fought in World War II in the Allied armies; I'm talking about the participation of the Jews in the war. And what remains of that in history? The Warsaw Ghetto Uprising! Because it was done under a Jewish banner. In the ranks of the Polish Uprising, there were perhaps a hundred or two hundred times more fighters, but our small group of less than twenty people was what inserted the Jewish banner into the Polish revolt. The Poles themselves note that. And we appeared there, from the first moment, as Jews. Although I wasn't known as a Jew, here and now, in this Uprising, I wanted them to know I was a Jew. Our group was a nationalist group, the only organized one. These were members of the Jewish Fighting Organization, fighting on the front of the Old City of Warsaw. Other Jews, even small groups of fighters, joined as individuals—and that's the difference. I must say that there were many Jews in the Uprising who were cited for bravery. The Poles tell of them in their literature. Apparently there were former soldiers and former officers of the Polish army among them; experts in various military areas, distinguished for valor, and whose memory is now evoked. Some were killed whose Jewish name isn't known; but they were known to be Jews. As I said, many Jews were murdered by members of AK. That didn't happen in the Old City, I think, because of us.

In the apartments on Pańska and at Leszno 18, we had weapons; we probably didn't take everything. Those were the weapons I had prepared and sent to various places from time to time, since I didn't intend to keep them in the arms cache. I would send them where I knew they were needed and could be used. I always had a store of pistols, grenades, and explosives. That "helped a lot" in the bombing of our archive when the Germans hit that house with their mortars.

I can't answer specific questions about the Uprising. I would meet with Jews, but not very much. My contact was always through couriers. I knew everything that was done, about every fortification that fell. I got daily, weekly, monthly reports; but I can't tell about Jews at all except for our own group. Before the Polish Uprising, that was the most wretched group in the sense that, though it was a fighting group, and in other conditions, in another place—in the ghetto, among Jews—it would have continued to fight and wouldn't have ended its war on May 10, 1943, with the burning of the ghetto, on the Aryan side, it was doomed to paralysis. The people couldn't do a thing. What could Zivia do? I cite her as an example because of her explosive temperament. She demanded things that couldn't be achieved. The force of her claim was that you always had to stand on tiptoe and even then couldn't reach. The same goes for Marek Edelman, whom I saw up close as a brave fighter, and in the Old City, too.

That was a fighting group in its soul, but paralyzed physically because of conditions. Now, in the Polish Uprising, that force was liberated. I don't have to be a psychologist to understand what took place in the souls of those people. I imagine they had always carried that dream in their heart—to fight the Germans. Now came August 1, 1944, and the Uprising freed them.

Here's a story from the days of the Polish Uprising: Jurek, our comrade Luba Gewisser's boyfriend, was a member of the Polish Scouts and friendly with Hubert Kaminski. On the day the Uprising began, Luba was on a mission to Praga beyond the Wisła River. By then, we were on Leszno Street. Luba's boyfriend was hiding in the apartment. When she left, she locked the door so it looked as if no one were at home. Remaining in the apartment, he tried to be quiet, not to run the water in the bathroom, and so forth. Certain rules had to be followed whenever no one was supposed to be at home. No one was prepared for the Uprising; certainly not that couple; there weren't any stocks of food in the house. When the Uprising began, she remained on the other side of the Wisła and he remained locked in the apartment. One day passed and then another. He heard shooting and understood what was going on and was probably happy. When he ran out of food, he started knocking on the door for someone to let him out. The neighbors came, opened the door, and arrested him. He tried to explain and even referred to his distinguished Polish friend Hubert Kaminski, one of the leaders of the AK underground, and hoped they would believe him. But the Poles took him to the Polish police, which was hastily beginning to organize in the conditions of the Uprising, and they executed him.

How many Jews were murdered? How many of the 20,000 in Warsaw were killed? Now I know how many were killed; in those days, I didn't. We fought in the Old City and I must say that if there are days of honor in Polish or Jewish history, they were the days of this war. When I passed by with my comrades, they would applaud us from both sides. Maybe such a thing also happened in 1863, during that Polish Uprising, too.[7] It didn't matter if we held some position; any other group could have done that. What was important was that it expressed the participation of a nation. The banner of the Warsaw Ghetto remains in historical memory, the banner of a Jewish war. Thousands of Jews fought in the Polish Uprising, but that group is engraved in history because it bore the Jewish banner, because it appeared for everyone as a Jewish fighting unit. I'm not judging the personal significance for everyone who participated in it, but the national significance. I don't have any thought or pretension that I have to save the honor of the nation; joining was simply an internal, emotional need: *Wherever they stand up against the German troops—there is our place!*

In the Uprising, we fought in many places throughout Warsaw. ZOB members, for example, weren't far from Okęcie, where our unit was, in the bunker where I visited them close to the start of the Uprising. The place was taken immediately by the Germans and the members there were captured and later executed. That was a group of Ha-Shomer Ha-Tza'ir who had come there in December 1943, from Ostrowiec. They had previously been in the forests and we brought them back from there. I encouraged their return because there weren't any chances for a partisan unit in those areas (about 100 kilometers from Warsaw). They weren't identified with either of the two underground groups and were hated by everyone around. Hatred for Jews and for anyone who tried to help them was abysmal there. For example, in Koniecpol, near Częstochowa, Poles who helped our group were murdered. Going to the forest in May 1943 resulted only from helplessness, from a lack of any other solution.

I must also state that, from the first moment, throughout Warsaw, we were among the few who didn't believe in the success of the Polish Uprising. When the Uprising began, and the Red Army cannons fell silent, we grasped the meaning of what was happening, and we realized that the AL didn't know the Uprising was about to start. We learned that they weren't coordinated with Moscow at all. In light of that situation, we didn't believe the Poles would overcome the Germans on their own.

7. The Polish insurrection of January 22, 1863, was against the policy of Count Aleksander Wielopolski, who supported a loyal union with Russia and planned to press the revolutionary youth of the Polish cities into the Russian army. The uprising was crushed after fifteen months and was followed by executions, confiscations, and deportations.

That period looks to me like a glorious period of the Jews among the Polish people. It seems as if only then did the Poles grasp the meaning of the Jewish Uprising in the ghetto and relate to us properly. It's too bad our fighting force wasn't in the center of the city. I'm not accusing the leadership. The people aren't alive anymore. One died right after the war (L. Feiner—"Mikolaj"). Another, a member of the Bund, died here in Israel. How did Jews get murdered there?! Why wasn't there an immediate Jewish representation? With us, in the Old City (*Stare Miasto*), there was an address right away where people could come, an address known both by the AK and the AL.

Many Jews joined the Uprising, including, for example, those imprisoned in Pawiak and released; Jews from Greece and other countries; some of our women couriers in the area at the time also joined (Inka Szwajger, for example, was a doctor in the AK hospital). Others of our couriers joined the Polish units of the AK and the AL. There were also some who didn't want to be exposed as Jews, since they didn't know how the Polish Uprising would turn out.

As a rule, most of those questions have no answer and it's better for me to be strict with myself than with others. Going to war was tantamount to suicide, but we went to that war fully aware that if that was the end, let it be so. Not that we thought from the first moment "I'm going to commit suicide," but a lot of things go through your mind.

In terms of practical matters, we were well off. We were organized in a military framework in which I had a respectable position, as, for example, participation in the military command staff of the AL. Given the conditions, I had everything I needed. And that was at a time when the civilian population was starving. Even if I had had the millions of Złotys that were lost at Leszno, what could I have done with them? Can you eat money? But I must say that a few weeks after the Uprising, it turned out that Jews needed help—and there was no money.

We went to that war of our own will, and we wanted to be in it as Jews.

As we know, there were a million and a quarter inhabitants in Warsaw before the war. Many Poles left for the villages and fled to various places. After the Uprising, and the murder of the half million Jews of Warsaw, 750,000 inhabitants were left, and during the two months of the Polish Uprising, every third person in Warsaw died or was murdered. That means that, from August 1 to September 30, *250,000 Poles were murdered*. The Germans did that, it happened in Warsaw. Right in the heart of the city. Fortunately for us, perhaps, we couldn't know about that when it was going on. We knew only what was taking place nearby. The Polish press says that our group didn't surrender. The truth is that we couldn't surrender, neither physically nor emotionally. We could not believe in the success of the Uprising, since we immediately grasped the nature of the situation. In conversation with Polish friends—and I had very good friends, mostly Communists—I explained to them that, from the Soviet point of view, it was an imperative and consistent position, no matter how painful it was.

We didn't go to war to die. We did everything to survive after the Uprising; but we knew that death was the likely outcome. One thing we did know—that we wouldn't surrender under any conditions. I don't think any other group of people was as conscious of what it could expect as we were. We were beyond all hope. We heard German voices where we were posted, from our barricade. We were the only ones who didn't go into a bunker or into hiding for twenty-four straight hours. Going into the cellar was one of the hardest things for us, like riding a tram. Later, I was assigned to rescue the Polish inhabitants of the cellars in our area, whose houses had caved in on them. The AL cellars weren't meant for housing. Meanwhile, I talked to the trapped people, I heard their voices and tried to cheer them; but we couldn't save them. That was a six-story building. After the war, they took the bodies out of the cellar and buried them in the center of the city. One of them was Major Nestek Matywiecki (a Jew), of the AL staff. Their commander was Grysza, an extraordinary gentile, who was only five years older than me, but was considered old.

AK members later did research and wrote books about the Polish Uprising. It was known that the participants weren't all made of the same stuff. There were Socialists and peasants as well as members of the NSZ, the Fascists; and there were also members of Sanacja. The story of the messenger supposedly sent by the Red Army to coordinate the operation with the AK was pure fiction, a political deceit. If they had appealed to Moscow, Moscow would have known what to reply; but they didn't. They wanted to anticipate, to confront Moscow with a completed fact. We knew the people and we also knew the Red Army from way back. After all, that was our second encounter with them. The battles in Warsaw went on for months and the Russians said: "Never mind. Let the Russian soldiers rest in peace on the banks of the Wisła and let 250,000 Poles rest in peace under the ruins of Warsaw." On the day of the Liberation, the soldiers who fought at Stalingrad said that that city was less devastated than Warsaw. What happened was a result of a cold calculation by Moscow. To my great sorrow, if I had to choose between "decadent democracy" and that "fresh socialism" I became acquainted with, I don't know which I would select.

They said that Stalin "rushed" to save Warsaw, just as the Allies hurried to save the people of Paris. But 250,000 human beings were murdered by the Germans and the city of Warsaw was destroyed. All the members of the Polish army were taken prisoner, to concentration camps, except for General Bór-Komorowski, the commander of the Uprising, who was left in the position of a defeated general, out of political considerations.

When Zivia and I were on vacation in Tel Aviv, I went to visit Aharon Carmi, who invited friends of his in Tel Aviv, members of the Jewish Fighting Organization, and we spent an evening talking. Pnina Grinspun, Haim Frimmer's girlfriend, was also there, and she said she remembered that I came to them the day before the Polish Uprising began, brought them money, and explained that I wasn't sure I could stay in touch, and they should have some money. She also told her own story, which is a tale in itself.[8] It's good to hear a real story without any embellishments.

That evening, I also mentioned the placed I had gone to visit one day before the Uprising. Pnina Grinspun-Frimmer may have been the only survivor. That day, I traveled by rickshaw, which I usually didn't do. That day, I was carrying a lot of dollars, and was very tense. I distributed the money to our groups at that time in case we were cut off. That was twenty-four hours before the Uprising began, and it was in the air. It started at about five o'clock in the afternoon, if I'm not mistaken. The Germans appeared and cut off entire suburbs, Praga, for instance. Our place overlooked the bridges.

I accepted the Uprising with a feeling I can't put into words: a feeling that, at last, the moment of revenge on the Germans had arrived. The next day, August 1, 1944, I wrote the famous proclamation in Polish, formulated very diplomatically. That is, no emotions or ideology, but an appeal to the remnant of the Jewish Fighting Organization and young Jews, who were armed, to join the Uprising for a free Poland, democracy, and so forth. I didn't say who to join. Although we had decided to join the AL, I wasn't authorized to act as a private person or as a representative of a small group. I met previously with fighters in that area of Leszno and Dzielna and I knew their position. First, I negotiated with the AK so everyone would know the Jewish Fighting Organization was joining, and second, that the Jewish Fighting Organization took full responsibility, not as an auxiliary organization, but as an organization that would appear in its own name. That proclamation was published in the press, which was no longer an underground. It appeared in the press of the London people and of the PPR, and in all kinds of other presses and that was significant. To this day, those facts are published in Poland. It expresses pride for the participation of Jews in the Uprising, even though, in fact, it was a symbolic participation. The Jews gave all they had, all that was left: that small group, the Jewish Fighting Organization; there was no more than that on the field.

8. See her book, *Our Days Were Nights* (Hebrew), 1984.

I negotiated with the AK and they put me off with hemming and hawing. I think the minutes of those meetings are in the Polish documentation. Apparently, Henryk Wołyński (Wacław), my Polish friend, in charge of Jewish issues in the AK, testified on that after the war. He said he had gotten word of appeals that weren't answered; that is, he confirmed that I didn't get a reply to my appeals. Nevertheless, I must state that as soon as the Uprising began, I came to the command staff of the AK in the Old City, close to Leszno and easy to get to, a ten-minute walk (before the area was occupied by the Germans, of course). On August 3, I published the proclamation to the Jews. I wrote it and Sak, an expert in the Polish language, formulated it and corrected the language.

Later, when I met with the command staff of the AL, I learned that, in the staff meeting of the AL, my friend Major Sanek Molecki (who had the same military rank as I) had opposed including the Jewish Fighting Organization in the Uprising. That stunned me since I had had friendly and brotherly relations with him in the underground years on the Aryan side of Warsaw. But he explained immediately that it would be too great an historical responsibility to send the few survivors of the Ghetto Uprising back to war. "We have to keep them in a museum, protect them," he said. Coming from him, that was a genuine reason, a human reason. It was an expression of the responsibility of a "gentile" Pole toward his Jewish brothers. I replied that neither I nor my comrades would accept the rejection. I said I would tell them about it and ask them, but I was sure they wouldn't accept it. And, fifteen minutes later, I confirmed what I had said; all my comrades at Leszno 18 rejected the idea of not participating in the Uprising. And our apartment immediately turned into a magnet for all those who learned of it and were eager to participate in the Uprising. I'm referring to Bundists as well as Yosef Sak, who joined immediately. The same goes for Stefan Grajek and Tuvia Borzykowski, who wasn't with us and we found him somewhere in the area; and David Klein of the Bund, and many others. Fortunately for us, the landlords had stocked the house with food. Now we were all together; we slept on the floor until we joined the fighters. That went on for three days. After the proclamation was published, we all went in a convoy to the AL command staff; our house was in firing range of the Germans from Pawiak, but we didn't take even one hit before we left. We left there to force the AL to accept us. They refused to send us to the barricades, but we insisted. So we were given an important position on Mostowa Street. I knew the central people of the AL since I always met with each of them separately; now I met them all together. They treated us well and were friendly to me, which they expressed by often including me in the command staff meetings even though I wasn't a member. In dark, critical times, when the situation was grave, I participated in those meetings of joint consideration and consultation. In his book, Tuvia Borzykowski tells of "our" barricades, one of the most difficult.[9]

We were quite skeptical about the results of the Uprising and, unlike the Poles, we didn't hope for victory. However, we fought properly and all Warsaw knew that.

We had side arms. I took the grenades with me, but I left the explosives in the apartment on Leszno, in the bunker with the dollars and all our documents. We took our side arms, but later we got the sort of weapons they had. They wanted to appoint me commander of that barricade, but I said: "Look, you know we're here as Jews and in the name of the Jewish Fighting Organization. On that barricade, we fight alongside members of the AL and also with the members of the AK—I'm not Stanisław Bagniewski here, but Yitzhak Zuckerman, and you have to take account of the fact that I'm fighting here as a Jew, because if something happens to the Polish fighters, they'll blame the Jews. Furthermore, they may not accept my authority. So, I request a demotion in rank (I was a major) to second lieutenant. (After the war, the Polish Ministry of Defense awarded me the rank of *Półkownik*, parallel to the rank of colonel.) I'm no longer a major, I'm one of the fighters." The reason to request a demotion was that, as a major, I couldn't fight under the command of a Polish lieutenant. But, for both the AK and the AL, I was the senior person among the Jews. Out of responsibility, I didn't want to accept command of that barricade on Mostowa Street. Across from us was the "Red House," famous in the history of the Uprising. It was on the western side of the Wisła and was held by the Germans (it was restored after the war). The commanders of the AL changed but they would always consult with me. The procedure was that, for twenty-four hours, that fighting barricade was in our hands, and for twenty-four hours, we went to rest in the rear. Twenty-four hours without sleep, until we were relieved. We erected the barricade in the street, perhaps a hundred meters from the "Red House," where the Germans were based. We heard their voices and looked at heaps of junk and rocks and a deep excavation. There were positions and observation points in the buildings, and we stayed on duty on the barricade. We were better off there than when we rested in the "rear," because at the barricade, we weren't hit by airplanes or artillery. The Germans couldn't shell us because of our proximity to their "Red House." The hard times were the twenty-four hours in the rear. We had retreat bases where there were houses that took us in. As we went from the barricade to the "rear" and back, all the "gentiles" knew that this was the Jewish unit. We didn't feel a trace of antisemitism. Perhaps for the

9. "It was one of the most dangerous posts in the Old City, located close to German posts on the [Wisla] River" (Borzykowski 1972:170).

first time in my life in Poland, since my childhood, I felt unrestrained admiration of us.

You have to understand that we weren't a decisive force, not even an important force; we were only a few dozen; but, morally, we were significant; we were proud of our participation in the Uprising. What can a single paratrooper bring with him? Almost nothing! But sometimes he brings encouragement, additional strength—that's what we brought to the Uprising. The Poles in the bunkers would sometimes salute us when we passed by on our way to the barricades; we threw kisses during the bombardment, when they went down to the bunker. Afterward, there were instances of genuine concern for us on the part of the AL. My personal relations with the staff were extraordinary, perhaps beyond the purely necessary. I was "Jewish Antek"; I joined the Uprising with my comrades, and they understood and appreciated our act. And those who survived the Uprising never forgot that.

Being in the rear was harder for us than anything else. Many buildings were destroyed by artillery; we had the strange luck that the buildings were destroyed while we were on the barricades and, by then, we didn't have anyplace to return to. But we always found shelter, someone to take care of us. After twenty-four hours of barricades, we would fall on the floor like corpses and sleep soundly. What saved us was perhaps that "dread of bunkers and cellars." It wasn't heroism, but rather the idea that you could be buried alive. And that's what happened later to the AL command staff. Buildings simply caved in from the bombardment. Incidentally, here's the error in the film,[10] since the Warsaw of the Jewish ghetto was perhaps the only city in the war that was burned down—a city destroyed not by tanks or artillery, but only by fire. But the film shows buildings caving in. Buildings collapsed in the Polish Uprising, not in the ghetto. I can't excuse this fake. It also changes the real nature of what happened in the ghetto. The explanations that that "was also Warsaw" and was close don't hold. The buildings that caved in were from the Polish Uprising, which is characteristic of it. The Germans brought their artillery by train from the front and positioned it there. Those were mobile cannons on tracks. They bombarded the area and the rebel fighters couldn't return fire because they didn't have weapons to use against them, and there weren't any antiaircraft guns either. When I visited there after 1945, I saw that Jewish Warsaw remained standing because the buildings were left on their foundations, even though they were burned down. But in the Polish Uprising, everything was destroyed. After the Ghetto Uprising, the Germans built a concentration camp on the site and brought Jews from Czechoslovakia and Greece along with groups of Polish women

10. That is, the film *The Eighty-First Blow*, produced by Beit Lohamei Ha-Getaot.

to dismantle the buildings and separate the metal and bricks. We were lucky; although the buildings in the Old City collapsed, we stayed there until it fell on the last day of August 1944.

We members of the Jewish Fighting Organization were stationed on our AL barricade with a lot of "gentiles" and AK fighters; the barricade was in a very dangerous sector. Our job was to prevent the penetration of the Germans. And we also went on offensive attacks, but with no success. We attempted to capture the "Red House." We had good weapons—machine guns, grenades, and rifles. One night, we engaged the Germans for a few hours of heavy battle and inflicted some casualties. But, ultimately, we failed and had to retreat. Evidently the Germans could fight.

Our losses on the barricade were caused at night. The moment came when the Old City was about to fall and there was a general retreat. The Uprising was hopeless; we had no illusions from the first. I remember saying harsh things to the members of the command staff, the Polish Communists: "You're not the ones who decided either on the Uprising or its date. So I may say that this is a political uprising against the Red Army and an armed uprising against the Germans. I figure we won't get help from the Red Army, they'll abandon the Uprising." It was hard for them to hear that, but it came true; we couldn't count on help from the Red Army.

The AL command staff didn't contact the Red Army; on August 3, they were still hesitating and didn't know how to behave. The leadership was no longer in Warsaw. Spychalski wasn't there. And Gomułka had also crossed the lines to the Red Army. Lublin was already liberated, and even before that, the leaders had left for the liberated areas of Poland. The London people wanted to confront the Russians with a fait accompli: that *they* liberated Warsaw; but that wasn't a correct consideration (there's no analogy with the Allies' relations with De Gaulle), since they were dealing with the Russians, who abandoned them, really abandoned them. It was painful to see how puny their position was afterward, when the Russians conquered Praga, from the other side of the Wisła, and they looked on helplessly as the Polish people were destroyed; and it was painful to see the buildings caving in and covering thousands of human beings with their debris.

The accounting I made earlier about Warsaw showed that every third person was killed; but if we subtract Praga, where the losses weren't so heavy, we can say that, on the western side of the Wisła with perhaps half a million people, every second person was killed. Such ratios of killing are truly catastrophic for a fighting people, and we must forget antisemitism for the moment and remember that these were people, families, children, who were murdered—and we should know that they were killed not only by bombings and shellings, but that many of them were taken to death like sheep, like the Jews.

By the time our house on Leszno was captured, we weren't in it anymore. We stood behind our barricade until it fell. If I want to be modest, I'll say that I was one of the last two on the barricade. And if I don't want to be modest, I'll say that I was the last one left on it. I was also wounded in the head there and it was only years later that they found the sliver that has remained in my head ever since. I knew I was wounded because I felt a sharp pain, and a strong flow of blood covered my head; but I didn't know they had left me a "souvenir." That was a moment before the retreat. Did we get an order to retreat? No. And I wouldn't have retreated under any circumstances. Why? If I had been just a fighter, I would have retreated; but I always remembered that I was also a Jew. That was my "complex." I didn't want them to say "that Jew," "that Antek." I've been scared many times in my life. The question was how to overcome fear. But those moments on the barricade were beyond fear. And it wasn't indifference either. I wasn't aware of what was going on all around, until the courier grabbed me by the sleeve and pulled me and then I saw that the unit was no longer in the area, and only the last of the retreating forces sent messengers to see if anyone was left.

The barricade was positioned on a narrow street. From the roof, you could see the Wisła, which was very close. We would see the Germans swimming near the bridge, and they paid with casualties for their dip in the water, when they were hit by our snipers. There were buildings on both sides of the barricades; it divided the street and connected the buildings.

Our "rear" base was a very big, multistoried building that served as a good target for the Germans stationed in the "Red House"; and we had exchanges of gunfire with pistols and machine guns or grenades. It went on like that until they began surrounding us with tanks as well. Because the street was narrow, they shelled and destroyed buildings all around; hence our defeat. They advanced very slowly because they didn't know we made a full retreat from that section. To the credit of the Poles, they were brave people who stuck to their guns. I didn't see any panic or running away. They stood firm to the end despite all their casualties. When the Germans started shelling the barricade hard and sent tanks, there was one low-ranking officer who ordered the men to leave and climb the barricade; but they didn't obey. You didn't have to be a strategist to understand that if they're shelling the barricade, there's no point being exposed and it's better to protect people. But I carried out the order. I stretched out on the barricade with my weapons facing the tank advancing toward me in a completely "ungentlemanly" way. All of a sudden, I felt pain and rolled from the top of the barricade into a pit. I felt my hand and saw it was full of blood.

At last, even that miserable commander understood we had no business being on the barricade and then we entrenched ourselves in the building, facing the tanks, until they penetrated the courtyard. I saw the tank in the courtyard, but we all stayed there. (Apparently, an order was given to stay and no one ran away.) At a certain moment, the courier pulled me to join the retreat. I hadn't heard the order to retreat because I was groggy from my wound. I was posted in an observation position, and when the courier pulled my sleeve, there wasn't anybody around me. We were close to our base on Freta Street and we retreated there. That was in our twenty-four hours of "rest." I don't know what happened afterward at the barricade. When I returned to the base, they began taking care of me, washing and bandaging my head. The next day, the bombing started. I was lying on the floor when the great bombardment began. I was in terrible pain and the building was shaking. There was an air raid.

I said we didn't like to go to the bunker. We had gotten used to that over the years; it wasn't indifference. Sometimes it was because we were a group of Jews and we forbade ourselves, and other times for some other reason. We had gotten used to the idea of not dying beneath the rubble. Then came such a heavy bombing! The building almost caved in. It was amazing that it didn't take a direct hit. But there was a blast nearby and the building began to topple. When the bombing stopped for a while, one of my officer friends came and asked how I was. I said "Terrific." And he said, "Antek, there was a terrible catastrophe. The building of the AL command staff was completely destroyed." That was the building opposite; I think it had six stories. The staff was in the bunker, underground. "Can you organize help?" he asked me. "All the high-ranking officers are buried in the bunkers." I went out and started organizing help.

The whole civilian population was at my disposal. No one asked any questions. The bombing continued, but no one stopped working. We stood in the bombing and began digging into the debris of the building that had collapsed and fallen down. We had to dig from the cellar to the entrance, we knew exactly where. That wasn't a bunker for people who wanted to hide, it was a cellar for storing things or such. If it had been built right, there had to be another exit. But everything was covered and the digging lasted for hours; whenever there was a very heavy bombing, it was interrupted. The Poles worked—soldiers and civilians. I stood there and talked with those imprisoned in the cellar. I don't know if they were all alive at the time. I encouraged them, I said: "In a little while, just a little while and we'll get there." The people toiled at great risk but, in the evening, the last voice fell silent. There were a few hundred tons of rubble, the entire collapse of the big building, which covered them. They died from lack of air. We couldn't see them through the opening we made; we only heard them. There wasn't enough time. I knew all those people personally. I used to sit in meetings with them, some of them were friends of mine.

We used to talk freely with the staff and maybe we infected them with our pessimism. We were convinced it was lost, since where would help come from? One of the staff members was a Jew, whose underground name was Nestek Matywiecki, and whose Jewish name was Menashe. He was a young attorney, a Communist. In the underground, he was involved with the Jewish issue and was active in the group that dealt with welfare. I had heard of him, but I had never seen him because he was connected with Dr. Berman; here, however, we did meet and became close—two Jews, Nestek and Antek. As I recall, he was from Kobryń (a "Jewish city"); he knew a little Hebrew. Here we became friends. He was very dear to me; and if the Poles on the command staff took care of us, how much more did Nestek! He was a captain, and received a posthumous promotion. My conversations with him were even more open. In a command staff meeting, I suggested setting up a base in the farthest rear echelon (at Leszno before it was conquered by the Germans) where we could transfer anyone who wasn't needed in the rear. It didn't occur to me that the Germans would destroy Warsaw. And that was decided on.

In the early days of the Uprising, the AK attacked Pawiak and the concentration camp in the area of the ghetto, which the Germans had built after the Ghetto Uprising; I think the camp was a branch of Maidanek. At any rate, administratively, it wasn't an independent concentration camp. There were Jews from Greece and Czechoslovakia there. Hundreds of Jews were liberated by the Poles during the Polish Uprising and came to various places, including the Old City, where the problem of these Jews suddenly emerged. Now their situation depended on whom they came upon. I was in the Old City then, and I must say with all modesty that that was significant. I wasn't in central Warsaw, where the fate of the Jews was different because, there, the AK sent the Jews to the barricades or to clear mines. In my area, as soon as I came across such a case, I immediately appealed to the AK commander; I brought a representative of those Jews, a Czech, to him. That man survived and, after the war, told one of the Shlikhim in Czechoslovakia that he remembered me well. There were hundreds of Jews like that.

In those days, we had no formal organization. Those Jews from the concentration camps seemed to come from another planet, without any foothold or family, and their lives were in danger. I appealed to the AK on their behalf and they agreed that we would appoint someone to

represent them; we named Yosef Sak who went to work immediately. He
was fit for that. He had good relations with those Jews, and knew how to
talk to the Poles, and looked imposing. Unfortunately, he and his group
were cut off from us. At that time, I wasn't a public person, I was a fighter.
But those Jews would come to me about food, the most basic things; and
I helped as much as I could. In fact, the AL would have given the Jews
food from their own stores. The Jews performed vital functions. They
identified with the Uprising. These weren't Polish Jews, but they worked
out of a sense of responsibility. When the Uprising was about to fall apart,
maybe a week before the end, I went to the AL commander of the
Uprising (not the general commander of the Uprising, who was a member
of AK). There was a truce between the AK and the AL. They divided up
the barricades. The big force was the AK. That AL commander was
Richard Kowalski. (His wife was a Jew, Jeaneta, whom I knew from the
Ghetto Uprising. She was the AL representative at the first meeting, when
I asked them to do something for the fighting ghetto.) At that time, in
1943, I was sent to Commander Bolesław Kowalski, who told me he was
sure we wouldn't hold out, but since we were "great experts in the sewers,"
he ordered me to organize the retreat through the sewers. It didn't help
when I said I had never been in the sewer and wasn't an expert in that.
But an order was an order. They put a big group at my disposal and I
prepared to go with them; when he learned about it, he called me in and
said: "A commander doesn't go!" And he forbade me to go. It turned out
indeed that going there didn't fit my height (over six feet). They didn't
find a way and crawled around through the sewers most of the time. I
couldn't have stood that. Kazik, who was an expert in those things, was
with them. I took care of every detail, I even gave them vodka for the trip,
for walking in water, in order to recover. Today they say that vodka isn't
good in the cold, but then we believed it was medicine for everything.
They were there for several hours and returned empty-handed. They
barely found the way back. That was a failure—my personal failure
because I was in charge of the operation.

The Polish Uprising failed. When I saw that all was lost, I went to the
AL commander and told him I wanted above all to take care of the Jews:
the big group of Jews from Greece and other Jews who were in danger
of being annihilated. He agreed and we gave them Polish guides to get
through to Zolibórz. It turned out that they didn't cross to Zolibórz and
later used the AK passages, since they had safer connecting roads. For
example, the AK controlled the connection to Zolibórz and the central
city, and had maps of passageways; and they did let them pass. Perhaps
they didn't know they were Communists. We sent hundreds of Jews on
those escape routes; but while escaping, they came upon an obstacle we
also encountered a few days later: the Germans dropped bombs into the

sewers through the manholes. The Jews in that group were the first to run into the bombs and, apparently, a few of them were hit. But, unfortunately, instead of waiting and trying again, they retreated in a panic and returned. All my coaxing, all my powers of persuasion were of no avail to explain to them that the Old City was about to fall and that, if they remained in that suburb, they could expect certain death from the Germans, whereas, this way, they might be saved. They were afraid to go again, and stayed in the Old City. And the Germans did indeed murder them; they also murdered the Poles, every last one, including the wounded in the hospital, the nurses, the doctors; they destroyed them all as in the ghetto. And the Jews, too, of course, except those who were clever enough to hide. Later, when the Uprising collapsed, I was called in a panic and informed that it was hard to remove all the fighters. I was asked to join the command staff temporarily, but I refused. I demanded first of all that, along with the fighting group, the whole Jewish periphery in the area must also be evacuated. They agreed and did it, even though they didn't take the Polish civilian population; they took the Jews in our area with them, the ones we knew about, and all those we managed to round up in a few hours.

I'll never forget that night. The Old City went up in flames and, the next day, the area was occupied by the Germans. They shelled and bombed. That Warsaw near us, the Old City, burned down, and we were about to enter the sewers in groups. I was in charge of a few hundred fighters and, when the signal was given, we went in. I went first, along with the guide, who led us the whole way. Entrance to the sewer system was from one of the streets, and we went straight into the central sewers. In some places, you had to bend over; but in others, you walked erect. We had to walk single file, or sometimes in two's. Our people walked behind me: Marek Edelman, followed by Zivia; Tuvia was with us all along. Dozens of people. We walked for hours. At dawn, we came to where the sewers split into three directions, and I discovered the malicious cleverness of the Germans: they had stretched a wire and everyone who went through the sewers had to touch it; but you didn't know you were touching it. When the wire was touched, a feather moved on the surface, so they knew when to throw grenades inside. I stood on the side and told the people to start walking, and the guide led the way. (Beams of light illuminated the path.) They went, except for those near me, including Zivia, who stopped with me. Thus I kept the people close to me with me. They splashed through a stream of water and we didn't know how deep it was. And when the wire moved, a grenade whistled and some people were hit; fortunately, only a few people at the site of the explosion were wounded lightly. A great turmoil ensued. Those behind retreated and began running away. We Jews didn't have anywhere to run or anywhere to return. We had to continue on. The guide refused to go into the water, which was deep in that place; and there was a waterfall that created a whirlpool. It was the strongest stream of sewer water in the city, which came to that junction, where it split off. Some people retreated because of the grenade. There we were when that Pole refused to go on. Then I got around him. I told him: "Fine. Just show us exactly what direction to walk in; I see three forks here and I don't know which one is the right one. We might get to a dead end." When he came close, I shoved him into the water and walked right behind him. It turned out that the place with the whirlpool was deep, and we had to cross it slowly and silently because the Germans and Ukrainians were lying in wait up above. Later, when I was on the other side of the dangerous place, it turned out that Marek Edelman who was walking behind me had saved Zivia who had slipped and almost drowned. Marek himself, apparently, wasn't a great swimmer. At the last moment, I pulled him up, the people came out and passed; some of them were wounded.

One of those with us was Zygmunt Taberman, an attorney, who was later in the Polish Attorney-General's office and had been a high official in the Judenrat; he turned out to be a fine fighter. I hadn't known him previously. People proved themselves in action and you sometimes learned about a person in a single moment what you hadn't known for years, as if he were illuminated by a sudden flash. He hadn't been a member of the Judenrat, just an official. But we had always been suspicious of him because he worked there. He was intelligent and spoke Polish. He turned out to be a brave and fine person.

Those who retreated and went back didn't survive. Some of them were "gentiles," who weren't in my group. Those Poles were under an illusion and were also murdered later, whereas we got through. Only later did we understand what dangers we had faced. We stepped on bodies in the water. I saw Zivia's condition; she was at the end of her rope, and I carried her on my shoulders. The water came up to my neck. She badly wanted to sleep, and she clasped her hands around my neck. I walked first and she floated in the water as she slept.

At noon, after a few hours of walking, we came to Zolibórz. The guide I threw in the water owes me his life, if he's still alive. He led us to the exit from the sewer in Krasinskiego Square, which was exactly where the fighters had been waiting for us. I don't remember any more if they were AK or AL. In hindsight, I can state that even if I had gone through the waterfall, I wouldn't have gotten there on my own because there were a lot of branches on the way. In the Polish film, *Canal*,[11] the people get to the Wisla, but the exit is blocked in front of them and that's the end, death.

11. Of Andzej Wayda.

When I shoved that gentile into the water, I didn't think I was taking him with us, but we realized we didn't know how to get him past the waterfall. Ultimately, he really did lead us where we wanted to go. On our way, we kept coming on forks in the road. Right, left, where? I could easily have fallen into the hands of the Germans. I could have come to the Gdansk railroad station, which was held by the Germans. You just had to be off by a hundred meters.

When we got to Zolibórz, people were waiting for us. The operation was carefully organized. They welcomed us as the heroes of the day. I especially impressed them: I was wearing a big bandage on my head; I had a bad headache. (Today I'm not surprised—with a lead splinter in my head!) And I was tired, like everybody else. They greeted us warmly and immediately found a place for us. We found the address of the members of the AL at once and re-established our fighting group.

Our whole fighting group came out of the sewers along with a few more Jews from other groups. Aside from the Jews I had insisted on adding, there were also a few Poles. Everyone who was strong enough to endure the difficulties of that trip arrived. What a "crossing" that was! Not simply walking through the sewers; it was a trip on bodies, treading on the remains of food, even though it didn't occur to anyone to look for something in the water. We trod on corpses, and ultimately we arrived.

Right after we arrived, we set up a base and got word to Adolf Berman and his wife (the Bermans were "guests" of the place). The care was nice, friendly, extraordinary. We were exhausted and hungry, and people waited on us and took care of us. Berman was very proud when he heard on the radio about our participation in the Uprising. First, because of my "voice in the wilderness" proclamation and then because of our participation in the battle. Politically, the fact that the Jews were fighters enhanced his power! That was a great source of pride, with a lot of symbolic value. Zolibórz was an idyllic, pastoral place, after the hell of the Old City. The Germans were busy with their conquest since they occupied the Old City that day, and then they started taking control of the central city; and they had time.

We emerged with all our side arms, rifles, and grenades. We went through the sewers with everything we had. Not a single drop of water got into our rifle barrels. We moved all our weapons. I scolded one of the fighters because he wanted to throw away a few kilograms of bullets. I told him: "If you have to throw something away, throw food." We got to Zolibórz at the beginning of the second month of the Uprising. It was relatively more comfortable and easier there, because of the shelling, of course. I gave myself the military rank of second-lieutenant. After the war, my Polish friends, who granted ranks, told me that every one of them rose a rank or two, and that I was promoted to the rank of colonel, but I again requested a document that my rank was second-lieutenant. They didn't understand me. They built their positions for their future in Poland, and they may have needed that. I didn't. A military-political committee awarded rank and all the members were my friends. They decided whatever they wanted. And they didn't think they were doing me a favor; many were promoted posthumously and those who survived had to perform a function with a suitable rank. They wanted to get me involved in issues that were important to them. But I didn't want every second-lieutenant to have to salute and stand at attention for me. The truth is that it didn't mean anything even to the Polish fighters. When I passed by, they would salute. For them, my position had nothing to do with rank. I was the commander of the Jewish Fighting Organization and that was enough. That didn't need any external insignia of rank.

The issue of rank is connected with responsibility, like responsibility for a barricade. I couldn't accept that responsibility from a Jewish-nationalist perspective, as I explained before. Even though I didn't feel a trace of antisemitism, I knew that everything that happened was liable to be put on my account, including blood libel. And that wasn't my own personal issue, since there were other Jews there, too.

When we came out of the sewers, no one asked me my rank. There was one man there who later filled senior positions in the leadership of the government in Poland, for good and for bad—Zenon Kliszko who was a close friend of Wacław, the party ideologue.[12] He was in Zolibórz at that time and served as my "commander" under all circumstances. The whole issue of rank was of no importance to either of us. But the existence of the Jewish fighting group made a great impression, as if a unit of paratroopers had come from Britain. Our appearance in Zolibórz had national significance, and all the officers and soldiers would salute me. I don't remember if we used insignia of rank. At any rate, I only had an AL insignia on my sleeve, which, as my friends later warned me about the AK, could have cost me my life. I had already been warned once, on the Aryan side of Warsaw, that they were liable to assassinate me because of the letter and the claims I addressed to Bór-Komorowski; and it wasn't particularly hard to kill me. As I recall, in the Old City, nobody paid attention to the AL stripes on my sleeve, whereas, in Zolibórz, I was warned specifically. In those days, I wasn't on the barricades; and I joined only when the Germans began their big attack on Zolibórz. In Zolibórz,

---

12. Zenon Kliszko (b. 1908): Member of the PPR Central Committee, 1944–1949. In 1948–1949, he was removed from the leadership with Gomułka. Reinstated in 1956, he was a member of the Polish Politburo and, in 1963, Chairman of the Ideological Commission of the Central Committee of the PZPR. Removed from power in 1970.

I had time for political activity on behalf of the Jews. Warsaw was still split between Germans and Poles, or at least the Old City was, and those were days of destruction.

Before we left the Old City, I sent a group of Jews (who were liberated from the concentration camp on Gesiówka) to Zolibórz through the sewers. They were attacked in the sewers and went back to the Old City. That dread of death in the sewers made them reluctant to go back in the sewers under any circumstances. All my talk about death lurking for them in the Old City as well and my attempt to convince them to try it again was in vain; you couldn't get that dread out of their hearts. Later, when the Old City was conquered, many of them were murdered. Fortunately for us, we got out of there right at the last minute, after the defense of the suburb collapsed. The Germans came into the area the next day and slaughtered the whole population. When I went to Czechoslovakia after the war, I was told that a few of those refugees survived.

Relative quiet prevailed in Zolibórz. Although there were shellings from the armored train people said was brought from the Stalingrad front, there was absolutely no comparison with the situation in the Old City. There were hours of calm, you could run across the streets, you could even sunbathe.

Dr. Berman turned my attention to the fact that there were many destitute Jews in and around Zolibórz and asked if I would lend a hand in that welfare operation. I consulted with the Poles and they expressed a willingness to do something for that civilian population. I divided my time between military activity and civilian welfare operations.

We couldn't give them any money since we didn't have any. It was here in Zolibórz that I realized—and I must emphasize this—that Dr. Berman was impeccably honest, because he didn't have to tell us what he had. But he immediately brought a large sum and gave it to us; and then we started gathering Jews. We couldn't help them with food. We were better off than the civilian population because the army controlled the German sources and warehouses and distributed what they found—first of all to the soldiers. The civilian population had to make do with a starvation ration. We had enough pull to get something for a few people but, even with a supreme effort, I couldn't help all of them. We could only give them a little money so that every one of them could look for means of subsistance.

How many Jews were there? We know of thousands. Zolibórz was a neighborhood of laborers and working intelligentsia, where the PPS, the Communists, and the Democrats were very influential. Naturally, it was more comfortable for a Jew to hide there than in other parts of the city. Dr. Berman lived in Zolibórz throughout the Uprising. He got information about what was happening to us. He poured money into aid and asked me to devote myself to it. So as long as relative calm prevailed in

Zolibórz, and we only had to guard the fortified heights, I could free myself from that without any problem. That went on until the final days, when the Germans began surrounding Zolibórz from all sides.

Polish units included in the Red Army were stationed on the other side of the Wisła. Those Poles were eyewitnesses to the destruction of Warsaw, during the suppression of the Polish Uprising. They were commanded by General Berling, commander of the Polish brigades in the Red Army, a brilliant military man and an energetic person, with a talent for making courageous decisions.[13] At a certain stage in the suppression of the Uprising by the Germans, he sent a small unit to assist the rebels. He took that step, apparently, without permission from the Russians. Unfortunately, the whole unit was wiped out. We heard the sounds of the assault and the roar of the battle. It was an unsuccessful attempt. As I recall, that was in mid-September. The war in the Old City raged for one month; and, in the second month, in Zolibórz. That was a quieter month, relatively speaking, until the storm came and lasted only forty-eight hours. The Germans began attacking from the Gdansk Railroad Station, and went on attacking from all sides—at a certain stage, we realized we were surrounded. I left everything else and joined my comrades; but I didn't stay with them, since we urgently composed a special unit, armed with anti-tank weapons. We weren't familiar with those weapons, which the Russians had parachuted to us. A mixed group of the AK and the AL was formed and I was appointed commander of it. We didn't know how to use the weapons, but I took a look or two and went out with them. It was the last day of the battle when German tanks appeared en masse and crushed the areas held by the rebels. For twenty-four hours, we used those weapons, and I wouldn't have known about the retreat at all if some Pole hadn't dragged me off. Before that, I saw a tank approaching us and, up above too, on the top floors of the buildings, the Germans were already setting up positions; I kept on shooting that antitank weapon, which was a kind of rifle mounted on a stand (they called it "Papanatz"); it fired big bullets, of two colors, red and green. One ignited and the other exploded. The echo of that shooting made me completely deaf for a few months,

13. Zygmunt Berling (b. 1896): Field officer until 1935 and in Soviet prison, 1939–1941. In 1941–1942, he was an officer in Anders's Army. In 1943–1944, he commanded the First Polish Army in the Soviet Union; was dismissed in December 1944. From 1949 to 1953, he was the Commander of the General Staff Academy. A document in the Polish Central Archive states that "Berling went up to the front and took command. . . . That was when he took the decision, irrespective of any military or political considerations. What counted was that Poles were fighting across there [in Warsaw] and they had to be helped. He realized that the landings could only be made by the Polish Army and that the sole function of the Red Army would be to assist them. The quarrel between the Polish Army and the AK was a matter for Poles alone" (Polonsky and Drukier 1980:454–455).

even though I knew the rule that you had to keep your mouth open, because I didn't have any cotton to stuff in my ears.

So they advanced and were approaching the barricade and I was pulled off of there only because of the Polish soldier who simply dragged me away. Until that moment, I didn't know what was going on all around. And only then did I see that my Polish soldiers, good and brave fighters, had disappeared. Our comrades were a fighting unit, which had fought on the barricades. But of course you couldn't sit on the barricades for forty-eight hours; shifts changed and we were in the nearby base for twenty-four hours. At first, I would come to the barricades to see what was happening; but I didn't participate in their missions as I had done in the Old City, except at the end of the final week.

At that time, Zivia was with the members of our group at one of the bases close to the German positions. On the night after the retreat, I was summoned to the AL command staff in Żoliborz and told that, at a signal agreed upon with the Red Army, at a fixed time, our units would try to cross the Wisła to the side occupied by the Russians, to Praga. Now, during the night, the units would withdraw from the forward bases to the center. The AL staff was busy preparing the retreat to the Wisła as soon as the signal was given. We weren't far from the river. One of those who went to bring the fighters from the forward bases was my friend, a young Jewish Communist lieutenant, whose name slips my mind. I told him that Zivia was there and asked him to make sure she got back. She was the only woman in that whole unit. He promised me to find her. He returned from his errand at night, without Zivia; the whole unit came back, except for Zivia; she disappeared.

In the morning, I was very worried. I wasn't a drinker, but I asked one of the gentiles to bring me some spirits to ease my worry and my head-ache. The Germans were constantly shelling. It didn't look simple: my friend the officer said the Germans were shelling as the unit was taken off its positions and the people in it could have been killed on the way. I waited until dawn and then we went out to search. I organized a few people and asked what route they had taken. Then they started exerting great pressure on me to get me to join those who were crossing the Wisła. To the credit of the Poles, I must say they did everything to convince me to go with them, and even ordered me to do it. They argued that I was the only one who knew how to use the antitank weapons; but at that stage, that wasn't important anymore. They wanted to take me with them and I kept resisting their demand until they left. Some of them did get across to the other side, not all. I don't know the details. There was a surprise attack by the Germans and only some of them got across the river. (Some time later, after the war, I met with them in London. One of those who got across was Kliszko.)

Meanwhile the rumor came that the AK had surrendered to the Germans! They didn't discuss that with the AL command staff. After the surrender, AL fighters could take off their AL armband and look like AK soldiers or civilians. We Jews couldn't do that. I exerted pressure on those in charge to get the members of our group across the river first, but in vain, because they didn't want to take them along—which was another reason for me not to go. But ultimately, they might have let me take the Jewish group. At any rate, I certainly wouldn't have deserted them and gone.

By now, it was four or five in the afternoon, and Zivia hadn't yet returned. Everything seemed lost, but we couldn't give up. Finally, we went out in a procession toward the Wisła. I was the highest in rank and led the way. As we approached, they greeted us with shellfire. With one thing and another, we didn't get to the Wisła because, until afternoon, the Germans controlled most of the area, and only a few people got across. Many of our people were killed. It was a disorganized and panicky retreat, and as a result, we returned to our starting point. There was confusion and we didn't know what to do with ourselves. The Poles began taking off. A few of us from the Jewish group remained. While we were still in Zolibórz, a German military delegation came there and negotiated with the AK about the surrender; and I must say that the AL didn't know anything about that. The AK simply didn't tell them anything or ask them anything.

At dusk, we saw two soldiers in German uniforms in the distance and, as they came closer, we realized that one of them was a woman. In fact, at that time, we all walked around in German clothes we looted from their warehouses, and just had the AL band on the sleeve. From various signs, we identified them as Poles, our people. When they approached, we realized they were Marek Edelman and Zivia!

What happened was that the unit commander, that special Polish gentile, went to look for the Jewish girl in his unit. He got to the unit base but didn't find her. Searching in one of the bases, he encountered Marek Edelman and the two of them continued looking for her. Ultimately, they found her! It turned out that the night when they came to withdraw the group, Zivia was guarding the base and, when they withdrew—they forgot her there. The entire group was brought back, and she was the only one who stayed to guard the empty base, holding a rifle (like the "Good Soldier Schweik"). So that officer didn't see her either and was sure he had brought them all, and I was sure that Zivia was with them and had been killed on the way, because many had indeed been killed in the shelling. That happened after the failed attempt to cross the Wisła. If the attempt hadn't failed, I don't know how we would have met Zivia or what would have happened, or if we would have met at all. If I were a poet,

I might be able to express that meeting, since I was a hundred percent sure she was dead.

Here, a new chapter begins: Zivia was reborn! After all, once, she had risen from the sewers when we came out of the ghetto. The second time, retreating from the Old City, I carried her on my back, after her strength gave out and she began drowning in the sewer water. That time, too, it was Marek Edelman who saved her. The hand of fate.

Under the current conditions, we couldn't put up our hands and surrender. Maybe only those of us who looked Aryan could do that. But it was almost certain that it wouldn't help because all of them, including the Poles, would be taken to a concentration camp anyway. The civilian population was taken out to Prusków where some of them were released. But many others were taken to a concentration camp, including the sick people and all the prisoners-of-war; only Bór-Komorowski was treated decently. But simple soldiers were sent to camps and murdered. And as for us Jews, there was no point at all of even thinking about surrender.

The terms of surrender were terms of captivity, which didn't include Jews. From the Germans' point of view, Jews weren't in that category at all; nor did the surrender include the AL; and revealing that there were Jews among them meant abandoning them to destruction. As usual, the Germans set conditions of surrender for the fighters; but for the masses, there was a great slaughter in Warsaw. In the two months of the Uprising, 250,000 Poles, including many Jews, were killed.

Because we couldn't surrender, we looked for a way of rescue and reached the bunker where two old Jewish women were hiding in Zolibórz, in the Promyka quarter. There was also a sick Polish woman there who had been abandoned by her family. (One of the women immigrated to Israel and worked for years in the Polish national bank.) We lived with the old women in that bunker, ten minutes from the Wisła. For six weeks, we hid in that bunker, which was small as a prison cell.

The situation was miserable in that bunker. I couldn't hear a thing and I was extremely sensitive. When I did something bad, they would pinch me and make signs to shut me up. That made me mad. It was an ideal situation to develop a complex of grudges against people. Headaches and deafness in both ears made it impossible for me to carry on with my functions. I was supposedly the commander: they gave me the best pallet to lie on, whereas everyone else slept on the floor; but I was completely isolated. It wasn't a matter of a day; it went on for weeks.

In those days, a true story was circulating about me. One day I claimed that we had to get to the Wisła at night and find a boat. I could swim, but not everybody else could. I said we had to try to cross to the other side, since there was no more Uprising and nobody was left in Warsaw. It didn't help. The shelling continued constantly. We would get the salvos of the Soviet cannons and hear the shooting of the German artillery. And another episode: one night, a few people, including Marek Edelman, went out to reconnoiter the area near the Wisła, and I went with Tuvia to answer the call of nature. I couldn't hear a thing. Later, he claimed that he yelled to me. When he heard footsteps, he disappeared and I was left in a situation that is hardly congenial. If they had been Germans, they would have finished me off.

In the first week, we were like Robinson Crusoe; some were emotionally upset and there was even a suicide attempt; and then we decided on a daily "seminar" schedule. Every day, there was a lecture to "lift morale" and there were lecturers on various subjects: for example, a physician and biologist lectured on biology; Zygmunt Wakhman, who was a lawyer, lectured on law and justice. Tuvia Borzykowski lectured on the Jewish labor movement, Jewish sociology, and Borochovism. I lectured on literature. Everyone had to sit still and listen. Afterward, we gathered together for an hour of jokes. Some of the jokes I know are from that time. So we structured the day. We slept during the day and were awake at night to search for food.[14]

I was very active in this area of "raising morale," but I was considered dead. I was even a hindrance because of my deafness. I always talked, even when we had to be quiet. I was very mad at Zivia; it seemed to me that she pinched me the hardest. When people laughed, I wanted to know why. And these were silly things. She had to shout (for me to hear), or there wasn't anything to tell, but I wanted to know; I was afraid I would be like that forever. But it passed. Incidentally, to this day, I still have a bit of it left. For instance, on hot days, for twenty-four hours, I hear a humming like a waterfall. When I came to Kibbutz Yagur, Dr. Ogen started taking me to specialists who examined me and said they could do an operation but it might endanger what was left. Tabenkin talked to me at that time (during the War of Independence) about joining the Palmakh.[15] But I'm sure they would have rejected me. I think my eyesight grew sharper at the expense of my hearing. Even now I hear better in my right ear. It depends on various things. Fatigue, for instance. When I'm

14. Tuvia Borzykowski described life in that bunker: "We decided to fill our days with some activity and we worked out a schedule. The day would start at about 8 o'clock with our 'radio announcer' announcing the day of the week and the date . . . During the time left between breakfast and lunch we heard a lecture given by one of the group, with a discussion following . . . The lectures were delivered in whispers, and the discussions, also in whispers, often lasted four or five hours . . . At 4 o'clock we had an hour of jokes, puzzles and similar entertainment" (Borzykowski 1972:208–209).

15. The strike force of the Hagana, actually under the influence of Tabenkin and Ha-Kibbutz Ha-Meuchad; founded May 19, 1941, and disbanded by Ben-Gurion in 1948.

with people, I feel that noise in my ears less. But at night—it doesn't let up.

But let's go back to searching for food and water. We assumed that despite the prevailing hunger, something had to be left in the buildings, like groats or something. And a few times, we did indeed find something. I say *we*, even though I wasn't in the search party. I was busy with something else. We found sacks of rusks which were dropped by the Russians. Although they weren't of the finest Western quality and were moldy, they did save us. The Russians dropped them in the area conquered by the Germans, but the Germans didn't want them. At night, we would collect sacks of rusks and that was what we lived on.

The water situation began getting serious, so we started rationing a quarter cup a day—because we had to wash a bit, maintain basic hygiene. We would wipe our faces with a wet rag. I persuaded two or three comrades to help me and together we tried to get to water by digging: but we couldn't because we didn't have any tools. And you could dig only during the artillery shelling since the Germans walked around the area all day, until the last week, which was critical. They set up a headquarters above us. A day before we left the place, they started digging some tunnel there, between one bunker and another.

Salvation came after forty-two days, in our sixth week in Promyka, near the Wisła. That night was a night of horrors. I had nightmares and then I woke up and realized it wasn't a dream at all: I dreamed that the Germans had burst in on us. We heard the banging of hammers on the wall I was lying next to. We prepared our weapons, the grenades, so they wouldn't take us alive, and we waited for them to break through. It was noon. We got dressed so we would be ready for the last moment. But the Germans stopped working at noon and, apparently, went to eat. Suddenly we heard a knock at the door and shouts: "Celina, Celina!" (That was Zivia's alias.) It was Dr. Ala Margolis, who later married Marek Edelman.[16]

The incident began when we went out to look for water. The local population had been expelled and removed and the houses were empty. We searched in the bathrooms of nearby houses and anywhere we could. Lodzia, Tuvia's girlfriend, also went out with one of the old women to the Wisła to bring water. Now and then, they were caught but were released. She was supposedly going out with her grandmother. Ultimately, the SS caught the two of them and started interrogating and demanding. So the

---

16. Ala Margolis: Born in Łódz. Was a courier for the Bund and the ZOB on the Aryan side. On October 15, 1944, a month and a half after the Polish Uprising, she led a Polish Red Cross rescue unit to the ruins of Warsaw and saved the ZOB members in Zolibórz. Currently lives in France.

Germans came to our bunker. We heard everything as we hid in the next room. They saw that there really were three old women there and the granddaughter; two days later, they brought a wagon and a donkey and took the old women and the "granddaughter" (Lodzia) out and we remained cut off from the world.

Before that, soldiers would visit the old women from time to time. (There were such human phenomena.) One day, they even brought cigarettes. When we didn't have any, we would dry leaves from the trees and smoke those. A few German soldiers who happened to be in the area knew about the three old women and would bring them all kinds of food. They thought they were Polish, but only one was Polish, two were Jews. They removed the women from the bunker and took them to Grodzisk, a few dozen kilometers from Warsaw, where there were many refugees, and a hospital close by. Lodzia met Ala Margolis in the hospital and told her story of a supposed AK officer (me) hiding in a bunker with a few other people. She had to be careful since she didn't know whom she was telling it to. But it turned out that the doctor, the director of the hospital, was one of the Righteous Gentiles. He and his comrades formed a delegation of six volunteers from the hospital who had Red Cross passes. Lodzia and Ala Margolis accompanied them. The hospital people brought stretchers. They were coming supposedly to rescue the "AK officer," but we got out all the people in the bunker. We covered Marek Edelman's face so his Jewish looks wouldn't give him away. Zivia and another woman disguised themselves as Poles who had come to search for their property in the deserted houses and thus they got out. Tuvia was with us and so was Zygmunt Wakhman, who was extraordinarily brave. He suffered from typhus in the bunker. After the war, he was a judge of the supreme court in Poland. He wasn't a Communist, but an assimilated Jew; he knew a little Yiddish.

We know exactly what happened after we left. The Germans were a few hours late. They weren't looking for us. It didn't even occur to them that there were people there. But after they broke through the wall and found traces, they understood that there had been people there, more than one. But they were too late. When we heard the shouts we wondered who it could be. We feared provocateurs who came with the Germans. "Celina, Celina!" was the shout. With unusual excitement, we organized in minutes and set out.[17]

17. Tuvia Borzykowski presents details of the three (in fact there were four) people hiding in that bunker in Zolibórz, on Promyka Street, the last street before the Wisła. There was a deaf and dumb Christian woman, who remained after the evacuation, because she couldn't move; Rena Laterner, a short Jewish woman, who was assimilated and had stayed away from Jews all her life. The third was Cecilia Goldman, a Jew who took care to obscure any Jewish trait she may have had. In addition, there was a fourth, Sabina, who was like a

Among those who responded to the call to save the rebel fighters were a man and a woman from the hospital (Dr. Zelikowicz and his wife). Later, I invited them to a festive dinner in Warsaw where the "wine was flowing," and they said that when they saw me, they were scared I suspected they were Jewish. It turned out that the man was a doctor and the woman, a nice blonde, was a nurse. So as not to give himself away, he worked as a nurse in the hospital and did all kinds of dirty work. They volunteered for the rescue not knowing they were rescuing Jews. They thought it was the AK commander. They volunteered together, along with a few Poles. But no one said a word. You had to be completely stupid not to see we were Jews. We did bandage Marek's face and carry him on a stretcher. Whoever could stand up walked. We sent Zivia and the blond nurse on ahead. We walked all the way, carrying the "sick people" on stretchers.

The Poles respected me and didn't let me carry stretchers; they knew a "commander" doesn't carry. On our way out of the city, we encountered Germans. The nurse (the doctor's wife) decided that walking was too much for us, and the Germans should provide a wagon. We saw Zivia and the nurse talking with the patrol and pointing to something; then we saw the Germans let them pass. The Jewish nurse persuaded the Germans that there were sick people and the Germans examined our shoes to be sure they weren't army shoes. Fortunately for us, at the last minute, Zygmunt Wakhman and I had exchanged our army shoes for some sandals we found. They gave us a cart and a driver who was blind in one eye. One of the women began talking with him to divert his attention, and we sat in back. The driver was a German soldier. She asked him where he had been wounded and he answered: in the Warsaw Ghetto Uprising. The Jews wounded him, he said; and there he was, driving us in the

---

mother to the three women and took care of their needs. She was vivacious and unafraid; she herself was about seventy years old (Borzykowski 1972:199–215). Additional details for an understanding of Antek's story are: The people were hiding in a bunker camouflaged in a cellar, which was entered behind a cabinet near the wall.

One other detail lacking in Antek's account is that before Lodzia left the bunker, Zivia made her swear to rescue the group if she got out safely and told her they would wait for two more days and, if help didn't come, they would get out by any means. Here is a list of the people hiding in the bunker on Promyka: (1) Rina Nowicka; (2) Cecilia (Regina Goldman); (3) the mother of the landlords; (4) Sabina; (5) Jasia (Tosia Goliborska); (6) Yitzhak Zuckerman (Antek); (7) Marek Edelman; (8) Zivia Lubetkin (Celina); (9) Tuvia Borzykowski (Tadek); (10) Lodzia Bokowska (Leah Zilberstein); (11) Joseph Ziemian (resistance fighter and patron of the children's gang of Cigarette Sellers of Three Crosses Square and author of a book of that name); (12) Zygmunt Warman; (13) Zosia Skarzewska (Renia Friedman); (14) Marysia Wachman (Bronka Feinmesser); (15) Yurek Fiszgrunt; (16) Andzia (Hannah Gorcweig); (17) Stasia (Adzia Kasztowska), Andzia's friend; (18) Vitek; (19) Edek. For a detailed account of the time on Promyka, see Leah (Lodzia) Zilberstein 1988.

wagon. I sat in back next to Tuvia and nudged his shoulder with joy. He said: "Don't say 'thanks' before we get through."[18] They brought us to the hospital and the director of the hospital, as we learned later, immediately sensed who we were (he thought we were a mixed group of Jews and Poles) and put us in a separate ward. And to keep the Germans, who were constantly coming and searching, from finding anything, he put a sign on the door saying "Typhus." We lay there and rested. As for me, all night long, I was "drunk but not on wine." I couldn't believe such a great miracle had happened to us: to come from killing and chaos to rest and food, and all at once.

The rumor about the "last of the rebels" spread like wildfire, and suddenly the local priest appeared to offer a solemn Sunday mass in honor of the fighters. It was a civilian hospital but was under German supervision. Every day they would come and snoop around and the doctor in charge of the hospital was extraordinarily brave to accept us. I didn't meet him again, but Tuvia found him afterward.[19] Apparently he thought I was a Pole. He suspected that the others were Jews, not to mention Marek Edelman who had a typical Jewish, Semitic face.

About that time, a Polish priest came who was interested in each of us and told about the solemn mass he was about to offer in our honor. Hence we decided I would leave at once to find us a place in Grodzisk. We told Lodzia where we would be and Kazik showed up. All that time, he had been with a group sent to our base on Leszno and now lived in Grodzisk. Along with Kazik, we began looking for a place and, in a few days, we removed the whole group from the hospital to the village of Wołochy, a small community, near Grodzisk. It was winter and our women comrades showed remarkable ingenuity in the rapid organization of living quarters.

At that time and after the war, Inka (Szwajger) was the girlfriend of the *Starosta* of the AK in the Old City (I don't know if they separated or not). He was a member of PPS. *Starosta* was a high rank in the government hierarchy; he was in charge of the Old City, and they entertained us in their house, except for a few people whom the gentiles there didn't like. He was a Pole, and Zivia and I and Marek found shelter with them. Lodzia had once found a place for Tuvia in that bunker on Promyka where a love affair started between the two of them, which ended here in Israel. After a few days of rest, the Bermans came and we began rounding up the survivors. Things were calm. Germans would indeed snatch people from time to time. I remember once sitting in a tavern and drinking a beer with somebody when a German showed up. We knew a man had been snatched

18. Borzykowski says that leaving the bunker on Promyka and going to the hospital in Bernerowa took place on November 15, 1944 (Borzykowski 1972:222).

19. This was Dr. Swital (Borzykowski 1972:219–223).

that day and I told him in Polish (he spoke a little Polish) that I was afraid
he had come to snatch us, but he said he had come to drink beer.

Complete calm prevailed until one day thousands of cannons suddenly
cut the silence: that was the Soviet assault on January 17, 1945, at twelve
o'clock. We were sitting down to lunch when the landlord came and said:
"Soviet tanks are in the city!" There was silence. I called Zivia. We had
a big, intelligent dog there, a wolfhound, who had belonged to the
Germans, but his owners had been killed and the *Starosta* had taken him
in; we were really fond of him. He was an unusually smart dog. He had
a mattress and, before he lay down on it, he would turn it over and shake
it. I used to walk with him, sometimes for kilometers, to get mail from
abroad on microfilm that came to Warsaw. In Warsaw, I would give them
to others to be decoded; but in Grodzisk, I had to do it myself. The AK
knew where we were and sent us the mail. Berman was also there; he had
an easier life and didn't go through everything we did. During those
weeks, he made contacts and carried out searches. The *Starosta* of course
knew we were Jews, but the landlord didn't. I think that he suspected,
though, since it was impossible not to suspect Marek.

I remember the moment: Zivia, the dog, and I went out to the square
and saw Soviet tanks, tank drivers with soot-blackened faces, joyful; and
suddenly, for the first time—*I started weeping*. We walked along with the
dog and, at dusk, we returned home. Near the house, I saw a Soviet
military car, with officers inside. They approached us and asked: who are
Antek and Celina? We were stunned. It turned out we were invited to a
celebration. The officer, a brigadier general, was a Jew. They knew our
names from Berman. They took us to their military base in Wołochy and
gave us whatever they had—battle rations and liquor—along with words
of blessing, love, and pride. Berman had told them I was the commander.
Suddenly, an officer came with an order to our hosts to move to the front.
We said goodbye to them after the commander supplied us with military
passes.

In those weeks in Grodzisk, we performed a very important function
for the AL. That was an historic opportunity to repay our debt to them.
They were completely crushed. Many of their people were slaughtered
by political opponents and we suddenly became capable, enterprising,
initiating. Lublin was liberated by then, but they didn't have contacts with
the new Polish government. They didn't have any strength or status. We
created contact with Lublin for them: we sent two people to Lublin, Kazik
and Irka Gelblum, who got through to there. We helped them with
money. We put them on the list of those we supported. Our contact was
through the secretary of the PPR in Warsaw, Alexander Kowalski. Most
of them were concentrated around Warsaw and they came to us. We did
all we could for them. I think that was our *moral obligation* to them, and

they appreciated it; and, thanks to that Kowalski, a lot of our misfortunes were solved after the war, because they remembered what we had done for them. After the war, Gomułka was secretary of the Warsaw district, before he was General Secretary; and when he was promoted, Kowalski replaced him. We were firm friends, from the time I was in Aryan Warsaw. He was a veteran Communist, older than I. If there had been a lot more like Kowalski, Poland would have been different. He clearly understood the problematic situation of the Jews. I never had to hide our situation from him. And I spoke as a Kibbutznik, a Halutz, on behalf of Eretz Israel. And he understood me very well. He wasn't a perverse "Jewish Communist." I often came to him when he was in an important function, in the Politburo of the PPR. He never refused to see me; a telephone conversation was always enough. Every matter was discussed frankly. We displayed all our troubles and fears because the UB began to control things.[20] I witnessed the arguments he had with the "great" Berman, Jakub Berman. Our messengers reached Lublin and created contacts with the AL, which had been crushed and was impotent.[21] By then, the Communists governed Lublin, but in the German occupation zone, they had been murdered and punished severely. They had many wounded, idle people, refugees. The AK withdrew and didn't help them at all; in fact, the AK beat them up and murdered them as much as possible. Communist Poland already existed, but the Russians didn't help the Uprising and abandoned the rebels to their fate. We knew the "great love" in Poland for the Communists throughout the years, so we were their saving grace. Nevertheless, we shouldn't say that the Jews lost anything by helping the Polish Communists with money and deeds.

A new period began. But for me, January 17, the day the Soviet forces entered Warsaw, was one of the saddest days of my life. I wanted to weep, and not tears of joy. This was the first time I wanted to weep. Apparently, that was a human weakness. Once when I was wounded in Krakow, I didn't have the strength to go the long way and I lost a lot of blood; only with difficulty and great effort did I get to my room in Warsaw and fainted on my bed. I was completely exhausted, but nevertheless, I did get home. And then I wasn't responsible for anything. Zivia and Marek Folman were there and took care of me until I recovered. But now, when I saw the masses shouting for joy, when I was there with Zivia and the dog, suddenly the knowledge that there was no Jewish people sliced through me like a knife. That feeling rose in me as the tank drivers kissed the crowd and flowers flew in the air; that jubiliation in contrast to our

20. UB (*Urząd Bezpieczeństwa*), Security Office, political secret police.
21. See Kazik 1984:132–134.

loneliness, we the orphaned, the last ones—what joy could we have? I was thoroughly crushed and broken. Until then, I had had to hold onto myself tightly, but now I could cry, be weak. Suddenly I asked: what am I and what is my strength? Ultimately, my own struggle for life had a limit. And not only me, everybody. There had always been a sense of mission that gave us strength; but now, it was over, as it were. People asked: why go on?!

Zivia had never seen me cry because I had never cried. Our comrades hadn't seen me in a state of depression. I had to live, to hold out; but on January 17, everything was shaken. Of course, other days followed: going out to the towns, searching. It's not easy to be the last of the Mohicans! We knew approximately how many Jews had been in Warsaw before the Polish Uprising—we estimated them at about 20,000. Twelve thousand got assistance in various forms. Of course those aren't exact numbers. We didn't get to many of them because they were afraid and didn't want us. And there were also many Jews who didn't know about us. A great many more were killed in Warsaw, killed as Poles were killed, and also killed by Poles and by Germans. They were also killed when they left Warsaw. People who didn't have documents also left Warsaw. They were in hiding and "surfaced" during the Polish Uprising. Now their houses were destroyed, many of them were murdered. The books say that in 1944, the AK had 300,000 members and the AL barely had a few thousand and that, in the Uprising in Warsaw, in August 1944, the AL mobilized altogether 500 people, whereas the AK stationed 46,000 fighters in Warsaw alone. But I can't believe those numbers. It's hard to assess forces in the underground; and we know that small groups sometimes make a bigger noise than big forces. But there is no doubt that the AK was the dominant force in the Uprising, although I think that the AK emphasized the number of their soldiers. It's hard to believe that a nation can put hundreds of thousands into underground action or even on the fringes of underground action without producing a great collapse. Here's the whole big camp of the Hagana and the Palmakh, as well as those involved in Brikha—how many were there? The English reports say 300,000; but even if I say that every member of Yagur was a potential member of the underground, I still don't believe the number is correct. I don't believe it was possible to estimate the number of members in the Polish underground. It was easier to estimate the members of the AL. But I don't think there were only 500 of them during the Uprising. For they also had partisan units and there were quite a few Communists. You can say that every Communist was a potential member of the underground. They probably had fewer fighters than the AK; but the AK didn't have 46,000 fighters. Nor do I believe they had weapons for so many people. But the

fact is that even on my barricade on Mostowa, there were joint forces of
the AK and the AL; and I don't know many barricades the AL could have
held on its own. The central role was played by members of the AK; but
there were other forces along with the AK and the AL, like the battalions
of the peasants party and others. So you have to add a little to the AL and
take away quite a bit from the AK; but the proportion was in favor of the
AK, no doubt about that—in Warsaw and everywhere else.

I can't say the AL hated the Russians because of their behavior during
the Uprising. There was general disappointment in the population, in the
AK and, of course, in the AL, too; but it's hard for me to talk about hatred
at that period. Because ultimately, help could come only from the east.
The "episode of Katyń Forest"[22] arose just when the Warsaw Ghetto was
destroyed. The Germans formed something like an international committee of journalists, those who collaborated with them, including Poles,
and brought them to Katyń, which started the propaganda against the
Russians about that incident.

In point of fact, I must say that for many years, both during and after
the war, I didn't believe the Russians murdered the Polish officers. A
cautious comment in the *Book of Ghetto Wars*, which I'm responsible for
(in 1953), says that the Germans murdered the Polish officers and blamed
it on the Russians. But later evidence (not because of a change in my
relations to the Soviet Union) has clearly shown that it really was done by
Stalin's order. I have no doubt that the great majority of the Polish people
believed the Russians did do that wicked act. You have to follow the
development in relations between General Sikorski and Moscow up to the
disruption in relations and, of course, that situation created a background
for the Poles' growing disbelief in the Russians and led many of them to
believe the Russians did do it, despite their great hatred for the Germans,
despite the fact that they saw with their own eyes what the Germans did
and were capable of doing. In this case, the simple Polish people believed
the killings were done by the Russians.

As for the abandonment of the Polish Uprising, until recently—I read
about it only a few weeks ago—the Poles claimed that when the Uprising
began, they relied on a Soviet officer sent by the advancing Russian army,
who came to AL headquarters. Afterward, it turned out he wasn't a
messenger, but a Soviet officer escaping from German captivity who
found shelter in Warsaw and came to the AL. The AL knew that and yet

22. Thousands of Polish officers who had fled from Poland to the Soviet Union when
the Germans invaded Poland in 1939 were executed at Stalin's order in Katyń Forest, near
Smolensk. The Germans publicized the incident in 1943, after the mass grave was discovered. The Soviet authorities denied it, accusing the Germans of the crime. Because of this,
relations between the Polish Government-in-Exile in London and the Soviet Union, deteriorated to the point of complete disruption.

their representatives met with him. But he didn't represent anyone. They used his name and rank so that the world would know that the Poles didn't begin the Uprising on their own but in conjunction with the Soviet army. If you take account of the Russian mentality, you don't have to be a genius politician to understand that they were capable of abandoning an ally, something the Americans couldn't do with De Gaulle.

It's true that just a day before the Uprising, they were defeated near Deblin and retreated some seventy kilometers, which was supposedly an excuse for their inability to advance. And a month went by until they reached the Wisła. Then they stayed on the other side of the Wisła, after they captured Praga. And they proved to the Polish people and its political leadership that neither the Poles in Warsaw nor the Polish authorities in England would conquer Warsaw with independent forces and confront the Soviets with a fait accompli. The claim that London asked them to give bases to the Allied planes is correct. The Russians didn't agree. They did everything in the most brutal fashion. They abandoned the Uprising, the rebels, the Polish people, and Warsaw. I don't think the Russians planned to destroy the Polish forces. Since even if 46,000 participated in the Uprising—that wasn't a big fraction of the 250,000 who were killed who didn't take an active role in the Uprising; and that wasn't what determined their decisions. It seems to me that their calculation was purely and simply political: Poland was to become a satellite of Moscow and was given an opportunity to determine only the hour when they approached the gates of Warsaw before the conquest. I have no doubt they had enough forces to help. This is not to say that this possibility was prevented because of some army that retreated seventy kilometers. They had an army of millions, and they were then at the height of their great momentum. That was likely to go on for another week and they would liberate Warsaw. At any rate, Warsaw wouldn't have given 250,000 victims and wouldn't have been destroyed as it was.

Soviet officers who had been at Stalingrad said that Warsaw was the most destroyed city in Europe. It was a clear political game and it teaches us that when politics are involved between warring forces, the forces stop at nothing. And when there is an enemy like the Soviet Union, you have to take that into account. I was naïve. I thought: to be so anti-human?! After all, they could have done something else: they could have crossed the Wisła after they let the Poles shed their blood for a month. They could have saved Warsaw in the second month. Even then they would have proved to the world that it was they who conquered Warsaw. But they broke the *Polish political force*. And afterward, it took years for the Communists to heal the break.

During the Katyń episode, they still hadn't taken into account the fact that they would form a Polish army on their own land to fight alongside the Soviet army. These were officers captured by the Russians; there were a lot of them and there was an argument that it wasn't clear if they could be trusted. Indeed, their commander, Berling, was a Communist. The division named for Kosciuszko[23] was composed of a Communist staff (including many Jews, even among the *Politruks*). But there were also many simple officers: junior officers, patriots, who couldn't join Anders's army for various reasons, or who really wanted to fight against the Germans. There were hundreds of thousands of Poles, including quite a few Jews. The Soviets were counting on the patriotic sentiment and hence, the division was named for Kosciuszko and not for some proletarian leader. So they introduced the Polish national anthem and the Polish cap. That was Russian politics—they emphasized patriotism. And there were a great many Polish officers who weren't at Katyń, in the collective catastrophe. But there were other Polish officers who simply wanted to fight. They weren't Communists, and not all were anti-Soviet; there were democrats among them; there were those who didn't have any obvious hatred for the Communists. Not all were members of the Endeks and the Sanacja; some were liberals. The Soviets were counting on that and so they formed the army. In point of fact, the help they gave the Russians was only symbolic. The Russians could have achieved victory without their help. But it was a wise policy. They behaved like that wherever they could form a local national army. And they deserve praise for that wisdom.

When I was in the Old City, I didn't sense antisemitism even once, neither from the civilian population nor from the AK; the opposite was true. The AL admired us and the AK showed us camaraderie. We were with them on the barricades and my comrades can testify to the fact that not once did we hear a hint of antisemitism.

They didn't even blame us for the fact that the Red Army remained opposite, although we were always blamed for all failures and catastrophes. But precisely in this case, they didn't blame us. I occasionally talked with simple soldiers of the AL, not to mention conversations with the command staff. Those who were realistic about this thing were the Jews who participated in the Uprising. They simply made a realistic assessment and concluded that the Soviets wouldn't help the Uprising and the Uprising would collapse. Our disillusionment began quite early. And that was the reason for the idea of setting up bases in Warsaw which hadn't yet been conquered so we would have routes of retreat; and that was agreed to in the command staff. So we tried and failed (to set up a base at Leszno 18).

23. A Polish national hero of the Polish uprising against the Russians in the nineteenth century; aided the Americans during the Revolution.

Clearly the Uprising had to fail since the Soviets wouldn't help. Our estimate was that the Soviets wouldn't aid the Polish Uprising aimed against them. That was logical. Although it was very brutal, that was war and "all's fair in war." They were used to that. They sacrificed millions of soldiers. They had twenty million dead—"so let a few more Poles die for the great cause of Communist Poland." However, the AL believed naïvely that the Soviets couldn't offer help; they believed the Red Army really had suffered a blow at Deblin and that that was the real justification for their behavior. They saw that as a temporary weakness during the Uprising which ended in two months. And that was one of the greatest catastrophes that befell the Polish people. In no uprising in Polish history did the Poles sacrifice so many victims—neither in 1831 nor in 1863, when they fought the Czar—as in this one.[24]

It's hard to summarize and assess the battle. As far as we were concerned, if there had been Polish forces in our area that continued the revolt in January 1945, we would have joined them. That was our attitude all along. From September 1939, I was always a "Polish patriot" to my comrades. I saw that war really as a Jewish war. I had no reason to be sympathetic to the Poles or their regime; but during the war, I forgot all the hatred. And if I had been in the Soviet occupation zone, I would have fought in the ranks of the Polish army. I have no doubt of that.

There is another accounting I have to make, which doesn't have anything to do with the account of the war against the Germans. Joining Anders's Army meant getting close to Eretz Israel, which was my heart's desire. Yet, if I had a choice of whom to go with—Anders who was an obvious antisemite or Wanda Wasilewska[25]—I certainly would have joined her because of the war with the Germans and, in particular, because of the nature and essence of the force I was joining: Communists, liberals, and such. Did I have to choose the members of the Sanacja, the Endeks? Did I have to join them in the war? That is all correct, if I don't take account of Eretz Israel. If I weren't Yitzhak Zuckerman, a Halutz facing toward Eretz Israel, I would probably have gone with Berling; but Yitzhak Zuckerman, the Halutz, needs an additional accounting. And that calculation has to do with Eretz Israel. That is, with the chance of getting to Eretz Israel and even fighting there. Incidentally, we knew about the Jewish

24. The Polish uprising of January–September 1831, against Czar Nicholas I, was fought to prevent sending the Polish army to fight against France and Belgium. It was quashed by the Russians.

25. Wanda Wasilewska (1905–1964): A Polish writer, one of the leaders of the Polish Communists in the Soviet Union and chairman of the Union of Polish Patriots from 1943 to 1946. In 1945, she married the Ukrainian writer O. Korneytshuk and settled in Kiev.

Brigade.[26] Ultimately, the consideration of the war against the Germans took priority over all other considerations.

After the great failure, after what we had gone through in January 1945, we faced the question of the continuation of the war, not only me but the entire group. If we could have fought where we were, we would have rejoined the war. But we were no longer needed and there was no war. Poland's force was broken; the AK was also close to breaking. They hadn't learned anything from what had happened to the AK in Vilna, when the Soviets conquered that city, where many of the local partisans belonged to the AK, and they paid a heavy price: Vilna became Soviet Vilna.

26. The Jewish Brigade: The only military unit in the British army (and in all the Allied forces) to serve in World War II as an independent national Jewish force. The Brigade existed from 1944 to 1946.

TWELVE

The Longed-For Liberation

The Central Committee
of the Jews in Poland
and the Beginning of Brikha

In July 1944, the Poles went from Russia to Lublin.[1] At that time, there was the Polish Committee of National Liberation (PKWN).[2] The Soviets conquered the eastern part of Poland and set up the provisional government in Lublin. The Poles were led by Berling and Rola Zymierski.[3] And it was the members of the leadership of PPR—Gomułka, Spychalski—who crossed the front lines and reached Lublin and Moscow. Gomułka wasn't in Warsaw during the Uprising. I met him in Praga, two days after the liberation of Warsaw. By then he was deputy head of the government.

As the Uprising approached, after the Soviets had advanced and conquered most of Poland, not all the party leadership came to Warsaw. (Zenon Kliszko was in Zolibórz.) Mieczyław Moczar, for example, wasn't in Warsaw at all, but was in the forests with the partisans. I learned of him and his position only long after the war. Roman Zambrowski[4] was in the Soviet Union along with Jakub Berman and was part of the Moscow

1. That is, a group of Polish Communist leaders, who remained in the Soviet Union throughout the war (or for part of it).
2. PKWN (Polski Komitet Wyzwolenia Narodowego): Established on July 20, 1944, to administer those parts of Poland liberated by the Red Army.
3. Michał (Rola) Zymierski (b. 1890): During the Occupation, he was in touch with the PPR. Director of the PKWN Defense Department. Promoted to Field Marshall in 1945. Minister of National Defense, 1945–1949.
4. Roman Zambrowski (b.1909): One of the organizers of the Polish army in the Soviet Union. From 1945, Politburo member of PPR. From 1941 to 1952, Deputy Speaker of the Sejm. Minister of State Control, 1955–1956. On March 20, 1956, Khrushchev declared that Zambrowski was unacceptable because of his Jewish origin. In 1957, he was removed from Party activities; in 1968, in the wake of an anti-Zionist crusade, he was expelled from the Party.

group. Witołd wasn't in Warsaw either or in the Old City; I think he also got to Lublin. In the Old City, there weren't any people of national stature of the leadership. One of those I knew, whose last name was Kowalski, was Richard; and there was also Bolesław Kowalski the AL commander in the Old City; and there was also Olek Kowalski, the secretary of the party in Warsaw (who replaced Gomułka in that job). There was also Zuta, Richard Kowalski's Jewish wife; and the wife of commander Witołd. After we went through the sewers, we realized that the entire military leadership had been killed, but I found others I knew, including Zenon Kliszko, in Zolibórz. None of the "greats" was there. Zenon Kliszko stayed in Zolibórz and crossed the Wisła on the day of the surrender. I was supposed to have crossed with him. He was one of those who tried to persuade me to join them in crossing the river.

The day the Red Army entered Warsaw, we felt like orphans; we had a sense that there was no Jewish people anymore. We had no estimate, we didn't know how many were left.[5] Our own people were also with us, Jews and non-Jews, who operated in Krakow. Later, we had contact with labor camps and concentration camps and we knew something about the Jews in them. We knew that with the advance of the Soviets, the Germans began sending the Jews to the west, and we suggested to the people in the concentration camps of Hasag in Częstochowa and other places to escape in light of the approaching front. Not to the west, but to the forests, during the evacuation. But during the Polish Uprising, we lost touch with what was happening in the occupied areas. A few weeks after we surfaced, I made my first contacts with A. Berman, after he had begun that work by himself. We decided to start assembling the remnants. We didn't reach most of the people either because the Jews couldn't find us or we couldn't find them. Instead of thousands, we now had hundreds. Quite a few were taken to the concentration camp at Pruskóv, near Warsaw, and sent from there to concentration camps in Germany. Since we didn't go through

5. In May–June 1944, the estimate was that in all of Poland 160,000–200,000 Jews remained. This included Jews in concentration and labor camps in Warsaw and other cities. According to our estimate, about 25,000 were in hiding, and the Jews in the concentration camps numbered about 80,000. It was also thought that about 80,000 Jews remained in Łódz Ghetto. Altogether, according to this, the number of surviving Jews is between 180,000 and 200,000. Meanwhile, many changes took place. During and after the Polish Uprising, in the few months between the Uprising and the Liberation, many Jews were murdered by Poles and thousands were captured by the Germans when they evacuated Warsaw. At that period, the Germans liquidated the remnant in the camps. In several dozen camps there were Jews, according to information we received from contacts with them. With the Soviet advance, the Germans evacuated the concentration camps and transported the Jews to the west.

We were the only group that didn't respond to the Germans, unlike the AK and the soldiers of the AL (in whose framework we also operated) who surrendered. (Testimony of Zuckerman at the Institute of Contemporary Jewry of the Hebrew University, 1964.)

that entire hell of mass exodus from Warsaw, that chapter is missing in my experiences.

As I said, we started collecting people. We contacted Kraków; we sent messengers. Some of our comrades—Stefan and Kazik—came to help us. We started organizing. In civilian terms and in terms of freedom of movement, after the Soviet conquest, we didn't have a status. I was a civilian named Stanisław Bagniewski. Those who weren't conscripted into the Polish or Red Army were civilians.

How did we contact Lublin? I already talked about the Soviet officers who came and took us, knowing we were fighters. I didn't know exactly how they knew that. Later I learned that they came to Wołochy, a town closer to Warsaw than Grodzisk, and the people there, perhaps Berman, told them that fighters who had played an important role in the Jewish and Polish war were at that address. So those officers came to us in their car. From then on, we dealt with the army and not with the civilian administration, since that was the day the Soviets occupied Warsaw and the surrounding area. They were the ones who gave us passes over the Wisła. There were pontoon bridges only for the army (they brought tanks west); but we got permission to cross. A Soviet military car took us to Warsaw and dropped us off at the Wisła, where we had to make it on our own. Zivia and I, along with Adolf and Batya Berman, crossed the bridge to Warsaw, where we learned that Gomułka was in Praga; so we crossed over there to meet him. I hadn't known him before that, since Witold, a military man, handled my affairs. When I went to the Aryan side of Warsaw in 1943, Gomułka was already in a high position—he was General Secretary of the party. Later, he was deputy head of the government. I met with his replacements as Party Secretaries in Warsaw. I had close relations with the last of them, Andzej, with whom I was friendly, until he was transferred to Kraków. Then I got word that he had been captured by the Germans there. He was replaced by Olek Kowalski, whom I met at least once a week.

So when we arrived in Praga, Berman and I went to meet with Gomułka, a very emotional meeting. He was really very glad to see Berman whom he knew better than me, but he also kissed me twice, in the Polish style, and gave us some information about what was going on in Lublin, and asked how he could help us. The only thing I requested was transportation to Lublin. He put a military auto at my disposal and, that day or the next, Adolf and Batya (Basha) Berman and Zivia and I left for Lublin. Before we left, we met with the Jewish organization in Praga, where there was a branch of the Jewish Central Committee and people I didn't know. For the first time, I met many Jews—dozens, maybe hundreds, who were looking for a place to sleep. Officials were functioning. These were people who had left for Praga in time, since Praga was liberated on October 2, 1944, and they managed to get organized.

In the house we went to in Praga, we found many people who knew about us; they didn't know us personally, but they did know the names of Antek and Berman. From Praga we left for Lublin, where we experienced our first meeting with Jews from other places. We got the first information from more reliable sources about what was happening in the eastern zones because western Poland was still under German control and in the thick of the Soviet army attack. The greatest experience was meeting the group of Ha-Shomer Ha-Tza'ir from Vilna—but not exclusively: there were also "Asians," that is, members of Ha-Shomer Ha-Tza'ir who had wandered or who had been exiled to remote areas of Russia, after the conquest of eastern Poland, and had spent most or part of the war there. It turns out we were half a year late, in terms of the first organization, and they had already managed to do something. There I met Abba Kovner after his adventures in Vilna, as well as Ben Meir and Yosef Sklar, Mordechai Rozman[6] who was later active in Brikha, and Leyb Lewidowski,[7] a member of Po'alei Zion–Z.S. And we also came across the first Jewish reorganization.

There were few members of He-Halutz or Dror among all those Jews. I think that Elhanan Magid[8] was there, but I didn't know him; there were very few of them. These were mostly members of Ha-Shomer Ha-Tza'ir and partisans, hundreds of Jewish partisans from the forests, who started gathering in Lublin, or from the eastern sphere; and some who went east in 1939 as refugees and now returned in the wake of the Liberation. The partisans came out of the forests, and those who didn't join the Soviet or the Polish army looked for Jewish centers and came to Lublin. Meeting the Jews was a profound experience. First of all, I learned that there were still Jews, comrades, Halutzim. Meeting Dr. Emil Sommerstein was a special experience.[9] He was then director of the War Compensation

6. Mordechai Rozman: Member of Ha-Shomer Ha-Tza'ir, one of the "Asians," who came to Lublin from the Soviet Union at the Liberation. Very active in Brikha. Accompanied convoys of survivors to exit ports.

7. Leyb Lewidowski: Member of Po'alei Zion–Z.S. Active in the underground in Baranowicz, partisan in the forests of Polesie. After the Liberation, one of the founders of the partisan organization in Italy. Active in Brikha in Italy.

8. Elhanan Magid: Born in Białystok. Member of FPO in Vilna; went with them to the Rudnicka Forests as a partisan. Lives in Israel.

9. Emil Sommerstein (1883–1957): Born in Hleszczawa, Tarnopol District. Zionist leader. Spent the war in a Soviet prison and was released in 1944, when he returned to Poland with the Red Army. Appointed to the Polish Committee for National Liberation in July 1944. Moved to Lublin in February 1945. In April 1946, he went to the United States with a delegation of Polish Jews, fell ill there, and remained. He died in New York.

Department of the PKWN. And when the provisional Polish government was established, he became Minister of Repatriation Affairs.

The only one I knew in that whole group was Abba Kovner. We had attended the same Gymnasium; as I recall, he was three grades younger than me. I was in He-Halutz and he was in Ha-Shomer Ha-Tza'ir. I don't remember if Vitka was with him then; I don't think so.[10] Before I talk about my conversations with them, I want to tell about my meeting with Dr. Emil Sommerstein who was instrumental in determining my direction for the long run. When we came to him and introduced ourselves, he hinted that he wanted to meet me in private. I hadn't known him before, but I knew that he was one of the leaders of Et Livnot. I knew he joined the Communist or pro-Communist government—as a rightist Zionist— and I was quite amazed. In my conversations with Dr. Berman, before we came, we had expressed our amazement at that. My conversation with Sommerstein was private. He might have heard not about the "split" (there was no split), but about two different perspectives—mine and Dr. Berman's.

The day before the Polish Uprising, before we said goodbye (we already heard the cannons approaching), at lunch in his house, in Bat-ya's presence, we started talking about the future. We weren't used to talking about the future, because we didn't know if there would be one. And all of a sudden, we heard those "merry cannons." Then we realized we had a difference of opinion. Obviously, the Red Army would enter, and obviously Poland annexed to the Soviet Union would be a different Poland, a Communist Poland. The argument had to do with our role in it.

It turned out that Berman wouldn't do anything illegal, he was an active Zionist, but "only with permission," and he believed that our participation in the underground with the AL, and his with the KRN (the underground leftist parliament) was an omen for the future.[11] He thought the Muscovite wedge in Warsaw granted us increased possibilities. I, however, didn't envision such a good situation. Nevertheless, I took into account the possibility that the Soviet presence would be good for the Jews—if anything could be good for the Jewish remnant. But, in Zionist terms, I didn't expect that we could function as we wanted. And since I had had a little experience in 1939 and early in 1940, I was also

10. Vitka Kempner-Kovner: Partisan, member of FPO in Vilna. In May 1942, she and two others blew up a German troop train headed for the front. In October 1943, from their base in Rudnicka Forest, she walked twenty-five miles to Vilna with a suitcase of explosives, blew up the power plant, and rescued sixty Jews from Kaylis Camp. Married Abba Kovner; lives in Israel.

11. KRN (Krajowa Rada Narodowa), National Council for the Homeland. Underground parliament, founded on January 1, 1944.

emotionally and ideologically ready for a Halutz Zionist underground. Apparently, we were divided on that.

When we were together in Zolibórz, we met a few times a day, but we didn't go on talking. Apparently in Lublin, Emil Sommerstein and the group of Ha-Shomer Ha-Tza'ir were told either by the Poles or the Jews that Zivia and I were on one side and Berman was on the other—that we didn't see eye to eye. So, Dr. Emil Sommerstein expressed his views concretely in his attitude toward us and toward Berman. It never occurred to me to suspect Dr. Berman's Zionist credentials, but the Ha-Shomer Ha-Tza'ir people especially the "Asians," and Abba Kovner as well, got scared when they saw me on the first two days associating with Berman. They viewed Dr. Berman as a *Yevsek*,[12] and that wasn't true. Dr. Emil Sommerstein treated him with the same attitude and with great caution.

Dr. Emil Sommerstein, a short, bespectacled Jew, with a rabbinical beard and gray hair, past middle-age, was now a minister in the provisional government of Poland. He hugged and kissed me and asked my forgiveness. For what? It seems that twenty-four hours before I arrived, he delivered a eulogy for me on the radio after getting word that I had been killed. The Poles had told him that and he thought it proper to deliver my eulogy. And here I was in front of him, alive and well. He had already met many Poles we had worked with in the underground, and they had told him of Berman and me. As for the eulogy, "that's a sign of long life," he said.

Then we had a frank discussion. I asked him how he had come to join the Communist government. Rather lightheartedly, he told me of his imprisonment and release from a Soviet jail. When the war broke out, he fled eastward. Some of his companions were executed; we knew about that, too. He, however, was interrogated and imprisoned in a Soviet concentration camp. One day, recently, one of the interrogators had come to him and asked which he chose—to stay in jail or to be a minister. He had to make a fateful decision and he did. They took him out of jail, dressed him, brought him to Moscow, and put him in the Polish Provisional Government. He understood that they did that not because of his merits but because they needed him so they could appear to the outside world with a government that included a Zionist representative, since they had to consider the United States and world Jewish opinion.

He understood all those intentions, accepted his fate, and did the best he could, he said; and now he was busy with a very important matter: the

12. Originally referred to a member of the Yevsektsia; but acquired a broader connotation of a Communist working in the Jewish sphere.

issue of repatriation and remuneration, since even then, they had to estimate the reparations Jews were entitled to receive. He also told me about the provisional government—in fact, at the time, it was just a committee of himself and his Polish comrades, summoned to Stalin at a reception in the Kremlin; he said it had been a very jolly and friendly meeting. Stalin received them warmly. He, Sommerstein, the Jew, was depressed and wanted to know what Stalin thought about the future of the Jews; but he didn't know how or when to ask. (I'm telling this from memory, but I think that I'm telling the story precisely.) Then, at the right moment, in a cheerful mood while drinking wine, he saw Stalin standing alone and looking out the window, and he went to him and said: "Generalissimo, I would like to ask you something." "Ask," Stalin replied. And he asked: "Here's what happened to the Jewish people and they were destroyed. Don't you think this question of the Jewish people, of those who survived, should be on the agenda of the international forum and receive an international solution?" He was afraid to utter the words "Eretz Israel" or "Palestine," and spoke only of the international significance of the Jewish problem. Stalin answered him with a single word; but, before that, Sommerstein said, Stalin twisted the right side of his moustache and then the left, and then he said a single word: "*Budyet*! (It will be done!)" Then Sommerstein addressed me: "Now, tell me, Antek, what did he say to me?" We laughed at how he reached his high position and about the conversation with Stalin. Now the interpretations began: why did Stalin say what he said—he didn't know and neither did I. But that was the truth; that was Stalin's answer: *Budyet*—it will be done.

According to Churchill's memoirs and the protocols of the Yalta and Casablanca conferences, Stalin spoke of the Jewish right of self-determination. Sommerstein told me things in a humorous way. After all, he knew who I was. He told me one more thing at that time and asked me not to talk about it because the preliminary arrangements hadn't yet been concluded. This was the negotiations between the provisional Polish government and Moscow on the repatriation of hundreds of thousands of Polish citizens, including about 200,000 Jews, according to his estimate. It still wasn't known precisely. But he hoped it would be settled soon. That was very exciting information for me because it didn't occur to me that so many Jews had found shelter in the Soviet Union; I had thought that only a few Jews had sought that shelter. Most of the Jews were condemned there as capitalists, anti-Soviets, and were taken out of their beds, their towns, their homes in the middle of the night, and led far away to the north and east. And by dint of that Stalinist brutality, they survived.

I kept that to myself, but I knew there was a solid basis for hope that hosts of Jews would come from the east. Furthermore, in meetings with the partisans, they also spoke of thousands of Jews who had fought in the forests. I hadn't known about that either until I came to Lublin. I had always thought that the number of Jews who survived was what I had estimated in the devastated areas of Poland. As I recall, even though the numbers weren't checked, the estimate was that about 15,000 to 20,000 Jews fought in the forests and that many of them survived. Indeed, when I was in Lublin, many Jewish partisans gathered and began organizing the group of Partisans, Soldiers, and Halutzim (PHH).[13] Most of them were young. (The real organization took place in Łódz a few months later.) That was very heartening news. I know what the situation was in western Poland because the Germans didn't surrender until May and they still carried on a military offensive from west of the Wisła. We didn't know what was going on fifty kilometers to the west; we didn't know that those liberated from the camps also came, even though there weren't many, fleeing from German captivity, when they were transported westward as the Germans retreated. Both Treblinka and Maidanek were in the hands of the Russians or the Poles; but not many Jews got out of there alive.

I got all that information from Sommerstein, who trusted me fully. I don't know if he told me everything he knew in that private conversation, but I think that everything he did tell me was correct. I don't think there were many people in Lublin who were close to him, which was why he chose me as his confidante. At that time, people were involved in the Jewish issue whom I hadn't known before and whom I didn't respect.

Sommerstein probably also tried to get close to the members of Ha-Shomer Ha-Tza'ir. But one day, two young people came to him, dressed in Red Army uniforms (but not regular army), and I later learned that one of them was the partisan Eliezer Lidovski. As soon as Sommerstein saw the uniform, a barrier sprang up between them, and even his form of speech changed. They also treated him as a member of the Judenrat, a collaborator—although not with the Germans but with the Russians. They rejected all such people out of hand and didn't make the necessary distinctions or take into account what everyone had gone through or the responsibility a person accepted along with the duties he performed. As for me—and I say this after his death—I have nothing but admiration and respect for Dr. Sommerstein. He was assigned the mission of a Jew; in that government, he had the position of a Polish minister. And in his sensitive situation, he performed his function in a very positive way. And I must say that he won my heart from the very first moment. I didn't see him as a member of the Judenrat or as an opportunist; he filled his obligation.

13. An organization formed in Poland in 1945, comprising about five thousand members. [Translator's note: I have used the initials of the Hebrew words for this abbreviation: Partisans, *Hayalim*, Halutzim.]

At the time, some people called him a "collaborator," but that was absolutely unjustified. He wasn't requested to betray or sacrifice his people.
He was assigned to work in general areas of Polish activity, while being
shown off to both the Jewish and the non-Jewish outside world, and he
also worked on the Jewish level, as chairman of the Central Committee
of the Jews in Poland.

Ha-Shomer Ha-Tza'ir saw him differently. The "Asians" (as they were
called), who had spent the Holocaust in the Soviet Union, all hated the
land of the Soviets. The justification for their attitude was what they had
gone through there and their knowledge of Soviet reality. The same was
also true of Abba Kovner, who distrusted everything about the Soviet
reality and the Communist world view. They rejected everyone in that
orbit including Dr. Emil Sommerstein and Dr. Berman, each for his own
"pedigree," even though they were members of Ha-Shomer Ha-Tza'ir—
in this case, perhaps precisely because they were.

What was the situation in organized Jewry? When I visited Dr. Emil
Sommerstein, he tried hard to persuade me to join the Central Committee
of the Jews in Poland. He didn't believe he would find anyone else from
the "old guard" and knew there were second- and third-class activists
in the area who wouldn't do honor to the nation. What happened was that
the committee was composed of Communists and a few people who were
"on hand." I don't know what had gone on in his meetings with Berman.
He probably wanted Berman to join the committee, too. I decided to join,
but it turned out that, on the one hand, there were Jewish Communists
and Bundists and, on the other hand, representatives of what was then
called *Ikhud*, including Po'alei Zion–Z.S., that is, remnants of all the
Zionist movements. A man named Mordechai Sonnschein, subsequently
one of the owners of the Menora Publishers in Israel, presented himself
as a representative of Po'alei Zion–Z.S., which was absurd. Berman really
was a member of Po'alei Zion Left and was entitled to represent them. I
realized that Sonnschein and his comrades, as well as Mendel Kossower,
a member of the General Zionists, were unwittingly carrying out functions convenient for the Communists. At that time, the Communists
wanted the representation of the Zionist movement to be united, so they
"united" us; and Sonnschein assumed the function of representing Po'alei
Zion–Z.S. (supported by the Bund and the Communists). The situation
dragged on and some days I would bang on the table—Dr. Emil Sommerstein wouldn't allow himself to do that—and threatened to storm out
of the committee if they didn't also put Yosef Sak on the Jewish Central
Committee, as a representative of Po'alei Zion–Z.S. I claimed that
Sonnschein could appear there on behalf of Ikhud, but Po'alei Zion–Z.S.
didn't belong to any Ikhud. I also argued that there was a group of active
comrades who weren't represented.

Ha-Shomer Ha-Tza'ir wasn't represented because its members left Lublin and emptied the center of Halutz forces. Later, they gradually came back. I tried to persuade them to leave at least one or two representatives, since there was no one to start working with. Ultimately, only Israel Sklar remained for them, and I fought to include him on the committee.[14]

When I began the struggle for the representation of Po'alei Zion–Z.S., those Ikhud people didn't have enough sense to say that one of them "with short pants" represented Ha-Shomer Ha-Tza'ir in order to increase our power base. I myself came in as former commander of the Jewish Fighting Organization, that is, without any connection to a party label. Dr. Berman joined, as I said, as a representative of Po'alei Zion Left. The representative of the Jewish Communists was Pawel Zalecki. I don't know what his Communist credentials were before the war. He has been in Israel now for a long time; I think he was one of the first Communists to join Mapai; he works in the Ministry of Trade and Industry. He came to me on the kibbutz and I welcomed him nicely. Ever since I came to Israel, I have entertained Bundists and Communists, as if nothing had happened between us.

This was the composition of the Central Committee of the Jews in Poland:

Melekh Biter and Pawel Zalecki of the Communists. There was one more but I've forgotten his name; he called himself "professor" and had moved to the Soviet Union back in the 1920s. When Poland was liberated, he was sent by the Communists as a Polish Jew to set up the Jewish Central Committee and was a member of it. I think he was a member of the NKVD. And I think he was corrupt (but he didn't get any payoffs from me; he waited a long time for a watch but never got it; he didn't even get a shotglass from me). I saw him as the embodiment of the corruption of the regime. Later, an important personage appeared: the Communist Shimon Zachariasz. The chairman was Dr. Emil Sommerstein. He was above the General Zionists, but was close to their group in Ikhud. There was also that Sonnschein I mentioned and Kossower and maybe somebody else.

Moshe Ishai's book tells about the committee and its composition and about their relations and claims to get a representative of Po'alei Zion.[15]

He-Halutz should have been represented on the committee by Zivia and I was very upset about that because Zivia wasn't there then, and she

14. Israel Sklar (Glezer): Member of Ha-Shomer Ha-Tza'ir. Reached liberated Lublin with the Asians in 1944. Worked to open escape routes to Romania. Moved to Warsaw in 1945. Represented the Halutz movement on the Central Committee of the Jews in Poland.
15. Moshe Ishai, *In the Shadow of the Holocaust*, 1973.

was indispensable. Zivia "disappeared" and I had to cover her absence with all kinds of excuses. The truth is she was sent on a secret mission to Romania, while I said she was sick in bed because of everything she had gone through; I even said I had put her in Otwock (a convalescent home near Warsaw). I had to be careful of denunciations which were frequent, even though I didn't think they would put me in jail.

I wanted to be on the Jewish Central Committee in order to have a place and an office and free transportation, and so I could appear in cities and towns under the aegis of a bureaucrat. I was the only one on the committee who refused a salary, and I didn't accept it up to the end. In the final accounting, I was a member of the Movement; if I had accepted a salary, I would have been obliged to account for expenses, to come every morning as a senior official of a respectable institution, if you could call the Committee of the Jews in Poland a respectable institution. I refused from the first and they couldn't convince me. I said I was here voluntarily or in an honorary position, and not as a functionary. Financially, I didn't have a problem. First of all, we still had a few thousand dollars left after I sent money to the Soviet Union to bring our comrades from there (Oskar Hendler, for example). And I said that, back in Grodzisk, Berman had given us money. And right after the war, when we met, he gave us another few thousand dollars. I lived modestly and whatever I had was more than enough for me, and even a few more people. And I also became the confidante of Guzik, the director of the Joint, and worked to transfer the Joint from Romania to Warsaw.

We used our seats on the Jewish Central Committee for the He-Halutz movement and for Zionism. When I came to some city, by authority of the Jewish Central Committee, I could obtain apartments wherever we decided to form the training kibbutzim. That was the time of unification between us and Ha-Shomer Ha-Tza'ir. We formed joint training kibbutzim. Our unity was based on belonging to He-Halutz, the labor movement, and the Histadrut.[16] As for the future, we said that when people went to Israel, we would allow them to choose either a Ha-Shomer Ha-Tza'ir kibbutz or Ha-Kibbutz Ha-Meuchad. There was even the inception of an idea of forming a special independent core group, distinct from the kibbutz movements in Eretz Israel.

I immediately left for the devastated cities in eastern Poland to look for Jews. This was possible because, in the eastern liberated part, committees had already been formed in various places and there was always somewhere to go. I followed the Red Army to Częstochowa where I accidentally came on some young Jews who later established the training kibbutz in Warsaw; they weren't from our Movement.

16. Histadrut: General Labor Federation in Israel, founded in 1920.

Kovner's group was motivated to go to Romania by their position that we shouldn't stay in Poland and should keep moving on. But they got into a dead end because there was no "on" from Romania. Later, they went through Italy, whereas our comrade Oskar Hendler came up with the idea of turning the stream of displaced persons returning westward to Germany. In this context, I must say that we asked the members of Ha-Shomer Ha-Tza'ir for help to bring Oskar from the east, since those who had already come from the Soviet Union initiated the transfer of Jews from there; and we even gave them money for that. The messenger who was sent did indeed bring Oskar to us. And Oskar came up with the idea of turning the thousands of displaced persons to Germany and setting up an exit base there. At first, the idea shocked me: on German soil, of all places?! But there was something to it. There were many camps there with Jews who knew they had nothing to look for in Poland, since their communities were destroyed. Then Oskar Hendler went to Germany and, after he sent us information, we started organizing groups and sending them to Germany instead of Romania, since the people there were stuck with no way out. We also sent people to Slovakia, Hungary, and even the American-occupied zone in Italy and Austria.

Lublin was a sort of independent country—there was no supervision or Soviet commissar there. When the Russians wanted their own man someplace, they put him in as they later put the Russian general Rokossowski, as a Pole, into the government of Poland.[17] In the Provisional Polish Government, there were Communists loyal to them, who had spent the war in Moscow: Bolesław Bierut,[18] who was from the Warsaw group and worked in the underground, apparently wasn't yet loyal enough to them in that period. Bierut was later president of Poland and Gomułka was Party Secretary, which is higher than the president of the state. But in the underground, Bierut was chairman of the KRN and one of those who formed that institution in January 1944. Bierut stayed in Warsaw and not until the approach of liberation did he and Spychalski cross the Wisła. He was not loyal to Moscow, but was a member of the Polish underground, which may have been why he didn't allow Moscow-style show

17. Konstanty Rokossowski (1896–1968): Soviet and Polish Marshall. A Russian of Polish origin. Member of the Red Army since 1917. Appointed Marshall, one of the leaders of the Soviet Army, in 1944. In November 1944, appointed commander of the Byelorussian front. In November 1949, he was sent to Poland as Minister of National Defense and Deputy Prime Minister. He was seen as a symbol of Soviet power in Poland.

18. Bolesław Bierut (1892–1956): Statesman and Communist leader, who came to be called the Stalin of Poland. From 1939 to 1943, he was in the Soviet Union and went to Warsaw in spring 1943. In 1948, he replaced Gomułka as chairman of the Party. He was Prime Minister from 1952 to 1954. He died in Moscow while attending the twentieth Congress of the Soviet Communist Party.

trials in Poland, thus proving his courage. I think Bierut should be thanked for that. If it had been up to Jakub Berman, our Dr. Berman's brother, I think there would have been trials.

The Joint developed after we brought them money from Romania and after Dr. Joseph Schwartz returned. We established close ties with him, which lasted long after I left Poland, even in matters not connected with Poland. All I had to do was talk with him to transfer money from the Joint for purposes we indicated. Although there was a debate between the Joint and the Committee of Jews in Poland, which wanted the money sent directly to them, we wanted to protect the Joint as an independent philanthropic American institution; and, when I came to Schwartz to ask "what about me?" he would also give considerable sums of money to Dror.

My status and relations with Schwartz at that time allowed me to come to him and say: "I need money for my Movement and for He-Halutz"— and he would respond. For example, in 1946, a member of our Movement in Tunis told me of their financial distress, and I went to Schwartz and got five thousand dollars for him. The same was true of Abraham Gewelber who was sent from Eretz Israel and walked around in an UNRRA[19] uniform and asked for my help; and I got five thousand dollars from Schwartz for matters he was dealing with. Some time later, when Moshe Kliger[20] appeared, he wanted to eat me alive; he claimed I didn't have the right to distribute money in such a way and that there "has to be order." The truth is that if a delegation had gone to Schwartz, it's doubtful he would have given anything. Guzik and Giterman were in charge of the Joint throughout the war; when Guzik went to Lublin and later to Warsaw, he went right to work. People who knew Guzik knew that he knew how you get money, and he immediately appealed to various places, sent telegrams to New York. That was before our legally recognized activity; he didn't have legal money. I am sure the Poles wanted contact with him and we must say that, from the first, we didn't meet the Soviets, but only the Poles. He gave me the money simply because of the friendship and loyalty we had maintained for a long time. Joseph Schwartz made a strong impression on me: a man who was familiar with Hebrew culture, I think he spent his childhood in Romania; then he was in the United States for some time. The Joint appointed him to his position first as director in Europe and then, in 1946, after Guzik's

19. UNRRA: United Nations Relief and Rehabilitation Administration, created on November 9, 1943, and discontinued in 1947.

20. Moshe Kliger (1913–1978): Central activist in He-Halutz Ha-Tza'ir in Poland. Immigrated to Eretz Israel in 1935. After the war, he organized extensive missions of Ha-Kibbutz Ha-Meuchad to Holocaust survivors in Poland, Germany, and Italy. He enlisted several Shlikhim in Brikha.

death, as general director. When I went to the offices of the Joint, a hint from Dr. Schwartz was enough to open all doors to me. The affinity was much stronger than it had been before or during the war. I think those relations helped later, during the time of Brikha, when he supported us. I don't feel comfortable talking about it, but the truth is that many gates were opened to me; the same goes for the Polish leadership. The members of the Jewish Central Committee also had to respect me; even if they wanted to throw me out, Sommerstein would have prevented them. I'm talking about the leaders of the conspiracies and intrigues, the Communists and Bundists and others, including Ikhud. None of them wanted me on the committee.

After the war, Marek Edelman went off to study medicine and was no longer with us. He told me of the gathering of the Bundists to restore their movement. Marek was an extraordinarily brave man, but not a contemplative or an articulate man. He told me his "speech" at that gathering. He got up and said: "Comrades, enough splashing around in piss!" That is, the Bund had nothing more to do. That was his whole speech. He went to study medicine since he had always been attracted to that profession. During the war, he worked in the hospital on Czyste as a nurse. Hence his friendship with the women couriers, Dr. Inka Szwajger and other nurses who were on Czyste. Through him, I took them for our underground work on the Aryan side of Warsaw. Marek Edelman had firm relations with us, which have been maintained to this day: he was loyal to us. I value him as a brave, frank, and reliable person.

At the outbreak of the Six Day War, he sent Zivia and me an encouraging telegram. In those days, that took courage in Poland. In my letters to him in Poland, I was always careful not to harm him in any way. And he was indeed badly hurt. He is a famous cardiologist in a hospital in Poland, and they demoted him and shoved him aside. They may even have forced him out of his important practice in those days after the Six Day War.

Some time ago, I got greetings from him from someone who had visited there and, a year ago, I got a letter from Wacław telling about his and his wife's fate. Among other things, he wrote that, if not for Dr. Marek Edelman, his wife probably would not have survived because of a serious heart condition. As for Marek himself, I hear he is a great doctor and heart surgeon. A lot of his comrades who studied with him are here, because the time came when they were thrown out of Poland or understood there was no place for them there.

One of the Bundists who died after the war was a member of the committee in Lublin, an educated man, who sometimes attended meetings and was later a legal advisor of the government of Poland. His son is in Israel. Another one who was active there was Salo Fiszgrunt, with whom we were always friendly and who also participated in the underground. He wasn't a fighter, but was one of their politicians since, because of his age, he wasn't suitable for the Jewish Fighting Organization. He was second in command, after Feiner. In the public struggles in the Jewish Central Committee, we maintained good relations, even though the harshest attacks against us came from the Bund. We can say of the Bund that they not only didn't learn anything, they didn't know anything either. The Jewish Communists at least knew what their Polish comrades would allow them to do now. Fiszgrunt set his course according to prewar Bundist ideology, whereas the Communists received practical instructions on how to behave. This was how it was during Brikha, when Brikha was given legitimation. And Fiszgrunt didn't know that Spychalski was behind that policy. He would yell and protest the exodus of the Jews, although without mentioning my name; but the Bund always meant me. Later came Zachariasz, who was a personality; in terms of his political development, he, like Finkelstein-Lewartowski, was a former member of Po'alei Zion. During the split in 1921, they left and went to the Yevsektsia. Zachariasz was an outstanding personality, a harsh and hard man but honest, a real "Bolshevik," but a genuine, convinced Bolshevik, until quite recently. I think he broke down somewhere. He visited Israel and I refused to meet him. He called me, wanted to come to "the Passover Seder," and came to Beit Katznelson. I tried not to be there because it was hard for me to talk with him; he gave us a lot of trouble. But he was the opposite of his predecessor, who was a careerist devoid of ethical principles. Sitting opposite him, I knew I was facing a hard enemy, a man who believed in what he was doing. He came on the scene quite late, controlled things, and guided his comrades behind the scenes.

Dr. Sommerstein was kept as chairman of the committee as long as necessary. Later, the Poles allowed him to leave Poland. He left for the United States, where he died. I have nothing to say against Dr. Emil Sommerstein. In my opinion, the nasty things said about him are baseless. I think he performed his function honorably; he didn't flee from Jewish life; he saw himself as responsible. He couldn't have fought the Zionist war; he couldn't have done it under any terms; but he wasn't two-faced. Everyone knew he was a Zionist, a member of the General Zionists. We respected each other. He may not always have been satisfied with me. As for me, I had complaints about his comrades, but not about Dr. Sommerstein himself.

The Jewish Committee sat in Lublin until it was decided to moved the Provisional Polish Government to Warsaw—there was a big struggle about the location of the government. I think that Bierut was one of those who forced that decision.

In his book on Brikha, Yehuda Bauer tells of a supposed ideological "symposium" held in Lublin when our Warsaw group arrived there.[21] Opinions were divided with Ha-Shomer Ha-Tza'ir on several issues: whether to participate in the restoration and reorganization of the Jewish communities.[22] Kovner's group was for taking revenge on the Germans and for the total escape of the Jews from Poland. Bauer claims there was a debate on the timing of the exodus from Poland and that "Zuckerman was of the opinion that the destroyed Polish Jewry, which had no leadership, should not be abandoned, and cadres should be left in place." And, according to him, "Zuckerman expressed opposition to the idea of revenge." There are also a few imprecise things there about unification. In the debates in Lublin, we didn't discuss revenge, either tacitly or explicitly.

That debate developed later, in Romania, when Zivia participated in those debates. She told me about the position of the comrades in those discussions. You can imagine only theoretically what I would have said if there had been such a debate in Lublin. I don't know of a single Jew who survived who didn't cherish the notion of revenge, and I say with full responsibility—and you also have to take into account the fact that of all the comrades who led the underground Halutz movement in Poland (Dror), Tuvia and I were the only ones left—and if I had had to choose in 1945 whether to go to Germany for revenge or to devote myself to organizing Jews who were assembling, I would without hesitation have chosen to organize the Jews. And I'm not discussing now if and how we should have taken revenge.

One of the fundamental causes of the debate was the position of Abba Kovner and his comrades, including the "Asians," about when to abandon Poland. As I recall, they appeared as a crystalized, unified group. They had a few months to think about those things because they were liberated before us. Their position was that there was no need for a special organization of the Halutz movement, or any other organizations: the Jewish people were one, the Jewish people were slaughtered, killed, murdered. Now the Jews had to join in a single, pan-Jewish organization. Neither Zivia nor I could accept that. We didn't see any contradiction, either then or now, between a movement, an ideological organization, and the existence of an independent organization of politically oriented people, participating in a broader framework and cooperating with other forces, without blurring their independent identity. That was the debate in Lublin.[23]

21. Yehuda Bauer 1970:24.
22. Bauer 1970:25.
23. Y. Bauer does affirm (1970:33; Hebrew edition) that Zuckerman "did think it would be irresponsible to abandon destroyed Polish Jewry. . . . He had to remain in Poland and set up frameworks by means of which every Jew would ultimately immigrate to Eretz Israel."

To introduce the subject of revenge at that time is to confuse things that happened later in Romania, not in Poland. Abba Kovner's people might have talked about that in Lublin, but not in Zivia's or my presence. The important debate in Lublin was on the question of *what do we do from now on?* The position supposedly attributed to me "to rebuild life in Poland" is utter nonsense. The question was whether to leave Poland *at once.* And that's just what they did. When we spoke about "what to do," I argued that, if we wanted to save our own lives, we could have done that before the liberation of most of Poland, since emissaries had come to us from Slovakia to rescue us (Zivia and me). We didn't agree to it then, when danger lurked at our door every day.

Could we agree to it now, in January 1945, before the war ended in Europe and when masses of Jews from the Soviet Union were about to return to Poland? Could we agree to leave Poland at that time? I think it would have been the greatest stupidity to reduce the forces we could have activated to help the Jews returning from the camps and those repatriated from the Soviet Union. In January 1945, there was, of course, no debate about whether we should organize and clear paths for Brikha. That was why a large majority of the Lublin Shomer group left for Romania in late January–early February 1945. One or two of them remained, and I pleaded with them to leave some members of Ha-Shomer Ha-Tza'ir behind in Poland, too, because more expatriates would come and there wouldn't be anyone to welcome and organize them. On that day, Zivia went with Abba Kovner.[24] They crossed the border, got to Romania, and formed the "brigade," later called the "Coordinating Committee." They set up the center in Romania.

There was a basic difference between the group that remained in Poland and the group that formed in Romania. The latter were political emigrants at a dead end. The hope that they could go on from there to the Black Sea and Eretz Israel proved false. That disappointment was a heavy blow for them. That was before the group decided to turn toward Italy.

However, there was the group that stayed in Poland, which soon grew strong and turned into a movement of many thousands: young people, partisans, soldiers. I say "grew strong," but you can't measure that phenomenon by prewar standards, since these were the remnants. That movement organized the youth, formed training kibbutzim, began Brikha even before instructions came from above, before we had any connection with Eretz-Israeli institutions or Shlikhim from Eretz Israel.

I used the term "political emigrants" before. I must say that emotionally, we were all "emigrants," including natives of Poland, because that

24. According to Bauer, they left on March 1, 1945.

was no longer our Poland, Jewish Poland, the Jewish streets; we were like driven leaves. But we had a lot of work ahead of us: to absorb the people, organize them, support them, set up training kibbutzim. The comrades who left for Romania, however, remained physically and emotionally isolated from all the problems facing those who stayed in Poland.

Young Jews sat together in Bucharest and other places, unable to advance, expecting and waiting, seeking ways to move on, sending emissaries; and for months they didn't know what to do with themselves. Their days were filled with stormy debates whereas the conditions we faced in Poland required a lot of work. Issues in Poland at that time have to be considered in the context of the period, of the murder of Jews returning from the concentration camps and returning to towns, and of Jews traveling the roads and riding the trains, Jews who were murdered by members of the Polish national underground who fought against the new regime. That reality was remote from the group that was concentrated in Romania.

The group of Ha-Shomer Ha-Tza'ir got itself into a dead end. I would call them, what the Germans called the governments that fled: *gefloygene Regierung* (a fly-by-night government). Here were strong, talented people, sitting for days and nights in Romania arguing about revenge. They created a mystical, sickly atmosphere around themselves, which was a hotbed for unrealistic dreams. Things reached such a pass that Zivia couldn't bear the nonsense and returned to Poland.

As for me, I was ostracized and excommunicated so completely that Zivia told me that when there were attempted pogroms and murders of Jews in Poland, they would point an accusing finger at me. Because I remained in Poland and didn't defend the Jews. Naturally, I considered that idle chatter.

As for our relations with the Soviet Union, Zivia's and my position came from our world view and our life experience. In 1939, for about half a year (a bit more for me than for Zivia), I worked in the underground in Lwów under the Soviet authorities; I didn't come across a concentration camp there, but rather the new regime which was beginning to take shape. My underground wasn't anti-Soviet. I was a member of the Zionist underground, and then I went through the Holocaust. During the Holocaust, I was in touch with Polish forces, and those who won our loyalty and helped us with their slim forces were the Polish Communists. In personal conversations with those people—since I often spoke with members of their party leadership about Zionism and Eretz Israel—I learned that their hearts were with us. They themselves suffered quite a bit from Stalinism: even before the war, the Komintern (i.e., Stalin) dispersed their party; lopped off their brothers' heads. Nevertheless, they saw the Soviet Union as the liberating force. They certainly forgot some of the account since human forgetting also exists. They hated the Poland of the fascistic *Sanacja* and sought someone to lean on. They included old-time Communists and those who joined them during the war out of a desire to see a different Poland. They were first of all Polish patriots who wanted to see a new Poland; and they were the only force we could rely on because of their attitude toward us, toward our Jewish group, their attitude toward those of us who survived. They didn't owe us anything and we talked freely, but they were sympathetic to the Zionist idea. We wanted to see a socialist Eretz Israel. We talked about that. We didn't lie. Even now, I would like to see a socialist Eretz Israel.

So I went through two different experiences: that of Polish Communism, as I saw it in those years, including the two years I stayed in Poland after the war. If I had been Polish, I would have joined them wholeheartedly, and not the other forces. The other experience was the *Zionist, Eretz-Israeli line.* But perhaps we shouldn't have deceived ourselves that a new Poland would be a different Poland. We thought that the experiences Poland had gone through and what had happened to Polish Communism might help them create a Communism with a "human face." After all, these are events before the "Prague Spring." The truth is that there were things we didn't know. Kovner and his comrades brought a completely different intellectual load, which perhaps was objectively correct. We heard shocking tales from members of Ha-Shomer Ha-Tza'ir. It's possible to argue about world views, but it's impossible to argue about the facts they brought with them. They weren't made up; these were people who had seen the Soviet reality as it was. They saw it in the partisan units and in the forests of the liberated Ukraine. In Kiev there was a pogrom when Khrushchev was the "boss" there; their ideas were based on fact. But our notions also had some justification. I thought I saw new forces rising which would have to rely on more liberal forces. Moreover, the Polish Communists themselves changed their aspect. During the Holocaust, their attitude toward the Jewish issue and toward our Zionist dream changed. But, the debate between us in Lublin began with concrete things and ultimately wound up in general issues that were quite significant to me.

I had known Abba Kovner in Vilna, but I didn't know he wrote poems; as I remember, we spoke Hebrew with one another. I think the Shomer group knew Hebrew and in their speech was an explicit expression of the Jewish existence: "The whole world murders us, all of us, the whole world hates us! Therefore, the whole nation must unite and come together in one brigade. We don't belong on the cursed ground of Poland! We have to leave Poland, we have to get up and go!"

That was the beginning of the great debate between us. These things were an expression of disappointment and despair. Some time later, the element of revenge was introduced into those discussions. But that wasn't in Lublin, but only later, in Romania. The fateful questions in Lublin were: first of all, whether all of us were leaving Poland. And whether we would blur our ideological, socialist Zionist essence because the Germans murdered everyone without distinction. The question was whether there was any distinction—I mean among that segment that bore an obligation, Jews organized into parties, youth movements—whether there was any distinction in the response of the victims. Did everyone say: self-defense? Weren't there collaborators? Were we now discussing an abstract world view or the concrete position of a group of Jews who behaved as they did because of the education they had received for years? And if He-Halutz sinned, if the Halutz movements sinned in their struggle, didn't we have to make an historical accounting? And is there any doubt that the Halutz movement was the leading Jewish force during the horror? It led the way to uprising, and self-defense. It wasn't the only force, but it was the initiating force. Should we blur that moral lesson?! That was the root of the debate between us. And something else. Abba Kovner and his friends said we should form *one organizational brigade*, with no distinctions, a single brigade with no accounting.[25] The whole nation was murdered, and it must join forces to go on from there. The second thing, according to them, was that if the border was opened, the whole leadership cadre would take off; anyone who wanted to go should go, since there was no chance of recovery for Jews here. Didn't Zivia and I say the same thing? But the first thing we said was that we weren't giving up our own ideological approach! Indeed, I should and could cooperate with the whole nation; after all, we had been educated for that and had worked for that in recent years. In Warsaw and in Poland, there was a general Jewish Fighting Organization in which we fought together. I didn't have to make an accounting with myself; after all, I worked with the Bund in almost every possible area. But that doesn't mean I now had to look for a new lowest common ideological denominator to be together. There was no need for ideological concessions. To this day, I think that the encounter between various movements was fruitful. You can do things in common without giving up your self-identity.

There was a difference of opinions on the second subject too. We said that all of us shouldn't leave Poland at this time. We had no doubt about the opening of borders, and there was nothing new in that. Back in 1940, we worked to open the borders to get out. We said there was no need to

25. The "Brigade" was originally called the "Brigade of the Remnants of Eastern Europe," and was established on April 26, 1945; it was to be the organic expression of Abba Kovner's desire for Jewish world unity. Yehuda Bauer states that Kovner didn't have any illusions either about Jewish world unity by means of the "Brigade." In his opinion, the movement was ethical and not political (see Bauer 1970:36–40).

teach that lesson to people who began working on it in 1939 in the Soviet zone. Although they themselves didn't escape, they had sent others to Vilna to pave the way; and they had also sent people to the Romanian border (some of whom were unfortunately captured and killed). Even during the German occupation we said we had to get across the borders and go. But we also knew you had to stay, and we had once refused to abandon the ghetto. So should we go now?! Didn't we have a national responsibility? The war wasn't yet over. What would happen to the Jews left in the concentration camps? And there was also a hope that many Jews were in the Soviet Union. But I didn't divulge what Sommerstein had told me about that.

Even before we got there, Ha-Shomer Ha-Tza'ir had sent Ruzka Korczak to Romania.[26] For some reason, our people were late in coming back from the Soviet Union and we didn't have anyone to send abroad. Most of the people I worked with in the underground weren't members of Dror and, although we had had five units in the Ghetto Uprising, very few of the members of Dror remained. (Although after the Russians captured Częstochowa, we added people.) Some of those who had been in the Jewish Fighting Organization were dispersed all over. Oskar Hendler was still in Russia, Dan Gelbard was already in Eretz Israel, at Alonim. Zvi Netzer was also in Eretz Israel. Most of the members of He-Halutz Ha-Tza'ir were still in Russia. So, in Lublin, in January 1945, Zivia and I were the only ones left. Tuvia, who played a central role, came later; but, in those weeks, he wasn't there. I used to joke with Zivia: *"General on an armey* (A general without an army);" later, the "army" also arrived. We divided up the jobs between us. The debates were extremely harsh. They were held in the Ha-Shomer Ha-Tza'ir commune in Lublin, where the "Asians" and others lived together. By the time of our second visit to them, Sak and Grajek were also with us.

Moreover, anyone who searches for the "fathers of Brikha," as Bauer does in his book, shouldn't focus only on the years of Brikha, but should go back to the late thirties in Poland. He will then realize that we never dropped the subject under any conditions and through all the years. We were all involved in it. Although I personally wasn't active in illegal emigration from Poland at the end of the thirties and was only on the fringes of practical action, I did know what was happening even if I didn't attend the meetings with Braginski and the other comrades who were active in those issues.[27] Every one of us who lived at Dzielna 34 or on Gęsia knew about it.

26. Ruzka Korczak left for Romania on November 7, 1944.
27. Yehuda Braginski, a member of Kibbutz Yagur, one of those responsible for illegal emigration from Europe in the late 1930s and in the 1940s.

When the war began, as soon as the Soviets entered eastern Poland, on December 17, 1939, we made our first attempt to go to Vilna, with the intention of going on to the Romanian border. The same goes for the German occupation zone from 1940 until the time of Brikha. This matter shouldn't be taken as a technical concept, as Bauer did. And you don't start the story from the moment Kovner and his friends appeared in Lublin. And I say this even though I'm not jealous of the various "parents" of Brikha—whether they're the "Wołyń fathers" or the "Lublin fathers." The subject of illegal emigration should be started in Poland in the late thirties.

I don't regret the decision to stay in Poland. It was made in good conscience. Even today, thirty years later, I would do the same. Not only am I not ashamed of it, I'm proud of it. Ultimately, under Zivia's and my influence, a few members of Ha-Shomer Ha-Tza'ir also stayed. I don't know what internal debates they had; I heard about them only later from Israel Sklar who worked with me on the Jewish Central Committee; he said they had bitter debates. I claimed that, if they left, it was their duty to leave a few people behind, for how could their own dedicated and loyal man, Mordechai Rozman, who was taking care of Brikha matters so well, suddenly disappear.[28] Jews come back and look for Mordechai and can't find him. Is this how Brikha will operate?! After all, the Jews have to be organized to leave, frameworks have to be set up. And when they described our position as a desire to resuscitate Jewish life in Poland, I was pained and sorry. Did any of us believe there was a future for the Jews in Poland?! But we had to organize frameworks for the young people, the older people, the partisans. Otherwise, how could there be Brikha? Would any Jew seek the border by himself? Would he look for Mordechai Rozman and Zvi Netzer? The organization was the force that directed and organized the great exodus, especially since it was illegal, when we had to be careful of ordinary Jews we didn't know. A framework of He-Halutz was established and in addition there were also frameworks of Ikhud and Oved. We formed communes of "Labor" and the organization of PHH (Partisans, Soldiers, Halutzim), which comprised 5,000 partisans and discharged soldiers. In May 1945 we didn't yet know how many Jews would come from the Soviet Union. No one knew. They talked of a quarter million Jews who crossed the borders. There are various reports and summaries, and all the statistics coincide with a specific day. But that was a migration of people. So revenge was not at the top of my agenda, which was occupied with the organization of Jews. We didn't know what we faced; it was a time of anticipation, a waystation.

28. According to Bauer (1970:28), the symposium of Lublin ended by appointing Mordechai Rozman to head Brikha activity.

The group that left for Romania set up an organization that didn't last long. It turns out that political and movement instincts came to the fore, for good and for bad, even in the Brigade they formed there. In point of fact, the Brigade was never established as an ideological organization. Early on, the Revisionists and other elements there began taking care of themselves. Everyone saw who was closer to him, in terms of movement and ideology. Cliques formed within the Brigade and mutual recriminations arose.

We who remained in Poland began organizing along different lines: two big movements—or, more precisely, two important core groups that survived—were Dror and Ha-Shomer Ha-Tza'ir. Even before other cores appeared—except for the groups that united in Ikhud, which absorbed various and strange elements—a combined movement of Dror and Ha-Shomer Ha-Tza'ir emerged. Together we formed branches and training kibbutzim. We took advantage of the possibilities opened to us, our membership in the Jewish Central Committee, which was meanwhile transferred from Lublin to Warsaw.

Back in Lublin, we had decided to send Zivia across the border to Romania. That was a very hard decision for us. Tuvia, as I said, was neutralized for a few months and Zivia's going meant that "half of the Movement" was leaving. But the decision had to be made. We had to formulate and organize Brikha and you had to be crazy to think that someone would sit in Lublin or Kraków and Jews would come to him. So Zivia and I decided she would go and I would stay. Some time later, Tuvia returned to work very energetically.

In Romania, Zivia was depressed because of various moves of Ha-Shomer Ha-Tza'ir against her because of our opinions. They were wary of her, as if she were a criminal. But there were a few members of the Jewish Fighting Organization in Romania who didn't belong to our Movement, who knew what was going on and reported to Zivia.

The group that coalesced in Romania degenerated for lack of activity. They sat and waited, got money, ate, argued, and, aside from that, didn't do anything from morning to night. They were waiting for some miracle from the sea. But there were no miracles. If they had stayed in Poland, they could have moved heaven and earth, organized, worked. Every one of them could have contributed. But they sat and argued. Revenge hadn't yet come up and they were supposedly concerned with transferring Jews and Brikha. But could you do that by sitting in Bucharest? After all, Mordechai Rozman got instructions and people from Warsaw, not from Romania. The people were to be sent from Łódz, Częstochowa, Warsaw, and Silesia. One of our first operations was setting up bases throughout Poland, which we called kibbutzim. To this day, the many people who did that have the right to boast of their handiwork.

I've already told of my first visit to Gomułka and how he helped us in those days. Afterward, we could manage even without going to him. Berman might have met with him; I'm not sure. Later, I had extremely unpleasant contacts with the "Great" Berman, Jakub Berman. Hilary Minc, also a Jew, was the economic advisor in the government of Poland, but I didn't know him and didn't meet with him. There were other members of UB whom I met with, but that was later. The Jewish center in Poland was housed in Praga. The Committee of Warsaw Jews was housed somewhere else. Jews began gathering around the two institutions. Most of them were then in Łódz and Silesia. At the center of our Movement was the kibbutz, which was housed in the same building where I had an apartment. My membership in the Central Committee of the Jews in Poland had certain advantages: wherever I went, the local committees were told to receive me. The local Communist committees ignored me and I returned the compliment.

I got on well. When I needed a vehicle, I got help from the Joint, and I could also ask the Central Committee of the Jews in Poland. Moreover, I rode the trains a lot, as many as returned to their routes. There were many difficulties, especially in winter. Unfortunately, it was important for the traveler to look Aryan, since there were murders on the roads. I traveled around a lot and my documents were Polish. The name Stanisław Bagniewski was a good disguise for my trips.

In those days, a special council was established to find Jewish children. At first, every group worked separately, but a little later, a coordinating committee was created. Leybele Goldberg from Eretz Israel was active in that. Sara Nishmit was active on our behalf.[29] The first children were discovered by chance. It happened on my first visit to Częstochowa; I was looking for an address. I had come from Warsaw (I think Zivia was still in Romania). On that trip, I looked for addresses and couldn't get a hold on anything. I was crossing a street in Częstochowa and thinking how to make initial contact with someone. I would usually go look for Jews and walk around the streets. For example, one day in Italy, I suddenly heard a partisan song and some Russian songs coming out of some building. I didn't think the singers were Polish because Poles didn't sing Russian songs much. I thought they were almost certainly Russians or Jews. I went in and there were Jews.

29. Sara Nishmit (b. 1913): Born in Suwalki District, Poland. Moved to Lithuania in 1925 and studied at the universities of Kovno and Vilna. When the Germans invaded, she was imprisoned, and escaped from a labor camp to the partisans in the forest; she remained with a Soviet partisan brigade until July 1944. From 1945 to 1947, she served on the Zionist Coordination to Redeem Children from monasteries and Christian homes in Poland. Member of Kibbutz Lohamei Ha-Getaot since 1955, wife of Zvi Shner, and author of several books and articles on resistance in the ghettoes and forests.

The same thing happened to me in Częstochowa. In the place I entered, I saw two adjoining rooms with a very small transom between them. Suddenly, I heard singing from the other room. I asked who was there and was told it was Jewish children, a group of Jewish sixteen-year-olds. I was curious, I went in, and asked where they were from. They told me they had been in hiding for a long time. The children had been in Camp Hasag and were now going to a Polish school. "What do you live on?" I asked them. And they said: "We steal!" They stole coal and bread. A wagon would pass by and they would steal from the back, like street urchins. They were all orphans. Their tale made a great impression on me. I shook hands with them and said: "Let's make a partnership—you'll be the thieves and I'll be the murderer." We started talking. I told them about Eretz Israel, about the youths. I said they didn't have a future here as Jews, since they were going to Polish school. I told them we were a Halutz movement, forming kibbutzim; and if they wanted, we would gladly take them. I gave them my address in Warsaw: Poznańska 39. Later, I found other Jewish youths and got in touch with the older fighters I found in Częstochowa. They could easily find me in Warsaw through the Central Committee of the Jews in Poland.

I returned to Warsaw. One day, a delegation of those young people showed up. They decided to form a kibbutz. That was a great joy for us. That group was the basis for the first kibbutz formed in that courtyard.[30]

A few words about my letter to the comrades in Romania from Kraków. Why and how was it written? Even though thirty years have passed, I keep trying to preserve the climate and experiences of those days—not to renew it but to tell what I thought and felt then. And I think I really am telling things as they happened. That's very important to me.

After re-reading the letter from Kraków (see below), it seems to me my thoughts also touched on things not directly connected to the letter but to experiences of the war, of that period. The letter was written in Yiddish so as not to offend our comrades who were then in Romania (who didn't know Hebrew). The letter was directed to our small core in Romania and was aimed against the idea of Abba Kovner's Brigade and against the

---

30. Here is a list of the comrades from Częstochowa who founded the kibbutz in Warsaw:
(1) Dorka Bram (Sternberg) (active in postwar Warsaw as a member of Dror; counselor in the Dror children's kibbutzim in Poland and in DP camps in Germany and Cyprus; member of Kibbutz Lohamei Ha-Getaot); (2) Ota Vargun (Grajek); (3) Zosia Zindman (Danieli); (4) Marysia Szajkowicz (Lefkowitz); (5) Mila Szajkowicz; (6) Hanka (Shapiro); (7) Andzia Kirshbaum; (8) Hanka Kirshbaum; (9) Netka Gold (active in postwar Warsaw; member of Dror and counselor in Dror children's kibbutzim in Poland and in DP camps in Germany and Cyprus; member of Kibbutz Ma'agan Michael); (10) Flusia Krakowska (Shapiro); (11) Dziunia (Weisenberg); (12) Menusia; (13) Jakobowicz; (14) Lilka Markowicz; (15) Jadzia Dankowska.

messianic and foggy words of many members of Ha-Shomer Ha-Tza'ir, which a few of our members also joined, those who were on the fringes of our Movement, including partisans; and was also against the talk of the "unity of all Jews," which I didn't believe in. I must say that, even today, I want to see national unity but, in any such unity, I want to see ourselves crystalized. It doesn't bother me at all to cooperate with all Jews, but with a conscious force, serious and firm in its opinion. That was my guiding idea then. It's hard for me to remember if the letter was sent before or after my trip to the borders; it is dated June 20, 1945, when my comrades were in Bucharest. Keep in mind that the war ended in May; so, it was close to the end of the war, that is, when Jews were beginning to come from the West, the camps, the concentration camps. That was also the time before the return of many Jews from the Soviet Union, but after Dr. Sommerstein had told me to expect them.

I must add that the messenger who took my letter also brought a letter from Guzik to the Joint in Romania, which opened the general Jewish connection, financially, between Poland and the United States, via the Joint office in Romania. My letter was addressed to our few comrades, including Zivia, who were then in Romania. I didn't have a clear address, and the letter shows I figured on the letter being forwarded to Eretz Israel, with which we didn't yet have contact. We thought that, first of all, we had to stand in the breach so the awareness and integrity of our little group in Romania wouldn't get blurred. In Poland, we didn't have such a problem—we were crystalized. The doubt concerned the people we sent to Romania. I don't think I'll be mistaken if I add that, at that time, our stream had already begun flowing westward, to Germany.

In the letter, I tried to emphasize to the best of my ability what was the central fighting force. That was in the city of Kraków. There was a crisis at the borders and I was called to come. I flew from Warsaw to Kraków, where I wrote that letter that was sent by special messenger.[31]

Here is the letter:

My dears,

Forgive me for two things this time, for writing at greater length today than ever before and for writing to you in Yiddish this time.

Today is my second day here in Kraków. I'm walking around in the streets of this ancient city and am reminded of many personal experiences from the days of the destruction and battles in my destroyed Vilna. Vilna speaks to me in her special tongue, even though I haven't seen her for awhile and probably never will see her again.

31. Zuckerman's letter was published in his earlier writings. We have decided to reprint it here because of the context and because the author considers it important and refers to it later.

And I accept this impression and write to you what comes into my pen.

How to begin? I've just come from Łódz, where we solemnly opened the first national council of the "Labor Faction of Eretz Israel." There were 163 delegates and more than 100 guests from ten cities in Poland—party members, He-Halutz and youth movements; delegates from our five kibbutzim that are already formed—in Warsaw, Łódz, Kraków, Sosnowiec, and the German city of Beuten [Polish:Bytom]; delegates from the partisan organization called "Partisans-Halutzim" from four cities—Lublin, Łódz, Chelm, and Beuten; and from the "Organization of Teachers" that has just now been formed in Łódz, and already numbers twenty teachers, who are also part of our group.

The opening of the kibbutz was also the opening of the council. We were welcomed by representatives of the Jewish Committee in Łódz, the representatives of the General Alliance of the Jewish Partisans, the Central Historical Committee, the Federation of Writers and Journalists, Po'alei Zion Left, Ikhud, representatives of the Polish youth of PPR and ZWP,[32] and representatives of the youth of PPS.

The day after the opening, an internal council was held. Sak opened with an expression of honor for our destroyed nation and the members of the Movement who were killed. He read a list of more than fifty commanders—of groups, of districts and of cities, as well as members of the high command of the Jewish Fighting Organization, members of our Movement who were killed in battle along with their groups.

I delivered the first lecture on "The Question of the Jews." [Israel] Sklar lectured on the "Questions of the Movement." Great differences of opinion weren't prominent in the discussions. The way of the Movement was accepted—the trend of internal unity in our Movement here and its functions in the unity of the Labor Movement in Eretz Israel. The question of *Aliya* was on every tongue. The word from Eretz Israel we were all awaiting never came.

I have no words to praise our group enough for the breadth of our operations, their great dedication despite our relatively small numbers, who, without isolating themselves from all that happened in the camps and bunkers, led the Movement and strengthened it and made it an important force among the survivors.

The central committee of the "group" was elected at the council and included Sheftel,[33] Sak, Streuweiss,[34] Manfeller, Grajek, Borochowicz, Sklar, Chaika Grossman, Tuvia Borzykowski, and me. A secretaryship of five members was also elected: Sak, Sklar, Michael, Tuvia, and I.

32. An umbrella organization that preceded the AK.

33. Arye Sheftel (1905–1980): Born in Vilna. Hebrew teacher, active in Po'alei Zion–Z.S. in Vilna, and member of FPO. He was sent to a labor camp in Estonia when the Vilna Ghetto was liquidated and survived the war. After the Liberation, he came to Poland and worked to restore the party. Immigrated to Israel, and was mayor of Rishon Le-Zion.

34. Haim-Leyb Streuweiss: Survivor of the Kraków Ghetto. Active in the Zionist Labor Movement. Worked with Holocaust survivors. Immigrated to Israel, where he died.

The partisan delegates expressed special difficulties in their report. They have positive and important fighting values, but an incipient demoralization of our current Jewish life in Poland is also evident in them. Incidents happen to them—"*tsum veynen un tsum lakhn* (you feel like laughing and crying at the same time)." For instance, a group of partisans riding a train threw a Polish gentile off a moving train because he insulted a Jew. They beat up a Polish *Ponucznik* (lieutenant), who didn't move aside for them in the street. A cloddish force and a hooliganism bursts from them. If our Movement can take them firmly in hand, they will bring us luck and blessings; if not, they are the first who are liable to turn into a terrorist gang in Eretz Israel and, even worse, God forbid, into criminals.

We are making efforts to bring them into a strong framework, but that isn't easily achieved. It's important to find people, on the way and further, who will bring them to the shore. Those fellows ("*di dozike yatn*") love Jews and are willing to die for them, but that doesn't prevent them from stopping a car with Jews and robbing them from head to foot. Of course, not all of them are like that. There are some good and serious fellows who have already found their way to us and these are the ones who are put in charge of the groups of partisans. They take orders from me. We also have to devote ourselves a bit to the Organization of Teachers.

I've expatiated on them because they can be important to us and because I love them very much.

Our kibbutzim now number 250 members. In two weeks, their number will double. This week, we're opening new groups in Będzin and Częstochowa; we're preparing to set up a kibbutz in the German city of Gleiwitz and in Katowice. We started negotiations to create two fishing groups on the seashore and that is progressing. If we had guides, we would set them up in Danzig and a few other German ports in Eastern Prussia. Right now, I don't have a map. Can you tell me what is the distance between our Polish shore and Sweden?

A large part of our people have been destroyed before our eyes. Why were so many millions destroyed? Because there were so many of us. And why were there so many of us? Because we are "*a paskudne folk*"[35]—"a contemptible people," who sleep when we should be working, work when we should be fighting, and with no sense of this small thing, which exists in the blood of every gentile—the sense of his own land.

But, nevertheless, what would have happened to Eretz Israel if, God forbid, the enemy had burst through the African front and conquered our land? I shudder! The foe would have destroyed every last Jew in Eretz Israel. He would have demolished and flattened our Tel Aviv and our Eyn Harod. In a word, wherever the enemy came, we would have been wiped out.

---

35. Allusion to a saying attributed to Chaim Weizmann: "*a kleyn folk ober a paskudne*"—"a little nation but a nasty one."

But the question is different: why were we annihilated *like that* and not otherwise? And right now, I'm not talking of the "heroic struggle of Polish Jewry" or of what we said on the radio about "our great part in the war, which gives us rights," and so on and so forth. Right now, I'm talking privately and with bleeding wounds in our heart, of a nation we belong to. Why, of 600,000 Jews in Warsaw Ghetto, did only 500 fight? But if the Germans had invaded our land in Eretz Israel, out of 600,000 Jews in Eretz Israel, 500,000 Jews wouldn't have fought and been killed in battle, but 150,000! Isn't that the truth?!

Indeed it is the truth that, in our conditions here (which are not enviable), the battle was difficult; yet, nevertheless, it was possible. Why could a revolt erupt in the Treblinka death camp when no more than a few hundred Jews were left alive—but was impossible when tens of thousands went to the crematoria there?! Here is the fundamental difference between our essential nature here and there. Moreover, there were rebellions nevertheless. After all, we fought and defended ourselves heroically. Small forces fought and performed miracles.

Who fought? Who carried on the battles? Of twenty-two battle groups in the Warsaw Ghetto, there was only one civilian group (of Zionist Youth) and the rest were groups of the Labor Movement; of these twenty-one groups of laborers and youth, 75 percent were ours! And who were the leaders? You know that.

In the January Uprising in the Warsaw Ghetto, only He-Halutz fought and no one else. Who defended our honor in Kraków? Our Movement and the splendid members of Akiba who were bound to us by thousands of threads during the war, to He-Halutz and to the Jewish group of the PPR—aside from them, no one! Who defended Częstochowa, Białystok? And who organized the battle organizations in the various camps? We can learn less from the revelations of the partisans' war, where chance mostly prevailed, whereas the fighters' organizations went to battle consciously, went deliberately to death for the sake of life.

In sum, if we ask: "Did our Movement stand up to the test of history?" It did! Was the education we received correct? It was! To know how to work in time of peace and to fight in time of war. And what are the conclusions? (1) There is still a little sap of life left in the nation; (2) laborers and youth are the ones who defended our honor; (3) 90 percent of the laborers and youth were killed with Eretz Israel under their head—the Eretz Israel of Eyn Harod and Mishmar Ha-Emek.[36]

In sum, did He-Halutz disappoint? Absolutely not! And the conclusion is that no other force has the power to exalt and raise the

---

36. Mishmar Ha-Emek: Kibbutz on the southwest rim of the Jezreel Valley, affiliated with Ha-Shomer Ha-Tza'ir. Eyn Harod is affiliated with Ha-Kibbutz Ha-Meuchad. Both were the symbols of their respective movements, hence both encompass the Halutz movement as a whole.

youth except He-Halutz. Instead of fading, we should reinforce its strength. The way of He-Halutz is the way of all Jewish youth. We want a working nation and a working youth; that is our lesson and our ambition.

As for Eretz Israel, we have educated ourselves to be laborers, that is our fate; and the building and creating part of the Yishuv are the Histadrut and the kibbutz. Is that demagoguery or truth? I think it is a great truth—and if the education of the Histadrut and the kibbutz gives wings to our members and leads them to battle, alone among all the Jews—that is truth!

Our fate here is to work and fight. Our fate is to be connected with the building and fighting part of the Yishuv in Eretz Israel, with the Histadrut. Only with the Histadrut! If this is decreed for us and must be, why not say it clearly: we want to bind our fate with the Halutz part of the Histadrut, with the kibbutz. Because we have learned plenty of lessons, because every one of us suffers the pain for millions of Jews, and now we want to work for the millions and for ourselves and for the children we shall have—why not give the maximum of ourselves where the maximum is demanded of everyone and where it is within reach?

From our work here, we Halutz, socialist movement of He-Halutz, have formed unified training groups and a unified group of activists, and we are creating the unified plans for our future. We're not yelling, but are speaking softly among ourselves and saying that we are united politically, and that the kibbutz movement in Eretz Israel should also unite. We are all very worried about the schism in Eretz Israel and want to see a United Halutz, socialist force, in all areas of life in Eretz Israel. That is our aspiration and our command to the Labor Movement in Eretz Israel. We would be more active and take more initiative. But we are far away and without personal contacts. And I must say, openly and honestly, we have been cut off from Eretz Israel for six years now and we don't know how to unite the kibbutzim.

We don't know the problems and we aren't familiar with the atmosphere of Eretz Israel. That's the job of the Shlikhim. They who knew us and our wounds up close will help us in this initiative. We have no impediment and we see it as our first obligation.———[37] I come to you with two proposals, and I don't know if you can carry them out:

1. Concerning the difficulties of youth education in our joint kibbutzim, where the issue is connecting youth with concrete ways of life, we educate them for the general concepts of kibbutz life, knowing and aware ourselves that we must present them not with an abstract concept but an example of a kibbutz united in Eretz Israel and that those will be their first subjects.

37. The hyphens here were in the text of the letter (which was copied on a typewriter) when it came from Romania to Eretz Israel. They might indicate a deletion done by those who received the letter in Romania.

Now we confront the question of preparing a new generation of teachers for the Movement, because there must be a continuation. We have decided to begin a seminar between July 5–10 in Łódz, attended by forty to sixty young comrades, which will go on for four to five weeks. The function of the seminar is not only to prepare a young group to take on the work but also to be the first generation to bear the banner of the unity of all Halutz organizations, both politically and in terms of the kibbutz. And without comrades from Eretz Israel, it won't be done. We want a Shaliah from Eretz Israel to come to us, at least during the seminar.

You yourselves understand the heavy responsibility we assume and, if it is done, it must be done well. We are waiting for the Shaliah.

2. The questions we touched on before also concern other countries besides Poland. The initiative to unify, first of all ourselves and then the Eretz-Israeli Labor Movement, should be in the hands of the Polish movement and the Romanian-Czech-Hungarian movement. I suggest a meeting in Kraków. The second transport might be used and, if it's impossible for all those parts to meet, let those come who can. We must once talk face to face and agree among ourselves.

We sum up for ourselves the situation of the Eretz-Israeli Labor Movement. All the Halutz movements of southeastern Europe, who stand on the base of the federation of workers and socialism, should not only talk, but should also act. And our speech must be clear both to us and to Eretz Israel. None of us is satisfied with the practical developments in Eretz Israel. And I've already written about that in my last letters.

Our contact with the Labor Movement in Eretz Israel cannot be doubted. If unity with nonsocialist groups, however, is presented, nothing will come of it. That's not just my personal opinion. Every turn to the right weakens the Halutz force and, for me, that is important and decisive. We cannot order Eretz Israel to do things; we know very little. But we are obligated—after things are clarified for us in all their breadth and depth—to present them to the Labor Movement and the kibbutz.

I am convinced that many elements in the Histadrut live on mistaken concepts about several issues. We must prepare a joint delegation from here which will include people from Poland as well as from central Asia. The latter are no less important. You know what I mean. And if, without knowing issues well, we're talking about the unification of the Labor Movement politically, and most important, the kibbutz movements (the first seems easier to me)—that is dictated to us by our intuition, everything we have gone through, and the lessons we derive from that. We are sure that is the order of the day. Especially when we prepare ourselves for state functions—the bearer must be fitting and strong. Who will do that, if the Labor Movement is not capable? After all, we face questions of mass immigration, of preparing the youth of the Diaspora for a Halutz life, for great settlement in Eretz Israel, for creativity. In another ten or fifteen years, another Hitler is liable to arise. March, march forward. The Labor Movement must be prepared!

——. Yitzhak

P.S.

While making a clean copy of this letter, I have taken out everything connected with Ikhud. They are carrying on a shocking propaganda against me here, but my back is not yet bent and my head is still erect toward the sky. Soon, they will accuse me of owning an orange grove in Eretz Israel and preparing myself for a career in Eretz Israel. If those wretched souls only knew what I was preparing myself for . . .

Now, remarks on Neustadt's letter and Moshe Kliger's comments:

I suggest that the publication of *Yizkor* wait until Zivia and I come to Eretz Israel.[38] Instead of publishing a distorted book, as Ber Mark did in Moscow, it's better to wait. And the material we sent isn't altogether precise either. I shall explain this some time.

I knew about the transports from Bergen-Belsen a year ago. I also knew that Dr. Natan Eck jumped [off the train] and is likely to be somewhere in Paris.

We went through the whole hell with Yitzhak Katznelson. I am very familiar with his life. We'll tell more details when the time comes. Find out where he is buried. I will arrange the required digging. We are now digging at Dzielna 34 and looking for our archive. Parts of Yitzhak's works are also there. I know all his words from the war. Here is an approximate bibliography: . . .[39]

Warm greetings to everyone in Eretz Israel. Most important—to the whole group from Poland: Abraham Gewelber, Mulka Barantshuk, Zvi Melnitzer, Perlis, etc., etc. Warm greetings to Yudke Helman. We have a few memories in common.

If there's something in my letter for Eretz Israel, extract it and send it to them. I shake hands with all of you.

Our situation in Poland, the killing of Jews, is a chapter in and of itself. About that, next time.

38. That is, the edition of *Yizkor* in *Destruction and Revolt of Warsaw Jewry*, prepared by Melekh Neustadt.

39. Here various details are presented of the literary works of Yitzhak Katznelson. The editors of the present volume decided to forego publishing here.

THIRTEEN

London Conference

Split in the Movement and Its Restoration

The representative of Ha-Shomer Ha-Tza'ir and I brought news of the United Halutz Movement to the Zionist conference in London, in August 1945. The people closest to me at the conference were Bar-Yehuda (Idelson) and Tsizling. By that time, we were working with Ha-Shomer Ha-Tza'ir, we formed joint kibbutzim, and brought that news to the conference. We didn't ignore the fact that such kibbutz unity didn't exist in Eretz Israel. When asked what would become of it, we replied whatever would be would be—we will bring the news; perhaps the unification of the kibbutz movement would come from that; if not—we would form our joint kibbutzim and see how things developed. The important thing was to bring the people to Eretz Israel. I thought then that the essential thing was to save the youth and that, only by joint forces, could we perhaps succeed in that mission.

Before the conference, I flew to Chaika Grossman in Białystok to persuade her to come to London with me. At that time, Ha-Shomer Ha-Tza'ir didn't have people in the central operations in Warsaw, and I thought she could join that delegation. Pesakh Burstein, the Bundist, who was assembling those who came out of the camps, still remembers my visit to Białystok in 1945. I convinced Chaika and she came to Warsaw, where we flew to London together. Afterward, she returned to Białystok for a long time and joined the work in the central operation later on. At the Ha-Shomer Ha-Tza'ir meetings in London, Meir Ya'ari and Yakov Hazan[1] told her explicitly that they didn't agree to any unification with

---

1. Yakov Hazan (b. 1899): Born in Poland. One of the founders and leaders of the youth movement, Ha-Shomer Ha-Tza'ir in Poland. Immigrated to Eretz Israel in 1923; one of the founders of Kibbutz Mishmar Ha-Emek. Ya'ari and Hazan were the leaders of the kibbutz

Dror. The split became a fact again and I felt that immediately in London. Until those internal meetings, we didn't have any Movement secrets. I would meet with Chaika Grossman and the two of us would coordinate our approach, what we would say. After she met with the leaders of Ha-Shomer Ha-Tza'ir in London, a wall went up. We left for London as one delegation and came back as separate delegations. On our return, we brought those things to the comrades for decision. It was Ha-Shomer Ha-Tza'ir that split. After London, the joint kibbutzim were disbanded.

When I spoke of unification there (in London and previously), I didn't mean the "unity of all Jews," in Abba Kovner's terms. I talked about the unity of the two Halutz movements, Dror and Ha-Shomer Ha-Tza'ir, and there's a difference. Kovner's idea was the unity of "all Jews," including the Revisionists and everybody else. We preserved our Halutz movement character, our education for certain values, the kibbutz. He talked of a brigade encompassing the Jewish people with all its trends—that's something altogether different. As for the Brigade that was formed in Romania in the spirit of Abba Kovner's ideas, Bauer should have talked to Zivia, who was there with them at that time, but he didn't. That wasn't done under the influence of the Shlikhim like Auerbach who was there during the liberation of Romania, or of the paratrooper Shlikhim, Dov Berger and Arye Fikhman who were in Romania after the Liberation and didn't interfere in the split. Their activity was only a positive and useful blessing. The split there (in the Brigade) took place because there hadn't been a common denominator. It was an artificial unification. Every bloc had intellectual and Movement baggage that it had also carried in the ghettoes. And you can't compose ideas for people artificially.

The split in the Brigade began from the inside. Mapai wanted to be built from such "Unities" and tried later to unite us by force. It caused splits with its compulsory unity (although it was a minority). For example, in Germany, where I went especially, motivated by the desire to unite, they split the partisans. There's a man in Israel who was their proxy in this, Dr. Atzmon, chief medical officer after 1948. He tried to split the partisans, since they would stoop to anything, including a threat to stop supplying UNRRA food packages to our comrades. Then I got instructions to come to Germany immediately because they were splitting the partisans and tormenting members of Dror.

Let's go back to the London conference (August 1945). That was the first Zionist conference after the war, and it was a kind of congress. In

---

movement of Ha-Shomer Ha-Tza'ir, Ha-Kibbutz Ha-Artzi, and of Mapam. Hazan was a representative to Zionist Congresses and a member of the Knesset from the beginning to the Eighth Knesset.

fact, it was a meeting between congresses. The Polish government immediately agreed to the trip; there weren't yet visas and they gave us a collective visa and an airplane to fly us from Warsaw to Paris. In Paris, a big delegation was waiting for us headed by the Polish authority (there wasn't yet a Polish ambassador in Paris), who came to the airport with his staff. They took us to a first-class hotel and we were invited to an official dinner. The next day, we flew to London in a French military plane. The only one who got a decent seat befitting a minister was Dr. Sommerstein (they put a chair in the plane), whereas we sat on metal benches along the walls. All the members of our delegation, including Dr. Sommerstein, threw up because we hit a storm over Germany and the plane was bounced around like a balloon in the wind. Only Yosef Sak was left next to me. I winked at him and he understood me. I took out a bottle and, while all of them were vomiting, we drank from the bottle and ate a sausage we had taken with us on the way; we went through the storm without any ill effect.

In London, we were welcomed and immediately taken to the conference. I then met for the first time the two representatives of Ha-Kibbutz Ha-Meuchad who were waiting for us since the Poles had told them of our expected arrival. We were greeted properly with warm words by Tsizling and Idelson (Bar-Yehuda), whose names I knew. Naturally, that was a very emotional meeting. They said that Tabenkin would never forgive himself for not coming. They had indeed demanded he come to this conference, but he refused, saying that the authorities probably wouldn't let the comrades from Poland come.

I agreed to spend the night with Tsizling and Idelson in a hotel, and they reserved rooms. As I was standing and talking with them, Ben-Gurion came up and invited me to be his guest. I didn't know what to reply and they said that they would yield, and I was Ben-Gurion's guest in a private apartment, where he and his wife Paula were staying. I don't intend to give a detailed report on my meeting with Ben-Gurion because there are some things that aren't complimentary to Ben-Gurion. But I must say that both Ben-Gurion and Paula were charming hosts. At the time, I had a problem with my leg because the wound had opened again. It hadn't troubled me for a long time, but late in 1945 (perhaps because of my exertions in Brikha), I was limping. Ben-Gurion didn't let me sit up after dinner and insisted that I lie down on a bed; he sat next to me and I talked with him. That went on all night.

Zivia didn't come to London with me; and I got there first. I told him about life in Poland and then about the Movement. I don't remember that he asked many questions about the Uprising. But he was very interested in current events. Among other things, I told him I had a dream I thought could be realized of training fishermen in Gdansk. I said I had gotten permission from Polish institutions and authorization from the Joint to buy fishing boats. They gave us a chance to scout with experts and choose a proper place for a training kibbutz; I thought that was necessary and important.

Ben-Gurion was very optimistic about it. At first, he was excited about naval training and was willing to authorize whatever I said, even if it concerned large expenditures of money; the same goes for Brikha. Everything was fine, until one day he learned that I spent "too much" time with Tsizling and Bar-Yehuda. Then his attitude suddenly changed: these things ceased to be important. The money wasn't given. This really depressed me—no naval training, no boats, no other plans, nothing. All castles in the air! These were things that could be carried out, and after all, I had gotten his "yes" at our first meeting. But the truth is he was extremely suspicious. As for me, I knew exactly where to go, to whom I belonged; but I didn't tell anyone, because I wanted to preserve the integrity of the Movement; that was before I found out about the split Chaika was bringing with her. Thirty years have passed since then. I hope they'll believe me that, as far as I was concerned, there was nothing sneaky, dishonest, or indecent in this matter. My idea was that our young students would come to Eretz Israel and decide on their path. It was enough for me to educate them for good deeds, the kibbutz, the Histadrut, a life of labor—that was my position.

Later, I learned that my comrades, Tsizling and Bar-Yehuda, differed with my position but respected my ideas. Ben-Gurion didn't say anything about that. Maybe he was dissatisfied that we were united only with Ha-Shomer Ha-Tza'ir. Anyway, a few days later, he ceased all contact with me and didn't meet with me anymore.

Israel Idelson (Bar-Yehuda) impressed me very much; he was a real phenomenon. The same goes for Tsizling. And they showed such friendship, such concern. In London, I lived somewhere else, which was better than their accomodations; the two of them lived in one room. One day, I recall, I came early and they were still in bed. The thin Idelson and the big hearty Tsizling. They were in their underwear, no pajamas. I laughed at the sight and they asked why. I told them they reminded me of a story by Gorky. I also told them what I had told Ben-Gurion about the new unified movement. They said that that was a fatal blow to Ha-Kibbutz Ha-Meuchad, since the Movement in the Diaspora was its last reserve. But they understood and didn't do anything against it. They would send their opinion to Eretz Israel and request the Shlikhim to respect our wish and not damage this issue of indefinition.

As for the so-called legend that Ben-Gurion compared me to Joseph Trumpeldor, what he really said was that I could have played a role like Trumpeldor's in his generation if I weren't friendly with "factionalists like

Bar-Yehuda and Tsizling." I'm amazed at only one thing: how did it leak out? Because I didn't tell anyone about it!

More precisely, Ben-Gurion greeted me nicely in London and spoke of my role in the history of the Diaspora, as a symbol of the Uprising. And, in the process, he said: "You're Trumpeldor." When Eliahu Dobkin came to Germany, he repeated Ben-Gurion's words in one of his speeches: "This is the man who could have been Trumpeldor . . . And he turned into a factionalist." That is, he robbed me of the "crown" and turned me into a factionalist.

I met with Tsizling and Idelson a lot in London. They told about the situation in Eretz Israel and Ha-Kibbutz Ha-Meuchad, and I repeat: I admired them. They didn't just accept me, but were very friendly. And they respected and appreciated what we had done.

After London, there was no longer a general framework. The members of Ha-Shomer Ha-Tza'ir once said that the generals were from Dror, but the local leaders were Ha-Shomer Ha-Tza'ir. And after all, it was their duty to transfer their ideological baggage to the students. And when the schism came, most of the people went with them. A few months passed until, by means of continual and successive seminars, we trained a loyal group of guides and succeeded in growing. Objectively, we had advantages over the others because of our good connections with the authorities and what could be achieved with them. It wasn't only a question of convenience, since we obtained everything we needed overnight. It was a bit harder for the others and they quickly learned that.

I shall tell another episode illustrating Ben-Gurion's suspicion in London. Limping on my leg, I walked with a disreputable-looking cane I had found in Poland. On the evening I was at Ben-Gurion's, he gave me a nicer cane than mine; but in the morning, when I left them, I forgot to take it; they had entertained me very amiably and warmly. But I forgot and took my old stick. On one of the days of the conference, Ben-Gurion came to me at the break and said: "You despise me that much; you're with Tsizling and Idelson all the time, and you didn't even take the cane I gave you!"

I was stunned and didn't know what to answer. Later, as I said, all his promises to finance our establishment of a base on the Baltic Sea turned out to be false. Incidentally, that plan of a naval base was printed in the journal, *Sea*, published by Shmuel Tolkowsky on behalf of the Sea Section. What I wrote on the subject was published on the first page; I saw those things in 1945.[2]

2. Shmuel Tolkowsky (1886–1965): Agronomist and Israeli diplomat. Active in various economic and social areas in Tel Aviv.

I had a few other ideas, but I requested money only for that. Ben-Gurion accepted the idea immediately, but because of Idelson and Tsizling, and "because of the cane," he changed his mind. I can say that I got the "cane on my head" from him, but I didn't get any money. That pervasive hatred of my leader depressed me.

Both Chaika and I appeared at the London conference. Quite a few attended that conference, but the hall wasn't full since it was right after the war and communications weren't very stable; and the delegation from Eretz Israel wasn't very big. Shertok (Moshe Sharett) stood up to respond to me.[3] I said bitter things at the conference and, even then, I hadn't yet said everything I felt because I knew there were attentive listeners and curious journalists and I didn't want to appear as someone handing down the judgment of history. I said: "I don't have complaints against Eretz Israel or our Movement during the war. I imagine they did all they could. But what we will not forgive you for is that right after the war, no one came to us to hold out a brotherly hand. We looked for you everywhere, we went to the Brigade, and we also came here."

I spoke in Hebrew. After I said that, Sharett stood up and said: "How was it possible to get into Poland?" In my opinion, that was a provocative question. Since there were people in the hall whose job was to listen to what was said. Could I answer him that getting out of Poland was also illegal? I told him: "Isn't it as possible to get in as to get out?" After all, thousands of Jews had already gotten in and out. It was then I knew there was a chasm between us—a broad chasm. After 1945, I always had a standard to compare and assess every difficulty: the years of war under German occupation. For, with the Germans, the answer to everything was death. Now, if Jews entered illegally, so what? What could happen to them now? Three days in jail, beatings. What else could there be?! And the Jews were leaving there by the thousands. But no one had yet come in from Eretz Israel. These things were very painful.

In London, in 1945, I became friendly with the Yiddish poet Itzik Manger and tried to persuade him to come to Poland.[4] I asked why he went on living in London. I said: "Jews are in Poland, and there's also as much vodka as you want. If you don't like it—come back." He didn't agree.

On the way back from London, something curious happened. I tell it to illustrate the difference in attitudes to danger. We crossed the English

3. Moshe Sharett (1894–1965): Israeli statesman and Zionist leader. First Foreign Minister of the State of Israel; succeeded Ben-Gurion as Prime Minister from January 1954 to November 1955.

4. Itzik Manger (1901–1969): Yiddish poet, dramatist, and novelist.

Channel, first in a boat and then in a train to Paris. I had some money
I had gotten, a few thousand pounds sterling, a rather large sum, but not
enough to solve all our problems. The treasurer, I think it was Ze'ev
Shind, gave the money on instructions from Ben-Gurion.[5] My arguments
about the size of the sum didn't help, all the treasurers said that those were
Ben-Gurion's instructions. He didn't even authorize me a tenth of what
I asked for. That was money for the whole Zionist movement in Poland.

On the train, we sat in the same compartment as Shlikhim from Eretz
Israel, including Yosef Shprinzak. As we approached the border, there
were searches because it was forbidden to take out currency, and some
other things were also prohibited. As we approached, I took off my shoes,
divided the bundle of money in two and put one in each of my shoes.
Shprinzak saw me do that and was terrified. He said he didn't want to sit
with me, and he left. We got to the border. The English asked all sorts
of questions. I asked one of my comrades to be my spokesman. They
asked me if I had anything and I answered that I didn't. I opened my
bundles for them. Shprinzak had five pounds sterling and they took it
away from him. We went out and crossed to the train going to Paris—
Shprinzak appeared. I invited him to sit down, but he disappeared. Later,
on the train to Paris, he came back to my compartment. I told him we were
going to eat in the dining car. He said he would go with us, but they had
taken his money. I invited him to eat on me.

When I came to Paris, I got a little money "on the side" there, too. That
was from Ruth Kluger, who helped me in those "dirty" deals.[6] I packed
the money nicely, like a box of candy. I came to the airport in Warsaw
with suitcases; I brought a lot of gifts with me. I didn't have money for
that—but Tsizling and Idelson took care of Zivia and also bought all kinds
of little presents for the comrades. And they might have got things from
somebody to be transported. At any rate, I was carrying a lot of things.
The porter appeared and took the packages from me, and the people
standing next to the airplane saluted me. So I walked along holding the
"candy box." My idea was that, even if they caught me, what would they
do to me? I'd be in jail for three months, no more. That is, my standard
was in comparison with what would have happened if we had been

5. Ze'ev Shind (1909–1953): A member of Kibbutz Ayelet Ha-Shahar; active in Hagana
and illegal immigration activities. Member of the Rescue Committee in Istanbul during the
war. After the war, was a member of the interorganizational Jewish Coordinating Committee for Rescue and on the War Refugee Board established by President Franklin D.
Roosevelt in January 1944.

6. Ruth Kluger (Aliav; 1914–1980): The only female member of Aliya Bet, the organization that smuggled Jews illegally into Eretz Israel. From 1942 to 1945, she worked with
the French and Dutch Resistance movements. Her book, *The Last Escape*, details her experiences from 1939 to 1941.

dealing with the Germans. And in fact, maybe I shouldn't complain about the comrades because they thought in completely different categories— but as I recall, in this period, everything could be done and you didn't expect a death sentence as under the Germans.

What I said to Moshe Shertok made a bitter impression at the time. Later, I had personal conversations with many people separately, with Shertok, Ignacy Schwartzbart,[7] and many others who were there. Weizmann invited me to lunch at a fabulous hotel.[8] I didn't know how to act since I wasn't used to such things. When I returned to Paris, the Jewish Agency gave me a room in a splendid hotel, near the Opéra, with a reception room and an enormous bedroom; the bathroom there was bigger than my whole apartment here in Kibbutz Lohamei Ha-Getaot. But I lay in the bed and couldn't fall asleep; it was so soft and comfortable, and I wasn't used to that, and I tossed and turned. I was a young man and I could usually sleep even standing up; but there, I couldn't fall asleep. So I got out of bed, locked the door, and lay down on the carpet. Then I fell asleep and slept all night.

In London, Chaika wouldn't talk to me about Movement issues. But I did meet with Yakov Hazan and Ya'ari, who said they were against that unity. Meanwhile, Chaika stopped meeting with me; by that time, I knew what had happened and was just waiting to hear it from her.

When we got back, I went to our comrades and said that news of the split was likely to come any minute. And, indeed, right after that, they held a separate meeting (up to then, we used to meet together). Before that, I had had been close to Israel Sklar and had told him things he needed to know; I did that out of movement camaraderie. He was one of the "Asians," a very good fellow, a member of Kibbutz Nir David, who was later killed in an automobile accident.[9] Chaika brought the verdict on the united movement to Poland. In hindsight, they did Ha-Kibbutz Ha-Meuchad a favor since, if they hadn't opted out, most of the members of the united movement would have gone to Ha-Shomer Ha-Tza'ir kibbutzim in Eretz Israel. I say that without accusing them of "evil intentions."

7. Isaac (Ignacy) Schwartzbart (1888–1961): Born in Chrzyzanów, Galicia. Completed his study of law at University of Kraków. A Zionist leader in Poland; one of the main founders of the General Zionists in 1931. In 1938, he was elected to the Polish *Sejm*. At the outbreak of the war, he fled to Romania and helped Jews escape. From 1941 to 1945, he was a member of the Polish Government-in-Exile in London and Paris. In 1946, he moved to the United States.

8. Chaim Weizmann (1874–1952): Chemist, statesman, and Zionist leader. Guiding spirit and leader of the World Zionist Organization; statesman instrumental in gaining acceptance among world leaders for statehood for Israel. First President of the State of Israel (1949–1952).

9. Nir David: A kibbutz at the foot of Mt. Gilboa in central Israel, affiliated with Ha-Shomer Ha-Tza'ir, founded in 1936.

A person is only a person and, naturally, follows those who took care of him personally, and that was decisive among youngsters. Their people would meet with the youth more than we did. Our activity focused more on the general level. And neither we nor Tuvia tended very much to any particular training kibbutz.

Tsizling and Idelson didn't know about the change that had taken place. But they did know that Ha-Kibbutz Ha-Artzi was against this unity. However, the conversations with Tsizling and Idelson were held before I met with Ya'ari and Hazan, whom I met with only in the last days of the London conference. They did go to Paris with me, but I was careful not to talk about that. The mood when I returned wasn't good; the feeling was unpleasant. My estimate was that we would suffer a great loss from the schism and, to our great surprise, within three months, the situation had totally changed.

Initially, the two movements held only joint seminars; and there weren't any separate activities since we were cut off from everything during the war and didn't know what was going on in Eretz Israel. And what we did know was only from the German press, which didn't choose to tell about happy events. Sometimes we would read the *Völkischer Beobachter*, sometimes other papers. I would read the *Deutsche Allgemeine*, which sometimes printed items about the Near East.

When I returned from London, an extremely serious seminar was held which included two men who knew about political life and the kibbutz in Eretz Israel and gave us a political forecast. This was the first time we heard things in such a context. One of them was Isser Ben-Zvi, whom I knew well enough to know I couldn't rely on him intellectually.[10] By the time I returned from London, I knew about the position of Ha-Shomer Ha-Tza'ir. That is, from the discussion with Ya'ari and Hazan, and from Chaika's behavior on the way back, I was sure those were the directives. But I didn't want to say anything, nor did I want to pressure her to tell me. But I knew she was bringing some kind of news. And, indeed, as soon as they returned, they assembled their members and informed them of the schism. We had no choice. We did try to persuade them, but even those who were most loyal to the idea of unity no longer hesitated even a minute. I don't think our people would have been convinced so easily if we had gotten such directives. But we never did get directives; apparently we were made of different stuff. Afterward, I saw how they fell in

10. Isser Ben-Zvi: Leader of Gordonia in Poland and Israel and He-Halutz activist in Lithuania. Immigrated to Eretz Israel in 1934 and was a member of Kibbutz Degania B. Served as Hagana Shaliah in Poland from 1945 to 1947 and led Brikha from there. Was head of the Youth Department in the Ministry of Defense after the rise of the State of Israel.

line ideologically. People who couldn't utter the name of the Soviet Union suddenly knew the Soviet Union better than I. They fell into line so the gentiles would know they were a "revolutionary movement," "more leftist."

These conflicts of opinion don't reflect life at that time or the difficulties we faced. Israel Idelson (Bar-Yehuda) and Aharon Tsizling are to be credited with telling me that that unity wouldn't strengthen Ha-Kibbutz Ha-Meuchad, but under no circumstances would they let anyone harm the unity we had made. They spoke in the name of Ha-Kibbutz Ha-Meuchad and said its Shlikhim would treat the unified Halutz movement as their own. That is not what happened in Ha-Shomer Ha-Tza'ir.

We didn't have any counseling forces. In Ha-Shomer Ha-Tza'ir, they would say that Dror has "generals," but the "corporals" are in Ha-Shomer Ha-Tza'ir. In every new kibbutz, the first counselor was a member of Ha-Shomer Ha-Tza'ir. As long as the Movement was united, it never occurred to me even once to examine what "defined" them. I must say there was a loyal cooperation between us. But when we came back from London, we suddenly realized we didn't have any "corporals." Then, we divided the "peckl" between us—as Zivia wrote to Eretz Israel, the "*orem peckl*" (the "poor sack of belongings").

The schism was done simply by dividing the Movement, first by personal affinities, which was also how bases were divided. Some knew whom they belonged to and defined themselves immediately; that was so with the old-timers. In that situation, we said that we, at least, would try to do it decently. And if there was to be a division of the "joint bundle," it should be according to the propensities of the people, the counselors and the students. There was a group of counselors from the joint seminars who went with us; and that was quite decisive. Almost all the counselors of the kibbutzim were members of Ha-Shomer Ha-Tza'ir. In the joint seminars, we could meet with the whole Movement; but not all the students came to the seminars, and some of them remained outside our sphere of influence. So there was a division according to influence—let's say, according to personal influence. The first thing we did after the schism was our central seminar and an assault on the kibbutzim. We showed up in full force. I don't know what charmed the members. But suddenly it was clear we were the dominant force. In two months, we were "back on our feet." You can say for sure that within half a year, Ha-Shomer Ha-Tza'ir realized that although they were an important force, we were the major force. Naturally, there were arguments between the movements about the estimated weight of each side. Then they started counting members, and each side would lie to the other. By then, there were Shlikhim from Eretz Israel in Poland.

One day they came to me and said they trusted my honesty and asked me to judge the numerical ratio. I examined the lists and saw that the numbers were much inflated, and I proposed at the start that each one reduce the number by one zero, that is, by one-tenth. But that didn't help. Every three months, we would send a joint council to count the members and, on the basis of that count, we would distribute the money we got. As I said, we were the dominant force. To this day, they can't forgive us for that. I see it in the literature of the period. They demanded more than us, but they never presented a basis for such an estimate. It was possible to count—and they did. This wasn't tens of thousands of people. Even during the war, they wanted to change the criteria. On what basis did they want to change now? We told them: fine, let's do it according to the members of the kibbutzim. There was a simple way to count the members in the kibbutzim: a joint committee would go through and count. At first they were very happy with the schism; but later, their enthusiasm waned when they realized that, materially, there was nothing we couldn't get. We could accomplish much more than they could in the area of apartments, bases, farms; we showed initiative and overcame difficulties. But we had to hurry and raise a generation of counselors, although a respectable share of the young people joined us.

One day Shaike Weiner, their emissary, came to us to negotiate a bigger share for them. I told him they were the ones who cut themselves off, not us. None of them could blame us; they made the schism because they wanted to—so they had to bear the consequences. I was correct with them, but that left a bad taste. To this day, I am on good terms with Shaike Weiner, their first Shaliah.

It was a bitter pill for us that our comrades of Ha-Shomer Ha-Tza'ir were so easily convinced by Ya'ari and Hazan and fell into line so fast. I think most of them, except maybe Chaika, had been definite enemies of the Soviet Union before they met with Ya'ari and Hazan, whereas I was then rejected by their comrades because of my sympathy for the land of the Soviets. I think if I had really been so sympathetic toward the Soviet Union, I would have formed a more leftist movement than Dror. But they fell into line. And it was strange—that adherence to the Movement, their factionalism. One person who didn't really fall into line and was rejected for it was Shalom Cholawski. I was glad he came to us, because I had known him back in Vilna. He studied in the teachers' college when I was a student in the Hebrew gymnasium. Afterward, we worked together. I was the secretary of He-Halutz in Vilna and he was a member of Ha-Shomer Ha-Tza'ir there. He told me his comrades didn't accept him.

So, within a month, they went from being in a joint movement with us to turning us into a "revolutionary movement," and Cholawski, with his opinions about the Soviet Union, was rejected by his comrades. When he came to me, I accepted him gladly and proposed that he be the commander of Partisans, Soldiers, and Halutzim, and he got into that. Even after the partisans assembled and the exodus from Poland began, each one of them was still isolated. We thought they should be united and turned into a force.

One day, one of the partisans came to me and introduced himself as Barukh Levin; I've told about him already. I could sit with him for days on end listening to his stories of the forests. The same goes for Yosef Kaplan (not to be confused with the member of the leadership of Ha-Shomer Ha-Tza'ir), whose son was later killed in the Yom Kippur War. Barukh Levin came from Zalodek (Vilna district), and was later in the Lida Ghetto,[11] but previously, in Lida, he kept calling on the Jews to rise up and defend themselves. He told us about his arguments with the members of the Lida Judenrat who argued that those who worked would survive. He didn't believe that and waited for the moment he would have weapons. When he did, he was careful to keep his weapons clean. He was a Jewish partisan, the only one in a unit of gentiles, in eastern Poland. He was a fighting man; he worked as a saboteur with the partisans. He learned the craft and later taught it to others. He would lead Russian paratroopers on operations. He became a legend among both Jews and non-Jews. Everyone should read his book.[12]

When I met him, I sold him on the idea of setting up PHH. He didn't want to stay in Poland for long and left. He remained loyal even during the attacks on me in Romania and didn't let them hurt me. To this day, we're great friends and maintain a mutual understanding.

Yosef Kaplan also came to me in those days; he said he was a member of Betar and I told him I didn't care about that and he still likes me for that to this day. I told him: "To me, you're a partisan!" But he didn't want to stay in Poland either. Others were looking for their relatives or the houses they had left. At any rate, a force of thousands took shape. And in those thousands, there wasn't a single person from either Ha-Shomer Ha-Tza'ir or Dror, except Shalom Cholawski. No one had taken care of them previously. They were organized into groups of ten and, on the basis of that arrangement, I would transmit instructions to them. Within twenty-four hours after receiving an order, they were to move; it was a very well-organized force. But it couldn't be used for defense since, when the gates were opened, our consideration was that, first of all, we had to get out.

They had some rights as partisans, but the Poles didn't yet grant them in those days. If they had stayed, they would probably have gotten those

---

11. Lida is a small town near Vilna.
12. Barukh Levin, *In the Forests of Revenge* (Hebrew), 1968.

rights as well as the medals they deserved. They assembled as partisans. They had an attachment to the general Histadrut in Eretz Israel which was expressed in their "oath"; but they didn't have contact with any party movement. In fact, some of them tried living on a kibbutz although PHH didn't steer or force them to do that. Barukh Levin also came to Yagur and was there during the time of the "Black Saturday,"[13] which is a story in itself: there he got his "eighty-first blow."

Partisans, Soldiers, and Halutzim included some very fine people, fearless fighters as well as others who later exploited it and received countless decorations and medals. Barukh Levin broke away from his Communism in Russia, during the war, in Minsk, I think, when medals were handed out; he was one of the candidates to be a Hero of the Soviet Union (I saw the relevant document). But he sent his documents and distinctions back to Moscow, as did other comrades. I then told everyone I could: "Don't do that because they'll throw them in the trash can and we may need them someday. You should keep these awards; it doesn't do any good to send them back." They say Barukh Levin blew up seventy German trains; because of his many merits, they treated him with great respect, and he was famous as a Communist and as a fighting man. Even in Byelorussian Minsk, he insisted on his desire to leave the Soviet Union and his right to go to Eretz Israel.

The partisans weren't only fighters; they also included educated people, members of movements, and they built PHH in Poland and Germany. There were also some rowdies among them. There was one partisan I despised. Another partisan in Lublin told me of an incident when Russian partisans captured a German and sentenced him to be executed; and that partisan I hated bribed the commander to let him hang the German with his own hands. His yearning to be a hangman revolted me. If he were just carrying out an order, fine; but to ask to be a hangman! I didn't want to see him. There were people like that. And there were others who were in the forests, in "family camps." Like Tuvia Bielski,[14] Moshe Beyrakh, or Borya Yudkowski who came later.[15] Barukh Levin was angry at Bielski and didn't forgive him for collecting Jewish non-

13. Black Saturday: On June 29, 1946, the most extensive British operation against the Yishuv took place, culminating in the arrest of the leaders of the Jewish Agency, and including thorough and violent searches in the course of which a Hagana weapons cache was discovered in Kibbutz Yagur.

14. Tuvia Bielski: Leader of Jewish partisans in Byelorussia, along with his two brothers, Zusia and Ashoel. Was commander of the Kalinin group of Jewish partisans in Naliboki Forests. He protected a large camp of Jewish families. Immigrated to Israel.

15. Borya Yudkowsky: Member of He-Halutz. Fled from his hometown near Slonim to the forests of Ivatzevitz in 1941 and led a partisan unit. Immigrated to Israel and was a member of Kibbutz Lohamei Ha-Getaot.

combatants, to save them. There were arguments about that, and I don't know if Levin has changed his mind in the meantime. As far as I'm concerned, Bielski was a man who did a lot for hundreds of Jews. I should add that they later formed a fighting group led by one of the Bielski brothers. Tuvia Bielski was a brave man; and don't think it was easy for a person to save Jews in the forest. Instead of appearing in his full stature as a fighter, he saved Jews. Everyone had rejected them; they included old people, women, children. I understood what he did and approved of him; I even looked for Bielski in those days. But at that time, there wasn't unanimous agreement on that. The family camps weren't accepted by agreement of all the partisans, but some partisans did help them. Barukh Levin couldn't accept or forgive that line.

My encounter with Tuvia Bielski in Israel was strange and surprising. One day I went from Haifa to Tel Aviv in a jitney cab. We passed the Netanya junction. The driver was sad and I sat next to him reading a newspaper the whole time. All of a sudden, I heard him humming a partisan song. I ask him: "Were you a partisan?" He says: "Yes, sir." "Where were you?" He answered something. "What's your name?" He answers: "Tuvia Bielski." I said to him: "I'm Yitzhak Zuckerman." He slammed on the brakes so hard all the passengers were jolted. We got out of the car and hugged. After a time in Israel where he worked hard, he left for the United States, where he still works hard. He didn't become a millionaire there. On a trip to Israel, several years ago, he visited me. I think he would have managed just as well in Israel as abroad, where he works as a truck driver. More agile men made a fortune, but not him. As far as I'm concerned, Bielski is a marvelous figure, even though there are all kinds of accusations against him—that he supposedly behaved either like a king or like a charlatan. There were moral charges about women. I can't judge because I wasn't there. Some people claim he killed a Jew, apparently for disobeying an order not to take loot. That was after they came out of the forest. There were still a lot of Germans in the forest then, wandering around in groups. And you had to be alert. The story has all sorts of variants. Others say that the Jew he killed had a lot to tell about Bielski and Bielski was scared of him. I don't know. True, he also killed Jews. Anyway, Tuvia Bielski is a marvelous character, he and his brothers, Zusia and Ashoel—three brothers who enhanced the honor of the Jews and saved Jews from destruction.

I have met many characters on my way. I could sit for days on end, listening to their tales. Some of them were liars. I immediately identified the ones who told the truth, people like Yosef Kaplan, Barukh Levin. And then there were those who made up lies, like Yosef Miller, who claimed to be a partisan commander, even though no one knew him or knew anything about him.

The transports of Jews which began arriving from the Soviet Union weren't directed either by the government of Poland or the Central Jewish Committee. True, there was a plan, but the Jews themselves in the trains were the directors, and it was they who bribed whomever had to be bribed to get to their destination. The government of Poland decided that these Jews should go straight to Gdansk, since there was a plan to concentrate Jews in Silesia, and the authorities would direct the trains there. But the Jews from the Soviet Union knew very well where they should go. We then had bases everywhere and, as soon as a train came, the whole city knew about it. There were also curiosities. One day, in Kraków, I met a member of the Warsaw branch of He-Halutz Ha-Tza'ir. (To this day, he works in Israel as a locomotive engineer and I sometimes meet him when I ride the train.) And I found out that he was in the Ikhud kibbutz. I said to him: "How come you're on an Ikhud kibbutz? There's a Dror kibbutz[16] here." He said: "I'll tell you the truth: when I came to the railroad station, I met young people in a cart and young people in a taxi, and I decided to ride in the taxi. It turned out they were from Ikhud and the ones in the cart were from Dror." That was how they grabbed people. The fellow, a member of our Movement, forgot his movement attachment and joined anyone.

Our people would stand at the railroad station and, when they saw young people coming, would take them along. That was very important for the young people who arrived, since they immediately had a house, a bed, and food. We would direct the older people to the refugee bases. PHH was a general movement, that is, attached to the Histadrut. There wasn't a partisan who didn't belong to PHH, first, because everyone was seeking warmth and wanted not to be alone, wanted to join a bloc group—and that was a movement. In Łódz, we found apartments, organized groups, clubs. You could come in, get warm, have a drink. They got used to counselors inserting a bit of movement spirit.

The members of PHH weren't poverty stricken. Many of them brought property and started dealing. Some of them lost their bearings, and some even went to Germany to trade. One day, one of those partisans (not the most pleasant) returned, and I asked him where he had been. He said his whole group had crossed the border on the way to Eretz Israel. He came late because he had been in Germany. As for what he was doing there, these were his words: "*Ikh hob a bisl farkoyft un a bisl batsolt, men hot mitgenumen farshidene trantes.* (I sold a little, paid a little. We took all kinds of junk with us.)" You could sell anything in Germany, there were shortages of everything. And he added: "*Un batsolt far shikses mit vemen ikh hob geshlofn.* (And I paid for gentile girls I slept with.)"

16. The one Havka Folman was then directing.

Leviteh,[17] who was then in Poland, said to him: "*Nit fayn. Nishto idishe meydlakh?* (Not nice. Aren't there any Jewish girls?)" And he answered: "*Vos iz mit aykh? Umgliklekh makhn idishe meydlekh?* (What's with you? How can you make Jewish girls unhappy?)" There were people like that, too.

The Joint started working right after Zivia went to Romania. Guzik was one of the last to be liberated. He was hiding in a bunker in Warsaw and had no idea that Warsaw was liberated. It was a few days before they found out. He was one of the few who was saved. He soon made his way to me and we began working together. It was no longer the same Guzik, the member of the Joint from the ghetto; and Yitzhak Zuckerman wasn't the same either, not the Yitzhak Zuckerman who would stand and wait in Guzik's corridor. These were two men who had once worked together in the underground. He was in my group receiving welfare on the Aryan side. Even though he charged me and Berman with depriving him, as it were, we remained friends.

He asked if I could help him transfer Joint money from abroad. He had sent a telegram, but he wasn't sure it had reached the Joint in New York, because he hadn't gotten an answer. I asked him where he wanted money transferred from, and he replied that he knew the Joint was operating in Romania; I said that if it was Romania, it could be done. I sent a special envoy with a letter from Guzik sewed into the lining of his coat. (He was sent from Kraków, as I said.) Even if he were captured at the border, he didn't expect a severe punishment—the Poles would probably put him in jail for a few weeks. But the envoy did get across and, on the basis of Guzik's letter (he probably used the code agreed upon between them during the war), he brought a considerable sum. The money was brought to me and I gave it all to Guzik and told him: "Count it and I want you to treat me as a partner." And he really did; and so did Schwartz who succeeded him. The two of them were very generous to He-Halutz and the Movement we represented.

Aside from that, we did financial transport operations. Some Jews returned home from Russia, sold their houses to Poles, and didn't know how to get their money out. Moreover, the Polish Złoty wasn't worth anything. But, for us, that money was important. We gave receipts and used the money we got for our needs. Eretz Israel was still silent. Neither money nor people had come from there yet. The argument that the war

17. Leyb (Lyova) Leviteh (1904–1976): Born in Minsk. Arrested as a Zionist in the Soviet Union and sentenced to exile in Siberia. Immigrated to Eretz Israel in 1924. Member of Kibbutz Eyn Harod and one of the leaders of Ha-Kibbutz Ha-Meuchad. Leader of the He-Halutz Shlikhim to Poland, 1934–1935 and 1939. In 1946, he was head of the delegation of the National Committee to Poland and Germany. Participated in illegal immigration activities. Served as political secretary of Mapai.

wasn't over was hollow because they didn't have to come from the West. They could have come from Romania, where the war already was over. It was only on German soil that the war continued until May 1945.

The members of the Brigade didn't come to us either. We sought and found the Brigade, when it moved, on its way to Italy. We found it when we met with Moshe Averbukh, a member of Kfar Giladi, who was a Shaliah from Eretz Israel. They could have sent money through him. Zivia did indeed transfer something when she was in Romania, but that wasn't what we needed. In the existing situation, there were German cities with no inhabitants, like Bytom in Silesia. But in other places, we had to look for apartments to house people. We formed branches in Kraków and Łódz. Many Germans had once lived in Łódz, but they escaped or were thrown out. Empty apartments were left and we could get along there. It was harder in Warsaw, but we managed, thanks to an apartment I got. In other places, we had to take care of the most elementary things like housing, beds, and so forth. Eretz Israel didn't seem to exist.

One of the greatest achievements of our Movement, and not just Dror, was that we soon consolidated, formed a movement, assembled thousands of young people and partisans, as well as older people and families in the labor framework. I don't know why Eretz Israel ignored us for so long. The Polish government would only help the Jewish Central Committee and we were helped by the Committee, but it didn't have enough money. The Joint did allot money to it, but there was always a controversy about that between the Joint and the Committee of the Jews in Poland. I remember only one big sum the Committee of Jews in Poland gave me to excavate on Dzielna Street, where we had buried our documentary material. They didn't give money for other needs. We started digging on Dzielna right after we returned to Warsaw. I must say I didn't believe we'd find anything, but Tuvia kept arguing we would. The building on Dzielna was a mound of debris—there was nothing there but a mountain of bricks from the building destroyed by the Germans. The nearby Pawiak was also destroyed; Tuvia claimed he knew where to search and he would get to it. Everything was buried in the ground in our cellar, under four stories that collapsed. We didn't find much. How Tuvia got to what he was looking for, I don't know. But he worked courageously, self-confidently. We needed money: our comrades and members of the Warsaw kibbutz worked on the excavation, and we had to support the kibbutz. But the Jewish Committee gave money only for the excavation. For other needs, we had to get money from outside.

As for antisemitism, when I arrived in Lublin, there had already been countless murders of Jews in Poland. I met a Jew there named Elvin—his real name is Levin—he was in the United States for many years and thought Elvin sounded better. He once studied at the university in Vilna and came to Lublin from the Soviet Union after a lot of wandering around. In Lublin, his son was murdered by the Poles—the ones fighting against the new regime. The source of the new antisemitism was first of all in the eternal antisemitism of the Poles, which was augmented by an ideological reason: not simply hatred of Jews qua Jews, but also because they were Communists, whereas the Communists were hated because they were Jews. Both were targeted for murder. However, they also murdered a great many Poles; but a Pole who was murdered was a Pole in a uniform; that is, he had to be famous since they didn't murder ordinary Poles, only well-known ones. But as far as they were concerned, with regard to the Jews, every Jew deserved death and it was a good deed to kill him. Moreover, a Jew was likely to ask for his property, his house back. And there were such cases. For example, Dr. Ishai tells of a Jew who came to get his property and got it with an axe.[18] As a rule, we can say that Jewish lives were unprotected.

The Communists were the only ones who tried to defend the Jews. This is true of both Witołd and Osóbka-Morawski.[19] I was in contact with them and I know they couldn't even protect the lives of Poles if they were Communists, Democrats, or Liberals, not to mention Jews. I believed them. Of course, incidents like the Kielce pogrom were aberrations.[20] In Kielce, I think it was precisely the local Communists who abandoned the Jews. But even if I wasn't close to their world view, I emphasize again that, as I knew them during the war in Poland—and I'm not talking about Soviet Communism, but about Polish Communism—they were the only ones who came out strongly, with decrees, instructions, and orders to the militia to avoid harming Jews; they were the only ones who sincerely wanted to defend Jews, but they didn't have much power. And I would say that, even if I were a sworn enemy of the regime. What to do? But after the pogrom in Kielce, what I said was the only correct thing to do: let the Jews leave Poland! You can imagine what would have happened to the last Jews of Poland if they had stayed. After all, it's clear that the AK would have destroyed them; they would certainly have killed Yitzhak Zuckerman.

Stanisław Mikołajczyk, who was active at that time and promised to support us, didn't keep his word. The clergy—including cardinals— disappointed us. In fact, the priests were against the Communists, which

18. Moshe Ishai was sent to Poland on a rescue mission from Eretz Israel by the Jewish Agency in 1945–1946. (See his book, *In the Shadow of the Holocaust* [Hebrew], 1973.)

19. Edward Osóbka-Morawski (b. 1909): Left-wing socialist activist. Prime Minister of the Polish Provisional Government and the Government of National Unity, 1947–1949, and Minister of Public Administration. Was expelled from the Party in 1949 and readmitted in 1956 without any function.

20. See chapter 15.

meant also against the Jews. So, in that period, to be a partner of the Communists was a Jewish national role, if only from the single perspective of Jewish existence. Even if only to get across the territory of Poland, the Jews first of all had to remain alive. And they were attacked and murdered on the roads, in the small towns, and in the big cities.

Many Jews went into government ministries because they were educated. I read the Polish journal, *Kultura*, published in Paris, the organ of the "good," anti-Communist, Democratic emigrés, which condemned the Arabs and has always been on Israel's side—it was really nice to read it. There was an article about how Communism in Poland is now without Communist ideology because they threw out the Jews and it was the Jews who carried the ideology. That's not a specifically antisemitic article, and there's also a reply by a woman of Jewish origin named Gerszonowicz who was thrown out of Poland. She replies, and it's interesting that they trusted the Jews. A Jew didn't have to be a Communist to fill an important position. It was enough for him to be a Jew to be trusted.

The Jews were on the side of the Communists, or they stood between the Communists and the Reaction, and they had to choose. And there was also an infamous referendum we knew was nothing but a fake,[21] a series of questions to be answered "yes" or "no." Obviously in other conditions, most of the Polish people would have answered "no." But I'm sure the Jews sincerely answered "yes"; there was a special appeal of the government to the Halutz movement; we worked as hard as we could for this fake.

In the Ukraine, there was opposition to the regime—not just in the cities, but it was stronger in the cities and the army was brought there from the Soviet Union, and they then formed their own militia which had to be loyal to the new government, although anti-Communist partisans also infiltrated it. There were also quite a few Jews among them, and they did unspeakable acts. The militia established order in the cities. One of our members, whose name I don't want to mention, was in the militia and knows what they did in the cities and districts they controlled. They simply killed like the Germans. That was a vicious struggle, a real civil war, except that the Jews were murdered as Jews. There's no need to add that, even among the Communists, quite a few murdered Jews. These weren't members of the leadership, which was very far from antisemitism; but there were some who murdered Jews and it didn't bother them as Communists.

The first major riot against the Jews was in Kraków. But there were murders every day in Lublin and Warsaw too. As I recall, there were outbursts in Kraków when I was in Lublin (1945); and there were also

21. Referendum made by the new Polish government on June 1, 1946.

pogroms in Radom and Częstochowa. The riot in Kielce was later, in 1946. Before that, individual Jews were murdered on trains, but not yet in an organized and bloody pogrom.

I left for London in August, for the first Zionist conference after the war. The units were arranged by their representatives; as I recall, we had a parity arrangement with Ikhud. They spoke in the name of Mapai, the General Zionists and their youth movements. We may have been a little bigger than they were. That didn't mean anything. My first meeting with people from Eretz Israel after those long years took place in London. The trip to London wasn't my first time out of Poland, since I had already gone to Germany, where I was called to come to Oskar Hendler and his comrades, who had formed a movement. Mapai was going crazy trying to destroy it. Members of the Brigade were there in those days, and I met them in Bavaria. I also went to Italy. I had no contacts with Germans while I was in Germany. I saw a devastated country that had little food. Those who "got along" were the Jews. The American military authorities were hostile and harsh to the Jewish DPs. One day, I went out; I took a car with a Jewish driver and went to the French occupation zone where the situation was even worse.

I visited the camp at Dachau which now accomodated prisoners-of-war, SS men, who basked in the sun and got good food. But the American guards were brutal to the Jews in the DP refugee camps. Later, in Germany, I met our people in UNRRA. That was my first visit.

At that time, I was assigned to go to Germany, Slovakia, Hungary, Austria, and Italy; that was in light of the scope of the collapse of our Movement. Zivia and Tuvia "landed" on Poland and I went through other countries, trying as much as possible to minimize the damage done to our Movement by Mapai in those countries.

On my trip to Italy, in Milan, I met Zvi Ze'ira[22] and Zvi Netzer, setting out for Poland. Netzer stayed in Italy and I took Ze'ira with me. Zvi Netzer came to work in Brikha. Isser Ben-Zvi, a member of Mapai, preceded him. I knew him from Vilna, when he was active in Gordonia there in the thirties.

In those days, there were almost no members of Mapai in Poland, which was their own fault. They were suspicious of us politically without any foundation, since we didn't bring into Dror any element of the dissension between Akhdut Ha-Avoda and Mapai in Eretz Israel and certainly no dissensions in Ha-Kibbutz Ha-Meuchad. After all, at that time, they were still in Ha-Kibbutz Ha-Meuchad; the schism in Ha-Kibbutz

22. Zvi Ze'ira: Member of Kibbutz Yagur. From 1945 to 1947, was Shaliah of the Histadrut and the kibbutz to Zionist educational operations in Poland and DP camps in Germany.

Ha-Meuchad happened later on. Our education in Dror was directed toward Ha-Kibbutz Ha-Meuchad and founded on its basic principles.

Brikha was a joint matter, not only of the youth movements, but of all the Zionists. A person who said he wanted to immigrate to Eretz Israel wasn't asked his political identification. There were certain cases when I refused to help. For example, Liber Brenner of the Bund asked me to get him out of Poland and said explicitly that he wanted to go to America.[23] I told him we didn't take care of those who go to America. I said if he declared he was immigrating to Eretz Israel, we would get him out. But in general, we didn't ask. Bundists left this way, and later decided whatever they wanted. But the kibbutzim served as concentration points and were based on Movement direction. If only we had had as many Jews then as we could get out of Poland in 1946, since the new government opened the borders, and the extent of the exodus depended on us, our organization. This situation existed after the Kielce pogrom. Before that, the situation was different—our contacts with the authorities concerning Brikha weren't yet so close or extensive.

You should read everything that's written against me in the book devoted to Polish Jewry. Gruenbaum does lavish praise on me, but there is also the accusation that, in the everyday work of Brikha, I supposedly "didn't exist." The truth is that, *in the big issues of Brikha, there wasn't a thing I didn't have a hand in*, and there was nothing they didn't tell me about. I was "infected" with a great love for Israel and I didn't ask a Jew for his identity in order to get him out. That period of 1946, until I left, is a time of gates opening wide.

But neither during the war nor right afterward when I came to London in January did I accept the new ideology of Ha-Shomer Ha-Tza'ir. I'm not a conservative by nature, and especially since I was then a young man, I was far from a settled conservatism. But when you're looking for a way to build strength, you have to build it on the basis of certain givens. And the issue we confronted turned into phraseology around *Unity!* Apparently, there's nothing nicer than that; but in certain times and circumstances, it becomes an empty word. The proof of that is what happened later, since the issue exploded internally and destroyed quite a few creative forces.

We were a handful of people who survived. So we wanted unity; but within unity, we wanted a kernel of a crystalized, ideological force that knew what it wanted. No doubt a united force was needed for joint action on Aliya, Brikha, and illegal entry, all those things—to do whatever was possible together but without anyone blurring his own independent char-

23. Lieber Brenner: Bundist in Częstochowa; a representative on the Central Committee of the Jews in Poland.

acter. That was the essence and content of the letter I wrote from Kraków. Today, I might write it a bit differently; but I wouldn't change any of the content. I might have been mistaken in thinking that kibbutz unity would come as a result of political unity. After all, I wrote about the political unity of the labor movement in the first line, and, in the second line, about kibbutz unity. Kibbutz unity seemed harder, since it turns out that the commandment of personal fulfillment and the reality of twenty-four hours of life together, in the various kibbutz movements, were harder than unity in a joint political framework. Although we were far away, cut off, you don't feel my bitterness in the letter at being isolated from Eretz Israel, something I can't accept to this day, since I can't understand it. That was unrequited love. We looked for the borders, we shaped the force, we . . . But Eretz Israel?! It's incomprehensible. To this day. Maybe there's a lesson in that.

I can conclude from this that the efforts on the part of Eretz Israel to reach us not only were insufficient, but also that there was a psychological chasm between us. There was a big gap in the awareness of what could and couldn't be done. I had a completely different measuring rod from the people in Eretz Israel. In fact, by now, I've also lost the measuring rod of those days, which set no barrier, except death, between the possible and the impossible. I was so used to that measuring rod because of the "university of the Hitler years" I went through, when everything you did had only one meaning: death! Death for going out of the ghetto, death for riding the train, death for everything; so that was my constant measuring rod. Life in Eretz Israel was completely different, however, measured by different standards: crossing borders, traveling—what will they say? How will they get in? That wasn't obvious. And that won't be forgiven! They should know that. I must say: Eretz Israel was my "eighty-first blow." Oh, my land, land of my dreams[24] . . . Velvele, silly, where are you going? To watch the cornflowers.[25]

People say it's different now; now there's a State, then there wasn't. State or no state, there was the Yishuv, which for me was as much an entity as the State later on. The State is nothing but a set of different instruments. And what does the State have to do with this? If someone has to get somewhere, is in danger, what difference does it make whether there's a State or not?! Weren't there people willing to do that in Eretz Israel then? During the Holocaust, if I had posted an announcement in every kibbutz saying, "Who is willing and able to go to Warsaw?", I maintain that

24. An allusion to two poems by the Hebrew poet, Shaul Tshernikhovski: "Oh, My Land! My Homeland!" and "They Say There Is a Land."
25. Zuckerman is quoting a line from a poem by Tshernikhovski, "Like the Heat of the Day."

hundreds of people would have come forward! But that idea didn't exist. So what difference does it make that there wasn't a State?! It wasn't a matter of possibilities; if it was a political possibility at all—Poland wasn't yet cut off. Poland wasn't yet recognized. But in that period, in those months in 1945, there was a migration of people in all directions. People from Hungary and Czechoslovakia and Belgium and France and Poland and Russia wandered all over Europe. Didn't Eretz Israel know anything about that? Didn't they understand that you could at least get to other countries of Europe bordering on Poland? You could—but there was some psychological abyss. I'm sure of that; I'm sure that thousands of people in Eretz Israel were willing; if they had been asked they would have come. If there had been such a movement, collective idea, with a State or without a State. I wasn't wrong when I warned against the return of Hitler. Fifteen years passed and everything was forgotten. Was he resurrected? Our film, *The Eighty-First Blow*, was shown to the security forces, to the army. I went through all that and I represent only a thousandth of the Jewish experience; since I belonged to the so-called "Jewish aristocracy" of the underground and didn't go through everything. There are ranks in this reality: there are those who didn't survive, who were killed; then there are the refugees of Auschwitz, the "other planet"; then members of the commando that burned the bodies; and those who were in the camp and escaped, and some survived to tell their tale; and there are those who didn't get to Auschwitz, like me. You can say I went through that war with relative ease. In the labor camp, my life was indeed in danger every minute. But in comparison, I went through the war extremely "elegantly." Of course, I wouldn't want to live through it again—and couldn't, it seems to me, perhaps because of my age or other things. But if there's no choice, I would say with full awareness, let it be again! Maybe I would live it differently, act differently, maybe correct many errors. Let me put it this way; in my life, since 1939, in its general direction, there are no errors. Yet there are many mistakes. We could have done everything a bit sooner, a bit differently. They say maybe that's no accident. I don't know. I can't blame anybody, except myself.[26]

26. Here, Yoske Rabinovitch, the interviewer, made the following comment:
Yitzhak, we know that Zivia doesn't tend to compliment you unless she has to. And, as soon as she came to Eretz Israel, in 1946, Zivia, Yitzhak Tabenkin and I spent two days and nights at Beit Oren on the Carmel, and she talked the whole time. On the first evening of our conversation, at a certain moment, she stopped talking and, after a brief silence, as if overcoming hesitation, she turned to us and said: "I want you to know something about Yitzhak. I'm his wife and we were together there in everything, and you can say that whatever I say is subjective . . . What can I do . . . I'm convinced it's the objective truth. By now, there are no witnesses left except me and I say things now, here, on my first day in Eretz Israel: if it weren't for Yitzhak,

As for what Zivia said, I can say that I was, by chance, the first one who got the information from Vilna in 1941; that was a strange combination of things. I left Warsaw to set up training camps, mainly in Ostrowiec, Częstochowa, and Sandomierz; and I met with an agent from Vilna and with Irena Adamowicz, and I was the first who heard the tidings of Job. In fact, what could I do? Should I have returned to the ghetto immediately? What did I do? I thought if I behaved like that, it would be weakness, and I had to examine myself and go on my way. It's hard for me to describe it, since it wasn't something abstract, but in my own hometown, in Vilna! Vilna wasn't just my hometown, where my family lived, it was everything to me. And I set out to go on and not to give in. That was stupid: I should have gone back to the ghetto immediately, but I spent a few days on the road. I never cried except at the end of the war, but my heart wept now. I went on with my work in order to get over it. What nonsense! I set up the training kibbutz in Ostrowiec, and that was even before the information about Chelmno—but in my heart I knew this was the end. Even if we say I was late by those two weeks.

I'm no masochist, but nothing helps—thirty years have gone by now. In my first years in Israel, I would hold.a trial for myself at night. I'm basically a happy person, I love brandy and mischief and laughter—and, here, for the first time, I say it: endless torments, even though I knew the truth: that I wouldn't have saved even one more person if I had gone back immediately, not one.

I'm very grateful to Zivia for what she said. I'm hearing that for the first time; I'm not used to such compliments. But I must say we were a very united group—I knew exactly what Frumka was thinking when she was in Wołyń or Będzin. There was extraordinary communication between us, even without the telephone or telegraph. We worked in different places. There was some emotional common denominator between us. I could say precisely what Zivia would do, what Frumka would do, what Mordechai Tennenbaum would do. With everyone, of course, things were reflected in his personal, emotional prism. But we had a common denominator. We were very crystalized, very united; the delusion and the easy belief that those Jews were destroyed in eastern Poland

---

we Halutzim would not have had the Warsaw Ghetto Uprising! Only one step—and we would have been swallowed up in the darkness of the Holocaust without any real trace. I don't say that easily, but more categorically: I say it for the first time and the last time. Zivia won't say that ever again." I think it necessary to tell what she said, as it is engraved on my memory, after I repeated it—to preserve it.

Later, Yoske comments:

Out of some internal impulse, I burst out with that story in the middle of Yitzhak's speech, while he was talking into the tape recorder in one of our last interviews.

"because they were Communists" or that other Jews in the West were destroyed "because they were residents of the Reich" was remote from us; it didn't take with us. Quite simply, we didn't seek delusions!

It was so hard for me that night that I was on the brink of madness. When I returned, it was as if I were standing on the abyss; I constantly saw the abyss facing me. Nobody wants to get killed, not even a member of the underground. And I must say that being a member of the underground was relatively easiest. And as a Pole, when I was with Poles, I always knew how to be careful, as opposed to the ordinary man next to me, the innocent neighbor—why was he killed? At least I knew why, and I knew how to protect myself: on the street, in the apartment, with every honking of a car at night, I was alert. That has stayed with me, even here. At Yagur, when a car passed by on the road at night, I would wake up and wait until I remembered I was at Yagur. In time, that passed. It was easier for a member of the underground in the sense that he was on guard all the time, twenty-four hours a day. And in those terms, too, I belonged to that pedigreed elite. A few million were murdered and you might think they were murdered because they were members of the underground. But that's not so. Simple, honest people were murdered, who hadn't done anything against the occupier, and yet they were murdered.

After the war in Poland, I rode the train and flew a lot because after the war, I was a respected person because of my personal connections in the underground. By dint of these contacts with members of the underground, I was received in all institutions without an appointment. And I used that to our advantage. Even when there weren't any airplane tickets, there was always a ticket for me. Whether it was a military or a civilian plane, it was always arranged. And in general, if things didn't work out, I would appeal to the security office or the militia where General Witołd was in command (later he turned into a "non-revolutionary" person), and things were arranged. When I came back from the flight to Kraków to the Central Committee of the Jews in Poland, a few members of the committee grabbed me (Zalecki, Biter, and others): "We're going to lunch!" At the time, there were two very fine restaurants in Warsaw; one was for the Soviet élite, with caviar and good Moscow vodka; and there, during lunch, they asked me: "Where were you?" I said: "You don't know where I was?" And they said: "We only know where you went. But where were you, really?" I enumerated for them the border points I had visited because I knew they had investigated me and knew I was in Kraków and at the border. I gave them our points I had visited, and I was sure they thought I was lying.

I told them that, after they *denounced* me, the secret was out anyway. Maybe I didn't express myself so sharply, but I did say something like that. Then, those two, Biter and Zalecki (who is in Israel) rushed to dissociate themselves from the others and kissed me, calling out: "Antek, what's with you!" And indeed, I read letters signed by Zalecki, which included spying on me. The Poles gave them to me. His secretary was more loyal to me than he was, and I knew what was in his desk drawer; and I also knew that the Poles now knew all the secrets. However, I never told that either to Isser Ben-Zvi or to Netzer who thought "they made an underground."

The Poles knew everything about us. But I never shattered that illusion. If the Poles had decided to close the border in 1945 or 1946 (after the pogroms in Kielce), they could have done it immediately. And if they decided to arrest someone, to give us a hint, they did it. I was aware I wasn't in the underground and every step I took was known to the authorities. One day, a man close to the PPR appeared in my apartment on Poznańska in Warsaw and told me he heard that they were going to raid my apartment and arrest me that night. (The man is in Israel.) I listened to him, but I decided not to leave the apartment for several reasons: (1) if I took off, someone was almost certainly waiting for me downstairs; (2) I thought that, as a member of He-Halutz, I simply couldn't run away. And there was also some weight to the delusion that they wouldn't arrest me. Maybe that wasn't a delusion then and they really wouldn't arrest me. That is, a little later, they certainly would have! And in that case, I would have spent a few years in the cellars of the UB. But in this period, I felt safe. First of all, I had close friends, Poles, people who always supported me, and who knew and understood I would soon leave Poland. I never denied the subject of Eretz Israel; on the contrary, I always appeared with that banner, especially during the underground days.

How many cities did I visit? How many Jews did I find? What does my soul glean from that postwar period? I can say that it destroyed me! The period of the war didn't wreak such devastation on my soul; and it took quite a long time until it reached to my consciousness. After all, I knew everything and yet . . . Everything was magnified then. But now it was as if I suddenly saw everything in detail with my own eyes.

I saw the abyss in front of me after the war more than in 1943 and 1944—without a people, without Jews, without a family, without friends (Zivia wasn't with me some of the time). That was very hard. It's no wonder that after the Shlikhim came and our center was in Łódz, I was perpetually wandering back and forth between Łódz and Warsaw, where I was working. Every single night on a truck. I had to leave from Marszałkowska and there was no regular transportation. I remember myself in winter shaking with cold, on bad roads, running at night to be with my comrades in Łódz to get up the next day at dawn and return to Warsaw. There, in Łódz, I warmed up a little.

I never had such a hard time, not even during the *Aktsias*. That sudden vacuum after the dread, that abyss. There was no dawn. Why live?!

Without that ideal, without Eretz Israel and the strength it inspired in me, I would probably have put an end to myself. Not if I had been a Communist, since the Communists after all still had some hope or delusion. It was Eretz Israel that saved me as a person. At any rate, I can't give a faithful description of my life in those years after the end of the war.

Moreover, in those days, all the Russian curses I knew were spread all over the east. That dreadful loneliness. An idealistic Pole, who started rebuilding his homeland from the ruins might have felt a sense of exaltation. He knew what he was building. It wasn't like that for me. If I had been a Communist, I would have given my all to the building! But I didn't belong to that land or that culture or that life. I was a Jew in all the bones and sinews of my body, a Halutz Zionist.

I must also add here my emotional background. Twice I was on the brink of total collapse. The first time was after the shock of Vilna and Chelmno. The second time was after the war, after May 1945, when the full scope of the disaster was revealed. I was one of the few who knew almost everything. But when I saw with my own eyes what was left, I broke down. I was drawn at that time to the ruined ghetto as by a magnet; I would occasionally take some food and a bottle and sit for hours in the debris. And after a visit to Lublin and Częstochowa—mainly in those cities—I collapsed: I stopped eating except when I was drinking hard. If not for Eretz Israel, I would have been a complete alcoholic. There was a sense of emptiness. Those sights, in Łódz and other places. Thousands of Jews had been there. The sight of the abandoned houses. There was a sick mood of cemeteries. The mass graves. I wasn't a boy anymore, I was twenty-nine years old; when the war broke out, I was twenty-four. After the war, I saw that let-down. I know very little about the wisdom of the soul. And I'm only trying to explain my situation. The incident in Kraków is always in my mind's eye, when I was wounded in the leg and ran away. I saved myself with the quiet emotional strength I mobilized and reached Warsaw. I passed through the ghetto and the wall and it was only when I got to my quiet room that I fainted. The same thing happened to me after the war. Before that, I never broke down; maybe only for a few hours, and then I would recover and get up. There was a collapse here and there, friends and relatives were killed. I knew that when I left home, I might not be alive five minutes later; and I endured that until the war was over. Then I fainted: I couldn't hold out anymore. As if I needed tremendous emotional forces to return to education, the Movement, creativity. Suddenly, after that great uproar, after the great dread—the quiet of the cemeteries. I tried to explain, but I don't know if I explained anything.

For two years, I studied pedagogy and psychology, and nothing's left of it; it was all formal study. The period I'm describing was the hardest time in my life. And if we add the loneliness and the isolation from Eretz Israel—no Shaliah, no letter. God, there were ways to get there! If I had decided, right after the war, to get to Eretz Israel, I would have reached our beloved land. That really was unrequited love. That won't be forgiven. The dynamic, pre-State kibbutz, the kibbutz of the Palmakh, of the illegal immigration, of activism—won't be forgiven!

This wasn't grace or favors. I never felt like a beggar. But many months passed, without a sound, without a sign. I don't understand it at all. If there had been even only twenty of us then, one of us would probably have left for Eretz Israel. But there were three of us altogether. And I've already said that Tuvia was neutralized for a few months after the war, for personal reasons. Zivia was half. Only Zivia and I were left—and then "50 percent" went to Romania. I was the only one left of our Movement. And ultimately, I wasn't some small peg in Jewish society, and yet I had to appear in public somehow. If I could have left, I would have. But there wasn't anyone to send and I couldn't leave. By then, I had made a few trips across the borders. I would go for two weeks maximum, to various places. But to go look for ways to Eretz Israel? You can't compare it to the prewar situation.

It turns out we made endless historical mistakes in Eretz Israel. By now, I'm a partner in them. I know that for sure, so I don't have any moral validity because, now, I personally should have behaved differently. There are the Jews of Syria, the Jews of the Soviet Union—and what am I doing about that? Drinking coffee and cognac, talking about it. Yes, I hear that there was a kibbutz council then in Kfar Giladi,[27] a few weeks after the end of the war, and Vanya Hadari came from Istanbul; they decided there that Leviteh should go to Poland, and Yoske [Rabinovitch] says that people there were afraid they wouldn't make it. Tabenkin said then that Leviteh should go to Poland immediately because he was the last one to part from the comrades, and Leviteh said he would have awful difficulties meeting with the comrades—how would he meet Zivia? And Vanya said it was impossible to get there. I know all that.

I'm trying to understand the psychology of the people there. Why wasn't it possible for them to come to us? A few people did get to Eretz Israel both from Poland and from Slovakia, even during the war. So why was it impossible for them to come? If a delegation of ten paratroopers,

27. Kfar Giladi: A kibbutz in northern Israel, founded in 1916.

for example, had come to us in the ghetto, it's true nothing fateful would have changed, but it would have been different. Sometimes I would tell Zivia we were lucky the Shlikhim didn't stay in Poland in 1939, since I would have had to look for bunkers to hide them, too. That wasn't so simple—one more worry. But the fact is they would come to us in our distress! And we know how much a letter or a telegram means—the fact of that contact in times of distress is immeasurable. Leviteh came to us before the pogroms in Kielce and, by the time they occurred, he had gone to Paris. He came with the leaders of a big delegation I welcomed at night. That was in 1946, a few days after Black Saturday in Israel (June 1946). The pogroms in Kielce were in July 1946.

A woman member of Ha-Shomer Ha-Tza'ir who was in Auschwitz in 1944 went out of her mind after the war. When she was in Israel, she visited me, hugged me, and called me Mordechai Anielewicz. I already told about the fellow in Kraków who was hidden by his sister. We once sent her to Auschwitz to try to save members who were interned there. But you couldn't get into Auschwitz. The purpose of her mission was to be close to the camp and try to organize Havka's escape. She got there just before the Polish Uprising in Warsaw. And when the Uprising began, she was stuck. Later, after the Uprising, Havka's mother got letters from her daughter; we kept sending her packages and taking care of the family, and I've already told about meeting her mother; I've told the story of that family. Incidentally, in one of Havka's letters to her mother from Auschwitz, she wrote that among photos of people who were killed by gas, she came across a picture of me. Her mother wrote her that I was alive. That was in 1944.

After the war, I couldn't meet frequently with Mother Folman. One day, she found me and told me that Havka was in Sweden. It turned out she was in one of Count Bernadotte's transports, and was taken to Sweden.[28] Havka wrote and asked what to do. Idelson was in Sweden after the war, and they wanted to send her to Eretz Israel. But she asked me what to do. And I wrote her to come back to Poland. A young girl, who had spent her best days in the ghetto and in the "university" of Auschwitz, her life was saved and she stayed in Sweden waiting for immigration to Eretz Israel. Then she gets a cruel letter from me to come back to Poland! I remember it as if it were today. It was a spring morning; I was still in bed, in my apartment on Poznańska, and a beaming blonde girl appears:

28. During the war, Count Folke Bernadotte (1895–1948) headed the Swedish Red Cross and took care of the liberation of inmates of German camps. Later on, in 1948, he was named by the UN to serve as mediator in the Jewish-Arab conflict. He was murdered by Lehi (the "Stern Gang") in Jerusalem in September 1948.

Havka! She got the letter and reported for duty. She came back to Poland, didn't go to Eretz Israel. Later, she played a central role in various operations. She was a counselor in Kraków, then she worked in the He-Halutz center. In Auschwitz in 1944, she was in contact with Lonka, and now we knew about Lonka and her death. I keep very nice things about Lonka in my heart, but I won't reveal them, lest I look like someone trying to raise a monument to himself rather than to erect a monument in memory of her, who deserved it.

Perhaps we will do well to ignore that now. In such a time of trial, sublime beauty and ultimate ugliness struggle in a person. So people remain in our hearts. For me, for Zivia, those people have remained to this day in their full glory. Even if I mention a person like Yosef Kornianski, who wasn't with us in the hardest time, he remains in our memory as a splendid person. And there are a few other people whom you could slander as much as you want—that doesn't detract from them in the least. I'm impervious, deaf to all those stories! That was a period of trial for people, a period of extraordinary friendship, of devotion, and not always for great things. You can't always live only for great things; but that simple friendship in everyday things, in taking care of friends, in the things a person can do for his friend in distress. Like their last bread my friends threw me when I was on the verge of death in Kampinos Camp. I got it every morning! I couldn't eat it because I was wounded and stunned and in pain. The issue isn't a piece of bread but that people stood the test of friendship! Although there always were some exceptions. That was true with us, with Ha-Shomer Ha-Tza'ir, Gordonia, the Bund, all the movements—but I know our Movement better.

Havka arrived on December 23, 1945, and immediately went to work in Kraków as a counselor in the kibbutz we established. (Incidentally, that was the same day [in 1942] that Havka fell into the hands of the Germans.) I surprised her by coming to Kraków suddenly. I took her out to a restaurant and taught her how to drink liquor. We spent time together and then, that same evening, she returned to the kibbutz, worried they would smell the alcohol on her breath. Despite my "complaints" against her, Havka was a fine person and still is.

After the war, they started coming back to Poland from east and west. A large part of the Jews came back and repatriation began. In this early period, it wasn't done officially; and later, there was a problem of how to get out to the West. Similarly, people from the camps came from the West. They came to look for their families or the remnants of them. Sometimes people came for materialistic reasons, to realize property. That was before the Poles started nationalization. Jews would come to a town and sometimes wouldn't return from it because they would be killed there.

They sold their houses, looked for their father, their mother, their children, their wives. In those days, the Jewish Central Committee played an important national role.

At first, the occupying armies (mainly the Americans and the British) tended to send people to their home countries. I think it was inspired by the English. Every Jew who survived was not a Jew for them, but a Pole or a Hungarian or a Romanian. They wanted to dismantle the camps because the people from all nations returned to their homelands. The Jews knew they were the last; they didn't want to return to their "homelands," but they were forced to. Then a wandering began, and the Jews started arriving by the thousands.

I remember one day, in Warsaw, Arye Sheftel showed up in my apartment, in camp clothes. I knew him from Vilna. I wasn't a party member, but I belonged to "Labor Eretz Israel," and I knew him from the days of my activity in He-Halutz. He was a Hebrew teacher, one of the few in the Yiddishist Po'alei Zion–Z.S. in Vilna who was a Hebraist. After many meetings and conversations, on that same day, I took him to a store and dressed him from head to foot. I didn't have a problem with money; in fact, I had never been so rich as in those days. I had the money of the Jewish Central Committee and the money of the Joint, and I wasn't limited.

Once, in Łódz, I met two sons of our former landlord in Vilna. (My family later moved to another place.) I saw them in their clothing and I naturally invited them immediately to lunch. I also wanted to buy them new clothes but it turned out they had lots of money and didn't need me. I can't say where they got money. They were agile and amassed a fortune. But many were destitute. Then the idea emerged among us that we should build our Movement, without consideration of age, and also on the collective base of partisans and older Jews in the style of the Labor organization. We set up the Labor Movement because many people arrived destitute and anarchy prevailed in Poland, great chaos reigned. That was the situation after the Soviet occupation and at the inception of the Polish government. The Communist minority assumed the management of the state, despite the hostility of the majority; we had to take care of the Jews. We brought all those who knocked at our gates into the Movement and we built collectives. I think that was how we saved people. We called every collective, which in fact was nothing but a soup kitchen, a kibbutz; but in that framework, people preserved a sense of self-respect. They didn't need to stand in line in public kitchens, with a bowl of soup. I don't know how we overcame the financial distress, but we did. The thousands who arrived later felt they were getting into a "trap." You have to understand that there was a difference between my emotional constitution, since I knew why I stayed, and those people, who wondered why they had come back and aspired with all their being to get out. That was the greatness of the Movement, that it organized the people and sent them as its emissaries to their destination.

The center moved to Łódz, but things were decided in Warsaw. I didn't live in Łódz, nor did any of the members of the Central Committee. I don't mean to praise myself when I say I was concerned with Jewish matters in political and social terms. Łódz then became a movement center as well as a Jewish center, since Warsaw was devastated and there weren't any intact houses there. In Łódz, however, which had been the second largest city before the war, and whose Jews were executed, the houses remained standing. The Germans who lived in the city were thrown out and whole quarters were empty. People streamed to Łódz where it was very easy to get an apartment, and so the city turned into a big center.

There was even an idea of moving the Provisional Government from Lublin to Łódz. Bierut, Osóbka-Morawski, and others decided that the government would be in devastated Warsaw; when I moved to Warsaw— that was quite early—and got an apartment, there wasn't a living soul around me in the entire big building where I lived; that was an apartment whose tenants were bugs and fleas. Indeed, that's what drove Tsizling away when he visited. He later sent us something to keep fleas away when he returned to Eretz Israel.

Housing was a good reason why people streamed to Łódz, since not only Jews came; and it was easy to get in there; but to live in Warsaw, you had to get special permission. The only part of Warsaw that remained standing was Praga, the suburb on the other side of the Wisła. Aside from that, the entire city was destroyed. After the Polish Uprising, the Germans had time to destroy the houses systematically. What attracted people to Łódz was simply houses.

So Jews also streamed there and the city became our center. There was no problem forming one or twenty kibbutzim there, as long as there were young people. Our kibbutz was formed on Połódniowa Street, and there was another kibbutz of the Zionist Youth, and after the movement split, Ha-Shomer Ha-Tza'ir established a separate kibbutz. You could do anything in Łódz.

FOURTEEN

Argument about Our Image

Our liberation from the German occupation took place in January 1945; and in February we decided that Zivia would go to Romania. We both agreed, and I remained in Poland in good conscience, but most of the leadership of Ha-Shomer Ha-Tza'ir left. And that led to an argument about whether all of us should leave or whether we had to fill some mission and whether there should be—as I thought—a continuation to our activity.

Did I need another legitimation for my Zionism? A confirmation that I was a Halutz, a man of Eretz Israel, and that Communist Poland didn't interest me? I didn't believe for a minute in the restoration of Jewish life in Poland. When there were millions of us, I didn't believe in it. Why should I believe in it after the war? But there was a *responsibility*. What happened to us in Poland was that, suddenly, in 1942, *with much delay*—if only we had reached that awareness earlier—we found ourselves as leaders. And I knew that truth which has a grain of pride—that we became the real leaders. And in 1945, I also knew that I had to stay in Poland out of responsibility to the Jews who remained—especially after I heard what Sommerstein said, and he knew more than I did; and especially after the Jews began coming. When was the argument with Abba Kovner in Lublin? They didn't know what was going on in Częstochowa. How could they think that history began the moment they were liberated and came to Lublin? We didn't know the fate of the Jews who survived. How could you get up and leave? They didn't even know what was going on in the towns around Lublin. It didn't even occur to them that you had to look for Jews!

I was never attracted to *Doikeyt*.[1] But to leave like that?! That wasn't "one of the things" we argued about. That was the main thing! I repeat: to save myself, I could have left in 1940; I really didn't have to go back from the Soviet occupation zone to the German occupation zone. I could have gone to Vilna with our party veterans. If I had decided to do that, the comrades wouldn't have accused me of desertion nor would I accuse others. Even afterward, there were still possibilities, or delusions—countless ones. All that we did during the war, we did deliberately. If not, I wouldn't hold my head up, but would be ashamed. That I didn't succeed in saving the nation, that there was a catastrophe—I'm not guilty of that.

As for "Revenge," that subject kept me awake nights especially since, later, they came and asked to me to lead "Revenge."[2] But my notion of revenge wasn't theirs. I was "dying for revenge," but I was remote from their idea, which bordered on madness. Could you annihilate a German nation of sixty million?! And if you did kill a thousand Germans, would that make you sleep better?! Could you think you had taken revenge for your nation? The issue kept pestering me, and even in Israel, I couldn't get rid of it—but I realized that their method was wrong. If I had devoted myself to revenge, I would have done it in good conscience and with full responsibility. My argument was that it couldn't be done by separating functions, separating forces. He who builds, educates, and shapes a force is also the one who devotes himself, partially, to the issue of revenge. For the emotional hygiene of those people, they should have been occupied with other things. In fact, they were given to dreams and visions for months, without relief, and without any communication.

Zivia's ostracism by the Romanian group infuriated me and was one of the reasons why I wasn't in on the secret of "Revenge." Zivia was a leader! One of the most important leaders in the war of the Jews of Warsaw, as well as in the formation of the Halutz movement. And what did they do with her! What rumors did they spread! And me too: if Jews were murdered in Poland, Yitzhak Zuckerman was to blame! They sat in quiet Bucharest and dared to say I wasn't defending the Jews in Poland. Apparently they thought I was appointed by the regime to defend the Jews. All that poisoned my days. I overcame it with a glass of cognac or vodka. Zivia wrote, but spared me and didn't reveal everything; but I heard things from the Shlikhim. In Romania, a mystical, messianic group

1. *Doikeyt* (Yiddish: Hereness): The Bundist position, seeing the main work in the Jewish Diaspora, in "work in the present" and not in the immigration of Jews to Eretz Israel.
2. "Revenge": An idea propounded by some former partisans (notably Abba Kovner) to take revenge on the Germans (in Germany) for the Holocaust.

took shape that could make people unbalanced. Their whole concept of revenge had no anchor in reality—neither in terms of the Movement nor in terms of the nation as a whole.

Some of them did indeed lose their emotional balance, primarily after Kovner withdrew. They got embroiled with one another and split up. Later, they accused Kovner of being a false messiah. As for Abba Kovner himself, it was a kind of aberration in his career. When he came to Eretz Israel, he fell into line with Ha-Kibbutz Ha-Artzi. I repeat that in our Movement such a thing couldn't have happened. If I had come to Eretz Israel in 1945 with an ideology like that of the "Asians," there was no way they could have silenced me! If Ha-Kibbutz Ha-Meuchad went against my conscience, I wouldn't have joined. I am even told that, some time later, some of that group became fanatics in the war against us in the united Mapam[3] and threw out individuals like S. Cholawski. It's shocking how the "Asians" fell into line. We're all human beings, but education apparently has an impact on intellectual collectivity. They could always make sure that in every framework and every unity no harm came to Ha-Shomer Ha-Tza'ir. It was different with us. What was dear to me was not Dror, not even Ha-Kibbutz Ha-Meuchad. Although, when there's a choice, I choose it.

Abba Kovner was extraordinarily influential, the life blood of Revenge. Of course he was also an outstanding poet. But if I had to choose a commander for the Jews of Vilna, I'm not sure I would have chosen a poet for that job. In my opinion, the commander could even have been a shoemaker. The quality of a poet or even the talent to compose a rousing proclamation wasn't necessarily the most important quality of a commander of the ghetto in such times.

As for that group, which was gripped by revenge, they were considerably influenced by their physical location. Those who stayed in Poland—in Łódz, Warsaw, Częstochowa—saw the destruction, the masses of Jews coming; and if they weren't corrupted, if they had a spark of humanity, they had to assist in the organization, clothing, consolation. But if you were in tranquil Bucharest, unemployed, with no real opportunity to immigrate to Eretz Israel, getting up in the morning, eating handouts, and talking endlessly, remote from Jewish reality—it's different. By staying in Bucharest, they could cut themselves off from death lurking every day, from Jews returning from the camps, from Jews coming back from

---

3. Mapam: United Workers' Party, a Halutz, left-wing, Labor Zionist Israeli political party, founded in 1945 from the parties of Akhdut Ha-Avoda (the former left wing of Mapai, based in Ha-Kibbutz Ha-Meuchad), Ha-Shomer Ha-Tza'ir (based on Ha-Kibbutz Ha-Artzi), and Po'alei Zion Left.

the east, from the whole Jewish existence of those days. The Romanian group, with its mysticism, is reminiscent of other periods in Jewish history. The war ended with a period like that of Shabbetai Zvi, of messianic yearning.[4] Young Jews were gripped by every glimmer of faith. And here were walking skeletons, depressed and mournful people, inspired with the breath of life only by the Movement. They didn't care about a few dozen "messiahs." They simply had to be lifted out of the dust.

We didn't intend to restore the Jews in Poland. We tried to shape a Jewish force, which we did with great toil and persistance. And the Jews believed in us. Why wasn't a single Ha-Shomer Ha-Tza'ir kibbutz established in Eretz Israel for the survivors? Because their leaders didn't believe in and were afraid of the survivors. Ha-Kibbutz Ha-Meuchad, however, did believe in them; and that inspired us with strength. I have a lot of criticism of Ha-Kibbutz Ha-Meuchad; but I also have a few words of praise for it.

Historians from Eretz Israel say it was Eretz Israel that split us, but that's not so. It's true that Tsizling and Idelson didn't want the unity we had formed with Ha-Shomer Ha-Tza'ir, because it was against the interests of Ha-Kibbutz Ha-Meuchad. But they understood "that nonsense of ours." (And, indeed, nothing came of it.) After all, my comrades and I went there and, as it were, cut off contact with our Movement in Eretz Israel. In fact, both the idea of "unity" and of "non-unity" came from the survivors. We mustn't blame Eretz Israel for that, we were against Ha-Kibbutz Ha-Meuchad and, as far as I know, Abba Kovner's comrades in Eretz Israel were also against his opinions. You have to take into account the fact that the local people had great influence, and no Shaliah would have held out against them; and there was no Shaliah who didn't respect the opinion of the local people. Leviteh came after the split. Our mission was to shape what existed. Although Leviteh was a consummate politician, neither he nor the other Shlikhim imposed the split of the B Faction in Eretz Israel on our Movement.[5] They didn't use their position for that. Maybe they themselves weren't so sure it was good. And they might have seen that the Movement was going in the right direction all by itself.

Back to Revenge. I was convinced that revenge operations should be carried out, and when I acceded at the meeting of the members of

4. Shabbetai Zvi (1626–1676): Most important of the "false" messiahs that have appeared in Jewish history. He initiated a mass movement that threatened rabbinical authority.

5. B Faction: In 1942, a leftist B Faction was organized within Mapai, led by the majority of Ha-Kibbutz Ha-Meuchad. Headed by Tabenkin, Idelson, and others, the B Faction split from Mapai in 1944 and formed the Akhdut Ha-Avoda party.

He-Halutz in Łódz and I agreed to lead that activity for a time, I intended to integrate these operations into the general operations of the Halutz movement, and not isolate it as a separate function. My definition was that the Movement was responsible for all operations, including revenge.

What was the role of the members of Dror in revenge? In truth, there was no such division of movements or political perspectives; the division was territorial, according to "climate," and psychology. A young Jew in Poland, in light of all the Jews who were coming, needed to help all the time. There were only a handful of activists and there were no parties. That is, they were only names without a following, barely a banner. Somebody was holding a banner without an army behind him. Only a small kernel remained of the Halutz movement. These days, the Communists write about the youth movement of that time (I read such an article in *Bleter far geshikhte*) stating that Dror was the biggest movement; but only individuals remained from it, too. At that time, a few people from our Movement came from Russia and not everyone who returned was the same person who had gone. After all, they went through a crisis! You couldn't ask my students or my young comrades in 1945 to pick up the threads of 1939 and go on, since something had happened to them.

The source of the contrast was the difference between the people who stayed in Poland and those who crossed the border to Romania. The latter had good intentions, but they hit on a dead end. And that, in fact, is the essence of Revenge. To me, that movement was like Shabbetai Zvi's movement (not Jakub Frank's, but Shabbetai Zvi's[6]); here they are! And they are going to do something great—to avenge the Jewish people! As for me, as I said, I was for revenge operations, but I absolutely refused to support what they did, things like poisoning wells, rivers, and such. Even after everything the Germans had done to us, Jewish humanism couldn't be destroyed. I wouldn't have taken part in "blind" operations against masses, acts of collective revenge. In my opinion, they should have taken means of individual retribution; and you could look for names of specific people who were notorious. Selectivity and judgment were required. The mass activities that were prepared weren't a response; they were just stooping to the level of the enemy. That was craziness.

In Poland, however, that wasn't the question because you couldn't do either one. If we had been united, it might have been different. But part of our forces were in Romania; we hadn't yet seen Shlikhim from Eretz Israel. If we had worked with all our might in all areas, revenge would

6. Jakub Frank (1726–1791): Jewish false messiah, who claimed to be the reincarnation of Shabbetai Zvi; Frank founded the antirabbinical Frankist sect, abandoning Torah for "a higher Torah," based on the Zohar; eventually, the movement joined the Polish Catholic Church.

also have been on the agenda and then, in my opinion, we would have directed it into other channels, carried out other kinds of operations. Keep in mind that we were in a country of pogroms, where Hitler's acts continued in a Polish version; where, on the one hand, there was a new government that wanted to defend us but couldn't, and could barely defend its own regime, whereas its best people, the Communists, were being killed every day. As far as they were concerned, the murder of Jews wasn't separate, but was part of their own problem.

As for me and my position, I was always opposed to collective, anonymous punishment, just because people belong to some group or other. For example, back in the days of the ghetto, there was an argument with Hirsh Berlinski who routinely expressed the notion of *avekleygn*! (Do away with him!) About everything: Do away with him! I thought then that if a person was guilty, he should be sentenced to death, but I couldn't participate in collective punishment, to this day.

After Abba Kovner left for Eretz Israel, the whole group of "avengers" remained in Romania like a flock without a shepherd. One day, a delegation of them from Germany came to me in Warsaw with two concrete issues: first, they asked me for information on the transport of money that was to come to the Joint. Since they were hard-pressed for means, they intended to rob the money to finance their activities. They also wanted me to give them dollars (which I had) to tempt a man in the black market to come to them for an exchange deal. Then, they planned to steal whatever money he had.

I must say that I responded sharply, although I started out speaking nicely: why rob money from the Joint? I asked them. Aren't there banks in Germany? You want to steal the money to help Jews? That's why you had to come to Poland?! And as for that black market speculator, I said: are we only talking about money? You've got guns; what if the speculator starts shouting? Will you kill him? The Poles are murdering Jews, the AK is murdering Jews, the NSZ is murdering Jews. And you too will murder Jews, for revenge?!

They appealed to me personally: they didn't have a leader and they came to me on behalf of the group to offer me the job. In my heart, I agreed; but I told them I would give them an answer later. Leviteh and other Shlikhim attended a meeting of Dror around that time, where I said that, since Abba Kovner had withdrawn, the group had been led by someone they didn't really accept and they had asked me to be their commander. The discussion concluded with a positive decision, but on condition that I go to Paris and meet with leaders of the Hagana. The Shlikhim also agreed.

I first visited Germany and met with people there, and went on to Paris, where I met with Nahum Shadmi, the Hagana man in Paris. I don't remember where we met, I only remember an apartment on the first floor. I told my tale and was asked if I obeyed the authority of the Hagana in Eretz Israel. When I said yes—now I'm quoting—he said: "As long as there is even one of that group in Europe, he is superfluous. If that's what they're trying to do, their immigration to Eretz Israel should be accelerated and the group should be dismantled."

If I had joined the revenge group, as commander, I would probably have been guided by another conception—my opinion was close to those who operated by searching for criminals and didn't work blindly. If I had thought you could annihilate the German people like that, I might have answered: if they annihilated us as a people, we will annihilate them. But to take revenge indiscriminately on a city, a village? And if I killed a thousand, even ten thousand, what would I accomplish?

If I had accepted the command, I would have tried to change the line. First, I would have set up an investigation to search for open and hidden Nazis who were swarming in Germany. In my mind's eye, I see the camp at Dachau, where SS men were imprisoned; I saw them playing basketball, football. How they looked! I would choose selectivity. But as I said, things didn't get to that. The envoys who came to me in Warsaw made a harsh impression on me. Incidentally, they didn't carry out their robbery plan after I warned them and even threatened them if they tried to touch the money intended to help Jews. And I remember the impression that group made on Leviteh, who told me about it: "The man was dressed altogether in a special way—his hat, his suit, everything about him seemed to say: I'm extraordinary, I'm different, I'm an avenger."

My tie to Revenge was broken. When I came to Eretz Israel, Yitzhak Sadeh[7] told me the secret of some of those issues: among other things, he wanted to consult with me after receiving an alarm from abroad where unsuccessful acts of revenge were committed and people were imprisoned. Ultimately, revenge was perverse romanticism, which totally unhinged a few people. It was simply a product of constant living with tension, ready for vengeance and killing—and not carrying it out. When there's no relief, there are complexes, emotional distress, which comes from inactivity, from a situation opposed to action. We also endured harsh conditions in Poland; but there was something to do for a young Jew: he organized seminars, set up training programs, aspired to immigrate to Eretz Israel. But for them, there were no bridges between vision and action that could be implemented by any individual. There was just thinking night and day about the great revenge. Such acts aren't done by groups; only individuals can do something. And those who did them

7. Yitzhak Sadeh (1890–1952): Creator of the Palmakh (the strike force of the Jewish underground) and its first commander.

should tell about them. They had partial successes and great failures. People came back to Poland broken and crushed. In sum, there was no revenge. There were words, there was talk that went on for months and filled their whole existence.

Did crossing the Romanian border solve the problems? Nothing was solved. On the contrary, the problems were just beginning.

I have often been asked about my trips to Germany. Did I see the Germans from a Jewish or a human perspective? Did I see them as the Germans of the time of the ghetto or as petit bourgeois paterfamilias? Was there a change in me? I must say that I saw the Germans all the time—and even to this day—as I saw them in the ghetto, in the *Aktsias*. I can't get away from that; perhaps that's my weakness. Oskar Hendler, who came to Poland from the Soviet Union with Abba Kovner, lived with me as before in Lwów when we shared a bed; now we lived in the same apartment in Warsaw. Day and night, I heard his stories of the Soviet Union; he concluded that the Jews had to go west from Poland, through Germany, to Eretz Israel.

Later I visited Germany a few times and, if I had to be there, I was forced to ignore the Germans so I could live so as to justify my life to myself, which means always being aware that I came there to the Jews, and that the Germans didn't exist for me; because if they did exist I would have to leave everything and devote myself to revenge. So I didn't see them, wasn't interested in them, didn't go to their cities, didn't see their glory, didn't see their museums. I saw the Germans, of course, since they lived in Germany; but my sights were fixed constantly on the Jews. I spent most of my time in the DP camps; I was in Munich, but I practically didn't see Munich. I went through many cities, and nothing of them remains in my memory.

I remember Italy very well—Milan, Via Ognana 5 and more. But nothing of Germany remains in my memory, except for the camps. To this day, I don't respond to greetings from a German, but I can't and won't take revenge the way they wanted to. Moreover, there won't be revenge; those are idle words. However, I don't have any contact with them; if a German, an anti-Nazi, writes to me personally, I answer him. If he hides behind some institution, I don't answer. I didn't answer a letter I got a month ago from a group of famous professors and scientists asking me to join some committee. If a German who came out of the camps himself or an anti-Fascist fighter writes to me, those are the letters I'm willing to answer. But when a German asks me for an article in a newspaper, I don't answer him. But I'm not willing to kill every German indiscriminately. I don't hate every German; but I have to know who the person is. Anton Schmidt, who was an Austrian, won my undying love.

Here's a story from those days. One day, probably in late January or in February 1945, I came to the Jewish Committee of Warsaw, not the Central Jewish Committee, but the house in Praga. I saw a gathering: in one of the rooms they surrounded a person with shouts. I didn't know him. I asked what happened, and they told me that the man had been a policeman in the ghetto. I knew two brothers, Jewish police in the ghetto during the *Aktsia*, who did fine service for the Germans.

I rescued that Jew from the shouting, the fists, and the curses, and an attempt to hurt him. I took him into a room and started talking with him: who are you? What are you? He said he didn't want to talk to me, but would talk with someone from the Jewish Fighting Organization. Well then, I said, you're talking with one. Then he panicked and started defending himself. When I heard his story, I said: you will tell all those things to the authorities. I called the UB and said I had a Jewish traitor, who had led Jews to death. A while later, some militiamen appeared and took him away. Within two weeks, one of the guards came to me (one of those who had helped the Jewish Fighting Organization), and said: You know, the man they arrested is free in Łódz.

I sent people to find out where he was hiding. We didn't know if he had escaped, but at any rate, he was walking around free. We caught him again in Łódz. I was there. This time, I decided not to give him to the Poles; the fact is they freed him. I got in touch with the staff of the Russian army, and again said there was a traitor here. Some time later, I learned that that policeman was once again walking around free. How? I didn't know. That was in April 1945, and I was sick. The first time after the war that I suffered from very strong pains, real torments. Apparently something was developing in my back and sides, and I was in terrible pain. A doctor friend of mine from the underground wanted to put me in the hospital, and other friends said nothing worked better than vodka. One day, I was also alone in my apartment on Poznańska. I always slept with a gun under my pillow since there were attacks by gentiles. My head was toward the door, and I didn't see who came in. A man entered and asked if he could talk to me; I said yes and he went to the window; I saw that it was that policeman I had arrested twice—once with the help of the Polish militia and once with the aid of the Russians—and he said to me: I came to you to judge me!

I didn't know what he wanted. He started talking and, with one hand, I pulled the pistol from under my pillow. He told me the story I later found was true: he bribed the Poles and Russians, escaped from Poland, and reached Czechoslovakia, where he had family. They were two brothers and one sister, and I don't know how they got to Czechoslovakia, back before the war. Apparently he did that contemptible work to save his mother. I asked him if he had saved his mother. He answered no. And the Germans took his brother, too.

He reached Prague, met with his sister who was one of the heroines of the underground. Her husband was on the staff of *Rude Prawo*, the Communist newspaper. He told me: I started hating myself; put an end to me! And he returned from Czechoslovakia to Warsaw and came to my apartment. I remember everything clearly. I was sick in bed. It was in April because I remember giving a speech on April 19, 1945, while I was sick and it was around that date. If he intended to murder me, he could have; I was weak, lying there with a fever and in terrible pain. When he finished, I said: "Get out of here fast!" No, I didn't forgive him, absolutely not.

Beginning at that time, early January 1945, I decided I wouldn't issue any more death sentences. Objectively, it was right to execute that person, definitely—yes! But there's no end to that, once you start. So I wanted to try him, but he escaped that. Now he came because his conscience oppressed him and he wanted to commit suicide. Should I have killed him? In those days, I was becoming increasingly aware that we had to put an end to issuing sentences and their partisan execution.

In those days, I also lectured at our seminars. And it's no distinction that I was one of the "important" lecturers. As I said, Tuvia Borzykowski played a first-class role in it.

The Shlikhim from the kibbutz arrived one by one, before the delegation of the Yishuv, which is a story in itself. Motl Tirosh came before Zvi Ze'ira, who was the first; and Zvi Netzer came later. I met with Zvi Netzer in Milan, where various problems came up. Two perspectives were popular at the time. According to one perspective, we should form a Halutz movement; and I was then in favor of a united Halutz movement of Dror and Ha-Shomer Ha-Tza'ir and perhaps other groups, too. At any rate, the idea was to shape a Socialist-Zionist Halutz force. I emphasize, even though the word seems loathsome to me today—*Socialist*. The other perspective was the path of the "unity of Israel," expressed by the Brigade in Romania and later in Poland as well, in Ikhud. They also tried to use the Bund to damage us; and even the Communists played a role in this because they wanted to see all Zionists with "all their eggs in one basket," so that all Zionist groups would have only one representative on the committee. Later, the NOHAM [No'ar Halutzi Meuchad] organization arose in Germany, and Mapai rode that wave. They thought if there was unity, it would lead to a Mapai framework. PHH was another story, an organization of fighters based on the broad principle encompassing all people (soldiers, partisans), whether they were Revisionists or Socialists.

I'm "known for my modesty," and I don't intend to deviate from it, but I must say that I was the initiator of PHH. The objective common denominator of that organization was Jewish fighting; the person was in PHH, whether he fought in the forest or in the ghetto—even without arms, since he might not have had the opportunity. PHH was established as soon as we began to aim at molding a force, in early 1945, when I came on partisans and saw who they were. Unlike the members of the Jewish Fighting Organization, who were all from the movements, with a movement, political, and educational "birth certificate," the people from the forest were mostly various kinds of random people who reached the forest by force of circumstance. They included Communists, Revisionists, Halutzim, and ordinary Jews who later returned to their "ordinariness," with all Jewish customs: underhanded trading, black marketeering, trips to Germany and back, that whole rotten situation they had been used to before the war—they returned to their evil ways.

When I saw that great mass of Jews—and, until I came to Lublin, I didn't know they even existed—I didn't know there had been such Jews fighting in the forests; my first thought was that they should be organized. The Communists didn't have to be organized because the party organized them. The question was how to organize that popular Jewish force, none of whom, in his own way, saw their place in Poland and wanted to leave. PHH unified them, but wasn't part of the idea of unity that arose among us. PHH was created simply in meetings with people who impressed me—it began in Lublin and I moved it to Warsaw, since I moved to Warsaw. In meetings, it turned out that although I knew a lot, I didn't know everything.

It turned out that the general values of the Histadrut and contact with Eretz Israel were the natural basis for the crystalization of thousands; there were about five or six thousand members in PHH, some of whom were also active in the movements. They also included Revisionists and Halutzim, as well as members of Dror, Ha-Shomer Ha-Tza'ir, Gordonia, and ordinary Jews who found their way to that movement; my dream was that those people would be fighters in Eretz Israel. They had gone through the Holocaust as fighters, and you didn't have to know exactly what was going on in Eretz Israel to foster such a dream. If you dreamed of a Jewish State of Israel—and that was in black and white, in our press back in 1941 and 1942—you knew the State wouldn't be given to us on a silver tray. At that time, we couldn't have said it so nicely; we did expect what was about to happen. And I hoped they would be fighters and settlers. Our members were the dominant influence within PHH. First, because they knew us as ghetto fighters, as an authority. We even found some of our old members, some of whom now live in Israel; not all of them went to the kibbutz. They weren't required to go to the kibbutz in PHH.

Legitimization to form that organization wasn't required in Poland, where any organization could be set up. For example, He-Halutz was given legitimation, and we published a newspaper. Later, printed material of PHH also appeared. In Germany and in Poland, a lot was published and is all in the archive of He-Halutz. The government of Poland did confiscate the archive, but the material is in Israel. Zvi Netzer made sure it got to us.

From that framework of PHH, people immigrated to Israel. And that's also part of Brikha. Could you manage Brikha so that someone stayed at the border or somewhere else and called on the Jews to immigrate to Eretz Israel? Brikha and the illegal immigration were realized by forces that crystalized into a framework, groups, units. We built PHH on the scale of the partisan unit. These were paramilitary frameworks. The common denominator was very general: the inclination toward the Labor Histadrut in Eretz Israel. Not the kibbutz, not the party, just the general Histadrut; that is, a constructive base. That was how we organized PHH and they streamed to us. They had to because each of them was fleeing his own isolation, since he had nothing; and those people knew how to get along; most of them were young. They could find their way somehow, but they were seeking a society. And we gave them the ideology, the shape. They didn't have to form PHH in order to drink vodka in a group and play cards. We gave them a bit of inspiration. They existed until they immigrated to Eretz Israel by forming kibbutzim. Who wanted to work? Gentiles didn't want to work at that time either. The Joint helped, and maybe a few did work, but most didn't. From morning to night, they were busy with speculation. You couldn't change much in their life style at that time. We closed our eyes to it, but we shaped them. Shalom Cholawski played the central role here; but his opinions weren't accepted by his comrades in Ha-Shomer Ha-Tza'ir. But I was happy he came; I had known him in Vilna. We met again during the "honeymoon" with Ha-Shomer Ha-Tza'ir. He was excited about PHH and invested himself in it, gave his all—first in Poland and later in Germany.

Thus we shaped a Halutz, movement, ideological force; and we molded a general, Jewish force, PHH. But, the moment they crossed the borders of Poland, going to Germany or Italy, they met members of Mapai who, with all their love of Israel and the majesty of Jewish unity they talked of, also held a whip. The keys to UNRRA were in their hands; and first of all, they began destroying the organization ideologically, thus damaging the weakest link—and everything was done in the name of unity. That hurt me terribly and does to this day: in the name of Jewish unity, in the name of Israel, how could they have brandished that whip! I'm willing to present this evidence against the members of Mapai to the whole world!

I don't know the Mapai central members who were active in that; but it's enough for me to mention the name of Z. Hering. Things didn't just happen, but came down from above. In Poland, they couldn't do anything because they were on the fringes; but the ones in Germany—Mordechai Sorkis,[8] Duvdevani,[9] and others—began knocking down the organization and so they occasionally called me to come urgently because everything was about to collapse. That hurt me a lot since we were putting things together and they were taking them apart. The greatest damage was in PHH since they forced the members to join Mapai, which made me mad because there were people in that organization who had belonged to us from the first, and I wasn't at all interested in that party side of things; I didn't even care that Yosef Kaplan, the partisan who was so close to me, was a Revisionist when I met him. I loved him as a partisan, as a Jewish fighter. But if someone had come along and tried to turn PHH into a Revisionist organization, could I have agreed to that? Mapai, however, wanted to bring the members into their party. So, I said: That's enough! And they didn't succeed.

I had already visited Milan after August 1945, apparently in September. They called me to come urgently and I came at once. That was only one of my trips. As I said, it was after the London conference. Suddenly, I was called to come urgently because they said Mapai was undermining the force we had shaped. I always left Poland with a passport in my real name. Those passports were provisional; you needed a special one for every trip. Poland didn't have diplomatic relations with every country and so, to reach my destination, I had to go to a country with diplomatic relations. For example, I could get to France and Italy, but I also had to go to other countries in Europe.

On a previous occasion, I was told that Reale, the Italian ambassador in Poland, wanted to see me; but I didn't go to him then. But this time, when I was in trouble because the French wouldn't give me a visa, I remembered Reale's invitation. I decided to find out where he was lodging and went to him. A secretary greeted me, and I said I wanted to see Mr. Reale. I was asked to wait because he was out. But I was also told I would receive an answer immediately. I was put in a room with a dark young woman, a real Italian, and was amazed when she hugged me and

---

8. Mordechai Sorkis (b. 1908): Born in Russia, immigrated to Eretz Israel in 1932. Member of the secretariat of Mapai. Mobilized in the British Army during World War II and served in the Jewish Brigade. One of the leaders of Brikha in Europe just before the establishment of the State of Israel. Served as mayor of Kfar Saba and as a member of the Knesset.

9. Yehiel Duvdevani: One of the founders of Kibbutz Giv'at Ha-Shlosha and active in Ha-Kibbutz Ha-Meuchad. Active member of the committee of volunteers for the Allied armies, worked with institutions of Holocaust survivors.

began speaking Yiddish. It turned out this was Reale's wife, who was the daughter of none other than Alter Kacyzne, the famous writer and photographer from Warsaw.[10] When I sat down, she served me coffee and refreshments; she told me her tale and I told her mine.

I'm not responsible for the accuracy of things; after all, it's been thirty years. I never saw her again, even though I did promise to visit her. I do know she was in Israel and looked for me, but I didn't get to see her. At that time, she told me she had been with her father during the war in Lwów, where he was murdered. Afterward, she was in a concentration camp, near an Italian army base, and the soldiers there helped Jews. She became friendly with one of the soldiers. When the Italians evacuated the rear for their German allies, the latter sent the Italian soldiers back home, and then her Italian friends decided to rescue her. They dressed her in a uniform and she returned with the Italian soldiers as if she were returning home. One of the soldiers who saved her was Reale, a veteran Communist. They got married and after the war, he was appointed Italian representative or ambassador in Poland.

Incidentally, a few years ago, the Poles published Reale's memoirs of Poland. For years, he was one of the distinguished representatives of the Communist Party, until, like many others, he resigned from the Italian Communist Party. He was a senator for many years. So that was the story of Alter Kacyzne's daughter. Reale's book was published here in Yiddish.

I got the visa within minutes, but our conversation went on a long time. I don't remember if I used the visa; but as I recall, because of the Italian visa, I also got a French visa. I usually left Poland legally, since I got the necessary visas. As for that case of Milan, I went to ask for a visa to Czechoslovakia and was told to come get it the next day; I was to get a passport that had to be renewed at intervals, and I would have to get a new one. When I came to get the passport, the secretary told me that the acting foreign minister, Modzelewski, wanted to see me.[11] I went in to Modzelewski, whom I knew from the underground; he asked some questions and began talking about the Jews, the situation; among other things, he asked me why the Jews were leaving Poland illegally. I gave him a diplomatic answer that I didn't know about that but, if it were true, it was apparently because they couldn't get out legally. Then he asked me where I was going, and I said I would be in France and perhaps some other countries.

10. Alter Kacyzne (1885–1941): Born in Vilna. Yiddish writer and photographer, lived in Warsaw. He tried to escape to Tarnopol in 1941, was caught by Ukrainian collaborators, and beaten to death. His daughter Shulamit Reale published the first volume of his collected works in 1967.

11. Zygmunt Modzelewski (1900–1954): Spent the war in the Soviet Union. From 1944 to 1947, Deputy Minister of Foreign Affairs; from 1947 to 1951, Minister of Foreign Affairs.

Then he told me I could inform the French government in his name that if the Jewish institutions could get French visas for Polish Jews, the Poles would give their holders unlimited permission to leave. They would have given permission even without that, he said, but the English were making trouble for them about releasing Polish gold in London, if the Poles allowed the Jews to leave illegally for Eretz Israel. They were holding them by the neck, and wouldn't release their gold; and he requested consideration of Polish interests. I said I would deliver the message. Incidentally, I heard similar things after the Kielce pogroms from Osóbka-Morawski. I conveyed that the same day, by telephone, to Paris. Modzelewski asked me if I would also be in Prague, and I answered yes. He asked if I would hold a press conference, and I answered that I wasn't planning to. Then he asked that, if I could hold a press conference, he had something I could express (although not on behalf of the government of Poland and its foreign ministry) concerning the conflict between Poland and Czechoslovakia; I was to hint that the Poles were willing to find a peaceful solution, through talks.[12] I promised to do that if I had a chance and if there was a press conference. But there was no press conference and my concern was devoted to other issues, because in Bratislava, I changed into the clothes of a refugee.

I didn't get to Prague at all, but made my way to Italy. Sometimes I would take another route, across Czechoslovakia, just not to go through Germany. This time, I went from Bratislava to Austria, which was divided among the Allies, and then to Italy. I came to Bratislava and changed my clothes to look like a refugee. I left my things in Czechoslovakia and joined a transport of Greek Jews and our young people who were on their way to Italy. That was the only time I traveled in a transport, since I usually traveled alone. My route this time was: Czechoslovakia–Hungary–Austria–Italy.

My visa was valid for a month, and I indeed wanted to return in a month. When they put us on the train for Hungary, we got instructions "not to talk Yiddish"—they only knew Greek. But we didn't know Greek, so we spoke Hebrew. Not all of our traveling companions knew Greek either. We tried to stick together, not to be among strangers. There were no windows in the train and it was cold; that was September. As night approached, I sat with a group of comrades and, as I said, we agreed not to let a stranger into our car; the train stopped and two Red Army soldiers appeared in the door, armed, pushing inside, and holding the door by force, with curses and shouts; and the train stood still. We had to let them

12. The conflict concerned control over the Cieszyn area, a small disputed area between Czechoslovakia and Poland, which Hitler gave to Poland when he dismembered Czechoslovakia in March 1938, but was returned to the Czechs after the war.

in. It was dark in the train, which started to move; everything was silent until, all of a sudden, one of the refugees decided he had "something to say," but speaking Yiddish was forbidden. So he said something like: "May redemption come from heaven," and so forth—those words from the prayer. And all of a sudden, one of the "Russian" soldiers turns on a flashlight and says to the other soldier in Yiddish—I thought I'd die laughing—"*Moyshe, ikh hob dir gezogt az zey zaynen yidn.* (Moyshe, I told you they were Jews.)" It turned out the two soldiers were Jewish speculators disguised as Red Army soldiers, in order to smuggle gold or dollars. So we went back to speaking Yiddish among ourselves.

In Hungary, I met with members of the movement for the first time, with Zvi Goldfarb[13] and Neshka, as well as with members of Ha-Shomer Ha-Tza'ir and all the Halutz group. I spent a few days with them and also did something for them with the Joint, relying on Dr. Schwartz. But I did get money for them, while they bought me "human-looking" trousers.

In Hungary, I got hold of a smuggler who took me to Austria. I came to Graz, where I was struck by terrible pains in my back and neck for the first time. I couldn't move and the group recommended one medicine: liquor. But the more I drank the worse the pains got. It had something to do with my spine, but I didn't know that then; the pain was dreadful. I was generally healthy; such things had never happened to me. But because the visa was limited, I hurried. Time was running out. I did a little bit in Budapest and a little bit in Graz. I wanted to hurry to Milan, where the refugees were concentrated and the people from Eretz Israel were. Suddenly, Mordechai Sorkis, whom I didn't know, came to me and was friendly and affectionate. I was about to leave illegally for Italy and he was opposed to it. This time I did have a visa to Czechoslovakia and, to get to Italy, I crossed all the Brikha points on the borders. Then Sorkis (someone else was with him) told me he absolutely refused to let me cross illegally and would make sure someone came to take me legally. It would take three or four days, but it would be organized by the Brigade. To this day, I don't know what Sorkis's intentions were because I never asked him. Later, I suspected he wanted me to stay in Austria and not go to Italy. The car with the blue-and-white flag of the Brigade didn't come, nor did anything else. I was abandoned, I watched the days running out, and I decided to leave illegally for Milan.

They put us in a transport. Things were arranged in Graz with a bribe. They would get a train car, put the refugees in the freight cars, close them

13. Zvi Goldfarb: Dror activist in occupied Warsaw. Sent to Slovakia in spring 1941. Prominent in Halutz underground and Dror in Hungary. Active in Brikha after the war. Died in 1977 at the age of fifty-six.

from outside, pass the English checkpoints, and get to Italy. The Italians were sympathetic to the Jews, beyond all expectations. I was put into the car with the others, and we rode and rode, until the train suddenly stopped and stood still for twenty-four hours. We heard the voices of the English. Then it turned out there was some holiday and so the train was stopped at the border and remained in the English zone. There were children and women on the train and no lavatories. Children began crying and then we heard dogs barking. The English discovered us and took us all out of the cars. Since my measuring rod was always in comparison with what would have happened to me if I had been captured by the Germans, this was only a minor episode for me. They kept us for some time and gave us something to drink; we didn't have any food because the people in charge were sure our trip wouldn't last long, and we would soon be in Italy.

I hurried to Milan. I had to get back to Poland; my time was running out. There were a few partisans with me, and I explained to them that I had a few Jewish acquaintances in the area and would soon try to get away and cross the border. There were mountains and rivers. I don't remember which partisan I told to accompany me. The rest were to make sure no one joined us, because I had to get across the border to Italy in an hour. The partisans did what I asked, and that man went with me. We went into the water, since I could swim; rocks and stones bruised my feet, but I crossed the river, and then I saw my companion drowning. He went into the water too, even though he couldn't swim, but we didn't think the water was so deep. I went back to him on the English side. There was some half-destroyed bridge there which we tried to cross, but the dogs caught us and the soldiers took us back and took him to the British command staff. I didn't know English, and only knew a special "Viennese" German. I said I was a refugee, a Greek (and I did have Greek documents), and that I spoke some German. They put the two of us in separate cells; I didn't see the other Jews, and I didn't know whether they crossed that day or were brought back and crossed later. In fact, the whole thing was just a game, child's play.

Afterward, they released the two of us. I was wet from my dunking, and hungry. A few hours later, they put us in a railroad car and closed it from the outside. I thought they were taking us back to Austria. There was nothing to do; we sat together in that freight car; I lay down and fell asleep. We rode without seeing a thing. All of a sudden, at one of the stations, the door opened, and there I was in Italy. Did they plan it, did they close their eyes? Or did they make a mistake? I didn't know. When the Italian railroad worker opened the door, I really started kissing him. From there, I got to Padua. I remember the name because of Rabbi

Moshe Haim Luzzatto who had lived in that city.[14] I had no money, no food; I decided to look for Jews. I started asking, in all kinds of languages, and I realized that the Italians didn't know German. Or maybe they didn't want to speak German. But somehow I got to the home of the rabbi and found the rabbi's wife. I started speaking. Yiddish they didn't know; German they didn't know; Hebrew they didn't know. Italian I didn't know. Then she led me to the big clock and pointed and said something about the Sabbath, *Sabbato*; and I understood I had come on the Sabbath.

I understood that if I came back in twenty-four hours, I would see the rabbi who was probably praying at that time. I left and started walking in the streets and, suddenly, I saw two men walking in front of me. I decided they were from Poland because of their hats, which were familiar. I tried to get close, but I didn't hear what language they were speaking. They walked and I followed them. Thus we came to some square, and it turned out they really were Jews from Poland. I wasn't mistaken. They were speaking Yiddish. I went up to those Jews and said: Look, I'm so-and-so, I haven't got any money, I have to get to Milan. A fellow appeared and said: I know you; I'll give you money and I'll order you a taxi. When you've got money, give it back to me. That fellow came from Poland, maybe he was a partisan or a fighter. Here, in Padua, he was involved in speculation.

That's how I got to Milan, like thunder on a fair day, to Via Ognana 5, the lodging of the Mapai Shlikhim. I didn't have more than forty-eight hours to stay in Milan, but I did meet Ada Sereni[15] and Yehuda Arzi, and we had a long talk with the members of the Movement and with the partisans. They returned the money to the Jew from Padua, paid him back all the expenses he had advanced me in Italian Lire. Then I also met with Zvi Netzer (Melnitzer). Interestingly, Zvi doesn't remember and denies that we met; despite the clear proof I have, he insists we didn't meet in Milan. Such things happen. It's very strange that such a meeting would be erased from his memory; but it's a fact. He was my student, even before the war, when he was a pupil in the Gymnasia; and I was the one who brought him to the Movement in Kowel, when he was still a student; he, Sheindl Schwartz, Yankele Zabludovski—that whole Kowel group. When I met him in Milan, he was on his way from Eretz Israel to a mission

14. Moshe Haim Luzzatto (1707–1746): Kabbalist, writer of ethical works, and Hebrew poet and playwright.
15. Ada Sereni: Wife of Chaim (Enzo) Sereni, head of the Eretz Israel paratroopers who landed in German-occupied territories; he descended into Yugoslavia, was captured and killed. After his death, Ada became a central figure in the organization of illegal immigration to Palestine through Italy.

in Poland, to work in Brikha. Isser Ben-Zvi was already in Poland; and about that time, another Shaliah, Zvi Ze'ira, came from Yagur. I met him in Graz when he was on his way to Poland.

How did I leave Italy? Yehezkiel Sakharov (now Sahar) was then a major in the Brigade. He didn't have a vehicle from Graz to Milan, but my return trip was arranged with great honor. I met Yehezkiel Sahar, to whom I am grateful to this day; and at his order, they dressed me in a uniform of the Brigade and brought a barber who turned me into an English officer. All I had to do was learn to act like an Englishman. A member of the Brigade was supposed to escort us across the borders. All the way, I learned my number, in English, and I got a stick, since British officers walked around with a stick under their arm; as soon as they stopped us, I forgot all my English. It was lucky I wasn't asked anything, and that they only asked the driver questions. I crossed the border and arrived elegantly in Graz where I changed clothes and became a refugee again—and I met Zvi Ze'ira. He had big suitcases, and he was short. We had to sneak across the border from the English zone of Austria, through the Russian zone of Austria, to Hungary. I saw Ze'ira's suitcases and, on the way to Poland, I said to him: "Don't just think of me in these clothes; in Poland I'll give you more than you have here. Throw the suitcases away." But he was loathe to lose his suitcases. I told him: "I can't help you carry them"—because I had a backache; moreover, in principle, I didn't like suitcases; but he hung on to them.

Thus we crossed the borders and approached the border of the Soviet occupation zone and already saw the lights beyond the border. It was night; there was a bridge ahead of us. The guide led the way; I followed, leaning on my stick. That helped me a little; I didn't feel well. I walked next to the ledge and held onto it with one hand. We crossed the bridge, and then we discovered that one man was missing; and we were on the border, in the Soviet zone. And falling into Soviet hands isn't like falling into English hands. It could end in Siberia. One person was missing! We had no choice, we lit a flashlight and discovered who was missing—it turned out Ze'ira wasn't there. We went back across the bridge to look for him, and there he was, in the water. The bridge had been damaged by a bomb; the pedestrian footpath was very narrow. Ze'ira had been walking in the middle and, now, he and his two suitcases were in the water. We fished him out because the water wasn't deep. He was saved from drowning, but his suitcases stayed there. So we reached the border station. I'll never forget that station in Hungary. I was in pain, broken, dirty. The smuggler took us to spend the night with some Jews, and the next day, we reached Budapest. And then the same way back to Poland. Apparently, I was forty-eight hours beyond the deadline of the visa. First there was a question of how to sneak Ze'ira in, and our people arranged that.

When I went to the Polish consulate in Prague to extend my visa for a few more days, they told me they didn't have the authority to do that; but I went back to Poland without any problem.

This whole story has skirted the real issue, which was to shape our forces, to prevent collapse, to keep up spirits in all those places. That was the first job: to preserve the force. Second, I wanted to experience personally the passage, in a transport of Jews, to go through the experience of transit with them.

Such were passages to Italy. Passage to Germany, where I visited many times, was similar. In Germany, the issue assumed another character: there was a large concentration of refugees, but I wanted to see how the passage was done. It interested me; it was part of the operation, the Jewish experience. I got to Germany on my way to France, and I would also go there especially—at any rate, I would always go "solo." In this way, I met with masses of Jews in the Movement, bound for Eretz Israel. That was before the Shlikhim came from Eretz Israel. The fact is I met the first Shlikhim (Netzer, Ze'ira) in Italy or Austria later, and the Shlikhim from Eretz Israel hadn't yet come. Eretz Israel hadn't yet found a way to us in Poland.

Then, as a result of the meeting with Tsizling and Bar-Yehuda, and maybe also with Sharett, the Shlikhim started coming. At the meeting in London, we didn't have a common language. Even though the Shlikhim came late, every Shaliah was worth his weight in gold because we didn't have comrades at such a level—active, independent. You couldn't create them from scratch—we didn't have time. We didn't have any like them, and now we felt we weren't alone. Now a central group of people from Eretz Israel and local people began to take shape. Leviteh, the central Shaliah, came later. Motl Tirosh was stuck in Switzerland; but within twenty-four hours after receiving a telephone call or a telegram, I arranged to get him into Poland. The problem of getting into Poland didn't exist—you could get in legally or you could get in illegally. Only Eretz Israel didn't understand that.

I also remember the arrival of the delegation from the Yishuv. I was sitting in my apartment on Poznańska in Warsaw; Zivia was in Łódz. I was planning to ride a truck to Łódz that night. All of a sudden, the door opened and Leviteh, Pinhas Rashish,[16] Moshe Kol,[17] and somebody else

16. Pinhas Rashish (1895–1978): One of the founders of Giv'at Ha-Shlosha. Immigrated to Eretz Israel in 1925. Was secretary of the World Center of He-Halutz and a delegate to Zionist congresses. In 1946, he was a member of the Yishuv delegation to Poland.

17. Moshe Kol (Kolodny; b. 1911): Born in Pinsk. Israeli politician and liberal Zionist. Moved to Palestine in 1932. Was head of the Youth Aliya Department of the Jewish Agency from 1948 to 1964, and was elected to the Knesset several times and was a minister in many Israeli governments.

from Ha-Shomer Ha-Tza'ir came in. I was speechless with joy! After the kissing and the hugging, I had to tell them I was planning to go to Łodz because Zivia didn't feel well. Leviteh told Rashish that he would go with me, and Rashish asked to come along. There was then a general curfew in Poland because of the antisemitic attacks throughout the country. I told them it was very hard for me to take responsibility for them because the roads were dangerous; but, finally, I got a taxi from the Center of Jews in Poland, since now it wasn't simply a trip. Leviteh looked unmistakably Jewish, and I couldn't go my usual way. So I got hold of a car and went with them. I sat next to the driver and held onto two grenades and a gun. It was about as far as from Tel Aviv to Haifa, maybe a little more.[18] But the road was bad. Trains weren't yet going everywhere. Autumn was coming on.

We came to Polodniowa where our commune was. Zivia wasn't there. Rashish was also with us—and I'm sorry, he got upset. We sat in the commune and I told Leviteh I had to go because curfew was coming—and I had to get to Zivia, who was resting in Lodzia's apartment. (Lodzia was Tuvia's girlfriend.) Leviteh replied that he also had to see Zivia no matter what, and he absolutely refused to wait until the next day. That was at night. I had to go and Leviteh wouldn't give in. The next day, when Rashish learned of it, there was an unpleasant situation. He couldn't forgive me for that for years. I didn't mean to offend him, but I couldn't endanger the people either. Zivia should tell about the meeting with Leviteh, which was an extraordinary experience. How can I tell what was between them? Am I a poet?

The next day, I moved on, in response to a call from Shalom Cholawski in Germany that they were undermining the PHH. I had previously set the date of my arrival there because I didn't know such an important delegation would come and that Leviteh would be with us. That night, I left Zivia and the next day, I was on the way to Germany. I was young, I picked up a stick, and I was off!

In Germany, I fell into a confrontation with Mapai, with their Shlikhim in UNRRA, including Dr. Atzmon, who did the work, along with the survivors, from Lithuania, members of Mapai. When I came to Munich, I offered to work peacefully with them: in Poland, we formed a bloc, on a broad ideological base, which wasn't politically undefined. And when they came to Germany, our people were forced, administratively, to join Mapai because UNRRA was in their hands; the money was in their hands; and the power was in their hands. That was how they treated the partisans, who included thousands with no political knowledge, who couldn't even distinguish between the political parties! I couldn't believe they were

18. That is, about seventy-five or eighty miles.

putting them into a political and party framework like that! I argued that it was impossible for us to do the general intellectual work in Poland and for them to turn everything upside down here and put people into a party cell. I wanted to reach a peaceful agreement with them. I offered various suggestions, but they were stubborn since they had control over things in Germany.

I stayed in Germany a few days. We called a conference of partisans who came en masse; if memory serves me right, the conference was held in Munich. The great majority dispensed with all that and left Mapai ashamed, after getting dumped on. The organization remained unaffiliated and continued to include all those who had fought.

Before my trip to Germany, I didn't know Aharon Berdyczewski, who wrote about the early years of He-Halutz Ha-Tza'ir. I had only come across his name from time to time. I once rode with Oskar Hendler, my host, in a car Oskar had gotten for that purpose. On the way, the car suddenly stopped next to a person, perhaps because of Oskar, who I think knew Berdyczewski. He was wearing an UNRRA uniform but looked anything but military. We had heard of each other. He was a member of Kibbutz Yagur. We hugged and kissed. That meeting was on one of the roads of Germany, on my travels. From there, I went to the Swiss border, to Saint Galen. Pino Ginzburg was then stationed in Switzerland and Saint Galen was on the Swiss side. At any rate, Oskar and I came to the border to help the movement in Germany and Poland. I crossed the border into Switzerland. We wanted to set up a kibbutz from the German side. There were many suitable places for setting up kibbutzim, but we were looking for a place to be a base for our contact with Switzerland, too. Now I learned that this German border town was ruled by a group of Jewish thugs, including many black marketeers from Vilna. When they heard the idea of setting up a base for the Halutzim here, they requested a meeting with us, at which they almost injured me physically. I stood alone opposite them—I remember to this day how Oskar sat pale as they waved their fists at me—these were underworld characters who were corrupt and degenerate after the war. I expected them to attack me since they controlled the place. Nothing I said to them helped, but ultimately, they didn't hurt me. They stood waving their fists at me, approached me, and I stood facing them and waiting. If they had wanted to, they could have hit me. Only Oskar was with me. We needed to set up our base there, because in the existing situation, Pino couldn't even transfer money to us. They bribed the Swiss guards; they controlled a bridge you had to cross to get across the border.

I left Germany, and I don't know if we set up a base there or not. I met with Pino Ginzburg in Switzerland, in the home of a local Jewish notable. When I entered that house, I was scared by the polished, gleaming parquet floor, as slippery as ice. They welcomed me nicely. Pino took care to advertise me as someone who was fond of a drink. We agreed in principle about helping our Movement in Germany.

That was one of my trips. I visited Germany several times with Oskar. I went to Italy and Austria only once.

The Jews made their way to Germany on foot. First were those who came from the camps, who knew they didn't have anything or anyone to look for in Poland; and they remained in Germany. They were exiled here by the Germans; even those who had been in labor camps or concentration camps until January 1945 were transferred to Germany by the Germans with the advance of the Russian army; they hurried them on foot, on trains, in cattle cars, with one purpose—not to let go of them. After the surrender, trains loaded with Jews were found standing on their tracks in Germany. But most of the camps were in Poland.

I didn't know some of these things. The war ended only in May, and Oskar came up with the idea of concentrating the Jews in Germany, even before the end of the war. The Jews did indeed behave as he expected. They had no reason to stay in Poland. There was no reason to go to Romania, since by then we had information that you couldn't go from there to Eretz Israel; and Oskar's idea was to concentrate Jews where we could lead them out—either to Italy or to France; in any event, to the sea! At the sea, there was a place of concentration. That was a correct idea, and then came the idea that a concentration of Jews in Germany would be mainly in the American zone, which was the most convenient for us. From our perspective, the worst, naturally, were the English. I visited all the zones; I toured all those camps. The treatment of Jews in those camps was brutal. True, it was hard for them to maintain control, but it was very hard to bear that treatment, after the Germans—the camp commanders, the armed guards, and the coarse, unrestrained language.

Life in the camps was degenerate, a life of idleness supported by charity. But there weren't any barbed wire fences; there was freedom. But no Jew would have escaped from there. In 1945 or 1946, the Jews were ready for that life. It wasn't hard for them to get used to it. For there was no direct emotional passage from 1939 to 1945. It was a passage from 1945 before the victory to May, after the victory, and the Jews got used to it. The movements, the Shlikhim had to plow deep, undertake a mighty educational work, in order to restore these people to humanity.

These were the conditions in which Yosef Rosensaft of Bergen-Belsen, now a millionaire, could amass a fortune.[19] Did he make his

---

19. Yosef Rosensaft (b. 1911): Born in Będzin. Prior to World War II, he was a scrap metal dealer; in 1943, he escaped from the train to Auschwitz and walked back to Będzin ghetto. Subsequently sent to Auschwitz and transferred to Bergen-Belsen, where he was liberated

money by working? Arye Palokh, who was sent from Łódz Ghetto to Auschwitz and came to Germany, is now a millionaire and they write about him in the papers. These were people who could make deals, every one of them was involved in profiteering, while carrying on negotiations with their "beloved" Germans. Of all people, the Jews were the sharpest mediators between the Germans on the one hand and the Americans and English on the other. It was the corruption of the Americans and of the Germans, but the Jews were in the middle, working as mediators.

Haim Gouri's story, *The Chocolate Deal*, tells of that reality.[20] And we have to say that all the movements did an extremely important Jewish national work. They gave something to the people, they gave them God, an inspiration.

The delegation that came to Poland in February 1946 was from the Yishuv in Eretz Israel; and it came officially, in terms of the Polish authorities. Every one of the members of the delegation had an entrance permit. They were received by the authorities, but they didn't have much to do. They didn't have anything to request from the authorities. The parties existed officially, so most of the members of the delegation returned; one of the few who stayed for a long time was Leviteh. Even the Bund held a reception for them, and they also met with the Central Committee of the Jews in Poland. I don't think the Bund really could have done anything against the delegation, even if they wanted to. The same goes for the Communists, since the delegation was received officially by the Communist state. At the same time, the Anglo-American Committee of Enquiry Regarding the Problems of European Jewry and Palestine also visited Poland and I also appeared before it.[21] The Jewish Communists also joined with the Zionist demands, since that was the position of the Polish Communist Party; today it's hard to understand that there was such a time. So you have to understand relations with the Communists at that time. I didn't accept the Jewish solution according to the Communists, but I'm talking now about a general way of life and the attitude about the Zionist solution. Some people don't understand and you can't explain to

---

in April 1945. Was chairman of the camp committee of Bergen-Belsen survivors and chairman of the Committee of Jewish DPs in the British zone of Germany until 1950. Helped smuggle Jews to Eretz Israel. Lived in the United States and Switzerland; president of the World Federation of Bergen-Belsen Survivors.

20. Haim Gouri (b. 1923): Born in Tel Aviv. Israeli poet and novelist. His novel, *The Chocolate Deal*, was published in Hebrew in 1968.

21. The Anglo-American Committee of Enquiry was appointed in November 1945. It recommended that the United States and Britain should try to find other places than Palestine for Jewish DPs and that 100,000 Certificates for Palestine should be issued immediately.

them how Yitzhak Zuckerman could have been an admirer of that regime in Poland. After recent years, it may be hard to describe that milieu, that atmosphere; but we must admit that the state of Poland was then on the side of the Jews, on the side of the national solution of the Jewish question.

The fact is that at that time, in all my conversations and meetings with the leaders of Communist Poland, various kinds of meetings, there was such an attitude. Not that all the Communists wanted it; on the contrary, I think the Jewish Communists went along reluctantly, following the orders of their party. I don't recall that the Anglo-American Committee held a referendum among the Jews of Poland as to whether they chose to remain in Poland or wanted to go to Eretz Israel.[22] But I have no doubt that, except for groups of Communists and the Bund and opportunists who got jobs or benefits, not a single Jew thought for even one moment of staying in Poland; there is no doubt that most of the Jews wanted to leave Poland, even though not all of them wanted to immigrate to Eretz Israel. The fact is that there was also a stream that flowed to the United States or other countries; many remained in France or Germany and renewed the Jewish community organization in Germany. Nevertheless, most of the Jews then wanted to immigrate to Eretz Israel, to be with Jews. Remaining in Poland was the last thing an ordinary Jew wanted.

I must say that the official position of the Bund was the sharpest and silliest position opposed to Zionism. Their words and acts were not only against Zionism, but also against themselves. It was self-destruction, but they didn't understand it. Most others had no choice, since they were Poles and Poland was their homeland; but the Bundists could have been Bundists in any free place in the world, and they didn't understand there wouldn't be room for the Bund in Poland. Their whole war against Zionism, against our people, was anachronistic; and the same goes for their opposition to the exodus of the Jews. The Jewish Communists were also opposed to the exodus initially but, as soon as they got the hint from the Party leadership, their position changed. That was still before the establishment of the PZPR—when the Communists and the PPS were separate parties.[23] The Bund's position was in "outer space," since the Jewish Communists knew by then not to oppose the exodus of the Jews, whereas the Bund was stuck with its old position. One day, I passed a decision in the Jewish Central Committee to establish bases for sleeping and eating on the borders—the Joint provided money—for Jews who

22. UNRRA did hold a referendum in the DP camps at the request of the Anglo-American committee. More than 95 percent of those asked answered that they wanted to migrate only to Eretz Israel, though, in fact, many of them eventually immigrated to Canada, the United States, and other countries.

23. In 1948, the PPR (Polish Workers' Party) and the PPS (Polish Socialist Party) forcibly merged to form the PZPR (Polish United Workers' Party).

were leaving. What made me bring up such a suggestion? I knew that the Polish Communists had gotten such orders from their Party, and so had the members of the Jewish Central Committee, which was controlled by the Communists; I also knew that the Joint had the permission of the Polish government to put up the money necessary for the Jews who were leaving. The Bundists were the only ones who didn't understand the reality they were living in. I made this proposal not because I was smarter, but because I already knew what was happening among the Communists; and I knew I had support; and I knew that if the Jewish Communists didn't yet know, they would know within twenty-four hours. For they would go denounce the exodus to the authorities and then they would find out the truth of the matter. So I knew from the start what answer the Jewish Communists would get when they went to protest the "injustices" the Zionists were perpetrating on the Jews of Poland and the state. The answer they got was: "When historical processes are taking place, the role of the Communist Party is to take the lead and not lag behind." Nor did the members of the Bund know everything I did. Nor were they aware of the situation even after the pogroms of Kielce, until they were told explicitly.

FIFTEEN

The Pogroms in Kielce and the Great Brikha

Departure from Poland

In my opinion, those who study Brikha, including Y. Bauer, would do well to devote more space to the sources of this phenomenon. Such a tendency would certainly demonstrate that through the years of the Halutz movement, either openly or underground, either in the German or the Soviet occupation zone, there were efforts to get to Eretz Israel. And there were quite a few failures, too. But the failures were also part of that effort. For example, for me, the uprising in Częstochowa is just as important as the Warsaw Uprising. The fellows in Warsaw who picked up guns and attacked the Germans did what they could; they had no more strength and they didn't have a better organization. But Częstochowa is not inferior to other places because of the way they acted; they are as good as the fighters in the Warsaw Ghetto.

The same can be said about the effort to get to Eretz Israel illegally. The principle is that you don't consider borders, laws, regulations. That's how it was before the Liberation and that's how it was after the Liberation. And even before the war, as far as I know, there were struggles in Eretz Israel between the leaders of the nation and the members of He-Halutz and the kibbutz about illegal immigration. That struggle within the Labor Movement existed even in the late thirties. One faction argued that illegal immigration hurt the political and diplomatic struggle. We shared the position that encouraged getting to Eretz Israel in every way.

As for the period beginning in January 1945, the period I know well, Brikha has to be divided into three stages: in terms of time, the number of people who took part in it, and the nature of Brikha.

In the first stage, there was the exodus of a few to Romania; first a delegation went which included Lidovski, Zivia, and Abba Kovner; and a few dozen followed in their wake—only a few dozen. I don't know if the total who assembled in Romania amounted to a hundred and fifty or two hundred people. I can only say that, from a historical perspective, there were few of them who went the wrong way, and there was an attempt to keep the action it completely secret from the Committee of the Jews in Poland.

That was in January and February 1945 (no longer during the war) and I had to invent all kinds of excuses for Zivia's disappearance. I would say she was sick, she was pregnant, I put her in the hospital someplace—until the Communists concluded that Zivia had left Poland. I don't know if they were also looking for Abba Kovner; I imagine they were. They knew him from Lublin and I knew they admired him. They tried to put him on the Jewish Central Committee, when the committee was based in Lublin, but he spared no effort to avoid it. I disagreed with him about that. Perhaps Dr. Emil Sommerstein didn't tell him what he told me. The main thing is to praise the people who organized Brikha for taking responsibility for it. They took responsibility for it! No one gave it to them. Did responsibility for the fate of the last Jews expire on the day of the Liberation? Remember, I have often emphasized that if our responsibility were "limited," we could have left Poland, even before the Vilna group, and crossed the border to Slovakia. But I don't know if we would have succeeded. That argument took place all the time, in several areas. If there had been a central committee, responsible for all issues—for Brikha and for organizing the survivors, and for revenge—then Zivia could have stayed with Abba Kovner and Yitzhak Zuckerman would have gone, and someone else could have led the revenge group. But that could only have been if there were general responsibility and a conception of general responsibility for everything. When those people left for Romania, I wanted Zivia to go with them. We were very isolated; keep in mind the war wasn't yet over; it was over for Abba Kovner, for Lidovski, even for Zivia, and for Yitzhak Zuckerman—but not for the Jewish people. Nor for the world. Berlin wasn't yet conquered. Sometimes we tend to forget the situation. We didn't know what was happening in the camps. We didn't know what was going on in the Soviet Union. I knew only from Dr. Sommerstein about the return of Polish citizens (not only Jews) from the Soviet Union. How would that develop? Would it have been an expression of responsibility if, on the day I was liberated, the national job was finished for me?! I couldn't do that. It broke my heart.

By then we realized that 180,000 Jews were returning to Poland from the Soviet Union—for us, that was decisive—and who would greet them? How would they be organized? You couldn't leave them alone. You didn't need ideology; you didn't need to preach disbelief in Jewish life in Diaspora, in Poland. That was self-evident in 1945. We had been convinced that "catastrophic Zionism" was correct back when we were sitting safely in our homes.[1] There was no need to explain to us that this was no longer Poland, but one big cemetery, with no room for Jewish life; these weren't only the people who wanted to immigrate to Eretz Israel. But we couldn't abandon the Jews, even ignoring ideological reasons and talking only about extending simple aid—food, clothing, housing. We had to organize; we had to be organized. We, that is, the Committee of the Jews in Poland, were the "Red Star of David"; we were first aid; I am not uttering a single word of criticism about what they did. But I would have criticized the "Asians" if they hadn't done what they did, even before I was liberated by the Red Army.

True, we, the active cadre, were at a crossroads. Some of us thought we should leave at once, or devote ourselves to vengeance and escape from Poland. Others thought we had to welcome the Jews, find work for them, build a Jewish community organization in Silesia or somewhere else, where there were houses the Germans had been thrown out of. But the first, elementary thing was to *organize the Jews*. I was familiar with that need back in January–February; it was imperative to set up shelters, soup kitchens, refugee housing. From these crumbs, these subhuman creatures, we wanted to build a force, immediately.

Wherever I went, I saw masses of humans, old people, young people, women, widows, orphans, all those who returned. In reality, one thing gives rise to another; the road led from the refugee shelters to some city, to the search for an apartment, to a workshop. Even the Polish Communists saw they couldn't be sent to factories and began forming cooperatives so the Jews would be in a Jewish environment, working "among their own"—with carpenters and tailors. There was nothing wrong with organizing them like this.

The argument among us had deep roots and had been going on for decades. It was the recognition of catastrophe which rose to consciousness after the war which gave us Halutzim the force to win people over to our way, to influence the Jews. Otherwise, it's doubtful that so many Jews would have left Poland. The fact is they didn't escape from every country. For example, I didn't see them escaping from Hungary or Romania, where there were no pogroms, and they could get along. Whereas here there was a real struggle. It seems that Poland was the only country where large organized forces, in fact a majority of the Polish people, were opposed to the new government. That was the first period of Brikha, when it was secret and only a few took part in it. Everyone who left at that time was cut off from the tempestuous and excited life of Polish Jewry.

1. "Catastrophic Zionism": The concept that Jews are threatened with disaster in Diaspora and should immigrate en masse to Eretz Israel to avert the ever-present menace.

Although Abba Kovner is a distinguished poet, I must say I didn't hear his voice during the period of Brikha. I don't think any Jew heard his voice at that time. Jews didn't even know that anyone had come out of Poland. What Jewish or general meaning did it have that Zivia Lubetkin, Abba Kovner, and a few other Jews crossed the border? It's more convenient for me to talk about Zivia Lubetkin: did it have any meaning at all? What did those names mean to people returning from the camps? Nothing.

The second stage began with the organization of the exodus at the border.

When groups formed, you could organize the exodus, not as an exodus of individuals, important as they might be, but of organized Halutz groups whose leaving had to be kept secret. Naturally, by then the secret was no longer secret. The border patrol knew about it, the authorities knew, the Communist Jews knew, and the Bund knew. They were followed, but the Poles treated them with leniency. Now and then, they hunted someone. I'm not talking about the guides or the uglier cases of Jews who sold arms to the Polish fanatics who fought the new government. Because there were characters who infiltrated our ranks and took advantage of the opportunities for profiteering and evil.

How was Brikha organized initially?

We put together a group of activists, members of the Movement, for this mission. The Brikha network was spread at the Czech border, and our members were responsible for staffing the crossing sites on both sides of the border. At the border, we set up legal training kibbutzim, which were also places to absorb those escaping. Our comrades on the border would inform the Central Committee of the number of people who could cross in the next few days. In accordance with that, groups were sent to the training kibbutzim to wait until the signal was given to start. The Czechs behaved nicely. That was still the illegal stage of Brikha. We also had problems of financing, and the number of those leaving wasn't very big. At any rate, there were thousands of "escapees."

Thus, we camouflaged Brikha from foreigners and from the Central Committee of the Jews in Poland. Whenever the Committee attacked us for concentrating people to sneak across the border, we would reply that there was a training kibbutz in that place. Of course the population of that kibbutz changed at regular intervals.

In the third stage of Brikha, the exodus encompassed hundreds of thousands. These were the Jewish masses who didn't belong to any organization or party—as distinct from the previous stage, when the backbone of the immigrants were Halutzim. The number of those leaving in the third stage can be put at about 280,000 Jews. An exodus of such scope absolutely could not have existed without fieldwork, organizational effort, and preparation. The organization not only encompassed the Halutz movements, that is not only the youth, but also the "Labor" Histadrut, on the prewar scale, that is families (including children), who were beyond the age of He-Halutz, thirty- and forty-year-olds. Instead of putting them in refugee houses and forcing them to organize in cooperatives, they had to be organized separately and supported.

Only a complete ignoramus or a villain could set the kibbutz in Eretz Israel or the prewar training kibbutz as a standard. Because in that period, we did everything *not* to strike roots where they were. Their common existence, and the help they got, even those who worked, who set up the agricultural farm in Friedland, even they couldn't live only on their work—they needed regular support. At a certain period, this support was given to every Jew in Poland directly by the Joint, or by the Committee of the Jews in Poland. We had to take advantage of funds in order to help Jews who were organized on their way to Eretz Israel. That was what we did.

The first stage of Brikha had no impact because it was small in scope and so secret that it had no resonance. The second stage didn't reach the masses of Jews but only the Jewish leadership and the Polish institutions. Only the third stage rose to such a mighty force that couldn't be controlled or checked. That was when many trains full of people came from the Soviet Union and turned north or south, depending on the destination of the Jews. Agents of the Jewish Central Committee would wait at the points where the Jews were supposed to arrive, but the train never came. That was a mighty force that took wing: *"Men geyt.* (We're going.)"

Leviteh saw that with his own eyes. I saw it, Zvi Netzer saw it more than anyone else. Day and night, he watched it at the borders. He played a central and highly responsible role in it. Of course, such things aren't done by one individual; I don't believe there is such a thing. Only a thinker sitting at a table with pen in hand can "create a situation"; but historical acts are done by multitudes. Without denigrating the "Wolyn Group" or the "Vilna Group," the value of their act is no greater than the acts of Shlomo Cygielnik and his comrades, at a time that was just as hard, when they tried to get across borders in 1940;[2] or the attempts of 1939 and 1940 to get to the Romanian border. It is both a methodological and an historical error to subtract from the whole description and research precisely those first links of getting across the borders. We should explain again that Brikha didn't "fall from the sky," but was an unrelenting process, which was in the blood of the Movement and the people throughout the war; it would be, for instance, as if I had bragged that the period of He-Halutz in my time was the beginning and origin of He-Halutz. If

2. See chapter 3.

I had gone to Romania at that time, I think it would have been a fatal error. And the same is true if other leaders of the Halutz movement had done that. I explained my position to Bauer in a long conversation, and it's too bad he didn't devote enough space in his book to this explanation.

The episode of the Kielce pogroms has an extremely significant connection with Brikha. How did things look in Poland in the summer of 1946? It began with information about the Black Saturday in Eretz Israel, the search in Yagur and other kibbutzim, the arrest of the leaders of the Yishuv and the members of the Palmakh in Latrun[3] and Rafiah.[4] We knew details of the search in Yagur, because they were published in a Polish newspaper and there was also a big article in one of the papers, sympathetic to the Jews and against the English. I don't remember if we learned of it from a telegram we got from Eretz Israel or from the Jewish Agency. At any rate, we did know about the events of June 29.

At the meeting of the Central Committee of the Jews in Poland, I put these events in Eretz Israel on the agenda, with a suggestion to request a political response from the Polish government. We didn't make a decision at once, but it didn't take long. In problems of principle, the PPR members on the Jewish Committee always waited for the response of their institutions, and the response was positive. The opposition always came from the Bund. At the meeting of the Jewish Central Committee a few days later, it was decided to go as a delegation to the prime minister, Osóbka-Morawski. And a delegation including, as far as I remember, Dr. Adolf Berman of Po'alei Zion Left, Pawel Zalecki of the Communists, and myself paid a call on him. There may have been another person, too. We came to Osóbka-Morawski in early July 1946 and told him about the events taking place in Eretz Israel and their significance; he knew something about it himself. We concluded with a request that the government of Poland make a public statement of its sympathy for the struggle of the Jewish people for Eretz Israel. Osóbka-Morawski's reply was extremely sympathetic, but he added things I had already heard a few times from important Polish elements like the Deputy Foreign Minister (who was in fact foreign minister) Modzelewski, who had explained to me their compulsions with regard to the English because of the Polish gold deposited in London. In the same spirit, Osóbka-Morawski also said that Poland would certainly respond in the most explicit and sympathetic manner to the Jewish issue, but he had to consider Polish interests in England—after

3. Latrun: Historical site and crossroads in the southern Ayalon Valley in Israel. During World War II, the British set up "Latrun Camp," where Jewish leaders and underground members were imprisoned in 1946.
4. Rafiah: A town near the Mediterranean coast, twenty-three miles south of Gaza, where the British built a detention camp in the 1940s.

all, this was a protest against Great Britain. But he added, nevertheless, he understood that the Poles had to respond in some way. So he suggested we write a draft declaration and he would check what could be done.

I remember the big hall, with a few telephones along the wall. We were sitting and chatting comfortably; he was the only one in his office—that is, there were no clerks or secretaries—and suddenly, at the other end of the room, the telephone rang. He went to it, listened, said something, and when he came back to us, he said: "Gentlemen, a great catastrophe, a pogrom in Kielce. A pogrom against Jews." He didn't know details, he only knew the army had been sent there. With that, the conversation was cut off.

By the time we left the Prime Minister's office, I was determined to go to Kielce. The comrades who had gone with me were all members of the Central Jewish Committee. They claimed I couldn't go to Kielce without holding an emergency meeting of the Central Jewish Committee. So we all went to the office of the Central Committee and started a discussion. I requested the car at the disposal of the Committee, which had a Polish driver, or a Jew who looked like a Pole, with "good documents." My identity document was in the name of Stanisław Bagniewski, as during the time of the Germans.

Some of the responses expressed in the Committee distressed me. For example, one member of the Bund, an active person who visited me here in Israel, asked what would happen if the car were caught by the rioters. I replied: "And what will happen to Yitzhak Zuckerman—that you don't ask?" My departure was delayed a few hours, since it was decided to take two truckloads of medicine, clothing, and whatever was necessary in such a case. We didn't yet know anything about what was going on in Kielce. Osóbka-Morawski didn't know any details either. The army hadn't yet arrived in Kielce.

I returned to my apartment. I always had grenades and guns at home. I took a gun and two or three grenades and stayed glued to the telephone, waiting for the two trucks that were to accompany us. I felt I was losing precious time, although I must admit that if I had gone to Kielce immediately, I would probably have been like the parachutist from Eretz Israel sent during the war who arrived in Hungary after the expulsions. At any rate, I was anxious to get to Kielce as soon as possible.

At sundown, the trucks and the car arrived. In the car was a Jewish driver with Polish documents and, with him, his girlfriend, who also looked gentile. I sat next to the driver and the trucks followed us. Of course, my car traveled much faster than the truck. At night, we stopped in Częstochowa to find out if the local Jewish Committee had more detailed information about events in Kielce. The chairman of the local Jewish Committee was L. Brenner, a Bundist (he came to Israel a few years ago). He was summoned and came with a few other members of the local Jewish Committee. They didn't know any details, but they did know a great catastrophe had happened there. He didn't think I should endanger the other people with me by going to Kielce at night. The drivers of the trucks were Poles, and that was a mistake, since when they heard what it was about, they refused to set out. It wasn't far, a few hours travel; and we could have arrived early if the roads of postwar Poland weren't destroyed. Polish roads were known to be bad. So we left before dawn (I remember sleeping on the car seat) and reached Kielce early in the morning. Kielce was a ghost town. We came to a place where there had previously been concentrations of Jews. I knew those places because I had been in Kielce a few times before the great catastrophe.

Outside, there was a large concentration of army troops. I was told that the name "Antek" was known here in various circles. But I wondered how the commander of the army and the UB knew it. Apparently, Warsaw had told them I was coming, which may have been a good thing; and they may also have given instructions to help me. At any rate, when I got there, the district army commander received me immediately. He saluted and told me dozens of Jews had been killed, and that all the Jews of the area were assembled in the big UB building with a large courtyard. I went there at once. The gate was closed. I rang. And once again, I was received without any introductions, and with all due respect. I was taken to the UB commander, Major Sobaczyński. I started asking questions, trying to clarify details. He didn't know much because, on the day of the pogrom in Kielce, it wasn't only the Jews of Kielce and the young people of the training kibbutz of the Zionist youth in the city who were attacked. The pogrom struck Jews in a radius of dozens of kilometers around Kielce—on the same day and at the same time, Jews were taken off trains and murdered.

That is, there was a well-organized plot. I felt uneasy listening to Sobaczyński's report. His answer to my question about where security forces had been at the time indicated that the army may not have been in the city. I realized later that he had been lying to me. I asked if the Jews used arms in the first moments of the pogrom. At that time, I didn't know what I learned a day or two later: that the day before the pogrom, members of the UB and the militia had come and collected weapons from the Jews, because the members of the training kibbutz had a few rifles and guns—and they came to take them away. The members of the kibbutz handed over the weapons out of innocence, since the authorities demanded them! So during the pogrom, the young people who had previously had a few weapons, now had nothing to defend themselves with! The lack of response by the security forces established beyond a shadow of a doubt that the UB was an accomplice, involved with the rioters. That is, the UB were among the elements in the bloodbath, and they abandoned the Jews of Kielce, knowingly and maliciously.

That Sobaczyński and his associates who helped prepare for the pogrom were never tried; he was even promoted. Later when I had left Poland, I heard he became head of the department of Jewish and immigration affairs. He was like his name, Sobaczyński (*Sobaka* in Russian means dog). That was how I saw the man, based on information I got from people who met him. He was an inveterate antisemite, even though he was a member of the Communist Party, of the PPR. According to his version, the pogrom was preceded by a provocation by a woman and the army tried to intervene—unsuccessfully. The whole thing turned out to be a lie.

When I left Warsaw, I got hold of a few hundred Złotys to distribute among the needy, but I didn't distribute the money. Among the survivors were some members of the local Jewish Committee, and I gave them the money and asked them to make sure that everyone who needed help got it. At least the minimum for basic necessities.

Then I went out into the streets of Kielce by myself. And once again, it looked like a ghost town. I returned to our base. The army was in its place—it wasn't clear what the army was guarding. I chatted with people in the building and yard in order to get eyewitness accounts. Everyone knew his own story. But these were the survivors. Some were our members and others were ordinary Jews. I didn't know the leaders of the local community. I asked to be taken to the morgue, where I saw dozens of bodies; and, meanwhile, more bodies of Jews killed on the roads were brought in. I saw pregnant women whose stomachs were ripped open. I can't describe the sight. And that wasn't in 1942, that was in 1946! There's no need to waste words on my feeling at that time in view of the sight of Jewish men and women, young and old, of all classes, laid out there, slaughtered.

In Kielce itself, there were forty-one dead; and, altogether, I think that close to sixty people were killed. In any case, I recall that there were more than fifty victims. The murders extended over a radius of dozens of kilometers. At sundown, Dr. A. Berman, officials, army people from Warsaw, and a group from the training kibbutz of the Zionist youth arrived by airplane. The question now was what to do with the Jews who survived. Berman, the *Wojewoda* (head of the district), the mayor, and I held a meeting to discuss the idea of removing all the Jews from Kielce to Łódz. Naturally, it was assigned to me. That night, we were guests of the city. They arranged a place for us to sleep, not in a hotel, but in a school where everything was prepared for us. In a conversation with the *Wojewoda*, whose name I don't remember, I told him I would take charge of this operation only on condition that a Red Cross train was ordered to

Kielce, and that I was given an escort from the city. For there were many wounded Jews in the hospital, and other Jews who had found shelter in the yard of the UB. I also insisted on fixing the time of departure of the train and commanding the troops that would accompany it. All my conditions were accepted. The train was about to arrive from Kraków on our second night in Kielce. The people from Warsaw flew back. My car and driver also returned to Warsaw, and I stayed to wait for the train.

When the train arrived, I was given an army unit to accompany the train and cars to transport the people. To the credit of the army or to the credit of the Polish civilian institutions, I must say that there were also tanks. Neither at the railroad station nor before did I tell anyone what train I was waiting for because I was afraid they would try to attack the train on the way from Kielce to Łódz. My suspicion that there were people inside who were in favor of another pogrom continued to bother me, and I calculated an attempted crime on the way, at one of the stations.

We removed the people from the hospital and set the departure of the train but not exactly at the regular time. When I came to the hospital, I had another shock, since no one there knew I was a Jew. I met with the director of the hospital. The army was ready outside in a caravan with an escort and tanks. I wanted to remove all the wounded Jews immediately, and this is where things got screwed up: one of the wounded Jews knew me, called me "Antek," and started speaking Yiddish to me. I immediately sensed an attitude of sabotage on the part of the doctors, the medics, and the nurses. What mockery, what cynicism! And every one of the wounded had to be carried on a stretcher from the hospital. What a walk that was! There was a moment when my nerves gave out and I couldn't maintain my poise. I pulled out a gun and ordered all the patients removed in fifteen minutes. The whole time, the ambulances waited outside and the behavior of the staff seemed organized. Now they began running and carrying out orders. The army obeyed my orders, and the patients were quickly loaded onto the ambulances. As the army escorted them from the hospital to the railroad station, I organized the departure of the Jews from the courtyard of the UB and, naturally, I couldn't persuade all the Jews to leave. Some decided to stay in the city to save whatever property remained in the houses. Whether they saved it or not, I don't know. I think most of the Jews of Kielce assembled and were taken to the Red Cross train. A lot of cars were hitched to the locomotive. In the train, the nurses, who were from Kraków, were warm and sympathetic. That was a different atmosphere, not like Kielce. Before the train left, a Russian officer reported to me; he was apparently appointed by the Polish council and spoke some Polish. He saluted and gave the number of Russian soldiers under my command. He was placed under my command until the train reached its destination.

I commanded the officer to concentrate all the Jews in the cars with the wounded. I found a quiet corner in the train from which I transmitted orders through the officer about where to stop and where not to stop. The train conductor in Kielce had previously received an order that the train was not to stop in the stations themselves, but ahead of them or past them. At every stop, we got out with the soldiers and surrounded the train to protect it. In the morning, we arrived in Łódz, where ambulances were waiting for us with members of the local Jewish Committee. I signed a printed form for the Russian-Polish officer, confirming that he had completed his job and that everything had gone well. Responsibility passed to the security forces and the local committee in Łódz. The wounded were taken to the hospital. My strength faltered and I could no longer stand on my feet. The dead remained in Kielce. What they did with the healthy ones, I don't know.

When the men and women were in trustworthy hands, I returned to Połodniowa and fell on the bed like a log, with my boots on. I don't know how long I slept until a woman doctor woke me up for some triviality. At dawn, I returned to Warsaw.

A special Soviet army plane with a Soviet escort flew to the funeral in Kielce. The plane carried government representatives and a few Jews, including me. As I recall, Berman and the chief military rabbi, David Cahana, were also there. All the parties of Kielce with their banners attended the funeral procession. It was a funeral sympathetic to the Jews. However, there is no doubt that those who participated in the pogrom also bore banners at the funeral. The army maintained order.

As we left Kielce after the funeral, the airfield was guarded by the Soviet army, an indication of how shocked the authorities were. They understood clearly that the pogrom wasn't only an assault on the Jews, but also an attempt to bring down the institutions of the new regime.

A trial was held, but that was later, after an investigating committee visited there. It took time for the trial to be prepared. I wasn't at the trial. F. Herzberg was there on our behalf and published a long article about the trial in *Nasze Słowo*.[5]

After the funeral I flew back to Warsaw in a military airplane. I was sitting next to the window, depressed, looking out. An officer of the security force sat next to me; during the trip, he turned to me and expressed amazement at my glum mood. I said to him: "I have no doubt the government of Poland sincerely wants the good of the Jewish sur-

5. Fishl Herzberg: Born in Łodz. Studied law and journalism. Spent the war in the Soviet Union. After his return to Poland, he was a member of Po'alei Zion–Z.S. institutions. He immigrated to Israel in 1948.

vivors; but I also have no doubt that, with all its will, it cannot guarantee the lives of the Jews in Poland; what happened is evidence of that. We are between the hammer and the anvil. On the one hand, we are not allowed to leave for various reasons. On the other hand, our lives can't possibly be protected. I'm not thinking only of the dead. What will happen to the living? They are killed on trains and everywhere else, and then there's a pogrom in Kielce! And there will surely be other places. Open the door for the Jews to leave!" He was a senior official and, at that moment, he didn't respond to what I had said. But within forty-eight hours, I got a phone call at the Committee of the Jews in Poland, not from that man himself, but from one of the senior members of UB, asking to meet with me. We made an appointment at a certain café.

That meeting began with a friendly conversation. I won't mention that man's name because I don't know exactly what his situation and fate are today, and I prefer to be cautious. And I don't know the real names of those who were involved, one of whom was a Jew. The two men I talked with said they had been told what I said on the plane, and they had a few questions about it and a few difficulties with it. First of all, even if they were sympathetic to the departure of the Jews for Palestine, they couldn't give permission for such a departure unless they had government support; and their question was whether I could meet with the foreign minister, since the support should be given by the Foreign Ministry. And if the Foreign Ministry adopted such a policy, they would make sure it was carried out. The foreign minister was Zygmunt Modzelewski.

They didn't deal with foreign relations, but it wasn't hard for me to tell them what Modzelewski had told me, and I knew that despite his sympathy, he would give me the same answer connecting this with Polish interests and relations with Britain. And I knew that even if he knew about the departure of the Jews, he would have to say he didn't. Then they started listing names of other members of the government. Maybe Osóbka-Morawski, the prime minister? I told them about my meeting with him on the day of the Kielce pogrom. Then one of them asked how my relations were with Marian Spychalski, who was then—if I'm not mistaken—deputy minister of defense. He was my friend from the underground when, even if we weren't seeing one another, each one knew what the other was doing. More precisely, I knew more about him than he knew about me since he and his friend, the engineer Turbyński, who was later mayor of Warsaw, were close friends of Wacek Folman, Havka's older brother, an architect. They had known one another before the war; and during the war, Turbyński had helped Folman when he came to the Aryan side. After the war, we had several meetings both about restoring the farm in Grochów and about the apartment I got, thanks to him. There were all kinds of things between us of no great importance; at any rate, I was sure of his sympathy and I said we could try that direction.

The second question was which one of us would be in charge of the departure. I had to give an immediate answer. I said I personally would take responsibility. And I added I had reliable people with me. Until the last minute, I didn't know if this was a trap. It wasn't simple, since the UB was in charge of the borders and if I said the He-Halutz organization was responsible (I don't remember if He-Halutz was legitimate then)—even if it was all right legally—if the authorities decided one day that someone on the border wasn't proper, He-Halutz would have to take the responsibility. So I answered that I personally would be responsible.

Two things stood out in their position: first, that they needed support and without it they couldn't help; and the support had to be political, from someone in the government. And in consultation, the lot fell to Marian Spychalski. The second thing was who on the Jewish side would take responsibility. It didn't occur to anyone on the Central Committee of the Jews in Poland that we confronted operations of such a nature and scope. However, I couldn't give He-Halutz that responsibility for fear we would be swallowed up. That was what motivated me to assume the responsibility myself.

They wrote down the summary and I said immediately that as soon as I got an answer from Spychalski, I would get in touch with them.

After first and second thoughts, I decided to let Dr. Adolf Berman in on the secret. I already said that toward the end of the war, before the Polish Uprising, in a conversation about what would happen in the future, I realized we had differences of opinion. He was a "legalist," and he declared that. He also believed in some delusions, like the establishment of a Communist State of Israel; and he also believed in the new relationship of world and Polish communism to the Zionist enterprise, if and when everything was done legally. That was his reservation. I didn't believe in those things. I told him that our people and I had already worked illegally on the borders of the Communist zone in 1939 and 1940, but I imagined that wouldn't be simple for us now. And I said that legalism couldn't be the reservation for our acts. When we met after the war, we didn't continue that discussion.

In 1944, that was a theoretical question, because we didn't know if we'd survive. Then there was the Polish Uprising. Nothing practical was to be decided, and the decision wasn't in our hands; the Germans were still in Warsaw. Even though I knew Berman's world, his points of view, I had no reason in January, after the Liberation, to start an argument with him on precisely that Zionist point and to reveal to him what we were or weren't doing. We confronted certain areas of activity where we had to work together, in the issues of Polish Jewry, in things done legally; but now we confronted the illegal departure, which we had started in January and February 1945; and Berman didn't know about those things since I never talked to him about them. I would meet with him at the Committee of the Jews in Poland and would also come to his home. After the Polish parliament was established, he was a member of it, we would meet in all kinds of places, as well as with the family, and we were friends. We talked about everything except Brikha and our illegal work.

Now I decided to talk with him. I saw him as the person closest to us on the Committee of the Jews in Poland. Moreover, to his credit or not, among the gallery of Zionist activists, he was best known among *the* Polish leaders because of his brother, Jakub Berman, the Communist. Yosef Sak, member of Po'alei Zion–Z.S., was also there; but at that decisive period of the underground, on the Aryan side of Warsaw, for various reasons, he was remote from issues and sat at home while the political representative on the Jewish National Committee was Dr. Berman. He knew the people I knew, like Gomułka and Spychalski, and had contacts with many others I didn't know.

Now in that conversation I initiated, I told him of how things had evolved. I also told him what Modzelewski, the foreign minister had told me and about my last conversation with the members of UB. I told him I had concluded, along with them, that the only one who might be able to consider these things globally and calculate Poland's relations with England and what that required was Marian Spychalski, and we knew him from the underground; he was reliable and imaginative. "Maybe that will work," I told Berman.

Berman agreed immediately. We got in touch with Spychalski and were accepted without delay. I'll never forget Spychalski's reaction—the meeting with him was warm. Like us, he was shocked by the pogrom in Kielce. As far as I'm concerned, all Spychalski's later sins in general issues and Jewish matters cannot obscure his sympathy toward us in this case. We didn't tell him about our conversations or the replies we had gotten from the prime minister.

On the spot, he called the general in charge of the borders, a Soviet military man whose name was Czerwiński. I realized immediately that he was a Russian of Polish origin. His Polish was very "Russified." He was commander of the border patrol, the military patrol in charge of all the borders of Poland.

Spychalski said one thing to Czerwiński in our presence: Do not under any circumstances use the northern borders, that is, toward Berlin; use the southern route, across the Czech border. Czerwiński told him, if I'm not mistaken, that the distance between the new Polish border (the Oder-Neisse line) and Berlin was only seventy kilometers and there was a Soviet garrison there, whereas the Polish army was on the southern border. A few of our comrades in Brikha didn't accept that warning and later cost us lives. Some of them behaved irresponsibly at a certain moment when they were under pressure; they thought they should and could "open" the northern border, too. This time, in terms of the army, the arrangement was completely legal. When we received the positive reply, a meeting was arranged with Czerwiński. I assumed a certain pretense and, as someone who dealt with people of ministerial rank, I said I would send my man to meet with Czerwiński. That man was Stefan Grajek. We also wanted to demonstrate that there was no need to negotiate with Czerwiński, but simply to fix border crossings. So Stefan Grajek was selected as the liaison with General Czerwiński. Right after I got Spychalski's positive answer and after he appointed the commander of the border patrol, Czerwiński, to deal with the matter, I gathered our members of Brikha, Isser Ben-Zvi, Zvi Netzer, and Yohanan Cohen, a member of the Labor Zionists, one of the independent liberals, who was also a Shaliah from Eretz Israel.[6] Without going into details, I proposed to them to indicate border crossings we would suggest to Czerwiński. I also suggested we not expose the places we had secretly used thus far; and, if this was a trap, or some day they decided to stop, we would always have the crossings we had used. I must add that it never occurred to me for a moment that the Poles didn't know we were sneaking across the border and where. I privately thought they were closing their eyes to it, that is, not legitimizing it, since they would occasionally catch and arrest somebody. If they had decided to stop it, they would have done so the day we started smuggling people. In general, that was their policy, not with regard to Jews, but with their struggles with the Polish reactionaries, because they wanted to prevent border crossings by AK and NSZ members who were attempting to smuggle their men and weapons. That is, their policy didn't result from hostility to us. In a conversation I later held with members of UB, this issue came up. We marked places for Stefan Grajek and told him what he had to know about Czerwiński, and they left for the border. Czerwiński passed the responsibility for the case to two colonels and Zvi Netzer agreed to be liaison with them. Now it concerned people who really were on the border. One of the two officers was a Jew, and the other was a Pole who is no longer alive. The Jew cooperated with Zvi Netzer for a long time. After many years, in a chance conversation with Zvi Shner,[7] he

6. Yohanan Cohen: Born in Poland. Immigrated to Eretz Israel in 1931. One of the founders of Kibbutz Tel Yitzhak. One of the first to go to Poland after World War II to set up illegal immigration activities. Served as Israeli General Consul in Boston and then as Israeli Ambassador to Romania.

7. Zvi Shner (1912–1984): Husband of Sara Nishmit. Born in Łódz. Studied law, widely educated. Belonged to Po'alei Zion–Z.S. Worked with the famous Jewish statistician and sociologist Yakov Lestshinski in YIVO. Served in the Polish army, 1934–1935. Went to

realized he knew the man, who was once connected with some job in YIVO. Not a very important job, but he was an ally who now became an officer in the Polish army, and he was sympathetic in all his concrete negotiations with Zvi Netzer.[8]

At the second meeting, the question of responsibility came up again: how to prevent reactionary Polish elements from taking advantage of the situation. That is, the fear that our free passage would also be used by Polish opponents of the regime. That was one of the things they were doing—pursuing profiteers, smugglers of gold and dollars.

I told them I couldn't accept that responsibility, that they had been responsible for it all the time anyway. Nevertheless, I suggested that our people who crossed the border receive a stamp on their transit document, which we would design ourselves. Thus the issue was settled. We made our stamp (after producing samples), and one of those stamps I brought with me is in our museum. It had the word "Repatriation" or something like that—which became a code accepted by the people at the Polish border. At the border, the Jew would show a document with our stamp, confirming that the person was one of our Jews.

As for the second subject, my answer was clear and harsh: I cannot be responsible for those who smuggle currency or go back and forth across the border to make a fortune. I didn't care if they caught them, because they weren't our people, nor were they Jews who wanted to get to Eretz Israel. I informed them clearly that those people wouldn't get our permission and stamp. Even today, I would repeat that because I don't think that currency smugglers should be entitled to endanger a national issue. Their fate and the fate of a few dozen others who could bring down disaster on the whole great enterprise didn't worry me. After that, the great departure began. After I left Poland in December 1946, Stefan Grajek continued his contacts with Czerwiński in accordance with our decision.

Another matter involved with Kielce was the issue of defense in Poland. This was on the agenda, even though the Jews were leaving Poland. That was a matter of the defense of Jewish lives. A special meeting of the Jewish Central Committee was held, and it was decided in principle to go in a delegation to General Witołd, Franciszek Jószwiak, who was then head

---

Russia when the Germans invaded and served in the Red Army, but was discharged along with other Western refugees. In 1946, he returned to Poland and worked in the Jewish community. In 1948, he immigrated to Israel and was one of the founders of Kibbutz Lohamei Ha-Getaot and its museum, Beit Katznelson, which he directed.

8. The Jewish colonel was Michael Radowski; see Zuckerman 1988:155. Radowski currently lives in France and has published chapters of his memoirs in the Yiddish press.

of the militia. I knew him well from our weekly meetings during the underground when he was the commander-in-chief of the AL; he was an elderly, veteran Communist, a handsome man, whom I hadn't met since then.

That was right after the Kielce incident, before the borders were opened wide, I think. Kielce was only a omen; there was information that nationalist underground forces in many other cities were preparing to fight the government by murdering Jews. Some defense of Jews was organized in the kibbutzim even before that, but without weapons. Only individuals had guns. At my house on Poznańska, for example, there was a collection of guns; but I never got legal permits for them, nor did I request them, and they remained there. Now, however, this was an initiative of the central institutions of the Jews to obtain legal weapons from the authorities for self-defense.

In the wake of the meeting of the Jewish Central Committee, there was apparently a special meeting of the PPR members on the committee with General Witold. Afterward, I was called to a top secret conversation with Communists, where they proposed me as commander of the defense. That amazed me since they had at least one other person fit for the job, a Jewish Colonel Gustaw. I asked why they chose me of all people and whom they had discussed it with. They said they had also spoken with Witold. I accepted the proposal and met with Witold who understood our request for weapons for defense. We were immediately given the quantities of rifles and guns we wanted. But now, troubles began. We sent weapons to all the organized places (after all, we couldn't give them to ordinary Jews), and to the training kibbutzim. The great Brikha began at about that time.

One day, the kibbutz in Bytom disappeared overnight. Although I knew they were expected to leave for the border, they didn't leave any traces of the weapons sent for their defense. And I was personally responsible for those weapons. Another group was supposed to come in place of those who left; and now there were no rifles or guns. Until my last day in Poland, I couldn't account for all the weapons. And I had heaps of trouble with the Poles about it. To this day, I don't know what happened to the weapons or where they disappeared.

For a long time after Kielce, I established my headquarters at the Jewish Central Committee. At that time, I could do anything. Someone was on duty there twenty-four hours a day and there was a direct telephone line to my apartment. We would get information from the local Jewish committees because self-defense was a central operation approved and recognized by the authorities. We would get warning calls and telephone appeals about the fear of outbursts here and there. In such a case, we would put all defense groups on alert. The authorities regarded them as a kind of popular militia for the defense of Jews. The Poles didn't interfere, and no one supervised us. The weapons were given to us in full trust. The Jewish Central Committee was responsible and I was responsible to the committee.

At a symposium on Yehuda Bauer's book at Ef'al, Leviteh asked me to take issue with a few things. He claimed that allowing Jews to leave en masse couldn't possibly remain the property of one branch of government and not be known to the general government institutions; and that it couldn't be concealed from the citizens of Poland, because the day after the agreement, the Jews began selling their possessions and moving and all Poland knew about it. No doubt such a thing couldn't have been done underground, vis-à-vis other branches of the administration. But as far as I know, the Foreign Ministry was cautious about giving the issue official public approval, which could have damaged Poland.

I must also say that as far as I know, there wasn't an agreement between various branches of government. I don't know what authority Leviteh had for his remarks. I must say that in that position, Spychalski didn't ask the Foreign Ministry. True, those things couldn't be kept secret. In fact, a person in a key position soon responded sharply to the issue. But at first, nothing was known about it. For a few days or weeks, it was kept secret—I don't know.

Leviteh also claimed there couldn't have been such an agreement without the knowledge of the Soviet authorities. Did the Russians know about Brikha, and what was their attitude? I don't know what happened at the cabinet meeting, what Modzelewski said, what they said among themselves, or what Moscow said. There may be all kinds of speculations, but I don't know the facts. What I can do is reconstruct the course of things. And I state here that the decision came at that stage, within a few minutes, in the conversation Dr. Berman and I had with Spychalski. If the Polish government wanted to ruin it, they would have. Jakub Berman knew about it, too. Not at that moment, but a few days later. If he had wanted, he could have ruined it. The same goes for Moscow. Jakub Berman certainly didn't keep quiet without asking Moscow. I reject Leviteh's thesis, at least in regard to the first stage, and I can't say how long it went on—one day or two weeks. *I think that there was an historical, fateful decision here, made by Spychalski.* If we hadn't gone to him, if we had gone to the minister or to another ministry that would have considered the case from another angle, I don't know if the Jews would have crossed the borders as they did.

Could Spychalski, who was acting Minister of Defense, have decided such a thing on his own? At any rate, the fact is that, when he accepted

Berman and me, he didn't know why we had come. And when he gave his positive answer—I'm certain of it—he didn't pick up the telephone to call the Ministry of Foreign Affairs or any other element in the government. He gave the approval of his own, without asking. Before I came to him, I sat with members of the UB, who gave me all kinds of advice: to appeal to the Ministry of Foreign Affairs or the Prime Minister—and I rejected it; and only then did Spychalski's name come up. So, Spychalski didn't know in advance why we came to him. At that time, there was not yet a bureaucracy that obliged Dr. Berman and Yitzhak Zuckerman to inform Spychalski in advance what they wanted to discuss with him. We asked for an audience and he agreed. And, in our presence, he didn't ask anyone for permission; and, on the spot, he called the main in charge of the borders. He didn't ask the Ministry of Foreign Affairs, he didn't ask the Party, not did he ask the opinion of the he Prime Minister. True, it was impossible to hide it, either from the Polish public or from the circles of Polish leadership. But the fact is they didn't know. For example, the "great Berman" (Jakub Berman) didn't know. Zvi Netzer could testify to that too.

So, it is conceivable to me that Spychaski did it on his own, perhaps out of naïveté, perhaps because of his attitude toward Jews, perhaps because of the proximity to the Kielce incident, or because of the clash between his Communist theory and the Polish reality. These things and God knows what else might have caused that. At any rate, he accepted it openly and immediately gave permission right then and there. True, nothing was written and no agreement, no document was signed; it was all an oral conversation.

All that I've told are facts. What I add will be in the nature of speculation. For example, there were a few days between my meeting with the members of UB and our meeting with Spychalski—the members of UB might have contacted elements that anticipated us with Spychalski and he might have been ready for our visit. It's also possible that Jakub Berman and the Ministry of Foreign Affairs knew, but avoided the issue and didn't take an official position, with the argument that they couldn't accept responsibility—the Ministry of Foreign Affairs because of foreign relations and Berman in terms of Moscow. Perhaps it was convenient for them to assign the case to Spychalski, that is, to an internal Polish body. But, as I said, all this is speculation. Right after that, I met with members of UB. Incidentally, I was the only one who maintained contacts with UB, at least all the time I was in Poland; and neither Berman not Stefan Grajek was involved in that. I don't know if Adolf Berman continued his involvement in those issues; perhaps he had contacts in other issues. In case of a hitch, I would get a summons to clear things up; the meetings, of course, were held in some café.

Then the Jews began going. I don't know how much time passed; at any rate, it wasn't many weeks until that day when I sat with Berman, in the House of Deputies of the KRN; we were served tea and cake and suddenly the telephone rang. I heard Dr. Berman's answers and saw him turn white as a sheet. It turned out that the whole incident was know to Jakub Berman, his brother, who began investigating and traced it to the Ministry of Defense. When the Ministry of Defense was asked, they said that Antek and Berman visited them. It was unintentionally understood that "Berman" was Jakub Berman, who was mistakenly involved in a political hot potato he didn't know anything about. After shouts on the telephone, Dr. Berman asked me what to do. I said there wasn't anything to do, and we should wait and see what happened.

That night, when I got back to my apartment on Poznańaska, I found a frightened and pale Zvi Netzer there. Apparently he had been sitting somewhere with the two officers in charge for the Poles. That place wasn't on the border, but in Warsaw. Suddenly, they got a panicky call to come to Czerwiński, who told them Spychalski asked them to meet with Jakub Berman immediately. Apparently he felt there was something not right here, not appropriate, and thought it wasn't worth his while to go to Jacub Berman, who drew his power from Moscow, and it was even said that he had a direct line to Stalin. Czerwiński cajoled his two members of the border patrol to go to Jakub Berman. The two naïve officers, who were with Zvi Netzer, told him to come along. And Zvi Netzer, a member of our underground, the center of Brikha activity, went with two officers to Jakub Berman; and when he asked questions, they answered that Czerwiński was in charge and they didn't know anything. Then Berman pointed to Zvi Netzer, who wasn't in uniform, and asked who he was. Zvi stammered something unclear and Berman began screaming at him, and he didn't know where to hide. That was the meaning of the furious phone call Dr. Adolf Berman got from his brother, Jakub Berman, whose rage was so hot because he had been credited with arranging the departure of the Jews and the crossing of the borders. Apparently it became known to the British intelligence services, and the English presented a "note" to the office of the prime minister of Poland.

Leviteh was right when he argued that if there had been principled opposition by Moscow to Brikha, those loyal to Moscow would have stopped it immediately, and it would probably have had grave consequences. In face, there were no consequences. That is, Jakub Berman apparently did some hollering because he didn't know anything about it, and was scared because his name was mixed up in the incident. I am sure Modzelewski also know abut it. But neither Modzelewski nor Jakub Berman was involved in the Polish decision on it. Leviteh is wrong about that.

Brikha continued and confronted our comrades with problems. As long as there were dozens of people, crossing every day or night, that is, not many people (although in time, the numbers grew to thousands), the problems weren't very serious. But when masses of Jews began streaming every day, the question of organizing and supporting that movement came up. For there weren't buildings close to the crossings, and you couldn't always take all those who were prepared across, and we needed assembly places. The attitude of the Czech authorities was extraordinary. I appealed to the director of the Joint who was then Bein, who replaced Guzik, who had been killed in an airplane accident in Czechoslovakia. Schwartz was the director of the Joint for all of Europe, but Bein was the director in Poland. My relations with Bein weren't the same as with Guzik, whom I had known for year. But our relations with Bein were frank and correct. When Dr. Joseph Schwartz visited Poland, we also established good relations with him.

In the organization of the mass Brikha, problems of transport also arose. Sometimes the people clearly couldn't be taken across where they had come and had to be taken across a few dozen kilometers away. Sometimes they had to go from city to city, and sometimes, other help was needed. The director of the Joint said he would make transportation available, and even finance it, but he couldn't do that without permission of the Jewish Central Committee. There was a conflict between the Jewish Central Committee and the Joint. The Jewish Central Committee wanted the "people" to think it gave the money, although everyone knew the money came from the Joint, from foreign Jews. The Polish government also helped, but those were only small sums, compared with the money from the Joint. Bein was afraid that in these circumstances, the authorities might close the Joint or conspire against its activity. There was an element of competition in it. I had no choice but to tell Dr. Adolf Berman the secret and bring the question to the Jewish Committee.

Both the Communists and the Bund were represented on the Jewish Committee. You couldn't convene only the Zionists on the committee to discuss the question. In general, when it came to a hard issue, the decision would be postponed to another meeting. One thing I did know; when Brikha was known, both the Poles and the Bundists, who may have been the last to know the Jews were crossing the border, would go the UB and the Party and denounce both the people and the acts. The Party response showed them the Party knew what was going on. Our representatives demanded help for those leaving from the Jewish Committee; by then, Brikha was known to all the Polish institutions. But the issue was never brought up officially to the Committee of the Jews in Poland. I already knew they had protested and denounced us, and I also knew what answer they got. That is, the timing corresponded with bringing up the issue. I don't remember anymore if it was at the first meeting or a few days later that we made the general decision in the Committee which made shelter and transportation available to those leaving, and that was the "door" through which the Joint entered. They came in with the knowledge of the Committee of the Jews in Poland, which might have appeared in a few places and pretended it was doing the work, but in fact, it was the Joint. Its members bought or rented cheap cars and worked on other matters. As for the Committee of the Jews in Poland, they put up shelters. The Joint gave food, beds, blankets, and transportation.

It turned out that Zvi Netzer was the "boss of the borders," and it's not bragging if he says that. He maintained very good relations with the officers (the "colonels") and the members of the border patrol. At any rate, concerning Brikha, I think he was the most successful Shaliah, who performed his mission intelligently, resourcefully, loyally, and devotedly.

It's hard for me to assess the position of the Russians or their reasoning; we know how they behaved in the areas and at the borders they guarded. And we know the story of what happened in the spring of 1945, when Abba Kovner, Zivia, and Eliezer Lidovski crossed the border to Romania and were captured on the Polish border which was guarded by the Russians. They crossed the border at Sanok and, apparently as the result of a denunciation, were captured by the Russians. They introduced themselves as Bulgarians, an idea of dubious wisdom since the Russian was liable to understand Bulgarian and expose their fraud. But fortunately for them, the officer who caught them was a Jew and he let them go. I remember crossing the borders in places guarded by the Russians, for example, in the Austrian area, under Russian control.

I assume that the Poles could have closed their eyes and not asked for Moscow's order, as long as the exodus was carried out in dribs and drabs—until Kielce. But it's absolutely impossible to think that the mass exodus of Jews, after Kielce, was allowed without the knowledge of Moscow. Perhaps the Russians were aware that in the struggle with the opponents of the regime in Poland, which was simply a civil war, the Jews didn't strengthen the government and could be dispensed with. Perhaps "high politics" was also at work here: in a situation of confrontation with Britain, the consideration might have been to "make trouble" for the English. There could have been all kinds of considerations. At any rate, the fact is that the Russians didn't bother us. But when they tried to direct Brikha to the northern border, the Russians responded very severely, they caught people and sent them back. There also included members of

Nezakh,[9] and there was another group, but the people in it should tell about it. I was very angry about it because the comrades who did that did it deliberately. I was warned and I warned then not to go north. In that it's clear that the Russians nevertheless did decide what they would allow and what they would forbid. I imagine there were enough Poles, loyal Stalinists, in that period, even though that doesn't mean all of them were Stalinists. Some were more loyal to Moscow and some less. Those who were loyal to Moscow were those who were in the Soviet Union during the war; those who assisted in self-liberation were probably less loyal. Incidentally, I read in the Polish emigré press about the death of Hilary Minc, a Jew, a brilliant economist, who was then in the leadership. I don't think they printed that in the newspaper in Poland (the *Kultura*). His death went unnoticed.

The memorial to the Ghetto Uprising was commissioned from the sculptor Natan Rappoport after I left Poland.[10] Initially, we set up another memorial, a big stone on the bunker at Mila 18. I gave a speech on behalf of the Jewish community at the unveiling of the tombstone, along with a Polish general, on April 19, 1945. There are photos of that scene. I was very sick, with a high fever, and it was raining that day. It was just a big stone with an inscription. That stone isn't there anymore because, afterward, they put up Rappoport's impressive memorial. I selected the site of the memorial, before I left Poland. Apparently, in such matters they valued my opinion and asked me to suggest the place.

I used to spend a lot of time in the destroyed ghetto. I would go there and sit. Sometimes, I'd take sandwiches and a small bottle and do some soul-searching. I'll describe the place in case someone knows the area; the square of Gęsia Street, which connects with Zamenhof Street—a small square, a kind of triangle. The Judenrat building here and the prison ("Gesiówka") remained standing. Part of the Judenrat building was destroyed but, as I recall, it was restored. It had a plaque because it's an historic edifice: here was the Jewish police and, opposite, in the yard, was our headquarters. I decided that the memorial should be in that square. One side of it housed the Jewish Fighting Organization and, opposite, on the other side, the Judenrat. The building that housed the headquarters of the Jewish Fighting Organization was destroyed, so the square could be expanded. The stone placed there before was closer to the Judenrat. Not everyone understood why I chose that precise place. The reason is

9. Halutz Scout Youth, a Ha-Shomer Ha-Tza'ir movement in the Soviet Union and in the Baltic state, which seceded in Israel, joined Mapai and set up an autonomous framework in Ha-Kibbutz Ha-Meuchad.

10. The monument was unveiled on April 19, 1948.

that it was the site of the command staff of the Jewish Fighting Organization, across from the Judenrat.

At Miła 18, the site of the last bunker, there is a memorial to this day. In 1948, we unveiled the memorial stone at Dzielna 34. There was a memorial stone there, with an inscription in Hebrew, Yiddish, and Polish: "Here the Jewish Fighting Organization was established," and the date. The commune was also there. That was in 1948, on a visit to Poland. Then they held the unveiling ceremony. At that time, I traveled in a delegation from Israel by invitation of the Poles; but later they took down the memorial, thus showing a contempt for the historic place. However, they did leave the plaque on the bunker at Miła 18.

When Zivia returned to Warsaw from Romania, we decided I should remain in Poland, whereas Zivia was to immigrate to Eretz Israel. She moved about for another month and stayed with me for some time in Paris. In June 1946, she arrived in Eretz Israel.

I returned to Poland for a few months. In December 1946, I left Poland for Eretz Israel. On the way, I stopped in Paris, and then I attended the Zionist Congress, then back again to Paris; I came to Eretz Israel in 1947, two years after the end of the war.

The past lives in the present and in the future; if not, it has no meaning. Building the "children's memorial" or shaping the "central hall"—another building, another wing, another museum exhibition—they're all meaningless if the lava of the extinguished volcano cannot be poured into them.

I am a happy man by nature, I enjoy drinking, company, but those things don't depend on me. I'm not the one who determines the timing and it bursts out of me and is part of me, my past—something like lava gushing out of the ground and sprouting up in your life, and you can't separate between "then" and "now."

It doesn't get easier or weaker with the years; on the contrary, it gets sharper. I ask myself: if I were a monk, if I beat my breast in penance, would that help me?!

Zivia was different. Life made us different, and that's good. If we were the same, life would have been impossible. When she came to Eretz Israel, she began to live her internal life anew, with and in spite of all the burden of the past.

But I couldn't get rid of the past. After the Holocaust, it gets worse and worse. At that time, during the Holocaust, I was like a drunkard or perhaps like a tightrope walker in a circus who doesn't fall down. I've already said—and don't think me arrogant—there were few people who knew the full scope and horror of what happened as I did. But, in January

1945, when I saw the vacuum left after the murder of my people, I broke down. And ever since, I've had enough time to take stock and to judge myself. And it doesn't matter if you were elected or if you appointed yourself. It doesn't matter, since you immediately find yourself working, taking responsibility.

Twenty, thirty years have gone by, and things still bubble up in you. Sometimes it's only the fate of one person.

But the basic question is: what should we have done that we didn't do? The decisive judgment is the historical judgment. If I were chosen to stand before such a judgment, I would say that I was late, I was late in everything. For we could have done everything a little sooner, a little different. They say maybe that's no accident. I don't know. I can't blame anybody but myself—that I'm allowed. . . .

I'm not afraid of any judgment that's not the judgment of history. But as the years go by, it gets harder. Only an intelligent, conscientious, moral person can weigh the truth. That ancient rule not to judge your fellow man until you're in his place is good and right. And maybe it can also mitigate my sentence.

But the judgment of history is being written and will go on being written by the historians. I don't care who my judges are.

And the essential thing, what is really important, is me confronting myself. . . .

BIBLIOGRAPHY

Adler, Stanislaw, 1982. *In the Warsaw Ghetto, 1940–1943*, trans. Sara Philip. Jerusalem: Yad Vashem.

Ainsztein, Reuben, 1974. *Jewish Resistance in Nazi-Occupied Eastern Europe*. New York: Harper and Row Publishers, Inc.

——. 1979. *The Warsaw Ghetto Revolt*. New York: Waldon Press, Inc.

Arad, Yitzhak, 1982. *Ghetto in Flames*. New York: Holocaust Library.

Auerbach, Rachel, 1954. *In the Streets of Warsaw* (Hebrew). Tel Aviv: Am Oved.

Avnon, Arye, ed., 1966. *Gordonia Press: The Underground Press of the Youth Movement "Gordonia" in Ghetto Warsaw* (Hebrew). Hulda: Archives of Gordonia-Maccabi-Hatzair.

Bauer, Yehuda, 1970. *Flight and Rescue: Brichah*. New York: Random House.

Ben-Gurion, David, 1971. *Israel: A Personal History*, trans. Nechemia Meyers and Uzy Nystar. New York: Funk and Wagnalls, Inc.

Berlinski, Hirsh, 1966. *Three* (Yiddish). Tel Aviv: Ringelblum Institute.

Berman, Adolf Abraham, 1971. *Underground Days*. Tel Aviv: Hamenora Publishing House.

——. 1977. *Where Fate Sent Me: With the Jews of Warsaw* (Hebrew). Israel: Ghetto Fighters House.

Berman, Batya Tabenkin, 1956. *Underground Diary* (Hebrew). Tel Aviv: Beit Lohamei Ha-Getaot.

Blumenthal, Nachman, and Kermish, Joseph, 1965. *Resistance and Revolt in the Warsaw Ghetto* (Hebrew). Jerusalem: Yad Vashem.

Borzykowski, Tuvia, 1964. *Between Tumbling Walls* (Hebrew). Tel Aviv: Hakibbutz Hameuchad Publishing House Ltd.

——. 1972. *Between Tumbling Walls*, trans. Mendel Kohansky. Tel Aviv: Beit Lohamei Hagettaot and Hakibbutz Hameuchad Publishing House.

Brand, Adam, 1954. *Man in the Ghettoes* (Hebrew). Merhavia: Sifriat Po'alim.

Brenner, Liber, 1950. *Resistance and Murder in Częstochowa Ghetto* (Yiddish). Warsaw: The Jewish Historical Institute.

Carmi, Aharon, and Frimmer, Haim, 1961. *From That Blaze* (Hebrew). Tel Aviv: Hakibbutz Hameuchad Publishing House, Ltd.

Celeminski, Yakov, 1965. "With the Slaughtered Nation" (Yiddish), *Undzer Tsayt*. New York: N.p.

Czech, Danuta, 1990. *Auschwitz Chronicle: 1939–1945*, trans. Barbara Harshav, Martha Humphreys, Stephen Shearier. New York: Henry Holt and Co.

Czerniakow, Adam, 1979. *The Warsaw Diary of Adam Czerniakow*, ed. Raul Hilberg, Stanislaw Staron, and Josef Kermisz; trans. Stanislaw Staron and the staff of Yad Vashem. New York: Stein and Day.

Dawidsohn, Gusta, 1953. *Justina's Diary* (Hebrew). Israel: Ghetto Fighters House.

Dobrosycki, Lucjan, ed., 1964. *Cywilna Obrona Warszawy we Wrzesnice 1939*. Warsaw: Panstwowe Wydawn Naukowe.

Doracz, Anna, 1972. "Memoirs" (Hebrew), *Moreshet*, November.

Dror, Zvika, ed., 1984. *Testimonies of Survival* (Hebrew). Tel Aviv: Kibbutz Lochamai Hageta'ot and Hakibbutz Hameuchad.

Dworzecki, Dr. Mark, 1948. *The Jerusalem of Lithuania in Battle and Defeat* (Yiddish). Paris: Union Populaire Juive.

Eck, Natan, 1960. *Wandering on the Roads of Death* (Hebrew). Jerusalem: Yad Vashem.

Engelstern, Ruth, 1973. *Written in a Barn*. Tel Aviv: Beit Lohamei Hageta'ot.

Ferencz, Benjamin B., 1979. *Less than Slaves*. Cambridge, Mass.: Harvard University Press.

Goldstein, Bernard, 1961. *Five Years in the Warsaw Ghetto*, trans. and ed. Leonard Shatzkin. New York: Doubleday and Company.

Grinspun, Pnina, 1984. *Our Days Were Nights* (Hebrew). Tel Aviv: Lohamei Ha-Getaot and Ha-Kibbutz Ha-Meuchad.

Grossman, Chaika, 1987. *The Underground Army: Fighters of the Bialystok Ghetto*, trans. Shmuel Beeri. New York: Holocaust Library.

Gutman, Yisrael, 1989. *The Jews of Warsaw, 1939–1943: Ghetto, Underground, Revolt*, trans. Ina Friedman. Bloomington: Indiana University Press.

Gutman, Yisrael, and Rothkirchen, Livia, eds., 1976. *Destruction of the Jews of Europe*. Jerusalem: Yad Vashem.

Helman, Yehuda, 1969. "Beginning of the Halutz Underground in Conquered Poland" (Hebrew), *Dappim Le-Heker Ha-Shoah Ve'Ha-Mered*, second series, collection A. Tel Aviv: Hakibbutz Hameuchad Publishing House, Ltd.

Höhne, Heinz, 1979. *The Order of the Death's Head*, trans. Richard Barry. New York: Ballantine Books.

——, 1976. *In the Cornfields of Grochów*. Tel Aviv: Beit Lohamei Hagetaot and Hakibbutz Hameuchad Publishing House.

Ishai, Moshe, 1973. *In the Shadow of the Holocaust: Memoirs of a Mission to Poland, 1945–1946* (Hebrew). Tel Aviv: Ghetto Fighters' House Publishers.

Kaplan, Chaim, 1973. *The Warsaw Diary of Chaim A. Kaplan*, trans. and ed. Abraham I. Katsh. New York: Collier Books.

Katznelson, Yitzhak, 1956. *Last Writings* (Hebrew). Tel Aviv: Hakibbutz Hameuchad Publishing House, Ltd.

Kazik (Simha Rotem), 1984. *The Past Inside Me* (Hebrew). Tel Aviv: Hakibbutz Hameuchad Publishing House, Ltd.

Klein, David, 1968. *Arm in Arm With the Angel of Death* (Yiddish). Tel Aviv: Y. L. Peretz Verlag.

Klonitski, Aryē, and Malwina, 1970. *Journal of Adam's Father* (Hebrew). Tel Aviv: Beit Lohamei Hagetaot and Hakibbutz Hameuchad.

Korczak, Janusz, 1983. *The Ghetto Years, 1939–1942*, trans. Jerzy Bachrach, Barbara Krzywicka, Avner Tomaschoff. Tel Aviv: Ghetto Fighters House, Ltd.

Korczak, Reizl, 1965. *Flames in Ash* (Hebrew). Tel Aviv: Sifriat Po'alim.

Krall, Hanna, 1986. *Shielding the Flame*, trans. Joanna Stasinska and Lawrence Wechsler. New York: Henry Holt and Company.

Landau, Ludwig, 1963. *The Chronicle of War*. Poland.

Lazar-Litai, Haim, 1963. *Masada of Warsaw* (Hebrew). Tel Aviv: Publishers of the Jabotinski Institute.

Levin, Baruch, 1968. *In the Forests of Revenge* (Hebrew). Tel Aviv: Lohamei Hagetaot and Hakibbutz Hameuchad.

Levin, Nora, 1973. *The Holocaust: The Destruction of European Jewry, 1933–1945*. New York: Schocken Books.

Lewin, Abraham, 1989. *A Cup of Tears: A Diary of the Warsaw Ghetto*, ed. Antony Polonsky; trans. Christopher Hutton. New York: Basil Blackwell, Inc.

Lubetkin, Zivia, 1981. *In the Days of Destruction and Revolt*, trans. Ishai Tubbin. Tel Aviv: Beit Lohamei Haghettaot, Hakibbutz Hameuchad Publishing House, and Am Oved Publishing House.

Meed, Władka, 1979. *On Both Sides of the Wall*, trans. Dr. Steven Meed. New York: Holocaust Library.

Mendelsohn, Ezra, 1983. *The Jews of East Central Europe Between the World Wars*. Bloomington: Indiana University Press.

Neudstadt, Melekh, 1947. *Destruction and Uprising of the Jews of Warsaw* (Hebrew). Tel Aviv: Published by the Executive Committee of the General Federation of Jewish Labour in Palestine.

Polonsky, Antony, and Drukier, Bolesław, 1980. *The Beginnings of Communist Rule in Poland*. London: Routledge and Kegan Paul.

Putermilch, Yakov, 1981. *In Fire and Snow* (Hebrew). Tel Aviv: Beit Lohamei HaGettaot and Hakibbutz Hameuchad.

Reitlinger, Gerald, 1961. *The Final Solution*. New York: A. S. Barnes and Company, Inc.

Ringelblum, Emmanuel, 1975. *The Journal of Emmanuel Ringelblum*, ed. and trans. Jacob Sloan. New York: Schocken Books.

———. 1986. *To Live with Honor and Die with Honor! . . . Selected Documents from the Warsaw Ghetto Underground Archives*, ed. and annotated by Joseph Kermish. Jerusalem: Yad Vashem.

Rufeisen-Schüpper, Hela, 1990. *Farewell to Miła 18* (Hebrew). Tel Aviv: Ghetto Fighter's House.

Schwersantz, Yitzhak, 1969. *Halutz Underground in Nazi Germany* (Hebrew). Tel Aviv: Lohamei Hagettaot and Hakibbutz Hameuchad.

Seidel, Hillel, 1973. *Man on Trial* (Hebrew). Tel Aviv: N.p.

Seidman, Dr. Hillel, 1947. *Diary of the Warsaw Ghetto* (Yiddish). Buenos Aires.

Shulman, Abraham, 1982. *The Case of Hotel Polski.* New York: Holocaust Library.

Steiner, Jean François, 1966. *Treblinka* (French). Paris: Librairie Anthème Fayard.

Stroop, Jürgen, 1979. *The Stroop Report: The Jewish Quarter Is No More*, trans. Sybil Morton. New York: Pantheon Books.

Suhl, Yuri, ed., 1975. *They Fought Back: The Story of the Jewish Resistance in Nazi Europe.* New York: Schocken Books.

Szwajger, Adina Blady, 1990. *I Remember Nothing More: The Warsaw Children's Hospital and the Jewish Resistance*, trans. Tasja Darowska and Danusia Stok. London: Collins Harvill.

Tennenbaum, Mordechai, 1947. *Pages from the Blaze* (Hebrew). Tel Aviv: Hakibbutz Hameuchad, Ltd.

Trunk, Isaiah, 1977. *Judenrat.* New York: Stein and Day.

Turkow, Jonas, 1969. *This Was Jewish Warsaw* (Hebrew). Tel Aviv: Mifaley Tarbut Vechinuch Ltd.

Wdowinski, David, 1985. *And We Are Not Saved.* New York: Philosophical Society.

Weichert, Michael, 1963. *The War* (Yiddish). Tel Aviv: Hamenorah Publishing House.

———. 1970. *After the Catastrophe* (Yiddish). Tel Aviv: Orli.

Ziemian, Joseph, 1977. *The Cigarette Sellers of Three Crosses Square*, trans. Janina David. New York: Avon Books.

Zilberstein, Leah, 1988. "Warsaw, Ghost Town," *Moreshet* 45 (June).

Zuckerman, Yitzhak, 1962. *The Fighting Ghettos*, trans. and ed. Meyer Barkai. Philadelphia and New York: J. B. Lippincott Co.

———. 1986. *In Ghetto and Uprising* (Hebrew). Tel Aviv: Ghetto Fighter's House, Ltd.

———. 1988. *The Polish Exodus* (Hebrew). Tel Aviv: Ghetto Fighters' Publishing House.

INDEX